HUMAN
RIGHTS
WATCH

WORLD REPORT

WITHDRAWN

2016

)F 2015

Front cover photo: *Asylum seekers and migrants disembark from a large fishing vessel that transported them from Turkey to the Greek island of Lesbos.*
© 2015 ZALMAÏ for Human Rights Watch

Back cover photo: *Thirteen-year-old Sifola in the home she shares with her husband and in-laws in Bangladesh. Sifola's parents, struggling with poverty, took her out of school and arranged for her marriage so that the money saved could pay for her brothers' schooling.*
© 2015 Omi for Human Rights Watch

Cover and book design by Rafael Jiménez

www.hrw.org

Human Rights Watch defends the rights of people worldwide.

We scrupulously investigate abuses, expose the facts widely, and pressure those with power to respect rights and secure justice.

Human Rights Watch is an independent, international organization that works as part of a vibrant movement to uphold human dignity and advance the cause of human rights for all.

Human Rights Watch began in 1978 with the founding of its Europe and Central Asia Division (then known as Helsinki Watch). Today, it also includes divisions covering Africa; the Americas; Asia; Europe and Central Asia; and the Middle East and North Africa; a United States program; thematic divisions or programs on arms; business and human rights; children's rights; disability rights; health and human rights; international justice; lesbian, gay, bisexual, and transgender rights; refugees; women's rights; and emergencies. It maintains offices in Amsterdam, Beirut, Berlin, Brussels, Chicago, Geneva, Johannesburg, London, Los Angeles, Moscow, Nairobi, New York, Oslo, Paris, San Francisco, Sao Paulo, Stockholm, Sydney, Tokyo, Toronto, Washington DC, and Zurich, and field presences in over 45 other locations globally. Human Rights Watch is an independent, nongovernmental organization, supported by contributions from private individuals and foundations worldwide. It accepts no government funds, directly or indirectly.

HUMAN RIGHTS WATCH

Table of Contents

COUNTRIES 53

Foreword

World Report 2016 is Human Rights Watch's 26th annual review of human rights practices around the globe. It summarizes key human rights issues in more than 90 countries and territories worldwide, drawing on events from the end of 2014 through November 2015.

The book is divided into two main parts: an essay section, and country-specific chapters.

In the introductory essay, "Twin Threats: How the Politics of Fear and the Crushing of Civil Society Imperil Global Rights," Human Rights Watch Executive Director Kenneth Roth details how fear drove two of the most important global developments of 2015. Fears of terror attacks and of the potential impact of refugee influx led to a visible scaling back of rights in Europe and other regions. Scapegoating Muslims and refugees, Roth argues, hurts and alienates populations crucial to counterterrorism efforts. Efforts to weaken encryption of communications and to intensify surveillance—the knee-jerk response of many governments to terror attacks—undermines privacy rights, can endanger critical infrastructure, and may distract from the focused investigative work that should be at the heart of counterterrorism efforts. In countries as diverse as China, Ethiopia, India, and Russia, another set of fears—in this case, fears that new digital communications platforms will energize social and political movements—helped to drive a less recognized but disturbing and destructive global trend: the adoption by many countries of repressive new nongovernmental organization laws and policies targeting individuals and groups that try to hold governments to account, including social media users, civil society groups, and the funders who back them. Roth traces the ways in which human rights law can and should guide responses to these major global developments. "We abandon it," he warns "at our peril."

Most people never question the "boy" or "girl" designation they receive at birth. In the next essay, "Rights in Transition " Neela Ghoshal and Kyle Knight examine the humiliating and violent treatment often endured by those who do. Across the world, transgender people are subject to discriminatory laws and policies that prevent them from accessing a range of rights and services, including health care, free expression, and privacy, and that in some cases ban their very existence. Years of advocacy by intrepid transgender activists, combined with recent international pressure—including from the United Nations and Council of Europe—has increased access to legal recognition for transgender people and eased the process by which they can achieve it. No new or special rights lie at the heart of such crucial efforts, argue Ghoshal and Knight, but rather a fundamental "commitment to the core idea that the state or other actors will not decide for people who they are."

Around the world, girls are forced into child marriages that are often ruinous for their personal growth and disastrous for their ability to realize basic human rights. Child marriage often means leaving school, domestic violence, a cycle of poverty, and an increased risk of serious health problems and death due to early childbearing. One in nine girls in the developing world marry before 15, and one in three by 18. The UN Sustainable Development Goals adopted in September 2015 aim to eliminate child marriage within 15 years, and many governments, donors, and civil society groups have rallied to the cause. But success, warns Nisha Varia, will not come easy and requires sustained political commitment to address social and cultural norms around girls' sexuality; coordination across multiple sectors; learning about what works and for whom; and empowering girls themselves with information and access to services so that they can realize a potential that so many of their mothers—themselves child brides—have been denied.

Finally, in "Children Behind Bars," Michael Bochenek looks at the global overuse of child detention. The UN Children's Fund, UNICEF, estimates that more than one million children are behind bars worldwide. Some of these children are serving excessively long sentences, others are held for skipping school, running away from home, and other acts that should not be crimes, and some have never been tried for their alleged crimes. Migrant children are often held in immigration detention. Children with disabilities may be institutionalized. All of these practices violate international standards. A UN study soon underway will hopefully result in increased attention to these abusive practices and greater compliance with international standards. But as Bochenek notes, governments do not need to wait for this study; they can and should act now to develop alternatives to detention and ensure that children who are locked up receive schooling, health services, and humane treatment.

The rest of the volume consists of individual country entries, each of which identifies significant human rights issues, examines the freedom of local human rights defenders to conduct their work, and surveys the response of key international actors, such as the UN, the European Union, the United States, and various regional and international organizations and institutions.

The report reflects extensive investigative work that Human Rights Watch staff undertook in 2015, usually in close partnership with human rights activists in the country in question. It also reflects the work of our advocacy team, which monitors policy developments and strives to persuade governments and international institutions to curb abuses and promote human rights. Human Rights Watch publications, issued throughout the year, contain more detailed accounts of many of the issues addressed in the brief summaries in this volume. They can be found on the Human Rights Watch website, www.hrw.org.

As in past years, this report does not include a chapter on every country where Human Rights Watch works, nor does it discuss every issue of importance. The absence of a particular country or issue often simply reflects staffing limitations and should not be taken as commentary on the significance of the problem. There are many serious human rights violations that Human Rights Watch simply lacks the capacity to address.

The factors we considered in determining the focus of our work in 2015 (and hence the content of this volume) include the number of people affected and the severity of abuse, access to the country and the availability of information about it, the susceptibility of abusive forces to influence, and the importance of addressing certain thematic concerns and of reinforcing the work of local rights organizations.

The *World Report* does not have separate chapters addressing our thematic work but instead incorporates such material directly into the country entries. Please consult the Human Rights Watch website for more detailed treatment of our work on children's rights, women's rights, arms and military issues, business and human rights, health and human rights, disability rights, international justice, terrorism and counterterrorism, refugees and displaced people, and lesbian, gay, bisexual, and transgender people's rights, and for information about our international film festivals.

Danielle Haas, senior editor in the Program Office, edited the World Report. Christina Kovacs, Program Office associate, coordinated production. Grace Choi, director of Publications, supervised the print and online publications of the World Report.

Twin Threats:
How the Politics of Fear and the Crushing of Civil Society Imperil Global Rights

By Kenneth Roth

Fear stood behind many of the big human rights developments of the past year. Fear of being killed or tortured in Syria and other zones of conflict and repression drove millions from their homes. Fear of what an influx of asylum seekers could mean for their societies led many governments in Europe and elsewhere to close the gates. Fear of mounting terrorist attacks moved some political leaders to curtail rights and scapegoat refugees or Muslims. And fear of their people holding them to account led various autocrats to pursue an unprecedented global crackdown on the ability of those people to band together and make their voices heard.

In Europe and the United States, a polarizing us-versus-them rhetoric has moved from the political fringe to the mainstream. Blatant Islamophobia and shameless demonizing of refugees have become the currency of an increasingly assertive politics of intolerance.

These trends threatened human rights in two ways, one well known, the other less visible. The high-profile threat is a rollback of rights by many governments in the face of the refugee flow and the parallel decision by the self-declared Islamic State, or ISIS, to spread its attacks beyond the Middle East. The less visible threat is the effort by a growing number of authoritarian governments to restrict civil society, particularly the civic groups that monitor and speak out about those governments' conduct.

The Western governments threatening to curtail rights include many of the strongest traditional allies of the human rights cause. Their voices are needed to counter the broader effort in countries throughout the world to squeeze civil society, jeopardizing human rights and efforts to uphold them.

Blaming Refugees or Muslims while Missing the Boat on Terrorism

The estimated one million asylum seekers who have fled to Europe by sea in the past year are among the more than 60 million people now displaced by war or repression—the highest figure since World War II. The biggest driving force recently has been the brutal conflict in Syria, due in part to atrocities committed by ISIS and other armed groups but foremost to Bashar al-Assad's government indiscriminately attacking civilian population centers in opposition-held areas. Some 4 million Syrian refugees initially fled to neighboring countries, including more than 2 million to Turkey and another million to Lebanon where they now comprise nearly a quarter of the population.

The million or so reaching Europe in the past year are just a fraction of the populations of the European countries where they are heading—some 1.25 percent of the population in Germany, where the largest group sought refuge in light of Chancellor Angela Merkel's remarkable leadership and welcome, or 0.20 percent of the total European Union population, if resettlement sharing occurs.

But the uncontrolled and at times chaotic refugee flow had sparked deep concern throughout Europe even before ISIS attacked Paris in November, using at least two attackers who may have entered Europe with the refugees. That attack intensified the EU's reaction: new wire-razor fences were erected, border restrictions mushroomed, fear-mongering and Islamophobia mounted, and the EU promised Turkey €3 billion in aid with the understanding that Turkey would curtail the flow. These steps reflect the EU's longstanding effort to push responsibility for refugees to others, despite having ratified the conventions to protect refugee rights, and despite Europeans having historically benefited from refugee protection as they fled Nazism and Communism.

To a large extent, Europe's preoccupation with the new refugees as a possible terrorist threat is a dangerous distraction from its own home-grown violent extremism, given that the Paris attackers were predominantly Belgian or French citizens. The roots of radicalization are complex but relate in part to the social exclusion of immigrant communities—the persistent discrimination, hopelessness, and despair that pervade neighborhoods on the outskirts of some European cities, and particularly the disjuncture between expectations and prospects among subsequent generations.

For some—and it takes only a few—these conditions can foster political violence. How to address these challenges—let alone, how to remedy the larger and related problems of inequality and unemployment—should be major parts of today's public debate.

Instead, public discourse has been filled with voices of hatred and fear of Muslims, for whom the refugees are surrogates. These messages need to be countered foremost because they are wrong. In the modern world of easy air travel and rapidly shifting populations, Muslims are part of almost every vibrant community. Like everyone, they should not face discrimination.

Vilifying entire communities for the unacceptable actions of a few is also counterproductive for the effort to prevent terrorism. It is exactly the divisive and alienating response that terrorist groups seek to generate more recruits. And it undermines the cooperation with law enforcement efforts that is essential for preventing terrorist attacks. By virtue of their community or neighbors, Muslims are often the ones most likely to learn of a terrorist threat based on radical Islam, best suited to dissuade others from such violence, and best positioned to report those who might be planning to use it. Tarring all Muslims risks discouraging them from these important forms of law enforcement cooperation.

We should learn from the abusive and self-defeating US response to the September 11, 2001 attacks—not only the notorious torture, enforced disappearances in CIA "black sites," and long-term detention without trial at Guantanamo Bay, but also the use of immigration and "material witness" rules to detain non-citizens because of their religion or ethnicity while circumventing more rights-protective criminal procedures.

Discarding rights or scapegoating people of a certain religious or social profile harms those people while distancing them from counterterrorism efforts. It is the opposite of what is needed. As painful experience shows, the smart counterterrorism policy is the rights-respecting one.

Protecting Refugees also Protects Recipient Countries

The desperate flight of refugees and asylum seekers from unending violence and abuse in countries such as Syria, Iraq, Afghanistan, and Eritrea, and their limited chance to secure adequate work, housing, schooling, and legal status in neighboring countries, will lead many to attempt to reach Europe one way or another. The question is whether they arrive in an orderly fashion that permits security screening, or chaotically through smugglers.

The effect of European policy so far has been to leave refugees with little choice but to risk their lives at sea for a chance at asylum. With boats arriving helter-skelter at various Greek islands, it is difficult to screen systematically to stop a would-be terrorist from slipping in. A safer and more humane alternative would be for the EU to increase refugee resettlement and humanitarian visas from places of first refuge such as Lebanon or Pakistan.

The United Nations refugee agency, UNHCR, if adequately supported, could increase its capacity to screen refugees and refer them to resettlement countries. With expanded resettlement programs, Europe could signal that its doors will not shut abruptly, so there is no urgent need for refugees to board rickety boats to cross the Mediterranean, where some 3,770 drowned in 2015, a third of them children. More orderly screening would also make Europeans safer.

In addition, greater capacity to process refugees in countries of first asylum would facilitate resettlement in the countries beyond Europe that should be doing more—not only traditional recipient countries such as the United States, Canada, and Australia, but also the Gulf states and Russia.

Not every asylum seeker will choose this more orderly route, nor as a matter of right should they be required to. Its success will depend in large part on its generosity: the more that refugees feel it provides a reasonable chance of resettlement without languishing for years in a camp, and the more they can lead normal lives while waiting, the less likely they are to embark on a dangerous alternative. A viable resettlement program would help to reduce the irregular flow that is overwhelming screeners on Europe's southern shores.

The asylum seekers who manage to enter Europe via Greece or Italy face similar chaos if, as most do, they continue to make their way north. The sluggish implementation of an EU plan for organized relocation combined with the proliferation of beggar-thy-neighbor fences in countries such as Hungary, Slovenia, and Macedonia has contributed to the massive, uncontrolled flow of people that is a gift for those who want to evade law enforcement scrutiny.

Here, too, a more orderly process, with all EU countries living up to their pledges to accept asylum seekers, would permit more effective screening, while providing a safer route as an incentive for asylum seekers to participate. It would also be the first step towards shared responsibility across the EU, which is needed for the common EU asylum system to function effectively and to avoid overwhelming individual EU countries. In addition, it could help to replace the current Dublin Regulation, which imposes responsibility for asylum seekers on first-arrival countries, which include some of the EU members least capable of managing them.

Europe is not alone in adopting a counterproductive approach to refugees, especially those from Syria. In the US, some officials and politicians have been denouncing Syrian refugees as a security threat even though the handful permitted into the US have gone through an intensive two-year screening process involving numerous interviews, background checks by multiple US agencies, and biometric data. That is hardly an attractive route for would-be terrorists, who are more apt to enter as students or tourists subject to much lower scrutiny. Of all people entering the US, refugees are the most heavily vetted.

Yet, 30 governors in the US tried to bar Syrian refugees from being resettled in their states. The idea was even floated (though broadly rejected) of blocking Muslim non-citizens from entering the country altogether. Canada, under its new prime minister, Justin Trudeau, offered a very different initial response: accelerating the reception of 25,000 Syrian refugees and spreading them to a largely warm welcome across all 10 provinces. Setting a tone of respect over fear and distrust, he personally greeted the first planeload of refugees at the airport.

Mass Surveillance Versus Smart Responses to Terrorism

Beyond scapegoating refugees, policymakers in the US and Europe have used the terrorist threat as an opportunity to seek greater law-enforcement powers, including mass surveillance, beyond the formidable array of tools that they already deploy.

In the US, CIA Director John Brennan used the Paris attacks to decry recent technical and legal restrictions on intelligence agencies' ability to engage in the mass collection of phone metadata, even though those restrictions are modest given the scope of mass surveillance revealed in 2013 by former National Security Agency contractor Edward Snowden. Moreover, two independent oversight bodies with access to classified information concluded that such metadata had not been essential to foiling a single terrorist plot, despite the enormous invasion of privacy involved in scooping up these often-intimate details of modern life.

FBI Director James Comey also used the Paris attacks to revive efforts to require Internet companies to include "back doors" to the strongest forms of encryption they use. Companies have strived to build more secure systems following public dismay at Snowden's revelations. But there is no back door that only the good guys can exploit. Criminals would inevitably have a field day, endangering critical infrastructure and the sensitive communications of ordinary users. And the terrorists will inevitably find their own encryption methods even if not from the mass market.

Some European officials, too, appear tempted to increase mass surveillance. France adopted a new intelligence law that bolstered mass surveillance powers. The United Kingdom is in the process of doing the same. Yet the perpetrators in a number of attacks in Europe have included people who were known to police but not pursued due to lack of police resources.

French President François Hollande seemed to recognize this problem by promising to add 8,500 more law enforcement officers to pursue leads, rather than simply accumulating more mass data without the means to follow up. Still, after the Paris attacks France also embraced potentially indiscriminate policing techniques, with its president declaring a state of emergency that allows security forces to conduct warrantless searches and arrests. The lack of court oversight makes profiling all the more likely—in this case of young Muslim men. Police stops based on such profiling have long plagued the very populations that should be cultivated to help counter violence.

Civil Society Empowered by Social Media

While Europe and the US worry about the nexus of refugees and terrorism, political and economic pressures have led authoritarian governments to fret about the combination of civil society and social media.

A vigorous civil society helps to ensure that governments serve their people. Isolated individuals find it difficult to speak loudly enough to be heard. Joining together in civic groups amplifies their voices and leverages their ability to influence governments. Civil society—the nongovernmental groups and associations that enable people to band together on matters of mutual concern—is an essential part of any democracy worth its name. Independent and vigorous civic groups help to guarantee that governments build schools, ensure access to health care, protect the environment, and take countless other steps to pursue their vision of the common good.

Yet some officials see popular input not as a guide to policy, but as a threat. When leaders are primarily interested in advancing themselves, their families, or their cronies, the last thing they want is an empowered public, able to link together and combine resources to investigate, publicize, protest, and rectify government corruption, malfeasance, or incompetence.

In a different era, autocrats might have dispensed with any pretense of democratic rule, but these days at least a facade of democracy is often a prerequisite for legitimacy. Yet just as authoritarian rulers have learned to manipulate elections to ensure their political longevity, so they are now working between elections to prevent an empowered public from impeding their authoritarian aims. By closing the political space in which civic groups operate, autocrats are trying to suck the oxygen from organized efforts to challenge or even criticize their self-serving reign.

In recent years, social media have made this competition between state and society more free-wheeling and volatile. Until recently, civil society had to work through traditional media to make its voice heard widely. The finite number of traditional media outlets in any country made censorship easier.

Today, the rise of social media, especially when readily available on mobile devices, means that people can bypass traditional media and speak to large num-

bers without a journalist intermediary. The result has greatly enhanced civil society's ability to be heard and, ultimately, to demand change. The impact of social
media is not all positive—users include purveyors of hate as well as "trolls"
funded or inspired by governments to reinforce official propaganda. Still, a public able to broadcast its concerns through social media is an important supple-
ment to mainstream media for challenging the government line.

The most dramatic manifestations of this evolution were the Arab uprisings that
began in late 2010, in 2014 the Maidan revolution in Ukraine and the Occupy
Central movement in Hong Kong. Each demonstrated the synergy between a rest-
less public and civil society activists adept at using social media to mobilize
people in the streets.

But the combination of civil society and social media has also been felt in less
spectacular ways. From China to Venezuela to Malaysia, it has forced governments that prefer to rule unconstrained from above to face pressure to be more
accountable to the people below. Repression, corruption, or simple indifference
are at greater risk when readily scrutinized by a more connected, better organized society.

The Autocrats' Reaction

Disinclined to accept such popular limits on their rule, autocrats are fighting
back, in what has emerged as an intense and self-reinforcing trend. As repressive governments learn from each other, refine their techniques, and pass on
lessons learned, they have launched the broadest backlash against civil society
in a generation.

The most common tools these days are efforts to deprive civic groups of their
right to seek funding abroad when domestic sources are unavailable and to
smother civil society with vague and pliable regulations. At risk is the promise of
more representative government that social media had brought to its more empowered civil society users.

To note this worrisome trend is hardly to spell the demise of civil society. Just as
the great potential of an empowered people has pressed terrified autocrats to try
to return society to a more atomized, malleable form, so that potential enables
civil society to fight back. But it is far from clear who will prevail in this duel be-

tween peoples' quest for accountable government and autocrats' desire for unfettered rule.

Key third parties in the contest are the many governments that profess belief in the principles of human rights underlying democratic rule. Their willingness to adhere to principle over the temptation to accommodate rich or powerful autocrats can be decisive in determining whether dictatorship or rights-respecting representative government prevails. But as Western powers violate rights in addressing refugees or terrorism, their ability to uphold the broader set of rights is compromised.

Reasons for Covering Up

When you scratch the surface, efforts to suppress civil society are often led by governments that have something to hide. For each offender, there are failures of governance that officials would prefer not be discussed, a record of misconduct they want kept in the shadows, a subject they want changed. Because restricting civil society is about avoiding accountability, the topics that governments choose to suppress are a good indicator of their deepest fears.

China and Russia, perhaps the two most influential offenders, are good examples. Each government made an implicit pact with its people: in return for strict limits on political participation, they promised rapid economic growth and enhanced personal opportunity. They are now having trouble keeping their side of the bargain.

In part that is because the lack of public scrutiny has led to poor economic policies. Russia's elite milked oil and gas revenue without the diversification of its hydrocarbon-dependent economy that more critical public scrutiny might have encouraged. The economy grew more precarious in the face of plummeting oil and gas prices coupled with sanctions imposed in response to the Kremlin's military activities in Ukraine.

In China, economic growth is hobbled by the same pathologies as the political system: the impulse to whitewash seemingly controversial information, such as how to respond to the August stock market plunge; the reliance on a court system that does the Communist Party's bidding rather than impartially adjudicating contracts or other disputes; and an anti-corruption campaign that doubles as a political purge.

These top-down policies, unconstrained by independent public debate, have contributed to economic slowdowns if not recessions. And as waning fortunes raise questions about the rulers' efficacy, both Russia and China have embarked on crackdowns not seen in decades.

First in response to the anti-Putin protests in 2011 and 2012, and accelerating as the Kremlin stoked nationalism to boost its vision of a new identity for Russia, the Kremlin has been crushing Russian civil society, one of the most important elements to have emerged from the demise of Soviet rule. The new, poisonous atmosphere helped the Kremlin to divert attention as Russia's economic woes deepened.

Meanwhile the Chinese government, recognizing at some level the need to meet people's rising expectations, speaks of the rule of law and selectively prosecutes officials for corruption, but is also arresting the lawyers and activists who have the audacity to pursue these goals outside of government control. Needless to say, a government-manipulated legal system is not the rule of law, while a selective government crackdown on corruption undermines the much-needed establishment of a functional, independent legal system.

Similar trends are evident elsewhere. For example, one feature often found behind efforts to repress civil society are officials' attempts to evade the threat of prosecution or other consequences of illegal activity:

- Turkey's then prime minister (now president), Recep Tayyip Erdoğan, began his crackdown—the most intense in at least a decade—after large street protests against his increasingly autocratic rule. He reinforced it when audio tapes emerged suggesting that he and his family were directly involved in corruption. When his party, in office for three terms, received a reduced plurality at the polls in June, the president intensified the crackdown on media and political opponents and was able to secure victory in a rerun of the election in November.

- Some senior officials in Kenya have attacked civil society organizations for supporting prosecution by the International Criminal Court (ICC) of those who allegedly directed the 2007-2008 post-electoral violence, including

Deputy President William Ruto. Kenya has also targeted civic groups that have documented security force abuses in the context of counterterrorism efforts against increased gun and grenade attacks in various parts of the country.

- Sudan expelled humanitarian organizations from Darfur in response to the March 2009 ICC arrest warrant for President Omar al-Bashir, and shut down groups that publicly promote justice and human rights.

- President Jacob Zuma's government in South Africa targeted the group that had obtained a court ruling against its welcoming of Bashir, whose ICC arrest warrants the government openly flouted.

- As global outrage mounted over its expanding illegal settlements, Israel adopted a law—affirmed in 2015 year in most elements by the Supreme Court—that could be used to penalize civil society groups, as well as individuals calling for cutting economic or other ties with settlements or Israel.

Other governments have acted when elections or term limits threaten their continuation in power:

- In Burundi, the government launched intense and often violent attacks on civil society after widespread protests against President Pierre Nkurunziza's decision to seek a constitutionally questionable third term. Most notably, a gunman shot and seriously wounded the country's foremost human rights defender, Pierre Claver Mbonimpa. Two of his close relatives were killed in separate incidents.

- In the Democratic Republic of Congo, human rights defenders and pro-democracy youth activists have been jailed, beaten, and threatened after organizing peaceful protests and speaking out against the possible extension of President Joseph Kabila's term beyond the constitution's two-term limit. Government officials claimed without foundation that the activists were plotting "terrorist activities" or "violent insurrection," while security forces used lethal force to disrupt the groups' peaceful demonstrations.

- Venezuelan President Nicolás Maduro harassed, arrested, and demonized critics and civil society groups in the months leading up to legislative elections—which he ultimately lost, most observers believe, because of his mismanagement of the economy.

- Ecuadorian police used excessive force against citizens demonstrating against a proposed constitutional amendment that would allow unlimited presidential re-election. President Rafael Correa's response was not to investigate the abusive police officers but to congratulate them for their "professionalism."

Some governments seek to exploit natural resources unimpeded by popular input or independent oversight. For example:

- Oil-rich Azerbaijan has been imprisoning civil society leaders to avoid public unrest over its eye-popping corruption and official mismanagement. Europe has been too busy buying its oil and gas and wooing it from Russia's influence to mount much protest.

- Uzbekistan, whose officials personally profit from the cotton sector, has attacked people trying to document and report on forced labor within the industry. The World Bank has boosted its investment in the industry, but has limited its expression of concern to private conversations of questionable utility.

Behind these varied motivations for cracking down on civil society is the autocrats' view equating organized public debate with a political threat. Better to prevent or hinder people from joining together, these governments seem to reason, than risk their discontent being widely heard and embraced.

From this fear of unfettered public debate comes a series of devices that have been used to restrict or stifle civil society. These include threats, violence, arbitrary arrests, trumped-up prosecutions, and two increasingly common techniques: restricting the right to seek foreign funding, and imposing arbitrary and oppressive regulations.

Restricting the Right to Seek Financial Support

Many countries are too poor to have a pool of donors capable of significant financial contributions to civic groups. Even when individuals are wealthy enough to make such gifts, autocrats can often dissuade them by attacking their business interests. Threatening a tax investigation, withholding necessary licenses, or restricting business with the government usually suffices to discourage financial support for groups critical of the authorities.

When would-be domestic donors are too frightened or lack the means to give very much, civic groups naturally exercise their right to seek support abroad. That right, in turn, has become a favorite target of repressive governments. Their first priority has been to cut off foreign sources of funding for groups that defend human rights or hold the government to account.

India, its democratic traditions notwithstanding, has been a long-time practitioner of this technique through its Foreign Contribution Regulation Act, which requires government approval before any civic group can receive a contribution from abroad. The government's willingness to allow such contributions tends to bear an inverse relationship to the "sensitivity" of the group's work. Service-delivery groups operate relatively unhindered while human rights groups are often restrained. Under Prime Minister Narendra Modi, environmental groups have been particularly victimized because of perceived challenges to official development plans. Another activist who was targeted was known for her work on the anti-Muslim riots of 2002 in Gujarat in which then Chief Minister Modi was implicated.

Russia has applied such restrictions aggressively—first tarring Russian groups that accept contributions from abroad as "foreign agents" (which in Russian has the unsavory connotation of "traitor" or "spy"), then banning certain donors as "undesirable foreign organizations" with criminal penalties applicable to anyone who cooperates with them.

Other former Soviet states are now emulating Russia. Kyrgyzstan's parliament is considering its own "foreign agents" law, which borrows heavily from Russia's. Kazakhstan adopted legislation that requires funding for civic groups to be channeled through a single government-appointed "operator" with discretion over the dispersal of funds. Belarus requires registering all foreign funding with a government agency that can reject it if its purpose is not on a narrow officially approved list. Azerbaijan opened a criminal investigation into a handful of the most prominent foreign donors, froze the bank accounts of dozens of their grantees, jailed key veterans of the human rights movement, and required government licensing of all foreign donors and official approval of each funded project.

Some of China's most important civil society organizations—particularly those that try to uphold human rights—are largely dependent on outside funding, but the government is expected soon to adopt a foreign NGOs management law that in all likelihood would enable it to exert tighter control of overseas sources of funding. Organizations that engage in advocacy rather than service delivery would be particularly vulnerable.

Besides India, Ethiopia pioneered such techniques in 2009 by restricting the foreign funding of any group working on human rights and governance to 10 percent of its revenue, effectively shutting down most monitoring organizations. Kenya, claiming that backers of ICC prosecution are promoting a "foreign agenda," is considering a similar 15 percent cap. Angola has banned funding from foreign entities that are not approved by a government body. Venezuela's Supreme Court ruled in 2010 that any group receiving foreign funding could be prosecuted for "treason," while the pro-government majority in the National Assembly prohibited international assistance to any group that would (in a transparent display of its fear) "defend political rights" or "monitor the performance of public bodies." Morocco is prosecuting five civil society activists for "harming internal security" for having accepted foreign funding to organize a workshop to empower citizen journalism through a phone app.

The Rationalization of Restrictions

Autocrats favor restricting access to foreign donors for civic groups that monitor their conduct because they can dress it up with nationalist rhetoric: how dare those foreigners "interfere" in our internal affairs! Yet the same governments that attack civic groups for seeking foreign contributions actively promote foreign investment and foreign trade deals. Many also eagerly solicit foreign aid to themselves and encourage it to service-delivery groups. And some engage in the same efforts to influence public debates abroad that they want to prohibit civil society from pursuing at home.

This inconsistency cannot be explained by the argument that civil society is somehow inappropriately engaged in public affairs. Businesses routinely lobby for beneficial laws and regulations and take part in debates about public policy. Foreign aid often goes to the essence of governmental functions, typically with conditions attached. Indeed, the amounts that civic groups seek tend to be miniscule compared with the foreign money flooding into a country through investment, trade, or aid.

So why is civil society singled out? Because of its capacity to mobilize a citizenry to challenge governmental malfeasance—especially when the message is amplified on social media. And where media are muzzled, as is often the case in these authoritarian contexts, civil society is the only remaining actor with the capacity to press officials to serve their citizens rather than themselves. An attack on the right of organizations to seek funding abroad is really an attack on organized efforts to hold government to account.

Governments offer various rationales for depriving civic groups of their right to seek funds abroad, often by comparing their restrictions to those in established democracies. For example, some democracies bar political candidates from receiving foreign contributions. Yet the restrictions preventing civic groups from receiving funds from abroad extend well beyond the electoral context. They limit civil society's ability to organize and speak out on a wide variety of issues that have nothing to do with elections.

Neither international human rights law nor any proper understanding of democracy permits it, as UN Special Rapporteur Maina Kiai explained in a recent report. Free popular participation is essential for citizens to give nuance to their periodic act of voting, enabling them to speak out and be heard on the plethora of issues that their officials address between elections.

Some autocrats also invoke laws in democracies such as the US Foreign Agents Registration Act, which requires those acting on behalf of a foreign government to register as its agent. Yet that law addresses only people or entities that act as "agents" of a foreign government or at its "direction or control." Few if any contributions to civic groups are so directive. There is no agency relationship that would warrant special disclosure, let alone prohibition. And in many cases, the foreign funder is not a government at all but a private individual or foundation.

Some governments, including Cambodia, Egypt, Tajikistan, and India, justify restrictions on foreign contributions to civic groups as necessary to fight terrorism. Countries such as China, Pakistan, and Bangladesh also invoked the terror threat in introducing draft measures containing similar foreign-donor restrictions. But since terrorist groups can as easily set up businesses as voluntary organizations to finance their crimes, the differential treatment again reveals other concerns.

The ultimate irony is that many of the same governments that restrict civil society's right to seek funding abroad themselves spend copiously on lobbyists or public relations firms to spruce up their own images overseas. Governments such as those of Russia, China, Egypt, and Azerbaijan have spent millions of dollars in Washington alone to put a benign face on their repression, while starving civil society as it tries to alleviate that repression at home. Their concern about cross-border funding influencing the public debate thus seems to depend on whether the funding contributes to scrutinizing or reinforcing the government line.

In sum, efforts to restrict civil society's access to foreign donors is not about transparency or good governance. It is about avoiding organized oversight of governance, about blocking what is often the sole source of independent funding for such efforts when domestic sources do not exist or have been scared off.

If governments really want to shelter their societies from foreign funds, they could emulate the reclusiveness of North Korea. In fact, they want a selective cutoff, enabling commercial funds and aid to themselves but restricting funds that might be used to hold them accountable. Any such governmental distinction between commercial and charitable funds, or between aid to themselves and aid to civic groups, should be seen for what it is: an effort to block their citizens' rights to freedom of expression and association, and the accountable government they foster.

Death by Regulation

Beyond restricting funds, autocrats are increasingly adopting laws and regulations to rein in civil society. These rules have the advantage of seeming ordinary, routine, apolitical. And some indeed are unobjectionable—for example, those requiring honest and transparent budgeting, respect for labor laws, or simple administrative registration. Yet autocrats seeking to stifle civil society have used legal constraints to accomplish far more: to undermine the very independence of civic groups.

A common method is to claim that civil society jeopardizes some vague, government-defined sense of the common good—usually meaning the government's continuation in power or policies favored by a powerful constituency.

- Russia criminalized revelations about military losses during "special operations," which just happened to include the Kremlin's military activities in eastern Ukraine. Critics of Russia's annexation of Crimea also faced prosecution.

- China enacted a series of laws on state security, cybersecurity, and counterterrorism that conflate peaceful criticism with threats to national security. The proposed Foreign NGO Management Law would broadly preclude civic groups from "endangering China's national interests" or "society's public interest," as well as "public order and customs."

- Kazakhstan has criminalized "inciting social, national, clan, racial, class, or religious discord," which it has used repeatedly to silence critics.

- Hungary used "fraud" charges to attack funding groups that addressed corruption and human rights.

- Turkey jailed journalists and closed media groups that showed themselves willing to scrutinize government policy and corruption, or report evidence of arms transfers to Syrian opposition groups.

- Uganda's parliament adopted an act that, if signed into law, would permit up to three-year prison sentences for leaders of independent groups that shirk broad and undefined "special obligations," including engaging in any act that is "prejudicial to the interests of Uganda or the dignity of the people of Uganda."

- Sudanese journalists and civil society activists who voice dissent face charges of "crimes against the state" that carry the death sentence.

- Cambodia shuts groups that "jeopardize peace, stability and public order or harm the national security, national unity, culture and traditions of Cambodian society."

- A Moroccan court ordered the closure of an association that promoted the rights of the population of the Ifni region on the grounds that it harmed Morocco's "territorial integrity."

- Ecuadoran President Rafael Correa gave his government the power to dissolve groups that "compromise public peace." It then used this power to shut down an environmental group challenging oil drilling in the ecologically sensitive Amazon.

- Bolivian President Evo Morales has signed a law and issued a decree in 2013 granting his government the power to dissolve any civil society organization whose legal representative is criminally sanctioned for carrying out activities that "undermine security or public order."

As Western governments intensify their efforts to stop terrorism, others have become adept at using vague language about terrorism to deflect criticism of their crackdown on civil society.

- Egyptian President Abdel Fattah al-Sisi said that crushing the Muslim Brotherhood and the threat it once posed to him at the ballot box is really about fighting terrorism. His ploy is backed with billions of dollars from the Gulf monarchs, who are terrified by a movement that combines the political Islam they claim to uphold with the electoral means they find anathema.

- Kenya included two human rights groups on a list of suspected supporters of terrorism. The two organizations documented abuses by security forces during counterterrorism operations. The organizations had to go to court for a judge to clear them of any links to terrorism and unfreeze their bank accounts.

- A draft Chinese law defines terrorism to include "thought, speech, or behavior" that attempt to "influence national policy-making." It also includes a catch-all prohibition of "other terrorist activities" that could be used to deem any activity a terrorist offense.

- A counterterrorism bill under consideration in Brazil contains overbroad and vague language that criminalizes "advocating terrorism" without any explanation of what that entails. Another provision could be interpreted to allow the prosecution as terrorists of protesters for "taking over" roads and buildings.

Behind these efforts to restrict civic groups to government views of the public good is a misconception of the role of civil society. In a rights-respecting society, people should be free to band together to pursue their own conception of the public good, subject only to limitations preventing direct harm to others. Many of these goals will differ from a government's; indeed, that is the idea. A government is most likely to meet the needs of its people if they are free to debate what those needs are and how best to pursue them. People joining together to advance their points of view, in whatever variations and permutations, is an essential part of the process.

When governments use vague laws about the public good or the national interest to constrain civil society, they restrict the scope of public debate—both through their own censorship and the self-censorship of groups struggling to understand what statements or activities are allowed. That not only violates the rights of those who want to join with others to make their voices heard. It also results in a government that is less likely to serve its people and more likely to serve the private interests of its leaders and their most powerful allies.

Convenient Homophobia

An increasingly popular method to crack down on civil society is to target organizations of lesbian, gay, bisexual, and transgender (LGBT) people or those that advocate on their behalf. Some repressive governments claim, much like their calls to limit the right to seek foreign funding, that LGBT people are alien to their culture, an imposition from the West. But no Western country is "exporting" gays or lesbians; they have always been in every country, with their visibility largely a product of the extent of local repression. The only imposition going on is the local government imposing dominant views about gender and sexuality on a vulnerable minority.

Like broader attacks on civil society, attacks on LGBT groups tend to be most intense when governments are most intent on changing the subject. Some of the world's most vocal leaders on repressive LGBT legislation—Russia's Vladimir Putin, Uganda's Yoweri Museveni, Nigeria's former President Goodluck Jonathan, and Gambia's Yahya Jammeh—tend to be under political pressure for failures of governance. Portraying themselves as guardians of "traditional values" against gays is a convenient way to avoid discussion of their own mismanagement. But because that ploy is unlikely to work indefinitely, official homophobia is often a prelude to a broader crackdown on civil society, the proverbial canary in the coal mine.

Closed Societies

The most severe autocrats do not settle for limiting civil society; they bar or dismantle it altogether. In countries of severe repression—North Korea, Uzbekistan, Turkmenistan, or Eritrea—there is no independent civil society to speak of. Organized commentary on government conduct is out of the question. In many other countries—Bahrain, Belarus, Egypt, Rwanda, Saudi Arabia, Sudan, the United Arab Emirates, Vietnam—forming a civil group to hold the government to account is a recipe for prison.

Yet today, many of the governments leading the charge to repress civil society want the benefits of calling themselves democratically accountable but not the actual organized oversight that civic groups foster. They are often the ones most likely to resort to the subterfuge of limiting access to foreign funds or imposing vague constraining regulations. Governments committed to a vision of democracy based on human rights should make clear that they see through this subterfuge and will condition normal relations on its end.

Rights as the Way Forward

As the global community becomes more connected—as travel and communication become easier—human rights issues rarely present themselves in the isolation of a single country. Atrocities in Syria or Afghanistan spark refugee crises in Europe. Europe's response, or lack thereof, affects the ability to build societies elsewhere that respect people of different cultures, religion, and sexual orientation. The ease and democratization of modern communication—the Internet and especially social media—challenge governments the world over to accept accountability to their people in a more active and piercing form.

Given the tumult in the world today, meeting these challenges is hardly easy. Change can appear threatening, whether to a community grasping nostalgically at memories of greater homogeneity, a nation confronting increased insecurity, or a dictator clinging to power.

But if the aim is to ensure communities that respect all their members, nations that secure the best strategy for their defense, or governments that most effectively serve their people, the wisdom enshrined in international human rights law provides indispensable guidance. We abandon it at our peril.

Kenneth Roth is the executive director of Human Rights Watch.

Rights in Transition:
Making Legal Recognition for Transgender People a Global Priority

By Neela Ghoshal and Kyle Knight

The process is as universal as it gets: when a baby is born, a doctor, parent, or birth attendant announces the arrival of a "girl" or "boy." That split-second assignment dictates multiple aspects of our lives. It is also something that most of us never question.

But some people do. Their gender evolves differently from their girl/boy birth assignment and might not fit rigid traditional notions of female or male.

Gender development should have no bearing on whether someone can enjoy fundamental rights, like the ability to be recognized by their government or to access health care, education, or employment. But for transgender people, it does—to a humiliating, violent, and sometimes lethal degree.

The Trans Murder Monitoring Project, an initiative that collects and analyzes reports of transgender homicides worldwide, recorded 1,731 murders of transgender people globally between 2007 and 2014. Many were of a shockingly brutal nature, sometimes involving torture and mutilation.

Outright violence is not the only threat to the lives of transgender people. They are as much as 50 times more likely to acquire HIV than the population as a whole, in part because stigma and discrimination create barriers to accessing health services. Studies in the United States, Canada, and Europe have found high rates of suicide attempts among transgender people, a response to systematic marginalization and humiliation.

Several countries, including Malaysia, Kuwait, and Nigeria, enforce laws that prohibit "posing" as the opposite sex—outlawing transgender people's very existence. In scores of other countries, transgender people are arrested under laws that criminalize same-sex conduct.

This data only gives a glimpse of the horrific variants of violence and discrimination transgender people face. Absent legal recognition in the gender with which they identify, and associated rights and protections, every juncture of daily life when documents are requested or appearance is scrutinized becomes fraught with potential for violence and humiliation, driving many transgender people into the shadows.

The demand for legal gender recognition provokes moral panic in many governments. But it is a crucial fight to wage. If transgender communities are to thrive, and if the rights to privacy, free expression, and dignity are to be upheld for all, the human rights movement needs to prioritize eliminating abusive and discriminatory procedures that arbitrarily impede the right to recognition. Governments should acknowledge that the state should no longer be in the business of denying or unjustly restricting people's fundamental right to their gender identity.[1]

Turning Tide

In recent years, transgender people around the world have made tremendous strides toward achieving legal recognition.

Argentina broke ground in 2012 with a law that is considered the gold standard for legal gender recognition: anyone over the age of 18 can choose their gender identity, undergo gender reassignment, and revise official documents without any prior judicial or medical approval, and children can do so with the consent of their legal representatives or through summary proceedings before a judge.

In the subsequent three years, four more countries—Colombia, Denmark, Ireland, and Malta—explicitly eliminated significant barriers to legal gender recognition. This evolution sets them apart from countries that either do not allow a person to change their "male/female" designation at all, or only allow them to do so when certain conditions have been met, which may include surgery, forced sterilization, psychiatric evaluation, lengthy waiting periods, and divorce. For the first time, people can change their gender marker on documents simply by filing the appropriate forms.

This progress, long in the making, has often come on the backs of courageous individuals willing to have their lives and identities adjudicated by often unfriendly courts.

For instance, Ireland's 2015 Gender Recognition Bill was the product of a 22-year legal fight by Lydia Foy, a now-retired dentist. Braving a gauntlet of legal procedures, she made her case to be recognized as a woman before Ireland's High Court in 1997, and again in 2007, backed by domestic and international human rights bodies that called on Ireland to institute a gender recognition procedure based on identity and human rights, not surgeries and expert opinions. Despite the consistent pressure, it was not until 2015, after an overwhelming victory on a same-sex marriage referendum, that the government instituted identity-based legal gender recognition.

In South Asia—where hijras, an identity category for people assigned male at birth who develop a feminine gender identity, have long been recognized culturally, if not legally—activists have pursued a related aim: the formal recognition of a third gender. Hijras' traditional status, which included bestowing blessings at weddings, had provided some protection and a veneer of respect. But rather than being viewed as equal to others before the law, they were regarded as exotic and marginal—an existence dictated by boundaries and limitations, not rights.

Nepal's Supreme Court, in a sweeping 2007 ruling, ordered the government to recognize a third gender category based on an individual's "self-feeling." The ruling rested largely on the freshly minted Yogyakarta Principles—the first document to codify international principles on sexual orientation, gender identity, and human rights. Armed with the ruling, activists successfully advocated with government agencies to include the third gender category on voter rolls (2010), the federal census (2011), citizenship documents (2013), and passports (2015).

Similarly, in 2009, the Supreme Court in Pakistan called for a third gender category to be recognized, and in Bangladesh, the cabinet issued a 2013 decree recognizing hijras as their own legal gender. In 2014, India's Supreme Court issued an expansive judgment recognizing a third gender, affirming "the right of every person to choose their gender," and calling for transgender peoples' inclusion in state welfare programs.

In a few countries, the very purpose of gender markers is now being interrogated. New Zealand and Australia now offer the option to have gender listed as "unspecified" on official documents, while the Dutch parliament has begun considering whether the government should record a person's gender on official identification documents at all.

A Matter of Dignity

The right to recognition as a person before the law is guaranteed in numerous human rights treaties, and is a fundamental aspect of affirming the dignity and worth of each person. However, even in countries that allow for people to be recognized in the gender with which they identify, the requisite procedures may subject applicants to humiliating and harmful treatment.

For example, transgender people in Ukraine who wish to be legally recognized must undergo a mandatory in-patient psychiatric evaluation lasting up to 45 days to confirm or reject a diagnosis of "transsexualism"; coerced sterilization; numerous medical tests, which often require extensive time commitment, expense, and travel, and that are unrelated to the legal gender recognition procedure requirements itself; and a humiliating in-person evaluation by a government commission to further confirm the diagnosis of "transsexualism" and authorize the change in legal documents. These procedures fail to respect the right to health and may expose transgender people to prohibited inhuman or degrading treatment.

Tina T., a 38-year-old Ukrainian transgender woman, told Human Rights Watch that during her stay in a psychiatric institution, the staff forced her to live in a high security male ward with bars and metal doors. She said she was only allowed to walk around the perimeter of a 30 square meter yard for 45 minutes each day; the restrooms did not have locks, making her feel unsafe; and doctors did not allow her to take female hormones while she was under their care.

It may seem obvious: subjecting people to unwanted or unnecessary medical procedures has no place in a recognition process for an identity. However, even in countries that consider themselves progressive with regards to LGBT rights, including some Western European and Latin American countries and the US, transgender people are still forced to undergo demeaning procedures—even sterilization—to change the gender marker on their identity documents. These negative consequences of seeking legal gender recognition seriously and harmfully limit individuals' ability to access crucial services and live safely, free of violence and discrimination.

A Gateway to Other Rights

Legal gender recognition is also an essential element of other fundamental rights—including the right to privacy, the right to freedom of expression, the right to be free from arbitrary arrest, and rights related to employment, education, health, security, access to justice, and the ability to move freely.

A Delhi High Court ruling in October 2015 lay out the intrinsic link between the right to legal gender recognition and other rights. Affirming a 19-year-old transgender man's right to recourse against harassment by his parents and the police, Justice Siddharth Mridul wrote:

> Gender identity and sexual orientation are fundamental to the right of self-determination, dignity and freedom. These freedoms lie at the heart of personal autonomy and freedom of individuals. A transgender [person's] sense or experience of gender is integral to their core personality and sense of being. Insofar as, I understand the law, everyone has a fundamental right to be recognized in their chosen gender.

Employment and Housing

Transgender people routinely report that they are turned down for jobs and housing when it becomes evident that their appearance does not match the gender marker on their official documents. In the US, a 2011 national survey by the National Center on Transgender Equality and the National LGBTQ Taskforce found that among respondents whose identification documents did not "match" the gender that they presented with, 64 percent said they had experienced discrimination in hiring, as compared to 52 percent of respondents who had updated the gender marker on their documents. Similar evidence of discrimination was found when transgender people without "matching" documents sought to rent or buy a home or apartment.

Sharan, a transgender woman in Malaysia, told Human Rights Watch that although she presents as a woman, the absence of legal gender recognition in

Malaysia means she must submit male identity documents when applying for a job. She described her experience at job interviews:

> When I go for an interview, if the interviewer is male, the first thing he asks me is, 'Are your breasts real? When did you decide to change?' I explain I'm a transsexual woman. 'Do you have a penis or a vagina? Do you have sex with men or women? Which toilet do you go to? Did you do your operation? Why did you choose to take hormones?' It's nothing relevant to the job..... And then they tell you they'll call you in two weeks, but you don't get any phone calls.

Education

Transgender children and young adults face abuses in school settings ranging from sexual assault, to bullying, to being forced to attend a single-sex school or wear a uniform based on the gender marker assigned at birth.

In Japan, junior high and high school students told Human Rights Watch that strict male/female school uniform policies that often do not allow children to change uniforms without a diagnosis of "Gender Identity Disorder" caused them extreme anxiety, leading to extended and repeated absence from school and even dropouts. Some said the country's legal gender recognition procedure, which mandates sex reassignment surgery, put pressure on them to undergo the full procedure before they became adults so that they could enter university or apply for jobs according to their gender identity.

In Malaysia, the Education Department of the Federal Territory (Kuala Lumpur) has an explicitly discriminatory policy that calls for punishment, including caning, suspension, and expulsion, for homosexuality and "gender confusion."

Malta has become a pioneer in recognizing transgender children's right to education: following its April 2015 legal gender recognition legislation, the government launched comprehensive guidelines for schools to accommodate gender non-conforming students, including through addressing issues related to uniforms and toilets.

Health Care

Absent identity documents that match their gender presentation, transgender people who seek health care are subjected to invasive questioning and humiliation. Erina, a transgender woman in Malaysia, was hospitalized for two days in 2011 for a high fever. She told Human Rights Watch that she was placed in a male ward because of the "male" gender marker on her identity card, despite her request to be placed in a female ward. Doctors and nurses quizzed her about her gender identity, asking questions unrelated to the condition for which she was seeking treatment.

Where transgender identities are criminalized, access to health care is even more fraught. In Kuwait, transgender women told Human Rights Watch that medical doctors have reported them to police after noting the gender on their government-issued IDs does not match their appearance and presentation, effectively limiting their access to health care.

After Uganda passed its notorious Anti-Homosexuality Act in February 2014, law enforcement officials and ordinary citizens targeted transgender people alongside lesbian, gay and bisexual people. Jay M., a transgender man, told Human Rights Watch that when he sought treatment for a fever,

> The doctor asked me, 'But are you a woman or a man?' I said, 'That doesn't matter, but what I can tell you is I'm a trans man.' He said, 'What's a trans man? You know we don't offer services to gay people here. You people are not even supposed to be in our community. I can even call the police and report you....'

In the end, Jay paid the doctor a 50,000 Ugandan shillings (about US$14) bribe and fled the office.

Travel

Simply moving from one place to another can be a dangerous and humiliating experience for people whose documents do not match their expression. The stakes are high, particularly for international travel, and range from fraud accusations and exposure to intense scrutiny and humiliation.

A transgender woman in the Netherlands told Human Rights Watch: "When I travel internationally, they often take me out of the queue for questioning: people think I have stolen my passport." A transgender man in Kazakhstan explained: "Every time I have gone through the airport in Almaty—all four times—the security officers have humiliated me." He described how "first, the guard looks at my documents and is confused; next he looks at me and asks what's going on; then I tell him I'm transgender; then I show him my medical certificates; then he gathers his colleagues around, everyone he can find, and they all look and point and laugh at me and then eventually let me go."

United Nations human rights experts have condemned such targeting of transgender people in security processes.

Access to Police Protection and Justice

The lack of basic recognition before the law impedes access to recourse for crimes, a significant problem for a population exposed to shockingly high rates of violence. Carrying documents that do not match appearance can mean abuse gets even worse when trying to report it to authorities.

In Mombasa, Kenya, a transgender woman, Bettina, told Human Rights Watch that vandals destroyed the market stall where she sold food during a wave of homophobic and transphobic attacks in October 2014. When Bettina reported the crime to police, they quizzed her about her gender identity and refused to give her a case number to follow up on her situation. "I left, because there was nothing there for me," she said.

Freedom from Violence

In many countries, transgender people in detention are placed in cells with persons of a gender that they do not identify with, exposing them to abuse and sexual violence. International guidelines on detention issued by the UN Office on Drugs and Crime warn that, "where transgender prisoners are accommodated according to their birth gender, especially when male to female transgender prisoners are placed with men due to their birth gender being male, this paves the way to sexual abuse and rape."

In the US, where most correctional facilities assign detainees to wards based on gender assigned at birth rather than identity, data indicates that one in three transgender detainees are sexually assaulted in prison.

Privacy

A government's refusal to recognize people in the gender with which they identify can amount to violation of the right to privacy. In a 2002 case in the United Kingdom, the European Court of Human Rights held that refusal to change identification documents and legal identities could amount to discrimination and violate the right to respect for private lives. In another case in 2003, that court found that Germany had failed to respect "the applicant's freedom to define herself as a female person, one of the most basic essentials of self-determination."

A Basic Right to Freedom

In too many countries, transgender people are criminalized simply for being who they are. Malaysia's state Sharia laws, which prohibit "a male person posing as woman" and, in some states, "a female person posing as a man," have resulted in countless arrests of transgender people for the simple act of walking down the street wearing clothing that state religious officials do not find appropriate to their sex as assigned at birth. They are sentenced to imprisonment, fines, or mandatory "counseling" sessions.

Nigeria, Kuwait, the United Arab Emirates, and Saudi Arabia have also carried out arrests for "cross-dressing" in recent years; although no law specifically criminalizes transgender people in Saudi Arabia, Saudi judges have ordered men accused of behaving like women to be imprisoned and flogged.

Laws prohibiting same-sex conduct are also used to arrest and otherwise harass transgender and gender non-conforming people—regardless of the fact that gender identity has no direct correlation to sexual orientation or sexual behavior—as Human Rights Watch has documented in Malawi, Uganda, and Tanzania.

Transgender people are also arrested under other pretexts, In Nepal, police arrested and sexually abused transgender women in 2006 and 2007 under the guise of cleaning up public spaces. Police targeted transgender women with arrests and forced evictions in India in 2008 as part of a similar "social cleansing" effort. In 2013, police in Burma arbitrarily arrested a group of 10 gay men and transgender women and abused them in detention.

For many of the victims of these abuses, a future in which they may be legally recognized—and in which they will no longer risk imprisonment for being themselves—may seem far off. Yet it is precisely the persecution these individuals face that lends urgency to the struggle for legal gender recognition. It highlights that states should not be in the business of regulating peoples' identity.

A Shift in Medical Thinking

The Yogyakarta Principles state that each person's self-defined sexual orientation and gender identity is "integral to their personality" and is a basic aspect of self-determination, dignity and freedom. They are clear that gender recognition may involve, "*if freely chosen* (our emphasis), modification of bodily appearance or function by medical, surgical or other means."

Put simply, the process for legal recognition should be separate from any medical interventions. But if an individual's personal transition process requires medical support, those services should be available and accessible.

In 2010, the World Professional Association of Transgender Health (WPATH), an international multidisciplinary professional association, stated: "No person should have to undergo surgery or accept sterilization as a condition of identity recognition." In 2015, WPATH broadened the scope of its claim and called on governments to "eliminate unnecessary barriers and to institute simple and accessible administrative procedures for transgender people to obtain legal recognition of gender, consonant with each individual's identity, when gender markers on identity documents are considered necessary."

The World Health Organization is considering major changes to its revised version of the International Classification of Diseases, due out by 2018, which will significantly transform the ways physicians around the world code and categorize transgender people's experiences. The proposed revisions, while still in draft form, would move transgender-related diagnoses out of the mental disorders chapter—an important step in destigmatizing transgender people.

A Transitioning Rights Paradigm

Learning from decades of transgender activists' assiduous work around the world, the international human rights movement has slowly begun to recognize human rights violations based on gender identity and expression, and has begun to document and condemn the abuses.

A landmark report by the Office of the High Commissioner for Human Rights in 2011 on violence and discrimination based on sexual orientation and gender identity noted that most countries do not allow for legal gender recognition, so that transgender people may face many difficulties, including applying for employment, housing, bank credit or state benefits, or when traveling abroad. The follow-up report, issued in 2015, identified progress in 10 countries, but found that the overall lack of progress continued to impact a wide spectrum of rights for transgender people.

Indicating both the groundswell of attention to legal gender recognition and its intersectional urgency, a joint statement in 2015 by 12 UN technical agencies—ranging from UNICEF to the World Food Programme—called on governments to ensure "legal recognition of the gender identity of transgender people without abusive requirements," such as forced sterilization, treatment or divorce. In April 2015, the Council of Europe issued a resolution, adopted by its Parliamentary Assembly, calling on governments to adopt quick and transparent gender recognition procedures based on self-determination.

***

The law should not force people to carry an identity marker that does not reflect who they are. Recognizing, in law, peoples' self-identified gender is not asking governments to acknowledge any new or special rights; instead, it is a commitment to the core idea that the state or other actors will not decide for people who they are.

Achieving the right to legal gender recognition is crucial to the ability of transgender people to leave behind a life of marginalization and enjoy a life of dignity. A simple shift toward allowing people autonomy to determine how their gender is expressed and recorded is gaining momentum. It is long overdue.

Neela Ghoshal is a senior researcher and Kyle Knight is a researcher in the LGBT Division at Human Rights Watch.

[1] While this essay focuses on transgender people, many of the law and policy reforms related to legal gender recognition that human rights obligations mandate might also improve the situation for intersex people. Intersex people, who are born with sex characteristics that to not fit typical binary notions of male or female bodies, also face unique challenges and rights violations, including being subjected to unnecessary surgical procedures for the purpose of trying to make their appearance conform to binary sex stereotypes.

Ending Child Marriage:
Meeting the Global Development Goals' Promise to Girls

By Nisha Varia

Sharon J.'s marriage at age 14 in Tanzania dashed her hopes for the future: "My dream was to study to be a journalist. Until today, when I watch news or listen to the radio and someone is reading news, it causes me a lot of pain because I wish it were me."

Around the world, marriage is often idealized as ushering in love, happiness, and security. But for Sharon and other girls, getting married is often one of the worst things that can happen. Roughly one in three girls in the developing world marries before age 18; one in nine marries before turning 15.

Human Rights Watch investigations in Afghanistan, Bangladesh, Malawi, Nepal, South Sudan, Tanzania, Yemen, and Zimbabwe have found that early marriage has dire life-long consequences—often completely halting or crippling a girl's ability to realize a wide range of human rights. Leaving school early both contributes to, and results from, marrying young. Other impacts include marital rape, heightened risk of domestic violence, poor access to decent work, exploitation doing unpaid labor, risk of HIV transmission, and a range of health problems due to early childbearing.

At present, unprecedented attention is being paid to child marriage globally. Prominent voices in and out of government—including those of Sheikh Hasina, the prime minister of Bangladesh, and Joyce Banda, the former president of Malawi—have publicly committed to fight child marriage in their countries.

But change is often incremental, and promises do not always lead to effective action. Despite setting a goal of ending child marriage in Bangladesh by 2041, Sheikh Hasina has also proposed legislation that would lower the age of marriage for girls to 16 from the current age of 18. In April 2015, Malawi adopted a new law setting the minimum age of marriage at 18; however, it does not override the constitution, which does not explicitly prohibit child marriage under 15, and allows 15- to 18-year-olds to marry with parental consent.

International donors, United Nations agencies, and civil society groups, including Girls Not Brides, a coalition of more than 500 organizations worldwide, have also rallied behind the cause. The challenges are formidable. Child marriage—fueled by poverty and deeply rooted norms that undervalue and discriminate against girls—will not disappear if the concerted attention it now enjoys subsides in favor of the next hot-button issue.

A recent development may help sustain attention: the UN Sustainable Development Goals adopted in September 2015 include eliminating child marriage as a key target by 2030 for advancing gender equality.

Meeting this target requires a combination of approaches that have proved difficult to achieve for other women's rights issues: a commitment of political will and resources over many years; willingness to acknowledge adolescent girls' sexuality and empower them with information and choices; and true coordination across various sectors, including education, health, justice, and economic development.

Tackling the Roots of Child Marriage

> I faced a lot of problems in marriage. I was young and did not know how to be a wife. I was pregnant, had to look after my husband, do housework, deal with in-laws, and work on the farm. My worst time was when I was pregnant; I had to do all this and deal with a pregnancy while I was just a child myself.
>
> Elina V., married at age 15, Malawi

The main causes of child marriage vary across regions and communities but often center around control over girls' sexuality.

In some countries, such as Tanzania, Human Rights Watch interviewed many girls who said they felt forced to marry after becoming pregnant. In other countries, such as Bangladesh, parents hasten a daughter's marriage to avoid the risk that she will be sexually harassed, romantically involved, or simply perceived as romantically involved, prior to marriage.

A common thread is that most girls—economically dependent, with little autonomy or support, and pressured by social norms—feel they had no choice but to
comply with their parents' wishes.

Discriminatory gender norms in many places, including traditions that dictate
that a girl live with her husband's family, while a boy remains with and finan-
cially supports his parents, contributes to perceptions that daughters are an economic burden while sons are a long-term investment.

Poor access to quality education is another contributing factor. When schools
are too far away, too expensive, or the journey too dangerous, families often pull
out their girls or they drop out on their own and are subsequently much more
likely to be married off.

Even when schools are accessible, teacher absenteeism and poor quality education can mean that neither girls nor their parents feel it is worth the time or expense. Girls may also be kept out of school because they are expected to work
instead—either in the home, or sometimes as paid labor from young ages. These
same drawbacks, combined with lack of support from school administrators or
from husbands and in-laws, often prevent married girls from continuing their education.

Many girls and their families cite poverty and dowry as another factor for marriage. The stress of "another mouth to feed" hastens some parents' decisions to
marry off their daughters early. In Bangladesh, where a girl's parents pay dowry
to the groom, the younger the girl, the lower the dowry—meaning that some poor
families believe that if they don't marry their daughters early they will not be
able to marry them at all.

In contrast, in South Sudan, the girl's family will receive dowry from the groom,
either in the form of cattle, an important economic asset, or money. For example,
Ayen C., from Bor County, said, "My husband paid 75 cows as dowry for me. We
never talked or courted before we got married. When I learned about the marriage, I felt very bitter. I told my father, 'I don't want to go to this man.' He said, 'I
have loved the cattle that this man has, you will marry him.'"

Many girls have miserably little access to sexual and reproductive health information and services—whether on how one gets pregnant, reliable contraception

methods, protection against sexually transmitted infections, prenatal services, or emergency obstetric care.

As a result, child marriage is closely linked to early—and risky—childbearing. The consequences can be fatal: complications from pregnancy and childbirth are the second-leading cause of death for girls ages 15 to 19 globally. In other cases, the stress of delivery in physically immature bodies can cause obstetric fistulas, a tear between a girl's vagina and rectum that results in constant leaking of urine and feces. Girls suffering this condition are often ostracized and abandoned by their families and communities.

According to 2013 data, 74 percent of new HIV infections among African adolescents are in girls, many of them in the context of marriage where limited agency in the relationship and pressure to have children contribute to lack of condom use.

Domestic violence is another risk of marriage, perpetrated by a girl's husband or in-laws, including psychological, physical, and sexual violence, such as marital rape. While not all child marriages are marked by domestic violence, the risk increases when there are large age gaps between a girl and her husband.

Many countries fail to criminalize marital rape, and even when it is a crime, child brides have little ability to seek help. And in general, limited information about their rights, lack of access to services especially legal assistance and emergency shelters, discriminatory divorce, inheritance, and custody laws, and rejection from their own families, can leave many trapped in abusive marriages with no means of escape.

Armed conflict heightens girls' risk of child marriage and other abuses. For example, forced marriage of girls is a devastating tactic of war used by extremist groups such as Islamic State (also known as ISIS) and Nigeria's Boko Haram. Human Rights Watch interviewed Yezidi girls in Iraq who gave harrowing accounts of being captured, separated from their families, and bought and sold into sexual slavery. One young woman who escaped described being taken to a wedding hall with 60 girls and women where ISIS fighters told them to "forget about your relatives, from now on you will marry us, bear our children."

Environmental factors also play a role. Poor families living in areas at high risk of natural disaster, including as a result of climate change, such as in Bangladesh, have cited the resulting insecurity as a factor pushing them to marry their daughters early. For example, flooding of crops or the loss of land can deepen a family's poverty, and parents said they felt pressure to hasten a young daughter's marriage in the wake of a natural disaster or in anticipation of one.

The Way Forward

While the harms caused by child marriage are grim, the benefits of ending the practice are transformative and far-reaching. Tackling child marriage is a strategic way to advance women's rights and empowerment in several areas, ranging from health, education, work, freedom from violence, and participation in public life.

But child marriage is complex and varies widely around the world. Governments committed to achieving the Sustainable Development Goals target of ending child marriage by 2030 will need to employ a holistic, comprehensive approach that is tailored to local contexts and diverse communities.

And while the rate of child marriage has begun to drop in some places, it has increased in others. For example, civil society groups report a growing incidence of child marriage among Syrian refugees in Jordan.

Adopting and implementing cohesive national legal frameworks that uphold international human rights standards is key. This includes making 18 the minimum marriage age, avoiding loopholes such as exceptions for parental consent, ensuring the laws require free and full consent of both spouses, requiring proof of age before marriage licenses are issued, and imposing penalties on anyone who threatens or harms anyone who refuses to marry.

Governments should ensure these protections are not undermined by religious or customary laws and traditions, and should regularly engage with religious and community leaders.

Learning about what types of interventions work—and for whom—is key. Only some of the proliferation of interventions have been adequately monitored or evaluated to know which deserve to be replicated and expanded. In a 2013 review, the Washington DC-based International Center for Research on Women found that only 11 of 51 countries with a prevalence of child marriage greater than 25 percent had evaluated initiatives that fight child marriage.

An assessment of 23 programs out of 150 found evidence supporting the effectiveness of: 1) empowering girls with information and support networks; 2) ensuring girls' access to quality education; 3) engaging and educating parents and community members about child marriage; 4) providing economic incentives and support to girls' families; and 5) establishing and implementing a strong legal framework, such as a minimum age of marriage.

The Population Council, an international action-research organization, conducted a rigorous, multi-year study that found offering families in Tanzania and Ethiopia economic incentives, such as livestock, to keep their daughters unmarried and in school led to girls ages 15 to 17 being significantly (two-thirds and 50 percent respectively) less likely to be married compared to those in a community not participating in the program.

In Ethiopia, in communities where girls 12 to 14 were provided free school supplies, they were 94 percent less likely to be married than a comparison group. Communities that engaged in sensitization programs about the value of educating girls and the harms of child marriage also had fewer married girls.

A particularly powerful message that communities and parents respond to is information about the harms of early childbearing. Correspondingly, access to information about reproductive and sexual health is key for adolescents to understand their bodies, promote respect and consensual conduct in relationships, and prevent unwanted pregnancies.

However, while governments have little problem promoting interventions that generally garner broad public support such as providing school supplies, many remain reluctant to introduce programs that might trigger a backlash. They avoid offering comprehensive sexuality education in schools or through other community mechanisms, and ensuring that adolescents, as well as adult women, get full information about contraception and affordable access to health services, including safe and legal abortion.

The effort to end child marriage cannot succeed without greater acceptance of adolescent girls' sexuality and their rights to make their own informed choices about their bodies, their relationships, and their sexual activity.

Governments and donors can rally around the idea that a 12-year-old girl should be in school rather than a marriage. Countries such as Canada, the Netherlands, the United Kingdom, and the United States have been lead donors in combatting child marriage. But the challenge will be whether they can make sure child marriage interventions are not standalone efforts disconnected from other undertakings to empower women and poor communities and promote education and health.

Governments, whether as donors or as implementers, need to address some tough questions if they are going to make genuine progress. Do their education programs include special outreach to married girls? Do national plans of action on gender-based violence and "women, peace, and security" include efforts/steps to end child marriage? Do their police training programs on gender-based violence include policing methods to fight child marriage, such as prosecuting local officials who sign marriage certificates for underage girls?

Such coordination is crucial to ensuring that critical opportunities are not missed when allocating resources and programming that will be dedicated across the expansive

Sustainable Development Goals Agenda

Efforts to end child marriage also mean the donors should press governments to meet their obligations under international law to eliminate the practice. Key international human rights treaties include the International Covenant on Civil and Political Rights, the Convention on the Elimination of All Forms of Discrimination against Women, and the Convention on the Rights of the Child. While there is growing evidence of the effectiveness of a number of community-level approaches, government cooperation, law enforcement, and national-level initiatives are key to scale and sustainability.

Too often, nongovernmental organizations and donors support innovative programs, but local government officials undermine their impact by ignoring or even facilitating child marriage (for example, by changing the age on a birth or marriage certificate in return for bribes) or local police fail to enforce laws that make child marriage a crime.

Similarly, critical opportunities are missed when government health workers cannot talk to adolescents about sexuality and contraception, or government school teachers and principals are not mandated or encouraged to reach out to girls dropping out of school to marry.

One of the most striking parallels across Human Rights Watch's research on child marriage is how girls who married young desperately long for a better future for their daughters.

Kalpana T., interviewed by Human Rights Watch in southern Nepal, is not sure of her age but said she married after she had three or four menstrual periods, and now has three daughters ages 5 and under. She never went to school.

"My sisters and I all had to work in the fields for the landlords for money from as soon as we were old enough to know about work," she said. "I had to marry because my parents wanted me to. I don't want this for my daughter. I am uneducated and I don't know how the world works…. I can't count money. I want my daughter to be educated and have a better life than what I have right now."

The Sustainable Development Goals target on ending child marriage could bolster Kalpana T.'s daughters' chances of having more opportunities than their mother. But a huge amount of coordination, willingness to tackle socially sensitive issues, and sustained commitment and resources is needed before this lofty goal can lead to meaningful change—both for girls in Kalpana T.'s village and elsewhere around the world.

Nisha Varia is advocacy director for the Women's Rights Division at Human Rights Watch

Children Behind Bars:
The Global Overuse of Detention of Children

By Michael Bochenek

Shortly after 16-year-old T.W. was booked into Florida's Polk County Jail in February 2012, his three cellmates punched him, whipped him with wet towels, and nearly strangled him with a pillowcase. They then urinated on him, sprayed his face with cleaning fluid, and stripped him naked before wrapping a sheet around his neck, tying the other end around the window bar, and pulling so tight he lost consciousness. They repeated this attack three times over the course of several hours without jail guards on regular rounds even noticing, a federal magistrate judge found.

Around the world, children languish behind bars, sometimes for protracted periods. In many cases, as with T.W., they face brutal and inhumane conditions.

The lack of record-keeping and a wide array of institutions means that the number of children held worldwide in such environments is not known. The United Nations children's fund, UNICEF, has estimated that more than 1 million children are behind bars around the world. Many are held in decrepit, abusive, and demeaning conditions, deprived of education, access to meaningful activities, and regular contact with the outside world.

Many of these children—and adults who were convicted of crimes committed when they were children—have received excessive or disproportionate sentences that violate international law, which requires that imprisonment of children be in "conformity with the law and shall be used only as a measure of last resort and for the shortest appropriate period of time."

Others are held for acts that should not be crimes at all, such as skipping school, running away from home, having consensual sex, and seeking or having an abortion. Some have never been tried for their alleged crimes; others are tried as if they were adults and, when convicted, sent to serve time in adult prisons.

Migrant children are also routinely held in immigration detention, contrary to international standards. Children with disabilities and others may be institutionalized in the guise of protection.

A UN study expected to be finalized in 2017 promises to put international focus on the detention of children and hopefully result in more systematic monitoring of abusive practices, increased compliance with international standards, and a dramatic reduction in the number of children deprived of their liberty.

But governments need not wait for this report; they can and should act now to establish genuine alternatives to detention and ensure that those children who must be detained are held in humane conditions and benefit from schooling, health services, recreational opportunities, and contact with the outside world.

Detention and Incarceration in Response to Crime

Most countries keep no accurate records of the numbers of children who are locked up for breaking the law. Furthermore, getting a sense of the numbers of children behind bars is complicated by the fact that some governments hold children in several kinds of facilities, including adult jails and prisons as well as juvenile detention centers.

We know that the United States leads the industrialized world in the number and percentage of children it locks up in juvenile detention facilities, with over 60,000 children in such facilities in 2011, according to data compiled by the Annie E. Casey Foundation, which works on juvenile justice and other children's rights issues. The US also sends an extraordinary number of children to adult jails and prisons—more than 95,000 in 2011, Human Rights Watch and the American Civil Liberties Union estimated—with few opportunities for meaningful education or rehabilitation.

Whatever the numbers, there are several reasons why many children around the world should not be locked up.

First, the Convention on the Rights of the Child requires that locking up children on juvenile or criminal charges be a matter of last resort. Too often it's the first, or even only, resort; there simply may be no alternatives in law or practice.

Second, children are too often charged and held for acts that shouldn't be criminal. For instance, street children are frequently presumed to be guilty of wrongdoing and arrested on vague charges—if they are charged at all, as Human Rights Watch has found in Cambodia and Uganda, among other countries.

Many countries place children in detention for disobeying their parents or for other "status offenses," acts that would not be crimes if committed by an adult. A Texas Public Policy Foundation study found that in the US in 2010, over 6,000 children were detained for acts such as truancy, running away from home, "incorrigibility," underage drinking, and curfew violations.

Girls may face specific restrictions on their freedom of movement, enforced by criminal law. In Saudi Arabia, for example, girls as well as adult women may be jailed, imprisoned, and flogged for the ill-defined offenses of "seclusion" and "mingling," which one official described to Human Rights Watch as a girl or woman "being in an apartment by herself, or with a group of others, or sitting in a place where it is not natural for her to be."

Children in some countries, including Peru and some Mexican and US states, may face criminal charges for consensual sexual conduct—in the case of the US, particularly if the partner is of the same sex. Anti-prostitution laws in many countries mean that children may also be arrested, imprisoned, and detained when they engage in survival sex (the exchange of sex for food, shelter, or money in order to meet basic needs). Girls who seek or procure an abortion may face criminal charges—even in cases where the pregnancy was the result of rape—in Chile, El Salvador, Ecuador, Peru, and the Philippines, among other countries.

Third, children may be imprisoned under sentences that are impermissible under international law. International law flatly prohibits sentences of death (as well as life sentences that do not allow for the possibility of release) for crimes committed under the age of 18.

Nevertheless, at least 160 individuals were on death row in Iran for crimes they were found to have committed when they were younger than 18, the UN secretary-general reported in February 2015. Since 2010, juvenile offenders have been sentenced to death in Egypt, Iran, Maldives, Pakistan, Saudi Arabia, Sri Lanka, Sudan, and Yemen. In Nigeria, some convicted before 2010 continue to be held under sentence of death.

International law also requires that children be detained or incarcerated for the shortest appropriate period of time, and they must receive sentences proportionate to the circumstances and gravity of their offenses, as well as their own individual circumstances and needs. Their sentences must be subject to early, regular, and meaningful review for the purpose of conditional release or parole. Nevertheless, children may receive life sentences in 73 countries, including the US and 49 of the 53 states in the Commonwealth of Nations, a 2015 study by the Child Rights International Network (CRIN) found.

Fourth, children from minority groups are frequently disproportionately subject to arrest and detention. In fact, the disparities between their treatment and that of children from groups that represent the majority may increase at every stage of the process, from arrest to bail determinations to sentencing to parole decisions, as studies of Aboriginal children in Australia's juvenile justice system and of minority children in the United States have found.

Fifth, prosecuting children as adults poses additional problems. Not every country has established a juvenile justice system, despite the requirement in international law to do so. As Human Rights Watch found in Zambia, for example, the absence of a dedicated juvenile justice system can mean that children may wait for months or even years for their cases to be concluded.

Of those states that do have a juvenile justice system, some nevertheless treat older children as if they were adults. This may be done systematically, by setting an age lower than 18 for the jurisdiction of the ordinary criminal courts, as is the case in Cuba, Ethiopia, Jamaica, Hong Kong, the Philippines, Ukraine, the Australian state of Queensland, and New York State, among other jurisdictions.

It may also be done arbitrarily, such as when judges decide to treat children as adults if they show signs of puberty, as is done in Saudi Arabia and other countries in the Middle East. In addition, in the US, every state and the federal criminal justice system allow some children to be prosecuted in the ordinary criminal courts, depending on their age and the seriousness of the offense with which they are charged.

Brazil and India were at time of writing each considering lowering the age of criminal majority, the minimum age for trial in the ordinary criminal courts, for some crimes. If these proposals are enacted in their current form, children ages

16 and over who are accused of serious crimes will be prosecuted in adult courts.

Detention as a Means of Immigration Control

When Beatriz L. fled to the US from Honduras with her 11-year-old son after gangs threatened to forcibly recruit him, they were locked up together in a US detention center for migrant families for over 10 months. Beatriz told Human Rights Watch that her son began to spend all day sleeping. He said, "Mom, I just want to sleep so that when I wake up we'll be free."

International standards provide that the detention of any asylum seeker, whether a child or an adult, should normally be avoided. Mandatory or indefinite detention of children violates the Convention on the Rights of the Child, which states that the detention of children should be used only as a matter of last resort and for the shortest appropriate period of time. The Committee on the Rights of the Child has urged governments to "expeditiously and completely cease the detention of children on the basis of their immigration status." Moreover, the detention of children solely because of their parents' immigration status violates the prohibition on arbitrary detention.

Nevertheless, many countries continue to detain children as a means of enforcing their migration laws.

Australia has operated a mandatory detention framework for all asylum seekers since 1992. Australia held 112 children in immigration detention in mainland detention centers as of October 31, 2015. A further 95 children were held in Australia's regional processing center in Nauru. Reviews by the UN refugee agency (UNHCR), the Australian Human Rights Commission, and other authorities have found serious shortcomings in the Nauru detention center, including severe shortages of water, footwear, and clothing, and unhygienic and crowded conditions that have resulted in outbreaks of lice, gastroenteritis, and bacterial skin infections. In 2015, disturbing reports emerged that children and adults had been sexually assaulted at the hands of staff and other detainees during the previous two years.

In the US in mid-2014, the Obama administration dramatically expanded family immigration detention capacity, from fewer than 100 beds to more than 3,000, for the stated purpose of deterring Central American migrants from crossing into the US from Mexico. The Obama administration has since backed away from that rationale of deterrence in custody determinations for individual cases. Nevertheless, it continues to argue in federal court that it requires the family detention system to deter further mass migration.

Thailand's immigration laws permit the indefinite detention of all refugees, including Rohingya and members of other ethnic groups from Burma, ethnic Uighurs from China, Pakistanis, and Somalis. Migrant children are held in squalid cells without adequate food or opportunity to exercise or receive an education. Children have told Human Rights Watch that immigration detention centers can be so crowded they must sleep upright. One mother said there were three toilets for 100 detained migrants, which her teenage daughter would avoid using because they had no doors.

Elsewhere in the world, Human Rights Watch and other groups have documented large-scale detention of migrant children in Indonesia, Malaysia, and Mexico.

Detention in the Name of National Security

Children deemed to be a security threat may be held under administrative or military detention, which have fewer checks than criminal and juvenile justice systems.

Such children include captured, surrendered, or demobilized child soldiers, even though international standards call for states to treat them primarily as victims and offer them rehabilitation. Children have been held in large numbers in Afghanistan, Democratic Republic of Congo, Iraq, Somalia, and Syria for alleged association with armed or extremist groups. The special representative of the UN secretary-general for children and armed conflict, Leila Zerrougui, expressed concern that children were detained for alleged involvement with armed groups in 17 of the 23 situations covered in her 2014 report.

Each year, Israel arrests, detains, and prosecutes in the military court system some 500 to 700 Palestinian children suspected of criminal offenses in the occupied West Bank, according to Defence for Children International/Palestine Section. Israel is the only country that automatically prosecutes children in military courts. In 2015, Human Rights Watch found that Israeli security forces used unnecessary force to arrest or detain Palestinian children as young as 11 in East Jerusalem and the West Bank, and have choked, beaten, threatened, and interrogated children in custody without parents or lawyers present.

Other countries also prosecute some children in military courts. In Egypt, for example, some of the dozens of children arrested in the last two years for political offenses have been tried in military courts.

Detention in the Name of Treatment or Care

Children are also detained in the name of "treatment" or "rehabilitation" from drug dependence or as a misguided means of managing disabilities.

In Cambodia, eight drug detention centers hold about 1,000 people at any one time. According to the last government figures made public, at least one in 10 is a child under the age of 18. Children face the same abuses as adults while confined, including cruel, inhuman and degrading treatment and even torture.

Romchoang was under age 18, for example, when he was held in a military-run drug detention center in Koh Kong province for 18 months. He was locked in a room, chained to a bed for the first week, and later made to perform physical exercises each morning. Soldiers, who beat him if he fell asleep, told him sweating would help him recover from drugs.

Laos and Vietnam also operate drug detention centers that hold large numbers of children; in Vietnam, detained children and adults are subjected to forced labor, beatings, and torture. In fact, the rationale for such drug detention centres is to lock up and punish the poor and marginalized. In Cambodia, these centers hold "street children" who do not use drugs but who are picked up and detained in operations to "clean the streets." Similarly, Lao authorities use the Somsanga detention center, which has received direct support from the US embassy in Vientiane in recent years, as a dumping ground for street children and others considered socially undesirable.

Elsewhere in the world, street children are frequently rounded up and detained arbitrarily, sometimes under vaguely worded criminal laws.

Many countries lock up children with disabilities, ostensibly for their care, but in reality due to a lack of community services and support for families. In Russia, for example, too often children with disabilities are whisked to institutions shortly after birth, where they may be tied to beds, receive little or no attention or education, and be denied health care and adequate nutrition. Human Rights Watch has found similar abusive practices in Croatia, Greece, and India, to name just a few recent examples.

Some children may also be locked up for perceived or actual psychosocial disabilities. Human Rights Watch documented the practice of shackling children as young as five years old—together with adults—in so-called prayer camps (or spiritual healing centers) in Ghana, where they were tied to a tree or wooden post with a heavy metal chain, denied food, water, and shelter, and separated from their families.

Impact of Detention and Imprisonment

Detention takes an enormous toll on children, particularly on their physical and mental health. Torture and other ill-treatment at the hands of guards is a risk for every form of detention, especially for children held on national security grounds.

Children may also face violence and other abuses from fellow detainees, sometimes instigated or condoned by staff. In Australia, for example, a damning report from the Northern Territory's Children's Commissioner that was made public in September 2015 revealed that children in detention were subjected to isolation in cramped quarters, sometimes for nearly three weeks, and to excessive force. In Florida, two children died in February and September 2015 after other juvenile detainees beat them, possibly in exchange for contraband food from guards.

Sexual assault is a specific risk for boys as well as girls, particularly when children are held with adults.

There are generally fewer detention facilities for girls, who are usually detained less often than boys. Many are held far from their families and communities, or shunted off to the adult system. Some detention centers lack adequate sanitation, and girls may lack the materials and privacy needed to manage their menstruation. The lack of privacy in areas for bathing or going to the bathroom exacerbates the risk of sexual harassment or assault.

Facilities where children are held are often little more than warehouses. Educational services are often not available to children who are held for acts of delinquency, on national security grounds, or for immigration control. Children who are deprived of their liberty in the name of protection or care, including children with disabilities, frequently do not receive the education and other services they need. Children held for acts of delinquency are too often placed in facilities that lack the staff and infrastructure necessary to provide anger management classes, life skills training, counselling, and other rehabilitative support.

Detained child asylum seekers in particular experience extremely high rates of anxiety, depression, and symptoms of post-traumatic stress disorder, as research in Australia, Britain, and the US has found. Immigration detention may also lead children to abandon asylum claims even though they need international protection.

Alternatives to Detention

To ensure that deprivation of liberty is really used as a last resort, governments should establish and employ true alternatives to detention.

In the justice system, these include diversion of children from the formal justice system through alternative procedures and programs, probation, mediation, counselling, community service, and, where appropriate, "semi-open" facilities that give children supervision and structure but allow them to attend schools in the community and return home for overnight visits.

For migrant children and families, community-based alternatives—housing in settings that allow asylum seekers, refugees, and other migrants to attend regular schools, work in the community, and otherwise interact regularly with others—are preferable in virtually every respect to immigration detention, as the experience of supervision and case-management programs in Australia, Canada, Indonesia, Thailand, the United Kingdom, and the US have shown.

They may be healthier, more cost-effective, and result in comparable rates of appearance at asylum or immigration hearings, research has found. States should also do more to facilitate placing unaccompanied and separated children with relatives in the destination country or in third countries.

Children who use drugs should receive appropriate treatment and care. Compulsory drug detention centers cannot be considered a form of "treatment" or an "alternative to imprisonment." In line with the calls of the UN special rapporteur on torture and 12 UN agencies, states should immediately close all drug detention centers.

Children with disabilities should enjoy their right to live in the community, with appropriate support for themselves and their families. When institutional treatment is necessary, it should follow strict therapeutic protocols, including strict safeguards on involuntary treatment. Children with disabilities should receive appropriate legal and other support to enable them to make important life decisions, including related to medical treatment, and should have meaningful opportunities to challenge institutionalization.

***

Recent years have seen some positive developments in the treatment of children who otherwise would have been detained. The number of children in juvenile detention centers in the US fell consistently and dramatically from 1996 to 2011, the last year for which complete data are available. In California, legislation enacted in 2014 offered the possibility of earlier parole for several thousand offenders who were under 18 at the time of a crime but who were tried as an adult and sentenced to an adult prison term, and a 2015 law extended eligibility for parole to those who were 22 or under at the time of the crime.

Several countries have agreed in recent years to end or sharply reduce detention of migrant children. Finland, Malta, and the UK have publicly committed to ending the practice, while policies in France and Israel limit the detention of migrant children to "exceptional circumstances." Panama, Japan, Turkey, and Taiwan have enacted legislation prohibiting detention of migrant children, and South Africa's High Court ruled in a series of decisions beginning in 2004 that migrant children may only be detained as a last resort.

In February 2015, a federal court required that US immigration officials begin individually evaluating asylum-seeking families for release. In June 2015, after sustained advocacy from Human Rights Watch and other organizations, US government officials committed to releasing a majority of detained families within weeks if they could make a facially legitimate asylum claim. Later in the year, another federal court found that children could not be housed for long periods of time in jail-like facilities that have no license to care for children.

In 2010, in response to information provided by Human Rights Watch, UNICEF investigated Cambodia's Choam Chao detention center, which it had funded since 2006. After finding abuses in the center, UNICEF called for the immediate release of all children from drug detention centers in Cambodia. In response, the government stopped admitting children to the center and closed it shortly thereafter.

Such steps show that governments can do more to reduce their reliance on detention and incarceration. Locking children up is frequently unnecessary, abusive, and counterproductive. It's time for states to recognize these facts and end these unlawful practices.

Michael Bochenek is senior counsel in the Children's Rights Division at Human Rights Watch.

HUMAN
RIGHTS
WATCH

PRECIOUS METAL, CHEAP LABOR

Child Labor and Corporate Responsibility in Ghana's Artisanal Gold Mines

HUMAN
RIGHTS
WATCH

WORLD REPORT
2016

COUNTRIES

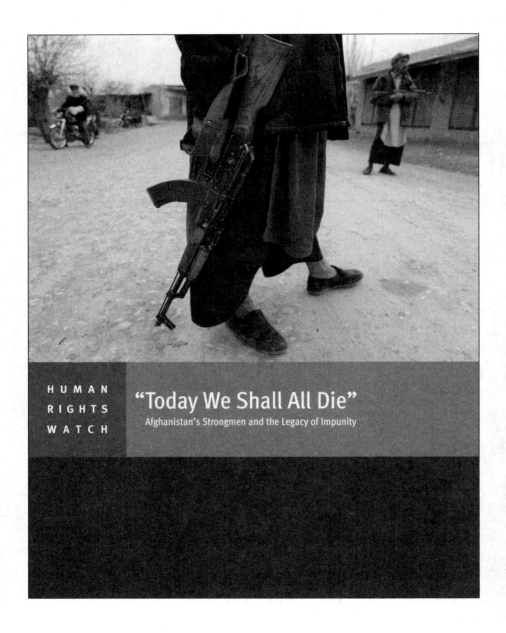

Afghanistan

Fighting between the Taliban and government forces in Afghanistan escalated in 2015, with the Taliban seizing control of Kunduz and holding the city for nearly two weeks before Afghan National Security Forces (ANSF), with United States air and ground support, regained control. The Taliban also seized a number of district centers and threatened other provincial capitals. The United Nations deemed nearly half of the country's provinces as being at high or extreme risk.

The upsurge in violence had devastating consequences for civilians, with suicide bombings, improvised explosive devices (IEDs), and targeted attacks by the Taliban and other insurgents causing 70 percent of all civilian casualties. The number of civilians killed during government military operations, particularly ground offensives, increased too.

While both President Ashraf Ghani and Chief Executive Abdullah Abdullah publicly affirmed the government's commitment to human rights, their National Unity Government (NUG) failed to address longstanding concerns, including violations of women's rights and attacks on journalists. The government launched an action plan to curb torture and enacted legislation criminalizing the recruitment of child soldiers, but impunity for both continued.

Parliamentary and provincial elections scheduled for 2015 were postponed indefinitely pending contested electoral reforms. More people became internally displaced due to conflict than in any previous year since 2002; the 100,000 new IDPs in 2015 brought the nationwide total to almost 1 million.

Armed Conflict

IEDs planted by insurgents remained a leading cause of civilian casualties. Such weapons function as anti-personnel landmines, and their indiscriminate use violates international humanitarian law. Hundreds of Afghan civilians were also killed and injured in suicide attacks.

With the Taliban insurgency appearing increasingly splintered—particularly following revelations that senior Taliban officials had kept the 2013 death of Mullah Omar, the movement's spiritual leader, a secret—it was impossible to attribute responsibility for many acts of violence.

In Nangarhar province, a group saying it was affiliated with the extremist group Islamic State (also known as ISIS) claimed responsibility for some attacks, although such claims were hard to verify, including an April 18 suicide attack on the Kabul Bank in Jalalabad that killed at least 30 people and injured more than 100. On August 7, insurgent attacks killed 50 people and injured 350 in Kabul, the bloodiest single day in the capital since 2001.

Targeted attacks on civilians by the Taliban also increased in 2015. In statements released in April and May, the Taliban vowed to kill government officials, specifically judges, prosecutors, and employees of the Ministry of Justice. The Taliban also identified Afghans and foreigners working for aid organizations as targets, a policy that helped make Afghanistan the world's most dangerous country for humanitarian aid workers.

Among those killed were nine Afghan staff members of the organization People in Need, including one pregnant woman, shot on June 2 in Balkh province. On May 13, 14 Afghan and foreign civilians were shot in an attack on the Park Palace guest house in Kabul for which the Taliban claimed responsibility.

Government forces were increasingly responsible for civilian casualties during ground offensives, mainly through the use of mortars and rockets used indiscriminately in civilian-populated areas. During fighting in Helmand in April, most civilian deaths were caused by mortar fire; journalists were blocked from traveling to the area at the time. On August 28, President Ghani issued an order to all security agencies to assess their operating procedures and take steps to reduce civilian casualties.

On February 2, Ghani signed into law a decree criminalizing recruitment by Afghan security forces of soldiers less than 18 years old. However, Afghan Local Police (ALP) and pro-government militias in some provinces continued to recruit children. The Taliban recruited boys as young as 14 to fight and carry out suicide bombings.

The UN also reported a significant increase in attacks against schools between April and June, mostly by the Taliban. Threats from both pro-government militias and insurgents led to school closures in Kunduz, Ghor, and Nuristan. In May, Afghanistan endorsed the global Safe Schools Declaration, thus committing to do more to protect students, teachers, and schools during times of armed conflict, including through implementing the *Guidelines on Protecting Schools from Military Use.*

As fighting intensified in northern provinces, Afghan officials reactivated pro-government militias to bolster security. In Faryab, Kunduz, and other provinces, these militia forces were accused of abuses against civilians.

The year also saw an increase in abductions and hostage-taking of civilians by insurgent groups, including two incidents in Zabul province: the November 9 kidnapping and killing of 7 civilians, and the February 23 kidnapping of 31 bus passengers, 19 of whom were released, with the fate of the others unknown. In both cases the victims were apparently targeted because they were ethnic Hazaras. Five employees of the nongovernmental organization Save the Children were kidnapped in Uruzgan on March 3 by the Taliban and killed when demands for the release of Taliban prisoners were rejected.

Women's Rights

When the Taliban took control of Kunduz, they looted the offices of women activists, shelters, and female-run radio stations, and issued threats that compelled dozens of activists to flee the city.

Early in the year, the new Ghani administration publicly affirmed its commitment to preserving and enhancing protections for women's rights. However, the government failed to take steps to improve enforcement of the Elimination of Violence against Women Law (EVAW) and to stop prosecutions of so-called moral crimes, which lead to imprisonment of women fleeing domestic violence and forced marriages.

A February report by the United Nations Assistance Mission in Afghanistan, UNAMA, concluded that 65 percent of cases filed under EVAW that involved battery and other kinds of serious abuse were resolved through mediation, while only 5 percent led to criminal prosecution.

The March 19 murder of Farkhunda Malikzada, 27, by a Kabul mob after she was falsely accused of burning a copy of the Quran galvanized women's rights activists, who launched public demonstrations demanding justice. Of the dozens of mostly young men who beat Farkhunda, ran her over, and then lit her on fire, 30 were eventually arrested; an unknown but large number remained at large.

HUMAN
RIGHTS
WATCH

"Stop Reporting
or We'll Kill Your Family"
Threats to Media Freedom in Afghanistan

The trial was held in haste, and some of the accused alleged that their confessions had been coerced. Of the 30, 18 were acquitted, 4 sentenced to death, and 8 sentenced to 16 years' imprisonment; the death sentences were later reduced to prison sentences. Of the 19 police charged, 11 were convicted, and 8 acquitted. Eleven police officers were sentenced to one year in prison for failing to protect Farkhunda.

The Afghan parliament delivered another setback to women's rights on July 8 when it rejected President Ghani's nominee for the Supreme Court, Judge Anisa Rasouli, head of Kabul's Juvenile Court and the nation's first-ever female nominee. Conservatives had campaigned against her, saying that a woman could not serve on the Supreme Court. Ghani promised to choose another woman for the post, but by November, no further nominations had been made.

On June 30, Ghani launched Afghanistan's National Action Plan (NAP) on Women, Peace and Security, which outlines how Afghanistan will implement Security Council Resolution 1325 and ensure women's "equal participation and full involvement in all efforts for the maintenance and promotion of peace and security."

To the frustration of activists and donors, the NAP was not accompanied by an implementation plan, and women were not included in the government's first "official" negotiations with the Taliban in Pakistan in July. At a September meeting with donors, Ghani reportedly agreed to develop an implementation plan for the NAP by the end of 2015 to be put into effect in the first half of 2016.

Accountability for Torture by Security Forces

In January, President Ghani launched a national action plan to eliminate torture. The working committee for the plan was not established until May 4, and progress on finalizing both policy and legislation was slow. On June 25, the National Directorate of Security (NDS), Afghanistan's security agency, issued an order reiterating the prohibition on torture, particularly its use in obtaining confessions.

However, documented cases of torture by police and NDS officials, which had declined slightly in some provinces in 2014, increased again in 2015. According to a UNAMA report in February 2015, one-third of detainees in Afghan detention facilities are tortured and unofficial detention centers continue to function, with four such centers in Kandahar alone. There were no reported investigations into incidents of torture documented by UNAMA, and no reported prosecutions.

A September 2015 amendment to the Criminal Procedure Code, imposed by presidential decree, allows Afghan authorities to detain for a renewable one-year period anyone suspected of "crimes against internal or external security," or believed "likely to commit such a crime."

Freedom of Expression

Despite modest progress in some areas, reporting restrictions and increasing violence against journalists meant that Afghanistan's media continued to function under threat in 2015. On May 5, the government scrapped the Media Violations Investigations Commission, a body long used to harass and intimidate journalists, and promised to consult with journalists and civil society groups in establishing a Mass Media Commission to adjudicate disputes over reporting. As of October 2015, the commission had not been established.

On March 1, the government imposed restrictions on reporting from combat zones and barred all government officials except police chiefs from speaking to the media about security issues. In August, on orders of the National Security Council, the NDS summoned six journalists for questioning on suspicion of running a popular and anonymous Facebook page dedicated to political satire.

Key International Actors

Although most international forces had withdrawn from Afghanistan by the end of 2014, approximately 10,000 US forces and military from other NATO countries remained without a combat role as part of NATO's Resolute Support training and support mission.

During an official visit to Washington by President Ghani and Chief Executive Abdullah in March 2015, the US agreed not to reduce its military presence any further through 2015. In October, Obama announced that the current number of US troops would remain through 2016, and be cut back to about 5,500 by the end of 2016 or early 2017. Germany, Turkey, and Italy agreed to keep their deployments in Afghanistan at current levels of 850, 760, and 500 troops, respectively, through 2016.

US Special Forces continue to carry out counterinsurgency operations in the country. Although US air support for Afghan government security operations officially ended in 2014, the US military bombed Taliban positions during a battle to retake the symbolically important district center of Musa Qala in August 2015. US drones also launched air strikes with greater frequency against targets believed to belong to the Taliban and those affiliating themselves with ISIS.

On October 3, a US warplane acting in support of Afghan and US ground forces repeatedly fired upon a hospital in Kunduz run by the aid organization Médecins Sans Frontières, leveling the building and killing at least 30, including 13 health workers and 10 patients, and wounding dozens more. The US military inquiry launched an investigation into the incident; by mid-November the findings had not been made public.

In August, the US reopened a criminal investigation into the 2012 murders of 17 civilians in Wardak province who had been detained by an Army Special Forces team. Previous investigations exonerating US forces had not interviewed family members and other witnesses.

The International Criminal Court continued its preliminary examination of allegations of serious international crimes in Afghanistan which it began in 2007.

At the London Conference on Afghanistan in December 2014 and the Senior Officials Meeting in Kabul in September 2015, most donors showed little enthusiasm for holding the government to specific human rights benchmarks, including those outlined in the Tokyo Mutual Accountability Framework, although several countries continued to push for specific indicators of progress on women's rights and media freedom.

While a number of donors have sought to maintain their support for Afghanistan, aid has fallen significantly in recent years, in part due to competition from other global crises, including the needs of refugees and migrants crossing into Europe, many of whom are Afghans.

Algeria

The government again failed in 2015 to introduce reforms promised since 2011 and severely restricted human rights. Authorities continued to stifle free speech and rights to freedom of association, peaceful assembly and protest, arbitrarily arresting and prosecuting trade union and human rights activists. They also continued to block the legal registration of several national and international human rights organizations. In July, communal violence in the Ghardaia region—600 kilometers south of Algiers—between local Sunni Arabs and members of the Amazigh, or Berber, minority left 25 people dead and more than 70 injured, mostly by gunfire.

Freedom of Assembly

The government continued to suppress peaceful protests by prohibiting all public gatherings held without prior approval. Article 97 of the penal code makes it a crime to organize or participate in an unauthorized gathering, even if it is peaceful, and imposes a penalty of up to one year in prison for demonstrating in public spaces.

The courts imposed prison sentences on at least nine labor rights activists convicted of engaging in peaceful protests in support of unemployed workers. On February 11, the First Instance Tribunal of Laghouat sentenced eight members of the National Committee for the Defense of the Rights of Unemployed Workers (Comité National pour la Défense des Droits de Chômeurs, CNDDC) to one-year prison terms, half of which it suspended, after convicting them of "unauthorized gathering" and "exercising pressure on the decisions of magistrates," under penal code articles 97 and 147.

Police arrested the eight union activists two weeks earlier when they gathered outside the court to protest against the trial of Mohamed Rag, a CNDDC activist arrested in January, who received an 18 month prison sentence for engaging in another protest. The sentences were all confirmed on appeal.

Freedom of Association

The Ministry of Interior continued to block the registration of several human rights and others organizations, impeding their ability to operate legally and exposing them to risk of dissolution. In 2012, the government enacted Law 12-06, which requires all associations—including those that had already successfully registered—to re-file registration applications and obtain a registration receipt from the Interior Ministry before they can operate legally.

In practice, however, the ministry refused to issue such receipts, without providing reasons, to a number of associations, thus making their legal status uncertain. Law 12-06 gives authorities wide discretionary powers to refuse to deny new associations legal status and to order the dissolution of associations that already have legal status.

For example, authorities can refuse to register any association whose activities they deem "contrary to public order, public morality, and the provisions of existing laws and regulations." They can also deny registration to a formerly registered association on vague criteria, such as deeming it to be "interfering with the internal affairs of the country" or "harming its sovereignty," or because it has received foreign funding without obtaining government approval or is deemed to be conducting activities not specified in its statute.

The Algerian League for Human Rights (*Ligue Algérienne des Droits de l'Homme*, LADDH) and Youth Action Rally (*Rassemblement Action Jeunesse*, RAJ) were among a number of formerly registered associations whose new applications for registration received no answer from the Ministry of Interior, leaving them in legal limbo.

Freedom of Speech

Although a new press law enacted in 2012 removed imprisonment as a penalty for defamation and other speech offenses—such as "contempt" of the president, state institutions, or courts—authorities continued to arrest, prosecute, and imprison critics using penal code provisions. They also threatened media deemed critical of the government.

Police arrested Rachid Aouine, a labor rights activist, on March 1 after he posted an ironic comment on Facebook in response to a government announcement that law enforcement officers who staged protests would face disciplinary action. Authorities charged him with "inciting an unarmed gathering" under article 100 of the penal code. On March 9, a court convicted Aouine and sentenced him to six months in prison.

In April, authorities censored "Weekend," a satirical talk show broadcast by the privately owned El Djazaira TV after the show's presenter in its April 17 edition referred to the Paris apartments of several Algerian ministers, hinting at possible corruption and embezzlement. The state Broadcasting Regulatory Authority promptly summoned the talk show's producer, Karim Kardache, and warned him of possible penalties against the TV station, and publicly accused the program of "sarcasm and mocking people including state symbols" and of breaches of professional ethics punishable under media and broadcasting laws.

On October 4, the general prosecutor in Al Bayadh tribunal brought charges against Hassan Bouras, a freelance journalist who has been critical of the government, for "insulting state institutions" and "attacks intended to overthrow the regime." He has been in detention since then. Algerian authorities have previously targeted him for alleging local corruption in al-Bayadh.

Terrorism and Counterterrorism

At least nine Algerian soldiers were killed in an attack on July 17 when their patrol was ambushed by members of the armed extremist group Al-Qaeda in the Islamic Magreb (AQIM) at Souq al-Attaf in northwestern Ain Defla province. The attack was one of the most lethal in the country since a mass hostage-taking by attackers linked to Al-Qaeda at the In Amenas natural gas plant in eastern Algeria killed 40 people in January 2013.

Algerian authorities arrested and prosecuted several political and minority rights activists on terrorism charges despite weak evidence. On July 9, police arrested Kameleddine Fekhar, an Amazigh activist and advocate of autonomy for the northern Sahara Ghardaia region who had previously accused the government of "complicity in crimes against humanity by Sunni Arabs against the Amazigh, or Berber," and 24 others. Authorities charged all 25 with participating in a terrorist act and inciting hatred during violent confrontations on July 7 between members of the Amazigh and the Arab communities in the Ghardaia.

Women's Rights

The People's National Assembly, the lower chamber of parliament, adopted a draft law in March to amend the penal code to criminalize physical violence against a spouse and sexual harassment in public spaces, but amid opposition from Islamist and conservative parties by September, the Senate had still to debate and vote on the proposed law. There is no other specific law on domestic violence that provides measures to protect individuals from domestic violence, including allowing authorities to issue temporary protection orders for victims. Marital rape is not explicitly recognized as a crime under Algerian law.

Accountability for Past Crimes

Perpetrators of human rights crimes and abuses during the internal armed conflict of the 1990s continued to enjoy impunity under the 1999 Law on Peace and National Reconciliation. This law criminalizes comments deemed to denigrate the security forces or state institutions for their conduct during the political strife of the 1990s, during which state forces committed torture, enforced disappearances, unlawful killings, and other serious abuses.

Associations representing the families of the disappeared continued to face official harassment and pressure to accept state offers of compensation provided under the same law, and to abandon their demands for details of the fate of those missing and for truth and justice.

Key International Actors

On March 29, for the first time in more than a decade, the European Parliament adopted a resolution on the "imprisonment of workers and human rights activists in Algeria," calling on the Algerian authorities "to ensure the safety and security of civil society activists and human rights defenders and their freedom to pursue their legitimate and peaceful activities."

The Algerian government has only permitted one United Nations human rights mechanism, namely the special rapporteur on the rights to education in early 2015, to visit Algeria since 2011. Pending requests for access included those of the UN special rapporteurs on torture and on freedom of peaceful assembly and of association, and of the UN Working Groups on Enforced or Involuntary Disappearances and on Arbitrary Detention.

65

Angola

The government of President José Eduardo dos Santos continued to violate human rights in Angola despite several new pledges to improve its record. In March, the Angolan government said it would accept many of the recommendations resulting from the Universal Periodic Review of the country held by the United Nations Human Rights Council in October 2014. In the same month, it passed a restrictive law regulating the work of nongovernmental organizations (NGOs). Security forces continued to crack down on independent media, human rights activists, and other critics through criminal defamation lawsuits, arbitrary arrests, unfair trials, intimidation, harassment, and surveillance. Two prominent human rights activists were sentenced to prison terms following unfair trials, sending a clear message that dissident voices would not be tolerated.

Security forces arbitrarily arrested and used excessive force against critics of the government, in addition to stopping a number of peaceful anti-government protests and other gatherings. In June, police arrested 15 activists who had gathered to read and discuss books on peaceful resistance. In Huambo province in April, police killed an unknown number of followers of a religious sect during an operation to arrest their leader.

Freedom of Expression

Freedom of expression continued to be severely restricted in Angola due to government repression, censorship, and self-censorship in state media and in private media outlets controlled by ruling party officials. There were some slight openings in 2015 when some media outlets, including state television TPA and private TV channel Zimbo, began to allow opposition and civil society groups to participate in their weekly live discussions on human rights, security, and youth activism. However, such public discussions on these sensitive topics remained extremely rare.

The government continued to regularly use criminal defamation laws and other abusive laws to silence journalists. In March, the minister of justice and human rights, Rui Jorge Mangueira, welcomed the concerns raised about the right to freedom of expression in Angola by the Human Rights Council, but insisted that current provisions on defamation in the country's constitution were compliant with international standards. The Angolan government defended the constitutional provisions on defamation, slander, and similar offenses, saying it protects the interests of the offended party and does not violate or restrict the right to freedom of expression.

Internet blogs and social media remained the main channels for open debate in Angola. In July, several people including José Gama, whom authorities believe is linked to the Club-K news website, and Rafael Marques, editor of Maka Angola news website, were questioned by the intelligence services about the content and origin of articles about the attorney general published on their websites. The articles suggested that the attorney general, Joao Maria Moreira de Sousa, was using his office to deliberately and unlawfully target a businesswoman.

In May, Rafael Marques, a prominent Angolan journalist and human rights activist, was sentenced to six-months' imprisonment, and suspended for two years, for criminally defaming seven high-ranking army generals in a book published in Portugal in 2011. The court ordered Marques to withdraw the book from publication and not translate it. Marques had accused the plaintiffs of involvement in torture, rape, and killings. The lawsuit proceeded despite that the legal time limit to present formal charges expired in June 2014. The Attorney General's Office shelved a complaint filed by Marques against the generals and business associates in 2012 and failed to investigate the allegations.

In June, a group of 15 prominent activists, most of them members of the Revolutionary Movement, were arrested in Luanda, the capital, following a meeting where they read and discussed books about nonviolent protest methods. Two other female activists were also questioned in August, but not jailed. All were accused of preparing acts of rebellion and plotting against the president and state institutions. If found guilty they could face heavy prison sentences.

At least four activists went on hunger strike to protest their arrest and detention. Henrique Luaty Beirão ended his hunger strike after 36 days following requests by his family and friends. A trial date was set for November. Some of the 15 jailed activists were kept in pretrial detention for more than 90 days before being formally charged, exceeding the 90 days allowed by Angolan law

Journalists covering protests in Luanda and elsewhere, including in the oil-rich enclave of Cabinda, were also harassed and detained by state security officials.

In August, Nelson Sul d'Angola from Deutsche Welle was briefly held by police in Luanda, after visiting the 15 jailed activists. Also in August, VOA's Coque Mukuta was detained in Luanda when relatives and friends of the 15 jailed activists attempted to hold a peaceful march. Police seized his equipment.

Right to Peaceful Assembly

Article 47 of the Angolan Constitution permits citizens to protest without prior authorization, provided they inform authorities in advance, but the government has continued to respond to any kind of peaceful anti-government protest with excessive force and arbitrary arrests, claiming that some of the protests were organized by people with the intent to destabilize the country. In 2015, there was no record of any peaceful anti-government protest or march that authorities permitted. Authorities banned attempts by supporters of the 15 jailed activists from the Revoluntionary Movement to hold vigils or peaceful marches.

Those who tried to organize protests were frequently arrested, detained, and tried in unfair judicial proceedings. In March, Arão Bula Tempo, human rights lawyer and president of the Cabinda Provincial Council of the Angolan Bar Association, was charged with rebellion for planning a peaceful demonstration against corruption. He was conditionally released pending trial. In September, Marcos Mavungo, a prominent human rights activist who had been arrested in March, was sentenced to six years in prison for attempting to organize a protest against bad governance and human rights violations in Cabinda province. In October, Cabinda authorities prevented the Association for Justice Peace and Democracy (AJPD) from holding workshops about transparency in the oil industry.

Conduct of Security Forces

Security forces continued to be implicated in excessive use of force. In April, the opposition party, National Union for the Total Independece of Angola (UNITA), accused the Angolan security forces of killing hundreds of members of a Christian religious sect, the Seventh-Day Light of the World, led by José Kalupetaka in Caala, Huambo province. Police said that during the unrest, 9 police officers and 13 of Kalupeteka's bodyguards were killed, but denied a massacre had taken place.

The authorities permitted media and MPs to visit the area, but only under police escort. Authorities refused requests from local human rights groups, opposition members of parliament, and the United Nations High Commissioner for Human Rights for an independent commission to investigate the events. In October, Kalupeteka was formally charged with crimes of murder, civil disobedience, and illegal possession of guns. He was awaiting trial at time of writing.

In a rare case of security officials being held to account, seven police officers and state security agents were sentenced in March to between 14 and 17 years in prison for the murder of two protest organizers, Isaías Sebastião Cassule and António Alves Kamulingue. The two men were abducted, tortured, and killed in 2012 after organizing a protest by former presidential guards and war veterans over complaints of unpaid salaries and pensions.

Civil Society

A new law regulating NGOs in Angola, Presidential Decree 74/15, went into effect in March and severely restricts civil society independence. It requires civil society organizations to register with multiple authorities including the Foreign Ministry before they can operate, obtain a "declaration of suitability" issued by the government, undertake activities that align with government policies, be subject to supervision by authorities, provide funding agreements for prior approval, permit authorities to determine the programs and projects they should carry out, and the location where projects should be undertaken.

During the 57th ordinary session of the African Commission on Human and People's Rights in Banjul, the Angolan secretary of state for external relations met with Angolan and international rights groups and pledged to resolve any "grey areas" of the decree.

In September, the director of the Open Society Foundation in Angola, Elias Isaac, was questioned by the Angolan police over allegations that the organization financed the website Club-K, which is critical of the government. Isaac had previously been accused by ruling party members of financing anti-government protests. The Open Society Foundation denied all accusations.

Key International Actors

Angola's oil wealth and military power continued to make it an influential power in Africa. Dos Santos played an important role in the region, most notably in conflicts in Africa's Great Lakes. In 2015, France hailed Angola as a stable presence in the region and the United States praised Angola's presidency of the International Conference on the Great Lakes Region (ICGLR). Angola continued to hold its non-permanent seat on the UN Security Council, a mandate that lasts until 2016

The Angolan government did not accommodate criticism from international partners. In May, following reports of the alleged massacre in Huambo, the Office of the UN High Commissioner for Human Rights (OHCHR) urged the Angolan government to conduct "a truly meaningful, independent, thorough investigation" into the events. The government accused OHCHR of violating its own procedures and demanded an official apology.

In September, following a European Parliament resolution on human rights in Angola that called on the authorities to investigate and end arbitrary arrests and detentions and torture by the police and security forces, Angola denied the allegations and said the resolution was based on a partial and subjective report by a European parliamentarian privately visiting the country.

Argentina

Argentina enjoys robust public debate, but existing and proposed laws threaten free expression, and harassment of judges threatens judicial independence. Prison conditions are poor, police at times use excessive force against demonstrators, violence against women is endemic, access to reproductive services is imperiled, and indigenous peoples do not enjoy the rights afforded to them by law.

Argentina continues to make significant progress regarding lesbian, gay, bisexual, and transgender (LGBT) rights and in prosecuting officials for abuses committed during the country's "Dirty War" (1976-1983), although trials have been subject to delays.

On December 10, Mauricio Macri began a four-year term as president after winning a run-off election in November.

Impunity for the AMIA Bombing

Twenty-one years after the 1994 bombing of the Argentine Israelite Mutual Association (AMIA) in Buenos Aires that killed 85 people and injured more than 300, no one has been convicted. From the outset, judicial corruption and political obstruction hindered criminal investigations and prosecutions.

The investigation stalled when Iran, suspected by the Argentine judiciary of ordering the attack, refused to allow Argentine investigators to interview Iranian suspects in Argentina. In 2013, Argentina and Iran signed a memorandum of understanding (MOU) to allow an international commission of jurists to review evidence and question Iranian suspects—but only in Tehran.

Because interviews conducted in Iran would likely not be admissible in an Argentine criminal court, a coalition of Argentine Jewish groups mounted a legal challenge against the MOU. The MOU has never been implemented. The perpetrators of the AMIA attack continue to go unpunished.

In January, Alberto Nisman, the prosecutor in charge of investigating the bombing, was found dead in his home with a single gunshot wound to the head. His body was discovered only days after he filed a criminal complaint accusing then-President Cristina Fernández and her foreign affairs minister of conspiring with

Iran to undermine the Argentine criminal investigation of Iranian suspects. A pistol matching the wound was found beside the body.

In May, a federal court dismissed Nisman's complaint, and as of November, the courts had not determined if Nisman was murdered or committed suicide.

In August 2015, a Buenos Aires court began the trial of several officials—including former President Carlos Menem, his head of intelligence, and a judge—for their alleged interference with the initial investigation into the bombing.

Judicial Independence

Government officials and supporters have harassed judges, threatening judicial independence.

In February, former President Fernández castigated the judges and prosecutors who were pressing for a rigorous investigation of Nisman's death, accusing them of being part of a "judicial party" seeking to "destabilize" the government.

A three-member panel of federal judges was expected to rule on the constitutionality of the MOU with Iran by the end of June. However, on June 25, government supporters in the Council of the Judiciary removed from office one of the three judges, Luis María Cabral, who had been expected to rule against the MOU.

The lawyer whom the council appointed to replace Cabral was suspended from his position weeks later by a higher court, following a legal challenge to the law the council had relied on in making the appointment. In November, the Supreme Court ruled the law unconstitutional, saying it did not provide for proper participation by the executive or legislative branches and undermined judicial independence. At time of writing, the courts had yet to decide on the constitutionality of the MOU with Iran.

Confronting Past Abuses

Several cases of human rights violations committed during the "Dirty War" waged by Argentina's military dictatorship (1976-1983) against political opponents were reopened in 2003, after Congress annulled amnesty laws that had been passed in the 1980s. In 2005, the Supreme Court ruled the amnesty laws unconstitutional, and federal judges subsequently struck down pardons favoring former officials convicted of, or facing trial for, Dirty War human-rights violations.

As of June 2015, courts had decided 142 cases of crimes against humanity committed by the dictatorship, resulting in 592 convictions. The Center for Legal and Social Studies (CELS) reported that, as of November, 56 suspects had been acquitted and 2740 had been charged.

Given the large number of victims, suspects, and cases, prosecutors and judges face challenges in bringing those responsible to justice while also respecting the due process rights of the accused. Other concerns include significant trial delays, the failure to capture two convicted military officers who escaped in 2013, and the unresolved fate of Jorge Julio López, a torture victim who disappeared in 2006—a day before he was due to attend the trial of one of his torturers.

Argentina has made significant progress both in identifying children of the disappeared who were illegally abducted and given to other families during the dictatorship, and in reuniting them with their biological families. As of November, 118 children illegally taken from their parents during the Dirty War had been found. The National Bank of Genetic Data, created by the government in 1987, has been of enormous help in his effort, but its usefulness was severely limited by a 2009 law. Local human rights activists have challenged the law, and the case was pending at time of writing.

Freedom of Expression

In December 2014, Congress adopted a law to regulate access to the Internet and telecommunication services. The law establishes that telecommunications are a "public service," granting the government broad regulatory powers, and creates an implementing body that would have authority to sanction service providers who do not comply with its terms.

An antidiscrimination bill being debated in Congress would grant authorities broad powers to punish "discriminatory acts," which are defined in vague terms, and would increase criminal penalties for such acts. The bill would also require online news outlets that allow users to post comments to "adopt necessary measures to prevent broadcasting of discriminatory content," opening the door to prior censorship.

The absence of transparent criteria for using federal funds, and in some provinces state funds, to purchase media advertisements creates a risk of discrimination against media that criticize government officials or policies. The Supreme Court has repeatedly ruled that while media companies have no inherent right to receive public advertising contracts, government officials may not apply discriminatory criteria when deciding where to place advertisements.

Argentina lacks a national law ensuring public access to information held by government bodies at all levels. A presidential decree ensuring access to information issued in 2003 applies only to the federal executive branch, though some provincial and local governments have adopted regulations for their jurisdictions. The public's access to information about the function of local, provincial, and national government remains piecemeal and haphazard.

In 2009, Congress approved a law that included provisions to increase plurality in the media, and four years later the Supreme Court established parameters regarding how the law should be implemented to protect free expression, including that a diverse range of perspectives should be heard in state-run media programming. So far, the federal agency in charge of implementing the law has not successfully addressed the overwhelmingly pro-government editorial line of state-run media. In 2014, the agency unilaterally tried to limit the number of broadcasting outlets owned by the Clarin Group, the biggest private media group in Argentina. The Clarin Group challenged the government's proposal, and the case remains pending before the courts.

Police Abuse

Police abuse remains a serious problem. Security forces ocassionally employ excessive force against protesters, despite a 2011 commitment by authorities in at least 19 of Argentina's 23 provinces to ensure that force would be used proportionately. In August 2015, dozens of protesters were injured when local police dispersed a largely peaceful demonstration in the province of Tucumán by firing rubber bullets and beating protesters with batons.

In May, a policeman in Buenos Aires province was convicted of torturing Luciano Arruga, a teenager who was arbitrarily detained in 2008 and whose whereabouts remained unknown until 2014, when his body was found buried in a cemetery in Buenos Aires.

Prison Conditions

Overcrowding, ill-treatment by guards, inadequate facilities, and inmate violence continue to be serious problems in Argentina's prisons. The National Penitentiary Office, an official body created by Congress, reported 33 deaths, including 17 violent ones, in federal prisons between January and September 2015. The office also documented 796 cases of torture or ill-treatment in federal prisons in 2014, and 241 cases between January and April 2015. In June 2015, a federal court convicted four officers of the Federal Penitentiary Service for their participation in the torture of a detainee in 2011.

Indigenous Rights

Indigenous people in Argentina face obstacles in accessing justice, land, education, healthcare, and basic services. Argentina lacks a law to protect indigenous peoples' right to free, prior, and informed consent when the government adopts decisions that may affect their rights.

A 2006 law that requires the government to survey land occupied by indigenous communities is being implemented slowly. Communities are reportedly being evicted from their lands even though the law, as amended, suspends evictions until 2017.

Women's Rights

Abortion is illegal in Argentina, except in cases of rape or when the life of the woman is at risk. But even in such cases, women and girls face numerous obstacles to obtaining an abortion. They also have trouble accessing reproductive services such as contraception and voluntary sterilization. These barriers mean that women and girls may face unwanted or life-threatening pregnancies and that they are subject to criminal prosecution for seeking abortions.

In a landmark ruling in March 2012, the Supreme Court determined that prior judicial authorization was unnecessary for abortion after rape, and urged provincial governments to ensure access to legal abortions. The Association of Civil Rights found that as of March 2015, more than half of Argentina's 23 provinces still had not adopted protocols that met the court's requirements.

Despite a 2009 law that includes comprehensive measures to prevent and punish violence against women, gender-based violence remains a serious concern, as manifested in June demonstrations throughout the country that were attended by thousands of people demanding reforms to curb such violence. In response, the government agreed to develop a national registry of "femicides and homicides aggravated by gender" and to provide official statistics on the number of women killed nationwide. No such database was available at time of writing.

Sexual Orientation and Gender Identity

In 2010, Argentina became the first Latin American country to legalize same-sex marriage. The Civil Marriage Law allows same-sex couples to enter into civil marriages and provides for equal rights and the legal protections of marriage afforded to opposite-sex couples, including adoption rights and pension benefits. Since 2010, nearly 12,500 same-sex couples have married nationwide.

In 2012, the landmark Gender Identity Law established the right of individuals over the age of 18 to choose their gender identity, undergo gender reassignment, and revise official documents without any prior judicial or medical approval. Surgical and hormonal reassignment procedures are covered as part of public and private health insurance.

In October 2015, Diana Sacayán, a transgender human rights defender, was found dead in her apartment, according to the Inter-American Commission on Human Rights. Former President Fernández condemned the killing and called for an investigation.

Key International Actors

As a member of the United Nations Human Rights Council, Argentina supported UN action to scrutinize human rights violations in North Korea, Sri Lanka, Belarus, Iran, the Occupied Palestinian Territories, and Syria. In 2015, Argentina co-led the development of the global Safe Schools Declaration, whereby states commit to do more to protect students, teachers, and schools during times of armed conflict, including through implementing the UN Guidelines for Protecting Schools and Universities from Military Use during Armed Conflict.

In March 2015, during an informal meeting at the UN Human Rights Council, Argentina and the International Committee of the Red Cross presented a "good practice guide" on the use of forensic genetics in investigations of human rights and international humanitarian law violations.

Prompted by a debt crisis, Argentina pushed for an international framework on debt restructuring, arguing that it would help governments to fulfill certain rights obligations. In September, the UN General Assembly adopted a resolution establishing a set of principles for sovereign debt restructuring, including that negotiations be transparent.

Armenia

Armenia's rights record remained uneven, with serious concerns related the government's interference in freedom of assembly. Other concerns include media freedom, poor prison conditions, including overcrowding and ill-treatment, and discrimination against lesbian, gay, bisexual, and transgender (LGBT) people.

In December 2015, Armenia held a referendum on constitutional amendments, proposed by the ruling party, to move from a presidential to a parliamentary system. Some critics said the amendments are intended to allow the party to remain in power, although the Council of Europe's Venice Commission said that the draft constitution was "in line with international standards." Following the referendum, some domestic and international observers reported allegations of large-scale vote-buying, ballot box stuffing, and intimidation and violence against observers.

Freedom of Assembly and Political Dissent

Authorities in several cases interefered with freedom of assembly in 2015, including by force. Some protesters faced violence. In September, Smbat Hakobian, of the Alliance of Freedom Fighters, an independent group critical of the government, was savagely beaten by several men he did not know, after a protest march. Police had charged three suspects in an investigation ongoing at time of writing.

On June 19, hundreds gathered in central Yerevan to protest a proposed 17 percent hike in electricity tariffs in round-the-clock demonstrations dubbed "Electric Yerevan." On June 22, demonstrators marched toward the presidential palace and, after police blocked them, occupied a central avenue until early June 23, when police issued warnings and then used water cannons to disperse the protest. Police officials told media that at least 25 people, including 11 police officers, were injured. Several protesters sought medical assistance. Activists and media reported that police attacked and detained numerous reporters, in some cases, smashing or confiscating cameras and deleting photos and videos of the events.

Police detained more than 200 demonstrators and held them for most of the day before releasing them without charge. In at least two cases, police refused access to lawyers. By evening, thousands gathered on the avenue to protest police actions. Police did not interfere. Many stayed until the police cleared them without incident on July 6. After an internal inquiry into the July 23 incidents, one officer was demoted and eight received reprimands for failure to demonstrate restraint. A criminal investigation into police conduct was ongoing, and no one had been charged at time of writing. Authorities eventually dropped a criminal investigation into "hooliganism" regarding the protests.

Police forcibly dispersed another peaceful protest against the rate increase on September 11, temporarily detaining approximately 50 protesters.

On April 7, Yerevan police arrested five members of the opposition movement Founding Parliament, including Chairman Garegin Chukaszyan, and Jirair Sefilyan, Varuzhan Avestisyan, Pavel Manukyan, and Gevorg Safaryan. The group had received permission to hold a rally in Yerevan on April 24, the 100-year anniversary of the Armenian genocide. Authorities charged the men with planning a mass disturbance, after searching their homes and office and seizing wooden bats, kitchen knives, a stun gun, and a publicly available pamphlet, as well as their laptops and flags. On April 10, a Yerevan court remanded all five to pretrial custody, but on May 4, the prosecutor general released them pending the investigation, which was ongoing at time of writing.

In 2015, appeals courts upheld the verdicts against controversial opposition leader Shant Harutyunyan and 13 of his supporters, who were arrested in 2013 after clashes with police during an attempted march on the presidential administration in Yerevan. In 2014, a Yerevan criminal court convicted them of violence against authorities and imposed prison terms of one to seven years.

Harutyunyan and activist Vardanyan alleged that police beat them following their detention.Tthe authorities refused to investigate the allegations. In June, penitentiary officials granted their petitions to serve their remaining sentences in solitary confinement, due to their fear of politically motivated violence in prison.

On September 15, a Yerevan court sentenced Hayk Kyureghyan to nine years in prison for shooting air pistols to protest the 2014 trial of Harutyunyan and his

supporters. Many local activists consider the sentence disproportionate, and retaliation for Kyureghyan's political views.

Freedom of Expression

Authorities continue to curtail media pluralism, and impunity for attacks on journalists, including by the police, remains the rule. The Committee to Protect Freedom of Expression reported that if the law on television and radio remains
unchanged, provisions will take effect in January 2016 limiting each region to
one television station, and at least 10 stations will have to close.

The committee documented 19 cases of violence against journalists in 2015, including 13 during the June Electric Yerevan protests, and, aside from the reprimands noted above, reported that no one was held responsible for any of the
attacks.

In a positive step, the Constitutional Court ruled in October that journalists are
not obliged to reveal confidential sources in cases not involving serious crimes.
The decision resolved a multi-year attempt by the Special Investigative Service to
force the Ilur.am news portal and *Hraparak* newspaper to disclose confidential
sources.

Torture and Ill-Treatment in Custody

Despite new guidelines issued to law enforcement officers, human rights groups
reported that torture and ill-treatment in custody remain serious problems in
pretrial and post-conviction facilities, especially to coerce confessions. Some
victims do not file complaints, fearing investigations will not be effective. Impunity for torture remains a key concern.

The Armenian Helsinki Association reported that, in April and August, appeals
courts in Yerevan upheld Aik Agamalyan's 10-year prison sentence for murder.
Authorities refused to investigate claims that investigators tortured and ill-
treated Agamalyan, 16 at the time of his arrest in 2013, and his relatives to coerce a confession.

According to the Helsinki Citizens' Assembly Vanadzor, a human rights monitoring group, in May, a woman in Yerevan rebuffed a police officer who whistled at
her. Four officers handcuffed her and took her to the station, where they insulted

HUMAN
RIGHTS
WATCH

"All I Can Do Is Cry"
Cancer and the Struggle for Palliative Care in Armenia

and ill-treated her for three hours. A forensic exam revealed bruises and psychological distress. Her appeal of the Special Investigation Service's decision to dismiss her complaint was under court review at time of writing. She was charged with insulting an officer, and two preliminary hearings on the charges had been held at time of writing.

Authorities opened an investigation into allegations that some witnesses were pressured to testify against Karen Kurngurtsev, whose murder trial was ongoing at time of writing, but refused to investigate Kurngurtsev's allegations that police ill-treated him after his arrest in 2013.

Military Service

Although Armenia has taken significant steps to correct long-standing problems with military service, including by providing for alternative service for conscientious objectors, Armenian rights groups reported that violence among conscripts and a high number of non-combat deaths remain concerns.

Palliative Care

Armenia continues to discuss reforming its complicated and time-consuming prescription and procurement procedures for opioid medications. A national action plan on palliative care remained pending for more than a year at time of writing. Current regulations obstruct the delivery of adequate palliative care, condemning most terminally ill patients to unnecessary suffering. Tight police controls on injectable opioids and restrictive policies on procurement, prescription, and disbursement are inconsistent with many of the World Health Organization's recommendations on palliative care.

Sexual Orientation and Gender Identity

Activists reported that LGBT people continue to face discrimination, harassment, and physical violence. Although the government dropped a proposed constitutional change that would have prohibited same-sex marriage, it has not addressed hate speech or discrimination against LGBT people. Gender identity and sexual orientation are not included in anti-discrmination or hate speech laws, limiting legal recourse for many crimes against LGBT people.

On October 17-18, the LGBT rights group PINK Armenia held the first Armenian forum to discuss problems faced by LGBT people. An article about the event and a photograph of participants posted on PINK Armenia's website and re-posted by various media outlets, received a slew of homophobic comments and threats in social media, including calls to burn and kill the forum participants. PINK Armenia filed a complaint with the Prosecutor's Office to investigate the threats and had not received a response at time of writing.

PINK Armenia reported that five men attacked two transgender sex workers in a Yerevan park in August, causing serious injuries, including brain trauma. The victims attempted to seek assistance from security officers, who refused to help them. The case was under investigation at time of writing.

In April, an appeals court rejected the appeal by 16 plaintiffs whose lawsuits against the *Iravunq* newspaper were dismissed by a court in October 2014. *Iravunq* had published several online articles calling for LGBT people and activists to be excluded from public life and for their families to shun them. One article included a "blacklist" of 60 such people, with links to their social media sites. The newspaper refused to publish a retraction.

Women's Rights

Following her April visit, Anne Brasseur, president of the Parliamentary Assembly of the Council of Europe, called for immediate action to combat violence against women and domestic violence, echoing the March report by the council's human rights commissioner. Despite evidence that violence against women remains common, Armenia has no law criminalizing domestic violence and has not become a party to the Council of Europe's Convention on Preventing and Combating Violence against Women and Domestic Violence.

Key International Actors

On June 23, following police assaults on journalists in Yerevan, Dunja Mijatovic, the Organization for Security and Co-operation in Europe's (OSCE) representative on freedom of the media, called for authorities to investigate the incident and ensure journalists' safety.

On June 24, Michael Georg Link, director of the OSCE's Office for Democratic Institutions and Human Rights, called on the Armenian authorities to respect the right to freedom of assembly and investigate the detentions of protesters.

In May 2015, the UN special rapporteur on the sale of children, child prostitution, and child pornography visited Armenia and noted gaps in awareness campaigns, detection, and reporting mechanisms for cases of abuse and violence against children.

In its March European Neighborhood Policy progress report, the European Union noted that "Armenia made limited progress on deep and sustainable democracy, human rights and fundamental freedoms," and urged it to adopt a comprehensive anti-discrimination law, and ensure accountability for attacks and threats against human rights defenders.

PACE adopted a declaration in January on the failure of the Armenian authorities to condemn incitement of hatred against LGBT people and to call for implementation of a Committee of Ministers' recommendation on combating discrimination.

Armenia underwent its second universal periodic review at the UN Human Rights Council in January, with the resulting recommendations calling on Armenia to strengthen children's rights protections, adopt comprehensive anti-discrimination legislation, and end impunity for attacks against journalists and human rights defenders, among others.

Australia

Australia has a solid record of protecting civil and political rights, with robust institutions and a vibrant press and civil society that act as a check on government power. However, the government's failure to respect international standards for asylum seekers and refugees continues to take a heavy human toll.

In 2015, Australia's practices of mandatory detention of asylum seekers, abuses related to offshore processing, and outsourcing of refugee obligations to other countries were heavily criticized by United Nations experts, foreign governments, and even some Australian government-funded inquiries.

However, senior government officials dismissed such criticism and even attacked and tried to discredit institutions such as Australia's Human Rights Commission (AHRC) and the UN. The government has also instituted overly broad and vague counterterrorism laws and has done too little to address indigenous rights and disability rights.

Asylum Seekers and Refugees

Australia outsources some of its obligations to asylum seekers and refugees to poorer, less well-equipped, and unsafe countries such as Nauru and Papua New Guinea (PNG). Australia has also returned several boats carrying migrants and asylum seekers to Sri Lanka and Vietnam, despite their poor rights records. Australia has also towed boats carrying asylum seekers back to Indonesia, endangering lives, and in May, Indonesian police and asylum seekers accused Australian officials of paying more than US$30,000 to people-smugglers to turn a boat back to Indonesia.

As of October 31, 2015, 929 asylum seekers and refugees were detained on Manus Island, PNG, while 621 were in a center on Nauru. Three years after Australia first started sending asylum seekers to PNG, not a single refugee had been resettled. In August, an asylum seeker detained on Manus Island for more than two years was persuaded and paid by Australian officials to return to Syria. He has said he was detained by intelligence officers upon arrival in Damascus, and in October, was injured by shelling.

AUSTRALIA AT THE
HUMAN RIGHTS COUNCIL
Ready for a Leadership Role?

The immigration department established an independent review of detention conditions in the Nauru center that found evidence that children and adults were sexually and physically assaulted. Thirty-three asylum seekers allege they have been raped or sexually assaulted at the center. A parliamentary senate inquiry found that the conditions on Nauru were "not adequate, appropriate or safe," and recommended that all children be removed from the center as soon as possible.

An AHRC report into conditions in Australian mainland immigration detention centers and facilities on Christmas Island in February found that mandatory and prolonged detention had profoundly negative impacts on the mental and emotional health and development of children. More than 300 children committed or threatened self-harm in a 15-month period in Australian immigration detention, and 30 reported sexual assault.

Following the report's release, senior government officials made personal and unsubstantiated attacks on the credibility and integrity of the president of the AHRC, Professor Gillian Triggs, including calling for her resignation. The chairman of the International Coordinating Committee, the UN body responsible for accrediting national human rights institutions, described these attacks as intimidating and undermining the independence of the AHRC.

In March, the UN special rapporteur on torture, Juan Mendez, concluded that by failing to provide adequate detention conditions, end the practice of detaining children, and put a stop to escalating violence in processing centers, Australia was in violation of the Convention against Torture. Former Prime Minister Tony Abbott responded by stating that Australia was "sick of being lectured" by the UN.

In September, the UN special rapporteur on the human rights of migrants postponed a visit to Australia due to the "lack of full cooperation from the government regarding protection concerns and access to detention centres." A High Court challenge on the legality of offshore detention centers was heard in October, and at time of writing was awaiting judgment.

In May, parliament passed the Australian Border Force Act, making it a crime punishable by two years' imprisonment for anyone who works directly or indirectly for the Department of Immigration and Border Protection, including contractors such as doctors and aid workers, to disclose information obtained by them while doing that work. Medical groups have spoken out against the new law.

Under a refugee transfer deal struck with Cambodia, four refugees agreed to be relocated from Nauru to Cambodia in June. A fifth refugee was relocated in November. To gain Cambodia's cooperation, Australia promised Cambodia A$40 million (US$29 million) in development aid and allocated a further A$15.5 million (US$11.2 million) to fund refugee resettlement in Cambodia.

The Migration Act continues to provide for the mandatory and indefinite detention of "unlawful non-citizens," including children. According to the December 2014 amendments to the Migration Act, non-citizens can have their visas canceled for committing certain offenses or failing a "character test," which is affecting migrants, long-term Australian residents (including those from New Zealand), and refugees. In November 2015, violence broke out on Christmas Island following the death of an Iranian refugee who escaped the center and whose body was found at the bottom of a cliff.

Counterterrorism Laws

Australia has adopted extensive and overly broad new counterterrorism laws in response to the threat of "home-grown terrorism." Amendments to the Australian Security Intelligence Organisation (ASIO) Act in October 2014 criminalize disclosure of information "that relates to a special intelligence operation" punishable by 5 or 10 years' imprisonment. The offenses will have a chilling effect on whistleblowers, human rights defenders, and journalists, and impede reporting that fosters legitimate public debate and is in the public interest.

In March, the government passed the Telecommunications Amendment bill, requiring telecommunications companies to retain metadata for a period of two years so that Australian intelligence organizations can access the data.

In June, the government introduced the Australian Citizenship Amendment (Allegiance to Australia) bill, which provides that dual citizens who act in a manner "contrary to their allegiance to Australia," including engaging in or supporting terrorist activities, will be stripped of their citizenship. The bill includes problematic provisions that operate retrospectively. Further legislation was introduced in

November, allowing control orders to be applied to children as young as 14, and introducing a new offense of advocating genocide.

Indigenous Rights

In February, the prime minister's "Close the Gap" report highlighted the continued disadvantages that indigenous Australians face. While there were modest improvements in education and health outcomes, there was little progress on closing the life expectancy gap. Aboriginal and Torres Strait Islander peoples still live on average 10-12 years less than non-indigenous Australians, have an infant mortality rate almost two times higher, and continue to die at alarmingly high rates from treatable and preventable conditions such as diabetes and respiratory illness.

Indigenous Australians continue to be disproportionately represented in the criminal justice system. Aboriginal women are the fastest growing prisoner demographic in Australia.

In November, the High Court upheld the Northern Territory's "paperless arrest" powers that allow police to detain individuals for up to four hours for minor, fine-only offenses.

A report from the Northern Territory's children's commissioner made public in September revealed serious shortcomings in juvenile detention practices in the territory. Youths in detention were subjected to isolation in cramped quarters, sometimes for nearly three weeks at a time, as well as to excessive use of force. In response to a disturbance in one Darwin juvenile detention center, staff used tear gas on six children, hooded and handcuffed them, including two who had taken no part in the disturbance, and temporarily moved them all to an adult prison.

Across Australia, Aboriginal and Torres Strait Islander children under age 18 are seriously overrepresented in youth detention facilities, representing more than half of child detainees. Indigenous children are often held in detention on remand, despite the international requirement that the detention of children be used as a last resort and for the shortest appropriate period of time.

Disability Rights

Women and girls with disabilities in Australia face higher rates of violence in the community and in institutional settings than other women and girls. Some face coerced sterilization and forced psychiatric interventions. To date, the Australian government has done little to address such violence.

In September, a school principal was fired for building a metal cage in a class-room and using it to restrain a 10-year-old boy with autism. The incident prompted an inquiry into how schools respond to students with "complex needs and challenging behaviors."

According to the AHRC, people with intellectual disabilities are overrepresented in the prison population and have limited access to justice. There is also a lack of community-based independent living arrangements and support services for people with disabilities.

Sexual Orientation

Australia does not recognize the right of same-sex couples to marry. There is in-creasing public support for same-sex marriage in Australia, and some parliamen-tarians are pushing for a plebiscite or referendum on the right of same-sex couples to marry.

Foreign Policy

Australia rarely raises concerns publicly about human rights violations in coun-tries with which it cooperates on border protection matters, or in countries with which it has significant trade relationships.

The public outcry over Indonesia's execution in April of Australians Andrew Chan and Myuran Sukumaran for drug trafficking pushed senior Australian officials and politicians to condemn the executions and reiterate Australia's stance against the death penalty more broadly. In July, the government established an inquiry to review how Australia engages internationally to promote the abolition of the death penalty.

In 2015, Australia announced its candidacy for a seat at the UN Human Rights Council in Geneva for the 2018-2020 term. To date, with observer status at the council, Australia has a mixed record, advancing certain thematic issues but not playing a leadership role on grave country situations globally. Australia has often responded dismissively to recommendations made by UN experts about its own domestic human rights record.

In November, Australia's domestic rights record was reviewed for the second time as part of the council's Universal Periodic Review process. More than 100 countries spoke up at the review, and nearly half of them—from every corner of the globe—criticized Australia's asylum laws and refugee policies and its treatment of indigenous people.

Because New Zealand citizens bear the brunt of changes to Australia's immigration laws and face detention and deportation, criticism from New Zealand has increased. In November, New Zealand Minister of Internal Affairs Peter Dunne called Australia's immigration detention policies "savage and inhumane" and stated that "the modern concentration camp approach Australia has taken is simply wrong."

Azerbaijan

The government's unrelenting crackdown decimated independent nongovernmental organizations (NGOs) and media. Courts sentenced leading human rights defenders, political activists, and journalists to long prison terms in politically motivated, unfair trials. Dozens more face harassment, have been imprisoned, are under criminal investigation, face travel bans, or have fled. The authorities denied entry to international human rights monitors and journalists.

Azerbaijan's international partners have expressed concern about the trials of government critics and the broader climate of repression, but they have yet to impose concrete consequences to secure rights improvements. Azerbaijan hosted the first European Games in Baku in June, but the European Olympic Committees did not act when Azerbaijan failed to respect Olympic Charter media freedom and human dignity guarantees.

Prosecuting Government Critics

The government continues to bring false charges against critics in politically motivated prosecutions to silence and imprison them. Common charges used by the government include hooliganism, drug possession, treason, and so-called economic crimes. This practice reached a peak in 2015, with dozens of human rights defenders, journalists, political activists, and other critics prosecuted, convicted, or remaining in prison in this manner.

Among those convicted this year and handed prison sentences ranging from six to eight-and-a-half years are human rights lawyer Intigam Aliyev; veteran human rights defenders Leyla and her husband, Arif; prominent investigative journalist Khadija Ismayilova; and human rights campaigner Rasul Jafarov. Others imprisoned on politically motivated charges include Seymur Haziyev, a columnist for the opposition newspaper *Azadlig*; Musavat members Siraj and Faraj Kerimlis; and Popular Front Party member Murad Adilov. Human rights activist Taleh Khasmammadov received a three-year sentence.

The Yunuses still face treason charges. Their serious, pre-existing health conditions worsened since their 2014 arrests. Both made allegations of ill-treatment in detention, which the government has not investigated. On November 12, the

Appeals Court released Arif Yunus on his own recognizance due to his deteriorating health, and in December the same court changed the sentences of both Yunuses to five years' probation and released Leyla Yunus.

Political analyst Ilgar Mammadov and journalist Tofig Yagublu remained in prison on charges of inciting violence, despite repeated calls by the Council of Europe to release Mammadov following a 2014 European Court of Human Rights (ECtHR) decision on his case, and a November 2015 ECtHR decision finding Yagublu's detention unlawful.

In August, the Supreme Court upheld a 2014 sentence of five-and-a-half years in prison against Anar Mammadli, the head of the Election Monitoring and Democracy Studies Centre (EMDSC), an independent election monitoring organization.

On March 18, President Ilham Aliyev pardoned 101 prisoners, including EMDSC co-founder, Bashir Suleymanli.

Persecution of Lawyers

Azerbaijan's bar association disbarred or punished several lawyers representing human rights defenders and activists. In several cases, prosecutors summoned lawyers as witnesses in the cases they were representing and removed the lawyers due to alleged conflict of interest. On July 10, a Baku court disbarred human rights lawyer Khalid Bagirov for alleged misconduct after questioning the court's decision against his client, Ilgar Mammadov. Also in July, a court disbarred Alayif Hasanov, following a defamation suit after he publicized alleged beatings of Leyla Yunus by her cellmate.

Freedom of Media

The closed trial of Rauf Mirgadirov, an outspoken formerly Ankara-based correspondent arrested in 2014 on trumped-up espionage charges, began in Baku on November 5.

In December 2014, authorities raided Radio Azadlig's Baku office, interrogated employees, seized equipment, and sealed off the premises. Several staff members fled the country. In February 2015, authorities forbade Radio Azadlig journalist Babek Bakir from traveling abroad due to a travel ban.

Around the June 2015 European Games, authorities deported or barred entry to several leading international journalists.

Emin Milli, director of Berlin-based Internet television station Meydan TV, alleged threats from Azerbaijan's minister of youth and sport for critical reporting. Meydan TV staff in Berlin also reported cases of harassment and threats against their relatives in Azerbaijan. On September 3, prosecutors questioned three Meydan TV freelance reporters about their coverage of protests and a death in custody. Also in September, a court sentenced Meydan TV journalist Shirin Abbasov to 30 days' detention for allegedly resisting police. Almost all Meydan TV journalists in Baku face travel bans.

Swiss authorities helped secure the departure of the founder of the Institute for Reporters' Freedom and Safety, Emin Huseynov, from Azerbaijan to Switzerland in June. Fearing a politically motivated arrest, in August 2014 Huseynov sought refuge in the Swiss embassy in Baku, where he remained until his departure.

The daily *Azadlig* faced imminent closure because of government restrictions on sales, the state-run distributor's refusal to pay debts to the newspaper, and accumulated defamation fines. In July, authorities detained three relatives of exiled *Azadlig* editor Ganimat Zahidov. Two were sentenced to 25 and 30 days' administrative detention on bogus charges. A third remains in custody on drug charges.

In December 2014, parliament approved amendments prohibiting foreign media funding and authorizing the court-ordered closure of any outlet that disseminates incorrect information twice within a year.

Freedom of Association

Dozens of independent NGOs have been effectively closed since 2014 following prosecutions on laws that severely interfere with NGO operations. A December 2014 report by the Council of Europe's Venice Commission found that amendments made to Azerbaijan's Law on NGOs since 2012 "restrict the operations of NGOs in Azerbaijan," through more stringent registration and reporting requirements, severe penalties, and bans on foreign funding.

Torture and Ill-Treatment

Torture and ill-treatment continue with impunity. On August 20, Bahruz Hajiyev died in a Mingechevir police station soon after police detained him for questioning. The Interior Ministry said that Hajiyev threw himself from a window. Hajiyev's relatives reported that his body showed signs of other violence.

In December 2014, Elshad Babayev died in prison. Babayev's sister released photographs of the body with apparent signs of violence. Authorities opened a criminal case, but no one has been identified as responsible for his death.

In July and August, Ilgar Mammadov publicly alleged he had been attacked by fellow inmates for refusing to sign a letter of repentance to President Aliyev. In August, the secretary general of the Council of Europe (CoE) sent a letter to the justice minister urging a thorough investigation. Mammadov said that prison officials beat him in October. Authorities failed to effectively investigate.

In April, the United Nations Subcommittee on Torture conducted a visit and found the government did not guarantee "all fundamental legal and procedural safeguards" to prisoners, "including access to a lawyer, a medical doctor, and to contact his or her family."

Elections

The Office for Democratic Institutions and Human Rights of the Organization for Security and Co-operation in Europe (OSCE/ODIHR) refused to send its observation mission to the November 1 parliamentary elections, citing the government-imposed restrictions on the mission. ODIHR had previously said that the election environment was negatively impacted by detentions, lawsuits, and other pressure on journalists. The European Parliament and the OSCE Parliamentary Assembly also refused to send observers. The Council of Europe Parliamentary Assembly's limited observation mission said the vote was "generally in line with international standards," but three of its observers dissented, citing the lack of "conditions for holding free and democratic elections."

Key International Actors

With the exception of the European Parliament, European Union institutions and member states have not mounted a unified response to Azerbaijan's human rights crackdown or imposed consequences for bilateral relations. Negotiations on an EU-Azerbaijan strategic partnership agreement are ongoing.

The EU's special representative for human rights did not use his February visit to Baku to secure substantive human rights improvements. The EU high representative for foreign affairs and security policy issued statements, including about "disproportionate" sentences, but stopped short of calling for the release of government critics, except for Leyla and Arif Yunus.

The EU's report on Azerbaijan's implementation of the European Neighborhood Policy found "regression" on human rights and fundamental freedoms.

The United States State Department issued several statements condemning prosecutions of human rights defenders. In May, media reports revealed that the state-owned oil company, SOCAR, had secretly funded a 2013 trip to a conference in Baku and expensive gifts for 10 US Congress members and 32 of their staff members. Ethics investigations found no evidence that lawmakers or staff knew the Azerbaijani government had funded the conference. Following the trip, a provision favorable to SOCAR and other oil companies was inserted into US legislation. After the investigations, participants returned the gifts.

In a June resolution, the Parliamentary Assembly of the CoE condemned "the crackdown on human rights in Azerbaijan" and called for an end to "systemic repression." The council's secretary general and the president of the parliamentary assembly issued statements concerning the trials. In October, the secretary general announced the organization's withdrawal from a human rights working group with Azerbaijan, citing the deterioration of the situation of human rights defenders.

The Council of Europe human rights commissioner intervened before the European Court of Human Rights on a number of cases, noting "a clear pattern of repression in Azerbaijan against those expressing dissent or criticism of the authorities."

At the June UN Human Rights Council, 25 states, led by Ireland, condemned the "systematic silencing of critical voices" in Azerbaijan, and called for "immediate and unconditional release" of government critics. On August 20, six UN experts issued a joint statement condemning the Yunuses' conviction as "manifestly politically motivated" and called for an end to "persecution against human rights activists" in Azerbaijan. In September, the UN high commissioner for human rights condemned the crackdown and called for the release of government critics.

The government forced the OSCE's already downgraded operations in Baku to close in July. The OSCE special representative on media freedom issued several statements about prosecutions of journalists, the raid on Radio Azadliq, and the death of Rasim Aliyev.

In March, the UN Committee on the Elimination of Discrimination against Women noted legal improvements, including a domestic violence law, and the institution of a minimum age of marriage at 18 years. The committee criticized the delay in ratifying the CoE's convention on violence against women; a lack of adequate measures to address violence against women and child marriage; as well as restrictive NGO laws and the arrest of and interference with women journalists and activists.

The Extractive Industries Transparency Initiative (EITI) downgraded Azerbaijan's standing from a "compliant" to a "candidate" country in April, insisting that the government ensure "civil society in Azerbaijan can participate in the EITI in a meaningful way."

HUMAN
RIGHTS
WATCH

"The Blood of People
Who Don't Cooperate"
Continuing Torture and Mistreatment of Detainees in Bahrain

Bahrain

In 2015, further evidence emerged of the torture and mistreatment of detainees, pointing to the ineffectiveness of institutions established since 2011 to safeguard detainees, and the persistent failure of authorities to hold officials accountable for torture and other serious rights violations.

Anti-government protests continued despite a ban on freedom of assembly, and police used excessive force to disperse demonstrators. Authorities continued to restrict freedom of expression, prosecuting high profile activists and opposition figures for speech-related offences and subjecting them to unfair trials. The government used repressive new legislation to arbitrarily strip rights activists and political dissidents of their citizenship, in some cases rendering them stateless. Authorities attributed the deaths of three police officers in two incidents to terrorist attacks.

Torture

Torture of detainees continued due to the failure of authorities to implement effectively recommendations for combatting torture that the Bahrain Independent Commission of Inquiry (BICI) put forward in 2011.

Individuals detained at the Criminal Investigations Directorate between 2013 and 2015 described a range of torture methods used there, including electric shock, prolonged suspension in painful positions, severe beatings, threats to rape and kill, forced standing, exposure to extreme cold, and abuse of a sexual nature.

In 2011, the BICI report had identified all of these methods of torture and concluded that the authorities "followed a systematic practice of physical and psychological mistreatment, which in many cases amounted to torture, with respect to a large number of detainees in their custody."

Bahraini lawyers complained about official practices that have the effect of circumventing the country's legislative safeguards against torture, particularly the authorities' failure to divulge the whereabouts of detained suspects, often for weeks at a time.

Former detainees and families of inmates held at Jaw Prison alleged that security forces firing tear gas and bird shot used disproportionate force to quell violent unrest among prisoners there on March 10, 2015. They then subjected inmates to torture and cruel, inhuman and degrading treatment, including forcing hundreds of prisoners to stay outside in open areas, where they beat and humiliated them. One prisoner described how security forces made inmates strip to their underwear and perform exercises while shouting chants in support of King Hamad bin Isa Al Khalifa.

Another described how officers broke an inmate's collarbone and then left him without medical attention. A group of inmates accused of encouraging the riot were taken to a separate building, where some were severely beaten in toilets and administration rooms, where there are no cameras.

The institutions that the authorities established in response to the BICI report findings and recommendations, in particular the Special Investigations Unit (SIU) and the Ministry of Interior Ombudsman, are still failing to hold security forces and high officials accountable for torture and serious mistreatment of persons in custody.

The SIU has not conducted investigations or prosecutions that have led to the conviction of any individuals for acts of torture in cases relating to Bahrain's political unrest. The ombudsman, who accepts individual complaints and directs them to the appropriate investigatory authority, did not provide details concerning the 83 cases his office referred to the SIU, so it is unclear how many may have related to allegations of torture.

Freedom of Expression and Fair Trial

Bahraini authorities continued to prosecute individuals, including high-profile activists and opposition figures, for exercising their right to freedom of expression.

In April, authorities arrested the prominent human rights activist Nabeel Rajab after he criticized the authorities on social media. Rajab had repeated allegations that authorities had tortured Jaw Prison inmates in the aftermath of unrest at the jail on March 10, and criticized the Bahraini military's involvement in the conflict in Yemen.

In May, a court of appeal upheld a six-month sentence Rajab received in late 2014 for "offending national institutions" after he criticized the government on social media for using counterterrorism laws to prosecute human rights defenders and said that Bahraini security forces foster violent beliefs akin to those of the extremist group Islamic State (also known as ISIS).

In July, authorities announced that King Hamad had pardoned Rajab for unspecified health reasons, but at time of writing he still faced charges relating to the comments that led to his arrest in April and remained under a travel ban.

In July, authorities arrested Ibrahim Sharfi, secretary general of the opposition National Democratic Action Society, and accused him of encouraging the government's overthrow and "inciting hatred" in a speech that consisted solely of peaceful criticism of the government and calls for political reform.

Authorities had released Sharif from prison two weeks earlier, nine months before the end of a five-year sentence. In 2011, a court found Sharif guilty of "terrorism" on the basis that he was one of a group of individuals who chose to "advocate the declaration of a republic in the country." At time of writing, Sharif remained in pretrial detention with a December 15 trial date.

On June 16, 2015, a Bahraini court convicted Sheikh Ali Salman, secretary general of the country's largest legally recognized opposition political society, Al Wifaq, of three speech-related charges and sentenced him to four years in prison. The presiding judge refused to allow Sheikh Salman's defense lawyers to present potentially exculpatory evidence, including recordings of speeches for which he was prosecuted, on the grounds that "the intent of them is to raise doubts about the substantiating evidence that has persuaded the court." At time of writing, Salman's third appeal hearing was scheduled for December 12.

In August, the Bahraini cabinet discussed a draft law on "criminalizing contempt of religions," which would also criminalize "any hate and sectarian discourse that undermines national unity." At time of writing, the cabinet had referred the draft to the Ministerial Committee for Legal Affairs for further study.

Revocation of Nationality

As a result of a 2014 amendment to Bahrain's citizenship law, the Interior Ministry can, with cabinet approval, revoke the citizenship of any person who, according to authorities, "aids or is involved in the service of a hostile state" or who "causes harm to the interests of the Kingdom or acts in a way that contravenes his duty of loyalty to it."

On January 31, the minister of interior revoked the citizenship of 72 Bahrainis stating that they had been involved in "illegal acts," including "inciting and advocating regime change through illegal means," "defaming brotherly countries," and "defaming the image of the regime."

The 72 individuals included former parliamentarians, doctors, politicians, human rights activists, and several Bahrainis alleged to have left the country to join ISIS. The government did not inform the individuals concerned, some of whom are living in exile abroad, of the specific reasons for revoking their citizenship.

Women's Rights and Sexual Orientation and Gender Identity

Law no. 19 of 2009 on the Promulgation of the Law of Family Rulings regulates matters of personal status in Bahrain's Sunni courts. It does not apply in the country's Shia courts, with the result that Shia women, who comprise the majority of women in Bahrain, are not covered by a codified personal status law.

In May, a parliamentary committee called for the repeal of article 353 of the penal code, which allows rapists to escape punishment if they marry their victim. The article was not amended by the end of 2015. In August, the king ratified the Law on Protection from Family Violence, which for the first time provides measures to protect individuals from domestic violence, including requiring authorities to investigate and assist domestic violence victims, and allows public prosecutors to issue temporary protection orders for victims.

In November, Bahrain's Supreme Council for Women announced the launch of a National Strategy for the Protection of Women from Domestic Violence.

Same-sex conduct is not criminalized in Bahrain. However, there is no law that prohibits discrimination on the grounds of sex, gender, sexual orientation, or gender identity.

Key International Actors

Bahrain joined the Saudi Arabia-led coalition that began attacking Houthi forces in Yemen in March. Coalition airstrikes caused thousands of civilian deaths and injuries in Yemen, while a coalition-imposed sea and air blockade threatened to cause widespread starvation.

In June, the United States State Department lifted restrictions on arms sales to Bahrain stating that the government had made "some meaningful progress on human rights reforms," while acknowledging that the human rights situation was not "adequate."

In September, 33 states, including the US and the United Kingdom, supported a joint statement at the United Nations Human Rights Council in Geneva—the fifth since June 2012—criticizing Bahrain and calling for the release of political prisoners and for the revision of laws that restrict freedom of expression. Both the US and the UK signed the statement.

On July 9, the European Parliament adopted an emergency resolution on the rights situation in Bahrain, and on the case of Nabeel Rajab in particular. Rajab received a pardon from the king four days later. The US and the UK had also criticized his original conviction.

HUMAN
RIGHTS
WATCH

"Whoever Raises their Head
Suffers the Most"
Workers' Rights in Bangladesh's Garment Factories

Bangladesh

Bangladesh headed in an authoritarian direction in 2015. Bangladesh has not had an effective parliamentary opposition since the Bangladesh Nationalist Party (BNP) boycotted national elections in 2014. In place of parliamentary debate, 2015 saw the BNP taking to the streets and the government under Awami League leader Sheikh Hasina cracking down on free expression and civil society.

In several instances, commuters were killed or injured when street protests turned violent. The frequent blockades and strikes also prevented many children from attending school or sitting examinations.

The government responded by deploying troops to quell the street violence, detaining thousands of opposition members, and restricting BNP leader Khaleda Zia to her office ahead of planned opposition protests. Key opposition leaders were arrested, accused of serious offenses, some of which were trumped up. Many remained in hiding, fearing arrest. Security forces committed serious abuses including killings, "disappearances," and arbitrary arrests, with few investigations or prosecutions of those responsible.

Freedom of speech came under increasing attack. Media critical of the government continued to face closure, and editors faced charges and arrest. Four bloggers with atheist sympathies were hacked to death. Instead of denouncing the attacks, the government called on bloggers to use restraint in their exercise of free speech. Civil society activists and journalists faced lawsuits from ruling party supporters for criticizing the government, and contempt of court allegations for criticizing unfair trials.

Bangladesh made some progress in ensuring better safety regulations in garment factories following the collapse of the Rana Plaza building, which killed and injured thousands of workers in 2013. There were some improvements to labor laws in 2015, including the removal of arbitrary legal hurdles to unionize, but some factory owners still used threats and violence against union leaders to stymie union formation.

Security Force Abuses and Impunity

The ruling Awami League entered office promising zero tolerance for serious human rights abuses, but such abuses have continued unabated and in some areas have increased. The Detective Branch of the police, the Bangladesh Border Guards (BGB), and the Rapid Action Battalion (RAB) have been responsible for serious abuses, including arbitrary arrests, torture, enforced disappearances, and killings.

Opposition BNP spokesman Salahuddin Ahmed was abducted on March 10, 2015, from a friend's apartment where he was in hiding. Witnesses said the abductors identified themselves as member of the Detective Branch, while other witnesses reported RAB vehicles in the area. In May, Ahmed was found in India and was charged by Indian authorities with illegal entry. He sought protection from the United Nations Refugee Agency (UNHCR), saying he had been abducted by unknown gunmen and feared for his life if returned to Bangladesh. The government failed to investigate the possible role of security forces in this and other disappearances, even in cases where family members identified the perpetrators to be members of RAB or police.

The opposition Jamaat-e-Islami party claims its activists were arrested and tortured by the police, including its Detective Branch, and says several members were killed by security forces. For instance, witnesses saw the police arrest Ahmadullah, a 22-year-old student supporter of the party, on January 31; his body was found the next morning. The police claimed that he was killed in crossfire between security forces and Jamaat supporters.

Several Jamaat supporters said that the police took them into custody and deliberately shot them in the knee or shin to disable them. Odhikar, a Bangladesh human rights group, documented at least 30 cases where people were shot in the leg—sometimes after arrest. The police claimed the shootings occurred during efforts to disperse violent mobs.

According to the Bangladesh human rights organization Ain O Salish Kendra, of the 135 people killed by security forces between January and September 2015, 90 were by the police, 33 by RAB, and the rest by other security agencies including the BGB.

In August, RAB was identified as responsible for the killing of three ruling party activists, leading to dismay among government supporters.

Attacks on Civil Society

The government increased its attacks on civil society organizations and critics in 2015, and drafted a new law restricting foreign funding to Bangladeshi groups.

The human rights organization, Odhikar, was regularly harassed, its access to foreign funding blocked. In August, after Odhikar published a report on extrajudicial killings, the police issued a statement warning that activities that harm the reputation of the security forces are considered acts of subversion. Criminal charges remain pending against its secretary, Adilur Rahman, and director, ASM Nasiruddin Elan, for allegedly publishing false information.

Ain O Salish Kendra (ASK), another prominent human rights organization, remained under pressure for reporting on enforced disappearances and extrajudicial killings. In May 2014, ASK reported an attempt by security forces to abduct its director of investigations, Mohammad Nur Khan. Groups working on indigenous and minority issues continued to report intimidating surveillance, and humanitarian groups working with the refugee Rohingya population faced ongoing restrictions.

Freedom of Expression

In several instances, critical editors and journalists were sued by government supporters. In August, university teacher Muhammad Ruhul Amin Khandaker was convicted for a 2011 Facebook comment blaming the prime minister for a rise in fatal traffic accidents. Later in August, journalist Probir Sikdar was arrested for a Facebook post that alleged to have "tarnished the image" of a ruling Awami League leader, a relative of Prime Minister Sheikh Hasina, and a member of her cabinet.

Journalists and civil society activists critical of Bangladesh's war crimes tribunal (see below) faced contempt charges and trials. Journalist David Bergman was found guilty of contempt for criticizing the tribunal. When a group of 49 civil society actors signed a petition against his conviction, they were charged with con-

HUMAN
RIGHTS
WATCH

**MARRY BEFORE YOUR HOUSE
IS SWEPT AWAY**
Child Marriage in Bangladesh

tempt as well. Most of them offered unconditional apologies to avoid convictions.

Several bloggers and their publishers were hacked to death by Islamist militants in 2015 for promoting secularism. Ansar Al Islam, an insurgent group linked to Al-Qaeda, claimed responsibility and threatened further attacks. Although Sheikh Hasina promised to take action against the attacks, she also warned the bloggers against "hurting people's religious sentiments." The killings of three foreigners in October and November, this time claimed by the armed extremist group Islamic State (also known as ISIS), heightened anxieties over what appeared to be increasing violence in the name of religion.

Labor Rights

Intense international and national scrutiny following the collapse of the Rana Plaza factory complex in April 2013 led to efforts to shore up safety conditions and workers' rights across the garment sector. International brands pledged to conduct fire and safety inspections across all factories they used in Bangladesh and to make their reports public. Concerns remained about inspections carried out by Bangladeshi authorities, however, as these were not made public. Union leaders and those seeking to join unions faced threats and opposition from factory managers and owners, including physical violence in some instances.

Labor conditions remain poor in other industries. The government continues its de facto policy of not enforcing labor and environmental laws against tanneries in Hazaribagh, a residential area of Dhaka. Workers in the tanneries continue to suffer from highly toxic and dangerous working conditions, and local residents complain of illnesses caused by the extreme pollution of air, water, and soil resulting from tannery operations. Some tanneries have begun to build new premises at a dedicated industrial zone in Savar, but production had not started, and the seriousness of the government's commitment to better regulating tanneries there remained unclear at time of writing.

Early and Forced Marriage

Bangladesh has the highest rate of marriage in the world for girls under 15. Sixty-five percent of girls in Bangladesh marry before age 18. While the legal age of marriage for women is 18, the law is almost entirely unenforced. Local government officials often facilitate child marriages by collecting bribes in return for furnishing forged birth certificates.

The government failed in 2015 to take decisive steps to end the practice. Eliminating child marriage will require ending associated school costs that lead to drop-outs, despite free tuition; making schools responsible for helping to prevent child marriages; taking appropriate action against government officials who facilitate child marriage; strengthening criminal justice responses to child marriage and sexual harassment and threats against girls; improving girls' access to information about family planning and to contraceptive supplies; and improving public awareness about the health and legal consequences of child marriage.

In 2014, Sheikh Hasina pledged to end marriage of children under age 15 by 2021 and under 18 by 2041. Her government subsequently proposed to lower the age of marriage for girls to 16.

Overseas Workers

Many Bangladeshis work in Persian Gulf countries as domestic workers. The government has sought to increase the recruitment of such workers without putting in place adequate protection mechanisms. Bangladeshi workers in the Gulf report being deprived of food and forced to endure psychological, physical, and sexual abuse. Bangladesh has set a minimum salary equivalent to around US$200, the lowest minimum salary of all sending countries—and its embassies in the region do not provide adequate protection and assistance to many Bangladeshi nationals there.

Refugees

Nearly 32,000 long-term Rohingya refugees live in camps administered by UNHCR along Bangladesh's border with Burma. These refugees, and another 200,000 stateless Rohingya in Bangladesh, face often terrible conditions, and humanitarian groups seeking to provide assistance to them in border regions face highly restrictive conditions.

War Crimes Trials

The International Crimes Tribunal (ICT), set up to address laws of war violations committed during Bangladesh's 1971 independence movement, continued its operations in 2015 without addressing serious procedural and substantive defects that lead to unfair trials.

In April, Mohammad Kamaruzzaman, a leading member of the Jamaat-e-Islami party, was hanged. His trial violated basic fair trial standards, arbitrarily curtailing the ability of the defense team to submit evidence, including witnesses and documents, and to challenge the credibility of prosecution witnesses by confronting them with prior inconsistent statements.

In July, the death sentence against BNP member Mir Qasem Ali Salahuddin Qader Chowdhury was upheld on appeal. Both he and Ali Ahmed Mohammed Mujahid were executed on November 21 after the president rejected their last-minute clemency petitions. Several other accused were awaiting final appellate judgments at time of writing, including Motiur Rahman Nizami, who was sentenced to death in October 2014.

Sexual Orientation and Gender Identity

Same-sex sexual behavior, dubbed "carnal intercourse against the order of nature," is criminalized in Bangladesh. Lesbian, gay, bisexual, and transgender rights groups reported continuing threats, particularly after homophobic public comments by Islamic leaders.

In 2013, the cabinet issued a circular indicating legal recognition of a third gender, called *hijra*, a traditional cultural identity for transgender people who, assigned male at birth, do not identify as men. The third gender status came with no official definition but could ostensibly accord *hijras* education, health, and housing rights. However, the decree did not indicate any process by which legal recognition as a third gender should be conferred. In December 2014, a group of 12 *hijras* were selected for a government employment scheme, and in early 2015 they were subjected to invasive and abusive exams as part of the hiring process. The *hijras* said they were asked humiliating questions about their bodies, and some reported that the physicians in charge of the exams called them "disgusting" and then instructed hospital janitors and security guards to conduct physical exams, which included touching their genitals. Shortly after the medical exams, the *hijras'* names were exposed in a newspaper article that declared them impostors because they were "really men." The 12 were denied their employment positions and report increased harassment from neighbors.

Key International Actors

In June, Bangladesh and India signed a border agreement which allowed the two countries to exchange small land enclaves; prior to the agreement, people living in the enclaves had been effectively stateless, many without legal title to their property.

Influential bilateral partners, including the United States, United Kingdom, and India failed to press for an end to government repression of the political opposition and civil society. These and other countries welcomed the government's efforts to curb extremist groups but failed to demand proof or challenge its claims that opposition political parties were engaged in "terrorism," a claim it used to justify attacks on opponents.

The US Department of Justice funded and trained an internal investigations program within RAB, but the program produced no human rights prosecutions or convictions, and the US said little publicly to signal the importance of RAB accountability.

India pledged in 2012 to prosecute members of the Border Security Force for serious abuses against illegal Bangladeshi migrants crossing the border, but made little progress in 2015.

After intense international and national scrutiny following the collapse of the Rana Plaza factory complex in April 2013, two large international cooperative agreements—one involving largely European companies (Bangladesh Accord) and the second involving largely North American companies (Alliance)—pledged to conduct fire and safety inspections across all factories they use in Bangladesh. However, when the accord pushed for labor law reforms, the government insisted that the accord's mandate was restricted to safety inspections. The US refused to reinstate Bangladesh's GSP plus status, arguing that it had not made sufficient improvements in labor sector reforms.

Belarus

President Aliaksander Lukashenka released on humanitarian grounds six opposition figures who had been imprisoned on politically motivated charges, but the overall human rights situation in Belarus in 2015 did not improve.

The death penalty remains in use. Officials pressure and arrest human rights activists and critics on spurious charges. Authorities regularly harass independent and opposition journalists. Legislative amendments further restricted freedom of expression, in particular Internet freedom.

Observers deemed the October presidential elections insufficiently transparent and flawed due to significant irregularities with vote counting. While Belarus held its first human rights dialogue with the European Union since 2009, authorities continued to refuse cooperation with the United Nations special rapporteur on Belarus. In a positive development, in September, Belarus signed the Convention on the Rights of Persons with Disabilities but has yet to take the necessary steps to become a full party to the treaty.

Death Penalty

Belarus remains the only European country to use the death penalty. In 2015, the country took no steps to introduce a moratorium or to abolish it. In April, at the Council of Europe's Parliamentary Assembly, a Belarusian parliamentarian stated that Belarus is "ready to discuss the issue of the abolition of the death penalty with the Council of Europe."

In July, an appeals court in a closed hearing upheld the March death sentence of Siarhei Ivanou, 21, for the murder of a young woman. In November, a regional court sentenced Ivan Kulesh to death for the murder of three women.

Arrests and Harassment of Human Rights Defenders and Critics

The authorities continue to routinely use arbitrary detentions, searches, and interrogations to harass government critics.

In February, authorities forced leading human rights lawyer Elena Tonkacheva of the Legal Transformation Center to leave the country after annulling her residence permit on spurious grounds. Tonkacheva, a Russian citizen who had lived in Belarus for more than 30 years, was barred from re-entering for 3 years.

In March, the police searched the Viasna Human Rights Center's Mahilau office, seizing computers in conjunction with a libel case against a local newspaper editor. Authorities did not return the computers until August, although the investigation was closed in April. The group's representatives believe that authorities searched the computers for information about their human rights work.

In February and March, Leanid Sudalenka, chairman of the Legal Initiative's Homiel branch, received death threats against him and his family, making specific reference to Sudalenka's human rights work. The authorities refused to investigate. In early April, the authorities searched the Social and Political Center in Homiel, which hosts Sudalenka's organization and other groups, as well as Sudalenka's home. Police seized computers and questioned Sudalenka under a criminal investigation for alleged distribution of pornography from his email. Sudalenka believes the investigation is in retaliation for his human rights work; he said that his email account had been hacked months before, and he stopped using it.

On August 22, President Lukashenka pardoned and released on "humanitarian grounds" six men sentenced in politically motivated trials: Mikalai Statkevich, Ihar Alinevich, Mikalai Dziadok, Yauhen Vaskovich, Artsyom Prakapenka, and Yuri Rubtsou. Like others convicted in political trials and released since 2011, the criminal records of those pardoned were not expunged, preventing them from occupying governmental jobs or standing in elections. Once released, such individuals remain on law enforcement "preventative watch lists," authorizing police to question them frequently. Some have also been forbidden, without explanation, from leaving Belarus.

On August 11, in Minsk, police detained five youth activists for graffiti in public places. Police released two of them, but detained and later charged Maksim Pekarski and Vadzim Zharomski with "hooliganism committed by a group of persons." Pekarski and Zharomski were released after confessing and paying damages, but the criminal investigation continues. A third man, Viachaslau

Kasinerau, was not charged, but was hospitalized with a jaw fracture, allegedly inflicted in police detention to pressure him to testify against the others.

Freedom of Expression

Authorities routinely harass and interfere with the work of independent and op-position journalists and bloggers. Law enforcement officials intensified prosecutions of independent freelance journalists for cooperation with unregistered foreign media, bringing 28 cases against 13 journalists through August, according to the Belarusian Association of Journalists. All resulted in significant fines.

December 2014 amendments to the law on mass media, hastily adopted without public discussion, authorized the Ministry of Information to block website access without judicial review after issuing two warnings, and made website owners responsible for unlawful content. In December 2014, the ministry blocked dozens of websites, including the largest independent information agency, the Belarusian Private News Agency, or BelaPAN, and opposition sites.

In the first half of 2015, the ministry denied access to 26 sites on the grounds that they were "distributing drugs," published profanity, or in one case, criticized the World War II Victory Day celebration and its participants. The latter involved an article calling on the authorities to use resources to assist war veterans, rather than organize a parade. Access was restored to two sites after they sought to remedy "the committed violations." December 2014 amendments to the criminal code introduced sentences of up to two years' jail for online defamation.

The ministry issued 30 warnings to 29 media outlets through August for violations such as using the acronym "RB" instead of the official Republic of Belarus in their materials. After two or more warnings, the ministry may request a court-ordered closure.

The December 2014 amendments also require distributors of print and broadcast media to register with the Ministry of Information and entitle the ministry to withdraw distribution rights on numerous grounds.

In December 2014, a draft law on "protecting children from information harmful for their health and development" was introduced in parliament. The law proposes to restrict dissemination of factually neutral or positive information about lesbian, gay, bisexual, and transgender people, blatantly discriminatory on the basis of sexual orientation.

Freedom of Association

Authorities continue to enforce legislation criminalizing involvement in an unregistered organization, and at the same time arbitrarily deny registration to and attempt to dissolve nongovernmental organizations (NGOs).

In March, the Ministry of Justice attempted to dissolve the only officially registered regional human rights organization, the Mahilau Human Rights Center, citing problems with its legal address. The group's representatives maintain that security service officials pressured their landlord to revoke their rental agreement. Authorities brought a similar lawsuit against the group in 2014. In April, the ministry withdrew the lawsuit.

In June, the Supreme Court deemed lawful the Ministry of Justice's refusal to register the Human Rights Association "For Fair Elections." The association's founders believe the grounds for refusal were minor and correctable, and that the denial, the third since 2011, was arbitrary and politically motivated.

On August 31, President Lukashenka signed a decree that the government said would improve procedures for NGOs receiving foreign donations. Belarusian NGO experts counter that the decree tightens reporting requirements and state control over use of foreign donations, and preserves existing restrictions, including wide latitude to refuse permission for foreign donations and severely penalize groups receiving unregistered foreign aid.

For the first time since 2001, the authorities invited monitors from the Parliamentary Assembly of the Council of Europe (PACE) to observe the October presidential election. In its pre-electoral statement, PACE emphasized that public broadcasters are obligated to ensure equal access for candidates without privileging the incumbent president. The Organization for Security and Co-operation in Europe's Office for Democratic Institutions and Human Rights (OSCE/ODIHR) also observed the elections. The OSCE observers found that significant problems, particularly during vote counting, undermined the integrity of the election and concluded that Belarus still has a considerable way to go in meeting its OSCE commitments for democratic elections.

Key International Actors

Belarusian authorities appeared to be seeking a political rapprochement with European governments and institutions, and hosted a number of high-level visits. Yet the European visitors failed to take full advantage of the opportunity to secure tangible rights improvements.

The government continued to actively oppose and refuse to cooperate with the mandate of Miklos Haraszti, the United Nations special rapporteur on Belarus, appointed in 2012. In June, the UN Human Rights Council extended the rapporteur's mandate for another year.

In February, authorities invited Andrea Rigoni, PACE rapporteur on the situation in Belarus, to visit. Rigoni met with officials, opposition activists, and NGO leaders. Rigoni called on PACE to seize the "favourable momentum" and encourage further initiatives to improve human rights and full normalization of Council of Europe (CoE) relations. Yet he stopped short of specifying what steps Belarus should take.

At the May UN Human Rights Council's Universal Periodic Review of Belarus, states raised concerns about the death penalty, politically motivated imprisonment, torture, and freedoms of assembly, association, and speech, but Belarus did not commit to specific reforms of its restrictive legislation. Belarus was urged to fully cooperate with UN human rights mechanisms.

In Brussels in July, the EU and Belarus held their second-ever human rights dialogue; the dialogue had been suspended since they first met in 2009. Topics included establishment of a national human rights institution; freedom of expression, assembly, and association; the death penalty; combating torture; and children's rights. The EU also raised the detention of human rights defenders and activists on politically motivated charges. There is no publicly available information on the government's response or any concrete outcomes.

On July 31, 24 Belarusian officials were removed from the EU's list of individuals subject to travel bans and asset freezes. In October, in response to the release of opposition figures and in the context of improving EU-Belarus relations, the EU suspended for four months restrictive measures applying to 170 individuals and three entities in Belarus.

Key international actors, including the EU, the CoE, and the United States, welcomed the release of six political prisoners in August, while making clear that further steps were needed for Belarus to move toward normalized relations.

Bolivia

Impunity for violent crime and for human rights violations remains a serious problem in Bolivia. Extensive and arbitrary use of pretrial detention—and trial delays—undermine defendants' rights and contribute to prison overcrowding, despite recent legal reforms.

The administration of President Evo Morales has created a hostile environment for human rights defenders that undermines their ability to work independently. Threats to judicial independence, violence against women, and child labor are other major concerns.

Impunity for Abuses and Violent Crime

Bolivia has prosecuted only a few of the officials responsible for human rights violations committed under authoritarian governments between 1964 and 1982, according to the United Nations Human Rights Committee. A contributing factor has been the unwillingness of the armed forces to provide information on the fate of people killed or forcibly disappeared during this period. In March, the deputy solicitor general announced plans to create a truth commission to investigate these crimes, but the government has not yet defined its scope.

Efforts to bring to justice those allegedly responsible for killings during violent clashes in 2008 between supporters and opponents of President Morales have made little progress. As of September 2015, a La Paz court had yet to rule in a case involving Leopoldo Fernández, former prefect of Pando Department, and three local officials charged in 2008 for their roles in the killing of 13 people.

The government has not reopened an investigation into the April 2009 killing of two Hungarians (one of Bolivian birth) and an Irishman who the government alleged were mercenaries involved in a separatist plot. Police shot them dead after storming into their hotel rooms in Santa Cruz. Independent reports suggest that at least two of the three may have been extrajudicially executed.

Prosecutors have yet to investigate fully allegations that police in 2011 gagged, stripped, and beat protesters when dispersing a largely peaceful demonstration against a proposed highway in the Isiboro Secure National Park and Indigenous Territory (known as "TIPNIS"). In April 2015, the Attorney General's Office dismissed the criminal case against a former vice minister of interior and at least 10 members of the National Police whom the Ombudsman's Office had implicated in the violations.

The lack of justice has led to mob attacks (or "lynchings") against citizens or police officers believed responsible for crimes. Ten people were killed in lynchings from January to November 2014, according to the UN High Commissioner for Human Rights. In September 2015, a mob tied a suspected criminal to a pole and beat him to death in El Alto, according to press reports. Impunity for lynchings remains the norm.

Military Abuses and Jurisdiction

Human rights violations against soldiers remain a problem. The Ombudsman's Office reported that four soldiers died on military premises between January and August 2015, and no one has been held accountable for their deaths.

The Constitutional Court ruled in 2012 that a civilian court should have jurisdiction in the case of a conscript who died in 2011 following a combat training exercise during which instructors allegedly beat him on the head and chest. The court urged lawmakers to reform Bolivia's military justice code to ensure that human rights violations are heard in civilian courts. In August 2015, a civilian court convicted three military officers for the conscript's death, but, at time of writing, the code had not been reformed.

Judicial Independence

The Bolivian justice system has been plagued by corruption, delays, and political interference for years. The 2009 constitution provided for judicial elections to overhaul Bolivia's highest courts, but the Plurinational Assembly selected candidates through a process that lacked transparency and did not adequately consider their qualifications. In January 2015, President Morales announced a new judicial reform process, but the government has not yet defined its scope.

Due Process and Prison Conditions

As of June, 78 percent of inmates in Bolivian prisons had not been convicted of a crime. Extended pretrial detention and trial delays have led to increased overcrowding and poor conditions in prisons. As of May, there were 13,793 inmates in prisons with a maximum capacity of 5,126.

A 2014 law decreased the maximum periods of pre-trial detention in most cases, but eliminated the maximums for certain crimes. Decrees adopted since 2012 allow the president to reduce the sentences of those convicted of crimes and pardon those in pretrial detention for minor crimes. As of August, more than 3,300 people had benefited from the changes.

Human Rights Defenders

Human rights defenders continue to face harassment and threats, including from government officials, undermining their ability to work independently.

In 2013, President Morales signed a law and adopted a decree granting the government broad powers to dissolve civil society organizations. Under the decree, any government office may request that that Ministry of Autonomy revoke an organization's permit if it performs activities different from those listed in its bylaws, or if the organization's legal representative is criminally sanctioned for carrying out activities that "undermine security or public order." As of September 2015, a case brought by the Ombudsman's Office challenging both provisions was still pending before the Constitutional Court.

In August 2015, Vice President García Linera accused four Bolivian NGOs of trying to "impede the development" of Bolivia; in June, President Morales said that any international NGO engaged in activities "detrimental to the exploitation of natural resources would have to leave Bolivia."

In 2013, the government expelled the Danish nongovernmental organization IBIS, which had worked with indigenous groups, accusing it of engaging in "political interference."

Freedom of Expression

While public debate is robust, the Morales administration periodically lashes out at journalists, accusing them without basis of publishing what it calls lies and politically motivated distortions. In September, the minister of the presidency accused local outlets of participating in an international conspiracy against Bolivia and President Morales.

Bolivia lacks transparent criteria for using government funds to purchase media advertisements, and some media companies have accused the government of discriminating against outlets that criticize government officials. There is no national law ensuring public access to information held by government bodies.

Indigenous Rights

The 2009 Bolivian Constitution includes comprehensive guarantees for the rights of indigenous groups, including collective land titling, intercultural education, prior consultation on development projects, and protection of indigenous justice systems. A 2011 law establishing jurisdictional boundaries between indigenous and ordinary justice systems has yet to be fully implemented.

Indigenous peoples' right to free, prior, and informed consent (FPIC) regarding legislative or administrative measures that may affect them is not fully embodied in Bolivian legislation. A current mining law limits FPIC to the exploitation phase of land concessions, but international standards call for FPIC through all stages of projects that impact on indigenous peoples' right to land and resources.

Gender-Based Violence and Reproductive Rights

Women and girls in Bolivia remain at high risk for gender-based violence, despite a 2013 law that sets forth comprehensive measures to prevent and prosecute violence against women. The law created the crime of "femicide" and called for the establishment of shelters for women, as well as special prosecutors and courts for gender-based crimes.

As of April 2015, a special police force created by the law had received some 60,000 complaints of gender-based violence, including 8,394 in 2015. In August, official sources reported that 115 "femicides" had occurred in Bolivia since 2013, and prosecutors had obtained convictions in 10 cases.

Women and girls face numerous obstacles to accessing reproductive health products, contraceptives, and services including abortion after rape (one of the few circumstances in Bolivia in which abortion is not penalized). Between 2008 and 2013, 775 women were criminally prosecuted for having an abortion, according to Ipas, a local nongovernmental organization, and thousands sought medical care for incomplete abortions.

In January 2015, the Health Ministry instructed public and private health services to comply with a 2014 Constitutional Court ruling that prior judicial authorization and prosecution of the alleged offender were not prerequisites for post-rape abortion.

Child Labor

In 2014, the Plurinational Assembly adopted legislation allowing children as young as 10 to work, violating international standards and making Bolivia the first country in the world to legalize employment at such a young age. In February 2015, the Ombudsman's Office said that 850,000 children worked in Bolivia, most of them less than 14 years old.

Sexual Orientation and Gender Identity

Impunity for acts of violence and discrimination on grounds of sexual orientation or gender identity persist. No one has been held accountable for the killings of more than 55 LGBT persons since 2004, according to local groups.

The 2009 constitution defines marriage as the union of a man and a woman. A proposal to legalize civil unions remained pending before the Plurinational Assembly at time of writing.

Key International Actors

President Morales announced in 2013 that he was "seriously considering withdrawing" from the Inter-American Commission on Human Rights, but Bolivia participated in hearings there in 2015.

In July, during its review of Bolivia's compliance with the Convention on the Elimination of Discrimination Against Women (CEDAW), the CEDAW Committee expressed concern at the prevalence of different forms of violence against women in Bolivia and the continuing impunity enjoyed by most perpetrators.

Bosnia and Herzegovina

Despite parliament's commitments for reforms, there was little change in 2015 regarding human rights for the people of Bosnia and Herzegovina. Severe floods in 2014 worsened the already bleak economic and social prospects for internally displaced people and those who returned home after the war.

Journalists remained vulnerable to intimidation and threats. The authorities failed to make progress on ending discriminatory restrictions political office candidacy for Jews, Roma, and members of other minority groups. Roma remain the most vulnerable group, subject to widespread discrimination. The 20th anniversary of the Srebrenica genocide highlighted the limited progress on justice for war crimes in Bosnia and Herzegovina.

Ethnic and Religious Discrimination

The government made no progress toward amending the constitution to eliminate ethnic and religious discrimination in candidacy for the national tripartite presidency and the House of Peoples. Currently, the constitution requires candidates for these institutions to come from one of the three main ethnic groups—Bosniaks, Serbs, and Croats. The European Court of Human Rights in 2014 ruled to affirm a previous judgment that this limitation in the constitution violates the European Convention on Human Rights.

Authorities failed again to make changes to the voting system in the city of Mostar, ordered by the Constitutional Court of Bosnia and Herzegovina. Residents of the city have been unable to vote in local elections since 2008.

Roma remain the most vulnerable group in the country, facing widespread discrimination in employment, education, and political representation. Lack of a free and universal birth registration system means that many Roma are not on the national public registry that records births, deaths, and marriages. This impedes their access to public services, including health care.

Accountability for War Crimes

The 20th anniversary of the Srebrenica genocide shone a spotlight on the limited progress toward justice for war crimes committed in Bosnia. While the International Criminal Tribunal for the former Yugoslavia (ICTY) has convicted 14 people of crimes committed at Srebrenica, and the trials of the alleged architects of the genocide continue in the Hague, progress in the national courts has been more limited.

At time of writing, the defense case in the trial of Ratko Mladic, the Bosnian Serb wartime general, was in progress at the international tribunal. Mladic has been charged with genocide, war crimes, and crimes against humanity, including in Srebrenica. In late 2014, ICTY judges granted the prosecution's request to re-open the case to put forth new evidence of a mass grave discovered in the village of Tomašica, in the Prijedor municipality, the presentation of which concluded in July. The trial judgment is expected in November 2017.

In July, Bosnian Serb wartime President Radovan Karadzic, also on trial at the international tribunal on many of the same charges as Mladic, demanded a new trial, citing unfair treatment and prosecution errors. His claim was rejected and his trial continued. Closing arguments were heard in late September and a verdict was expected in the first quarter of 2016.

The Bosnian government remained slow to implement the national war crimes strategy, adopted in 2008 to improve the prosecution of domestic war crimes. Prosecutors still lack sufficient capacity and funding, particularly at the district and cantonal levels. According to current estimates by the Organization for Security and Co-operation in Europe, there is a backlog of more than 1,200 cases in Bosnian courts involving several thousand suspects.

By September 2015, the War Crimes Chamber of the State Court of Bosnia and Herzegovina had reached 15 verdicts (3 acquittals, 9 convictions, and 3 partially acquitting verdicts) at the first instance in relation to 24 defendants, and 18 verdicts (1 acquittal, 15 convictions, and 2 partially acquitting verdicts) at the second instance in relation to 27 defendants, increasing the total number of completed cases to 290 since the court became fully operational in 2005. Throughout 2015, Zeljka Cvijanovic, prime minister of the Republika Srpska entity, repeatedly challenged the legitimacy of the state court and the state prosecutor's office.

The State Court sentenced two Bosnian Serb soldiers to 10-year prison terms in June for rape during the 1992 to 1995 conflict, and in a landmark ruling, granted financial compensation to the victim. Previously, rape survivors have had to seek compensation through the civil court.

The Appeals Division of the Court of Bosnia and Herzegovina in February revised the sentence of Milorad Trbic in relation to his criminal conviction for genocide, from 30 years to 20 years in prison. Trbic was among dozens of people convicted of war time abuses whose sentences were vacated or convictions were quashed by the Constitutional Court of Bosnia and Herzegovina, following a 2013 European Court of Human Rights ruling that Bosnian courts had wrongly applied law not in force during the war, when the offenses were committed.

In August, the Prosecutor's Office of Bosnia and Herzegovina indicted Naser Oric and Sabahudin Muhic for war crimes related to the killing of three prisoners during the war. In October, the Prosecutor's Office indicted Dzordze Ristanic for war crimes committed against several hundred Bosniaks and Croats in the territory of Brcko.

National Security

Imad Al Husin, a naturalized Bosnian from Syria detained in 2008, remained in indefinite detention on national security grounds, despite a 2012 European Court of Human Rights ruling that required Bosnia and Herzegovina to charge him, release him, or find a safe third country in which to resettle him.

Zeyad Khalaf Al Gertani, an Iraqi citizen, detained without charge on national security grounds from 2009 until 2014, remained under a supervision order confining him to the Bosnian town of Banovici, away from his family. At time of writing, the conditions of his release were under review by the Constitutional Court of Bosnia and Herzegovina.

Freedom of Media

Journalists continued to face threats and intimidation. As of July, the national journalists' association registered 52 cases of violations of media freedom and expression, including 4 physical attacks and death threats, and 12 cases of threats and pressure. Local and national political authorities interfere with journalists' work, subjecting some media outlets to bogus financial and other governmental inspections. State response to these threats and intimidation is often ineffective, and police investigations rarely yield results.

Freedom of Assembly and Expression

No progress was made on the allegations that police in Sarajevo and Tuzla used excessive force during protests in February 2014, as well as during the subsequent detention of protesters.

Sarajevo Open Centre, the lesbian, gay, bisexual, and transgender rights organization, documented 75 cases of hate speech, 15 cases of hate crimes, and 6 cases of discrimination based on sexual orientation or gender identity in the first 9 months of 2015. There was no progress in the police investigation into a 2014 attack on a film festival organized by Sarajevo Open Centre.

Key International Actors

In August, the Council of Ministers adopted a strategy for the implementation of the Council of Europe's Convention on Preventing and Combating Violence against Women and Domestic Violence, which was ratified by Bosnia and Herzegovina in 2013. The convention creates a comprehensive legal framework to tackle all aspects of violence against women and girls.

In April, on the occasion of International Roma Day, the Organization for Security and Co-operation in Europe (OSCE) called for greater efforts by Bosnia and Herzegovina to end Roma exclusion. The organization emphasized that institutions in Bosnia and Herzegovina should allocate funding necessary for the implementation of OSCE action plans on housing, education, health, and employment for Roma.

The Committee on the Elimination of Racial Discrimination of the Office of the United Nations High Commissioner for Human Rights in its concluding observations urged Bosnia and Herzegovina to amend the constitution as well as the electoral law to abolish discriminatory treatment on the basis of ethnicity. Additionally, it called upon the state to ensure the sustainable reintegration of returnees and to combat direct and indirect discrimination against minority returnees.

The United States State Department annual report on human rights in Bosnia and Herzegovina, published in June, highlighted the considerable number of allegations of torture and other cruel, inhuman, or degrading treatment or punishment. Additionally it underline harsh, and sometimes life-threatening, conditions in prisons and detention centers.

In its annual progress on Bosnia and Heregovina published in November, the European Commission highlighted the inadequate legal and institutional framework for the observance of human rights, intimidation of journalists, deterioration in the conditions for freedom of expression, and ongoing threats and attacks against the LGBTI community.

Brazil

Chronic human rights problems plague Brazil, including unlawful police killings, prison overcrowding, and torture and ill-treatment of detainees. Some recent efforts to reform the criminal justice system aim to address these problems, but others would exacerbate them.

The judiciary in 2015 worked with state governments toward ensuring that detainees are promptly brought before judges after their arrest, as required by international law. But in August, the Chamber of Deputies approved a constitutional amendment that would allow 16- and 17-year-old children to be prosecuted as adults for serious crimes, in violation of international standards. At time of writing, enactment of the amendment still required two additional votes by the Senate.

Internationally, Brazil continued to lead efforts to strengthen protections for the right to privacy in 2015, but its overall record at the United Nations Human Rights Council (HRC) was mixed. Between 2010 and 2015, the number of refugees admitted in the country doubled, reaching a total of 8,400 people.

Public Security and Police Conduct

The number of killings by police officers, including those off-duty, went up by almost 40 percent in 2014 to more than 3,000, according to official data compiled by the nongovernmental organization (NGO) Brazilian Forum on Public Security. In Rio de Janeiro—the state with the highest rate of killings by police—569 people died at the hands of on-duty officers from January to October 2015, an increase of 18 percent over the same period in 2014. In Sao Paulo, on-duty officers killed 494 people in the first nine months of the year, an increase of 1 percent over the same period in 2014.

Police routinely report these deaths as the result of shootouts with criminals. While some of these killings result from legitimate use of force, others do not, as Human Rights Watch and other groups have reported and Brazilian criminal justice officials have recognized.

Police officers in several states have also been implicated in death squad-style killings. In the state of Para, 10 people were killed in November 2014 after the

killing of a police officer who—according to an investigation carried out by the state legislature—had led a death squad. Prosecutors have accused 14 military police officers of failing to help the victims or pursue the killers. In Amazonas, 12 police officers and 3 civilians were detained for allegedly forming a death squad that killed at least 8 people in July, during a weekend in which 36 people were murdered in Manaus, the state capital. In Sao Paulo, 8 police officers were de-tained on charges of involvement in the killing of 19 people—including 2 chil-dren—within a few hours after the August killing of a police officer.

Also in Sao Paulo, 3 police officers were detained in connection with the Sep-tember killing of two 16-year-old children and two 18 year olds. Police investiga-tors believe that the killings were an act of revenge against the youth for allegedly stealing the purse of the wife of one of the detained officers.

Prison Conditions

Many Brazilian prisons and jails are severely overcrowded and plagued by vio-lence. The number of adults behind bars jumped 80 percent in the past decade, and in June 2014 it exceeded 600,000 people—over 60 percent more than the prisons were built to hold—according to the latest data from the Ministry of Jus-tice's Integrated System of Penitentiary Information (InfoPen).

Overcrowding and lack of sufficient staff hinder prison authorities from main-taining control within the prison grounds, leaving inmates vulnerable to violence and gang activity. The crowded conditions also impact prisoners' health. The prevalence of HIV infection in Brazil's prisons is 60 times—and of tuberculosis almost 40 times—that of the overall population, according to InfoPen. A lack of adequate medical screening, prevention, and care, along with poor sanitation and ventilation, contribute to the spread of disease among inmates.

With support from the National Council of Justice (known as CNJ, using the Por-tuguese acronym), which oversees the judicial system, all of Brazil's states have begun to bring detainees before a judge promptly after arrest, as required under international law, although the programs only apply to certain geographic areas in each state for now. In the absence of those "custody hearings," detainees may wait many months for a first hearing with a judge, contributing to prison overcrowding.

Maranhao was the first state to begin the practice, in October 2014. According to data published by the CNJ in November 2015, in 50 percent of the custody hearings held in the state, judges determined that pretrial detention was not warranted and ordered the detainees released pending trial. In contrast, when custody hearings were not held, judges ordered pretrial release in only 10 percent of the cases, according to the state´s judiciary. At time of writing, Brazil's congress was discussing a bill to make custody hearings mandatory throughout the country.

Those hearings also allow judges to detect torture or mistreatment of detainees, a major problem in Brazil. In Rio de Janeiro, almost 20 percent of detainees who had a hearing during the first month of the program said that they had been mistreated by police, according to the state's Public Defender's Office.

In March, the National Mechanism for Preventing and Combating Torture started work, designing a plan of action to monitor detention centers. Its 11 members are authorized to conduct unannounced visits to any detention center and to make recommendations to authorities. The mechanism is part of the National System to Prevent and Combat Torture, created by law in August 2013.

Children's Rights

In two votes in July and August 2015, the Chamber of Deputies approved a constitutional amendment that would allow 16- and 17-year-old children accused of serious crimes to be tried and punished as adults. The proposal, which would need to be approved by the Senate in two votes to be enacted, would violate international norms calling on states not to prosecute people under 18 as adults.

In July, the Senate passed a bill that would increase the maximum time a child can be confined in a juvenile center from three to 10 years. If approved by the Chamber of Deputies, the bill would aggravate overcrowding. Juvenile centers held close to 22,000 children in 2014, but facilities only had capacity for about 18,000, according to the latest data published by the National Council of the Prosecutor's Office, which inspects those units.

Freedom of Association and Expression

In October, the Senate approved a counterterrorism bill that contains overbroad and vague language that could be misused to prosecute as terrorists demonstrators and others engaged in dissent. A vote at the Chamber of Deputies was pending at time of writing.

At least seven journalists and bloggers had been killed in 2015 at time of writing. Two were tortured before they were executed. All had reported on corruption or crime and had criticized local politicians. During the past five years, at least 17 journalists have lost their lives in direct relation to their work, according to the Committee to Protect Journalists, an international press freedom group.

Reproductive Rights

Abortion is prohibited except in cases of rape, anencephaly—in which the fetus has a fatal congenital brain disorder—or when necessary to save a woman's life. In 2015, conservative members of Congress pushed a bill and a constitutional amendment that would eliminate those exceptions by awarding embryo and fetal rights. Both proposals are under discussion in the Constitution, Justice and Citizenship Commission of the Chamber of Deputies.

Women and girls who obtain an abortion illegally face sentences of up to three years in prison, while people who perform abortions face up to four years in prison. Abortions performed in clandestine clinics put women at high risk. For example, Tatiana Camilato, a 31-year-old mother raising three children alone in Rio de Janeiro, died in July 2015 during an unsafe procedure, according to press interviews with her relatives.

Disability Rights

In June, Congress approved a disability rights law that requires public agencies to give priority to people with disabilities when providing services related to health, education, work, housing, culture, and sport. The law also instructs cities to adapt sidewalks and public spaces for people with disabilities.

Sexual Orientation and Gender Identity

In March, the Supreme Court upheld the right of same-sex couples to adopt children, on the basis of the Court's 2011 approval of same-sex marriage. In 2013, the National Council of Justice ordered all notary publics to register same-sex marriages. But a committee of the Chamber of Deputies was, at time of writing, debating a bill that would define a family as a union between a man and a woman.

The national Human Rights Ombudsman's Office received 522 complaints of violence and discrimination against lesbian, gay, bisexual, and transgender persons in the first half of 2015.

Labor Rights

Since 1995, the Ministry of Labor has documented more than 48,000 cases of workers being subjected to forced labor, degrading working conditions, and other abusive working conditions that under Brazilian law rise to the level of "slave-like" working conditions. From May 2013 to May 2015, 420 companies faced penalties for employing people in "slave-like" conditions.

In December 2014, in response to a petition by a trade group, the Supreme Court ordered the federal government to stop publishing the list of companies penalized by the Ministry of Labor for employing workers in abusive conditions. Local NGOs have been able to get around that order by using the Transparency Law to request that the Ministry of Labor release the data.

Rural Violence

Rural activists and indigenous leaders involved in conflicts over land continue to face threats and violence. According to the Pastoral Land Commission, a Catholic NGO, 46 people involved in land conflicts were killed from January to November. Many of those killings, the commission noted, were allegedly ordered or carried out by large landowners or illegal loggers.

For instance, in Mato Grosso do Sul, the Guaraní-Kaiowá people, who are fighting to regain rights to their ancestral land, in 2015 suffered violent attacks by militias linked to landowners, according to the Indigenous Missionary Council of the Catholic Church. A member of that indigenous group was killed in August after a group of landowners arrived at a piece of contested land occupied and claimed by the Guaraní-Kaiowá. At time of writing, the police had not publicly identified any suspect in the killing.

Confronting Military-Era Abuses

In December 2014, a national truth commission published its final report after more than two years of work investigating human rights violations from the military rule of 1964 to 1985. The commission found that violations were "widespread and systematic" and were planned by officials at the highest level. The report identified 377 individuals responsible for human rights violations, including torture, killings, and enforced disappearances.

The perpetrators of these crimes have been shielded from justice by a 1979 amnesty law. In April 2010, the Supreme Court reaffirmed lower court rulings that the amnesty law barred most prosecutions of state agents involved. Six months later, the Inter-American Court of Human Rights ruled that this interpretation violated Brazil's obligations under international law.

Federal prosecutors have pursued some cases against former military officers for killings during the military era. Federal courts in Rio de Janeiro and Sao Paulo have allowed the prosecution of at least two cases against former military officers for killings during the military era. The Supreme Court, in decisions in 2014 and 2015, temporarily halted both cases, pending its reexamination of the validity of the amnesty law.

Key International Actors

After an August visit to Brazil, the UN special rapporteur on torture and other cruel, inhuman, or degrading treatment or punishment called on the government to address prison overcrowding and show a "genuine commitment" to combating torture. In September, after a visit to the country, the UN special rapporteur on minority issues urged Brazil to "fulfill promises of equality" for minorities.

In a joint statement issued in November, four UN rapporteurs criticized the counterterrorism bill approved by the Senate, saying that it is "too broadly drafted and may unduly restrict fundamental freedoms."

Also in November, two UN rapporteurs said the steps taken by the Brazilian government and two mining companies to prevent harm after the collapse of a tailing dam, which contained waste from mining operations, were "clearly insufficient." The accident killed at least 15 people, left 4 people missing, and released toxic chemicals into the Doce River. Brazil's government considers it the biggest environmental disaster in the country's history.

As a member of the UN Human Rights Council, Brazil was inconsistent, abstaining on a key resolution by the council on Syria in March, but voting in June to condemn Syrian human rights violations. Brazil abstained on a resolution to renew the mandate of the special rapporteur on Iran, who has denounced human rights violations there.

Brazil continued to lead on privacy rights in the digital age, co-authoring with Germany a resolution approved unanimously by the Human Rights Council to appoint a special rapporteur to promote and protect the right to privacy worldwide. Brazil was also a sponsor of Human Rights Council resolutions condemning racism and highlighting the corrosive impact of institutional corruption on human rights.

In May, Brazil endorsed the global Safe Schools Declaration, thereby committing to do more to protect students, teachers, and schools during times of armed conflict, including by implementing the *Guidelines on Protecting Schools from Military Use*. The 2014 guidelines were developed by representatives from 14 countries as well as human rights and humanitarian organizations.

The number of refugees admitted to Brazil has doubled over the past five years to a total of more than 8,400 in 2015, according to the Ministry of Justice. About a quarter of those admitted since 2011 have been Syrians. Brazil renewed a resolution that facilitated issuing humanitarian visas to Syrian citizens and developed new policies to better respond to the needs of refugees, especially for obtaining identity papers.

Burma

The transition from military to civilian rule in Burma that started in 2011 slowed down and reversed in some sectors in 2015. Despite a significantly improved environment for freedom of expression and media, in key areas the government's commitment to improving its human rights faltered or failed. The landslide victory of the opposition National League for Democracy (NLD) in November elections, the first relatively open national elections in 25 years, seemed poised to reenergize reforms in some areas, but it was too early to gauge at time of writing.

Elections

Nationwide parliamentary elections were held on November 8, with 91 parties and hundreds of independent candidates contesting over 1,100 seats. The NLD won a majority of seats in both national houses of parliament and in regional and state assemblies, with more than 85 percent of seats.

The Union Electoral Commission (UEC) lacked independence and impartiality in the lead-up to elections. Its chairman repeatedly said he hoped for victory by the military-backed ruling Union Solidarity and Development Party (USDP), and the commission itself issued guidelines prohibiting political parties from criticizing the military in policy platform speeches broadcast over state-controlled media.

Due to changes in political party laws and enforcement of the draconian 1982 Citizenship Law, the applications of more than 50 Muslim candidates were disallowed during candidate eligibility screening, including those of two sitting ruling party members of parliament who identify as Rohingya Muslims. Neither the USDP nor the NLD fielded a Muslim candidate anywhere in Burma, and no Muslim citizen was voted into parliament nationwide.

The nationwide repeal of temporary citizenship cards (the so-called white cards) disenfranchised over 800,000 people who had previously been permitted to vote in the 2008 constitutional referendum and the 2010 elections, many of them Rohingya in Arakan State.

Despite these serious defects, the two-month campaign was surprisingly open, with few reports of intimidation, violence, or irregularities. Party rallies were conducted peacefully throughout the country, and there were no significant curbs on

HUMAN
RIGHTS
WATCH

STATELESS AT SEA
The Moken of Burma and Thailand

freedom of expression or media. Polling was conducted in a transparent manner with large numbers of domestic and international observers, and political parties observing the count. The UEC acted professionally through the tallying period with daily updates on results.

Constitution

Despite calls from ethnic communities and opposition parties, the Burmese military refused to permit consideration of any amendments to the 2008 constitution in the national parliament in June and July. The constitution allocates 25 percent of parliamentary seats to the military and requires 75 percent of parliament to vote to approve constitutional changes, giving the military an effective veto.

Amendments that were rejected included a proposed change to section 59(f) on eligibility for the presidency, which bars opposition leader Aung San Suu Kyi from the position because she has children that hold foreign citizenship, and proposed changes to sections 261 and 262, giving the president rather than state and regional assemblies the authority to select the influential chief ministers of 14 of Burma's 15 states and regions.

Religious Minorities

Discrimination and threats against the Muslim minority in Burma, a manifestation of growing ultra-nationalism, intensified in Burma in 2015 with the increased prominence of the Buddhist-monk-led Association for the Protection of Race and Religion, known by its Burmese acronym *Ma Ba Tha*.

Ma Ba Tha successfully urged the government to draft and pass four so-called "race and religion protection laws": the Population Control Law, passed in May; and the Buddhist Women's Special Marriage Law, the Religious Conversion Law, and the Monogamy Law, passed in August. The four laws are discriminatory and violate religious freedom by, for example, creating special rules for Buddhist women who marry—or seek to marry—non-Buddhist men; introducing vaguely defined acts against Buddhism as grounds for divorce, forfeiture of child custody and matrimonial property, and potential criminal penalties; and empowering authorities to limit the number of children that members of designated groups can have.

In contrast, the parliament did not pass the comprehensive Violence Against Women Law, a bill that would have strengthened women's rights protections.

Burmese civil society organization leaders who publicly criticized the laws were accused of being "traitors" by senior *Ma Ba Tha* officials and some reportedly faced death threats. In September, nine embassies in Rangoon made a public statement against the misuse of religion in the 2015 elections, sparking a rebuke from the Ministry of Foreign Affairs.

While some political parties, notably the NLD, voted against the laws, other political figures promoted the laws as protecting Burma from Muslim threats. President Thein Sein took credit for the laws in a social media video as election campaigning began in September. *Ma Ba Tha* held a series of nationwide victory rallies lauding the laws as protecting the Buddhist faith against an Islamic "invasion" and in some cases declared its support for the USDP, marking its growing involvement in electoral politics.

Prominent *Ma Ba Tha* member and leader of the "969" anti-Muslim boycott movement *U Wirathu* threatened the UN special rapporteur on Burma, Yanghee Lee, during her January visit to Burma, calling her a "bitch" and a "whore," and exhorting followers to assault her. The government took no steps to respond to this incitement, and no prominent public figure in Burma has openly criticized the rising discrimination and threats endorsed by *Ma Ba Tha* or its intimidation of civil society.

Freedom of Association and Assembly

The numbers of political prisoners in Burma rose in 2015 as the government's commitment to ending the imprisonment of activists waned. At year's end, an estimated 112 people were incarcerated for alleged violations of the flawed Peaceful Assembly Law and other political offenses, a notable rise in cases since the large prisoner amnesties of 2012. At least 486 more were facing trial.

The leadership of the joint committee overseeing political prisoner releases— composed of representatives of the government, former political prisoners, and political parties—was changed in February with the hardline deputy minister of home affairs, a serving military officer, made chair. Prominent activist Ko Bo Kyi was removed from the committee.

On March 5, plainclothes police auxiliaries, suspected to be members of the *Swann Arr Shin* (Masters of Force), which had not been deployed against protesters since 2007, assaulted a small group of student protesters and activists from the 88 Generation Peace and Open Society Group who were peacefully assembling to criticize the government's education law. Police then arrested the protesters.

Five days later, on March 10, security forces blocked a small group of student protesters in the town of Letpadan from marching on Rangoon. When students attempted to tear down the barricades, police forces abandoned all discipline and violently assaulted the students, arresting over 80 of them. Students who were injured in the assault say they received only rudimentary medical care. At time of writing 50 students remain in custody in Tharrawaddy Prison on charges of rioting, assaulting police officials, and illegal assembly.

After the March violence, the European Union, which has been providing technical assistance to the Burma police force as part of a community policing and crowd control project, criticized the authorities and called for an investigation. In September, the Myanmar National Human Rights Commission issued a report calling for abusive police to be punished, as well as any student demonstrators who may have acted to provoke officials. No police officers had been prosecuted at time of writing.

Land rights activists in Burma are regularly arrested and charged with unlawful assembly and trespass for protesting land appropriation and displacement. Authorities arrested a number of land rights activists and farmers in Karen State in June and August who had been calling for compensation and redress for land they claim was unlawfully seized. Prominent activists such as Su Su Nway were also arrested in 2015, and authorities sentenced a number of leaders of the long-running protests in the Letpadaung copper mine case in Monya, including veteran activist Naw Ohn Hla, to four years in prison for peaceful protests they led outside the Chinese embassy in Rangoon.

Rising intolerance against Burma's LGBT communities was voiced by senior government officials, including a security minister in Mandalay Region who called on police to arrest and "educate" transgender people.

Refugees

The maritime exodus of Rohingya Muslims dramatically increased in 2015, with Rohingya families departing from Burma and Bangladesh on smuggling vessels, at times joined by large numbers of Bangladeshi migrant workers.

The United Nations estimates that 94,000 people made the journey between January 2014 and May 2015. In May 2015, some 5,000 people on boats were abandoned by smugglers and denied entry to Thailand, Malaysia, and Indonesia, with at least 70 dying during the ordeal. After intensive international media coverage, Malaysia and Indonesia finally permitted boats to land, and then promptly interned the new arrivals.

Thailand did not formally allow landings, but when boats made it to shore anyway, authorities detained those on board. Boats intercepted by authorities in Burma were towed to Maungdaw in Arakan State, and Bangladeshi citizens were repatriated back to Bangladesh.

A regional conference in Bangkok on May 29 hosted by Thailand and attended by 17 countries failed to adequately address the dispossession and abuse of Rohingya in Arakan State that continues to fuel the maritime crisis. At time of writing many observers were forecasting a resumption in maritime flight by desperate Rohingya, accompanied by serious human rights abuses, starting again in late 2016, when sailing conditions improve in the Bay of Bengal and the Andaman Sea.

Some 140,000 mostly Rohingya Muslims remain in internally displaced person camps in Arakan State, subject to strict restrictions on movement and access to basic services. Although access by humanitarian agencies to the camps improved somewhat in 2015, allowing for provision of limited health and education services, the situation remains dire. Poor conditions in the camps and the threat of renewed violence against the Rohingya are an important driver of maritime exodus. On the positive side, the government assisted an estimated 10,000 internationally displaced persons (IDPs) in 2015, helping them rebuild homes in the areas from which they had been displaced in 2012.

An estimated 110,000 refugees who fled Burma during decades of civil war remain in nine camps in northwest Thailand. UNHCR, international and national nongovernmental organizations, and the Thai government continue to discuss a plan for voluntary repatriation of members of this group. Refugees continue to express concerns about insufficient participation in planning for their return and the uncertain security situation in Burma, including the prevalence of land mines in some of the areas to which they may return.

Ethnic Conflict and Forced Displacement

Armed conflict between the Burmese military and non-state armed groups escalated in 2015. Clashes between the Burmese army and Kachin Independence Army (KIA) troops continued sporadically, reportedly involving disputes over natural resource extraction.

In northern Shan State, fighting between the army and the Ta-ang National Liberation Army (TNLA), often in conjunction with insurgents from the Arakan Army and Shan State Army-North, continued throughout the year and several thousands of civilians were displaced by conflict. In central Shan State, fighting between the Burmese army and Shan rebel forces escalated around the November elections, displacing some 6,000 civilians.

On February 17, two volunteers from the Myanmar Red Cross Society were injured when their convoy was attacked by unknown assailants. They were part of a marked Red Cross convoy that was evacuating civilians displaced by fighting in Shan state. Four days later, a Myanmar Red Cross volunteer was injured in an attack on a marked Red Cross convoy traveling from Laukkai.

In March, fighting began in the northern Shan State special region of Kokang between the army and forces of the Myanmar National Democratic Alliance Army (MNDAA). Burmese forces used airstrikes and heavy artillery bombardments, allegedly indiscriminately, during the fighting against the MNDAA. Tens of thousands of civilians were displaced in Kokang areas, with many fleeing to China.

The government sought to conclude a nationwide ceasefire with 16 non-state armed groups in 2015. Instead, conflict escalated to levels not seen since before the fighting in Kachin State entered an uneasy truce in 2013. Some 130,000 Kachin civilians remain internally displaced in camps, with many IDPs in KIA-controlled areas receiving little international assistance, largely due to Burmese army obstruction.

Child Soldiers

The Burmese military continues to recruit and use child soldiers, as do many paramilitary and militia forces under Burmese army command, and child soldiers have reportedly been recruited and deployed by many non-state armed groups as well. The Burmese military has maintained its support for the 2012 Action Plan agreed to with the UN and international groups to end child soldier recruitment, and has allowed monitors to visit army and militia camps.

Key International Actors

Influential bilateral partners of Burma including the United States, United Kingdom, European Union, and Australia maintained their support for the limited reforms of the Thein Sein government despite increased concerns over renewed assaults on basic freedoms. Numerous governments praised the relatively open November elections and the conduct of parties and the UEC.

The EU continued to sponsor Burma resolutions in the UN Human Rights Council (HRC) and General Assembly in 2015. In July, the HRC passed a resolution condemning persecution of Rohingya and other minorities in Burma and called on the government to ensure human rights protections for all groups.

China did not raise human rights concerns in 2015 but sharply criticized Burma for its failure to stem fighting in Kokang that spilled over the border, particularly for air strikes that killed a number of Chinese civilians.

Russia continues to sell Burma conventional arms, and there are reports that Burma and North Korea maintain military links. The US, UK, and Japan engaged in limited military-to-military engagement with Burma in 2015.

Burundi

Burundi's progress toward democracy and stability has suffered serious set-backs, as political upheaval and widespread killings by security forces and armed opposition groups gripped the country.

In April, demonstrations broke out in response to the news that President Pierre Nkurunziza would seek election for a third term. Police used excessive force and shot demonstrators indiscriminately, killing and injuring scores of people.

The government launched a crackdown against civil society activists and journalists and closed the four most popular private radio stations. Leading human rights activist Pierre Claver Mbonimpa was seriously injured in an assassination attempt.

Around 200,000 Burundians fled the country, most to Tanzania and Rwanda. Dozens of journalists, civil society activists, and opposition party members remain in exile.

Killings escalated after July's presidential election that returned Nkurunziza to power. Most opposition parties boycotted the election. Government forces, armed opposition groups, and unknown assailants killed more than 100 people in the second half of the year.

Abuses by Security Forces

In late April, the announcement by the ruling National Council for the Defense of Democracy-Forces for the Defense of Democracy (CNDD-FDD) that Nkurunziza would stand for a third term ignited protests in the capital Bujumbura, and later in other locations. Many Burundians complained that the president's third term violated a 2000 peace agreement that sets a maximum of two five-year presidential terms. Police suppressed the protests violently, shot dead dozens of demonstrators, and injured many others.

Following a failed coup d'état by a group of military officers on May 13, the government intensified its crackdown on protesters. Police arrested hundreds of people, including suspected opponents, many arbitrarily, and detained them for prolonged periods without trial.

Police and intelligence agents ill-treated or tortured scores of those arrested, in some cases making them stand on their heads, and beating them with electric cables while naked to force them to admit they were leaving the country to join an armed rebellion. Members of the ruling party's youth league, known as *Imbonerakure*, also arrested and beat people, despite not having legal powers of arrest.

Attacks by protesters against the police prompted police to seal or raid some neighborhoods of the capital. Men in police uniforms then entered these areas, allegedly searching for weapons, and shot dead a number of unarmed residents, in some cases indiscriminately.

Senior ruling party officials used inflammatory and apparently threatening language in public speeches and statements. In a speech to local officials on October 29, Senate President Révérien Ndikuriyo repeatedly used the word *"gukora,"* which means "to work" in the Kirundi language. The same word was used to incite people to mass violence before and during the 1994 Rwandan genocide.

President Nkurunziza warned on November 2, that anyone who failed to hand over weapons by November 7 would be "punished in accordance with the anti-terrorist law and fought like enemies of the nation." He told security forces they could use all means at their disposal to restore security. Search operations began on November 8.

Violence by Armed Opposition Groups

While anti-Nkurunziza demonstrations were initially peaceful, some demonstrators resorted to violence, throwing stones and Molotov cocktails and shooting marbles with sling shots at the police. On May 7, demonstrators in Bujumbura killed an *Imbonerakure* by throwing stones at his head and hitting him with clubs. They then put a tire around his body and burned him.

Government opponents in certain Bujumbura neighborhoods stepped up their violence after the July elections, throwing grenades at police patrols and attacking police stations. At least 26 police were killed and many others injured.

There were persistent reports of an armed rebellion, elements of which were believed to be based in Rwanda, others inside Burundi. Cross-border incursions led to clashes between these groups and the security forces, notably in Kayanza and Cibitoke provinces.

Other Killings

In August and September, unknown gunmen shot dead several high-profile people in Bujumbura, including Adolphe Nshimirimana, the former head of the intelligence services; Jean Bikomagu, former army chief-of-staff; and Patrice Gahungu, spokesperson for the Union for Peace and Development-Zigamibanga (UPD) opposition party, whose president, Zedi Feruzi, was killed in May.

Members of the opposition Movement for Solidarity and Democracy (MSD) and National Liberation Forces (FNL) parties were also killed, as were several members of the ruling CNDD-FDD, in what appeared to be reprisal attacks. Army Chief-of-Staff Prime Niyongabo escaped an attack on September 11. Some of his bodyguards were killed in the attack.

In the second half of the year, dead bodies were discovered on the streets of Bujumbura, and in other locations, on an almost daily basis. Some had been shot in the head. Others bore injuries or scars indicating they may have been tortured. Many victims remained unidentified.

Civil Society and Media

On January 20, Bob Rugurika, director of the private station *Radio publique africaine* (RPA), was arrested, days after his radio station broadcast a series of reports about the September 2014 murder of three elderly Italian nuns in Bujumbura. He was charged with conspiracy to murder, violating confidentiality in criminal investigations, harboring a criminal, and failing to uphold "public solidarity." The Court of Appeal ordered his release on bail on February 18.

In late April, soon after protests against Nkurunziza's third-term bid started, the government closed RPA. It also stopped two other private stations, Radio Isanganiro and Radio Bonesha, from broadcasting outside the capital, disabled their telephone land lines, and prohibited all three stations from broadcasting live from demonstrations.

The day after the attempted coup d'état, on May 14, people presumed loyal to the president attacked the offices of RPA, Radio Bonesha, Radio Isanganiro, and

Radio-Television Renaissance. Armed men in police uniforms threw a grenade in Radio Bonesha's office and destroyed its broadcasting equipment. The pro-ruling party Radio Rema FM was also attacked. The government announced an investigation into these attacks, the results of which are not known. The radio stations remained off the air at time of writing.

The prosecutor general set up a commission of inquiry into the demonstrations. The commission's report, published in August, described the protests as an "insurrectional movement." It claimed the damage to the radio stations was the result of "mutineers who guarded the stations" and that the director of Radio Bonesha, Patrick Nduwimana, had asked insurgents and military putschists to destroy Radio Rema FM.

The report named 24 civil society activists and several opposition politicians as having participated in the "insurrection" and said casefiles had been opened against some of them. The commission failed to investigate the use of excessive force by police during demonstrations.

On August 3, an unknown gunman on a motorcycle shot leading human rights activist, Pierre Claver Mbonimpa, in the face, when he was in his car. Mbonimpa survived with serious injuries. An outspoken critic of government abuses, Mbonimpa, president of the Association for the Protection of Human Rights and Detained Persons (APRODH), had been arrested and detained for four months in 2014. Mbonimpa's son-in-law, Pascal Nshimirimana, was shot dead outside his house in Bujumbura on October 9, and his son, Welly Nzitonda, was shot dead on November 6, after being stopped by the police.

On August 2, members of the intelligence services severely beat Esdras Ndikumana, correspondent for Radio France Internationale and Agence France-Presse, as he was taking photographs at the murder scene of former intelligence chief Nshimirimana.

Antoine Kaburahe, director of the independent newspaper *Iwacu*, was summoned to the prosecutor's office in Bujumbura twice in November in connection with his alleged complicity in the May coup attempt.

On November 23, the interior minister suspended the activities of 10 Burundian civil society organizations, including APRODH, after the prosecutor general ordered their bank accounts to be frozen.

Extrajudicial Executions in Cibitoke

In late December 2014 and early January 2015, the Burundian National Defense Force and police, assisted by armed *Imbonerakure*, committed at least 47 extra-judicial executions following a clash with an armed opposition group in Cibitoke province. Cibitoke borders the Democratic Republic of Congo where some Burundian armed opposition groups are believed to operate. The victims were members of the armed group who had surrendered, following gun battles with the security forces. Police, military, or *Imbonerakure* then shot or beat many of them to death.

The prosecutor general set up a commission of inquiry to investigate these allegations, but the commission members failed to talk to key witnesses. Some local authorities intimidated witnesses, especially those who they believed had spoken to "foreigners", and warned them not to talk about these events. The commission's report, published in April, was deeply flawed and misrepresented information collected from some witnesses. It claimed that almost all the combatants died during the fighting, with the exception of three who were killed by policemen acting on their own initiative. It stated that these policemen were arrested.

Key International Actors

Many governments and intergovernmental organizations, including the African Union (AU), the United Nations, and the European Union, expressed strong concern at the deteriorating human rights situation. Partly in response to the extrajudicial executions in Cibitoke, the United States and the Netherlands, as well as other European countries, suspended part of their assistance to the Burundian military and police.

The EU announced a review of its aid to Burundi in the framework of the Cotonou agreement. In September, the EU imposed sanctions on three senior police and intelligence officials and one opposition member who took part in the failed coup. In November, the US imposed sanctions on the minister of public security, the deputy director general of the police, and two leaders of the failed coup.

On November 12, the UN Security Council unanimously adopted a resolution strongly condemning human rights violations in Burundi, urging a rejection of violence, and calling for the resumption of dialogue. The UN High Commissioner for Human Rights also issued several strong statements of concern.

The UN Electoral Observation Mission in Burundi (MENUB) was set to withdraw by the end of the year. A team of the Office of the UN High Commissioner for Human Rights remained in place in Burundi, and the AU deployed human rights observers. In September, the UN Human Rights Council unanimously agreed to consider the human rights situation in Burundi at its three main sessions in 2016.

Cambodia

Prime Minister Hun Sen's government launched new assaults on human rights in Cambodia, especially during the second half of 2015, arresting and jailing members of the political opposition and activists, and passing a draconian new law on nongovernmental organizations (NGOs) that the government rushed through the National Assembly on July 13. Other repressive laws were also proclaimed or proposed, including laws or regulations on the Internet, as Hun Sen, who has ruled since 1985, increasingly undermined fundamental human rights.

Opposition leader Sam Rainsy attempted to establish a "culture of dialogue" with Hun Sen and the ruling Cambodian People's Party (CPP), but his initiative failed to stem arrests or attacks on the opposition, and on November 13, 2015, a politically motivated arrest warrant was issued for him based on a conviction for peaceful expression in 2011.

Land confiscations also continued in 2015, and corruption remained rampant. Cambodia is a party to the United Nations Refugee Convention, but authorities refused to register more than 300 Vietnamese Montagnard asylum seekers for determination of their claims and summarily deported at least 54 of them to Vietnam.

Politically Motivated Prosecution and Assault

On July 13, a Phnom Penh court launched an investigation to consider bringing defamation and interference with justice charges against prominent NGO figure Ny Chakriya, who had raised questions about the independence of the judiciary in a land-grabbing case.

On July 21, 11 opposition Cambodia National Rescue Party (CNRP) organizers, on trial since 2014 on trumped-up charges of leading or participating in an anti-government "insurrection," were suddenly convicted and sentenced by a Phnom Penh court to 7 to 20 years in prison. Despite the absence of evidence connecting them to any criminal acts, they were found responsible for crowd violence that erupted when government security forces broke up a peaceful CNRP-led demonstration calling for the reopening of Phnom Penh's "Freedom Park" on July 15, 2014. The convictions were accompanied by official warnings that seven

HUMAN RIGHTS WATCH

"Work Faster or Get Out"
Labor Rights Abuses in Cambodia's Garment Industry

CNRP National Assembly members also charged with insurrection in connection with the same incident could be convicted and imprisoned despite their parliamentary immunity. Following this, Hun Sen convened a closed meeting of almost 5,000 of the top CPP security force officials at which he issued an "absolute order" that security forces must "ensure there would be no color revolution" in Cambodia by "eliminating acts by any group or party" deemed "illegal."

On August 4-5, following Hun Sen's public call for more arrests of those allegedly responsible for the July 2014 Freedom Park violence, police detained three CNRP activists who were then charged with participating in the purported insurrection, while arrest warrants were issued for several others.

On August 13, Hun Sen ordered the arrest of Hong Sok Hour, an opposition party senator who the previous day had posted a video clip on Facebook including footage of the Cambodia-Vietnam border and of a badly translated excerpt from the 1979 Cambodia-Vietnam friendship agreement. Disregarding the senator's parliamentary immunity, a "counter-terrorism" security force contingent under the authority of Hun Sen's son-in-law detained him. More arrests followed between late August and early October 2015, including of a student who posted a Facebook message advocating a "color revolution."

On October 26-27, following public encouragement by Hun Sen to conduct anti-CNRP demonstrations, elements of the prime minister's bodyguard unit and others in civilian clothes brutally assaulted two CNRP parliamentarians outside the National Assembly. Three persons were arrested and charged with the attack, but others involved who were photographed were not taken into custody. The CNRP thereafter stopped attending National Assembly sessions, citing security concerns.

On November 13, following repeated warnings by Hun Sen that Sam Rainsy was liable to criminal prosecution, the Phnom Penh court issued an arrest order to belatedly enforce a judicial ruling of March 2013 confirming a two-year sentence related to Rainsy's allegation that Cambodian Foreign Minister Hor Namhong was implicated in crimes committed when the Khmer Rouge ruled Cambodia. The French Supreme Court, citing international human rights standards, had previously ruled that these comments were a legitimate exercise of freedom of expression. On November 19 and December 1, the Phnom Penh Court targeted him with additional new trumped-up criminal actions.

Legislation Restricting Civil Society

The new NGO law allows the authorities to arbitrarily deny NGOs registration and shut them down. The law is aimed at critical voices in civil society and could seriously undermine the ability of many domestic and international associations and NGOs, as well as community-based advocacy movements, to work effectively in Cambodia.

Its restrictions on the right to freedom of association go well beyond the permissible limitations allowed by international human rights law. The law gives the interior, foreign affairs, and other ministries sweeping, arbitrary powers to shut down domestic and foreign membership groups and organizations, unchecked by judicial review, and allows them to prohibit the creation of new NGOs. It requires registered groups to operate under a vaguely defined obligation of "political neutrality," on pain of dissolution, and criminalizes activities by unregistered groups.

After passage of the law, Hun Sen and other government officials launched a campaign against human rights-oriented NGOs, including those focusing on land disputes and women's rights. The authorities began to insist that grassroots civil society activities could no longer be carried out unless those involved had registered with the government in accordance with the new provisions, giving the government wide authority to decide what activities can and cannot take place.

On August 19, the government issued a sub-decree upgrading the status of an anti-cybercrime unit and empowering it to "investigate and take measures in accordance with the law with regard to actions via the internet of instigation, insult, racial discrimination, and generation of social movements," particularly those that might lead to a "color revolution."

On November 30, the government put a draft telecommunications law before the National Assembly, even though doing so was not inscribed in the legislature's agenda. The draft had never been made available for discussion by concerned civil society organizations. The CPP adopted it without parliamentary debate. The law gives government authorities arbitrary powers to issue orders to telecommunications operators, to secretly monitor and record telecommunications, and to imprison people for using telecommunications in a manner deemed to endanger "national security."

Arbitrary Detention, Torture, and Other Ill-Treatment

The authorities, especially in Phnom Penh, launched repeated street sweeps that detained hundreds of alleged drug users, homeless people, beggars, street children, sex workers, and people with disabilities in so-called drug treatment or social rehabilitation centers. Detainees never saw a lawyer or a court, nor had any opportunity to challenge the legality of their detention. Detained individuals received no meaningful training or health care, and faced torture, ill-treatment, and other abuses including, in some centers, forced labor. During 2015, at least three died in suspicious circumstances.

Khmer Rouge Tribunal

Numerous public statements by Cambodian officials and the start in June of publication of previously confidential court materials revealed numerous instances of government non-cooperation with the United Nations-assisted Extraordinary Chambers in the Courts of Cambodia (ECCC), set up to prosecute those most responsible for crimes committed by the Khmer Rouge from 1975-79.

While the government allowed a trial of two former leaders of the Khmer Rouge government, Nuon Chea and Khieu Samphan, on charges of crimes against humanity, genocide, and war crimes, it refused to carry out orders by a UN secretary-general-nominated investigating judge to arrest two other former Khmer Rouge leaders, Meas Muth and Im Chem.

This violated the 2003 UN-Cambodia agreement establishing the ECCC and continued a long pattern of opposition by Hun Sen to additional prosecutions. The government's non-cooperation has seriously undermined possibilities for investigating suspects whom Hun Sen, himself a former Khmer Rouge commander, does not want brought to justice.

Asylum Seekers and Refugees

Since late 2014, a wave of Montagnard ethnic minority asylum seekers from Vietnam has arrived in Cambodia. Most of them practice forms of Christianity that

HUMAN RIGHTS WATCH

30 YEARS OF HUN SEN
Violence, Repression, and Corruption in Cambodia

Vietnamese authorities characterize as "evil way" religion. In early 2015, Cambodia recognized 13 as refugees but refused to allow more than 300 other Montagnards to register as asylum seekers. At least 54 were summarily returned to Vietnam in violation of the Refugee Convention, while those remaining in Cambodia faced the threat of similar deportation, and some decided their best option was to return "voluntarily" to Vietnam.

In June 2015, the government implemented a deal with Australia to resettle some of the refugees held on the island of Nauru, but conditions for refugees in Cambodia were so inadequate that only four refugees agreed to relocate. In September, one of the four decided to leave Cambodia.

Key International Actors

China, Vietnam, Japan, and South Korea were Cambodia's leading foreign investors in 2015, while Japan, the European Union, and the United States were the leading foreign donors. Vietnam was by far Cambodia's most important partner in security matters, followed by China. The US provided limited military training, and was more outspoken than others about human rights violations in Cambodia. The EU only rarely commented on human rights in public, and almost all others were silent.

The World Bank, which suspended new lending to Cambodia in 2011 because the government had forcibly evicted people in a manner violating the bank's policy, considered resuming funding for government land projects in 2015 but at time of writing had not done so. The bank said nothing publicly about government repression of land rights advocates.

Canada

Canada's global reputation as a defender of human rights was tarnished by the failure of the Stephen Harper government, in power until October, to take essential steps to remedy serious human rights problems. Particular areas of concern include the rights of indigenous peoples, the legal status of sex work, restrictive counterterrorism measures, the impact of Canada's extractive and garment industries abroad, and the rights of asylum seekers and migrants.

Violence against Indigenous Women and Girls

Growing public concern over missing and murdered indigenous women and girls has led to numerous calls from provincial leaders, opposition political parties, civil society, and in 2015, two United Nations committees, for a national inquiry into the violence.

The UN Committee on the Elimination of Discrimination against Women concluded that Canada had committed a "grave violation" of the rights of indigenous women by failing to promptly and thoroughly investigate the high levels of violence they suffer. The committee also called attention to their mistreatment by the police, an issue that Human Rights Watch documented in its 2013 report *Those Who Take Us Away*.

The UN Human Rights Committee expressed similar concern over the violence facing indigenous women and girls, as well as Canada's failure to provide adequate and effective responses. Both UN committees recommended that Canada conduct a national inquiry to address the issue, a recommendation the Harper government rejected but which the newly elected Liberal government of Justin Trudeau has pledged to implement.

In October 2015, eight police officers of the Sûreté du Québec (Quebec Provincial Police) faced suspension over allegations of abuse of indigenous women in the mining city of Val-d'Or. At time of writing, the province had no plans for an independent civilian investigation of the allegations, but had appointed a civilian auditor to oversee an investigation by the Montreal police, a separate municipal organization.

Rights of Indigenous Peoples

During the 19th and 20th century, approximately 150,000 indigenous children were removed from their families and communities and placed in residential schools, where they were forbidden to speak their own languages or practice their culture. Many also suffered physical and sexual abuse.

In 2015, the Truth and Reconciliation Commission, mandated to provide former students and others affected by residential schools with an opportunity to share their experiences, found that the Canadian government pursued a policy of "cultural genocide" using residential schooling as a central element. According to the commission, the government's goal was to divest itself of its legal and financial obligations to indigenous peoples and to gain control over their land and resources.

The commission made a number of recommendations to uphold indigenous peoples' rights and to promote reconciliation. The UN Human Rights Committee subsequently endorsed the recommendations in 2015, but the Harper government did not accept them.

Indigenous groups have criticized Canada for failing to respect land agreements with indigenous communities or to consult adequately with them, including with regard to resource extraction plans on traditional lands. The government has yet to pay adequate attention to severe poverty, housing, water, sanitation, healthcare, and education problems in indigenous communities, particularly those in remote and rural areas. Inadequate access to clean, safe drinking water continues to pose a major public health concern in a number of indigenous communities.

Sex Work

Following the 2013 ruling by the Supreme Court of Canada striking down previous restrictions that the court deemed violated the rights and security of sex workers, the parliament in December 2014 passed the Protection of Communities and Exploited Persons Act, which criminalizes communicating for the purposes of selling sexual services in public, or buying, advertising, or benefitting from the sale of sexual services. As sex workers, researchers, and human rights groups outlined in testimony before parliament, the act severely limits sex workers' abilities to take life-saving measures, such as screening clients. Criminalizing communication disproportionately impacts street-based sex workers, many of whom are indigenous, poor, or transgender, forcing them to work in more dangerous and isolated locations.

Counterterrorism

In June 2015, Canada passed the Anti-Terrorism Act, a law that imperils constitutionally enshrined human rights, including the freedoms of expression and association.

Vague and overbroad provisions in the law empower the Canadian Security Intelligence Service to engage in operations that could disrupt legitimate acts of dissent and even violate Canada's Charter of Rights and Freedoms with virtually no oversight. The law's authorization of unfettered information-sharing among 17 government agencies invites violations of rights to privacy and procedural protections to prevent torture and ill-treatment. The act also denies meaningful due process to persons placed on Canada's no-fly list and to non-citizens facing deportation. Its new criminal offense of "advocating terrorism" could undermine free speech. It also significantly lowers the threshold and lengthens the period for detaining a suspect without charge.

The UN Human Rights Committee expressed similar concerns about the act, calling on Canada to refrain from adopting legislation that imposes undue restrictions on the exercise of civil and political rights.

Mining Industry Abuses

Canada is the mining industry's most important global financing hub, home to a majority of the world's mining and exploration companies. These firms have an enormous collective impact on the human rights of vulnerable communities worldwide. Yet the Canadian government neither regulates nor monitors the human rights practices of Canadian mining companies at work abroad.

In 2013, Human Rights Watch documented allegations that Vancouver-based Nevsun Resources' flagship Bisha gold mine in Eritrea was partly built using forced labor deployed by the local state-owned contractor Segen Construction. The following year, three Eritreans filed a lawsuit against Nevsun in a Canadian court, alleging that the company was complicit in the use of forced labor by Segen at the Bisha mine. The plaintiffs claim that they worked at the mine against their will, that they were forced to work long hours, and that they lived in constant fear of threats of torture and intimidation.

In 2015, the UN Commission of Inquiry on Human Rights in Eritrea reported that it had collected evidence that most workers at the Bisha mine were in fact conscripts performing their national service. Nevsun has rejected all of these allegations.

In 2011, Human Rights Watch documented widespread violent abuses, including brutal incidents of gang rape, carried out by employees of Canadian mining giant Barrick Gold at the Porgera gold mine in Papua New Guinea. The company has taken numerous steps to prevent further abuses and in 2015 provided remedy packages to more than 100 women who suffered abuse at the hands of company employees. The company has commissioned an independent assessment to evaluate the extent to which that program conformed to international norms and positively impacted the women involved.

In 2015, the UN Human Rights Committee called on Canada to enhance the effectiveness of existing mechanisms to ensure that Canadian corporations respect human rights standards when operating abroad, to consider establishing an independent mechanism with powers to investigate human rights abuses by such corporations abroad, and to develop a legal framework that affords legal remedies to victims.

Garment Industry Abuses

Canada is among the top four markets for garments and textiles from Cambodia, where garment workers often work in discriminatory and exploitative labor conditions. Workers, who are mostly young women, have trouble asserting their rights, and labor under short-term contracts that make it easier to fire and control them, with poor government inspections and enforcement and aggressive tactics against independent unions.

Canadian clothing brands have a responsibility to promote respect for workers' rights throughout their supply chains, including both direct suppliers and subcontractor factories. As documented in the 2015 Human Rights Watch report *Work Faster or Get Out*, not all Canadian companies have fully lived up to these responsibilities.

In spite of abuses, Canada has not introduced regulations to provide incentives or require international apparel brands domiciled in Canada to make non-financial, human rights-related disclosures, such as the names of their suppliers and subcontractors, to facilitate labor rights compliance throughout the supply chain.

Asylum Seekers' and Migrants' Rights

In 2012, parliament passed Bill C-31, which permits the government to designate a group of incoming migrants as "irregular arrivals," subjecting them to mandatory detention with limited judicial review and risking the prolonged detention of refugees and children 16 and older. Bill C-31 created a Refugee Appeal Division, but asylum seekers from 27 "designated countries" that have a history of respecting human rights are not allowed to appeal their denials, although the Federal Court may review their denials. C-31 also places a five-year ban on "irregular arrivals" from applying for permanent residence, which impinges upon the right of separated refugee families to reunite.

In July, the Federal Court held that denying applicants from "designated countries" the right to appeal a rejected claim violates equality rights under Canada's Charter of Rights and Freedoms. Three people had challenged the constitutionality of the policy: a gay man from Croatia and gay partners from Hungary, who all feared persecution based in part on their sexual orientation. The government is appealing the decision.

Also in 2012, Canada modified the Interim Federal Health Program to limit access to essential healthcare services to many asylum seekers, a decision that a Canadian court subsequently declared a form of "cruel and unusual treatment," and thus unconstitutional. In response, the federal government introduced a temporary health program providing partial health care coverage for some refugees.

In 2015, the UN Human Rights Committee urged Canada to refrain from detaining "irregular migrants" for indefinite periods, to ensure that detention is used as a measure of last resort, and to provide refugee claimants from "designated countries" with access to an appeal. The committee further recommended that Canada reinstate essential healthcare services to all refugee claimants, irrespective of their status.

Central African Republic

A transitional government led by interim President Catherine Samba-Panza struggled to establish security in the Central African Republic. The Bangui National Forum, held in May, set the country on a path toward elections, but there was little progress on reconciliation, disarmament, and the reassertion of state control.

Although the capital, Bangui, was relatively calm for the first half of the year, renewed sectarian violence gripped the city in late September. In 2015, at least 100 people died, of which at least 45 were civilians, shot at point blank range or stabbed to death or had their throats slit. Over 400 people were injured.

Sectarian violence and attacks on civilians were widespread in central regions of the country, most notably in Ouaka province, where predominantly Muslim Seleka rebels and largely Christian and animist anti-balaka militias continued to fight each other. By the end of 2015, thousands had been killed on both sides and hundreds of villages burned. An estimated 456,000 people, the majority Muslim, remained refugees. A further 447,000 remained displaced internally.

The United Nations peacekeeping mission, MINUSCA, deployed across many parts of the country, after taking over from African Union (AU) peacekeepers in 2014. They worked alongside French peacekeepers, known as Sangaris, to attempt to protect civilians and re-establish order. Their efforts were hampered by accusations that international peacekeepers were involved in sexual abuse of civilians, including children. Special representative of the secretary-general, Babacar Gaye, who led MINUSCA, resigned over the scandal.

Impunity remained a serious challenge, although there was new hope with steps taken toward the establishment of a Special Criminal Court in the national justice system. The International Criminal Court (ICC) prosecutor continued investigations started in September 2014.

Attacks on Civilians

The Seleka ("alliance" in Sango, the country's principal language), a predominantly Muslim rebellion made up of loosely affiliated factions, fractured into several different groups after infighting over political agendas and resources. The various factions continued to attack civilians, killing hundreds, often under the pretext of searching for and protecting themselves against the anti-balaka.

Seleka rebels also burned or otherwise destroyed villages and engaged in widespread looting. For example, in late 2014 and early 2015, Seleka fighters from the Union for Peace in the Central African Republic *(l'Union pour la Paix en Centrafrique)*, a former Seleka group, killed at least 120 people and burned hundreds of homes on the road between Kouango and Bianga, in Ouaka province.

The anti-balaka, a collection of predominately Christian and animist armed fighters who harbor hatred against Muslims, fought the Seleka and targeted Muslim civilians as well as, increasingly, others who were seen as being too close to Muslims or were not supporting the anti-balaka. In central regions, the anti-balaka killed scores of civilians and burned homes. For example, in late March, anti-balaka fighters killed at least 14 ethnic Peuhl herders outside Kaga Bandoro as they were moving their cattle. Ten of the victims were children, aged between one and nine years old, and three were women. The Peuhl scattered into the bush and several others went missing and are presumed dead.

Some anti-balaka fighters also held ethnic Peuhl hostage for ransom, raped Peuhl women and girls and, in some cases, held them as sex slaves. MINUSCA helped to facilitate the rescue of over 90 Peuhl held hostages in the southwest for many months.

Refugees and Internally Displaced Persons

The situation for internally displaced persons and refugees remained difficult and few returned to their homes. After the September violence in Bangui, a further 37,000 people were displaced in the capital. Many displaced people, such as those in Ouaka and Ouham provinces, had little or no humanitarian assistance. Human Rights Watch documented the deaths of 142 people from January to June in Ouaka province who had sought safety in the remote forests and savannah bush and later died from malnutrition and disease. This is likely only a fraction of the total.

In western parts of the country there was some improvement for 36,000 Muslims who resided in enclaves protected by international peacekeepers since the violence of 2013 and 2014. Hundreds of Muslims in Yaloké enclave who lived in dire conditions and were blocked by the transitional government and UN peacekeepers from leaving, were provided with more appropriate humanitarian aid and were finally permitted to leave for refugee camps in Cameroon or elsewhere in April. During the 16 months they had lived in Yaloké, 53 people had died from malnutrition and disease, the majority children. Muslims in other enclaves had some freedom to move around safely, though the sectarian violence in Bangui in late September was a serious setback.

Elections

In June, the transitional parliament voted to block refugees living outside the country from voting in upcoming national elections, which would have disproportionally affected the minority Muslim population, many of whom remained refugees. This decision was overturned by the transitional constitutional court in July. Registration for refugees began in September.

A constitutional referendum, scheduled to be held on October 4, was delayed due to the violence in Bangui, and was scheduled for December 13. On October 8, the president of the national electoral authority resigned saying credible elections could not be held before the end of 2015. The first round of elections was scheduled to be held on December 27. The former president, Francois Bozizé, on whom the UN imposed sanctions for his role in the 2013-2014 violence, and Patrice Edouard Ngaissona, one of the leaders of the anti-balaka, were among the 44 candidates for president. On December 8, the transitional constitutional court ruled that Bozizé and Ngaissona were not eligible to stand, along with 12 other candidates.

Peacekeeper Abuses

In May, revelations of sexual abuse of children by French and other international peacekeepers strained peacekeeping efforts. The revelations were based on a leaked UN report from 2014 which detailed sexual abuse by peacekeepers, of boys as young as nine. French authorities said they dispatched a team to Bangui soon after learning about the allegations, but had been unable to conclude their investigations due to lack of information. As a result of the public pressure, French authorities ordered a new investigation.

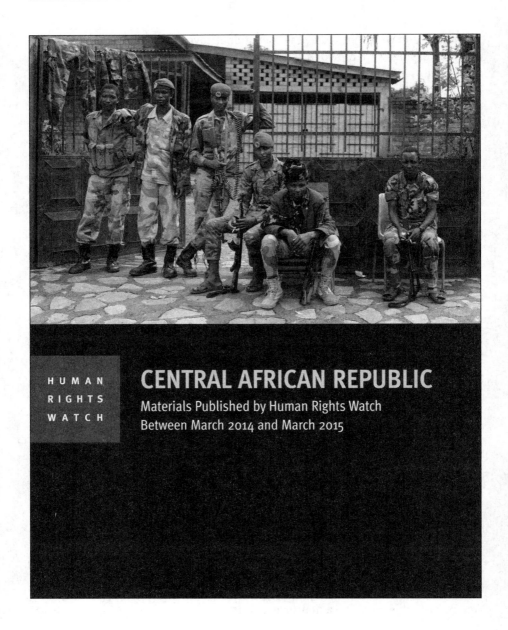

HUMAN
RIGHTS
WATCH

CENTRAL AFRICAN REPUBLIC

Materials Published by Human Rights Watch
Between March 2014 and March 2015

In August, MINUSCA peacekeepers and UN civilian staff were also accused of multiple cases of sexual abuse in the country, including the alleged rape by a UN peacekeeper of a 12-year-old girl. UN Secretary-General Ban Ki-moon demanded the resignation of Babacar Gaye, then-head of MINUSCA, and reiterated the UN's zero tolerance policy. In June, he also established a panel to review the UN's response to sexual exploitation and abuse and other serious crimes committed by peacekeepers not under the UN's command in the Central African Republic. After a delay the panel was due to release its report on December 17.

In June, the UN High Commissioner for Human Rights found that AU peacekeepers from the Republic of Congo were responsible for the enforced disappearance of at least 11 people in Boali in March 2014. In December 2013, AU peacekeepers allegedly beat to death two anti-balaka fighters they had detained in Bossangoa. No action had been taken regarding these findings at time of writing.

National and International Justice Efforts

Impunity remained one of the main challenges in addressing horrific past and ongoing atrocities. In September, some 600 prisoners escaped from the main prison in Bangui with the help of government soldiers. Prison breaks also occurred in other parts of the country.

In June 2015, Samba-Panza promulgated a law creating a Special Criminal Court, a hybrid court within the national justice system that will focus on grave international crimes committed since 2003, and will include both national and international judges and prosecutors. Government authorities and the UN started preparations to secure funding, technical support, and international experts.

The ICC continued investigations into war crimes and crimes against humanity committed since 2012. The ICC's case against the Lord's Resistance Army (LRA), a Ugandan rebel movement active in several countries across the region, was given new life in January when commander Dominic Ongwen surrendered in Obo, in the southeast of the country. The LRA had been operating in the country since 2008. Ongwen faces 67 counts of war crimes and crimes against humanity for crimes committed in Uganda. The LRA continued to threaten and abduct civilians in eastern parts of the country, though with less frequency than in past years.

The ICC trial of Jean-Pierre Bemba Gombo, a Congolese national and former vice president of the Democratic Republic of Congo accused of failing to control his militia—allegedly implicated in murder, rape, and pillage in Bangui in 2002 and 2003—rested at the end of 2014, and during 2015 the judges deliberated on the evidence. At time of writing they had not yet rendered a judgement. A second ICC trial against Bemba and three accomplices on charges of tampering with witnesses opened in September 2015.

Key International Actors

International actors paid less attention to the crisis than in previous years, although the UN Security Council renewed the mandate of MINUSCA, increased the troop ceiling, and specifically asked the mission to monitor human rights abuses against persons with disabilities. France reduced the number of peacekeepers from 2,000 to 900 troops and urged that elections be held before the end of the year. The European Union, the largest donor, provided €22 (US$24) million in humanitarian assistance and €141.6 (US$ 154) million in development assistance. The United States provided US$116 million to peacekeeping and humanitarian aid.

The Republic of Congo continued to act as the chief mediator in the crisis under the auspices of the *Central African Economic and Monetary Community*.

Chile

Chile's parliament in 2015 debated laws to strengthen human rights protection, as promised by President Michelle Bachelet, but none had been enacted at time of writing. These included measures to reform Chile's counterterrorism law and to decriminalize abortion in limited circumstances. Other long-needed reforms, however, including an expected bill to end the jurisdiction of military courts over alleged human rights abuses by the Carabineros—the police responsible for public order and crime prevention—had not been introduced as of November.

While courts continue to prosecute individuals for abuses committed during military rule, the Supreme Court has used its discretionary powers in many cases to reduce sentences against human rights violators, resulting in punishments incommensurate with the gravity of the crimes.

Confronting Past Abuses

In March 2015, the chief justice reported that 1,056 cases of human rights violations committed during military rule (1973-1990) were under investigation, 112 of them for torture. According to the Ministry of the Interior's human rights program, as of December 2015, 344 individuals had received final sentences for human rights violations, including killings and enforced disappearances. One hundred and seventeen were serving prison sentences.

While some individuals convicted of extrajudicial executions initially receive long prison sentences, the Supreme Court's criminal chamber has in many cases reduced the penalties on final appeal on the basis that the time elapsed since the crime justifies a lesser, or even a non-custodial, sentence. Two of the five judges on the panel have consistently dissented from this position.

In addition, the prison service and appeals courts have granted benefits such as day release and parole to individuals convicted of crimes against humanity, which the Supreme Court has upheld.

Gen. Manuel Contreras, who commanded Pinochet's secret police, the DINA, died in a military hospital in August 2015. Contreras was responsible for summary executions, enforced disappearances, and torture that claimed thousands of victims during the early years of the dictatorship. At the time of his death, he was serving accumulated sentences of 529 years, and other cases against him were pending.

Secrecy continues to cast a shroud over past human rights crimes. The problem was dramatically demonstrated in 2015 following the publication of a former soldier's testimony that an officer had set fire to two teenagers, Rodrigo Rojas and Carmen Gloria Quintana, after their detention during a 1986 street protest. Rojas died of his injuries in hospital; Quintana was left permanently disfigured after multiple operations for her burns.

The official version, based on military witnesses who allegedly had been instructed and intimidated, was that the victims had accidentally burned themselves with a Molotov cocktail. In November 2014, a former soldier testified that a patrol commander had ordered them to be doused with gasoline and set on fire, confirming Quintana's account of what happened. Based on this testimony, in July 2015 Judge Mario Carroza charged 12 former soldiers with first degree murder.

In August, the minister of defense formed a human rights unit, headed by a former judge, to coordinate and facilitate military cooperation in cases under judicial investigation.

Counterterrorism Law

A bill presented by the government in November 2014 to replace Chile's counterterrorism law was still under discussion in the Senate at time of writing. The current law lacks sufficient due process protections, and its definition of terrorism is overly broad. The 2014 bill would update and narrow the definition of terrorism, excluding crimes against private property, which had previously formed the basis for terrorism prosecutions of Mapuche indigenous activists. It would also strengthen due process guarantees, giving defense attorneys the right to be informed of the identity of protected witnesses, question them about their evidence, and probe their credibility.

Military Jurisdiction

Military courts continue to exercise jurisdiction over abuses committed by the uniformed police, the Carabineros, who are military officers on active duty. Criminal proceedings in military courts lack the independence and due process guarantees of ordinary criminal proceedings. Investigations are secret, the proceedings are conducted mainly in writing, and lawyers have limited opportunities to cross-examine witnesses.

Many legitimate complaints of human rights abuses that are filed with military courts are dismissed. Sentences are often inappropriately reduced by the military appeals court. Both the Constitutional Court and the Supreme Court have opposed military jurisdiction in such cases.

In May 2014 the minister of defense promised to present draft legislation before the end of June 2015 that would overhaul the military criminal code and end military jurisdiction over crimes committed against civilians by the armed forces (including Carabineros). At time of writing, the bill had still not been presented.

Police Abuses

In May 2015, a student, Rodrigo Avilés, was knocked off his feet by a police water cannon and severely injured when his head struck the sidewalk during a street protest in Valparaíso. The Carabineros initially denied responsibility, but after a video on state television showed Avilés being hit by a jet of water fired by police at short range, the Carabineros dismissed the officer responsible. They also announced that disciplinary action would be taken against two officers shown in a video to have struck a teenage girl without provocation during the same demonstration, leaving her unconscious on the ground.

Appeals courts have repeatedly called on the Carabineros to observe strict protocols on the use of force when entering Mapuche indigenous communities in the context of land conflicts in southern Chile. In February 2015, the Supreme Court ordered the Carabineros to respect the right to liberty and personal security (*amparo*) of three Mapuche teenagers who were allegedly pursued, detained, and beaten by police in October 2014. Cases of brutality and the disproportionate use of force, however, continue to be reported. Women and children have been among the victims of these abuses.

Torture

Torture by police and prison guards is a recurrent problem. Following Supreme Court rulings against military jurisdiction over alleged abuses by Carabineros, some cases were, at time of writing, under investigation by civilian prosecutors and were expected to be heard by civilian courts. Chile's criminal code still lacks a specific reference to torture as defined in international instruments. President Bachelet promised in her state of the nation address in May 2015 to present a bill to rectify this.

Prison Conditions

Despite measures adopted in 2010-2013 to reduce the prison population, many of Chile's prisons are still grossly overcrowded. Conditions remain poor, and violent abuses by prison guards are common. A survey of more than 2,000 prisoners conducted in 2013 by the Gendarmería, the Chilean prison service, revealed that more than a third claimed to have suffered violence from prison guards and more than a fifth said that they had been tortured. In January 2015, 18 prison guards were given suspended sentences of 61 days for beating a group of 57 prisoners in Rancagua prison following an escape attempt.

Reproductive Rights

Chile is one of four countries in Latin America (the other three being El Salvador, Honduras, and Nicaragua) with an absolute prohibition on abortion, even in the event of medical necessity or rape. In January 2015, President Bachelet presented legislation to decriminalize abortion in cases of rape or fetal unviability, or where there was a risk to the life of the woman or girl.

In August, the Chamber of Deputies' Health Committee approved the legislation in principle, the first stage of the parliamentary approval process. However, the bill was opposed by the Catholic Church, which exercises great influence in Chile, by sectors of the Christian Democrat Party, and by legislators of the opposition Alliance for Chile, who said they would challenge the bill in the Constitutional Court.

Sexual Orientation and Gender Identity

A "civil union" bill presented by former President Sebastián Piñera in 2011 that provides legal recognition and protection for same-sex couples became law in April 2015 and went into effect in October. Another bill tabled by five senators from different parties in May 2013 to achieve legal recognition of the gender identity of transgender people was under discussion in the human rights committee of the Senate at time of writing.

Human Rights Defenders

In April 2015, three opposition members of the Chamber of Deputies presented a motion proposing that the chamber ask the Supreme Court to dismiss the director of the National Human Rights Institute (INDH), Lorena Fries, for "manifest and inexcusable negligence." Their action followed a complaint by the chief of police about a school text on human rights distributed by INDH, which argued that Carabineros made numerous arrests during street protests in part to deter marchers from exercising their freedom of assembly.

The questioned passage was supported by official statistics showing that the number of arrests in demonstrations far outnumbered the individuals actually charged with an offense. After hearing Fries' defense, the Chamber of Deputies in June rejected the dismissal request by a two-to-one margin. The dismissal request and chamber vote—a disproportionate reaction to the INDH's criticism of the police—showed the agency's vulnerability to political reprisals.

Key International Actors

In July 2015, the UN Committee on Economic, Social and Cultural Rights published its concluding observations on Chile's fourth periodic report to the committee. The committee called on Chile to strengthen its legislation against discrimination and to increase the resources provided to the INDH. It also recommended that Chile expedite adoption of the pending abortion bill and consider broadening the circumstances in which abortion is permitted to ensure the bill's compatibility with women's right to health and life.

Also in July, the UN special rapporteurs on freedom of assembly and association, freedom of opinion and expression, and human rights defenders sent a joint letter to Chile's ambassador to the UN expressing concern at the action taken by legislators against the INDH's director.

In May, Chile endorsed the global Safe Schools Declaration, committing to do more to protect students, teachers, and schools during times of armed conflict, including by implementing the *Guidelines on Protecting Schools from Military Use.*

China

Ruled by the Chinese Communist Party (CCP) for more than six decades, China remains an authoritarian state, one that systematically curtails a wide range of fundamental human rights, including freedom of expression, association, assembly, and religion. While there were a few modest positive developments in 2015—authorities, for example, reduced the number of crimes eligible for the death penalty from 55 to 46 and issued directives guaranteeing students with disabilities "reasonable accommodation" in university entrance exams—the trend for human rights under President Xi Jinping continued in a decidedly negative direction.

Senior Chinese leaders, perceiving a threat to their power, now explicitly reject the universality of human rights, characterizing these ideas as "foreign infiltration," and penalizing those who promote them. Freedoms of expression and religion, already limited, were hit particularly hard in 2015 by several restrictive new measures.

Individuals and groups who have fought hard in the past decade for human rights gains were the clearest casualties of an aggressive campaign against peaceful dissent, their treatment starkly contrasting with President Xi's vow to promote "rule of law." Between July and September, about 280 human rights lawyers and activists were briefly detained and interrogated across the country. About 40 remain in custody, most in secret locations without access to lawyers or family, some beyond the legal time limits; most have been accused of being part of a "major criminal gang" that "seriously disrupts public order." The government has shut down or detained staff of a number of nongovernmental organizations (NGOs) and arrested and imprisoned many activists.

The government also proposed or passed laws on state security, cybersecurity, counterterrorism, and the management of foreign NGOs; these laws conflate peaceful criticism of the state with threats to national security. For example, the second draft of the Foreign Non-Governmental Organizations Management Law imposes an onerous supervisory framework and restrictions on staffing and operations of these organizations, and gives police an expansive role in approving and monitoring their work. Although close scrutiny of NGOs is not new for a government that has long labeled peaceful criticism as a threat to state power, the

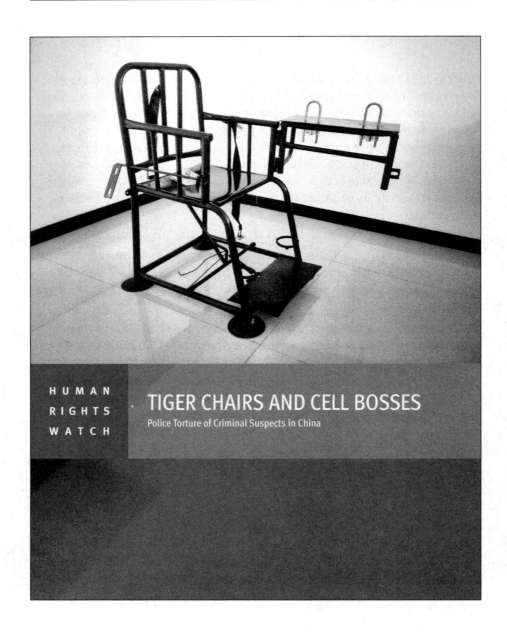

HUMAN
RIGHTS
WATCH

TIGER CHAIRS AND CELL BOSSES
Police Torture of Criminal Suspects in China

proliferation of laws authorizing such intrusion provides officials with even more ammunition to intimidate or punish activists.

President Xi's domestically popular anti-corruption campaign continues to feature prosecutions that violate the right to a fair trial. In June, former security czar Zhou Yongkang was given a life sentence following a closed-door trial and months of unlawful and secret detention. At the same time, anti-corruption activists involved in the New Citizens Movement, including legal scholar Xu Zhiyong, continue to languish in jail.

Human Rights Defenders

Activists seeking to defend human rights have faced a surge in reprisals under Xi, at times enduring arbitrary detention, enforced disappearance, politicized prosecutions, and torture by authorities in response to their work.

Various NGOs have been closed and their staff detained on bogus charges. In late 2014, authorities detained Guo Yushan and He Zhengjun, the director and administrative manager of the prominent Beijing-based public policy think tank, Transition Institute, accusing them of "illegal business operations;" they were released on bail in September 2015. In June, two former directors of Zhengzhou Yirenping, a group affiliated with the prominent anti-discrimination organization Beijing Yirenping, were taken into custody. They were subsequently released, but a government spokesperson vowed to "punish" Yirenping for unspecified "unlawful activities." Other NGOs, even lesser-known ones or ones working on subjects considered less politically sensitive, such as the Shenzhen Christian Guan'ai Home for the Homeless, faced closure and arrests.

In addition to the nationwide round-up of about 280 lawyers and activists in 2015, human rights lawyers were increasingly subject to physical assault, including by court officials. In August, lawyer Zhang Kai was detained for providing legal advice to Christians in Zhejiang Province who had resisted the authorities' forced removal of crosses on church buildings. Other lawyers, including Pu Zhiqiang and Tang Jingling, detained in separate cases since May 2014, remain in custody pending trial or verdict.

The government has increasingly used vague public order charges to silence human rights defenders. At time of writing, Guo Feixiong, a prominent Guangdong activist, was still awaiting a verdict after being tried in November 2014 for "gathering crowds to disturb social order."

A number of activists, including elderly journalist Gao Yu, Pu Zhiqiang, Uighur scholar Ilham Tohti, and anti-corruption activist Liu Ping, continue to be detained or imprisoned without adequate medical care.

Freedom of Expression

The Chinese government tightly restricts freedom of expression through censorship and punishments. While the Internet has offered a marginally freer space, the government censors politically unacceptable information through means such as the "Great Firewall." Despite media censorship, journalists and editors have at times pushed the limits of acceptable expression.

In 2015, government agencies such as the State Internet Information Office issued multiple new directives, including tightened restrictions over the use of usernames and avatars, and requirements that writers of online literature register with their real names. The government has also shut down or restricted access to Virtual Private Networks (VPNs), which many users depend on to gain access to content otherwise blocked to users inside the country.

In March, authorities also deployed a new cyber weapon, the "Great Cannon," to disrupt the services of GreatFire.org, an organization that has worked to undermine China's censorship. In July, the government published a draft cybersecurity law that will requires domestic and foreign Internet companies to practice censorship, register users' real names, localize data, and aid government surveillance. In August, the government announced that it would station police in major Internet companies to more effectively prevent "spreading rumors" online.

In January 2015, Education Minister Yuan Guiren told universities to ban teaching materials that promote Western values and censor speech constituting "attack and slander against the Party."

In April, prominent journalist Gao Yu was sentenced to seven years in prison for allegedly leaking an internal CCP document calling for greater censorship of liberal and reformist ideas. She was forced to confess, and the confession was aired on state TV long before criminal investigations against her ran their course.

Financial reporting has often appeared less tendentious than political journalism. But in August, the government took the alarming step of detaining Wang Xiaolu, a financial reporter, for having written about the authorities' deliberations over withdrawing stabilizing measures in response to the sharp declines in the Chinese stock market crash in June and July.

Also in August, the Urumqi government tried two brothers of Shohret Hoshur of Radio Free Asia, a reporter based in the United States, on state security charges; the brothers likely were being punished for Hoshur's critical reporting on conditions in Xinjiang, a sensitive minority region in western China. In September, a computer programmer was sentenced to 12 years in prison for placing anti-CCP slogans on TV.

Women's Rights

While the CCP is rhetorically committed to gender equality, its lack of respect for human rights means that women continue to face systemic discrimination on issues ranging from employment to sexual harassment. Family planning policies, which control the number and spacing of children people can have, continue to impose severe restrictions on women's reproductive freedoms. In October, authorities announced an end to its decades-old "one-child" policy; couples may now have two children.

In March, at least 10 women's rights activists were taken into custody by police for plans to post signs and distribute leaflets to raise awareness about sexual harassment in three Chinese cities. Five were soon released, but the others were held for 37 days on charges of "picking quarrels," sparking a widespread international outcry. Though the five were released on bail, continuing restrictions on their movements and police harassment led them to close their organization, the Weizhiming Women's Center in Hangzhou.

In March, the Supreme People's Court and other agencies issued instructions requiring judges to consider domestic violence as a mitigating circumstance in criminal cases against victims of such violence. In August, China's legislature reviewed a draft of the long-awaited Law against Domestic Violence. While a step in the right direction, the draft falls short of international standards, particularly in its definition of domestic violence. Cases of domestic violence in which local authorities fail to respond appropriately continue to occur with worrying regularity. In July, for example, a woman was killed by her husband during a mediation session in a police station.

Freedom of Religion

The government restricts religious practice to five officially recognized religions and only in officially approved religious premises. The government audits the activities, employee details, and financial records of religious bodies, and retains control over religious personnel appointments, publications, and seminary applications.

In 2015, authorities continued their campaign to remove crosses from churches, and in some cases demolished entire churches in Zhejiang Province, considered the heartland of Chinese Christianity. The campaign is publicly described as an effort to remove "illegal structures" that do not comply with zoning requirements, but according to an internal provincial directive, it is designed to reduce the prominence of Christianity in the region.

At least a hundred Christians have reportedly been briefly detained for resisting the demolitions since the start of the campaign in early 2014. At least one church leader, Huang Yizi, was convicted of "gathering crowds to disturb social order" and in March given one year in jail for speaking out against the removals.

In June, a top CCP official told religious leaders that "hostile forces" are using religion to infiltrate China, and that they must "Sinicize religion" to ensure that religious worship contributes to national unity.

The government classifies many religious groups outside its control as "evil cults," such as Falungong, and membership alone can lead to criminal and extra-legal punishments. Another group, Buddhist sect Huazang Dharma, has been targeted for arrests, and its leader, Wu Zeheng, was sentenced to life in prison in October for "using cults to sabotage law enforcement," extortion, and other charges.

In August, the National People's Congress approved proposed changes to article 300 of the Criminal Law, which punishes individuals for organizing and participating in cults. The potential penalty range has been lengthened to include life imprisonment.

Disability Rights

China ratified the Convention on the Rights of Persons with Disabilities (CRPD) in 2008, but persons with disabilities continue to face barriers and discrimination, including lack of access to education.

More students with low vision and blindness took the national university entrance exams, or gaokao, this year, following the Education Ministry's 2014 decision to make Braille and electronic versions available. In April, the ministry also promulgated new regulations requiring exam administrators to provide "one or more" forms of "reasonable accommodation," such as extending the time allowed for completing exams and providing sign language services to students with disabilities taking the gaokao. Given that other laws and regulations do not clearly require education institutions to provide such students with "reasonable accommodation" as defined in the CPRD, the April decision is a significant step forward.

Regulations drafted in 2013 on access to education for people with disabilities have still not been adopted. Official guidelines continue to allow universities to deny enrollment in certain subjects if the applicants have certain disabilities. Consequently, although more students with disabilities can now take the gaokao, many universities continue to deny them entry to their chosen field of study or entry to the university altogether.

The 2013 Mental Health Law stipulates that treatment and hospitalization should be voluntary except in cases where individuals with severe mental health conditions pose a danger to, or have harmed, themselves or others. In April, however, a Shanghai court ruled against Xu Wei, the first patient ever to invoke the law to challenge his confinement. Xu Wei has been held against his will for over a decade for schizophrenia.

Sexual Orientation and Gender Identity

Homosexuality was decriminalized in 1997 and removed from an official list of mental illnesses in 2001. There is still no law protecting people from discrimination on the basis of sexual orientation or gender identity, however, and there is no legal recognition of same-sex partnership.

A 2014 report by a Chinese lesbian, gay, bisexual and transgender (LGBT) organization revealed that very few Chinese textbooks portray LGBT people using objective and non-discriminatory language.

In what could be a sign of growing social acceptance of same-sex relationships, Chinese social media lit up with discussion and debate following the June US Supreme Court decision legalizing same-sex marriage in the US. In July, a Sun Yat-Sen University student donned a rainbow flag at a graduation ceremony and received gestures of support from the chancellor; state media widely covered the story.

LGBT groups and individuals continue to file lawsuits that challenge discrimination. In April, a man sued his Shenzhen employer for firing him after a video revealing his sexuality went viral online. In August, a university student in Guangdong Province sued the provincial education department for officially approved textbooks that depict homosexuality as an illness.

Tibet

The 6th Tibet Work Forum meeting in late August, held to determine central government policy for the region for years to come, emphasized the imperatives of security and "stability," but authorities failed to address systematic ethnic and religious discrimination and restrictions, or the profound socioeconomic changes brought by massive re-housing and resettlement campaigns in which Tibetans were compelled to participate.

Central government authorities continue to deploy officials in villages and monasteries and have expanded surveillance mechanisms to the grassroots level, a development which appears to have contributed to more frequent arrests of local community leaders, environmental activists, villagers involved in social and cultural activities, and writers and singers whose works are considered sensitive.

In July, Tenzin Delek Rinpoche—one of Tibet's highest-profile political prisoners—died in detention. In violation of the relevant regulations, authorities refused to release his body or investigate the circumstances of his death. Also in July, Lobsang Yeshe, a village head imprisoned for his role in a local anti-mining protest in May 2014, died in prison following reports that he had been mis-

HUMAN
RIGHTS
WATCH

ONE PASSPORT, TWO SYSTEMS
China's Restrictions on Foreign Travel by Tibetans and Others

treated. Another high profile prisoner, a young Lhasa NGO worker Tenzin Choedrak, died in December, two days after he was abruptly released early from detention.

Protests, particularly against mining and land acquisition, continue despite threats from local authorities. Security forces beat and arrested peaceful protesters in Chamdo in April and in Gannan in June. Following mass protests against mining in a supposedly protected part of Qinghai in 2014, mining operations were reportedly closed down, although the reasons for this remain unclear. After public outcry over corruption in the school exam system, authorities in the Tibet Autonomous Region and Qinghai introduced tighter regulations and prosecuted offenders.

Seven more Tibetans self-immolated in 2015, bringing the total since 2009 to 143.

Xinjiang

Xinjiang, home to 10 million Uighurs, continues to be the site of pervasive discrimination, repression, and restrictions on fundamental human rights. Opposition to central and local policies has been expressed in peaceful protests, but also through violent incidents such as bombings, though details about both protests and violence are often scant as authorities keep an especially tight hold over information in Xinjiang.

Chinese authorities in 2015 continued the counterterrorism campaign they launched in Xinjiang in mid-2014, deploying more security forces to the region, and implementing new laws and regulations that further criminalize dissent and restrict religious practice for the region's Muslim ethnic Uighur population. Since mid-2014, authorities have detained, arrested, or killed increasing numbers of Uighurs alleged by police to have been involved in illegal or terrorist activities, but the authorities' claims are impossible to verify independently. In June, a group of people attacked a police traffic checkpoint in Kashgar with small bombs and knives. Between 18 and 28 people reportedly died, including 15 suspects killed by police as well as several bystanders.

Xinjiang authorities promulgated comprehensive yet vaguely worded new religious affairs regulations in January. Those prohibit "extremist" attire and ban "activities that damage the physical and mental health of citizens." In recent years, authorities have used similar official and unofficial directives to discourage or even ban civil servants, teachers, and students from fasting during Ramadan. In March, a Hotan court convicted 25 Uighurs of "endangering state security" for their participation in "illegal" religious studies—in this case, private religious classes.

Hong Kong

Although Hong Kong is guaranteed autonomy in all matters other than foreign affairs and defense, and enjoys an independent judiciary and other civil liberties, Beijing appears to be encroaching on the rights to political participation, expression, and assembly there.

In June, Hong Kong's legislature rejected a Beijing-backed proposed electoral reform package for the region's chief executive. The proposal, which would expand the franchise but allow a Beijing-dominated nominating committee to screen out candidates it did not like, was opposed by many Hong Kong residents and in 2014 had sparked the months-long "Umbrella Movement" protests.

About 1,000 people were arrested in connection with the "Umbrella Movement," though most were released without being prosecuted. Authorities have charged student leader Joshua Wong Chi-fung, among others, with "unlawful assembly, and inciting others to take part in an unlawful assembly," despite those laws' incompatibility with international freedom of assembly standards. The Independent Police Complaints Council said it had received 159 complaints from demonstrators alleging police assault and abuse that it deemed "required investigation," but the only police who had been arrested at time of writing were police caught on film beating pro-democracy protester Ken Tsang.

Concerns about freedom of expression in Hong Kong persist, especially for media seen as critical of Beijing. In January, an attacker threw a Molotov cocktail outside the residence of pro-democracy media owner Jimmy Lai. No one was injured, but no one was arrested. In August, two assailants of former *Mingpao* editor Kevin Lau Chun-to were sentenced; one admitted that they had been paid to stab Lau to "teach him a lesson."

In July, Reverend Philip Woo Siu-hok was summoned to Shenzhen by religious affairs authorities to warn him against preaching to mainlanders who come to Hong Kong.

Key International Actors

Few governments exerted any substantial pressure on China over its worsening human rights record in 2015, instead limiting their interventions to bilateral human rights dialogues with the Chinese government and occasional public expressions of concern.

Some, such as the United Kingdom, went so far as to urge legislators in Hong Kong to accept Beijing's undemocratic electoral package, arguing that "something is better than nothing." New European Union High Representative for Foreign and Security Policy Federica Mogherini failed to publicly raise human rights abuses with Chinese leaders at a summit in May, as did US President Barack Obama during a state visit by Xi in September.

A remarkable diversity of governments, business and trade associations, universities, and other international organizations voiced concern through statements and submissions to the National People's Congress regarding China's draft foreign NGO management law after a second draft of the law was made public in May.

In August, the International Olympic Committee awarded Beijing the 2022 Winter Olympic Games despite international concerns about the current crackdown on rights and the lack of accountability for human rights abuses that accompanied, and in important respects were fueled by, China's preparations for the 2008 Summer Olympic Games in Beijing.

Foreign Policy

Under the leadership of Xi Jinping, China continues to aggressively advance its territorial claims in Asia, causing particular alarm by building structures on small reefs in the South China Seas that could one day accommodate military outposts. At the Security Council, China joined Russia in May 2014 in vetoing a resolution that would have referred the situation in Syria to the International Criminal

Court (ICC); in December, it tried to block discussion of the human rights situation in North Korea.

China continues to allow United Nations rapporteurs to visit on a highly selective basis; the rapporteurs on the freedom of religion, freedom of peaceful assembly and association, human rights defenders, health, extrajudicial executions, independence of judges and lawyers, and the freedom from torture all continue to await a response to their requests to visit. While not playing a visibly assertive role at the UN Human Rights Council, China continues to act as a spoiler, blocking greater scrutiny of human rights situations in other countries, including Belarus, Iran, North Korea, Syria, and Ukraine.

Concerns continued to be raised regarding reprisals against Chinese citizens participating in UN processes. The UN secretary-general noted that China had still not replied to communications about the death in custody of human rights defender Cao Shunli, who had been campaigning for greater civil society participation in the UN's universal periodic review, and both the UN Committee on the Elimination of Discrimination against Women and Committee against Torture (CAT) expressed concern at attempts to limit civil society participation in the treaty body reviews. Chinese officials provided few meaningful answers during its November CAT review.

The Chinese government marked the 70th anniversary of the end of World War II with a massive parade in Beijing. Sudanese President Omar al-Bashir, who is wanted by the ICC for genocide, war crimes, and crimes against humanity, attended at Beijing's invitation.

Beijing stepped up pressure on other governments to return allegedly corrupt officials to China; at least a dozen governments with politicized judicial systems complied and returned several dozen in 2015. China also pressured its neighbors to forcibly return refugees from China. In July, shortly after it had allowed nearly 170 Uighur women and children to resettle in Turkey after more than a year in detention, Thailand forcibly repatriated nearly 100 Uighur men to China, placing them at grave risk of imprisonment and torture.

Colombia

Civilians in Colombia continue to suffer serious abuses perpetrated by guerrillas, as well as by successor groups to paramilitaries that emerged after an official paramilitary demobilization process a decade ago. Violence associated with Colombia's internal armed conflict has forcibly displaced more than 6.8 million Colombians, generating the world's second largest population of internally displaced persons (IDPs) after Syria. Human rights defenders, trade unionists, journalists, indigenous and Afro-Colombian leaders, and other community activists face death threats and violence, but perpetrators are rarely held accountable.

The Colombian government and Revolutionary Armed Forces of Colombia (FARC) guerrillas have engaged in peace talks in Cuba since 2012, and at time of writing had reached an agreement on four of the six items on their negotiating agenda. In June, the government and FARC agreed to create a "Truth Commission" to carry out non-judicial investigations of gross human rights violations and serious violations of international humanitarian law committed during the conflict.

In September, the government and FARC announced an agreement that would create a new Peace Tribunal to try those responsible for gross human rights violations committed during the armed conflict. Under the agreement, those responsible for crimes against humanity and serious war crimes who cooperate with the new judicial system and confess their crimes would spend between five and eight years under "effective restraint of liberty" but face no prison time.

Exploratory talks between the government and National Liberation Army (ELN), Colombia's second largest guerrilla group, continued at time of writing.

Guerrilla Abuses

FARC guerrillas continue to attack civilians, although credible evidence suggests that abuses decreased during two unilateral ceasefires agreed on with the government starting in late 2014. There are credible reports that FARC continued to engage in serious abuses, including killings, forced displacement, and threats against civilians in the municipality of Tumaco in 2015. In June, an attack on an oil pipeline in Tumaco left almost 200,000 people with limited access to water for several days and led to complaints of lingering health problems.

The ELN also continues to commit serious abuses against civilians. In the province of Chocó, for example, the ELN has been responsible for kidnappings, killings, forced displacement, and child recruitment. In March, ELN guerrillas released a mayor from that province whom they had kidnapped in December 2014.

The FARC and ELN continued to use antipersonnel landmines in 2015. The government reported that landmines and unexploded ordnances killed 17 people and injured 113 between January and July 2015. In May, after an agreement reached in Cuba, members of FARC and the army started demining the El Orejón zone in Antioquia.

Paramilitaries and their Successors

Between 2003 and 2006, right-wing paramilitary organizations with close ties to security forces and politicians underwent a deeply flawed government demobilization process in which many members remained active and reorganized into new groups.

Successor groups, often led by members of demobilized paramilitary organizations, continue to commit such widespread abuses as killings, disappearances, and sexual violence.

In Buenaventura, a largely Afro-Colombian port on the Pacific coast, atrocities by paramilitary successor groups that include dismembering victims continued in 2015 despite a "special intervention" initially announced by the government in May 2014 to dismantle the groups. The municipality has one of the highest rates of forced displacement in Colombia, with 22,383 residents fleeing their homes in 2014, and 1,385 between January and September 2015.

Successor groups have also engaged in gross abuses in Medellín. In October, the National Institute of Legal Medicine and Forensic Sciences reported that 24 people had been dismembered in that city in 2015, presumably by successor groups.

Paramilitary successor groups have at times benefited from the tolerance and even collusion of state agents.

Implementation of the Justice and Peace law of 2005, which offers dramatically reduced sentences to demobilized paramilitary members who confess their crimes, has been slow. As of August 2015, only 115 of the more than 30,000 paramilitary troops who officially demobilized had been sentenced under the law, and over 1,000 remained in pretrial detention. The convictions cover a small portion of the nearly 70,000 crimes confessed by the more than 4,000 defendants seeking the law's benefits.

In November 2014, the Attorney General's Office obtained its first conviction in a case it designated "high priority" two years earlier. Twelve leaders of a paramilitary group responsible for hundreds of crimes between 1994 and 2004, including enforced disappearances, homicides, and rape, were convicted and sentenced to eight years in prison.

"Parapolitics" investigations into current and former members of Congress accused of conspiring with paramilitaries continued in 2015. As of August, 63 legislators had been convicted of crimes related to "parapolitics" since 2006.

Abuses by Public Security Forces

Between 2002 and 2008, army brigades across Colombia routinely executed civilians. Under pressure from superiors to show "positive" results and boost body counts in their war against guerrillas, soldiers and officers abducted victims or lured them to remote locations under false pretenses—such as with promises of work—and killed them, placed weapons on their lifeless bodies, and then reported them as enemy combatants killed in action. There has been a dramatic reduction in cases of alleged unlawful killings attributed to security forces since 2009, though credible reports of some new cases continue to emerge.

The government does not keep statistics for "false-positives" as a category of crime distinct from other types of unlawful killings. However, as of May 2015, the Attorney General's Office was investigating more than 3,700 unlawful killings allegedly committed by state agents between 2002 and 2008, and had obtained convictions for over 800 of them. Authorities have failed to prosecute senior army officers involved in the killings and instead have promoted many of them through the military ranks.

In June and October, the Attorney General's Office summoned a total of nine generals, including former army commander Mario Montoya, to testify on their alleged role in false-positive cases. At time of writing, no charges had yet been brought against any of them.

In July, the government replaced the army's top commander, Gen. Lasprilla Vilamizar, who commanded a brigade allegedly responsible for 48 extrajudicial killings. General Rodríguez Barragan, however, continued at time of writing to command the armed forces despite strong evidence implicating him in false-positive killings.

Peace Negotiations and Accountability

In September 2015, the government and FARC announced an agreement to create a new peace tribunal to try those responsible for gross human rights abuses committed during the armed conflict.

Under the agreement, those responsible for crimes against humanity and serious war crimes who cooperate with the new judicial system and confess their crimes would spend between five and eight years under "special conditions" that would entail "effective restraint of liberty" but no prison time. While the details of the agreement had not been finalized at time of writing, such "special conditions" could fail to provide punishments that reflect the gravity of the crimes as required under international law.

Other parties to the armed conflict would also benefit from the agreement, likely including members of the armed forces responsible for false-positive cases. The government announced that members of the armed forces could participate in the process under terms that are "differentiated" but "equitable" to those governing participation by guerrillas.

In April, the government dropped legislation intended to expand military jurisdiction, which could have derailed the ongoing prosecution of false-positive cases.

Internal Displacement and Land Restitution

More than 6.8 million Colombians have been internally displaced since 1985, government figures reveal. The government registered more than 180,000 newly displaced people in 2014, and over 37,000 from January to October 2015.

The government's implementation of land restitution under the Victims' Law continues to move slowly. The law was enacted in 2011 to restore millions of hectares of abandoned land and land stolen by armed groups and civilians to internally displaced Colombians. At the time, the government estimated that more than 150,000 land restitution cases would be settled by the end of 2015, but as of November, the government had obtained rulings in just 2,983 of the nearly 85,000 claims it had received.

Dozens of land restitution claimants have been murdered, and no one has been held accountable for the majority of those killings.

Gender-Based Violence

Gender-based violence (GBV) is widespread in Colombia. Lack of training and poor implementation of treatment protocols create obstacles for women and girls seeking post-violence care and can impede timely access to essential medical services. Perpetrators of GBV crimes are rarely brought to justice.

In 2014, the government enacted a law to improve access to justice and protection for sexual-violence survivors. A challenge by four nongovernmental organizations to a provision of the law making it optional for health providers to use post-rape protocols remained pending before the Constitutional Court at time of writing.

In July 2015, the government enacted a law that created the crime of "femicide"—defined as a murder of a woman because of her gender—and established comprehensive measures to prevent and prosecute GVB, such as creating a special unit at the Attorney General's Office and establishing victims' right to free and specialized legal assistance.

Human Rights Defenders, Journalists, and Trade Unionists

Rights advocates and journalists continue to be targeted with threats and attacks. Despite an Interior Ministry program that assigns guards to protect human rights defenders, trade unionists, and journalists, local groups report that dozens of rights advocates and community activists were killed in 2015.

The Foundation for Free Press (FLIP), a respected Colombian NGO that monitors press freedoms, reported that two journalists were killed and 60 were threatened between January and October 2015. As of August, no one had been charged in the 2013 shooting attack against investigative journalist Ricardo Calderón.

As of February, the government had reported 121 trade unionist killings since 2011, and the Attorney General's Office had achieved convictions in only six. The National Labor School, Colombia's leading labor rights NGO, reported 17 new killings between January and August 2015.

The Inspector General's Office continued its disciplinary investigation against Senator Iván Cepeda, a prominent victims' rights advocate, for collecting information about possible paramilitary abuses. The investigation, which relates to Senator Cepeda's interviews of ex-paramilitaries about former President Uribe's alleged ties to paramilitaries, appears to be entirely unfounded and could have a chilling effect on others who seek accountability for human rights abuses.

Sexual Orientation and Gender Identity

In 2011, the Constitutional Court determined that, if by June 2013 Congress had not passed a law recognizing same-sex unions, such couples could go before notary publics and judges to "formalize and solemnize" their union. In the face of congressional inaction and the still unclear status of such unions, the court held a follow-up hearing in July 2015 to address whether same-sex couples should be granted the right to marry under Colombian law. It had not issued a ruling at time of writing.

In November, the Constitutional Court ruled that sexual orientation could not be used to prohibit someone from adopting a child.

Key International Actors

The United States remains the most influential foreign actor in Colombia. In 2015, it provided approximately US$280 million, mostly in military and police aid. A portion of US military aid is subject to human rights conditions, which the US Department of State has not enforced; in September, it again certified that Colombia was meeting the conditions.

The Office of the Prosecutor (OTP) of the International Criminal Court (ICC) continues to monitor Colombian investigations of crimes that may fall within the ICC's jurisdiction. In November 2015, the OTP reported that it would "carefully review and analyse the provisions of the agreement [with FARC], in particular with respect to the restrictions of liberty in special conditions and the inclusion of state agents," and expressed its concern about limited progress on prosecutions of sexual and gender-based crimes in the ordinary justice system.

In November 2014, the Inter-American Court on Human Rights condemned Colombia for enforced disappearances committed by military troops after the recapture of the Palace of Justice in 1985.

In March 2015, the United Nations Committee on the Rights of the Child expressed concern about the continuing recruitment of children by non-state armed groups and successor groups of the paramilitaries. In May, the UN Committee Against Torture called on Colombia to ensure that military courts do not try military members accused of human rights abuses.

Côte d'Ivoire

Alassane Ouattara won a second term in the October presidential elections, deemed free and fair by international observers—another step towards recovery from the 2010-2011 post-election crisis. In the lead-up to the elections, however, clashes between ruling party and opposition activists, particularly supporters of the former president, Laurent Gbagbo, left at least three people dead and dozens injured. The government's prohibition of several opposition protests, and the subsequent arrest of dozens of demonstrators, threatened freedom of assembly. Several opposition activists were held in unauthorized detention facilities without access to legal assistance.

Côte d'Ivoire's strong macroeconomic growth continued and led to some gradual improvement in social and economic rights, such as access to education and basic healthcare. However, the government has made insufficient progress in tackling corruption and strengthening the judicial system. Members of the security forces continued to be implicated in illegal detentions and torture, albeit less often than in previous years, but extortion and racketeering by security forces was pervasive. Gender-based violence remained widespread, although the government's September 2014 adoption of a national strategy against sexual violence led to some positive steps to address it.

The Ivorian judiciary made progress in investigating atrocities committed during the 2010-2011 post-election crisis, although concerns persisted about the government's willingness to prosecute pro-Ouattara forces.

Land dispossession remained a key driver of inter-communal tensions and local-level violence in western Côte d'Ivoire. The 1998 land law, designed to increase certainty over land ownership by converting customary claims to legal title, is largely unimplemented.

Côte d'Ivoire's key partners—France, the United Nations, the European Union, and the United States—continued to favor private advocacy to push the government to pursue accountability for past crimes. The International Criminal Court (ICC) is scheduled to begin the trial of former President Gbagbo and Charles Blé Goudé, a former youth minister and leader of a pro-Gbagbo militia, in early 2016. However, the ICC made little progress in the investigation of crimes by pro-Ouattara forces.

HUMAN
RIGHTS
WATCH

"To Consolidate This Peace of Ours"
A Human Rights Agenda for Côte d'Ivoire

Accountability for Past Abuses

The Special Investigative Cell, the body responsible for investigating crimes committed during the 2010-2011 post-election crisis, in late 2014 received sufficient funding to conduct effective investigations. In 2015 it charged more than 20 perpetrators in relation to human rights abuses committed during the crisis, including commanders from President Ouattara's side.

However, no individual has yet been tried in national civilian courts for atrocities committed during the 2010-2011 post-election violence. Former First Lady Simone Gbagbo, as well 78 of President Gbagbo's former allies, were tried by a civilian court in early 2015: she was convicted, along with 59 others. However, this was for offenses against the state, not human rights crimes. Concerns about evidentiary weaknesses in the case also raised doubt about Ivorian courts' capacity to fairly try human rights cases. The beleaguered military justice system tried several cases involving killings of civilians by pro-Gbagbo soldiers during the post-election crisis, but discontinued a case against two commanders for indiscriminate shelling after the prosecution failed to produce sufficient evidence.

In March 2015, the National Assembly passed legislation amending the criminal code and criminal procedure code to ensure conformity with the Rome Statute of the ICC. However, the government refused to transfer Simone Gbagbo to the ICC to face trial for crimes against humanity committed during the 2010-2011 crisis, despite in May 2015 losing an appeal at the ICC against the admissibility of the case against her.

The much-criticized Dialogue, Truth and Reconciliation Commission presented its final report to President Ouattara on December 15, 2014. However, the government had not yet publicly released the report at time of writing, although President Ouattara has pledged to make 10 billion CFA (US$16.5 million) available for the indemnification of victims. The first group of victims began receiving financial and medical assistance in August 2015, but victims' groups criticized the lack of transparency of the reparations process.

Judicial System

Ongoing efforts to strengthen the judicial system continued throughout 2015, including the rehabilitation of court buildings and detention facilities, and training

HUMAN
RIGHTS
WATCH

MAKING JUSTICE COUNT

Lessons from the ICC's Work in Côte d'Ivoire

of judicial personnel. However, more fundamental problems, such as political interference in the judiciary and corruption, persisted. Prolonged pretrial detention remained the rule rather than the exception, and most prisons are overcrowded and lack adequate nutrition, sanitation, and medical care.

Conduct of Security Forces

Security forces continued to be implicated in arbitrary arrest and detentions and, less frequently, mistreatment and torture of detainees. They were also frequently implicated in criminal conduct, notably extortion. Very few security forces members faced judicial or disciplinary actions for these violations. Several commanders credibly implicated in atrocities during the 2010-2011 crisis remained in key positions in the security forces.

The military justice system is severely under-resourced, with one military tribunal in Abidjan for the whole country, and needs reform to strengthen its independence from the executive.

Cote d'Ivoire's Disarmament, Demobilization and Reintegration (DDR) program officially ended on June 30, 2015, and the government claims to have reintegrated almost 60,000 former combatants. The DDR process, however, has been one-sided, mostly benefitting forces who fought on President Ouattara's side during the post-election crisis. Former rebel commanders who fought with Ouattara had particularly close control over which ex-combatants obtained jobs as customs, prison, and forestry officers.

Corruption

Security forces continued to plunder revenues through smuggling and parallel tax systems on cocoa, timber, diamonds, and other natural resources. In its April 2015 report, the UN Group of Experts, appointed by the UN Security Council to monitor the sanctions regime in Cote d'Ivoire, identified several army officers involved in the illicit exploitation of natural resources, including gold and cocoa.

Extortion by security forces at illegal checkpoints remained an acute problem, particularly on secondary roads in rural areas. A specialized anti-racket unit has been undermined by inconsistent financial support from the government and the failure of the military tribunal to consistently prosecute perpetrators.

Land Rights

Land dispossession remains a key driver of inter-communal tensions and local-level violence between ethnic groups in western Côte d'Ivoire. Although customary authorities and local officials have successfully mediated many cases related to the 2010-2011 post-election crisis, the outcome of mediation often allows those who acquired land in bad faith to remain and frequently discriminates against women. Those implicated in illegal land sales are rarely prosecuted.

In 2013, the Ivorian government passed several reforms to land tenure and nationality laws designed to facilitate implementation of the 1998 land law, which seeks to convert customary land ownership into a land certificate and eventually legal title. However, the procedure for obtaining a certificate is too complicated and expensive, and so few landowners have applied for one. The government is considering reforms to simplify the process.

Violence against Women

Gender-based violence remained widespread, although the government has taken some positive steps to address it. In the first five months of 2015, the UN secretary-general's report on the UN Operation in Cote d'Ivoire (UNOCI) reported at least 80 cases of rape and other sexual abuses, fewer than in previous reporting periods.

In September 2014, the government launched a national strategy against sexual violence, with a strong commitment to prosecute perpetrators, and has conducted sensitization trainings for the security forces. In March 2015, the Ministry of Justice, Human Rights and Public Liberties instructed law enforcement officials that a medical certificate is not required to open a rape investigation, although fear of stigmatization still prevents victims from reporting rape cases. The cour d'assises mandated to try rape cases rarely functions, and many cases are downgraded to indecent assault, which carries a more lenient penalty, in order to be heard in regular courts.

Trafficking of women and girls, often from Nigeria, into Côte d'Ivoire for commercial sexual exploitation continues to be a problem.

Sexual Orientation and Gender Identity

Côte d'Ivoire does not criminalize same-sex conduct. However, same-sex couples can be prosecuted for public acts of indecency. Additionally, the penal code codifies discrimination by establishing a higher age of consent for same-sex couples. No law prohibits discrimination on the grounds of sexual orientation, gender identity, or intersex status.

Police have failed to arrest anyone in relation to a series of attacks in January 2014 on Alternative-Côte d'Ivoire, a nonprofit working on LGBTI rights and HIV prevention.

Human Rights Defenders

International and national human rights groups generally operate without government restrictions. In June 2014, the government passed a law that strengthened protections for human rights defenders, described as the first as its kind in Africa, though the government has so far failed to adopt a decree to facilitate the law's implementation.

Key International Actors

France, the European Union, and the United States continued to be the Ivorian government's main partners on justice and security sector reform, along with UNOCI, whose mandate the UN Security Council extended until June 30, 2016. The UN's new independent expert on capacity-building and technical cooperation with Côte d'Ivoire in the field of human rights published his first report in April 2015. The report praised the government's efforts to pursue sustainable economic development, but underscored the need to prosecute human rights crimes committed by both sides in the post-election crisis.

Cuba

The Cuban government continues to repress dissent and discourage public criticism. It now relies less on long-term prison sentences to punish its critics, but short-term arbitrary arrests of human rights defenders, independent journalists, and others have increased dramatically in recent years. Other repressive tactics employed by the government include beatings, public acts of shaming, and the termination of employment.

In December 2014, President Barack Obama announced that the United States would ease restrictions on travel and commerce and normalize diplomatic relations with Cuba. In exchange, the Cuban government released 53 political prisoners and committed to allow visits by international human rights monitors. The two governments restored diplomatic relations in July 2015.

Arbitrary Detention and Short-Term Imprisonment

The government continues to rely on arbitrary detentions to harass and intimidate people who exercise their fundamental rights. The Cuban Commission for Human Rights and National Reconciliation, an independent human rights group that the government views as illegal, received more than 6,200 reports of arbitrary detentions from January through October 2015. While this represented a decrease from the number of detentions during the same 10-month period in 2014, it was still significantly higher than the number of yearly detentions prior to 2012.

Security officers virtually never present arrest orders to justify the detention of critics. In some cases, detainees are released after receiving official warnings, which prosecutors can use in subsequent criminal trials to show a pattern of delinquent behavior.

Detention is often used preemptively to prevent people from participating in peaceful marches or meetings to discuss politics. Detainees are often beaten, threatened, and held incommunicado for hours or days. Members of the Ladies in White (Damas de Blanco)—a group founded by the wives, mothers, and daughters of political prisoners and which the government considers illegal—are routinely harassed, roughed up, and detained before or after they attend Sunday mass.

Lazaro Yuri Valle Roca, a blogger and videographer who often covers the Sunday demonstrations of the Ladies in White, wrote that police arbitrarily detained him on June 7 and drove him 30 miles from Havana, where they took him from the car at gunpoint, made him kneel on the grass, and put the gun to his neck, telling him he was "on notice" to stay away from the demonstrations.

The artist Tania Bruguera was arrested on December 30, 2014, hours before her planned performance art piece in Havana's Revolution Square, in which she was to have invited passersby to walk up to a podium and express themselves at a microphone for one minute. Security officials confiscated her passport and computer. Bruguera was released the following day but was detained and released twice more during the next two days. Cuban dissidents and independent journalists who had planned to attend the event—including Reinaldo Escobar, Eliecer Avila, and Antonio Rodiles—were also arrested on December 30. Bruguera was again detained in May during the 12th Havana Biennial Art Exhibition. She was released the same day.

On August 9, a few days before US Secretary of State John Kerry was to attend a ceremony to mark the opening of the US embassy in Havana, 90 people—including an estimated 50 Ladies in White—were arrested and detained after Sunday mass in the Havana neighborhood of Miramar during a peaceful march against political repression.

During the visit of Pope Francis in September, police detained some 100 to 150 dissidents to prevent them from seeing him. Miriam Leiva, a freelance journalist and blogger and a founder of the Ladies in White, was invited by the Papal Nuncio in Havana to greet the Pope twice, on September 19 and 20, but was detained for several hours each time, preventing her attendance.

Political Prisoners

Despite the release of the 53 political prisoners in conjunction with the agreement to normalize relations with the US, dozens more remain in Cuban prisons, according to local human rights groups. The government prevents independent human rights groups from accessing its prisons, and the groups believe there are additional political prisoners whose cases they cannot document.

Cubans who criticize the government continue to face the threat of criminal prosecution. They do not benefit from due process guarantees, such as the right to fair and public hearings by a competent and impartial tribunal. In practice, courts are subordinated to the executive and legislative branches, denying meaningful judicial independence.

Graffiti artist Danilo Maldonado, known as "El Sexto," was arrested in December 2014 and charged with "contempt for authority" for attempting to stage a performance involving two pigs painted with the names "Raul" and "Fidel"—a satire of the current and former heads of state. He was released on October 20.

Freedom of Expression

The government controls virtually all media outlets in Cuba and restricts access to outside information, severely limiting the right to freedom of expression.

A small number of journalists and bloggers who are independent of government media manage to write articles for websites or blogs, or publish tweets. However, the government routinely blocks access within Cuba to these websites, and those who publish information considered critical of the government are subject to smear campaigns and arbitrary arrests, as are artists and academics who demand greater freedoms.

Only a fraction of Cubans are able to read independent websites and blogs because of the high cost of, and limited access to, the Internet. In July, Cuba increased Internet access by opening 35 Wi-Fi hot spots in parks and city boulevards nationwide. The US$2-an-hour Wi-Fi connection fee is expensive in a country where the average wage is approximately $20 a month.

Travel Restrictions and Family Separation

Reforms to travel regulations that went into effect in January 2013 eliminated the need for an exit visa to leave the island. Exit visas had previously been used to deny the right to travel to people critical of the government—and to their families. Since then, many people who had previously been denied permission to travel have been able to do so, including human rights defenders and independent bloggers.

Nonetheless, the reforms gave the government broad discretionary powers to restrict the right to travel on the grounds of "defense and national security" or "other reasons of public interest." Such measures have allowed the authorities to deny exit to people who express dissent. For example, José Daniel Ferrer, the leader of the Patriotic Union of Cuba (Unpacu), was denied the right to travel abroad in August for "reasons of public interest," authorities said.

The government restricts the movement of citizens within Cuba through a 1997 law known as Decree 217, which is designed to limit migration to Havana. The decree has been used to prevent dissidents from traveling to Havana to attend meetings and to harass dissidents from other parts of Cuba who live there.

Prison Conditions

Prisons are overcrowded. Prisoners are forced to work 12-hour days and punished if they do not meet production quotas, according to former political prisoners. Inmates have no effective complaint mechanism to seek redress, and those who criticize the government or engage in hunger strikes and other forms of protest are subjected to extended solitary confinement, beatings, restrictions on family visits, and denial of medical care.

While the government allowed select members of the foreign press to conduct controlled visits to a handful of prisons in April 2013, it continues to deny international human rights groups and independent Cuban organizations access to its prisons.

Labor Rights

Despite updating its Labor Code in 2014, Cuba continues to violate conventions of the International Labour Organization that it has ratified, specifically regarding freedom of association, collective bargaining, protection of wages and wage payment, and prohibitions on forced labor. While the formation of independent unions is technically allowed by law, in practice Cuba only permits one confederation of state-controlled unions, the Workers' Central Union of Cuba.

Human Rights Defenders

The Cuban government still refuses to recognize human rights monitoring as a legitimate activity and denies legal status to local human rights groups. Government authorities harass, assault, and imprison human rights defenders who attempt to document abuses.

Key International Actors

In January, a month after announcing plans to normalize diplomatic relations with Cuba, President Obama called on the US Congress to lift the economic embargo of Cuba imposed more than four decades ago. The United Nations General Assembly has repeatedly called on the United States to end the embargo, most recently in October by a vote of 191 to two.

At time of writing, Cuba had yet to allow visits to the island by the International Committee of the Red Cross or by UN human rights monitors, as stipulated in the December 2014 agreement with the US.

The European Union continues to retain its "Common Position on Cuba," adopted in 1996, which conditions full EU economic cooperation with Cuba on the country's transition to a pluralist democracy and respect for human rights. After a meeting in April 2014 in Havana, EU and Cuban delegates agreed on establishing a road map for "normalizing" relations. A fifth round of negotiations towards an EU-Cuba Political Dialogue and Cooperation Agreement took place in Havana in September 2015, and a sixth round was scheduled for late November.

In November 2013, Cuba was re-elected to a regional position on the UN Human Rights Council, despite its poor human rights record and consistent efforts to undermine important council work. As a member of the council, Cuba has regularly voted to prevent scrutiny of serious human rights abuses around the world, opposing resolutions spotlighting abuses in North Korea, Syria, Iran, and Ukraine. However, Cuba supported a landmark resolution the council adopted in September 2014 to combat violence and discrimination based on sexual orientation and gender identity.

Democratic Republic of Congo

In 2015, security and intelligence officials in the Democratic Republic of Congo clamped down on activists and political opponents who opposed political maneuvers to allow President Joseph Kabila to stay in power beyond his constitutionally mandated two-term limit, due to end in December 2016. Security forces shot peaceful demonstrators, jailed activists and political party leaders, and shut down media outlets, as the government increasingly resorted to violent acts of repression.

In the country's east, the security situation remained volatile. Numerous armed groups carried out deadly attacks on civilians, while government security forces also committed serious abuses.

Freedom of Expression and Peaceful Assembly

In January, security forces brutally suppressed demonstrations in the capital, Kinshasa, and other cities by those opposed to proposed changes to the electoral law requiring a national census before national elections could be held, effectively extending Kabila's term for several years.

Police and Republican Guard soldiers fatally shot at least 38 protesters in Kinshasa and 5 in Goma, in eastern Congo. Dozens were wounded and at least five people in Kinshasa were forcibly disappeared. Soon after a delegation of political opposition and civil society leaders visited wounded protesters at Kinshasa's General Hospital on January 21, Republican Guard soldiers entered the hospital and fired indiscriminately, wounding at least three visitors.

In the lead-up to the demonstrations, the government shut down two television stations that had aired messages calling on people to demonstrate: Canal Kin Television (CKTV) and Radio Television Catholique Elykia (RTCE). RTCE was reopened in June while CKTV remained blocked at time of writing. During the January demonstrations, the government also shut down text messaging services and Internet access for several days.

The same week, security forces arrested nearly a dozen prominent political party leaders and activists. Most were first detained by Congo's National Intelligence Agency *(Agence Nationale de Renseignements, ANR)* and held without charge for

HUMAN
RIGHTS
WATCH

"Our School Became
the Battlefield"
Using Schools for Child Recruitment and Military Purposes
in Eastern Democratic Republic of Congo

weeks or months with no access to lawyers or family members. In March, the ANR arrested about 30 youth activists and others attending a workshop in Kinshasa to promote the democratic process.

At time of writing, human rights defender Christopher Ngoyi, youth activists Fred Bauma and Yves Makwambala, and political party leaders Jean-Claude Muyambo, Ernest Kyaviro, and Vano Kiboko remained in detention at Kinshasa's central prison. On September 14, Kiboko was convicted and sentenced to three years in prison on trumped up charges of racial hatred, tribalism, and spreading false rumors. On September 18, Kyaviro was convicted and sentenced to three years in prison for provoking and inciting disobedience toward public authorities. Trials based on politically motivated charges were ongoing for the others at time of writing.

In Goma in March and April, the authorities arrested and later released at least 15 activists from the LUCHA youth movement who were demonstrating peacefully to demand the release of their colleagues detained in Kinshasa. Some alleged that intelligence agents beat or tortured them through a form of near-drowning. In September, four of them were convicted of inciting disobedience to authorities and sentenced to a suspended 6-month prison term and a 12-month probation period. Twelve other people were arrested during a peaceful LUCHA demonstration in Goma on November 28. Nine remain in detention at time of writing, including two LUCHA activists.

During an opposition rally in Kinshasa on September 15, a group of thugs hired and instructed by members of the ruling political party and senior officials in the security services attacked demonstrators with clubs and wooden sticks, injuring more than a dozen. Only when demonstrators turned on the assailants—beating some so badly that at least one later died of his wounds—did the police intervene.

After seven senior politicians from Kabila's political coalition, known as the G7, sent a public letter to Kabila on September 14, demanding he respect the constitution's two-term limit, security forces surrounded many of their homes, intimidated their supporters, and shut down a radio station that belonged to Christophe Lutundula, a signatory of the letter.

Attacks on Civilians by Armed Groups

Dozens of armed groups remained active in eastern Congo. Many commanders controlled forces responsible for war crimes, including ethnic massacres, killing of civilians, rape, forced recruitment of children, and pillage.

In February, the army launched military operations against the Democratic Forces for the Liberation of Rwanda (FDLR), a largely Rwandan Hutu armed group. The FDLR has been responsible for some of the worst atrocities in eastern Congo over the past decade. United Nations peacekeepers, who were closely involved in planning the military campaign, withdrew their support following the government's last-minute appointment of two generals to lead the operation. Both have been implicated in past human rights violations. The government then suspended military cooperation with UN peacekeepers. The FDLR military leader, Sylvestre Mudacumura—sought on an arrest warrant by the International Criminal Court—remained at large.

In Beni territory, North Kivu, unidentified fighters continued to commit sporadic massacres of civilians, killing dozens. Further north, in Ituri province, the Patriotic Resistance Front in Ituri (FRPI) rebel group also committed serious human rights abuses, particularly rape and pillage. In Rutshuru territory, North Kivu province, bandits and armed groups kidnapped dozens of civilians for ransom.

In Nyunzu, in the north of former Katanga province, ethnic Luba fighters attacked a camp for displaced people on April 30. The assailants killed at least 30 civilians from the marginalized Batwa community, known as "Pygmy," with machetes, arrows, and axes and burned down the camp. Dozens of others remained missing and feared dead. The attack followed deadly raids on Luba by Batwa militias.

Justice and Accountability

Mathieu Ngudjolo, the first defendant to be acquitted by the International Criminal Court (ICC), returned to Congo on May 11. On September 2, the ICC opened the trial of Bosco Ntaganda, who faces 18 counts of war crimes and crimes against humanity allegedly committed in Ituri province in 2002 and 2003. He faced no charges for alleged crimes later committed in North Kivu province. The ICC prosecutor has said that her office is continuing investigations in Congo.

On December 19, two Congolese rebel leaders convicted at the ICC, Germain Katanga and Thomas Lubanga, were returned to Congo to serve the remainder of their ICC sentences in Kinshasa. Katanga faces national war crimes charges in Congo that were filed against him before he was transferred to the ICC.

On September 28, a court in Stuttgart, Germany, convicted Ignace Murwanashyaka and Straton Musoni, respectively the former president and vice president of the FDLR, and sentenced them to 13 and 8 years in prison. Murwanashyaka was found guilty of war crimes in relation to five FDLR attacks in eastern Congo and of leading a terrorist organization. Musoni was found guilty of leading a terrorist organization but acquitted of war crimes and crimes against humanity.

From April 27 to May 2, the Congolese Ministry of Justice and Human Rights convened a large conference in Kinshasa to evaluate its judicial reform program and recommend priority reforms that should be implemented, including the establishment of specialized mixed chambers to prosecute war crimes and crimes against humanity committed since the 1990s.

In August, the civilian Appeals Court in Lubumbashi opened a trial against 34 members of the Luba and Batwa communities in northern Katanga for crimes against humanity and genocide, a first for Congo's civilian courts.

FRPI leader Justin Banaloki, known as Cobra Matata, was arrested in Bunia on January 2 and charged with war crimes and crimes against humanity. At time of writing, he had not been brought to trial.

Ntabo Ntaberi Sheka, wanted on a Congolese arrest warrant for crimes against humanity for the mass rape of nearly 400 people in 2010, remained at large at time of writing. His troops continued to commit serious abuses.

No progress was made in bringing to justice those responsible for the summary executions of at least 51 young men and boys and the enforced disappearance of 33 others during a police campaign in Kinshasa, known as Operation Likofi, from November 2013 to February 2014, or for the summary executions during the January demonstrations.

The government failed to exhume the mass grave in Maluku, a rural area about 80 kilometers from Kinshasa, where it admitted burying 421 bodies on March 19. On June 5, family members of those forcibly disappeared or executed by Con-

HUMAN
RIGHTS
WATCH

JUSTICE ON TRIAL
Lessons from the Minova Rape case in the Democratic Republic of Congo

golese security forces during Operation Likofi and the January demonstrations filed a public complaint with the national prosecutor requesting exhumation.

Key International Actors

Little progress was made in implementing the "Framework Agreement" signed in February 2013 by 11 African countries (later joined by two other countries) to end the rebellion of the M23—an abusive Rwandan-backed armed group defeated in November 2013—and address other regional security issues. Many former M23 fighters and commanders remained in Uganda and Rwanda, including six former officers sought on Congolese arrest warrants for war crimes and crimes against humanity who are also listed on UN and US sanctions lists.

In July, the US State Department appointed Thomas Perriello as new US special envoy for Congo and the Great Lakes Region, succeeding Russ Feingold. Perriello and other senior US officials continued to raise concerns publicly about the importance of national elections being held on time to prevent further violence, repression, and instability.

The UN, US, and European countries publicly condemned the arrests of pro-democracy youth activists, and in July, the European Parliament adopted an urgency resolution calling for their immediate release and condemning other acts of political repression.

In October, UN Secretary-General Ban Ki-moon appointed Maman Sidikou, a former foreign minister of Niger and senior African Union official, as his special representative in Congo and head of MONUSCO, succeeding Martin Kobler. Sidikou will be tasked with implementing MONUSCO's strong mandate in support of human rights and the rule of law during what is likely to be a volatile elections period in Congo.

Dominican Republic

The Dominican Republic's treatment of Haitian migrants and Dominican citizens of Haitian descent dominated human rights developments in 2015. Government authorities are still responding to a 2013 Constitutional Tribunal ruling that stripped citizenship from tens of thousands of Dominicans of migrant descent, mostly of Haitian origin, by dual policies of re-registering denationalized citizens and carrying out mass deportations. At the same time, the government began its first comprehensive effort to regularize the status of undocumented migrants, mostly Haitians.

In November 2014, the Constitutional Tribunal also broadly jeopardized human rights protections when it declared the government's 1999 accession to the jurisdiction of the Inter-American Court of Human Rights (IACrtHR) unconstitutional. The decision created a legal limbo that remains unresolved.

Arbitrary Deprivation of Nationality

A 2013 ruling by the Dominican Constitutional Tribunal retroactively stripped Dominican nationality and citizenship from tens of thousands of people. According to estimates by the United Nations High Commissioner for Refugees, the decision affected more than 200,000 people, though the government says the number is closer to 100,000.

In 2014, President Danilo Medina's administration adopted a Naturalization Law designed to mitigate the ruling. While the law was meant to restore various citizenship rights to those affected by the 2013 decision and provided a promising legal framework, its implementation has been fraught with flaws. Many eligible people have been unable to resolve their citizenship status and remain at risk of deportation.

Migration and Deportations

Between June 2014 and June 2015, the government also implemented a national "regularization" plan to legalize the status of hundreds of thousands of undocumented migrants—mostly Haitians—who had been living and working in the Dominican Republic before 2011. By the end of the regularization period in June

2015, more than 288,000 individuals had submitted applications to regularize their status.

Officials reported that, in the summer of 2015, more than 66,000 immigrants voluntarily returned to Haiti. Rights groups, however, have challenged the "voluntary" nature of these returns, as some migrants report having been forcibly removed, or having fled the country for fear of mob violence. Acts of vigilante violence against Haitians punctuated the regularization process, including the lynching of a Haitian man in February and the murder of another Haitian man in August.

Rights groups have also raised concerns regarding the lack of clear deportation protocols and the possibility of racial profiling in the deportation process.

Prison Conditions

While the government has created "model prisons" as part of a program to improve prison

conditions, the majority of inmates remained in severely overcrowded traditional facilities. As of August, more than 26,000 prisoners were held in a system with an intended capacity of 14,000. La Victoria, the largest prison in the country, had an official capacity of 2,000 yet holds more than 8,000 inmates.

Violence against Women

Violence against women and girls remains a problem. The National Police has a dedicated unit to respond to such cases. However, between January 2008 and October 2014, the National Police reported more than 1,300 deaths due to gender-based violence. A bill proposing a series of judicial reforms to address the problem was still pending before the lower house of Congress at time of writing.

Reproductive Rights

In late 2014, the Dominican Republic decriminalized abortion in cases of rape, incest, certain fetal malformations, and when the pregnancy threatens the life of the woman. In December, the High Court ruled that the reform was unconstitu-

HUMAN
RIGHTS
WATCH

WE ARE DOMINICAN
Arbitrary Deprivation of Nationality in the Dominican Republic

tional and reinstated an absolute criminal prohibition on abortion dating from the 19th century.

Sexual Orientation and Gender Identity

The constitution of 2010 defines marriage as between a man and a woman. The law offers no comprehensive provisions against discrimination against lesbian, gay, bisexual, and transgender (LGBT) people. In 2015, LGBT rights groups reported instances of discrimination and violence, including murder, particularly against transgender individuals.

Key International Actors

In November 2014, the Constitutional Tribunal ruled that the Dominican Republic's 1999 accession to the jurisdiction of the IACrtHR was unconstitutional because it was enacted by a presidential decree and not ratified by lawmakers. Such a ratification was not required by the constitution then in force.

National and international legal experts decried the ruling as a violation of the country's obligations under the American Convention on Human Rights. The government has not formally withdrawn from the convention, nor has it ratified the jurisdiction of the IACrtHR, creating a situation of legal uncertainty that calls into question the juridical security of all treaties in the Dominican Republic.

Ecuador

The administration of President Rafael Correa has expanded state control over media and civil society and abused its power to harass, intimidate, and punish critics. In 2015, thousands of people participated in public demonstrations against government policies. Security forces on multiple occasions responded with excessive force. Abuses against protesters, including arbitrary arrests, have not been adequately investigated.

Other ongoing concerns include limited judicial independence, poor prison conditions, and women's and girls' limited access to reproductive health care due to fear of prosecution.

Conduct of Security Forces

Ecuadorian security forces repeatedly used force against peaceful protesters in 2015. In August, a minority of participants in largely peaceful nationwide demonstrations attacked security forces with rocks, sticks, spears, and Molotov cocktails, leaving 116 officers injured. Security forces responded with at times unnecessary and unlawful force, beating or arbitrarily arresting dozens of demonstrators and bystanders, and illegally entering the homes of people who were not participating in the protests.

French-Brazilian journalist and academic Manuela Picq, for example, was demonstrating peacefully in Quito when police officers kicked and beat her. Picq was detained and left the country after her visa was arbitrarily revoked. Manuel Asunción Poma Poma, a resident of Saraguro, Loja Province, said he was leaving a store close to where a demonstration was taking place when security forces attacked him with batons, knocking out five teeth and damaging his jaw.

Authorities charged 130 people for their alleged responsibility in violent incidents but appear to have made no serious effort to investigate officials who used brutal force to disperse anti-government protests, according to information provided by the Attorney General's Office in October. President Correa congratulated security forces for their performance.

In recent years, prosecutors and judges in Ecuador have charged anti-government protesters with "terrorism" and "sabotage." A new criminal code that entered into force in August 2014 narrowed the previously vague and overly broad definitions of both offenses, but judges failed to act promptly to use the new provisions to review unjust convictions in cases where high-level government officials signaled satisfaction with the convictions.

In October, the National Court of Justice sentenced five protesters to 18 months in prison for paralyzing public services, accusing them of forcibly entering the offices of Ecuador TV, the public television channel, during a police mutiny in September 2010. The protesters were demanding an opportunity to speak to the public after the government had ordered all stations to transmit Ecuador TV's programming. Among those convicted was a student who did not enter the building but was accused of supporting the group's actions with his applause.

Freedom of Expression

A 2013 communications law gives the government broad powers to limit free speech. The law requires all information disseminated by media to be "verified" and "precise," opening the door to censorship by allowing the government to decide what information meets these vague criteria. It also prohibits "media lynching," defined as "repeatedly disseminating information with the purpose of discrediting or harming the reputation of a person or entity." In addition, it prohibits what it terms "censorship," which, under the law's definition, includes the failure of private media outlets to cover issues that the government considers to be of "public interest."

The Superintendency of Information and Communication (SUPERCOM), a government regulatory body created by the 2013 Communications Law and separate from the Communications Ministry, has in dozens of cases ordered media outlets and journalists to "correct" or retract reports, or publicly apologize for their contents, including in opinion pieces and cartoons. SUPERCOM has also accused outlets of engaging in "censorship" by not publishing information officials deemed important.

The Correa administration repeatedly used the communications law to order media outlets to publish information favorable to the government. In July, the newspaper *El Mercurio* reproduced an article by the Spanish news agency EFE on the Pope's visit to Ecuador with the heading: "Extraordinary Welcome in Quito to Pope Francis and Loud Whistling against Correa." The communications minister ordered *El Mercurio* to publish a correction under the headline "Correa Was Not in Papal Motorcade." SUPERCOM has repeatedly imposed high fines on media outlets that refuse to publish corrections using the exact terms ordered by the Communications Ministry.

Journalists, media outlets, and social media users who openly criticize the government have been subjected to harassment and threats from anonymous sources. In February, an Ecuadorian activist who had posted satirical memes on Facebook and Twitter, including one picturing President Correa at a shopping mall in Europe, received an anonymous death threat after President Correa revealed his identity during the president's weekly television show; the threat came in a note with a floral arrangement delivered to the house where the activist was staying. The president had previously called on his followers to "join the fight to end abuses in social networks."

In September, an Ecuadorian TV producer who had worked on multimedia campaigns questioning government policies received anonymous death threats on Twitter and in a note delivered with a floral arrangement to his home. The Attorney General's Office has failed to adequately investigate the two incidents.

Criminal defamation remains a concern, despite a 2014 legal reform narrowing the definition of the crime. In May, President Correa had a criminal case for contempt opened against three men who he said had slandered him in 2010. They had asked the attorney general to investigate whether the president had broken the law when he ordered an armed assault on a hospital during a 2010 police mutiny. The three fled to avoid prison sentences of up to 18 months, but one turned himself in after his mother became sick and served his six-month sentence. None paid the $180,000 fines they had also been assessed.

The government frequently requires private media outlets to transmit official broadcasts responding to unfavorable news coverage. During several of the 2015 demonstrations, the Communications Ministry ordered radio stations to transmit live broadcasts of pro-government marches, speeches by President Correa, and government-produced spots. Private radio and TV news broadcasts were interrupted to transmit mandatory broadcasts accusing private media of "conspiring" against the government in their protest coverage.

Judicial Independence

Corruption, inefficiency, and political influence have plagued Ecuador's judiciary for years. President Correa received a popular mandate in a 2011 referendum to fix the problems. As part of his sweeping judicial reforms, however, the Council of the Judiciary appointed and removed hundreds of judges, including all magistrates of the National Court of Justice, through highly questionable mechanisms that have undermined judicial independence.

A 2014 report by three international nongovernmental organizations (NGOs)—the Due Process of Law Foundation, Dejusticia, and the Institute for Legal Defense—documented routine executive interference with judicial decisions, misuse of the penal system to target individuals who question the government's policies, and misuse of the judiciary's internal disciplinary system to punish judges whose rulings are inconsistent with the Correa administration's policies.

Human Rights Defenders and Civil Society

In 2013 President Correa issued an executive decree that grants the government broad powers to intervene in NGO operations, to the point of dissolving groups on the grounds that they have "compromise[d] public peace" or have engaged in activities that are different from those they identified when registering with the government. That December, the government dissolved the Pachamama Foundation, a highly regarded NGO that had engaged in environmental and human rights advocacy.

In August 2015, President Correa adopted a new decree that maintains his broad powers to regulate and dissolve groups. In September, the Communications Ministry opened an administrative process to dissolve Fundamedios, a local group that monitors free expression, on the grounds that it had engaged in "political" activities by publishing tweets linking to blogs and news articles criticizing the government. Weeks later, after several international monitors, including rapporteurs from the United Nations and the Inter-American Human Rights systems, urged authorities to halt the dissolution process, the ministry withdrew the proceeding. However, in October, it ruled that Fundamedios could not state in its statute that one of its purposes was to defend freedom of expression, arguing that only the state has the power to "respect" and "protect" basic rights.

Activists continue to be subject to prosecution for openly questioning government policies. In February, Javier Ramirez, an activist from Intag, Imbabura Province, who opposes a mining project there, was accused of attacking workers of the mining company, despite compelling evidence that he was home receiving treatment for a knee injury on the day of the attack. He was convicted of "rebellion" and sentenced to 10 months in prison. He was released on the day of his conviction since he had already served his sentence during pretrial detention.

Human rights defenders and lawyers have reported anonymous threats and acts of intimidation. Juan Pablo Alban is a lawyer who represents several victims of abuse during the current and previous governments; a note showed up at his Quito office in October 2014 telling him to "lay off our glorious army and police," and warning him, using a crude insult, that he would be killed. He told Human Rights Watch that he has noticed cars following him and that, although he is formally under a state-run program to protect witnesses, victims, and lawyers, he has never met or seen any indication of the officers supposedly assigned to protect him.

Right to Privacy

In July, news sources leaked what appear to be classified government documents showing that the National Intelligence Secretariat conducted illegal surveillance of human rights defenders, environmentalist activists, indigenous groups, academics, and political opponents of President Correa. Under Ecuadorian law, surveillance can only be authorized by a judicial order. The leaked documents include evidence that the intelligence agency sought to trace foreign funding of NGOs and indigenous organizations.

Prison Conditions

Prison overcrowding and other poor prison conditions are long-standing problems in Ecuador. Since 2012, the government has spent millions of dollars to construct new detention centers, but their distant locations and strict and limited visitation rules impede prisoners' contact with family members. Some visitors have reportedly been subjected to vaginal and anal inspections.

Accountability for Past Abuses

Progress has been slow on efforts to hold Ecuadorian officials to account for human rights violations committed from 1984 to 2008, the period covered by a truth commission set up by the Correa administration. In 2010, a special prosecutorial unit was formed to investigate 118 cases of abuse involving 456 victims, including 68 victims of extrajudicial execution and 17 of enforced disappearance.

At time of writing, prosecutors had brought charges in seven cases, including two in which suspects were convicted, and the National Court of Justice was set to begin hearing Ecuador's first-ever trial for crimes against humanity.

Reproductive Rights

The right to seek an abortion is limited to instances in which a woman's health or life is at risk, or when a pregnancy results from the rape of a "woman with a mental disability." Fear of prosecution drives some women and girls to have illegal and unsafe abortions and impedes health care and services for victims of sexual violence. Fear of prosecution also hinders detection and prevention of sexual and gender-based violence. Official statistics show that one in four women over 15 years old in Ecuador has been a victim of sexual violence.

Key International Actors

The government refused to participate in all but one public hearing before the Inter-American Commission on Human Rights and stated that it would not comply with the commission's recommendations.

In March, the United Nations Committee on the Elimination of Discrimination against Women expressed its concern about women's limited access to therapeutic abortion and their consequent resort to unsafe abortions, in addition to breaches of confidentiality by health care personnel who report to authorities women who seek an abortion or health care after a miscarriage.

In May, Ecuador endorsed the global Safe Schools Declaration, committing to do more to protect students, teachers, and schools during times of armed conflict, including by implementing the *Guidelines for Protecting Schools and Universities from Military Use*.

In June, Ecuador donated US$1 million to the Inter-American Court of Human Rights. A month later, members of the Organization of American States appointed Patricio Pazmiño, an Ecuadorian lawyer who continues to serve as a judge on Ecuador's Constitutional Court, to the court.

In August, the UN special rapporteur on the rights of indigenous peoples called for a fair and impartial investigation into all acts of violence during the August 2015 protests, including claims that police and military forces used excessive force.

In September, the Inter-American Court ruled that Ecuador had violated the rights of a three-year-old girl who was infected with HIV at a public hospital in 1998. The court ordered the government to adopt measures to prevent or address discrimination faced by persons with HIV/AIDS, especially children.

In October, the UN General Assembly elected Ecuador to become a member of the Human Rights Council between 2016 and 2018.

Egypt

President Abdel Fattah al-Sisi, who took office in June 2014—a year after ousting Mohamed Morsy, Egypt's first freely elected president—leads a country still in crisis. Authorities have imprisoned tens of thousands, effectively banned protests, and outlawed the country's largest opposition group, the Muslim Brotherhood. Courts have sentenced hundreds to death, including Morsy, after unfair trials.

In the northern Sinai Peninsula, fighting between the government and an affiliate of the armed extremist group Islamic State (also known as ISIS) escalated, despite Egypt's commitment of significant additional forces. The government claimed that the army killed thousands of "terrorists" in the Sinai but allowed no independent observers into the conflict area, and residents said the army had killed an unknown number of civilians.

Al-Sisi issued a sweeping counterterrorism law that expanded the authorities' powers. Law enforcement forces, especially the Interior Ministry's National Security Agency, committed torture and enforced disappearances, and deaths in custody continued. Mass trials mostly targeting Brotherhood members failed to establish individual guilt. At least 3,000 people were charged or sentenced in military courts.

The authorities continued to restrict freedom of expression and association by investigating independent nongovernmental organizations (NGOs), arresting people suspected of being gay or transgender, and prosecuting those accused of defaming religion.

Armed Groups and Counterterrorism

A constellation of insurgent groups throughout Egypt, including the ISIS affiliate, known as Sinai Province, escalated their attacks dramatically, from an average of 30 per month throughout 2014 to 100 per month between January and August 2015, according to the Washington, DC-based Tahrir Institute for Middle East Policy. Though civilians were rarely the target of attacks, in 2015 they were killed at three times the rate of the previous year, the Tahrir Institute found. A June 29 car

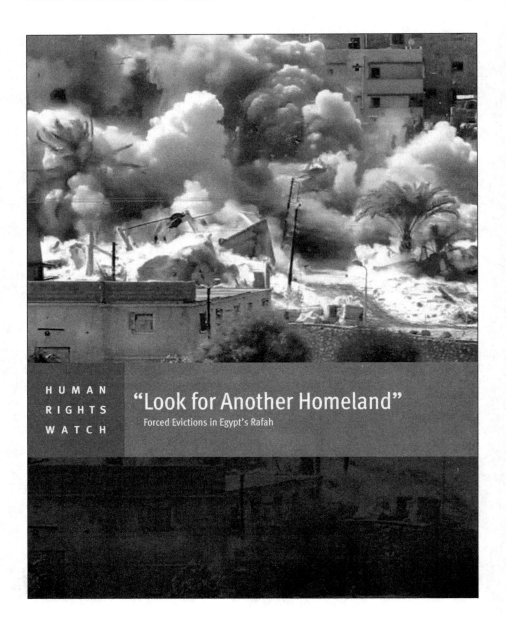

bombing in Cairo killed General Prosecutor Hisham Barakat, the first high government official to be assassinated since 1990.

The Egyptian government said that its counterterrorism operations in North Sinai killed at least 3,091 "terrorists" between January and July 2015. The government did not allow independent observers into the area of fighting and did not acknowledge any civilian deaths in the Sinai. In September, Egyptian security forces killed 12 civilians, including eight Mexican tourists, in the Western Desert region after apparently mistaking their sightseeing convoy for ISIS fighters. Prosecutors investigating the incident imposed a media gag order four days later.

Between October 2014 and August 2015, the armed forces demolished 2,715 buildings and evicted thousands of families on the border with the Gaza Strip, violating human rights law and possibly the laws of war. The government claimed that a "buffer zone" there would eliminate the smuggling of weapons and fighters from Gaza.

Al-Sisi—who governed in the absence of a parliament for most of the year—issued a counterterrorism law in August that gave prosecutors greater power to detain suspects without judicial review and to order wide-ranging and potentially indefinite surveillance of terrorist suspects without court orders. The law authorized a US$64,000 fine and possible one-year work ban for anyone who publishes news regarding terrorism that contradicts the Defense Ministry's official statements.

Security Force Abuses

On July 1, a special police unit acting on information from the Interior Ministry's National Security Agency raided an apartment in a Cairo suburb and killed nine Brotherhood officials. The government claimed the nine belonged to a "special operations committee" and died in a shootout, but relatives said the men did not carry weapons, and Human Rights Watch found that the deaths may have constituted extrajudicial executions.

National Security officers were responsible for dozens of enforced disappearances, often targeting political activists. Human Rights Watch documented the cases of five forced disappearances and two likely forced disappearances between April 2014 and June 2015. Three of these cases resulted in death. The

Egyptian human rights group Freedom for the Brave documented 164 enforced disappearances between April and June.

The National Security Agency banned scores of Egyptians—including activists, politicians and academics—from traveling. It did so with little or no oversight from judges or prosecutors and did not provide those who were banned with any way of challenging the decision, violating the fundamental international right to freedom of movement.

Police regularly used torture in their investigations. A January 2015 report by an Egyptian human rights law firm said its lawyers had interviewed 465 alleged victims of police torture and ill-treatment between October 2013 and August 2014 and filed 163 complaints to prosecutors, of which only seven reached the courts.

Accountability

On June 11, an Egyptian court sentenced a lieutenant in the Central Security Forces to 15 years in prison for the killing of Shaimaa al-Sabbagh, a member of a socialist political party shot dead when police dispersed a small protest in a downtown Cairo square on January 24. The verdict in al-Sabbagh's case marked the first time since Morsy's ouster in July 2013 that a law enforcement officer in Egypt received a prison sentence for killing a protester, despite hundreds of such deaths.

At time of writing, no government official or member of the security forces had been charged for the killing of at least 817 protesters in Cairo's Rab'a al-Adawiya Square on August 14, 2013—a likely crime against humanity. On August 13, a court halved a 10-year prison sentence handed to a police officer who participated in the tear gas suffocation of 37 people whom police had arrested from Rab'a Square.

Detentions

In October, the Interior Ministry announced that nearly 12,000 people had been arrested on terrorism charges in 2015, adding to the 22,000 people security officials said had already been arrested as of July 2014. The actual number is likely higher; the Egyptian Center for Economic and Social Rights documented more than 41,000 arrests, indictments, or sentencings between July 2013 and May 2014.

On September 23, al-Sisi pardoned 100 prisoners, including youth activists—some in poor health—and Al Jazeera journalists Mohamed Fahmy and Baher Mohamed, but many political prisoners did not receive pardons, including Ahmed Maher and Mohamed Adel, founders of the April 6th Youth Movement; Mahienour al-Masry, a human rights lawyer from Alexandria; and at least 18 journalists, including photographer Mahmoud Abu Zeid, whom police arrested in August 2013 and whose trial began in December.

The Egyptian Coordination for Rights and Freedoms, an independent group, documented 47 deaths in custody between January and June and said in an October report that 209 detainees had died due to medical negligence since al-Sisi took office in June 2014.

Due Process Violations and Mass Death Sentences

On June 16, a criminal court sentenced Morsy and 114 others to death in two related cases based almost entirely on the testimony of security officials, who claimed that Morsy and the Brotherhood had conspired with Hamas and Hezbollah to break out of prison during the 2011 uprising and had killed police officers in the process. Human Rights Watch found that prosecutors presented no evidence to substantiate the security officials' testimony and that the case appeared to be politically motivated.

Since Morsy's removal, courts have handed down at least 547 initial death sentences in cases connected to political violence, most involving Brotherhood members. Nearly all those sentences remained on appeal in 2015. The state carried out one execution in a case of political violence in March and executed another six men—accused of belonging to a militant cell and killing army officers in a shootout—in May following an unfair military trial.

Mass trials also involved those not belonging to the Brotherhood. In February, a judge sentenced activist Ahmed Douma, women's rights defender Hend al-Nafea, and 228 others to life in prison for participating in a December 2011 protest.

Between January and September 2015, authorities charged or sentenced at least 3,164 people—most of them alleged Brotherhood members—in military courts.

Freedom of Association, Expression, and Assembly

The government did not follow through on a November 2014 ultimatum to force independent NGOs to register under an onerous 2002 law but increased pressure on such groups. In June, government investigators visited the office of the Cairo Institute for Human Rights Studies and asked for registration and financial documents. National Security agents banned Mohamed Lotfy, executive director of the Egyptian Commission for Rights and Freedoms, from travel to Germany in June to attend a roundtable at the German Parliament.

Freedom of Religion

In February and March, courts handed prison sentences to two men, who later went into hiding, for allegedly supporting atheism online. In June, prosecutors in Beni Suef governorate ordered a local man arrested for allegedly posting cartoons online that insulted the prophet Mohamed. In October, an appeals court upheld a five-year sentence against TV presenter Islam al-Behery for contempt of religion, but al-Behery appealed the ruling to a higher court.

In June, the Egyptian Initiative for Personal Rights, an independent group, released a study documenting 51 sectarian attacks since the 2011 uprising that were resolved through "customary reconciliation," an extrajudicial process sponsored by the security services that does not abide by Egyptian law and often allows the security services to impose conditions on Coptic Christians.

Violence and Discrimination against Women

On January 26, an Egyptian court for the first time issued a conviction for female genital mutilation (FGM), which remains widely practiced despite being made illegal in 2008. The court sentenced the doctor to two years in prison for manslaughter and the father to a three-month suspended sentence.

In April, the government released its five-year national strategy to combat violence against women. The strategy included more shelters for women, better information collection in government ministries, and a new training manual for prosecutors and law enforcement officers. But the strategy also defined rape as "having sexual intercourse with a female against her will," which does not include anal rape or penetration with an object, and made no mention of sexual assault by multiple offenders—an enormous problem in Egypt—or sexual assault by law enforcement officers.

Sexual Orientation and Gender Identity

In January, a court acquitted 26 men who had been accused of debauchery in connection with a raid on a bathhouse allegedly used by gay men, but in February, morals investigators arrested seven allegedly transgender people who had met at a Cairo club to celebrate a friend's birthday. Police also arrested two allegedly transgender people on prostitution charges in May and 11 allegedly gay men, also accused of prostitution, in September.

Egyptian authorities routinely subject allegedly gay men arrested for "debauchery" or "insulting public morals" to forced anal exams, which amount to torture.

Refugees, Asylum Seekers, and Migrants

Egypt was home to 236,090 refugees and 25,631 asylum seekers as of December 2014, the most recent date for which the United Nations High Commissioner for Refugees (UNHCR) provided figures. About 130,000 of those refugees were Syrians, UNHCR said. Egypt has yet to develop national asylum procedures and institutions, and the country's political strife puts refugees and asylum seekers at risk of arbitrary arrest, deportation and harassment, according to UNHCR.

On several occasions, Egyptian security forces fired on refugees attempting to embark from the country's northern coast on smuggling boats across the Mediterranean Sea. In August, an 8-year-old girl, thought to be Syrian, was reportedly killed in one such incident.

About 3,000 to 4,000 Palestinian refugees from Syria who fled the country since 2011 remained in Egypt as of September, according to UN sources.

Key International Actors

In March, the United States announced it would resume the delivery of major military equipment that it had placed on hold after Morsy's removal. The decision allowed the US to send 12 F-16 fighter jets, 20 Harpoon missiles, and 125 M1A1 tank kits. The US earlier delivered 10 Apache helicopters in December 2014 to aid Egypt's counterterrorism efforts. But President Barack Obama announced that he would end Egypt's ability to buy US equipment on credit and restrict military aid to four sectors—Sinai Peninsula, counterterrorism, border security, and maritime security—beginning in 2018.

In August, the US held its first strategic dialogue with Egypt since 2009. Following the meeting in Cairo, Secretary of State John Kerry said that Egypt and the US were returning to a "stronger base" but that he had been "crystal clear" on human rights concerns and had raised the issue of radicalization "that can take place through imprisonment."

Over the course of the year, al-Sisi visited Berlin, Paris and London. In July, France began delivery of 24 Rafale fighter jets that Egypt purchased in February. In September, Egypt bought two Mistral class French warships—some of the most advanced in any Middle Eastern navy.

In March, Egypt joined the Saudi Arabia-led military intervention in Yemen's conflict, sending four warships to the Gulf of Aden. The extent of Egypt's troop commitment to the intervention remained unclear, and the military denied deploying ground forces.

In February, an ISIS affiliate in Libya beheaded 20 Egyptian Coptic Christians whom it had abducted over the prior two months. Egypt responded by launching air strikes against ISIS-affiliated forces in Derna that killed at least seven civilians.

Eritrea

Two key developments in 2015 highlighted the consequences of President Isaias Afwerki's authoritarian rule: the continuing flow of Eritreans escaping the country, and the publication of a scathing 453-page report by a United Nations commission of inquiry describing the serious human rights violations prompting thousands to seek refuge outside Eritrea.

The United Nations High Commission for Refugees reported at the end of 2014 that 416,857 Eritreans have lodged asylum claims or are registered as refugees, over 9 percent of the country's population. UNHCR released no comprehensive figures for 2015 but reported about 39,000 Eritreans had applied for asylum by October in 44 industrialized countries alone. In October, 10 members of Eritrea's national soccer team sought asylum in Botswana.

The commission of inquiry concluded that grave human rights violations "incite an ever-increasing number of Eritreans to leave their country." Based on over 500 interviews, the UN commission found that the Eritrean government engages in "systemic, widespread and gross human rights violations," and that the abuses occur in the "context of a total lack of rule of law" with the result that it "is not the law that rules Eritreans, but fear."

After refusing the commission entry into the country, the government protested its findings as not based on first-hand in-country observations. The government has never allowed any UN special mechanism investigators into the country.

In June, the UN Human Rights Council extended the commission's mandate until mid-2016, instructing it to further investigate whether some abuses constitute crimes against humanity.

Indefinite Military Service and Forced Labor

By law, each Eritrean is compelled to serve 18 months in national service starting at 18. In practice, conscripts serve indefinitely, many for over a decade. One escapee, echoing many others, told Human Rights Watch, "I don't mind military service but in Eritrea it never ends and you have no rights." Most Eritreans begin military training as part of the last year of high school, but children as young as

15 are sometimes conscripted. Assignments include forced labor for government-owned construction firms, farms, or manufacturers.

Conscripts receive inadequate pay to support themselves, much less a family. They are subject to military discipline and are harshly treated throughout their long service. Perceived infractions result in incarceration and physical abuse often amounting to torture. Military commanders and jailers have absolute discretion to determine the length of incarceration and the severity of physical abuse. Female conscripts are often sexually abused by commanders. There is no mechanism for redressing abuses; protest can result in more severe punishment.

Senior government officials told foreign visitors and diplomats in 2015 that the government intended to release the current and future classes of conscripts after they serve 18 months, but President Isaias made no public announcement of a change in policy, nor was there any other independent corroboration of the claim. Yemane Gebreab, the president's political adviser, admitted to a foreign reporter that demobilization hinged on whether the economy could absorb those released.

When conscripts have been "released" from national service, some have been forced to work for the government, rather than being allowed to choose their own careers and jobs, although at somewhat higher pay than conscripts. Older former conscripts are compelled to participate in the "People's Army," including periodic military training and weekly participation in public works projects, guard duty, or security patrols, all without pay.

Arbitrary Arrest, Prolonged Detention, and Inhumane Conditions

Arbitrary arrests are the norm. A prisoner is rarely told the reason for the arrest; often prison authorities are not informed. Detainees are held indefinitely. Releases are as arbitrary as arrests. Few detainees are brought to trial.

Prisoners are held in vastly overcrowded cells, underground dungeons, or shipping containers, with no space to lie down, little or no light, oppressive heat or cold, and vermin. Food, water, and sanitation are inadequate.

Beatings and other physical abuse in detention have frequently been reported, sometimes resulting in deaths. The commission of inquiry concluded that the prevalence of torture is a "clear indicator of a deliberate policy" to "instill fear among the population and silence opposition." Many prisoners simply disappear.

Freedom of Speech and Association

President Isaias rules without institutional restraint. A constitution adopted in 1997 remains unimplemented. No national elections have been held since independence. Eritrea has had no legislature since 2002. The court system is subject to executive control and interference. Nongovernmental organizations are not permitted.

The commission of inquiry noted the government's rampant use of spies through a "complex and militarized system of surveillance." Family members are often punished for the actions of close relatives, usually by having coupons and licenses necessary to receive government services cancelled; sometimes family members are fined or jailed.

The government owns all media. The Committee to Protect Journalists identified Eritrea as the most censored country in the world. Sixteen journalists remain imprisoned without trial, some since 2001. Six government journalists were granted bail in 2015, almost six years after being jailed without trial. No reason was given for their arrests or provisional releases.

In March, authorities in Adi Keyh, a town southeast of Asmara, bulldozed a number of "unauthorized" houses. When townspeople and students at the nearby College of Arts and Sciences protested, some with sticks and stones, security forces fired at them. Two people were killed and others injured. According to the UN's special rapporteur on Eritrea, houses were also destroyed near the capital, Asmara, rendering about 3,000 people homeless.

Freedom of Religion

The government persecutes citizens who practice religions other than the four it recognizes —Sunni Islam, Eritrean Orthodox, Roman Catholic, and Lutheran churches. Prayer meetings of unrecognized religions are disrupted and participants are arrested. A condition for release is usually a signed statement by the prisoner recanting his religious affiliation.

Jehovah's Witnesses are especially persecuted. Three arrested in 1994 for refusing to serve in the military remain imprisoned 21 years later. As of mid-2015, they were among 56 jailed Jehovah's Witnesses.

The government also interferes with the practices of the four religions it recognizes. The government appointed the Sunni imam in 1996, deposed the patriarch of the Eritrean Orthodox Church in 2005, and appointed his successor. The deposed patriarch remains under house arrest 10 years later.

Refugee Policy

In 2014, the Danish Immigration Service issued a report suggesting that human rights conditions in Eritrea were better than reported and that no harm would come to Eritreans who were returned from countries where they sought asylum. In 2015, the report was repudiated by two of its three authors amid growing questions about the credibility of the report's methodology. One of the report authors contended that quotations in the report were taken out of context by his superiors to achieve a political goal of discouraging Eritrean asylum seekers.

Despite widespread criticism of the Danish report, the United Kingdom's Home Office changed its guidance about Eritrea in early 2015 to assert that asylum-seekers "who left [Eritrea] illegally are no longer considered per se to be at risk of harm or mistreatment amounting to persecution on return."

Key International Actors

Eritrea's relations with neighboring Ethiopia and Djibouti remain severely strained. Fifteen years after a bloody border war, Ethiopia occupies slivers of territory identified by a boundary commission as Eritrean, including the town of Badme where the war began. President Isaias uses the pretext of "no-war, no-peace" to keep his countrymen under totalitarian control.

In September, Molla Asghedom, head of an armed Ethiopian opposition group, the Tigray People's Democratic Movement (TPDM), long given sanctuary in Eritrea and reportedly used to round up draft evaders and to protect President Isaias, fled to Ethiopia via Sudan, accompanied by several hundred followers. Eritrea continues to host other armed Ethiopian opposition groups.

The UN Security Council maintained an arms embargo on Eritrea for another year after receiving a report from its Monitoring Group on Somalia and Eritrea that found no evidence Eritrea was still supporting Al-Shabaab rebels in Somalia, but complained Eritrea had not cooperated in Monitoring Group investigations and had not provided information about Djiboutian prisoners of war captured in border clashes in 2008.

Much of Eritrea's foreign exchange income comes from foreign gold/copper mining company projects in which the Eritrean government holds a 40 percent stake. In 2015, a mine, majority-owned by China's Shanghai Corporation for Foreign Economic and Technological Cooperation (SFECO), began operations, joining the Bisha mine, majority- owned by Canada's Nevsun Resources. A third mine, bought in late 2015 by Chinese state-owned Sichuan Road & Bridge Mining Investment Development Corp. (SRBM) from a Canadian majority-owner is expected to begin operations in late 2016. Based on Nevsun's experience, there are concerns that new mining projects will be compelled to use government-owned construction firms for infrastructure development and thereby indirectly use conscript labor.

China is Eritrea's largest trading partner, investor, and contractor. One company, China Harbor Engineering Co., is engaged in a US$400 million project to modernize Eritrea's primary port, Massawa.

At time of writing, the European Union was reportedly considering a five-year €200 (US$216) million aid package designed to address "the root causes of migration."

Ethiopia

In Ethiopia in 2015 there were continuing government crackdowns on opposition political party members, journalists, and peaceful protesters, many of whom experienced harassment, arbitrary arrest, and politically motivated prosecutions.

The Ethiopian People's Revolutionary Democratic Front (EPRDF), the ruling party coalition, won all 547 parliamentary seats in the May elections, due in part to the lack of space for critical or dissenting voices. Despite a few high-profile prisoner releases ahead of the June visit of United States President Barack Obama, there was no progress on fundamental reforms of the deeply repressive laws and policies constricting Ethiopian civil society organizations and media.

Elections and Political Space

May's federal elections took place in a general atmosphere of intimidation, and concerns over the National Electoral Board's lack of independence. Opposition parties reported that state security forces and ruling party cadres harassed and detained their members, while onerous registration requirements effectively put opposition candidates at a disadvantage.

Opposition parties reported that government officials regularly blocked their attempts to hold protests and rallies in the run-up to the election by denying permits, arresting organizers, and confiscating equipment.

These restrictions, alongside the absence of independent media and civil society, meant there was little opportunity for dissenting voices to be heard or meaningful political debate on key issues ahead of the elections.

Freedom of Peaceful Assembly

Eighteen individuals identified as leaders of the Muslim protest movement that swept across Ethiopia from 2012-2014 were convicted in July under the Anti-Terrorism Proclamation and sentenced in August to between 7 and 22 years each after closed, flawed trials. Authorities detained them in July 2012 when some Muslim communities were protesting against perceived government interference in their religious affairs.

An unknown number of ethnic Oromo students continued to be detained, many without charge, after protests throughout Oromia in April and May 2014 against the planned expansion of Addis Ababa's municipal boundary into Oromia. Security personnel used excessive and at times lethal force, including live ammunition, against protesters in several cities, killing at least several dozen protesters, and arrested hundreds.

There have been no investigations by Ethiopian authorities into the deaths and the use of unlawful force. Those released said they were tortured or otherwise illtreated in detention. Ethnic Oromos make up approximately 45 percent of Ethiopia's population and are often arbitrarily arrested and accused of belonging to the banned Oromo Liberation Front (OLF).

Freedom of Expression and Association

Media remained under government stranglehold, with many journalists having to choose between self-censorship, harassment and arrest, or exile. At least 60 journalists have fled into exile since 2010. Tactics used to restrict independent media included targeting publishers, printing presses, and distributors.

In June, journalist Reeyot Alemu and five other journalists and bloggers from the Zone 9 blogging collective were released from prison ahead of President Obama's visit to Ethiopia, On October 16, the remaining four imprisoned Zone 9 bloggers were acquitted of terrorism charges after 39 hearings and 539 days in detention. A fifth charged in absentia was also acquitted. Many other journalists, protesters, and other political opponents continued to be prosecuted under the Anti-Terrorism Proclamation, and many journalists including Eskinder Nega and Woubshet Taye remain in prison.

The 2009 Charities and Societies Proclamation (CSO law) continues to severely curtail the ability of independent nongovernmental organizations to work on human rights. The law bars work on human rights, good governance, conflict resolution, and advocacy on the rights of women, children, and people with disabilities if organizations receive more than 10 percent of their funds from foreign sources.

The government regularly monitors and records telephone calls of family members and friends of suspected opposition members and intercepts digital com-

HUMAN RIGHTS WATCH

"Journalism Is Not a Crime"
Violations of Media Freedom in Ethiopia

munications with highly intrusive spyware. Leaked emails from Milan-based Hacking Team, which sold spyware to the Ethiopian government, reveal that despite warnings of the risk of Ethiopia misusing their spyware, they issued a temporary license to Ethiopia while they began negotiations in April on a new contract worth at least US$700,000.

Torture and Arbitrary Detention

Ethiopian security personnel frequently tortured and otherwise ill-treated political detainees held in both official and secret detention centers to give confessions or provide information. At its UN Universal Periodic Review in 2014, Ethiopia accepted a recommendation to "adopt measures which guarantee the non-occurrence of cases of torture and ill-treatment in places of detention," but there is little indication that security personnel are being investigated or punished for carrying out these abuses.

The Liyu police, a Somali Regional State paramilitary police force without a clear legal mandate, continued to commit serious human rights abuses in their ongoing conflict with the Ogaden National Liberation Front (ONLF) in Ethiopia's Somali Region, with reports of extrajudicial killings, arbitrary detention, and violence against civilians who are accused of supporting or being sympathetic to the ONLF.

Andargachew Tsige, a United Kingdom citizen and secretary-general of the Ginbot 7 organization, a group banned for advocating armed overthrow of the government, remains in detention in Ethiopia after his unlawful 2014 deportation to Ethiopia from Yemen while in transit. He had twice been sentenced to death in absentia for his involvement with Ginbot 7. UK consular officials visited Andargachew only three times, amid growing concerns about his mistreatment in detention. In April, the UN Working Group on Arbitrary Detention called on Ethiopia to release and compensate Andargachew.

Forced Displacement Linked to Development Programs

Some donors, including UK's Department for International Development (DFID) and the World Bank, rechanneled funding from the problematic Protection of Basic Services (PBS) program in 2015. PBS was associated with the abusive "villagization program," a government effort to relocate 1.5 million rural people into permanent villages, ostensibly to improve their access to basic services. Some of the relocations in the first year of the program in Gambella region in 2011 were accompanied by violence, including beatings and arbitrary arrests, and insufficient consultation and compensation.

Some Gambella residents filed a complaint in 2013 to the World Bank's Inspection Panel, the institution's independent accountability mechanism, alleging that the bank violated its own policies on indigenous people and involuntary resettlement. The Inspection Panel identified major shortcomings in the PBS program in its November 2014 recommendations, although the World Bank Board largely rejected the findings in February. A translator who worked with the Inspection Panel in Gambella was arrested in March and charged under the Anti-Terrorism Proclamation in September 2015.

In February, in the course of a court hearing on a complaint by an Ethiopian farmer that the UK violated its partnership principles by supporting the PBS program, DFID announced that it was ending support to the PBS program. DFID cited concerns over Ethiopia's civil and political rights record, including concerns related to "freedom of expression and electoral competition, and continued concerns about the accountability of security services."

There are ongoing reports of forced displacement from development projects in different regions, often with minimal or no compensation and little in the way of prior consultation with affected, often indigenous, communities. Allegations have arisen from commercial and industrial projects associated with Addis Ababa's expansion and the continued development of sugar plantations in the Lower Omo Valley, which involves clearing 245,000 hectares of land that is home to 200,000 indigenous people. Communities in Omo have seen their grazing land cleared and have lost access to the Omo River, which they relied on for crops. Individuals who questioned the development plans were arrested and harassed.

Violent incidents, both between different ethnic groups and between the government and ethnic groups, increased in 2015 partly due to the growing competition for grazing land and other resources. The reservoir behind the Gibe III dam began filling in January 2015, reducing the annual natural flood that replenished the agricultural lands along the banks of the Omo River.

Key International Actors

Ethiopia enjoys strong support from foreign donors and most of its regional neighbors, based on its role as host of the African Union and strategic regional player, its contribution to UN peacekeeping, security and aid partnerships with Western countries, and its progress on development indicators. The African Union(AU)—the only international body that monitored the May elections—declared the elections "credible" despite the severe restrictions on opposition political parties, independent media, and civil society.

Ethiopia continued to facilitate negotiations between warring parties in South Sudan, and its troops maintained calm in the disputed Abyei Region. Ethiopia deploys troops inside Somalia as part of the AU mission, and in 2015 there were growing reports that abusive "Liyu police" forces were also deployed alongside the Ethiopian Defense Forces. Ethiopia continued to host hundreds of thousands of refugees from South Sudan, Somalia, and Eritrea.

Ethiopia is one of the largest recipients of donor aid in Africa, receiving almost $3 billion in 2015 despite allegations of human rights abuses associated with some development programs, including forced displacement in Gambella and the Omo Valley. There are no indications that donors have strengthened the monitoring and accountability provisions needed to ensure that their development aid does not contribute to or exacerbate human rights problems in Ethiopia.

European Union

In a year marked by horrific attacks by armed extremists in Paris in January and November, and a deepening refugee crisis, the European Union and its member states struggled to develop an effective and principled response to the hundreds of thousands of asylum seekers and migrants who reached Europe. Narrow government interests too often displaced sound policy responses, delaying protection and shelter for vulnerable people and raising questions about the union's purpose and limits.

Migration and Asylum

Poor management and disagreements among EU member states escalated a crisis, as large numbers of migrants and asylum seekers reached Europe, most by sea. At time of writing, more than 850,000 people had crossed the sea during the year to reach Europe. The vast majority—an estimated 82 percent—of people crossed the Aegean Sea, from Turkey to Greece, and only 17 percent crossed the central Mediterranean, from North Africa to Italy, historically the most common sea route.

According to the United Nations Refugee Agency (UNHCR), 84 percent of those arriving by sea came from the refugee-producing countries of Syria, Afghanistan, Eritrea, Iraq, and Somalia. Nigerians, Gambians, Sudanese, Pakistanis and Malians together made up seven percent of the new arrivals.

The EU tripled the budget and resources of patrol operations in the Mediterranean following the deaths at sea of more than 1,000 people in a single week in April. Frontex, the EU's external border agency, began patrolling in international waters near Libya and increased patrols in the Aegean Sea, carrying out search-and-rescue and border enforcement activities. While tens of thousands of people were rescued throughout the year, including by private humanitarian initiatives, more than 3,500 migrants died or went missing at sea.

Many of those who reached Greece by sea continued their journey over land through the Western Balkans, encountering police abuse in EU candidates Serbia and the Former Yugoslav Republic of Macedonia and EU member Hungary, and appalling detention conditions at times in Macedonia and Hungary.

In September, thousands of migrants and asylum seekers were stuck at various borders with inadequate shelter, unable to proceed with their journeys but with no genuine alternative, and at times dispersed by tear gas and water cannons. Hungary effectively closed its border with Serbia to asylum seekers and migrants in September, and with Croatia in October. Slovenia and Croatia at times blocked access for asylum seekers and migrants in September and October. In late November, Slovenia, Croatia, Serbia and Macedonia imposed border restrictions for asylum seekers and migrants, allowing only certain nationalities, including Syrians, to enter.

EU governments worked fitfully over the course of the year to implement a set of proposals on migration and asylum policy that the European Commission made in May. An EU-wide refugee resettlement scheme was established, with countries pledging over 22,000 places over the next two years. Following a fractious debate and over the objections of Hungary, Czech Republic, Slovakia, and Romania, EU governments agreed to a program to relocate over the next two years a total of 160,000 asylum seekers who had landed in Italy, Greece, and potentially other countries experiencing significant arrivals. The United Kingdom opted out. At time of writing, only 159 asylum seekers had been relocated from Italy and Greece to other EU member states under the scheme.

The majority of the commission's proposals focused on measures to limit arrivals, strengthen border controls, and accelerate returns of people not granted the right to remain in the EU. The EU took some positive action, including pledges of increased aid to countries hosting large refugee populations and to humanitarian assistance organizations. Yet efforts to intensify immigration cooperation with origin and transit countries raised concerns about enabling rights abuses and denying people effective protection. Combating smuggling networks remained central to the EU approach, with a naval mission in the Mediterranean poised, beginning in October, to board, seize, and divert vessels used by smugglers.

The full package of recast directives making up the Common European Asylum System entered into force in July, imposing revised common standards and rules with respect to procedures and reception conditions. Asylum seekers continued to face a protection lottery, with wide disparity among EU member states in recognition rates, accommodation, and integration measures. The European

Commission stepped up its own enforcement, opening 74 infringement proceedings against 23 member states for failure to abide by EU asylum laws.

Discrimination and Intolerance

Attacks by armed extremists in Paris in January left 20 people dead—12 staff members of the satirical weekly *Charlie Hebdo*, four people taken hostage in a kosher supermarket, a police officer, and three attackers. In Copenhagen in February, attacks on a free speech debate and a synagogue left three people dead, including the attacker. The attacks underscored the serious problem of anti-Semitism in the EU. An October report by the EU Agency for Fundamental Rights showed that many EU governments fail to collect adequate data on hate crimes against Jews, a finding that reflects a wider failure to collect disaggregated hate crimes data.

Hate crimes against Muslims are also a serious problem, with spikes in incidents reported in France and the UK. The acceptability of intolerance against Muslims was demonstrated in September when several EU leaders said they only wanted Christian, as opposed to Muslim, refugees in their countries.

In September, the UN high commissioner for human rights, Zeid Ra'ad Al Hussein, criticized ongoing forced evictions of Roma and Travellers in several European countries in recent years. He highlighted France's "systematic national policy to forcibly evict the Roma" and urged Bulgaria to halt forced evictions, "which are devastating to the affected communities."

By enacting the Gender Recognition Bill in July, Ireland became the fifth country in the world to offer legal recognition to the gender of people's choice, excluding children under the age of 16. Ireland brought into effect a law permitting same-sex marriage in November following a successful constitutional referendum guaranteeing marriage equality in May.

Following its review of the EU, in September the UN Committee on the Rights of Persons with Disabilities (CRPD) raised concerns about children with disabilities living in institutions in EU countries who have no access to mainstream inclusive education. The committee also expressed concern about the negative effects of austerity measures on services for families with children with disabilities. The committee also noted concerns about the detention of refugees and migrants with disabilities, and the fact that many persons with disabilities have their legal capacity restricted, affecting their ability to make their own decisions.

Counterterrorism

The November attacks in Paris, the most deadly in Europe in more than a decade, prompted emergency measures in France (see below), a major security operation in Belgium, stepped-up border checks, including inside the Schengen free movement area, and a renewed push for stronger EU security and intelligence cooperation. Past experience of major attacks in Europe raised concerns that human rights protections would again be weakened in the name of security.

The publication in December 2014 of a redacted version of a report by the United States Senate on torture by the US Central Intelligence Agency (CIA) again threw a spotlight on the complicity of EU states with programs of rendition and torture and their limited progress towards accountability. The European Parliament civil liberties committee in February decided to resume its investigation into EU states' complicity in torture.

Lithuanian prosecutors announced in April that they had reopened an investigation into allegations that their country hosted a secret CIA detention facility. Romanian authorities continue to deny that their country hosted a secret CIA facility, despite an admission in April by the former President Ion Iliescu that he authorized a CIA site. There were few signs of progress during the year in investigations in Poland and the UK into complicity by state officials in torture and rendition (see below).

In March, the Council of Europe's human rights commissioner raised concerns about plans in several European countries to increase surveillance powers of security services without prior judicial authorization.

In July, the UN Human Rights Council appointed Joseph Cannataci as the first special rapporteur on the right to privacy. His mandate includes reviewing government policies and legislation on interception of digital communications. In August, Cannataci criticized the weakness of the UK's surveillance oversight mechanism.

Croatia

More than 441,931 asylum seekers and migrants entered Croatia by the end of November. Almost all stayed only for a short period before going on to Hungary (until it closed its border) or Slovenia. Croatia struggled to meet asylum seekers' and migrants' basic needs and at times closed border crossings from Serbia and restricted entry at its borders to certain nationalities in November.

Fewer than 5,000 people have claimed asylum in Croatia since 2006, and as of July 2015, only 165 had been granted some form of protection, 32 of them in 2015. Long-term asylum seekers and refugees face difficulties in accessing housing, health services, and education. Unaccompanied migrant and asylum-seeking children continue to be placed in a residential home for children with behavior problems and in reception centers for adults, without adequate guardianship or specific protection.

While the Croatian government made some progress in protecting the rights of people with disabilities, the guardianship system continues to deny roughly 18,000 people with disabilities the right to make decisions about their lives. Implementation of a 2011 deinstitutionalization plan progressed slowly and excludes people with disabilities in psychiatric hospitals and foster homes for adults. More than 7,500 people remained institutionalized as of September. In April, the UN Committee on the Rights of Persons with Disabilities urged the Croatian government to ensure that its domestic laws protect the rights of people with disabilities.

More than 220 war crimes cases have yet to be addressed by national courts. In February, the European Court of Human Rights (ECtHR) ruled that Croatia violated the fair trial rights of a dual Croatian-Serbian national convicted in his absence of war crimes and unable to obtain a retrial.

In April, the UN Human Rights Committee adopted concluding observations on Croatia, including concerns about discrimination and violence against members of ethnic minority groups, particularly Roma and Serbs.

Serbs stripped of tenancy rights during the war faced ongoing difficulties in benefitting from the 2010 government program that permits the purchase of property at below-market rates.

Stateless Roma faced particular difficulties accessing basic state services, such as health care, social assistance, and adequate housing. Roma children are de facto segregated in the education sector.

Estonia

Estonia ranks 10th in terms of stateless populations worldwide. According to the Interior Ministry, as of June 2015, about 6.3 percent of the country's population of 1.3 million is stateless.

In 2015, the government adopted measures to decrease child statelessness and simplify the naturalization process for older people. In January, the government amended the Citizenship Law to allow children born to stateless parents to automatically obtain Estonian citizenship at birth; previously, parents had to apply. Parents can reject Estonian citizenship on behalf of their children within a year. The amendments also exempt people 65 and older from the written portion of the mandatory Estonian language exam for naturalization.

Language test requirements remain the most significant naturalization challenge for the country's Russian-speaking population. The cost of naturalization, including application and language exam preparation, and the income requirements for citizenship, continue to disenfranchise poorer long-term residents, and have contributed to statelessness among the Russian speakers. The up-front cost of language classes to prepare for the test poses a considerable financial obstacle for non-citizens with modest or no income. The state reimburses language class fees only after the applicant passes the test.

Stateless residents do not enjoy full employment rights and are barred from occupying several professions, such as posts in the national and local civil service, police, and customs, and they may not become prosecutors, judges, or notaries.

The government has not taken sufficient steps to prepare for implementation of the Co-habitation Act, which was passed in October 2014 and enters into force in 2016. The act extends the rights of married couples to unmarried—including same-sex—couples.

Estonia maintains a minimalist refugee policy. The government agreed to accept 329 asylum seekers over a two-year period under the EU relocation scheme, but at time of writing, no one had yet been relocated. Asylum seekers encounter serious obstacles in receiving translation support in their language during refugee status determination interviews.

France

France suffered deadly attacks in January and November. Multiple attacks in Paris and the suburb of Saint-Denis on November 13 killed 130 people and wounded hundreds. On November 20, parliament passed a law extending by three months the state of emergency declared by President François Hollande following the attacks. The law also expanded the government's emergency powers including to conduct searches without a warrant and to place people under house arrest without judicial approval, raising concerns about the rights to liberty, freedom of movement, and freedoms of association and expression.

Over three days in early January, attacks on the satirical magazine *Charlie Hebdo*, a police officer, and a kosher supermarket left 20 dead, including the three attackers, who died in shootouts with the police. A surge in Islamophobic acts followed, and the government recorded over 50 attacks and threats against Muslims between January 7 and 12.

On January 12, the minister of justice instructed prosecutors to respond with criminal law to speech "glorifying terrorism" and anti-Semitic and racist speech in relation to the Paris attacks. By March 24, the French judiciary had opened 298 cases involving "glorification of terrorism"—an overly broad term that can include speech that does not incite violence —including 185 cases in which it was the only offense.

Anti-Semitic acts, including violent attacks and threats, increased by more than 100 percent in 2014 compared with 2013, according to the annual report of the National Consultative Commission of Human Rights published in April.

In a June review of France, the UN Committee for the Elimination of Racial Discrimination expressed concern about discrimination against migrants and "people of foreign origin" in access to employment, housing, culture, and health care, and difficulties they face in education.

In September, the UN high commissioner for human rights criticized France's "systematic national policy to forcibly evict" migrant Roma. According to rights groups, between January and September 2015, 8,714 Roma were evicted from 79 places in France, in most cases without alternative accommodation.

According to official estimates, around 4,500 asylum seekers and migrants lived in unsanitary conditions in a makeshift camp in Calais with limited daytime access to showers, electricity, and food in a center equipped to serve 1,500. In November, the Council of State ordered the government to equip the camp with water taps, toilets, and garbage collection, and to ensure emergency services can access the site if needed.

A law passed by parliament in July requires authorities to register asylum claims within three days of an asylum seeker lodging an application, or ten working days if there are large numbers of simultaneous claims. The law also ends the detention of unaccompanied children in transit zones if they intend to seek asylum in France, but provides for exceptions, such as when children are from a country the authorities consider to be "safe." Other unaccompanied children who do not assert an intent to claim asylum can continue to be detained for up to 20 days in a seaport or airport.

In July, France enacted a law permitting the government to conduct sweeping digital surveillance on broad grounds and without prior judicial authorization, in breach of the right to privacy. Following a July review, the UN Human Rights Committee urged France in August to ensure surveillance activities are necessary and proportionate and subject to judicial approval and oversight. In November, the French parliament passed a law permitting the surveillance of electronic communications sent or received from abroad.

In five ground-breaking rulings in June, the Paris Court of Appeal ordered the state to compensate victims of discriminatory identity checks. The court found that the failure to record checks deprived victims of an effective remedy. The government has failed to introduce stop forms, a key measure in addressing abusive identity checks, despite President Hollande's commitment to fight against abuses during such checks when he was a presidential candidate in 2012.

In a February report on his visit to France in September 2014 on a range of human rights concerns, the Council of Europe's human rights commissioner found France "lagging significantly behind" in making public places and transportation accessible to persons with disabilities, and noted high unemployment among persons with disabilities.

Germany

Authorities increased staff and budget of the federal asylum office in response to a significant increase in new asylum applications, and created new reception centers around the country. The government estimated Germany would receive one million new asylum applications by year's end.

In October, the Federal Parliament adopted legislation to accelerate asylum procedures, improve integration measures, replace cash support with benefits in kind, and expedite construction of new accommodation. Lack of unified, binding standards meant wide disparities in quality of asylum accommodation, including lack of safeguards to protect women and children from harassment and abuse.

The legislation adds Albania, Kosovo, and Montenegro to the list of safe countries that already includes Bosnia and Herzegovina, Serbia, and Macedonia. Syrians were the largest national group of asylum seekers, followed by Albanians and Kosovars. Nationals from countries considered safe are presumed not to need international protection and are subject to accelerated procedures, raising concerns about the quality of individual examinations and the consequences for the many Roma applicants from the Western Balkans.

Federal police registered 473 attacks on asylum accommodations in the first nine months of the year, more than double the total for 2014, and expressed concern about the rise of right-wing extremist groups. Anti-migrant protests flared throughout the year, particularly in the east.

The UN Committee on the Elimination of Racial Discrimination expressed concern in May about broad police stop-and-search powers leading to ethnic profiling and inadequate investigations of racially motivated attacks. In July, a law entered into force giving prosecutors greater powers to investigate racially motivated crimes, now subject to more severe punishment.

Germany's constitutional court ruled in March that a 2004 ban in North Rhine-Westphalia on teachers wearing the headscarf violated religious freedom and

**HUMAN
RIGHTS
WATCH**

A DIFFICULT PROFESSION
Media Freedom Under Attack in the Western Balkans

was discriminatory. The ruling renders unconstitutional similar bans in other states.

A new data retention law attracted concerns of unjustified interference with privacy rights and the criminalization of whistleblowing. The federal commissioner for data protection said the law was unconstitutional.

The UN Committee on the Rights of Persons with Disabilities said in May that Germany's system of guardianship denies equal recognition under the law and expressed concern about the widespread institutionalization of persons with psychosocial disabilities.

Greece

Political uncertainty, mass immigration, and instability marked Greece's year. In June and July, the UN independent expert on foreign debt and human rights urged the European institutions, the International Monetary Fund, and the Greek government to ensure that new austerity measures did not undermine human rights.

Thousands of migrants and asylum seekers arriving on Greece's Aegean islands and also in Athens faced appalling reception and detention conditions. Poor registration systems on the islands failed to identify people with special protection needs, including people with disabilities or medical conditions, and women and children, exacerbating risks for these groups.

At time of writing, almost 726,000 people, mainly from Syria and Afghanistan, have taken the sea journey from Turkey to Greece since the start of 2015. According to the International Organization for Migration, at least 588 died crossing from Turkey in 2015.

There were continuing allegations that Greek border guards engaged in collective expulsions and pushbacks of migrants and asylum seekers at the land borders with Turkey. In October, the authorities indicated they were investigating 20 such allegations brought by human rights groups. Unidentified armed masked men disabled boats carrying migrants and asylum seekers in the Aegean Sea, pushing them back to Turkish waters.

HUMAN
RIGHTS
WATCH

"As Though We Are Not
Human Beings"
Police Brutality against Migrants and Asylum Seekers in Macedonia

Asylum-seeking and migrant children registered as unaccompanied minors by the authorities were often detained much longer than adults or children traveling with their families, while authorities sought shelter facilities for them. There is no reliable estimate of the number of unaccompanied migrant children who entered Greece during the year.

In February, the government revoked a ministerial decision that had allowed detention of migrants beyond the 18 months permitted by EU law, and announced the immediate release from immigration detention of vulnerable categories of asylum seekers, as well as of people whose detention exceeded a six-month period. Conditions in immigration detention remain poor.

The ECtHR held Greece responsible for inhuman and degrading treatment in immigration detention in five separate cases since December 2014.

Despite improvements in the asylum system and significant increases in Greece's protection rates, asylum seekers face serious difficulties in accessing the asylum procedure. According to the Greek Asylum Service, only 10,718 people had applied for asylum in Greece as of the end of October. The authorities have yet to clear the backlog of asylum appeals under the old system operated by the police.

Attacks on migrants and asylum seekers and LGBT people continued, with a network of nongovernmental organizations (NGOs) recording more than 460 incidents over the last four years. In October, an Athens court published its written judgment in a 2014 conviction and sentence of life imprisonment for two men for the murder of a Pakistani man. The judgment clarified that the court found that the murder was racially motivated, the first such case in Greece for a serious offense.

In May, the UN special rapporteur on contemporary forms of racism urged Greece to set up efficient mechanisms for victims of racist attacks to seek remedies and ensure their access to justice as well as the due punishment of perpetrators. A law adopted in July introduced residence permits on humanitarian grounds for undocumented victims and witnesses of hate crimes.

In April, the government repealed a health regulation used in 2012 to round up dozens of women alleged to be sex workers who were then forced to take HIV tests. In early February, the new government of Alexis Tsipras announced the end of Operation Xenios Zeus, a police operation that targeted migrants and foreigners. However, the police continued to stop, arbitrarily detain, and harass homeless people and those who use drugs and sell sex, interfering with their ability to access health care and support services.

In a report published in February, the European Commission against Racism and Intolerance noted discrimination and police harassment toward LGBT people, notably against transgender persons.

Hungary

Hungary saw an enormous increase in asylum applications in 2015, stressing a flawed and inefficient asylum system. By late August, authorities had registered over 150,000 asylum applications since the start of the year, a tenfold increase compared to 2014.

In response, the government erected a fence along its border with Serbia, completed in September, and erected a fence on its border with Croatia in October. Through legal changes in July and August, authorities also introduced a new border regime, criminalizing irregular entry and establishing Serbia as a "safe third country," thus permitting the quick return of asylum seekers transiting through that country. As of late October, more than 500 people had been convicted of irregular border crossing and placed in immigration detention pending deportation, in most cases to Serbia.

Further changes included an accelerated asylum procedure, which jeopardizes due process rights, and a three-day limit for judicial reviews, which undermines the right to effective remedy. A September law authorized the army's deployment to the border and allowed soldiers to use non-lethal force, including tear gas grenades and rubber bullets, against migrants and asylum seekers.

In September, Hungarian border and counterterrorism police used tear gas and water cannons against asylum seekers protesting the closure of a border point with Serbia, some of them violently. The UN high commissioner for human rights criticized the use of force by police as disproportionate.

Police also beat three international journalists with batons, dragged them from Serbian to Hungarian territory, arrested them for 24 hours, and charged them with irregular border crossing. Charges were later dropped.

During the first part of 2015, the government engaged in an anti-migrant campaign, including a biased questionnaire to Hungarian citizens that linked migration and terrorism in April, and an anti-migrant billboard campaign in May.

The government also continued to restrict media freedom. In January, the CEO of RTL Klub, the independent broadcaster, moved his family abroad and hired bodyguards after being threatened with violence. In July, the Office of Immigration and Nationality denied Hungarian media access to refugee reception centers, arguing that the presence of journalists could impinge upon the personal rights of asylum seekers.

The Council of Europe's Venice Commission issued an opinion in June on Hungary's media stressing ongoing concerns about vague broadcast content regulation, particularly the ban on criticizing religious or political views and on content that violates privacy rights.

By October 31, 2015, 71 homeless people were charged with misdemeanors under local decrees banning the homeless from residing habitually in public spaces, a significant decrease from 234 reported by end of November 2014. In late January, the High Court annulled sections of a municipal decree that banned the homeless from living in the streets of certain areas of Budapest, effective May 31.

Roma continue to face discrimination and harassment. In May, the Supreme Court ruled that evictions of Roma in 2014 constituted unlawful discrimination. The European Roma Rights Center documented a pattern of police fining Roma for petty offenses, such as lack of bicycle accessories, and sometimes jailing those unable to pay. In September, Hungary's Equal Treatment Authority found the practice discriminatory.

Italy

By the end of November more than 143,000 migrants and asylum seekers had reached Italy by sea. Their main countries of origin were Eritrea, Nigeria, Somalia, Sudan, Syria, and Gambia. New asylum applications decreased compared to 2014 because most new arrivals quickly transited out of Italy.

Italy faced ongoing challenges providing accommodation to asylum seekers. As of August, 86,000 asylum seekers were staying in official centers and hundreds of temporary facilities. The government committed to creating 10,000 additional places in special shelters for asylum seekers and refugees. Residents in neighborhoods hosting emergency asylum centers periodically protested, sometimes violently.

An EU-supported screening center—a "hotspot"—began operating in Lampedusa in September, with four more planned to be fully operational by the end of the year. Rights groups reported concerns over triage procedures, with certain nationalities effectively prevented from applying for asylum and ordered to leave the country.

In May, the UN special rapporteur on migrants' rights expressed concerns about access to, and conditions in, asylum centers, as well as inadequate protection for unaccompanied migrant children. According to Save the Children, at least 7,600 unaccompanied children arrived in the first eight months of the year. The UN Subcommittee on Prevention of Torture conducted a week-long visit in September to assess treatment and conditions of detained migrants.

The ECtHR ruled in July that Italy's failure to provide any kind of legal status to same-sex couples violated the right to privacy and family life. At time of writing, parliament had yet to adopt a long-debated bill to recognize same-sex civil unions.

In September, the ECtHR ruled that the 2011 detention of a group of Tunisians, first in Lampedusa and then on ships, and their subsequent expulsion to Tunisia, violated their rights to liberty and security, to an effective remedy, to protection from inhuman or degrading treatment in detention, and against collective expulsion.

Latvia

Latvia has a large population of stateless people. According to the UNCHR, as of late 2014, more than 12 percent of the country's population is effectively stateless (those referred to by the authorities as "noncitizens"). Despite a 2013 reform to address the status of children who are born and live in Latvia without a nationality, 7,800 children in Latvia were stateless as of early 2015, according to a report by the nongovernmental organizations European Network on Statelessness and Latvian Centre for Human Rights.

Discrimination persists against Russian speakers, particularly in the spheres of employment and education. Latvian non-citizens are barred from occupying certain posts in the civil service and other professions. They also face restrictions on owning land.

State-imposed limits on Russian as a language of instruction in schools continue to impact the quality of education in regions where Russian speakers live. In Latvian public secondary schools, at least 60 percent of the curriculum must be in Latvian.

In 2015, the authorities continued efforts to sanction individuals and organizations, including a museum and a local council member, for alleged failure to use Latvian in professional communications.

In June, the Latvian capital Riga hosted EuroPride 2015, an annual European event celebrating LGBT pride, hosted by a different European city each year. It was the first time EuroPride had been held in a former Soviet state. However, also in June, the Latvian parliament voted to require schools to provide "constitutional morality education" to schoolchildren in line with the constitutional definition of marriage as a union between a man and a woman.

Netherlands

In an April resolution, the Committee of Ministers of the Council of Europe reaffirmed a 2014 decision by the European Committee of Social Rights that the Netherlands must offer decent humanitarian conditions to rejected asylum seekers until they leave the country. That same month, the government announced a "bed, bath, bread agreement" providing temporary shelter at night, a shower, and two meals a day. But the agreement is limited to the five largest municipalities and can be terminated if the person refuses to cooperate with removal from the Netherlands.

In August, the UN Committee on the Elimination of Racial Discrimination criticized the government's approach, saying that basic needs of migrants should be provided unconditionally. In November, the Dutch Council of State, the highest administrative court, said the Dutch government is generally entitled to place conditions on the provision of shelter to rejected asylum seekers, such as their cooperation with removal from the Netherlands, other than in exceptional circumstances, such as those related to the person's psychological state.

In June, the UN Committee on the Rights of the Child noted with concern the deportation of children in "vulnerable situations" to their countries of origin, where they may end up in orphanages, and urged the authorities to take measures to prevent such deportations.

In August, the UN Committee on the Elimination of Racial Discrimination expressed concerns over racial profiling by Dutch police and urged the Netherlands to adopt measures to ensure that stop-and-search powers are not exercised in a discriminatory manner. The committee also expressed concerns over reports that citizens seeking to protest peacefully against portrayals of the traditional "Black Piet" (Zwarte Piet) figure of the Sinterklaas festival have been denied authorization to conduct such protests at a meaningful time and place and have been subjected to violent attacks and other forms of intimidation, which have not been adequately investigated.

In June, the Netherlands paid compensation to relatives of victims of the Srebrenica genocide in 1995 who were forced to leave a UN compound by Dutch peacekeepers. A court in the city of Arnhem ruled in April that a former Dutch commander and his two adjutants would not be prosecuted for complicity in war crimes and genocide at Srebrenica.

In November, the Netherlands ratified the Council of Europe's Convention on preventing and combating violence against women and domestic violence (known as the Istanbul Convention).

Poland

There was little sign of progress in the Krakow Appellate Prosecutor's longstanding criminal investigation into a secret CIA detention and interrogation program. Following the release of the US Senate torture report, former President Aleksander Kwasniewski acknowledged authorizing a secret CIA detention facility. In February, the ECtHR upheld its decision of July 2014 concerning Poland's complicity in the detention program, and confirmed its order that Poland pay compensation to two former "black site" detainees. In September, a Polish court rejected an application for victim status in the case brought on behalf of a Saudi former detainee at Guantanamo Bay.

In May, the prosecutor general published a report on racist and xenophobic crimes. Despite a significant rise in the number of reported cases, convictions remained low. In June, the European Commission against Racism and Intolerance urged Poland to take further measures in addressing racial crimes, hate speech, and discrimination based on sexual orientation and gender identity.

Draft legislation on introducing civil partnership was again rejected by parliament's lower house in August.

Access to reproductive and sexual health rights continued to be restricted, with limited access to legal abortion and comprehensive sex education. In October, the Constitutional Tribunal considered the legality of elements of the "conscience clause," a code allowing medical personnel to decline to provide reproductive health services if that conflicts with their personal values or beliefs. The Constitutional Tribunal ruled that the legal obligation to refer the patient to another medical professional in the event of such a conflict is unconstitutional.

In October, parliament failed to override the president's veto on legislation that would have significantly improved the legal recognition process for transgender people.

In February, parliament enacted a law ratifying the Istanbul Convention. Violence against women remained a serious problem, and continued underreporting of cases limits survivors' access to services and justice.

Spain

Changes to Spain's immigration laws entered into force in April, allowing for summary expulsions from the country's enclaves in North Africa, Ceuta, and Melilla. Access to asylum offices established at the borders remained difficult for many, with Morocco at times closing the border, including to Syrians. An ECtHR challenge to the summary return of migrants from Melilla in 2014 was pending at time of writing.

A Melilla judge closed the cases against eight border guards on charges of degrading treatment, and against the local Guardia Civil chief on charges of obstruction of justice, in relation to use of force to return a group of migrants to Morocco in October 2014.

In April, the European Committee for the Prevention of Torture renewed its concerns about prison-like conditions in immigration detention facilities and criticized severe overcrowding in the center for migrants in Melilla.

A revamped criminal code and a new public security law, in effect since July, include provisions that define terrorism offenses in overly broad terms and infringe on the rights to freedom of expression and peaceful assembly—including steep fines for spontaneous protests and "lack of respect" for law enforcement officers, and stiffer penalties for resisting authority in the context of a protest. UN experts earlier warned these measures could lead to disproportionate or discretionary enforcement. The new criminal code introduced the crimes of stalking and forced marriage.

In September, parliament passed legislation requiring parental or guardian consent for 16- and 17-year-old girls to receive an abortion, despite protest and UN concerns over interference in the right to privacy and autonomy. The UN Committee on the Elimination of Discrimination against Women expressed alarm, in July, at the prevalence of violence against women and urged a series of reforms in legislation and practice.

In July, the UN Human Rights Committee expressed concerns about ongoing ethnic profiling by law enforcement bodies, despite some positive legislative reforms, excessive use of force by such bodies, and discrimination against immigrants and minorities, including Roma. The committee renewed its recommendation that Spain abrogate incommunicado detention, as well as the 1977 amnesty law that prevents accountability for torture, enforced disappearances, and extrajudicial executions during the Franco regime.

In September, the UN Committee on Economic, Social and Cultural Rights found that Spain violated the right to adequate housing in the case of a woman unable to contest a mortgage foreclosure on her home.

UK

In May, the newly elected government announced that it would propose legislation for a "British Bill of Rights" to replace the Human Rights Act, which incorporates the European Convention on Human Rights into domestic law. Statements by ministers suggest the new bill could weaken human rights protections.

A committee tasked by the government in December 2013 with conducting an investigation into UK involvement in renditions and overseas torture had yet to report at time of writing. Criminal investigations in UK officials' alleged involvement in several rendition cases involving Libya were ongoing.

In March, parliament passed the Modern Slavery Act with the aim of combating slavery, trafficking, forced labor, and servitude. However, the law fails to adequately address abuse of migrant domestic workers, whose immigration status is tied to their employer. An independent review of the domestic worker visa, commissioned by the government, had yet to report at this writing.

In November, the government proposed a bill that would enshrine broad government surveillance practices in law and expand them further, with only limited judicial involvement. In a June report, the UK's independent reviewer of terrorism legislation called for judicial authorization of interception warrants.

The London Metropolitan Police recorded respective increases of 22 percent and 46.7 percent in anti-Semitic and Islamophobic crimes in London between January and July 2015, as compared with the previous year.

In August, UK forces killed three members of the armed extremist group Islamic State (also known as ISIS) in a drone attack in Syria. Prime Minister David Cameron announced the attack was lawful under international law but refused to publish the legal guidance used to authorize the strike.

The Counter-Terrorism and Security Act 2015, enacted in February, allows authorities to confiscate passports of persons suspected of intending to travel abroad to participate in terrorism-related activities and to prevent UK citizens suspected of involvement in terrorism-related activities from returning to the UK for up to two years, making them de facto stateless for that period.

In August, the UN Human Rights Committee urged the UK to bring its counterterrorism laws in line with the International Covenant on Civil and Political Rights.

In July, the government suspended the "detained fast track," an accelerated procedure for assessing claims that UK authorities consider can be decided "quickly." In June, the Court of Appeal had ordered its suspension after the High Court ruled the procedure was unlawful and structurally unfair for appellants. In November, the Supreme Court refused an application by the government to appeal the June ruling.

Gambia

The government of President Yahya Jammeh, in power since a 1994 coup, frequently committed serious human rights violations including arbitrary detention, enforced disappearance, and torture against those who voiced opposition to the government. The repression and abuses created a climate of fear within Gambia, generating increased attention from the international community.

State security forces most frequently implicated in violations were members of the National Intelligence Agency (NIA), a paramilitary group known as the "Jungulers," and the Gambian Police Force. Those targeted included journalists, political opponents, and lesbian, gay, bisexual, and transgender (LGBT) people, many of whom fled Gambia out of fear.

Some of the worst abuses followed a failed coup attempt on December 30, 2014. In the days that followed, dozens of family members and friends of the alleged plotters were rounded up and held incommunicado, some for months. Three alleged coup plotters died in suspicious circumstances after being captured. In February 2014, a secret court martial, violating due process rights, convicted six soldiers of treason-related offenses. On March 30, the court sentenced three of them to death and three to life in prison.

Despite widespread allegations of serious abuses committed by the security forces over the last two decades, no members of the state security or paramilitary groups are known to have been convicted or otherwise held to account for torture, killings, or other serious violations.

In July 2015, in an unprecedented act, President Jammeh pardoned and released over 200 prisoners, including many political prisoners. Despite this, many Gambians remained in detention or are feared forcibly disappeared.

Draconian anti-gay legislation and persecution of LGBT people focused global attention on other aspects of the government's human rights record. Gambia's partners, notably the European Union, the United Nations, the United States, and the Economic Community of West African States (ECOWAS), were increasingly willing to denounce or take steps to address the rights climate, including by issuing public statements and conditioning assistance.

HUMAN
RIGHTS
WATCH

STATE OF FEAR
Arbitrary Arrests, Torture, and Killings

Enforced Disappearances

In January 2015, shortly after the attempted coup, Gambian authorities forcibly disappeared dozens of friends and relatives of the alleged coup plotters, including elderly parents and a 16-year-old boy. They were held incommunicado, deprived of contact with family, and denied access to lawyers for up to seven months.

The government refused to acknowledge the whereabouts or even the detention of many of them, effectively holding them outside of the protection of the law. A dozen of these family members were released as part of presidential pardons announced on July 22, the anniversary of President's Jammeh's 1994 coup.

In the past decade, Gambian security forces have been implicated in dozens of enforced disappearances, including of a journalist, two American-Gambian citizens, and a former army chief, all of whom remain unaccounted for.

Arbitrary Arrest and Detention

Arbitrary arrest and detention by the security services, especially the NIA and the Serious Crimes Unit within the police, continued. Among those arbitrarily detained and held beyond the 72-hour legal limit in 2015 were journalists—including Alagie Abdoulie Ceesay, the manager of Taranga FM radio station—as well as senior civil servants, ministers, and members of the security services. Many of those in detention were subjected to torture and enforced disappearance.

Torture and Other Ill-Treatment

During 2015, as in past years, numerous real or perceived government opponents were subjected to severe torture and other ill-treatment by members of the Gambian security forces and paramilitary groups. Much of the abuse appeared designed to intimidate or secure forced confessions from perceived government opponents, or to punish those who criticize the president or highlight the current administration's policy failures.

In January, six soldiers implicated in December's coup attempt and some of their family members were severely beaten while in detention at the NIA. In July, while arbitrarily detained at NIA headquarters for 11 days without charge, journalist

Alagie Abdoulie Ceesay was forced to drink cooking oil on several occasions and beaten until he lost consciousness.

Torture methods used included severe beatings with wooden clubs, metal pipes, cables, and electric wires; slicing with bayonets; near suffocation by tying a plastic bag over the head of the victim; trampling with boots; electroshock of body parts, including genitals; and dripping melted plastic bags onto the skin. Many victims were subjected to psychological abuse such as prolonged periods in solitary confinement, mock execution, and repeated threats of torture and death.

Sexual Orientation and Gender Identity

Gambians who identify as lesbian, gay, bisexual, or transgender (LGBT), or who are perceived as such, have increasingly become the target of hate speech from the president, as well as of discriminatory laws, arrest and prosecution by the authorities, and sometimes violent abuse in custody.

On October 9, 2014, the government introduced a series of new "aggravated homosexuality" offenses that impose sentences of up to life in prison. The new offenses criminalize anyone having "unlawful carnal connection with any person of the same sex," where the person commits the offense more than once or is living with HIV, and where the "victim" has a disability. These clauses criminalize and discriminate against LGBT people living with HIV and imply that persons with disabilities cannot consent to sex.

Weeks after the new law passed, state security rounded up dozens of people on suspicion of homosexuality. Several people detained by the NIA were abused and threatened with physical violence in an attempt to force them to provide names of LGBT Gambians. The security services conducted door-to door-searches for suspected homosexuals. In a May 2015 speech, Jammeh said he would "slit the throats" of gay people in Gambia. Two men, detained for over three months at the NIA before being tried for "unnatural acts," were acquitted in July 2015 for lack of evidence.

Freedom of Expression and Association

In 2015, the authorities continued to persecute journalists for investigating stories critical of the government, exposing human rights abuses, or producing coverage of the opposition in a seemingly favorable light. Since 1994, dozens of journalists have fled Gambia after being arbitrarily detained and often tortured. Since 2004, two journalists have been murdered or forcibly disappeared.

After the December 2014 coup attempt, state security closed down the Taranga FM radio station—regularly the target of such government closures—for four days in January. On August 5, journalist Alagie Abdoulie Ceesay was put on trial for sedition for sending an image on his mobile phone of the president, deemed by authorities to "raise discontent, hatred, or disaffection among the inhabitants of the Gambia." In August, Al Jazeera journalists were denied permission to film and were reportedly asked to leave the country.

While many private radio and print news outlets operate in the country, editors regularly engage in self-censorship out of fear of being shut down by the government. There is no international media presence in Gambia.

Since 2013, the government has used a series of increasingly repressive laws to muzzle freedom of speech, affecting not only journalists but anyone communicating across any media, including the Internet, social media, telephones, and even in private conversations.

Gambian human rights and pro-democracy groups have very limited space to promote good governance and respect for human rights. Due to a climate of fear and highly restrictive legal and administrative frameworks, very few nongovernmental organizations operate freely in the country. Those that do avoid monitoring and reporting on rights abuses.

Key International Actors

Two United Nations special rapporteurs conducted missions to Gambia in November 2014 to investigate allegations of torture and ill-treatment, in addition to extrajudicial and unlawful killings. Both rapporteurs issued highly critical reports stating that Gambia is characterized by widespread disregard for the rule of law, infringements of civil liberties, and the existence of a repressive state apparatus.

They said they encountered an atmosphere of fear and were denied access to detention centers, including the security wing of Mile 2 Prison in Banjul.

In March 2015, Gambia rejected many recommendations from the UN Human Rights Council in Geneva during its last Universal Periodic Review, including abolishing the death penalty, decriminalizing homosexuality, and removing restrictions on freedom of expression.

In February and March 2015, the UN Working Group on Enforced or Involuntary Disappearances transmitted seven cases under its urgent action procedure to the Gambian government on behalf of seven people abducted in January 2015, allegedly by the NIA.

In December 2014, EU assistance to Gambia was frozen over concerns about the country's dire human rights situation. In June 2015, Gambia cut ties with the EU, declaring its representative in Banjul persona non grata. However, plans for resuming EU aid were under negotiation at year's end.

The Banjul-based African Commission on Human and Peoples' Rights adopted a resolution in February on the deteriorating rights situation in Gambia, calling on the government to invite the commission to conduct a fact-finding mission into events after the December 2014 attempted coup.

In May 2015, US National Security Advisor Susan Rice said she was "deeply concerned about credible reports of torture, suspicious disappearances and arbitrary detention at the government's hands," adding that the US government was "reviewing what additional actions are appropriate to respond to this worsening situation."

In 2015, ECOWAS pressed Gambia to improve its human rights record and to establish a credible human rights commission.

Georgia

Georgia's human rights record remained uneven in 2015. The numerous investigations into alleged crimes by former officials raised questions as to whether they were being pursued on the merits of the cases, or were the result of selective justice and politically motivated prosecutions.

Law enforcement officers continued to use torture and ill-treatment and in many cases were not held accountable for abuses they committed. Media pluralism was threatened by the closure of several political debate programs and a dispute involving past and present high-level officials' alleged interference in the ownership and management of the most-watched television station, Rustavi 2. The prosecutor of the International Criminal Court (ICC) requested the court's authorization to investigate war crimes and crimes against humanity allegedly committed during the August 2008 war with Russia.

Justice

The Georgian Dream coalition government continues to investigate dozens of criminal cases against former officials who served under the previous government, led by the United National Movement (UNM) party. Authorities selected these cases from thousands of complaints citizens filed after the UNM was voted out of office in 2012. UNM members and supporters allege that the prosecutions are politically motivated, pointing to the absence of clear criteria for determining which cases to prosecute, and that investigations overwhelmingly target UNM members.

In September, the Tbilisi city court sentenced Gigi Ugulava, the UNM leader and Tbilisi ex-mayor, to four-and-a-half years in prison on misappropriation charges. Ugulava was acquitted of separate money laundering charges. The verdict came the day after his release from pretrial detention following a Constitutional Court decision that Ugulava's 14-month detention exceeded the constitutionally mandated limit of 9 months.

In October, a court in the city of Kutaisi ordered pretrial detention for three activists from the UNM party and its affiliated nongovernmental organization (NGO), Free Zone, following a confrontation with a Georgian Dream parliamentarian during a protest in front of parliament. Georgia's public defender, Ucha Nan-uashvili, called the court decision to remand them into custody "excessive," and accused the courts of selective justice. He noted that courts had not taken pro-government suspects into custody in similar cases, involving violent attacks against opposition UNM parliamentarians.

Also in October, police briefly detained Tabula television station's chief and pro-ducer, as well as an activist, as they hung posters criticizing government negoti-ations with Russia's energy giant, Gazprom, on a fence and street lamp in Tbilisi. The three faced misdemeanor charges. Tabula is known for criticism of officials.

Targeting Political Opposition

In October, pro-government groups, including local municipal employees, held rallies outside UNM party offices in at least 19 towns. The groups variously nailed or welded doors shut, shattered windows, painted graffiti, and splattered red paint on UNM offices. Media reported that police present at some locations of the attacks did not intervene.

Following the group attacks, Prime Minister Irakli Garibashvili publicly called the UNM a "criminal organization," and said that "aggression" against the party is "natural." Some NGOs said Garibashvili's remarks effectively condoned the vio-lence.

The attacks on UNM offices occurred after the online publication of a graphic video of prison officials sexually abusing two detainees in 2011, when UNM was in power. The videos appeared after polls showed a decline in public support for the ruling Georgian Dream coalition, leading to UNM accusations that the au-thorities may have leaked the videos to distract public attention.

Pro-government supporters organized public outdoor screenings of the video in downtown Tbilisi and Zugdidi on October 18. Local officials from the ruling coali-tion participated in the Zugdidi screening. Georgia's public defender and NGOs condemned the screenings.

In September, pro-government groups held multiple rallies outside the private residences of the constitutional court chairman, condemning the court's deci-sion to release former Tbilisi Mayor Ugulava from pretrial detention, threatening the chairman and his family, and throwing tomatoes and eggs at his home.

Under Georgian law, threatening a judge is a criminal offense, and holding a protest outside a judge's residence is a misdemeanor. In October, the chairman informed the authorities of the threats, but police did not respond.

Torture and Ill-Treatment

Georgia does not have an effective, independent mechanism to investigate crimes committed by law enforcement officials, resulting in frequent impunity. The Georgian Young Lawyers' Association (GYLA), a leading human rights group, received at least 41 allegations of torture and ill-treatment in 2015 through October; 23 of them concerned abuse by police, and 18 by prison staff. According to GYLA, the authorities failed to effectively investigate those allegations.

In November, a lawyer, Giorgi Mdinaradze, said that he was beaten at a police station by five policemen, including the station chief, after advising his client to exercise his right to silence. Authorities arrested the police chief on charges of abuse of office with use of violence.

In June, the prosecutor's office brought defamation charges against Giorgi Okropiridze, a pretrial detainee in Tbilisi, for allegedly providing false testimony to the public defender about ill-treatment in custody. A court imposed additional time in pretrial detention following the defamation charges. The public defender said the decision undermined trust in his institution and violated international obligations to prohibit official retaliation when people provide information to the national mechanism for the prevention of torture.

Freedom of Media

An ownership dispute over Georgia's most-watched television broadcaster, Rustavi 2, raised concerns about ongoing government interference in media. Kibar Khalvashi, Rustavi 2's owner from 2004 to 2006, filed a lawsuit in August to reclaim his shares, saying that in 2006, then-UNM government leaders forced him to sell. In November, the Tbilisi City Court ruled in Khalvashi's favor, and also appointed interim management for Rustavi 2, a move local human rights groups criticized as an attempt to effect the channel's editorial policy. A week later, the Constitutional Court suspended the civil procedure code clause that had allowed the appointment of temporary managers. Rustavi 2's current owners allege that the lawsuit is a government-orchestrated move to take over the opposition-minded station and plan to appeal the court decisions. Rustavi 2 claimed significant financial and logistical constraints from the lawsuit, including a court-ordered asset freeze against it and its majority shareholder company.

In October, Rustavi 2 Director Nika Gvaramia alleged that a government official threatened to leak a personal video of him if he refused to "step aside" from the station. Prosecutors initiated an investigation into the alleged threat. A few days later, secret recordings appeared online, allegedly of Gvaramia receiving instructions from former Georgian President Mikheil Saakashvili, to prepare for possible "physical confrontation" with the authorities to defend the station.

Many of Georgia's international partners expressed concern about the Rustavi 2 case, including the United States Department of State and the Organization for Security and Co-operation in Europe (OSCE) representative on freedom of media.

In August, Imedi TV, the second most-watched station, suspended its political talk shows. Inga Grigolia, a host of one and co-host of another talk show, alleged interference from authorities in the decision.

Sexual Orientation and Gender Identity

In October, the Tbilisi City Court acquitted a Georgian Orthodox priest and three other men on charges of disrupting an anti-homophobia rally in Tbilisi in May 2013, citing lack of evidence to prove the defendants' guilt beyond a reasonable doubt. Thousands of counter-demonstrators, including some Orthodox clergy, had violently disrupted the peaceful rally. Although police evacuated rally participants to safety, they failed to contain the mob, which threw stones and other objects at a van carrying participants.

In August, a court acquitted a man of premeditated murder after he stabbed to death a transgender woman, Sabi Beriani, and set her apartment on fire, apparently to cover up the crime, in November 2014. The court sentenced the defendant to four years' imprisonment for violence and property damage. Rights groups urged the prosecutor's office to appeal the decision and recognize hate as an aggravating circumstance in the crime.

Key International Actors

The ICC prosecutor requested the court's judges to authorize an investigation into alleged crimes committed during the 2008 conflict between Georgia and Russia, including by South Ossetian forces (in some cases, with the possible participation of Russian forces) and also by Georgian forces.

In its March European Neighborhood Policy progress report, the European Union noted some improvements, but also highlighted the need to ensure separation of powers and judicial independence, avoid "political retribution, confrontation and polarization," and increase the accountability of law enforcement.

In March, the United Nations special rapporteur on torture visited Georgia. He noted progress, but also highlighted areas for improvement, including more contact between prisoners and family members and prisoners' access to recreation.

In an October resolution, the Parliamentary Assembly of the Council of Europe criticized Georgia for "abuse of pretrial detention," including to "discredit or otherwise neutralize political competitors."

Also in October, the assembly's co-rapporteurs for Georgia issued a statement following a country visit highlighting key issues, including media freedom, criminal justice reform, and the electoral system.

In a November statement, the US-Georgia Strategic Partnership Commission, the primary bilateral dialogue to deepen cooperation between the countries, commended Georgia's reform efforts, but called for improvements, including in elections, media freedom, and judicial independence.

Guatemala

President Otto Pérez Molina resigned in September after being implicated by the United Nations-backed International Commission against Impunity in Guatemala (CICIG) in a million-dollar tax-fraud scandal. The commission was established in 2007 to investigate organized crime and reinforce local efforts to strengthen the rule of law in Guatemala. In 2015, after the Guatemalan Congress voted to strip both President Pérez Molina and Vice President Roxana Baldetti of their immunity, prosecutors charged them and more than 35 other government officials with corruption.

Guatemala's efforts to promote accountability for human rights atrocities committed during the 1960-1996 civil war have had mixed results. While the Attorney General's Office has successfully prosecuted several high-profile cases, the vast majority of victims have not seen any form of justice for the violations they endured.

Accountability for Past Human Rights Violations

Former Guatemalan head of state Efraín Ríos Montt was found guilty in May 2013 of genocide and crimes against humanity. He was sentenced to 80 years in prison, but several days later the Constitutional Court overturned the verdict on procedural grounds. The retired general had led a military government from 1982 to 1983 during which period the military carried out hundreds of massacres of unarmed civilians.

In August 2015, a trial court declared Ríos Montt mentally unfit for retrial, ruling instead that he should be represented by his lawyers in a special closed-door proceeding that is scheduled to start in January 2016.

In October 2015, an appellate court rejected a two-year old petition by Rios Montt's attorneys to apply a 1986 amnesty decree that would put an end to his prosecution. The court ruled that the decree, applicable to "all political and related common crimes" committed between March 1982 and January 1986, does not apply to genocide and crimes against humanity.

Guatemala's Congress passed a resolution in May 2014 denying that acts of genocide were committed during the country's civil war, despite findings to the contrary by a UN-sponsored Truth Commission in 1999.

In addition to pursuing the case against Ríos Montt, the Attorney General's Office has, in recent years, convicted several other former members of security forces for human rights crimes committed during the war. Five members of the army's special forces received lengthy sentences for their role in the 1982 Dos Erres massacre of more than 250 people, and former National Police Chief Héctor Bol de la Cruz received a 40-year sentence for ordering the disappearance of a student activist in 1984.

In July 2014, Felipe Solano Barillas became the first ex-guerrilla to be convicted in connection with atrocities committed during the country's civil war. Found guilty of ordering the massacre of 22 residents of the town of El Aguacate in 1988, he was sentenced to 90 years in prison.

In November 2014, the government approved a reparations policy and allocated funds to address human rights violations suffered by the communities that were displaced by the construction of the Chixoy Hydroelectric Dam in 1975.

In January 2015, former Police Chief Pedro Garcia Arredondo was sentenced to 90 years in prison for a raid on the Spanish embassy in 1980 in which 37 people burned to death.

The Guatemalan judiciary inaugurated a third "high-risk court" in October 2015 to hear cases of grave crimes, including genocide, war crimes, and crimes against humanity, among others. The new court was opened to help resolve cases more quickly and effectively, and ease the workload of the two existing high-risk courts.

Public Security and the Criminal Justice System

Violence and extortion by powerful criminal organizations remain serious problems in Guatemala. Corruption within the justice system, combined with intimidation against judges and prosecutors, contributes to high levels of impunity. Gang-related violence is also one of the principal factors prompting people, including unaccompanied youth, to leave the country. Frustrated with the lack of criminal law enforcement, some communities have resorted to vigilantism.

Despite such problems, prosecutors in recent years have made progress in cases of violent crime, as well as some cases of extrajudicial killings and corruption—due in significant part to support the Attorney General's Office has received from CICIG.

In April, a CICIG investigation uncovered a US$130 million tax fraud scandal involving more than 50 high-ranking members of the government that led to charges against then-President Otto Pérez Molina, Vice President Roxana Baldetti, and 35 others.

Attacks on Human Rights Defenders, Journalists, and Trade Unionists

Acts of violence and intimidation against human rights defenders, journalists, and trade unionists remain a serious problem. More than 70 trade unionists were killed between 2004 and 2015 according to the International Trade Union Conference.

In 2014, 39 journalists were victims of violence, according to the human rights ombudsman. Between January 1 and March 10, 2015, another 20 journalists were subject to attack, the ombudsman reported, and in March, 2 journalists were shot dead by a pair of gunmen in Mazatenango, Suchitepéquez. A third journalist was injured in the attack. At time of writing, three men were awaiting trial for their participation in the killings.

Key International Actors

The UN-backed CICIG, established in 2007, plays a key role in assisting Guatemala's justice system in the prosecution of violent crime. The CICIG works with the Attorney General's Office, the police, and other government agencies to investigate, prosecute, and dismantle criminal organizations operating in the country. It is empowered to participate in criminal proceedings as a complementary prosecutor, to provide technical assistance, and to promote legislative reforms.

The CICIG's mandate was scheduled to terminate in September, but in April, then-President Pérez Molina announced that he would request that the UN extend the mandate for an additional two years. The UN confirmed the extension in May.

The Office of the UN High Commissioner for Human Rights has maintained an office in Guatemala since 2005. The office monitors the human rights situation in the country and provides policy support to the government and civil society.

In Spain, despite a recent ban on universal jurisdiction cases, Judge Santiago Pedraz has said that he will continue investigations of eight Guatemalan officers implicated in human rights abuses during Guatemala's civil war.

The US State Department, in February, requested that Congress allocate $1 billion in assistance for Central America for 2016, which would represent a nearly three-fold increase in foreign aid to the region. More than 90 percent of the proposed $220 million earmarked specifically for Guatemala would go to civilian institutions to address the underlying risk factors that lead to crime and violence, and to strengthen "rule of law institutions."

The US continues to restrict military aid to Guatemala on human rights grounds. Before full aid is restored, the US Consolidated Appropriations Act 2014, requires the Guatemalan government to take "credible steps" to implement the reparations plan for communities affected by construction of the Chixoy Dam. It also requires the government to support the investigation and prosecution of military officers implicated in past atrocities and to ensure that the army's role is limited to combating external threats.

Guinea

Violence in the months leading up to and following the October presidential elections resulted in some 10 deaths, deepened ethnic tensions, and exposed ongoing concerns about abuses by the security forces. However, during 2015, there was some progress in strengthening the judiciary and rule of law and addressing the serious human rights problems that characterized Guinea for more than five decades.

The 2015 presidential election, won by incumbent president, Alpha Conde, was plagued by serious logistical problems but deemed largely free and fair by international observers. Local elections, not held since 2005, failed to take place, further stoking political tensions.

Reports of human rights violations by security forces declined. However, security forces were implicated in numerous incidents of excessive use of force and unprofessional conduct, including theft and extortion, as they responded to election-related protests.

The government made some progress in the dispensation of justice and in ensuring accountability for past atrocities, including the 2009 stadium massacre of unarmed demonstrators by security forces. However, concerns about prison overcrowding, unprofessional conduct by judicial personnel, and the lack of judicial independence remained.

International actors—notably the European Union, United Nations, France, the Economic Community of West Africa States (ECOWAS), and the United States— actively focused on resolving election-related disputes between the ruling party and the opposition, though they were reluctant to push for progress on accountability. Donors supported programs to address the aftermath of the Ebola health crisis, strengthen the rule of law, and improve discipline within the security sector.

Impunity and Accountability for Crimes

Since 2010, the judiciary has opened several investigations into serious violations by security forces, including the 2007 killing of some 130 unarmed demonstrators, the 2009 massacre and rape of opposition supporters in a Conakry stadium; the 2010 torture of members of the political opposition; the 2012 killing of six men in the southeastern village of Zogota; and the 2013 killing of demonstrators protesting the delay in holding parliamentary elections.

In 2015, investigative judges took steps to move most of these investigations forward, but their efforts were hampered by the failure of some members of the army, gendarmerie, and police to respond to judicial summons. At year's end, no trials had taken place.

Justice for the 2009 Stadium Massacre

More than six years on, domestic investigation continued into the September 2009 massacre of opposition supporters at a rally in Conakry, largely by members of the elite Presidential Guard. Security force members are implicated in the killing of some 150 people and rape of over 100 women during military rule under Moussa Dadis Camara.

Since legal proceedings began in 2010, the panel of judges appointed to investigate the massacre has made important strides, having interviewed more than 400 victims and charged 14 suspects, including several high-level members of the security forces. Meaningful steps taken in 2015 included the charging of former coup leader Moussa Dadis Camara and his then-vice president, Mamadouba Toto Camara.

Judiciary and Detention Conditions

Some steps were taken to reverse the striking deficiencies in the judiciary, despite the low operational budget, which remained at around 0.5 percent of the national budget. Unprofessional conduct in this sector, including absenteeism and corrupt practices, contributed to persistent detention-related abuses.

Prisons operate far below international standards. Prison and detention centers in Guinea are severely overcrowded as a result of the systematic use of provisional detention, weak case management, and the failure of the Cour d'Assises—which hears matters involving the most serious crimes—to meet regularly. Guinea's largest detention facility, designed for 300 detainees, regularly accommodated more than 1200. An estimated 60 percent of prisoners in Conakry are held in prolonged pretrial detention.

Meaningful progress in 2015 was evident in the February adoption of a 2015-2019 judicial reform plan; improved conditions for judges; the sanctioning of several judges for corruption and unprofessional conduct by the newly established Superior Council of Judges (*Conseil Supérieur de la Magistrature*); progress in the revision of key legal texts—including the penal code, the Code of Criminal Procedure, and the Code of Military Justice—to bring them in line with international standards; the recruitment of some 50 new magistrates; improvements in case management; improvement in the delivery of water and healthcare in Guinea's largest prison; and the construction, underway, of a new prison envisioned to address overcrowding. The Military Tribunal was also established, though it had yet to begin hearing cases at time of writing.

Efforts to ensure justice for mob and communal violence were accompanied by allegations of a lack of judicial independence. In April 2015, a court sentenced 11 people to life in prison for the mob killing of eight health workers, local officials, and journalists in Womey village, in Guinea's southern forest region, during the 2014 Ebola outbreak.

However, human rights groups said the judiciary failed to investigate the attacks or hold to account members of the security forces implicated in rape, pillage, and other abuses in the Womey incident aftermath. Similarly, 13 convictions of men implicated in a deadly spate of 2013 communal violence in the southern region of N'Zérékoré, which left some 200 people dead, failed to investigate the role of several politicians perceived to be close to the ruling party in the violence. Judicial bailiffs, responsible for the execution of many judicial decisions, denounced the frequent political interference with their work.

Legislative and Institutional Framework

Human rights progress in the legislative framework was evident in the late 2014 adoption of the National Strategy for Justice Sector Reform; the January 2015 establishment of an independent human rights institution as mandated by Guinea's 2010 constitution, albeit not in line with the Paris Principles; and the June 2015 passage of the Public Order Bill strengthening civilian control over the security services.

Guinea has still not ratified the Optional Protocol to the Convention against Torture and other Cruel, Inhuman or Degrading Treatment or Punishment, or the Optional Protocol to the Convention on the Elimination of All Forms of Discrimination against Women. Furthermore, Guinea has yet to codify the crime of torture into its penal code. Guinea has also not ratified the protocol to the African Charter on Human and Peoples' Rights on the Establishment of an African Court of Human and Peoples' Rights.

The Ministry for Human Rights and Civil Liberties, created in 2012, actively promoted respect for human rights, despite budgetary constraints. Minister Gassama Kalifa Diaby visited prisons, liaised with civil society, and advocated for strengthening the judiciary and respecting freedom of the press.

Security Forces

Discipline within and civilian control over the security forces appeared to have improved, and authorities seemed to show slightly increased willingness to sanction those implicated in violations and ensure security force personnel response to judicial summons. The military hierarchy ensured that the army and presidential guard remained in barracks, and those mandated to respond to civil unrest—the police and gendarmerie—did so proportionally and subject to civilian control.

However, in 2015, members of the security forces were implicated in numerous incidents of excessive use of lethal force, resulting in the deaths of several protesters, abusive conduct and the mistreatment of detainees as they responded to protests and criminality. The security forces were also implicated in numerous acts of extortion, bribe-taking, outright theft and banditry, and, to a lesser extent, torture and rape.

The security forces have long demonstrated a lack of political neutrality evident in the use of racial slurs, and failure to provide equal protection to citizens of all ethnic and religious groups, notably those supporting the political opposition.

Key International Actors

Guinea's key international partners, notably the UN, ECOWAS, the EU, France, and the US largely focused on keeping the presidential elections on track, while donors supported programs to address the aftermath of the Ebola health crisis, strengthen the rule of law and improve discipline within the security sector.

These actors rarely issued public statements pushing for progress on accountability.

The EU, Guinea's biggest donor, financed projects in justice, security sector reform, transport, and Ebola relief. In the aftermath of the 2014 Ebola crisis, multiple international donors significantly increased their development aid to Guinea. Additional funding announced in 2015 included €450 (US$749) million from the EU and $37.7 million from the International Monetary Fund, as well as $650 million from the World Bank for Guinea, Liberia, and Sierra Leone. The EU and the UN Development Programme took the lead in providing support to strengthen Guinea's judicial system and in security sector reform.

The country office of the UN High Commissioner for Human Rights regularly documented abuses, monitored detention conditions, and supported the Human Rights Commission, but failed to publicly denounce human rights concerns. In September, UN Special Representative on Sexual Violence in Conflict Zainab Bangura whose office continued to support accountability for crimes committed during the 2009 stadium massacre and rapes, visited Guinea to encourage further progress on investigation.

Guinea underwent Universal Periodic Review at the UN Human Rights Council in January 2015. UPR recommendations addressing torture, enforced disappearance, unlawful detention, prison conditions, judicial and security reform, impunity within the security forces, and women's and children's rights were accepted by Guinea in June.

The UN Peacebuilding Commission funded programs supporting security sector reform, reconciliation, and conflict prevention in Ebola-affected regions. After the February killing in Conakry of the UN peacebuilding fund coordinator in what the government alleged was a criminal assault, the PBF deployed a mission to Conakry to push for the killing to be investigated.

The International Criminal Court (ICC), which in October 2009 confirmed that the situation in Guinea was under preliminary examination, continued to engage the national authorities on progress in the investigation and the importance of conducting proceedings within a reasonable time frame. ICC Prosecutor Fatou Bensouda visited the country in July to assess progress, marking the second visit by her office in 2015.

Haiti

The terms of the majority of lawmakers in Haiti ended in January 2015 without new elections to replace them, shutting down the parliament. While President Michel Martelly governed pursuant to constitutional provisions permitting government institutions to continue operations, the lack of a legislature and protracted political stalemates over elections hindered the Haitian government's ability to meet the basic needs of its people, resolve longstanding human rights problems, or address continuing humanitarian crises.

As of June, only 3 percent of internally displaced persons (IDPs) living in camps in the aftermath of the 2010 earthquake remained, according the International Organization for Migration. Authorities, however, failed to assist many of the remaining 60,000 IDPs to resettle or return to their places of origin, and many continued to face environmental risks and the threat of forced evictions.

Haiti's cholera epidemic, which has claimed more than 9,500 lives and infected over 770,000 people in five years, surged in the first four months of 2015 following a significant decrease in 2014. There were more than 20,500 suspected cases and 175 deaths as of August 1.

A controversial regularization plan for foreigners in neighboring Dominican Republic caused an influx of thousands of Haitians and Dominicans of Haitian descent into Haiti; authorities were ill-prepared to meet their humanitarian needs.

Elections

At time of writing, nearly all elected national and local positions were open or filled by appointees; the only exceptions were the president and one-third of Haiti's senators. Negotiations between the provisional electoral council, executive branch, and political parties culminated in a March presidential decree mandating three election dates: first-round legislative elections on August 9; second-round legislative, first-round local and municipal, and presidential elections on October 25; and a presidential run-off election on December 27.

Haitian human rights groups raised concerns about some acts of violence in the pre-election period. They also documented irregularities in the August elections, leading to a repeat of first-round legislative elections in 22 of 119 districts, held concurrently with the first-round presidential elections.

The October 25 elections were mostly nonviolent, but were marked by low voter turnout. Approximately a quarter of registered voters participated and some electoral monitors and watchdogs raised concerns about voter fraud and transparency at voting centers and at the tabulation center where votes were counted. Police fired tear gas at and arrested protesters at recurring protests contesting the first-round presidential results. On November 18, two presidential candidates alleged that police fired on them at a protest, one saying he was struck in the head by a rubber bullet.

Election authorities rejected calls for an independent commission to verify the first-round presidential election votes. Eight presidential candidates, including first-round second place finisher Jude Célestin, issued a joint statement on November 29 stating that fair elections could not take place without reforms to the electoral commission and police, and that, absent such changes, the December 27 elections should be cancelled and a transitional government established to conduct a national dialogue, draft a new constitution, and prepare for free and fair elections at a much later date. The government's response to the joint statement and outcome of the December elections were not known at time of writing.

Criminal Justice System

Haiti's prison system remains severely overcrowded with many inmates living in inhumane conditions. Analysts trace much of the overcrowding to high numbers of arbitrary arrests and overuse of pretrial detention (according to the United Nations, more than 70 percent of suspects are held pending trial), which is often prolonged as cases take a long time to come to trial. The UN and other international partners have supported a number of initiatives to address this, including opening new legal aid offices and computerizing the case registry system in one jurisdiction in Port-au-Prince.

The limited capacity of the Haitian National Police (HNP) contributes to overall insecurity in the country. While the government and the United Nations Stabilization Mission in Haiti (MINUSTAH), the UN peacekeeping operation in the country, have made police reform a priority, there have been difficulties training sufficient numbers of entry-level cadets. Training of 1,500 new cadets began in August, along with screening of another 7,700 candidates, suggesting the target number of police could be met by the 2016 deadline.

Barriers to Education and Illiteracy

Approximately one in two Haitians age fifteen and older is illiterate. The UN independent expert on Haiti said in 2015 that action to eradicate illiteracy is one of the top human rights priorities in Haiti.

The quality of education in Haiti is generally low, and 90 percent of schools are run by private entities. Human Rights Watch found in 2014 that even some newly constructed schools lack adequate water and sanitation facilities. The minister of education said in September that the national education budget needed to at least double if his reform efforts were to survive.

Accountability for Past Abuses

Former President Jean-Claude Duvalier, who returned to Haiti in January 2011 after nearly 25 years in exile, was accused of financial and human rights crimes allegedly committed during his 15-year tenure as president from 1971 to 1986.

When the Port-au-Prince Court of Appeal ruled in 2014 that the statute of limitations could not be applied to crimes against humanity, and ordered additional investigation into the charges against Duvalier, victims of serious human rights violations, including arbitrary detentions, torture, disappearances, summary executions, and forced exile, hoped that they might finally see justice. However, Duvalier died six months after the ruling, without ever having been brought to trial. The Human Rights Committee and the UN independent expert on Haiti have both called on Haiti to continue the investigation and bring to justice all those responsible for serious human rights violations committed during Duvalier's tenure. At time of writing, a reopened investigation into crimes committed by Duvalier's collaborators was still pending.

Violence against Women

Gender-based violence is a widespread problem. Haiti does not have specific legislation criminalizing rape, domestic violence, sexual harassment, or other forms of violence suffered by women. The shutdown of parliament in 2015 prevented any progress towards consideration of a draft law to address this gap in protection.

Child Domestic Labor

Use of child domestic workers—known as restavèks—continues. Restavèks, most of whom are girls, are sent from low-income households to live with wealthier families in the hope that they will be schooled and cared for in exchange for performing light chores. Though difficult to calculate, some estimates suggest that 225,000 children work as restavèks. These children are often unpaid, denied education, and physically or sexually abused.

Haiti's labor code does not set a minimum age for work in domestic services, though the minimum age for work in industrial, agricultural, and commercial enterprises is 15. Most of Haiti's trafficking cases are restavèks. In 2014, Haiti passed legislation outlawing many forms of trafficking, including hosting a child for the purpose of exploitation.

Key International Actors

MINUSTAH has been in Haiti since 2004 and has contributed to efforts to improve public security, protect vulnerable groups, and strengthen the country's democratic institutions. In January 2015, permanent representatives of the UN Security Council traveled to Haiti for the first time in three years on a mission led by US Ambassador to the UN Samantha Power and Chilean Ambassador Cristian Barros Melet.

In March 2015, MINUSTAH began reducing its personnel, operations, and geographical presence in accordance with a drawdown plan adopted by the Security Council in October 2014. The UN Security Council extended MINUSTAH's mandate through October 15, 2016.

In March and September 2015, the UN independent expert visited Haiti and highlighted the poor conditions that Haitians deported by the Dominican Republic face in camps on the border between the two countries.

In 2012, a member of the 2011 Independent Panel of Experts on the Cholera Outbreak in Haiti convened by the UN secretary-general stated that "the most likely source of the introduction of cholera into Haiti was someone infected with the

Nepal strain of cholera and associated with the United Nations Mirebalais camp."

Responding to the UN's dismissal of claims for compensation from 5,000 victims of the epidemic, the victims' representative, the Institute for Justice and Democracy in Haiti, and the Bureau des Avocats Internationaux filed a lawsuit in 2013 before a US court. In January 2015, the case was dismissed. At time of writing, an appeal was pending. To date, there has been no independent adjudication of the facts surrounding the introduction of cholera and the question of the UN's involvement.

According to figures from the UN Office of Internal Oversight Services, at least 102 allegations of sexual abuse or exploitation have been made against MINUS-TAH personnel since 2007, including 7 between January and July 2015.

Honduras

Rampant crime and impunity for human rights abuses remain the norm in Honduras. Despite a downward trend in recent years, the murder rate is among the highest in the world. Efforts to reform the institutions responsible for providing public security have made little progress. Marred by corruption and abuse, the judiciary and police remain largely ineffective.

Journalists, peasant activists, and lesbian, gay, bisexual, and transgender individuals are among those most vulnerable to violence. Government efforts to investigate and prosecute violence against members of these groups made little progress in 2015.

The Council of the Judiciary has ignored due process guarantees in suspending and dismissing judges, thus increasing their vulnerability to political pressures. In December 2012, Congress arbitrarily dismissed and replaced four Supreme Court judges.

Police Abuse and Corruption

The use of lethal force by the national police is a chronic problem. Investigations into police abuses are marred by inefficiency and corruption; little information about them is made public; and impunity is the rule.

Efforts to address endemic corruption within the police force have made little progress. According to police documents cited by the newspaper *El Heraldo*, some 20 top officers who had been fired for failing confidence tests—including criminal background checks and polygraphs—were in service in mid-2015, as were several officers convicted of criminal activities.

President Juan Orlando Hernández has expanded the military's role in combating violent crime, although military intervention was first announced in November 2011 as a temporary intervention pending reform of the national police. Allegations of human rights abuses by the military have increased notably since then. Military police were accused of involvement in at least nine killings, more than 20 cases of torture, and about 30 illegal arrests between 2012 and 2014, a Reuters investigation found, and at least 24 soldiers were under investigation in connection with the killings.

Judicial Independence

Judges face politically motivated intimidation and interference. In December 2012, Congress voted to remove four of the five justices in the Supreme Court's Constitutional Chamber after the justices ruled that a law aimed at addressing police corruption was unconstitutional. A month after the appointment of four replacements, in January 2013, the new court rejected a legal challenge by the dismissed justices.

In April 2015, at the petition of ruling party legislators, the court struck down a long-standing constitutional prohibition of presidential re-election. The decision will allow President Hernández to run for a second term in 2017 if he chooses to do so. A proposal by former President Manuel Zelaya to call a referendum seeking to revoke the same constitutional prohibition was one of the main reasons the military gave for overthrowing Zelaya in 2009.

The replacement of the four Supreme Court justices was part of a broader pattern of interference. In 2015, lawyers' groups accused the Council of the Judiciary, which has the authority to appoint and dismiss judges, of using the threat of disciplinary action to intimidate judges and influence judicial decisions.

The selection process for the council, which was established by a 2011 constitutional reform, lacked safeguards to protect against political interference, according to the International Commission of Jurists, and irregularities included the exclusion of representatives from one of Honduras's two judicial associations. By December 2014, the Council had fired 29 judges and suspended 28, according to the Inter-American Commission on Human Rights (IACHR), although the basis for disciplinary action and the applicable penalties had yet to be defined by law.

Attacks on Journalists, Lawyers, and Human Rights Defenders

Journalists, legal practitioners, and human rights defenders continue to suffer threats, attacks, and killings. Forty-three journalists were murdered between 2010 and 2014, according to the National Human Rights Commissioner (CONADEH). The IACHR received reports of eight more murders of journalists between January and July 2015. In most cases, authorities fail to investigate and prosecute crimes against journalists. By the end of 2014, only 12 cases had been brought to trial, according to the government.

In February 2015, Carlos Fernández, a news presenter for Channel 27—whose offices are on the island of Roatán—was shot and killed on his way home from work. A candidate in local elections in 2013 and a critic of the 2009 coup, Fernández was a member of the opposition party LIBRE and was reported to have received threats in connection with his reporting.

The IACHR received reports of the killing of 86 legal practitioners and 22 human rights defenders between 2010 and 2014.

In May 2015, the government enacted a law to protect human rights defenders, journalists, and legal practitioners. The law creates a 14-member National Council for the Protection of Human Rights Defenders, with representatives from human rights organizations, press associations, and associations of lawyers, judges, and prosecutors, as well as a "protection system" headed by the Secretariat of Justice, Human Rights, Governance, and Decentralization.

Rural Violence

More than 90 people have been killed in recent years in land disputes in the Bajo Aguán Valley, most of them since 2009, according to a March 2013 report by CONADEH. Scores more have been victims of attacks, threats, abductions, and police brutality.

The land disputes often pit international agro-industrial firms against peasant organizations over the rightful ownership of lands transferred following a 1992 reform to the country's agrarian law. While most victims have been peasants, private security guards have also been killed and wounded.

Honduran authorities have been ineffective at investigating abuses or providing protection for those at risk. A Human Rights Watch investigation in 2013 into 29 cases of homicides and two abductions committed in Bajo Aguán between 2010 and 2012 found that none of the cases had been successfully prosecuted. In April 2014, a special prosecutorial unit was set up to investigate the crimes. The unit's chief prosecutor stated in an August 2015 press interview that it had yet to solve any of them.

Indigenous leaders active on environmental concerns have also suffered violent attacks carried out with impunity. In April 2015, Luis de Reyes Marcía, a member of the Tolupan indigenous community in Locomapa, Yoro–which has opposed local logging and mining activities–was stabbed to death at night in his home. Three other leaders from the same community were shot dead in 2013, and their alleged killers remained at large at time of writing. De Reyes' wife, Dilma Consuelo Soto, was one of 18 community members who received protection measures from the IACHR following the 2013 killings.

Sexual Orientation and Gender Identity

Homophobic violence is a major problem. The IACHR received reports of 174 bias-motivated killings of lesbian, gay, bisexual, transgender, and intersex people from 2009 to 2014. In August 2013, the government set up a special unit in the attorney general's office to investigate and prosecute such killings and those of members of other vulnerable groups. According to official figures, 10 people had been convicted of such crimes by October 2014; 42 cases had been brought to court.

Violence against Children

Children experience high levels of violence, largely perpetrated by armed gangs. Many are recruited into these gangs or are frequently under pressure to join them, according to press reports. Fear of violence drives hundreds of other children every year to leave their homes and head north, often unaccompanied, to Mexico and the United States. A 2014 report by the United Nations Refugee Agency (UNHCR) found that 43 child migrants from Honduras (out of a sample of 98) identified violence by organized armed criminal actors as a motive for leaving their home country. Some migrants who had been deported back to Honduras told Human Rights Watch they were living in hiding and were afraid to go out in public.

Prison Conditions

Inhumane conditions, including overcrowding, inadequate nutrition, and poor sanitation, are systemic in Honduran prisons. Designed to hold up to 8,600 inmates, the country's jails were holding more than 15,000 in February 2015 according to the prison service. Corruption among prison officials is widespread. Prison guards in many facilities have effectively relinquished control and discipline to the inmates, which has led to abuses, extortion, and violent confrontations.

Key International Actors

In May 2014, Honduras's human rights performance was assessed as part of the United Nations Human Rights Council's periodic review process. Honduras agreed to consider a US recommendation that it comprehensively reform its police forces and phase out the involvement of the military in policing duties.

In March 2015, the UN special rapporteur on violence against women, who visited Honduras in July 2014, reported that, despite government reforms, women continued to be discriminated against and subject to violence and sexual and reproductive rights violations.

In June 2015, the Committee on the Rights of the Child published its concluding observations on Honduras's combined fourth and fifth periodic reports. The committee recommended that Honduras strengthen measures to investigate, prosecute, and sanction cases of death and extrajudicial killings of children.

In October 2015, the Inter-American Court of Human Rights found Honduras to have violated the rights of four judges who were dismissed for opposing the 2009 military coup against former President Zelaya. The court ordered the judges reinstated.

In January 2015, in response to an influx of unaccompanied child migrants to the US, President Barack Obama asked the US Congress to approve an unprecedented US$1 billion in aid to Central American countries. Three hundred million dollars of the aid was aimed at improving police efficiency, backing community-led plans to tighten security, and strengthening prosecutorial capacity to deal with violent crime.

In a 2014 report based on interviews with 35 Honduran migrants in detention in the US or recently deported to Honduras, Human Rights Watch found that virtually all were summarily deported. Of those who expressed fears to US Border Patrol officials about returning, fewer than half were referred for a further assessment of whether their fears were "credible" or "reasonable."

India

India, the world's largest democracy, has a strong civil society, vigorous media, and an independent judiciary, but also serious human rights concerns. The government did little in 2015 to implement promises by newly elected Prime Minister Narendra Modi to improve respect for religious freedom, protect the rights of women and children, and end abuses against marginalized communities.

Even as the prime minister celebrated Indian democracy abroad, back home civil society groups faced increased harassment and government critics faced intimidation and lawsuits. Officials warned media against making what they called unsubstantiated allegations against the government, saying it weakened democracy. In several cases, courts reprimanded the government for restricting free expression.

Religious minorities, especially Muslims and Christians, accused the authorities of not doing enough to protect their rights. Some leaders of the ruling Bharatiya Janata Party (BJP) made inflammatory remarks against minorities and right-wing Hindu fringe groups threatened and harassed them, in some cases even attacking them.

There was encouraging progress on security force accountability in 2015, with the army confirming life imprisonment for six soldiers for a 2010 extrajudicial killing of three villagers in the Machil sector in Jammu and Kashmir states. The rare guilty verdict was delivered by a military court in November 2014 and was confirmed in September 2015.

However, the government failed to repeal laws that provide public officials and security forces immunity from prosecution for abuses without prior authorization. Lack of progress in implementing long-overdue police reforms showed the unwillingness among public officials to make the force more accountable and free from political interference.

Dalit rights groups welcomed progress toward enactment of the Scheduled Castes and Scheduled Tribes (Prevention of Atrocities) Amendment Bill; if passed, the bill will strengthen protections for Dalit and tribal communities, and make it easier for them to pursue justice.

Treatment of Minorities

Four Muslim men were killed by Hindu vigilante groups in separate incidents across the country in 2015 over suspicions that they had killed or stolen cows for beef. The violence took place amid an aggressive push by several BJP leaders and right-wing Hindu groups to protect cows, considered sacred by many Hindus, and for a ban on beef consumption.

Churches were also attacked in several states in 2015, prompting fears of growing Hindu nationalist militancy under the BJP government. Anti-Muslim rhetoric by several BJP leaders, including members of parliament, further stoked insecurities among religious minorities.

The authorities did not press robustly for prosecution of those responsible for violent attacks on minorities, and impunity for the assailants contributed to a sense of government indifference to growing religious intolerance.

Dozens of writers protested against sectarianism and the silencing of dissent by returning prestigious literary awards bestowed by the Sahitya Akademi, India's National Academy of Letters. Artists, academics, filmmakers, and scientists also added their voices to the protest. Economists and business leaders warned that the Modi government risked losing domestic and global credibility if it failed to control Hindu extremism and restrictions on freedom of expression.

A Delhi court in March acquitted all 16 policemen accused in the 1987 killing of over 40 Muslims during communal riots in Uttar Pradesh state, citing lack of evidence. The verdict exposed the inability, or unwillingness, of investigators to secure evidence for proper prosecution of such crimes.

The government failed to implement policies to protect Dalits and tribal groups from discrimination and violence. New revelations by an investigative news website on 6 major incidents of violence against the Dalit community in the 1990s in Bihar state—in which at least 144 people were killed by an upper-caste militia— once again triggered dismay over the difficulty marginalized communities face in obtaining justice.

Several commanders of the militia group admitted their complicity in the killings on camera and also implicated senior political leaders, even as courts acquitted nearly all of them due to lack of evidence, highlighting the failure of the prosecutorial authorities. Lack of protection for witnesses, who often refuse to testify or turn hostile because of threats and harassment from powerful perpetrators, remains a serious problem.

Impunity

In May, the northeastern state of Tripura revoked the draconian Armed Forces Special Powers Act (AFSPA), citing a decline in insurgency. However, it remains in force in Jammu and Kashmir and in other northeastern states. AFSPA has been widely criticized by rights groups and numerous independent commissions have recommended repealing or amending the law, but the government has not done so in the face of stiff army opposition.

A May report by the United Nations special rapporteur on extrajudicial, summary, or arbitrary executions noted that "impunity remains a serious problem" and expressed regret that India had not repealed or at least radically amended AFSPA.

Proposed police reforms again stalled in 2015 even as police committed serious violations including arbitrary arrests, torture, and extrajudicial "encounter" killings. In April, police killed 20 men in the forests of Andhra Pradesh, alleging they were smugglers and claiming they fired in self-defense. On the same day, five terrorism suspects in Telangana state were killed in custody as they were being transported from jail for a court hearing. Investigations are pending in both cases; rights groups say there is evidence that police staged both sets of killings.

In 2014 and 2015, several police officials were reinstated in Gujarat despite having been implicated in the alleged 2004 "encounter" killing of 19-year-old Ishrat Jahan and three others, raising concerns about the government's commitment to police accountability.

Women's Rights

Violence against women, particularly rape and murder, made headlines throughout 2015. While legal reforms introduced in response to the 2012 Delhi gang rape and murder gave prosecutors new tools for pursuing such crimes, they also expanded use of the death penalty. The Indian government does not appear to have a mechanism in place to track the efficacy of the reforms in preventing and punishing sexual violence. It has also failed to take effective measures to reduce sexual harassment and improve women's access to safe transportation.

In August, village leaders in Uttar Pradesh state allegedly ordered the rape of two Dalit sisters to pay for the "sins" of their brother who had eloped with a higher-caste woman. These unofficial village councils, called *Khaps*, made up of men from dominant castes who often enjoy political patronage, are known to issue edicts restricting women's mobility and rights, and condemning couples for marrying outside their caste or religion.

Children's Rights

In May, the lower house of parliament passed amendments to the Juvenile Justice Act to permit prosecution of 16 and 17-year-olds in adult court when charged with serious crimes such as rape and murder. A parliamentary standing committee, children's rights activists, and the National Commission for Protection of Child Rights all strongly oppose the amendments.

In May, the cabinet cleared amendments to the prohibition of child labor law. If passed by parliament, they would prohibit most employment of children under 14, but would permit them to work in family enterprises after school hours. This amendment, in the absence of effective implementation of the right to education law, could actually push more children into child labor.

Government statistics show that two out of five children drop out of school before completing eighth grade. The numbers are even higher for children from poor and marginalized communities because of discrimination based on caste, religion, and ethnicity. Those who drop out often end up being subjected to child labor and early marriage.

Sexual Orientation and Gender Identity

LGBT individuals continue to face harassment, extortion, intimidation, and abuse, including by the police. In December 2013, the Supreme Court upheld the constitutionality of section 377 of the Indian penal code, which criminalizes same-sex conduct between consenting adults. An appeal was pending at time of writing.

The upper house of parliament approved a proposed law in April that, if enacted, would protect the rights of transgender people. In 2014, the Supreme Court mandated legal recognition of transgender people as a third gender and ruled them eligible for special education and employment benefits.

Disability Rights

The Mental Health Care Bill and Rights of Persons with Disabilities Bill, both pending in parliament at time of writing, would advance the rights of people with disabilities, though still fall short of international standards. Further steps are needed to fully protect the rights of such individuals. In early 2015, the Indian government initiated it's first-ever survey on the condition of women living in mental health institutions across the country.

Restrictions on Free Speech

In a big win for online expression, in March the Supreme Court struck down section 66A of the Information Technology Act, which criminalized a broad range of speech and had been used by authorities to pursue critics of the government.

In several cases, interest groups that claimed to be offended by books, movies, or works of art pushed for censorship or harassed authors. The government often allowed them a "heckler's veto" rather than protecting those under attack. In January, a Tamil author decided to give up his writing career after being coerced by state authorities to tender an unconditional apology to calm down angry mobs unhappy with one of his books.

Overbroad and vaguely worded sedition, criminal defamation, and hate speech laws were used to harass and prosecute those expressing dissenting, unpopular, or minority views. In October, authorities in Tamil Nadu state arrested a folk singer under the sedition law for two songs that criticized the state government. The same month, Gujarat police arrested Hardik Patel, who is spearheading protests to demand quotas in education and government jobs for his community, and charged him with sedition in two separate cases.

Civil Society and Freedom of Association

Authorities in 2015 intensified their crackdown on civil society by using the Foreign Contribution Regulation Act (FCRA), a law regulating grants from foreign donors, to harass organizations that questioned or criticized government policies. The government cut off funds to organizations, including Greenpeace India, and put restrictions on others, including the Ford Foundation.

Authorities labeled activists "anti-national" when they questioned government infrastructure and development projects or sought justice for victims of the 2002 communal riots in Gujarat. Such tactics had a chilling effect on the work of other groups. The government's nationalist rhetoric was echoed by conservative media, creating an increasingly hostile environment for human rights groups.

In January, the government barred Priya Pillai, a Greenpeace India activist, from boarding a flight to London where she was to speak to members of the British Parliament, alleging that her testimony would have portrayed the government in a negative light abroad at a time when it was looking to attract foreign investment. In March, the Delhi High Court ruled that authorities had violated Pillai's rights to travel and to freedom of expression. In November, authorities in Tamil Nadu state, where Greenpeace India's registered office is located, cancelled the organization's registration.

Indian authorities also targeted activist Teesta Setalvad and her husband, Javed Anand, in what appeared to be acts of politically motivated intimidation, accusing them of violating the FCRA and receiving funds illegally, among other allegations. In September, the government suspended the registration of their organization, the Sabrang Trust, under the FCRA, and moved to cancel the license. Setalvad is well-known for her work supporting victims of the 2002 Gujarat riots and for seeking criminal charges against scores of officials, including Prime Minister Modi for his alleged involvement in the riots as the state's then chief minister.

Death Penalty

On July 30, 2015, India executed Yakub Memon for his involvement in a series of bombings in Mumbai in 1993 that caused over 350 deaths. Memon's execution sparked a debate in India over the merits of retaining the death penalty. Memon was the third person to be hanged since the government lifted an unofficial moratorium on capital punishment in 2012.

In August, the Law Commission submitted a report calling for abolition of the death penalty for all but terrorism-related offenses and "waging war" against the state.

Palliative Care

Millions of Indians with life-limiting illnesses continue to suffer needlessly from pain and other treatable symptoms. Amendments to the Narcotic Drugs and Psychotropic Substances Act adopted in February 2014 were expected to help improve access to opioid analgesics for patients suffering from severe pain, but it took until May 2015 for the government to issue partial implementation rules; without adequate guidance, implementation of the amendments had still not begun at time of writing.

India's Foreign Policy

Acknowledging expectations that India play a more prominent leadership role in global affairs, Prime Minister Modi urged diplomats to "shed old mindsets" and act proactively on issues such as climate change and threats to global peace.

Despite its democratic traditions, however, India has not yet emerged as an effective proponent of human rights. For instance, in October, when India invited all 54 leaders of the African Union to a summit in New Delhi, it ignored calls by the International Criminal Court (ICC) to arrest Sudan's president, Omar Hassan al-Bashir, who faces charges of war crimes and genocide in Darfur.

India responded swiftly to provide aid and relief to Nepal after a series of deadly earthquakes there killed over 9,000 people. But relations between the neighbors soured after India criticized Nepal's new federal constitution, which failed to address the concerns of ethnic communities living along the border with India.

In June, Modi visited Bangladesh where he signed several agreements, including a border agreement that allowed the two countries to exchange small land enclaves that had left the people living there effectively stateless. India also met with Sri Lankan officials to promote post-conflict reconciliation and justice.

In visits to China in May and Russia in July, Modi discussed trade agreements but failed to speak publicly on human rights concerns. However, during an August trip to the UAE, Modi visited a labor camp in Abu Dhabi, indicating concern about the welfare of migrant workers in the Gulf.

Relations with Pakistan deteriorated after scheduled talks broke down in mid-2015, prompting UN Secretary-General Ban Ki-moon to call for a direct dialogue between the neighbors to de-escalate tensions.

India was a weak proponent of human rights at the UN in 2015. In March, India voted in support of a Russian-backed resolution to remove benefits for same-sex partners of UN staff. India abstained on Human Rights Council resolutions on Syria, North Korea, and Ukraine, and voted against resolutions on Iran and Belarus.

In July, India abstained on a UN Human Rights Council resolution that called for Israeli accountability in the 2014 Gaza War. The Indian government said it had abstained from voting because the resolution included a reference to bringing Israel before the ICC, which India considered "intrusive."

Key International Actors

Several world leaders visited India in 2015, or hosted the prime minster in their capitals, evincing renewed global interest in trade and investment. Few foreign officials showed any willingness to raise human rights concerns publicly, deferring all too readily to India's sensitivity to perceived intervention in its domestic affairs.

However, at a speech in New Delhi, US President Barack Obama sent a strong message warning of the dangers of religious intolerance and urging the government to uphold religious freedom. In May, the US ambassador to India expressed concerns over the challenges faced by civil society organizations in the country and the "potentially chilling effects" of the "regulatory steps focused on NGOs."

Indonesia

President Joko Widodo's record during his first year in office was mixed. His administration signaled it would more actively defend the rights of Indonesia's beleaguered religious minorities, victimized by both Islamist militants and discriminatory laws, but made few concrete policy changes. He granted clemency in May to five of Papua's political prisoners and released another one in October, but at time of writing had not freed the approximately 70 Papuans and 29 Ambonese still imprisoned for peaceful advocacy of independence.

In May, the president—commonly referred to as Jokowi—announced the lifting of decades-old restrictions on foreign media access to Papua but then did not follow through, allowing senior government officials to effectively defy the new policy without consequences. In August, Jokowi announced that the government would form a "reconciliation commission" to address gross human rights abuses of the past 50 years, but left out the details.

Jokowi's outspoken support for the death penalty and his decision to make execution of convicted drug traffickers a symbol of his resolve reflected serious backsliding on his reform agenda. Indonesia executed 14 convicted drug traffickers in 2015, including a Brazilian who reportedly had severe mental disabilities, in the face of intense international criticism. Under Jokowi's predecessor Susilo Bambang Yudhoyono, Indonesia had executed only 20 people in 10 years.

Indonesia's two largest Muslim organizations, the Nahdlatul Ulama and Muhammadiyah, declared their commitment to promote human rights, campaign against violence committed in the name of Islam, and dampen Sunni-Shia sectarian divisions.

Starting in August and continuing through November, thick haze from fires set during annual forest clearing produced an environmental and health crisis in Sumatra, Kalimantan, Singapore, and Malaysia. In response, the National Police arrested seven plantation executives, including one from Singapore-based Asia Pulp and Paper, and fined dozens of other palm oil companies.

Religious Freedom

There were 194 incidents of violent attacks on religious minorities in the first 11 months of 2015, according to the Setara Institute, a nongovernmental organization that tracks religious intolerance. That number equals the total for all of 2014, demonstrating that religious violence remains a serious problem.

Minister of Religious Affairs Lukman Saifuddin took steps in 2015 to more actively counter harassment of religious minorities, a welcome change after a decade of passivity and at times complicity by officials. In January 2015, Saifuddin took to Twitter to defend an academic in Aceh province who had been falsely accused of committing blasphemy on campus. In August, Saifuddin announced that his ministry was drafting a bill to ensure religious freedom for all Indonesians, "including those outside the six main religions of Islam, Catholicism, Protestantism, Hinduism, Buddhism and Confucianism."

On June 15, after the Aceh Ulama Council declared the Gerakan Fajar Nusantara sect to be "heretical," the Banda Aceh district court convicted the sect's leader and five members of blasphemy, sentencing them to prison terms of three to four years. In October, local authorities in Singkil regency, Aceh, forced Christians to close 10 churches after Muslim militants burned down one church. A Muslim was shot to death in a clash outside one of the churches.

Also in June, the Constitutional Court rejected a petition to allow inter-religious marriage, ruling that the 1974 Marriage Law was valid because it legalized marriage "in accordance with the respective religious beliefs of the bride and groom."

On July 8, the South Jakarta district administration ordered the closure of an Ahmadiyah mosque in Bukit Duri in response to pressure from Sunni militants. That same month, three churches were forced to close in Bandar Lampung, Yogyakarta, and Samarinda.

On July 17, ethnic Papuan Christian militants demanded that a mosque in Tolikara district, Papua, not use a loudspeaker to broadcast its Idul Fitri prayer, burning down the mosque and dozens of nearby food stalls when mosque authorities refused to heed their demand. Security officers fired at the protesters, killing one and wounding 11 others.

On September 2, the Islamic People's Forum (Forum Umat Islam), a militant group connected to the Indonesian Ulama Council, declared that Sapta Darma traditional faith believers in Rembang, Central Java, were "blasphemers" and forced them to stop renovations to their temple. Police and government officials refused to intervene and instead persuaded the Sapta Darma to delay the renovations for an unspecified period of time.

Women's and Girls' Rights

Indonesia's official Commission on Violence against Women reported that as of October, national and local governments had passed 31 new discriminatory regulations in 2015, leaving Indonesia with 322 discriminatory local regulations targeting women.

The Indonesian armed forces and police require female applicants to undergo abusive, discriminatory, and unscientific "virginity tests." After Human Rights Watch research put a spotlight on the issue in 2015, some officials criticized continued use of the tests but did not ban them. "We need to examine the mentality of these [female] applicants. If they are no longer virgins, if they are naughty, it means their mentality is not good," said Indonesian military spokesman Maj. Gen. Fuad Basya.

In July, the Ministry of Defense issued a regulation allowing male employees to take second wives if their first wives are unable to bear children. The regulation forbids female personnel from practicing polygamy. The United Nations Human Rights Committee has emphasized that "polygamy violates the dignity of women," constitutes "inadmissible discrimination against women," and "should be definitely abolished wherever it continues to exist."

In June, the Constitutional Court rejected a petition to increase the minimum age of marriage for girls from 16 to 18. Only one judge, the sole woman on the nine-member panel, dissented. The Convention on the Rights of the Child, which Indonesia ratified in 1990, defines a child as anyone under age 18, and the CRC Committee has determined that 18 should be the minimum age for marriage regardless of parental consent.

Papua

The Jokowi government has sought to take a new approach to the provinces of Papua and West Papua ("Papua"), home to a low-level insurgency and a larger peaceful pro-independence movement. On May 9, Jokowi visited the Abepura prison and released five political prisoners, promising to release other Papuans imprisoned for political crimes in consultation with the parliament. There were at least 45 political prisoners in Papua at the end of September, according to the monitoring group "Papuans Behind Bars." Papua's most famous political prisoner, Filep Karma, was released in October.

Meanwhile, suppression of the rights to freedom of expression and association in Papua continued. On May 20-22, police detained dozens of activists of the West Papua National Committee, a pro-independence group, during peaceful rallies in the cities of Jayapura, Manokwari, and Merauke. Police subsequently arrested four of those activists—Alexander Nekenem, Yoram Magai, Mikael Aso, dan Narko Murib—on charges of "public incitement." In November, they were sentenced to one-and-a-half year jail terms.

New incidents of security force violence also continue to be reported. Two allegedly drunken soldiers opened fire on a crowd in Koperapoka, Mimika regency, on August 27, killing two people and wounding two others. In December 2014, security forces allegedly shot and killed five peaceful protesters in the town of Enarotali; a year later, the government had still not released the results of official investigations into the shootings or arrested any suspects.

On May 10, President Jokowi announced the lifting of restrictions on foreign media access to Papua. A month later, the Foreign Ministry announced the abolition of the "Clearing House" that had screened Papua access applications of foreigners for decades. But numerous senior government and security forces officials balked and openly resisted the change. In August, the Ministry of Home Affairs unveiled a new regulation that would have imposed onerous new reporting restrictions on foreign media nationwide. Jokowi ordered its cancellation the next day. However, the National Police still require accredited foreign journalists to apply for a travel permit to visit Papua, and the Ministry of Foreign Affairs also still requires such journalists "to notify" the ministry of their schedules and activities in Papua.

Military Reform and Impunity

In June, the government announced it would establish a "reconciliation commission" to seek a "permanent solution for all unresolved human rights abuses," including the 1965 anti-communist massacres that killed an estimated one million people and numerous other gross human rights violations since that time.

The government did not provide details about how the commission would work, apart from saying it would not conduct investigations into specific abuses but focus on creating a "settlement mechanism" for victims and their survivors. As such, it appeared highly unlikely it would include powers to pursue criminal accountability for the most responsible senior officials, despite continuing demands for justice from victims.

In August Brig. Gen. Hartomo was promoted to become governor of the Military Academy in Magelang. In 2003, Hartomo, then Special Forces commander in Papua, was tried and convicted by a military tribunal for his involvement in the killing of Papuan leader Theys Eluay.

Disability Rights

Tens of thousands of Indonesians with psychosocial disabilities spend their lives chained or locked up in homes or institutions instead of receiving community-based mental health care. The government passed a new mental health law in 2014 to address Indonesia's dire mental health care situation but has yet to implement it.

The Rights of Persons with Disabilities Bill, pending in the Indonesian parliament at time of writing, was expected to pass in 2016. While the bill represents a major advancement, activists say it does not fully comply with the Convention on the Rights of Persons with Disabilities, which Indonesia ratified in 2011.

Refugees and Asylum Seekers

In May, the government acceded to international pressure and began rescuing boatloads of ethnic Rohingya from Burma and Bangladesh stranded at sea for weeks on poorly provisioned, unseaworthy vessels. Although Indonesia agreed to bring rescued asylum seekers and migrants ashore, it said that they would only be sheltered temporarily and would need to be resettled to third countries after a year.

As of August, there were 13,110 refugees and asylum seekers in Indonesia, all living in legal limbo because Indonesia is not a party to the Refugee Convention and lacks an asylum law. This included 1,095 children detained in immigration centers, of which 461 were unaccompanied minors.

Key International Actors

The United States, an important trade partner, continued to seek closer military ties with Indonesia. President Jokowi made his first state visit to the US in October, but it was cut short because of the Asian haze crisis, and neither side publicly addressed human rights issues. Jokowi focused largely on attracting US-based companies to invest more in Indonesia. In April, the US Commission on International Religious Freedom again placed Indonesia in Tier 2, the second worst category, where it has been since 2003.

In June, the Melanesian Spearhead Group, a regional organization largely made up of southern Pacific island nations, gave observer status to the United Liberation Movement for West Papua, the umbrella organization of pro-independence Papuans.

Brazil and the Netherlands recalled their ambassadors after Indonesia executed citizens of the two countries on January 18 for drug crimes. Australia similarly recalled its ambassador after Indonesia executed two Australians, Andrew Chan and Myuran Sukumaran, on April 29.

Iran

Repressive elements within the security and intelligence forces, as well as the judiciary, retained wide powers and continued to be the main perpetrators of rights abuses. Executions, especially for drug-related offenses, increased sharply from previous years. Security and intelligence forces arrested journalists, bloggers, and social media activists, and revolutionary courts handed down heavy sentences against them.

Death Penalty and Torture

Authorities executed at least 830 prisoners by hanging as of November 1, 2015, with almost 700 executed in the first six months of the year. Officials also carried out amputations of limbs for crimes such as theft.

Under Iranian law, many crimes are punishable by death, including some that do not involve violence, such as "insulting the Prophet," apostasy, same-sex relations, adultery, and drug-related offenses. Convicted drug offenders sentenced after flawed trials in revolutionary courts formed the majority of prisoners executed in 2015.

On August 1, a revolutionary court in Tehran sentenced Mohammad Ali Taheri, the leader of a new age spiritual and healing group, to death on the charge of "spreading corruption on earth." The judiciary had previously sentenced him in 2011 to five years' imprisonment, 74 lashes, and fines for the same activities.

According to unofficial sources, at least four prisoners executed in 2015 may have been child offenders aged under 18 at the time of the murder and rape crimes for which they received death sentences. Dozens of child offenders reportedly remained on death row and at risk of execution, including Saman Naseem and Salar Shadizadi. Iranian law allows capital punishment for persons who have reached the official age of puberty: nine for girls, 15 for boys.

Alleging ties to armed opposition groups, the revolutionary courts have also handed out death sentences on charges of moharebeh ("enmity against God"). Dozens of others sentenced on terrorism-related charges, including many Iranian Kurds and Baluch, were on death row following trials rife with due process violations. On March 4, prison authorities in Rajai Shahr Prison in Karaj hanged

Hamed Ahmadi and five others. A revolutionary court had sentenced all six to death for moharebeh following unfair trials.

On August 26, officials executed Behrouz Alkhani, an Iranian Kurd that a revolutionary court had convicted of moharebeh for his alleged involvement in the assassination of a prosecutor on behalf of the PJAK armed opposition group. The Supreme Court still had to rule on Alkhani's appeal at the time of his execution.

Freedom of Expression and Information

Security authorities continued to clamp down on free speech and dissent, and revolutionary courts handed down harsh sentences against social media users, including death sentences in some cases. As of December, according to Reporters Without Borders, Iran held at least 50 journalists, bloggers, and social media activists in detention.

In April, an appeals court in Tehran sentenced six social media users to five to seven years in prison for their Facebook posts on charges of "assembly and collusion against the national security" and "insulting the sanctities." On July 13, 2014, a Tehran revolutionary court had previously sentenced eight Facebook users to a total of 127 years in prison for allegedly posting messages deemed to insult government officials and "religious sanctities," among other crimes.

On June 1, another revolutionary court sentenced Atena Farghadani to a total of 12 years and 9 months' imprisonment in connection with a critical cartoon she drew and posted on her Facebook page in August 2014 that depicted members of Iran's parliament as animals. The charges against Farghadani included "assembly and collusion against the state," "propaganda against the state," and insulting public officials. Although by law she should serve no more than seven-and-a-half years, the heaviest single sentence she received, the judiciary compounded her sentence.

On June 8, authorities announced a wave of arrests of social media users and activists who "published illegal invitations on social networks … [and] had anti-security tendencies."

On October 11, 2015, a judiciary spokesman announced Washington Post reporter Jason Rezaian's conviction. As of December, court authorities had refused to provide clarification about the specific charges for which he was convicted or the details of his sentence. The sentence came after unidentified agents arrested Rezaian, his wife Yeganeh Salehi—also a journalist—and two unnamed people—a photojournalist and her spouse—on July 22, 2014, and detained them without charge for months without allowing them access to a lawyer. Authorities released Salehi in September 2014.

Authorities continued to block websites, including Facebook and Twitter, based on arbitrary and unlawful content-based criteria.

Freedom of Assembly and Association

Scores of people held for their affiliation with banned opposition parties, labor unions, and student groups were in prison. The judiciary targeted independent and unregistered trade unions, and security and intelligence forces continued to round up labor activists and leaders.

Police arrested independent labor activist Reza Amjadi in the Kurdish-majority city of Sanandaj on April 25, Mahmoud Salehi and Osman Esmaili in Saqqez on April 28, and two members of the Union of Workers of the Tehran and Suburbs Bus Company, Ebrahim Maddadi and Davood Razavi, in their homes on April 29.

On July 22, authorities arrested approximately 130 teachers who planned a demonstration in front of the parliament building in Tehran to protest the recent arrest of Esmaeil Abdi, the head of a teacher's guild, who was arrested for his peaceful activities on June 27. They later released all the teachers without charge.

Political Prisoners and Human Rights Defenders

The authorities continued to imprison dozens of activists and human rights defenders, such as lawyers Mohammad Seifzadeh and Abdolfattah Soltani, on account of their peaceful or professional activities. Judiciary officials continued their efforts to further erode the independence of the Iranian Bar Association and restricted the right of criminal defendants to access a lawyer of their own choosing during the investigation phase of national security cases.

On May 5, authorities arrested Narges Mohammadi, a member of the banned Center for Human Rights Defenders, reportedly because of her continued peaceful activism against the state. In 2010, a revolutionary court sentenced Mohammadi to six years in prison for her rights-related activities, but authorities released her due to a serious medical condition that she still suffers.

On May 10, a revolutionary court informed Atena Daemi, a child and civil rights activist, that it had sentenced her to 14 years in prison on charges that included "assembly, collusion and propaganda against the state" and "insulting the Supreme Leader and religious sanctities" for her peaceful activism.

On August 19, a court acquitted former Tehran Prosecutor Saeed Mortazavi of charges related to the torture and death of three protesters held at Kahrizak detention facility following their arrest during the 2009 post-election protests. Mortazavi has so far escaped criminal punishment despite allegations implicating him in a range of serious rights abuses during his time in public office.

Prominent opposition figures Mir Hossein Mousavi, Zahra Rahnavard, and Mehdi Karroubi—held without charge or trial since February 2011—remained under house arrest.

Women's Rights

In 2015, authorities sought to introduce or implement discriminatory laws, including restricting the employment of women in certain sectors and limiting access to family planning as part of official measures to boost Iran's population. On April 22, the Guardian Council, an unelected body of 12 religious jurists, approved a controversial bill that empowers voluntary Basij paramilitary forces to "promote virtue and prevent vice," including enforcement of the strict Islamic dress code, or hijab, for women. If passed, the bill would empower individuals to act outside of any official capacity and without any parameters for holding them legally accountable.

In August, Iran's judiciary prevented the release from prison of women's rights activist Bahareh Hedayat although an appellate court had ordered it. A revolutionary court sentenced Hedayat to seven-and-a-half years in prison in January 2010 for her peaceful activism on charges of "acting against the national security" and insulting public officials.

Iranian women face discrimination in many aspects of their lives, including personal status matters related to marriage, divorce, inheritance, and child custody.

Authorities prevent girls and women from attending certain sporting events, including men's soccer and volleyball matches.

Regardless of her age, a woman cannot marry without the approval of her male guardian, and generally cannot pass on her Iranian nationality to a foreign-born spouse or to her children. Child marriage—though not the norm—continues, as the law allows girls to marry at 13 and boys at age 15, as well as at younger ages if authorized by a judge.

Treatment of Minorities

The government denies freedom of religion to Baha'is, Iran's largest non-Muslim religious minority, and discriminates against them. At least 74 Baha'is were held in Iran's prisons as of November 20, 2015. Security and intelligence forces also continued to target Christian converts from Islam, Persian-speaking Protestant and evangelical congregations, and members of the home church movement. Some faced charges such as "acting against the national security" and "propaganda against the state."

Authorities restrict political participation and public sector employment of non-Shia Muslim minorities, including Sunnis, who account for about 10 percent of the population. They also prevent Sunnis from constructing their own mosques in Tehran and conducting separate Eid prayers.

On July 29, municipal employees destroyed a Sunni prayer hall located in the Pounak district of Tehran that they alleged was functioning without the required permits. The government continued to target members of Sufi mystical orders, particularly members of the Nematollahi Gonabadi order.

The government restricted cultural as well as political activities among the country's Azeri, Kurdish, Arab, and Baluch minorities. In April, police and security agents rounded up and detained scores of Ahwazi Arabs, including several children, in Khuzestan province. In July, the University of Kurdistan announced it had opened a new department of Kurdish language and literature studies that would accept students for the 2015-16 academic year.

Sexual Orientation and Gender Identity

Same-sex conduct between men in Iran is punishable by flogging or the death penalty. Same-sex conduct between women is punishable by flogging. Lesbian, gay, bisexual and transgender people are subjected to official harassment, arbitrary arrest and detention, prosecution, and ill-treatment or torture. Although Iran permits and subsidizes sex reassignment surgery for transgender people, no law prohibits discrimination against them.

Refugees

Afghan refugees and migrant workers, estimated at between 2.5 and 3 million in number, continued to face serious abuses. Authorities reportedly allowed Afghan children, including undocumented ones, to register for schools after Supreme Leader Ali Khamenei issued a ruling reaffirming the need for universal education.

However, Afghans continue to face barriers to receiving other forms of social services; are at higher risk for arbitrarily being stopped, questioned, and/or detained by authorities; and have little recourse when abused by government or private actors.

Key International Actors

On July 14, the United Nations Security Council's five permanent members, along with Germany and Iran, announced that they had reached a comprehensive agreement to monitor Iran's nuclear program. The deal paves the way for gradually removing financial and economic sanctions against Iran. On July 28, during EU Foreign Affairs Chief Mogherini's visit to Tehran, Iran's foreign minister said Iran and the European Union had agreed to hold talks "over different issues, including ... human rights."

The government continued to block access to Iran by the UN special rapporteur on the human rights situation in Iran, Ahmed Shaheed, and other UN rights experts.

Iraq

Armed conflict between the armed extremist group Islamic State (also known as ISIS) and an array of Kurdish and central Iraqi government forces, pro-government militias, and a United States-led international air campaign dominated the human rights situation in 2015.

According to the United Nations, summary executions, car bombs, assassinations, artillery shelling, and aerial bombardment killed and injured over 20,000 civilians. Pro-government militias carried out assassinations, property destruction, and enforced disappearances. Since June 2014, the conflict has displaced close to 3.2 million Iraqis, and interrupted school for over 3 million children as well as access to medical care, food, and clean water.

Government forces recaptured the area around Tikrit in March and Beiji in October, and Kurdish forces took Sinjar in November, while ISIS took Ramadi on May 17. Ongoing battles for Ramadi, areas north of Tikrit, and in Diyala, Kirkuk, and Niniveh continue to inflict heavy casualties on both sides.

Islamic State Abuses

ISIS claimed responsibility for two devastating bombings that killed over 115 people in Khan Bani Saad, north of Baghdad, on July 17, and 67 people at Jamila Market in Baghdad's Sadr City, on August 13.

Iraqi media reported ISIS agents killing of thousands of people, sometimes in staged summary executions. On August 7, the forensic medicine department in Mosul said ISIS requested death certificates for 2,070 persons executed in Nineveh province since June 2014. Victims included candidates or elected members of local or national bodies, police, and military. Those executed included scores of former security officers, tribal leaders, and others who refused to pledge allegiance to ISIS, or whom the group suspected of cooperating with the Iraqi government.

On July 1, ISIS reportedly executed 22 members of the Jubur tribe in Badush, north of Mosul.

HUMAN
RIGHTS
WATCH

AFTER LIBERATION
CAME DESTRUCTION
Iraqi Militias and the Aftermath of Amerli

The reported execution of ISIS' own fighters also increased in 2015. On May 10, ISIS reportedly executed 20 of its Kurdish fighters in Sinjar and Tell Afar, and on July 10, 40 of its fighters in Hawija for weakness in battle.

ISIS also executed persons for allegedly violating what it claimed were crimes against Islamic law, including persons for alleged homosexuality, adultery, "insulting" God, and sorcery. ISIS repeatedly executed men accused of homosexual conduct, although Iraqi law does not criminalize homosexual conduct.

ISIS often executed persons by extremely cruel and painful methods such as burning, drowning, electrocution, and stoning.

In 2015, ISIS recruited children for suicide missions and to carry out executions. In June, Anbar Provincial Council Member Farhan Muhammad told reporters ISIS had abducted 400 children for military training.

Abuses by Pro-Government Forces

Mostly Shia militias fighting ISIS, such as Badr Brigades, League of the Righteous, or Imam Ali Battalions, carried out widespread and systematic violations of human rights and international humanitarian law, in particular, demolishing homes and shops in recaptured Sunni areas.

Militia fighters as well as Iraqi security forces in late August 2014 succeeded in driving ISIS fighters from the Shia Turkmen and Sunni Arab town of Amerli and subsequently raided several dozen neighboring Sunni villages driven by revenge and expelled Sunni Iraqis to alter the area's demographic. Kurdish Peshmerga fighters told Human Rights Watch of 47 villages that Shia forces methodically destroyed. Raids included looting, burning, and demolition by explosives, as well as the abduction of at least 11 local men.

After recapturing Tikrit in March 2015, militia forces torched and blew up hundreds of buildings and destroyed large sections of neighboring al-Dur, al-Bu 'Ajil, and southern al-Alam. Militias also forcibly disappeared some 200 men and boys.

Peshmerga forces of the Kurdistan Regional Government (KRG) also carried out, or failed to prevent, destruction of Arab homes and looting of shops in areas recaptured from ISIS. Witnesses implicated Peshmerga forces in the wholescale destruction of the village of Barzan, in Zumar district, in September 2014, as well as in nearby Bardiya town, where KRG forces, at a minimum, allowed Kurdish civilians to raze Arab houses.

Displacement and Movement Restrictions

The central government and KRG, militias, and ISIS on different occasions barred people from fleeing to safer areas. Following ISIS' capture of Ramadi on May 17, government security forces blocked many of the over 100,000 fleeing residents from crossing into Baghdad province without a local guarantor.

KRG authorities required fleeing Arab Iraqis to have local Kurdish guarantors to enter Kirkuk province, and, from there, Sulaimaniya, Erbil, or Dohuk provinces. In late 2014, KRG authorities required Arab Iraqis to obtain renewable residency permits and issued temporary permits for travel between Kurdistan's provinces.

Peshmerga and Asayish forces barred some Arab residents from returning to their villages and towns after they had cleared the area of ISIS. In some areas, such as Rabi'a in Nineveh, returnees required permits.

ISIS tightened its grip on Fallujah and Mosul and prohibited anyone from leaving. Some managed to leave, citing medical reasons and paying bribes of up to tens of thousands of US dollars, or leaving family behind who faced execution if the person failed to return.

Freedom of Assembly and Expression

ISIS executed over one dozen journalists, including Firas al-Bahar on May 19, Jasim al-Jubur, on May 20, and Suha Radhi on July 7, all in Mosul, the Iraqi Observatory for Press Rights said. In late May, ISIS named five "mercenary so-called journalists led astray," threatening their lives. In August, ISIS forces tied dozens of Rutba residents to light poles for several days as punishment for publicly protesting the execution of a fellow tribesman, several Iraqi media outlets reported.

KRG authorities arrested and prosecuted critics. On February 2, Asayish security forces detained and charged Sabah al-Atrushi with terrorism over public comments critical of senior Peshmerga commanders. On August 4, intelligence agents of the ruling Kurdistan Democratic Party arrested Esa Barzani over pictures on Facebook supporting Kurdish leaders rivaling KRG President Masoud

Barzani. On October, KDP authorities shut down NRT and Kurdish News Network, two opposition TV stations, and banned Muhammad Yusif Sadiq, the speaker of parliament from the opposition Change Movement, from Erbil, the seat of parliament.

Iraqis who publicly criticized officials and corruption faced threats and prosecution. In June, the Publication and Media Court awarded Ala' Rasul Muhi al-Din, inspector-general of the Electricity Ministry, 3 million Iraqi dinars (US$2,696) for "defamation" by Ibrahim Zaidan, a journalist, after he questioned the inspectorate's integrity. On July 25, Ala' al-Subaihawi, a correspondent for Sumeria Satellite TV, faced charges of "spreading false news" for reporting that Maysan's police chief had resigned. On August 20, 2015, Najaf Deputy Governor Tala Bilal physically attacked Dhiya' al-Gharifi, editor-in-chief of *Najaf Now* magazine, because he disliked his article two weeks earlier about workers protesting to be paid.

Since July, Iraqis in large numbers have peacefully protested against a lack of services and corruption. On August 14, several journalists at anti-corruption demonstrations in Baghdad reported that security forces instructed media to stop live coverage. Journalists in Dhi Qar and Karbala governorates received similar orders. On August 21, thugs claiming to be with the Popular Mobilization Forces, the official militia umbrella organization, attacked reporters and camera persons for the TV channels Mada, Sharqiya, and Baghdadiya covering the Baghdad protests. On August 24, the Iraqi Observatory for Press Freedoms registered eight cases of assault, expulsion, threats, and incitement to murder against journalists in Basra, Samawa, Baghdad, and Diyala covering the demonstrations.

Accountability and Justice

Iraqi courts continue to impose the death penalty. In October 2014, the United Nations Assistance Mission for Iraq (UNAMI) and the Office of the United Nations High Commissioner for Human Rights (OHCHR) reported with regard to the death penalty that "persistent and serious flaws remain in the ... criminal justice system, notably ... violations of due process and fair trial rights."

In the first KRG execution since instituting a moratorium in 2008, Kurdish authorities in August executed a man and his two wives for the abduction and murder of two schoolgirls in 2011 and 2012. In July, Iraq's cabinet proposed for parlia-

HUMAN
RIGHTS
WATCH

RUINOUS AFTERMATH
Militia Abuses Following Iraq's Recapture of Tikrit

mentary ratification procedural changes to speed up executions by empowering the justice minister to ratify execution warrants if the president has not done so within 30 days. In August, President Fuad Masum signed 21 execution warrants, but also expressed reservations about the cases of some of more than 700 persons on death row.

In July, Iraq's Central Criminal Court tried 28 persons for participating in the June 2014 ISIS massacre of up to 1,700 Shia military cadets. The trial lasted only a few hours, and the court sentenced 24 to death, despite defendants claiming their confessions were extracted under torture and that they could not choose defense lawyers.

Accountability for grievous crimes remained weak. There was no accountability for the abduction and murder of Sheikh Qasim Janabi in February 2015 by suspected Shia militants posing as security officials. Armed men grabbed Janabi, a Sunni sheikh engaged in intersectarian dialogue, in plain daylight with eight others, including his nephew, who survived. Prime Minister Abbadi ordered an investigation, but no suspects had been named or apprehended at time of writing. In Baghdad and Diyala, criminal gangs who Sunni victims say are affiliated with the Iraqi security services and Shia militias carried out uninvestigated assassinations and threats.

In one case, courts held Shia militiamen accountable. Baghdad's Rusafa Criminal Court in May sentenced to death an unknown number of defendants for their role in the August 2014 massacre of 30 Sunni worshippers at the Musab bin Umair mosque in Diyala province.

Women's and Girls' Rights

ISIS continued to sexually enslave and abuse Yezidi women and girls. By September, over 2,000 Yezidi women and girls had escaped, but over 5,200 remained in the hands of ISIS, according to Vian Dakhil, a Yezidi member of Iraq's parliament. Human Rights Watch documented a system of organized rape and sexual assault, sexual slavery, and forced marriage by ISIS forces. Yezidi women and girls told Human Rights Watch how ISIS members forced them into marriage; sold, in some cases a number of times; or given as "gifts" to ISIS fighters.

325

In 2015, ISIS reportedly forced Muslim women into marriage with fighters, imprisoning or executing those who refused, and instituting a female "Khansa," or morality, department to enforce morality codes among women of Mosul.

In June, the Karamsha and Shawi tribes of Basra agreed to settle their dispute over the murder of a Karamsha woman by the Shawi tribe handing over 10 unmarried tribeswomen as compensation. Karamsha men could then marry these women. Civil society pressure and tribal and official negotiations did not undo the agreement, and though no women had been handed over by September, they continued to remain at risk of forced marriage.

The government did not introduce measures to combat illegal arrests, due process violations, and assaults of women, to which security forces subjected many of the over 1,000 women in detention.

The KRG banned female genital mutilation by law in 2011, and several campaigns have since contributed to a decline in its prevalence, although its use continues for about half of all girls in Iraqi Kurdistan, German-Iraqi campaign group WADI reported.

Key International Actors

The United States and Iran supported Baghdad's military campaign against ISIS with equipment, training, intelligence, and advisors. Lebanon's Hezbollah group and Iran's Islamic Revolutionary Guard Corps-Al-Quds Force sent forces into combat in Iraq.

The US-led coalition bombing ISIS positions included France, the United Kingdom, the Netherlands, Belgium, Denmark, Canada, and Australia. Denmark and the US reviewed several airstrikes following allegations of civilian casualties. Germany, Hungary, Italy, and the Czech Republic, among others, also provided military equipment, including to Peshmerga forces. The US remained the largest provider of military equipment to Iraq.

Iraqi militias implicated in human rights abuses used US and Iranian weapons in their operations. The US State Department's 2014 annual report on end-use monitoring provides only cursory information on withheld military export licenses. Washington has not made available any further information, despite legal requirements that the government make information about suspended units public, to "the maximum extent practical." In its annual report on export controls for 2014, the European Union noted three denials of licenses to Iraq based on human rights and international humanitarian law concerns.

The US FY16 National Defense Authorization Act tightens obligations on the Defense Department to report on its security aid to the Iraqi government—including on end-user monitoring, suspending support for certain Shia militias, and addressing grievances related to the illicit arrest, detention, and unfair trials.

The UN Human Rights Council in March condemned abuses by ISIS after an OHCHR report earlier that month found that the group may have committed genocide, crimes against humanity, and war crimes. It failed to condemn possible war crimes by government forces.

Israel/Palestine

Israel continued in 2015 to enforce severe and discriminatory restrictions on Palestinians' human rights, and to build unlawful settlements in and facilitate the transfer of Israeli civilians to the occupied West Bank. Israeli authorities also arbitrarily detained peaceful Palestinian demonstrators, including children.

There was a sharp rise in killings and injuries related to Israeli-Palestinian hostilities beginning in October. Overall, Palestinians killed at least 17 Israeli civilians and 3 Israeli soldiers, and injured 87 Israeli civilians and 80 security officers in the West Bank and Israel as of November 27. Israeli security forces killed at least 120 and injured at least 11,953 Palestinian civilians in West Bank, Gaza, and Israel as of the same date, including bystanders, protesters, and suspected assailants.

In the West Bank, including East Jerusalem, Israeli authorities took inadequate action against Israeli settlers who injured 84 Palestinians and damaged their property in 130 incidents as of November 23, the United Nations reported. Israeli security officers arrested three Israelis in connection with an arson attack, which killed a Palestinian couple and their toddler.

Israeli authorities destroyed homes and other property under discriminatory practices that severely restrict Palestinians' access to construction permits and forcibly displaced hundreds of Palestinian residents in West Bank areas under Israeli control, as well as Bedouin citizens of Israel. Israeli courts have been unwilling to rule on the legality of the settlements under international law.

The Palestinian Authority arrested students allegedly for their affiliation with Hamas or political criticism, some of whom alleged mistreatment in detention. Hamas security forces allegedly tortured or ill-treated 258 people as of July 31, and Palestinian armed groups launched 20 rockets into Israel from Hamas-controlled Gaza as of October 31.

Neither Israeli nor Hamas authorities have prosecuted anyone for alleged crimes committed during the 2014 Israel-Gaza war, which, according to the UN, killed 1,462 Palestinian civilians, including 551 children, and 6 civilians in Israel, including one child. Israel and Egypt have maintained their partial but highly damaging closure of Gaza's borders, an unlawful act of collective punishment; they impeded the rebuilding of Gaza's devastated economy by severely restricting exports from Gaza.

Palestine also acceded to the International Criminal Court treaty and became an ICC member in April. Following a January 2015 declaration by the Palestinian government giving the ICC a mandate back to June 13, 2014, the ICC prosecutor opened a preliminary examination to determine whether the criteria have been met to merit pursuing a formal investigation.

Gaza Strip

Israel

In 2015, the Israel Defense Forces conducted 50 military incursions in Gaza as of November 23, according to the UN.

As of the same date, Israeli forces had killed 21 people in Gaza, including those shot during demonstrations at the border fence and those killed in air strikes, and injured more than 100. They also continued to shoot at Palestinian civilians in the "no-go" zone that Israel imposes just inside Gaza's northern and eastern borders and at fishermen who venture beyond six nautical miles from the shore—the area to which Israel restricts Gaza fishing boats.

In June, a UN commission of inquiry released a report regarding the 2014 Israel-Gaza war that found Israeli forces committed serious laws-of-war violations, including attacking residential buildings without an apparent military target, using artillery and other high explosive weapons indiscriminately in populated areas, and apparently targeting civilians not participating in hostilities.

Israel's military advocate general launched criminal investigations into 10 incidents, some of which he closed without indictments, even where the commission found credible evidence of violations. He indicted three soldiers, but only on charges of looting. Citing overly broad security grounds, Israel barred Gazans who had complaints that its forces had unlawfully killed their relatives from traveling to Israel to testify in court cases.

Closure

Israel's punitive closure of the Gaza Strip, particularly the near-total blocking of outgoing goods, continued to have severe consequences for the civilian population and impeded reconstruction of the 17,000 housing units severely damaged or destroyed during the 2014 conflict.

Egypt also blocked all regular movement of goods at the crossing it controls, and imposed increased restrictions on the movement of people. More than 70 percent of Gaza's 1.8 million people are forced to rely on humanitarian assistance.

Israel allowed incoming goods to Gaza that amounted to less than half of 2006 pre-closure levels. From the August 2014 ceasefire until September 2015, 2 million tons of construction material entered the coastal strip through the only functioning crossing point for goods—about 9 percent of the total need, according to the Israeli rights group Gisha. As of September, Gaza was unable to build some 250 new schools needed to adequately serve the population, according to Gisha.

Egypt's military-backed government maintained tight restrictions on the movement of Palestinians at the Rafah crossing between Gaza and Sinai, citing attacks by armed groups in the Sinai against Egyptian security forces. The crossing has been closed, including for humanitarian assistance, since October 24, 2014, except for 37 days of partial openings, according to the UN.

A monthly average of about 2,000 Gaza residents passed through the crossing, down from 20,000 in 2013. Egypt did not permit regular imports or exports of goods through Rafah and destroyed or closed many of the tunnels beneath the border that have been used for smuggling, leading to increased prices and unemployment, particularly in the construction sector.

Hamas and Palestinian Armed Groups

The UN Commission of Inquiry report released in June regarding the 2014 Israel-Gaza war found that Palestinian armed groups committed serious violations, including firing mortars and rockets into populated areas of Israel, and unnecessarily firing from within or near civilians in Gaza, putting them at risk.

In 2015 Palestinian armed groups launched 20 rockets into Israel from Gaza as of October 31, causing no casualties but generating fear in affected cities and towns. These rockets cannot be accurately aimed at military objectives and amount to indiscriminate or deliberate attacks on civilians when directed at Israeli population centers. Hamas, which has internal control over Gaza, is responsible for policing the border and acting to ensure that illegal attacks do not take place.

The Hamas internal security agency and police allegedly tortured or ill-treated 258 people as of July 31, according to complaints received by the Independent Commission for Human Rights (ICHR), a Palestinian rights body.

West Bank

Israel

In the West Bank, as of November 27, Israeli security forces and settlers fatally shot at least 96 Palestinian civilians and wounded at least 10,854, including those suspected of attacking Israelis, according to UN and Human Rights Watch monitoring.

In July, an Israeli colonel fatally shot Mohammed al-Kasbeh, 17, apparently while he was fleeing after throwing a rock at the colonel's vehicle. In August, Israeli forces killed Falah Abu Marya and shot his son in the legs during a raid on the family's home in Beit Ummar. According to witnesses, the soldiers did not face serious danger at the time of the shooting.

During an escalation in violence that began in October, Israeli security forces and settlers killed 8 protesters and 28 others suspected of attacking Israelis. In some cases, video footage and witness accounts strongly suggest that excessive force was used. In some cases, security forces appeared to shoot multiple times suspected attackers who were lying on the ground, apparently neutralized, raising concerns of extrajudicial killings.

Israeli authorities took inadequate action against Israeli settlers who injured Palestinians and destroyed or damaged Palestinian mosques, homes, schools, olive trees, cars, and other property. As of November 23, the UN reported 130 such attacks in which settlers injured 84 Palestinians.

In July, an arson attack, apparently carried out by Israelis, against two houses in the Palestinian village of Duma killed a toddler, Ali Dawabshe, and both his par-

HUMAN
RIGHTS
WATCH

RIPE FOR ABUSE
Palestinian Child Labor in Israeli Agricultural Settlements
in the West Bank

ents. In December, Israeli security officers arrested three Israelis in connection with the attack.

Settlements, Discriminatory Policies, Home Demolitions

Israel continued to provide security, administrative services, housing, education, and medical care for around 560,000 settlers residing in unlawful settlements in the West Bank, including East Jerusalem.

It also increased its settlement activity, authorizing construction work on 566 new settlement housing units, 529 of which were completed during the first quarter of 2015, an increase of 93 percent in housing starts and 219 percent completions over the same period in 2014, according to Israel's Central Bureau of Statistics.

Building permits are difficult or impossible for Palestinians to obtain in East Jerusalem or in the 60 percent of the West Bank under exclusive Israeli control (Area C). Palestinians in these areas have limited access to water, electricity, schools, and other state services, all of which the state makes readily available to the Jewish settlers there.

As of November 23, Israeli authorities demolished 481 Palestinian homes and other buildings in the West Bank (including East Jerusalem), displacing 601 people, including 296 children. In August, Israel demolished 22 homes in four communities in an area that Israel has designated for future settlement construction, called E-1. These communities are among 46 Bedouin villages Israel has earmarked for forcible "relocation" to three sites in the West Bank.

In May, the Israeli Supreme Court permitted the demolition of Susya, a Palestinian village in the south Hebron Hills in the West Bank with about 340 residents. The villagers built their homes on their agricultural land after Israel forcibly displaced them and designated the village as an archeological site.

Freedom of Movement

Israel maintained onerous restrictions on the movement of Palestinians in the West Bank, including checkpoints and the separation barrier. Settlement-related movement restrictions forced Palestinians to take time-consuming detours and restricted their access to agricultural land.

Israel continued construction of the separation barrier around East Jerusalem. Some 85 percent of the barrier falls within the West Bank rather than along the Green Line, isolating 11,000 Palestinians on the western side of the barrier who are not allowed to travel to Israel and must cross the barrier to access livelihoods and services in the West Bank. Palestinian farmers in 150 communities on the eastern side of the barrier were separated from their lands on the other side, the UN reported.

Arbitrary Detention and Detention of Children

Israeli military authorities detained Palestinian protesters including those who advocated nonviolent protest against Israeli settlements and the route of the separation barrier.

Israeli security forces continued to arrest children suspected of criminal offenses, usually stone-throwing, in their homes at night, at gunpoint; question them without a family member or a lawyer present; and coerce them to sign confessions in Hebrew, which they did not understand. The Israeli military detained Palestinian children separately from adults during remand hearings and military court trials, but often detained children with adults immediately after arrest.

As of September 30, Israel held 315 Palestinian administrative detainees without charge or trial, based on secret evidence. Israeli prison authorities shackled hospitalized Palestinians to their hospital beds after they went on long-term hunger strikes to protest their administrative detention.

Palestinian Authority

Complaints of torture and ill-treatment by West Bank Palestinian Authority security services persisted. The ICHR reported 113 complaints as of July 31.

PA security services arrested students for their alleged affiliation with Hamas or political criticism, some of whom alleged mistreatment in detention. In January 2015, police arrested Bara al-Qadi, a media student at Birzeit University, and held him for 13 days for criticizing a PA official on Facebook. In April, police arrested Jihad Salim, a student representative of a Hamas-affiliated student group at Birzeit University in Ramallah, following the group's victory in the student council election. Salim said officers beat him and held him for about 24 hours.

Palestinian governing authorities in the West Bank, as well as in Gaza, delegated jurisdiction over personal status matters such as marriage and divorce to religious courts. In practice, women seeking marriage and divorce suffered discrimination. Courts required Muslim women to obtain a male relative's consent to marry and to obtain the husband's consent to divorce, except in limited cases.

Israel

During an escalation of violence beginning in October, Palestinian civilians killed 18 Israeli and other civilians and 3 Israeli soldiers and injured 138 civilians in Israel and the West Bank as of November 30, according to the Israeli Security Agency and Human Rights Watch's monitoring.

In Israel, Israeli security forces acting alongside Israeli citizens killed five Palestinians suspected of attacking Israelis.

In two separate attacks in June in the West Bank, Palestinian civilians shot at Israelis in their car. In August, an Israeli military prosecutor indicted seven Palestinian men in connection with the attacks. Two additional Israeli civilians were killed in attacks by Palestinians in April and September.

Israel passed a number of laws that risk violating rights. A law approved by Israel's Supreme Court in April makes it a civil offense to advocate for a boycott of Israel or settlements. Two laws passed in July permit the force-feeding of hunger-striking prisoners

Bedouin citizens of Israel who live in "unrecognized" villages suffered discriminatory home demolitions on the basis that their homes were built illegally. Israeli authorities refused to prepare plans for the communities or approve construction permits, and rejected plans submitted by the communities themselves. In May, the Supreme Court approved the state's plan to raze the entire Bedouin village of Umm al-Hiran, displacing between 750 and 1,000 residents, to implement plans to build a Jewish neighborhood on these lands.

According to the Negev Coexistence Forum for Civil Inequality, Israeli authorities demolished 32 Bedouin homes in the Negev, and destroyed the crops of nine unrecognized Bedouin villages (two villages' fields were destroyed twice). In al-Araqib, an unrecognized village that has been embroiled in a years-long legal battle with the state, authorities demolished all the shacks seven times.

HUMAN
RIGHTS
WATCH

A RAW DEAL
Abuses of Thai Workers in Israel's Agricultural Sector

Israel continued its openly stated policy of applying coercive measures to make the lives of about 40,000 Eritrean and Sudanese "miserable" and "encourage the illegals to leave," in the words of former Israeli Interior Ministers Eli Yishai and Gideon Sa'ar, respectively. These measures include branding them "infiltrators" under Israeli law; prolonged detention; freedom of movement restrictions; rejecting 99.9 percent of Eritrean and Sudanese asylum claims; ambiguous policies on permission to work; and severely restricting access to health care. Between January 2013 and July 2015, 5,316 Sudanese and 3,039 Eritreans left Israel.

In August, the Israeli High Court ruled the authorities could require "infiltrators" to live in the Holot "Residency Center"—a de facto detention center located in Israel's Negev desert—but required the state to reduce the maximum time from 20 months to a more reasonable policy.

Pending a new policy, it held that anyone detained for 12 months or more should be released. Authorities officially banned all released detainees from living and working in Eilat and Tel Aviv, violating their free movement rights.

Israel continued to delegate jurisdiction over marriage, divorce, and some other aspects of personal status to Jewish, Muslim, Christian, and Druze religious courts. In practice, women seeking divorces suffered discrimination, such as refusal of divorce by state-funded Jewish religious courts without the husband's consent in up to 3,400 cases per year, according to women's rights groups. The government did not publish figures of spouses denied divorce, but women were reportedly the vast majority.

Key International Actors

The United States allocated US$3.1 billion in military aid to Israel in 2015 and $441 million in assistance to Palestinian security forces and economic support to the PA.

In January 2015, the Palestinian government lodged a declaration, giving the ICC jurisdiction dating back to June 13, 2014, for crimes committed in or from Palestine. It subsequently acceded to the Rome Statute, becoming an ICC state party in April. Based on its policy for when it receives declarations accepting the court's jurisdiction, the ICC Office of the Prosecutor opened a preliminary examination into the situation in Palestine to determine whether the criteria have been met to merit pursuing a formal investigation into crimes committed in and from Palestine.

The US criticized Palestine's accession to the ICC, and Israel in January froze the transfer of $473 million in tax revenues it collects on behalf of the Palestinian Authority for more than four months.

Israel and the US successfully pressured the UN not to include Israel on its annual list of countries responsible for grave violations against children in armed conflict, even though the draft 2015 report prepared by the secretary-general's special representative for children and armed conflict recommended adding Israel and Hamas to the list due to their repeated violations against children. The UN also did not include Hamas on the list.

Jordan

Jordan hosted over 633,000 Syrian refugees in 2015, although authorities tightened entry restrictions and limited new refugee arrivals. The government curtailed freedom of expression, detaining and bringing charges against activists, dissidents, and journalists, sometimes under broad and vague provisions of the country's counterterrorism law. Authorities replaced the heads of major security agencies in May, but did not publicly demonstrate police accountability for abuses.

Freedom of Expression and Belief

Jordanian law criminalizes speech deemed critical of the king, foreign countries, government officials and institutions, as well as Islam and speech considered to defame others.

Jordanian authorities increasingly used counterterrorism provisions to detain and prosecute activists, dissidents, and journalists for speech offenses, relying largely on 2014 amendments to its counterterrorism law that broadened the definition of terrorism and included acts such as "disturbing [Jordan's] relations with a foreign state."

In February, Jordan's State Security Court sentenced a senior Muslim Brotherhood figure, Zaki Bani Irsheid, to 18 months in prison after convicting him of "disturbing [Jordan's] relations with a foreign state," based on a Facebook post he authored criticizing the United Arab Emirates (UAE). In June, authorities arrested Eyad Qunaibi, a university professor, over Facebook comments criticizing what he considered un-Islamic social phenomena in Jordan and its cooperation with Israel.

Jordan curtailed media freedom in 2015 by detaining and bringing charges against at least nine journalists and writers, sometimes under broad and vague provisions of the country's counterterrorism law. These included Jamal Ayoub, a freelance columnist, whom authorities arrested between April 22 and August 17 for writing a column that criticized Saudi Arabia's bombing campaign in Yemen, and Seif al-Obeidat and Hashem al-Khalidi, journalist and publisher respectively with the Soraya News website, jailed between January 28 and March 8 after the site posted an article on negotiations between Jordan and the armed extremist group Islamic State (also known as ISIS) over the release of captured pilot Mu`ath al-Kasasbeh.

In 2015, a Ministry of Justice committee issued a proposed penal code overhaul that would amend at least 180 articles of the 1960 law. The draft amendments provided alternatives to imprisonment, such as community service, for the first time, but did not amend or remove articles long-used by authorities to limit free expression.

Freedom of Association and Assembly

Since the amended Public Gatherings Law took effect in March 2011, Jordanians no longer require government permission to hold public meetings or demonstrations. However, Amman hotels and other venues continued to seek the General Intelligence Directorate's permission to host public meetings and events.

The State Security Court delivered judgments in cases against political activists and demonstrators arising from protests and social media activism. In most cases, the court threw out the charge of "undermining the political regime," a terrorism charge under the penal code, and issued convictions on lesser charges carrying three-month jail sentences, which can be substituted with a fine under Jordanian law.

Refugees and Migrants

By November 2015, over 633,000 persons from Syria had sought refuge in Jordan since 2011, according to the United Nations High Commissioner for Refugees (UNHCR). Of these, approximately 79,000 were housed at the Zaatari Refugee Camp in northern Jordan, down from over 200,000 in 2013; 27,000 lived in Azraq Camp, 100 kilometers east of Amman; and 6,300 others were at the Emirates Jordan Camp in Zarqa Governorate. The rest were living outside refugee camps.

Beginning in March 2015, Jordanian authorities severely restricted informal border crossings in the eastern part of the country, stranding hundreds of Syrians in remote desert areas just inside Jordan's border for days and weeks with limited access to food, water, and medical assistance.

Jordanian authorities in 2015 initiated a "re-verification process" for all Syrians living in urban communities, requiring Syrians to prove they had proper documentation and legal status in order to obtain a service card that will later be required to receive humanitarian assistance, access medical care, or enroll children in public schools. The re-verficiation process adversely affected undocumented Syrians and those who left refugee camps irregularly, leading to cases of forced encampment in largely-closed refugee camps.

In 2015, Jordanian security forces continued to turn away Palestinian refugees seeking to enter Jordan from Syria at the country's borders. Security forces also detained and deported Palestinians who entered at unofficial border crossings using forged Syrian identity documents, or who entered illegally via smuggling networks.

In May, Jordan endorsed the Safe Schools Declaration, committing to do more to protect students, teachers, and schools during times of armed conflict, including implementing the *Guidelines on Protecting Schools from Military Use.*

Jordan hosted around 80,000 migrant domestic workers in 2015, mostly from the Philippines, Sri Lanka, and Indonesia. Nongovernmental organizations repeatedly referred domestic workers who had suffered multiple abuses to labor ministry investigators who, however, rarely classified them as victims of the crime of trafficking. Instead, they treated each aspect of abuse, such as non-payment of salaries, separately, sometimes even detaining workers for "escaping" employers.

Women's and Girls' Rights

Jordan's personal status code remains discriminatory despite a 2010 amendment that included widening women's access to divorce and child custody. Marriages between Muslim women and non-Muslim men, for instance, are not recognized.

Article 9 of Jordan's nationality law does not allow Jordanian women married to non-Jordanian spouses to pass on their nationality to their spouse and children. In 2015, authorities began extending special privileges to non-citizen children of Jordanian women, including free education and access to health services in government institutions, as well as provision of Jordanian ID cards and drivers' licenses. The privileges, however, did not apply to children whose mothers had not resided in Jordan for a minimum of five years.

Penal code articles 98 and 340, which allow reduced sentences for perpetrators of "honor crimes," remained in force. News reports indicated that at least 10 women and girls were killed by male family members in 2015, including a woman shot four times by her father after leaving her family home and reportedly having a relationship with a man her family refused to let her marry. Authorities arrested her father at the scene.

Criminal Justice System and Police Accountability

In December 2014, Jordan revived capital punishment by executing 11 Jordanian men by hanging, ending an eight-year de facto moratorium on the death penalty. Courts had previously convicted all 11 men of murder. On February 4, only hours after ISIS released a video showing its murder of a captured Jordanian pilot, Jordan executed two Iraqis, both long-term death row inmates affiliated with Al-Qaeda in Iraq (AQI), the precursor group to ISIS. All executions were carried out at Suwaqa prison, 70 kilometers south of Amman.

Perpetrators of torture or other ill-treatment appeared to enjoy impunity due to the authorities' reliance on special police prosecutors and judges to investigate allegations against, prosecute, and try fellow officers. At the Police Court, where many such cases are heard, two out of three sitting judges are serving police officers appointed by the police, and authorities rarely release information on the results of Police Court trials. To date, Human Rights Watch has not received evidence that a police or intelligence officer has ever been convicted of torture under article 208 of the penal code.

In May, Jordan announced the resignation of the heads of major security bodies, including the minister of interior, head of the Public Security Directorate, and head of Gendarmarie Forces. A Jordanian security official told Reuters that the high-level changes stemmed partly from the "heavy-handed police crackdown" in the southern city Maan in recent years, as well as the death of a detainee, Abdullah al-Zoubi, in early May, for which authorities arrested four police officers and later charged three.

Local governors continued to use provisions of the Crime Prevention Law of 1954 to place individuals in administrative detention for up to one year in circumvention of the Criminal Procedure Law. The National Center for Human Rights reported that 20,216 persons were administratively detained in 2014, some for longer than one year.

Key International Actors

In August 2015, the European Union granted Jordan €55 million (US$59 million) to help offset the impact of the Syrian refugee crisis in the education sector.

In February, Jordan signed a non-binding, three-year memorandum of understanding with the United States, in which the US pledged to provide $1 billion in aid to Jordan annually, up from $660 million in recent years. The US did not publicly criticize human rights violations in Jordan in 2015, except in annual reports.

In March, Jordan joined the Saudi Arabia-led coalition that launched airstrikes and other military action against Houthi forces in Yemen. Jordan remained a participant in US-led attacks against ISIS and other extremist groups in Iraq and Syria.

In May, the Saudi Development Fund signed two grant agreements with Jordan worth $80 million to finance infrastructure projects for new industrial estates. The grants were part of the $5 billion promised to Jordan by Gulf Cooperation Council countries in 2011 for development projects.

Kazakhstan

Kazakhstan took few meaningful steps to tackle a worsening human rights record in 2015, maintaining a focus on economic development over political reform. Snap presidential elections in April extended President Nursultan Nazarbaev's heavy-handed 24-year rule for another five years. Opposition leader Vladimir Kozlov remains imprisoned after an unfair trial.

Authorities continued to close newspapers, jail and fine people for holding peaceful protests, ban peaceful religious practice, and misuse the vague and overbroad charge of "inciting social, national, clan, racial, class, or religious discord." Workers' rights are restricted and the adoption of a new trade union law in 2014 resulted in some trade unions unable to reregister in 2015.

Elections

President Nazarbaev won snap presidential elections on April 26 with 97.7 percent of the vote. The election monitoring mission of the Organization for Security and Co-operation in Europe's Office for Democratic Institutions and Human Rights (OSCE/ODIHR) noted that "reforms for holding genuine democratic elections still have to materialize," and that "serious procedural deficiencies and irregularities" took place. OSCE/ODIHR also found a lack of genuine opposition and a restricted media environment.

Civil Society

On September 17, France's prime minister signed a decree approving the extradition of government critic and former banker Mukhtar Ablyazov to Russia. Ablyazov remains under threat of extradition pending review of his appeal at France's supreme administrative court.

On April 13, a court imposed restrictions on Saken Baikenov of the Antigeptil group, known for protesting Baikonur rocket launches, for two years after his Facebook posts were found to "incite ethnic discord." On November 9, authorities arrested Bolatbek Blyalov, also of the Antigeptil group, on suspicion of "inciting social discord."

On October 12, police arrested activists Ermek Narymbaev and Serikzhan Mambetalin on suspicion of "inciting national discord" after Facebook posts about writings attributed to Murat Telibekov, another civil society activist who is under criminal investigaton on the same charges.

Prison officials put opposition leader Vladimir Kozlov into isolation in mid-July and again in mid-August for prison regime violations. In July, additional restrictions were placed on his visitation, telephone, and parcel rights for six months. In 2015, PEN International and Maina Kiai, the United Nations special rapporteur on the rights to freedom of peaceful assembly and of association, expressed serious concern about Kozlov's imprisonment and called for his release. Kiai visited Kozlov in prison in January.

Civil society activist Vadim Kuramshin continues to serve a 12-year prison sentence, despite procedural violations during his trial and concerns that his sentencing in December 2012 was retribution for public criticism of the government.

Participants at the fourth annual meeting of the Civil Society Platform, a gathering of Central Asian activists outside Astana, were subject to intimidation when plainclothes officers attempted to attend their meeting and police demanded to see a list of attendees.

In November, UN bodies and international and local human rights groups expressed serious concern after parliament adopted a draft law on nongovernmental organizations (NGOs), which would impose government control over the distribution of foreign grants.

Media Restrictions and Freedom of Expression

Kazakhstan highly restricts media freedoms. Independent journalists and media outlets face harassment and interference in their work, and outlets have been shut down in recent years. Authorities brought criminal libel charges against Amangeldy Batyrbekov, a civil society activist, who was jailed in October for 18 months. In November, after four years, authorities unblocked access to LiveJournal, a blogging platform. A new access to information law was adopted in November.

In July, a Radio Free Europe/Radio Liberty journalist was detained while covering a peaceful protest in Astana. In October, journalist Yaroslav Golyshkin was imprisoned for eight years on charges of "blackmail." In September, Reporters Without Borders criticized his arrest and called for his release.

In December 2014, an Almaty court closed down ADAM bol, an independent journal, prompting OSCE Media Freedom representative Dunja Mijatovic to voice concern over the "drastic and disproportionate measures ... which endanger pluralism in Kazakhstan." In October, ADAM bol's successor publication, ADAM, was shuttered for a language violation.

Freedom of Assembly and Association

Authorities continued to exercise strict control over peaceful assembly, and broke up and detained people for even small-scale peaceful protests. Narymbaev, the activist, was on two occasions, in June and August, sentenced to 15 days' administrative arrest for violating a restrictive peaceful assembly law.

UN Special Rapporteur Kiai concluded after his visit to Kazakhstan in January that "the government's approach to regulating assemblies renders that right meaningless." He called on Kazakhstan to adopt a new law on peaceful assembly that complies with international standards.

Kiai also expressed serious concern about restrictions on public associations, political parties, religious groups, and trade unions. In August, an Almaty court closed down the opposition Communist Party of Kazakhstan for failing to meet membership requirements, a decision that the party head described as politically motivated.

Torture

Despite some efforts by the government to tackle torture, including by prosecuting some officers, torture remains a pressing issue and impunity is the norm. There have been no further steps to credibly investigate allegations of torture made by persons detained in connection with the 2011 violence in the town of Zhanaozen. The NGO Coalition against Torture in Kazakhstan reported 80 complaints of torture in the first half of the year.

In 2014, the UN Committee against Torture (CAT) found Kazakhstan responsible for torturing Rasim Bairamov. Bairamov was apprehended for alleged robbery and severely beaten by police and prison personnel in 2008. In partial implementation of the CAT decision, Kazakhstan granted Bairamov compensation and opened a criminal investigation into his treatment in custody. However, in September, authorities closed the case for lack of "evidence of a crime." As of May, five other complaints against Kazakhstan are pending before CAT.

Freedom of Religion

Some religious groups continued to be subjected to fines and short-term detention for violating a restrictive religion law, and some individual members faced criminal charges. A mosque in the city of Petropavlovsk has been repeatedly denied registration, according to Forum 18, an international religious freedom watchdog.

In July, Saken Tulbaev was imprisoned for almost five years for "inciting religious discord" and "membership in a banned religious organization." He was banned from "activity directed at meeting the religious needs of believers" for three years after his release. In January, alleged members of Tabligi Jamaat were imprisoned for belonging to a banned religious organization. Four were sentenced to 20 months in prison, and another to 18 months.

In November, an Astana court sentenced Ykylas Kabduakasov, a Seventh-day Adventist, to seven years' restricted freedom for "inciting religious discord." Officials raided a children's Bible camp in August, claiming the organizers had violated the religion law.

Labor Rights

A 2014 trade union law restricts the right of workers to join trade unions of their choice and to freely determine their structure. In 2015, some unions, including the Confederation of Free Trade Unions of Kazakhstan (KSPK), were unable to re-register in accordance with the new law. Worker members expressed serious concern about the law at the June session of the International Labour Organization (ILO). The government failed to attend the session, prompting heavy criticism from the ILO.

Other legislation governing the financing and collective bargaining rights of trade unions remains restrictive. A new labor code was adopted in November. Oil

HUMAN
RIGHTS
WATCH

"That's When I Realized I Was Nobody"

A Climate of Fear for LGBT People in Kazakhstan

unions expressed concern that the draft labor code would restrict workers' rights.

Sexual Orientation and Gender Identity

Lesbian, gay, bisexual, and transgender (LGBT) people in Kazakhstan live in a climate of fear fuelled by harassment, discrimination, and violence. On the rare occasions when LGBT people report abuse, they often face indifference and hostility.

In March, parliament passed bills that sought to introduce a broad ban on "propaganda of non-traditional sexual orientation," but final drafts were not made public and the end-stage of the legislative process was non-transparent. In May, the "propaganda" legislation was found unconstitutional for being too vague, but the Constitutional Council did not address the bills' discriminatory elements.

Key International Actors

Despite the absence of meaningful political reform in Kazakhstan, and European Union pledges to link upgraded relations to human rights improvements, the EU and Kazakhstan initialed an Enhanced Partnership and Cooperation Agreement on January 20. In April, following presidential elections, the EU issued a rare public message urging Kazakh authorities to "enhance their efforts to honour their international commitments regarding democratic principles and human rights."

The United States continues to be largely silent on publicly registering human rights concerns in Kazakhstan, and the bilateral relationship focuses prominently on security, nuclear nonproliferation, the economy, and trade.

During his June trip to Kazakhstan, UN Secretary-General Ban Ki-moon called on the government to continue to make human rights progress and remember that "all religious and minority groups should be guaranteed [freedom of religion] on an equal footing."

In April, Baskut Tuncak, the UN special rapporteur on human rights and hazardous substances and waste, concluded after a mission to Kazakhstan that the government was not properly implementing or enforcing environmental legislation and needed to protect people from hazardous waste, including in Berezovka, a village whose residents, particularly children, continue to live in a toxic environment and suffer chronic health problems.

In April, Kazakhstan ratified the Convention on the Rights of Persons with Disabilities and in August, signed on to the Safe Schools Declaration, a political commitment to better protect students, teachers, schools, and universities in armed conflict.

In its October concluding observations on Kazakhstan, the UN Committee on the Rights of the Child issued comprehensive recommendations, including on the prohibition of torture and ill-treatment, corporal punishment, and sexual violence against children, and addressing the needs of children with disabilities.

Kenya

Kenya's human rights environment faced serious challenges in 2015 as the security crisis escalated. Persistent deadly attacks by Al-Shabaab, the Somalia-based Islamist armed group, culminated in the April 2 massacre of 148 people, including 142 students, at Garissa University in the northeast. The government responded to Al-Shabaab attacks with efforts to expand police and security agency powers, and curtail basic rights through new legislation. Government policies have targeted human rights organizations for closure, tried to stifle media, and threatened refugee communities with forced returns to Somalia.

Security forces continued to be implicated in extrajudicial killings, torture, disappearances and arbitrary detentions, particularly during counterterrorism operations in Nairobi, Mombasa, the coast and in the northeast, and rarely faced investigations or prosecutions.

At least 28 bills necessary to implement the 2010 constitution had not been passed by the five-year deadline on August 27. The constitution was negotiated after the 2007-2008 post-election violence as key in addressing past injustices. There has been no tangible progress on accountability for crimes committed during the post-election violence, which left at least 1,100 dead and 650,000 displaced.

Key security sector, land, and accountability reforms identified in 2008 as crucial to address Kenya's political crisis have also not been implemented. Throughout the year, human rights activists and civil society groups reported harassment and threats for their work on justice and accountability.

Abuses by Al-Shabaab

Suspected Al-Shabaab fighters targeted and killed at least 226 unarmed people between November 2014 and July 2015, along the coast and in the northeast. During three separate attacks on quarry workers and on a bus in Mandera county and in another attack on Garissa University, Al-Shabaab fighters singled out and killed those who could not recite an Islamic creed.

INSULT TO INJURY

The 2014 Lamu and Tana River Attacks and Kenya's Abusive Response

HUMAN RIGHTS WATCH

hrw.org

KENYA HUMAN RIGHTS COMMISSION

www.khrc.or.ke

Conduct of Security Forces

Following alleged Al-Shabaab attacks in Lamu and Tana River counties in June and July 2014, security officers from multiple agencies raided communities, beating, harassing and extorting money from residents. Hundreds of predominantly Muslim and ethnic Somalis were targeted and detained without charge for periods well beyond the 24-hour limit set by Kenyan law.

After Al-Shabaab's massacre in Garissa in April 2015, the military and police were again implicated in kidnapping, killings, and disappearances of terrorism suspects in Garissa, Wajir and Mandera, in northeast Kenya.

There have been no investigations into at least 10 cases of extrajudicial killings and other cases of disappearance of terrorism suspects by the Anti-Terrorism Police Unit (ATPU) in Nairobi in 2014.

Security Laws Amendments

In December 2014, the ruling Jubilee administration proposed the Security Laws Amendments that expanded police stop and search powers, introduced new criminal offences with harsh penalties, limited the rights of defendants, and restricted freedoms of expression and assembly. The High Court in February struck down eight potentially repressive clauses as unconstitutional. However, other provisions were left intact, such as allowing pretrial detention of terrorism suspects for up to 90 days with court orders.

Accountability

Kenya has made no progress on accountability for post-2007 elections violence, including for sexual violence, but authorities continued with attempts to undermine the International Criminal Court (ICC) cases on Kenya by seeking to politicize the proceedings.

Many women and girls who survived sexual violence after the 2007 elections have serious physical injuries, illnesses, and psychological disorders and require medical care, financial, and psychosocial support.

In December 2014, the ICC prosecutor withdrew crimes against humanity charges against President Uhuru Kenyatta due to insufficient evidence that the prosecu-

HUMAN
RIGHTS
WATCH

"There is No Time Left"

Climate Change, Environmental Threats, and Human Rights
in Turkana County, Kenya

tor blamed on noncooperation by Kenyan authorities and widespread witness interference. Kenyatta's deputy, William Ruto, and former radio journalist Joshua
arap Sang are standing trial on similar charges. Victims in the Kenyatta case are
seeking to challenge the prosecution's decision to suspend investigations.

Both sets of Kenyan cases at the ICC have been dogged by claims of witness tampering. The trial chamber in the Ruto and Sang case found sufficient evidence of
tampering to admit into evidence the prior statements of six witnesses who subsequently refused to cooperate with the prosecution, setting off a new effort in
parliament to seek Kenya's withdrawal from the ICC. In early September, the
court unsealed arrest warrants against two Kenyans on accusations of attempting to bribe prosecution witnesses in the case against Ruto and Sang. The arrest
warrants against lawyers Paul Gicheru and Philip Kipkoech Bett come two years
after an arrest warrant was unsealed against journalist Walter Barasa on similar
charges. There has not been any progress on investigations by Kenyan authorities into the late 2014 disappearance and death of Meshack Yebei, who was
claimed as a witness by Ruto's defense team.

In late 2014, an ICC trial chamber indicated that the government of Kenya had
not met its obligations to cooperate in the prosecution's investigations in the
Kenyatta case but decided not to send a formal finding of non-compliance to the
court's Assembly of States Parties for enforcement. The Office of the Prosecutor
appealed the decision, and in August 2015, the Appeals Chamber referred the
matter back to the Trial Chamber for review.

In March, President Kenyatta said that a report of the Office of Director of Public
Prosecutions indicated that, due to lack of evidence, it would not be possible to
prosecute cases arising out of the 2007-2008 post-election violence and that
"restorative" approaches should be used instead.

Kenyatta issued a general apology for human rights violations committed by the
government and instructed the treasury to set aside Ksh10 billion (US$9.5 mil-
lion) over the next three years for victim reparations for past injustices dating
back to 1963, including victims of the recent post-election violence, as recommended in the report of the Truth, Justice and Reconciliation Commission.

Although the Independent Policing Oversight Authority (IPOA) has made some
progress with groundbreaking investigations into reports of police abuses since

it was founded four years ago, Jubilee Party legislators have called for its disbandment, accusing it of inhibiting counterterrorism efforts with demands for police accountability.

The Kenya National Commission on Human Rights, Commission on Administrative Justice and IPOA lack adequate financial support to achieve their mandates. Their reports and recommendations on human rights abuses are largely ignored by the key government officials including the president.

Civil Society and Human Rights Defenders

Reports of intimidation and harassment of nongovernmental organizations (NGOs) and activists continued in 2015. In April, the Inspector General of Police included two prominent human rights groups, Haki Africa and Muslims for Human Rights (MUHURI)–known for their work in exposing security forces' abuses at the coast–in a list of 86 individuals and organizations alleged to have terrorism links. The government also froze the organizations' bank accounts, paralyzing activities. Kenya Revenue Authority raided their offices on April 20 and 21, seizing documents and hard drives in connection with possible tax evasion investigations. In June, a court cleared the organizations of any links to terrorist activity, but their bank accounts remained frozen. They only managed to access their bank accounts after a court order in November.

The government also froze the organizations' bank accounts, paralyzing activities. Kenya Revenue Authority raided their offices on April 20 and 21, seizing documents and hard drives in connection with possible tax evasion investigations. In June, a court cleared the organizations of any links to terrorist activity. Their bank accounts remained frozen at time of writing, despite a court order in November that the accounts should be unfrozen.

The Jubilee party continued attempts to introduce tough legislative and administrative measures seemingly aimed at controlling NGOs. In 2014, the administration proposed amendments to the Public Benefits Organizations (PBO) Act, 2013, a bill seeking to amend the PBO Act to increase executive control over the public benefits authority. Parliament rejected the amendments in December that year.

In 2015, the government created a task force to gather public views to begin another process of amending the PBO Act. The Nongovernmental Organizations Coordination Board, the government regulatory body, has been drafting fresh amendments since July 2015. In October, the board said it would deregister more than 900 NGOs, alleging failure to comply with regulations and links to terrorism, but the decision was later suspended by the minister overseeing the board to allow more time for the organizations to comply.

Treatment of Refugees

Hostile and inflammatory rhetoric against Somali refugees from public officials increased, particularly in the wake of the April attack in Garissa. Authorities have, without any clear evidence, repeatedly blamed Somali refugees for security challenges facing the country.

On April 11, Deputy President William Ruto gave the United Nations an ultimatum to close Dadaab refugee camp within 90 days or the government would shut it down. Kenya backed down on the threat after a visit by the UN High Commissioner for Refugees in early May.

Sexual Orientation and Gender Identity

Homophobic groups violently attacked two gay men in Kwale County in February 2015. Both required hospitalization but feared filing statements with police.

In February 2015, police in Kwale county arrested two men on charges of "carnal knowledge against the order of nature"–the only instances in which this colonial-era penal code provision, understood to criminalize sex between men, has ever been used. Police submitted them to forced anal exams in order to compile "evidence," a degrading and illegal practice. The criminal case against them continued at time of writing. The National Gay and Lesbian Human Rights Commission (NGLHRC), an NGO, filed a petition in September challenging the constitutionality of anal exams.

In April, the High Court overturned the NGO board's refusal to register NGLHRC on the grounds that the penal code "criminalizes gay and lesbian liaisons." The victory followed three 2014 court judgments that recognized rights for transgender and intersex people. Deputy President Ruto responded to the ruling by say-

THE ISSUE IS VIOLENCE
Attacks on LGBT People on Kenya's Coast

ing, "There is no room for gays and those others in Kenya." In a rare comment on LGBT rights, President Kenyatta said in July that "gay rights are a non-issue."

Key International Actors

Kenya plays a prominent regional role particularly regarding counterterrorism efforts. Kenyan forces remain in Somalia as part of the African Union forces. President Kenyatta also actively participated in peace negotiations in South Sudan.

Anti-Western rhetoric by Kenyan public officials declined, and relations between Kenya and Western countries improved after the ICC dropped crimes against humanity charges against President Kenyatta in December 2014. Previously, President Kenyatta and Deputy President Ruto had claimed that Western governments supported the ICC cases against them.

Despite having made little progress on accountability for the post-election violence, international pressure on the Kenyan government to do so has diminished.

In July, US President Barack Obama visited Kenya for the first time as president, a significant sign of improved dialogue between the two countries. Obama used the opportunity to voice concerns about human rights abuses and simultaneously pledged new security sector support worth $65 million to several African countries, including Kenya. He also hosted a meeting with civil society and emphasized the importance of not suppressing independent voices.

Kenya did not accept critical recommendations that several countries made during the examination of its rights record under the Universal Periodic Review at the Human Rights Council in June, such as working to eliminate all forms of torture, ill-treatment, and disappearances of persons.

Kuwait

The government aggressively cracked down on free speech throughout 2015, using provisions in the constitution, the national security law, and other legislation to stifle political dissent, as well as passing new legislation criminalizing or increasing penalties for various forms and means of expression.

In an effort to curb local terrorism, according to authorities, Kuwait became the first country to pass a law requiring that all Kuwaiti citizens and residents provide DNA samples, in violation of the right to privacy.

Freedom of Expression

Kuwaiti authorities have invoked several provisions in the constitution, penal code, Printing and Publication Law, Misuse of Telephone Communications and Bugging Devices Law, Public Gatherings Law, and National Unity Law to prosecute over a dozen people over the last few years for criticizing in blogs or on Twitter, Facebook, or other social media the emir, the government, religion, and the rulers of neighboring countries.

Those prosecuted have faced charges such as harming the honor of another person; insulting the emir or other public figures or the judiciary; insulting religion; planning or participating in illegal gatherings; and misusing telephone communications. Other charges include harming state security, inciting the government's overthrow, and harming Kuwait's relations with other states. From January to October, courts convicted at least five of those charged, imposing prison sentences of up to six years and fines.

In June 2015, Kuwait passed a new cybercrime law that includes far-reaching restrictions on Internet-based speech. Article 6 of the law imposes prison sentences and fines for insulting religion and religious figures, and for criticizing the emir on the Internet. Article 6 also prohibits Internet-based statements deemed to criticize the judicial system or harm Kuwait's relations with other states, or that publicize classified information, without exceptions for disclosures in the public interest.

Article 7 imposes a punishment of up to 10 years in prison for using the Internet to "overthrow the ruling regime in the country when this instigation included an enticement to change the system by force or through illegal means, or by urging to use force to change the social and economic system that exists in the country, or to adopt creeds that aim at destroying the basic statutes of Kuwait through illegal means." The law empowers authorities to close for one year all outlets or locations in which these crimes are committed and confiscate devices used in committing them.

Treatment of Minorities

At least 105,702 Bidun residents of Kuwait remain stateless.

After an initial registration period for citizenship ended in 1960, authorities shifted Bidun citizenship claims to administrative committees that for decades have avoided resolving the claims. Authorities claim that many Bidun are "illegal residents" who deliberately destroyed evidence of another nationality in order to receive benefits that Kuwait gives its citizens.

Members of the Bidun community frequently take to the streets to protest the government's failure to address their citizenship claims, despite government warnings that Bidun should not gather in public. Article 12 of the 1979 Public Gatherings Law bars non-Kuwaitis from participating in public gatherings.

In media interviews during the year, government officials suggested that Kuwait may "solve" the Bidun community's nationality claims by paying the Comoros Islands to grant the Bidun a form of economic citizenship, thus regularizing them as foreign nationals in Kuwait and rendering them liable to legal deportation from Kuwait—possibly violating their right to family life.

Migrant Workers

About 2 million of Kuwait's 2.9 million population are migrant workers. Abuse and exploitation of migrant domestic workers—who comprise a large proportion of the migrant worker population—continued to be reported, including withholding of salaries, and physical and sexual abuse.

In June 2015, Kuwait passed a new law giving domestic workers enforceable labor rights for the first time. The law grants domestic workers the right to a weekly day off, 30 days of annual paid leave, a 12-hour working day with rest, and an end-of-service benefit of one month a year at the end of the contract, among other rights.

However, it has only unspecified "hours of rest" and lacks other key protections found in the general labor law, such as an 8-hour day; one hour of rest after every 5 hours of work; and detailed provisions for sick leave, including 15 days at full pay.

The domestic worker law also falls short by failing to set out enforcement mechanisms, such as labor inspections. It prohibits employers from confiscating workers' passports, a common abuse, but fails to specify penalties. The new law does not guarantee the right to form a union. It came into force on July 26, 2015, when it was published in the Official Gazette. The Interior Ministry is required to issue regulations to implement the law by January 2016.

Women's Rights, Sexual Orientation, and Gender Identity

Women continue to face discrimination in many aspects of their lives, and large legal gaps remain in protections for them. Kuwait has no laws prohibiting domestic violence, sexual harassment, or marital rape. Legislation proposed in April 2014 to penalize sexual harassment was not passed in 2015. Kuwaiti women married to non-Kuwaitis, unlike Kuwaiti men, cannot pass on their citizenship to their children or spouses. Kuwaiti law also prevents a woman from marrying a partner of her choice without her father's permission.

Same-sex relations between men are punishable by up to seven years in prison. Transgender people can be arrested under a penal code provision that prohibits "imitating the opposite sex in any way."

Counterterrorism

In July 2015, in response to a suicide bomb attack on the Shia Imam Sadiq Mosque that killed 27 people, Kuwait became the first country to pass a law requiring that all Kuwaiti citizens and residents provide DNA samples to the authorities as part of a new counterterrorism law.

Death Penalty

Kuwaiti authorities are currently seeking the death penalty for 11 suspects in the Shia Imam Sadiq Mosque bombing. In 2013, they carried out five executions, the first time the country had applied the death penalty since 2007.

Key International Actors

In the 2015 US State Department annual Trafficking in Persons report, the United States classified Kuwait as Tier 3—among the most problematic countries—for the ninth consecutive year. The report cited Kuwait's failure to prosecute, convict, or sentence a single trafficking offender during the reporting period.

It found that the government failed to develop procedures to identify trafficking victims among vulnerable populations or a referral mechanism to provide adequate protection services to victims.

Kyrgyzstan

Unaddressed human rights problems and new setbacks marred Kyrgyzstan's rights record in 2015. Authorities targeted and harassed some human rights groups, journalists, and lawyers. Impunity for ill-treatment and torture persist, and there is still no justice for victims of interethnic violence in 2010. Human rights defender Azimjon Askarov is still wrongfully serving a life sentence.

Domestic violence against women and girls is prevalent, and multiple barriers hinder survivors from accessing help or justice. Lesbian, gay, bisexual, and transgender (LGBT) people face discrimination and harassment. Draft laws discriminating against LGBT people and restricting the work of nongovernmental organizations (NGOs) advanced further in parliament.

Kyrgyzstan held parliamentary elections in October, which international observers found to be "competitive." In August, Kyrgyzstan became a member of the Eurasian Economic Union, a common market of five Eurasian states, led by Russia.

Parliamentary Elections

The election monitoring mission of the Organization for Security and Co-operation in Europe's Office for Democratic Institutions and Human Rights (OSCE/ODIHR) found that October's parliamentary elections were "competitive and provided voters with a wide range of choice," but had concerns about the inclusiveness of the voter list, ballot secrecy, and significant procedural problems.

In November 2014, rights defenders challenged the constitutionality of a 2014 law requiring citizens to submit biometric data as a prerequisite to vote. Parliament in May dismissed Klara Sooronkulova, a judge in the Constitutional Chamber of Kyrgyzstan's Supreme Court, after she was accused of publicly sharing her views on the law before the Constitutional Chamber issued its ruling. In September, the Constitutional Chamber found the law constitutional. The president of the Council of Europe's Venice Commission called on Kyrgyzstan to introduce guarantees for the independence of constitutional judges and to review Sooronkulova's dismissal.

Access to Justice

The authorities continue to deny justice to victims of the June 2010 interethnic violence in southern Kyrgyzstan. Ethnic Uzbeks were disproportionately killed, subjected to arbitrary detention, ill-treatment, and torture, and house destruction. In April, Mahamad Bizurukov, an ethnic Uzbek on trial since 2011 in connection with the 2010 violence, was sentenced to 13 years' imprisonment for murder. He was released in August on parole. A handful of other June 2010-related cases are still under judicial review.

In June, during a Central Asia visit, United Nations Secretary-General Ban Ki-moon called on authorities to investigate human rights violations related to the June 2010 violence, prosecute those responsible for serious crimes, review convictions tainted by torture, and work with civil society "to promote interethnic reconciliation," including through transitional justice and reparations for victims.

On the fifth anniversary of the violence in June, the OSCE high commissioner on national minorities noted that "a sense of insecurity is still prevalent among the ethnic Uzbek community" and "little progress" has been made in investigating cases related to the June 2010 violence.

Torture

Authorities acknowledge that torture is a problem and, in May, created a specialized investigative unit in the Prosecutor General's Office. Nevertheless, the National Center for the Prevention of Torture, an independent, specialized anti-torture body, reported that "measures are not being taken to prevent and eradicate torture."

Human rights groups and lawyers say that criminal investigations into allegations of ill-treatment and torture are rare, often delayed, and ineffective, as are trials. After a four-year trial, an Osh court in October acquitted four police officers charged with torture after the death of Usmanjon Kholmirzaev, an ethnic Uzbek who, in 2011, died of injuries sustained in police custody. According to information provided by the Prosecutor General's Office to the Coalition Against Torture, a group of NGOs working on torture prevention, authorities declined to

HUMAN RIGHTS WATCH

"Call Me When He Tries to Kill You"
State Response to Domestic Violence in Kyrgyzstan

open criminal investigations into 146 of 180 registered complaints of torture between January and June.

Civil Society

Despite widespread local and international criticism, parliament adopted in its first reading a "foreign agents" bill, which would require organizations that receive foreign funding and engage in broadly defined political activities to register as "foreign agents" or risk fines and closure. At time of writing, the bill was still under parliamentary review.

In March, the State Committee on National Security (GKNB) searched the homes and offices of two human rights lawyers in the city of Osh. Officials confiscated confidential client material, computers, and other equipment. The lawyers sued the GKNB, and in June, the Supreme Court of Kyrgyzstan upheld a ruling finding the GKNB's searches unlawful.

Human rights defender Azimjon Askarov, who is serving a life sentence after a prosecution and trial marred by serious violations of fair trial standards and allegations of torture that were never investigated, received the United States Department of State Human Rights Defender Award in July. The complaint he filed in 2012 with the UN Human Rights Committee remains pending.

Violence against Women

Domestic violence against women and girls remains a serious problem. Despite a 2003 domestic violence law, the absence of services and the authorities' inaction or hostility toward victims obstruct survivors' access to protection and justice. Police do not systematically enforce protection orders and few domestic violence complaints reach the courts. Pressure to keep families together, stigma, economic dependence, and fear of reprisals by abusers hinder some women from seeking assistance. The government is currently drafting a new domestic violence law.

In their 2015 reviews of Kyrgyzstan, the UN Committee on the Elimination of Discrimination against Women and the UN Committee on Economic, Social and Cultural Rights (CESCR) raised concerns about the prevalence of domestic violence and called on the government to provide adequate shelter and access to justice for survivors and to train law enforcement and judicial officials.

Human Rights Institutions

Parliament considered a draft law limiting the activities of and curbing the independence of the National Centre for the Prevention of Torture. Dissatisfied with the human rights ombudsman's annual report, parliament dismissed him in June, in breach of stipulated procedures. The United Nations in the Kyrgyz Republic issued a statement that "the principles of independence and pluralism of Ombudsman Institutions are not sufficiently guaranteed" by law.

Freedom of Expression

Article 19, an international media freedom rights group, published a statement noting "how government officials frequently prevent journalists from accessing information of public interest," despite an access to information law. In June, a court awarded 2 million som (US$27,750) in damages after the Prosecutor General's Office, on behalf of President Almazbek Atambaev, sued a local journalist for defamation, after the journalist wrote about the June 2010 events.

Some journalists face interference in their work. In March, national security officials arrested Umar Farooq, an American freelance journalist, in southern Kyrgyzstan, and accused him of possessing "extremist" material, charges he denied. Farooq was deported on March 29 for working without accreditation.

Sexual Orientation and Gender Identity

LGBT people in Kyrgyzstan experience ill-treatment, extortion, and discrimination from both state and non-state actors. There is widespread impunity for these abuses. In April, assailants firebombed the office of the LGBT rights group Labrys; no one was hurt. On May 17, International Day Against Homophobia, nationalist youth groups raided a private LGBT event at a café in Bishkek, threatening and filming those present at the event. The police opened an investigation on charges of hooliganism.

Parliament continued to consider an anti-LGBT bill banning "propaganda of non-traditional sexual relations," which appears aimed at silencing anyone seeking to openly share information about same-sex relations in Kyrgyzstan. When discussing the draft law, public officials used homophobic and discriminatory rhetoric.

Freedom of Religion

The government has escalated its efforts to combat religious extremism, but many investigations have been accompanied by violations of detainees' rights, according to local rights lawyers. Members of ethnic minorities are more vulnerable to abuse. In October, a court convicted popular Imam Rashot Kamalov to five years in prison on charges of inciting religious hatred and disseminating extremist material. His sentence was increased to 10 years in prison on appeal. Kamalov and his supporters believe he was targeted after publicly criticizing the police in December 2014.

According to Forum 18, an international organization that promotes religious freedom, a new draft religion law appears not to address a Constitutional Chamber ruling from September 2014 finding components of the existing law unconstitutional, such as a restriction that a religious organization can only carry out activities at its legal address. Forum 18 also decried police abuse of Jehovah's Witnesses, for example, during and after their gathering at a café in Osh in August.

Key International Actors

In January, Kyrgyzstan underwent its second Universal Periodic Review at the UN Human Rights Council. States commended Kyrgyzstan's adoption of a new constitution in 2010 and of a national preventive mechanism against torture, but raised concerns about violence against LGBT people, draft "foreign agents," and anti-LGBT "propaganda" bills, and the disproportionate prosecution and conviction of ethnic Uzbeks following the June 2010 violence.

In April, the UN Committee on the Protection of the Rights of all Migrant Workers and Members of their Families identified discrimination against migrant workers, especially in employment, education, and health. It urged Kyrgyzstan to raise awareness among migrants to Russia, who "are often targets of hate crimes," and provide consular assistance there.

In May, the European Union held its annual human rights dialogue with Kyrgyzstan. Officials raised the case of Azimjon Askarov and discussed problematic draft legislation, but missed other opportunities to publicly register concern about Kyrgyzstan's poor rights record, including on the fifth anniversary of the June 2010 events.

On July 21, Kyrgyzstan terminated a 1993 Kyrgyz-US cooperation agreement, after the US State Department granted Askarov a human rights award.

In its July concluding observations, the UN CESCR issued recommendations to the government, including: end persistent discrimination on ethnic and other grounds in accessing employment and health care; withdraw anti-gay "propaganda" and "foreign agents" bills; address gender inequality, domestic violence, and bride-kidnapping; and ensure evictions are carried out in strict compliance with international human rights law.

Lebanon

Lebanon's political institutions were paralyzed as the country remained without a president, and parliamentary elections—initially planned for June 2013 and then November 2014—were postponed again until 2017. The government's failure to provide basic services, including garbage removal, led to a wave of protests starting in August. In some instances, security forces used excessive force to quell these protests.

New entry regulations in January 2015 seriously restricted Syrian refugees from accessing Lebanese territory, while stringent residency renewal regulations rendered many Syrian refugees without legal status in Lebanon. With limited international support, the government struggled to meet refugees' needs. Draft laws to stop torture and improve the treatment of migrant domestic workers stalled in parliament.

Lengthy Pretrial Detention, Ill-Treatment, and Torture

Amid increased security threats, the Lebanese Armed Forces and Internal Security Forces (ISF) arrested suspects in relation to attacks on civilians in Lebanon or involvement with armed groups in Syria. Some of these suspects have suffered from lengthy pretrial detention and told Human Rights Watch that security forces had beaten, severely whipped, and tortured them, including with sticks, cigarettes, batons, and rifle butts.

In the context of conducting security operations, forces also targeted Syrian refugee settlements, sometimes arbitrarily detaining all adult males and later ill-treating or torturing some of them.

In June 2015, leaked videos showed ISF members torturing inmates in Roumieh prison north of Beirut following a prison riot. The interior minister confirmed the authenticity of the videos. Media reports said that 12 ISF members were referred for investigation; no update was provided regarding the outcome of the investigations.

Lebanon has not yet established a national preventive mechanism to visit and monitor places of detention, as required under the Optional Protocol to the Convention against Torture, which it ratified in 2008. Legislation to create such a body has stalled in parliament for several years.

Refugees

By November 2015, approximately 1.1 million Syrian refugees in Lebanon were registered with the United Nations High Commissioner for Refugees (UNHCR). In 2015, Lebanon set new entry regulations for Syrians that effectively barred many asylum seekers fleeing Syria from entering Lebanon, save for those who qualified for entry under exceptional humanitarian criteria.

In April, the Ministry of Social Affairs requested that UNHCR deregister all refugees who entered Lebanon after January 5 as part of ongoing governmental efforts to decrease the number of Syrian refugees in the country. Since May, UNHCR suspended the registration of Syrians in compliance with the government's request. Lebanon is not a signatory to the 1951 UN Refugee Convention, and refugees lacking legal status therefore risk detention for illegal presence in the country. Approximately 70 percent of Syrian refugees in Lebanon reportedly fall below the poverty line and rely on aid to survive.

Human Rights Watch also documented a few isolated incidents of deportations of Syrians and Palestinians back to Syria, putting them at risk of arbitrary detention, torture, or other persecution. Two Syrian inmates disappeared following their transfer into the custody of General Security in October and in November 2014; their relatives fear they have been forcibly deported to Syria.

Approximately 45,000 Palestinians from Syria are living in Lebanon, joining the estimated 400,000 Palestinian refugees already in the country. In 2015, Palestinians from Syria were still banned from entering the country. As of July, UN Relief and Works Agency for Palestine Refugees in the Near East (UNRWA) suspended its cash assistance for housing to Palestinians from Syria due to a shortage of funds.

Freedom of Assembly and Expression

In August and September, police used excessive force in a number of instances to disperse protesters demonstrating against the government's failure to resolve a trash removal problem, as well as corruption. On August 22 and 23, Lebanese security personnel used rubber bullets, tear gas, water cannons, rifle butts, and batons to control protesters. Security forces also fired live ammunition in the air. On August 19 and 29, and September 1 and 16, police officers also beat and arrested protesters.

Lebanon's State Prosecutor Samir Hammoud tasked a military prosecutor, who under Lebanese law has jurisdiction over crimes involving the security forces, to investigate the violence. Detained protesters charged with violence have been referred to military trials.

While freedom of expression is generally respected in the country, defaming or criticizing the Lebanese president or army is considered a criminal offense that can carry a jail sentence.

In January, Lebanese authorities summoned Al Jazeera journalist Faisal Qassem over charges of insulting the army in Facebook posts and, given his failure to show up to two hearings, issued an warrant of search and inquiry against him.

In October, political activist Michael Douaihy was released after General Security arrested and held him for nine days, and ordered him to pay a fine of $200 over a Facebook post criticizing the agency. Douaihy was indicted under article 386 of the Lebanese penal code that criminalizes libel and defamation against the president, public officials, and private individuals. Also in October, journalist Mohammed Nazzal was sentenced for six months in abstenia and fined US$666 for a Facebook post criticizing the Lebanese judiciary.

Migrant Workers

Migrant domestic workers, primarily from Sri Lanka, Ethiopia, the Philippines, and Nepal are excluded from the labor law and subject to restrictive immigration rules based on the *kafala* system, visa sponsorship that ties workers to their employers and puts them at risk of exploitation and abuse.

The most common complaints documented by the embassies of labor-sending countries and civil society groups include non-payment or delayed payment of wages, forced confinement to the workplace, refusal to provide time off, and verbal and physical abuse. Migrant domestic workers suing their employers for abuse face legal obstacles and risk detention and deportation due to the restrictive visa system.

HUMAN
RIGHTS
WATCH

UNEQUAL AND UNPROTECTED
Women's Rights Under Lebanese Personal Status Laws

In December 2014, six Lebanese workers submitted a request to the Labor Ministry to form a union for domestic workers. With support of the International Labour Organization (ILO), the International Trade Union Federation (ITUC), and the Federation of Trade Unions of Workers and Employees in Lebanon (FENA-SOL), approximately 350 domestic workers of various nationalities gathered for the union's inaugural congress on January 25, 2015.

The Labor Ministry denounced the formation of a domestic workers union on the grounds that it was illegal, as domestic work was not covered by the labor law. According to union members, the application for the union had yet to be decided at time of writing.

Starting in May 2014, nearly a dozen female migrant workers, many longstanding residents of Lebanon, reported being denied residency renewal for themselves and their children. Some were told their children were not allowed to remain with them in Lebanon and were given a short period of time to leave the country.

In March 2015, after months of advocacy by Human Rights Watch and other international and local nongovernmental organizations, General Security reversed this decision and migrant workers and their children are once again being issued residency renewals.

Women's Rights

Despite women's active participation in all aspects of Lebanese society, discriminatory provisions remain in personal status laws, nationality laws, and the criminal code.

Judges have issued scores of temporary protection orders since the enactment of the 2014 Law on the Protection of Women and Family from Domestic Violence. The new law establishes important protection measures and related policing and court reforms but leaves women at risk, as it still fails to criminalize all forms of domestic violence, including marital rape. Some women continued to report that police were unwilling to investigate their complaints, and the fund to assist victims of domestic violence has not yet been set up. Women continue to face obstacles in pursuing criminal complaints of domestic violence, mostly due to lengthy delays.

Under the 15 various Lebanese personal status laws, which are determined by an individual's religious affiliation, women across religions continue to suffer discrimination, including unequal access to divorce, child custody, and property rights. Unlike Lebanese men, Lebanese women cannot pass on their nationality to foreign husbands and children and continue to be subject to discriminatory inheritance laws.

Sexual Orientation and Gender Identity

Lebanon's penal code punishes "any sexual intercourse contrary to the order of nature" with up to one year in prison. In recent years, authorities conducted raids to arrest persons allegedly involved in same-sex conduct, some of whom were subjected to torture.

Legacy of Past Conflicts and Wars

Lebanese authorities continue to take no meaningful steps towards acting on proposals to set up an independent national commission to investigate the fate of people forcibly disappeared during the country's 1975-1990 civil war and its aftermath.

In October 2012, Justice Minister Shakib Qortbawi put forward a draft decree to the cabinet to establish a national commission to investigate the fate of the "disappeared," but no further action was taken. In September 2014, the government finally provided the families of the disappeared with the files of the Official Commission of Inquiry that had been appointed in 2000 to investigate the fate of the kidnapped. These showed that the government had not conducted any serious investigation.

Key International Actors

Syria, Iran, and Saudi Arabia maintain a strong influence on Lebanese politics through local allies and proxies, and increasingly so as the conflict in neighboring Syria drags on.

Many countries, including the United States, United Kingdom, members of the European Union, Canada, and various Gulf countries, have given Lebanon extensive, albeit insufficient, support to help it cope with the Syrian refugee crisis and to bolster security amid spill-over violence.

The Lebanese Armed Forces and ISF also receive assistance from a range of international donors, including the US, EU, UK, France, and Saudi Arabia. Some of these actors have taken steps to improve the compliance of these forces with international human rights law, but more pressure by the international community remains necessary.

Libya

Amid tenuous United Nations-led peace talks, Libya's political and security crisis deepened as two rival governments competed for legitimacy, control of vital institutions, and international support. Despite some factions signing a political deal in December, there was no end in sight to the crisis. As armed clashes continued, the country edged towards a humanitarian crisis, with almost 400,000 people internally displaced and increasing disruption to basic services, such as power and fuel supplies.

Forces engaged in the conflict continued with impunity to arbitrarily detain, torture, unlawfully kill, indiscriminately attack, abduct and disappear, and forcefully displace people from their homes. The domestic criminal justice system collapsed in most parts of the country, exacerbating the human rights crisis.

Armed groups that pledged allegiance to the extremist group Islamic State (also known as ISIS) continued to commit serious human rights abuses, including unlawful killings and summary executions, and succeeded in expanding and gaining control over towns in the center of the country, including Sirte.

The widescale breakdown in law and order enabled tens of thousands of migrants, refugees, and asylum seekers to transit through Libya as they made their way towards Europe. In Libya, they faced violence, ill-treatment, and forced labor, while at least 3,100 died attempting to cross the Mediterranean in flimsy boats provided by networks of criminal people smugglers. Over 143,500 people arrived in Italy by boat from North Africa, the vast majority from Libya, between January 1 and end of November 2015.

Armed Conflicts and War Crimes

Armed conflicts continued to rage in the east, west, and south. In Benghazi, forces loyal to the internationally recognized government battled against a coalition of Islamist militias, including ISIS and Ansar al-Sharia. Some civilians remained trapped in the areas of fighting. In the west, forces allied with the self-declared government in Tripoli continued to clash with opposing groups based in western coastal areas. In the south, Tebu and Tuareg militias clashed intermittently.

Warring factions indiscriminately shelled civilian areas, arbitrarily seized people, tortured and looted, burned, and otherwise destroyed civilian property in attacks that in some cases amounted to war crimes. Some forces also used cluster munitions and antipersonnel landmines, which are internationally prohibited weapons.

Political Process

An UN-sponsored dialogue that spanned a year sought to achieve agreement on the formation of a government of national unity and an end to fighting.

In December, some factions signed a political agreement in Skheirat, Morocco, designating a prime minister and a presidential council with a view to establishing a national unity government, and the UN Security Council passed a resolution recognizing this new entity as the sole legitimate Libyan government. However, by December the new entiy was operating from Tunisia due to key factions in Libya opposing the deal. In November, Martin Kobler took over as chief UN negotiator and special representative of the secretary-general in Libya.

Those engaged in the dialogue included in the east, members of the internationally recognized government, the House of Representatives (HoR), Libyan National Army, and affiliated militias, and in the west, members of the rival Tripoli-based Government of National Unity, as well as the rump General National Congress (GNC) and a host of armed militias affiliated with the Libya Dawn alliance.

In practice, the rival authorities continued to operate parallel institutions from al-Bayda and Tripoli, effectively creating two separate administrations, with the former also creating its own national oil company, investment authority, and national bank.

In May, Abdullah al-Thinni, head of the internationally recognized government, said he survived an assassination attempt in eastern Libya.

In October, the HoR, the legislature of the internationally recognized government, voted to extend its term of office, which legally expired on October 21, without conducting new elections, leaving a possible constitutional vacuum.

HUMAN
RIGHTS
WATCH

"The Endless Wait"

Long-term Arbitrary Detentions and Torture in Western Libya

Constitution and Legislation

Libya remains without a permanent constitution. The Constitution Drafting Assembly, elected in February 2014 to draft a new constitution, hampered by political infighting and a boycott by Amazigh groups, published a first draft in September 2015. Some political groups called for readopting the 1951 Constitution of the Libyan monarchy.

The HoR failed to amend the counterterrorism law that it adopted in September 2014, although several provisions could be used to curtail free speech and rights to peaceful assembly and movement. The law prescribes harsh punishments for vaguely defined acts "that harm national unity," includes an overly broad definition of "terrorist acts," and stipulates life imprisonment for establishing or leading a "terrorist organization" and 10 years with hard labor for joining a "terrorist organization," without requiring any evidence of violence.

In July, the HoR passed a General Amnesty Law. It stipulates that those who commit crimes of terrorism, rape, torture, corruption, and murder by race or ethnicity may not receive an amnesty. However, it fails to rule out amnesties for other serious human rights crimes, such as forced displacement, enforced disappearances, and unlawful killings.

Arbitrary Detention, Torture, and Deaths in Custody

In what may amount to a crime against humanity, prison authorities and militias continued to arbitrarily detain thousands of Libyans and foreigners—including some held since 2011—without charges, trial, or due process rights, and ill-treat them in detention.

Human Rights Watch gained rare access in April to detainees in facilities controlled by the military and Interior and Justice ministries in eastern Libya and in September interviewed detainees in prisons run by the Justice Ministry of the self-proclaimed government in Tripoli and Misrata. Although conditions varied, in most facilities, detainees reported torture and other ill-treatment, and in some, deaths in custody caused by abuse.

In August, an online news site leaked video tapes in which officials and guards at al-Hadba Prison in Tripoli seemed to ill-treat several detainees, including al-

Saadi Gaddafi, one of the sons of former leader Muammar Gaddafi. The General Prosecutor's Office announced an investigation into the incident.

Criminal Justice System

The criminal justice system collapsed or was dysfunctional: in the east, there were no prosecutions or trials, and in Tripoli, the Supreme Court's ability to exert judicial oversight and afford impartial remedy was threatened by the effective division between two rival authorities and deteriorating security conditions. ISIS-affiliated groups suspended the criminal justice system in the coastal city of Sirte and installed their own Islamic Court based on Sharia law.

International Justice and the International Criminal Court

Authorities failed to surrender Saif al-Islam Gaddafi to the International Criminal Court (ICC); he is wanted there for crimes against humanity related to the 2011 uprising that overthrew his father, Muammar.

The ICC prosecutor failed to open a new investigation into the grave and ongoing crimes within the court's jurisdiction being committed in Libya.

Death Penalty

More than 30 articles of the penal code still provide for the death penalty. Since Gaddafi's overthrow in 2011, civil and military courts around the country continued to impose death sentences. At time of writing, however, authorities had not carried out any judicial executions. The total number of people sentenced to death is unknown.

On July 28, Tripoli's Court of Assize convicted 32 former Gaddafi officials on charges of alleged crimes committed during the 2011 uprising. The court sentenced Saif al-Islam Gaddafi in absentia and eight other defendants to death, including former intelligence chief Abdullah Sanussi, and former Gaddafi-era prime ministers, al-Baghdadi al-Mahmoudi and Abuzaid Dorda. Serious due process violations, including denial of access to legal counsel for defendants, undermined the trial. In September, Human Rights Watch gained rare access to al-Hadba detention facility in Tripoli and met with Sanussi, Dorda, al-Mahmoudi and another son of Gaddafi, al-Saadi.

Women's Rights

The HoR failed to amend penal code provisions that deem sexual violence a crime against a woman's "honor" rather than the woman herself. The code continues to permit a reduced sentence for a man who kills his wife or another female relative because he suspects her of extramarital sexual relations. Libyan law inadequately prohibits domestic violence.

Abductions and Enforced Disappearances

Militias and criminal groups throughout Libya continued to abduct and forcibly disappear hundreds of civilians, including civil society activists, politicians, and nongovernmental organization (NGO) workers with impunity.

According to the Libyan Red Crescent, at least 600 people went missing in such circumstances between February 2014 and April 2015. Those still missing in November 2015 included four Italian oil company workers abducted in western Libya in July 2015, Suliman Zubi, a former GNC member abducted by Zintan groups in July 2014, and Abdelmoez Banoon, a Tripoli-based activist who disappeared in July 2014.

Freedom of Speech and Expression

Armed groups continued to harass, attack, and kill journalists. Victims included Muftah Al-Qatrani, who worked for a media production company prior to his murder on April 21 in Benghazi. Some international journalists reported harassment by Tripoli authorities, including questioning over contents of reports and threats of expulsion.

The fate of Sofiane Chourabi and Nadhir Ktari, two Tunisian journalists who went missing in September 2014 while on assignment in Libya, remains unclear. Groups affiliated with ISIS claimed in April that they had killed both men.

In November, the NGO Reporters Without Borders (RSF) said there were 31 individual attacks against journalists in Libya in 2015. The NGO also said that Libya ranked 154 out of 180 countries on the 2015 press freedom index.

ISIS and Other Extremist Groups

ISIS-affiliated groups continued to commit serious rights abuses while extending their presence and control of territory within Libya. They remained present around Derna and in Benghazi in the east, in the Tripoli area in the west, and in the south, and took total control of Sirte and its environs.

In January, ISIS militants attacked a Tripoli hotel, killing at least 12 people, mostly civilians, including foreign nationals. They also claimed responsibility for attacks on the Iranian ambassador's residence and the embassies of Algeria, Morocco, and South Korea. In September, ISIS-affiliated groups attacked a militia-run prison within the Mitiga airbase in Tripoli, which resulted in the reported deaths of at least three prison guards.

In Derna, ISIS militants maintained a reign of terror from January until June marked by public lashings and summary, extrajudicial executions of residents who opposed them, as well as at least four LGBT men. On February 20, ISIS said it carried out car bomb attacks in al-Qubba, a town near Derna, which killed at least 45 people, mostly civilians. In June, the Derna Mujahideen Shura Council (DMSC), an Al-Qaeda affiliated militia, forced ISIS militants to withdraw from Derna's center, but in November armed clashes continued. In October, ISIS militants killed one man after forcing him to dig his own grave, and killed another by dragging him through streets.

ISIS militants took control of Sirte and the nearby villages of Harawa and Nawfaliyah, and in February 2015, issued a video showing them beheading 21 mostly Egyptian Copts in Sirte. Another ISIS video issued in April appeared to show the killing of at least 30 Ethiopian Christians in separate incidents in Sirte and southern Libya. In August, ISIS militants established a public administration and an Islamic Court in Sirte. Armed clashes between local residents and ISIS-affiliated groups resulted in at least 29 reported deaths, mostly fighters but also some civilians.

In October, masked members of ISIS publicly beheaded two men accused of sorcery, and crucified an elderly Sufi Sheikh.

HUMAN
RIGHTS
WATCH

WAR ON THE MEDIA
Journalists under Attack in Libya

Internally Displaced People

The local council of Misrata and affiliated militias continued to prevent 40,000 residents of Tawergha and residents of Tomina and Karareem from returning to their homes in what amounts to a crime against humanity, and collective punishment for crimes they say were committed by some Tawergha residents during the 2011 revolution. Those displaced remained scattered in makeshift camps and private housing around the country, but continued to face harassment and arbitrary detention. Libyan authorities failed to end this ongoing crime, while perpetrators continued to benefit from impunity since 2011.

According to the United Nations, around 400,000 people remained internally displaced due to the ongoing armed hostilities in all parts of the country, which forced them to leave their homes.

Migrants, Refugees, and Asylum Seekers

Significant numbers of refugees, asylum seekers, and migrants reached Europe from Libya by sea in 2015. Over 143,500 arrived in Italy from North Africa, the vast majority from Libya, by the end of November. However, at least 3,100 others perished at sea during the same period. In May, the European Union significantly increased search and rescue missions in the central Mediterranean.

Libya's remaining active coast guard provided only limited search and rescue operations, citing a lack of resources.

The Directorate for Combatting Illegal Migration continued to detain asylum seekers and migrants found without official residence documents and hold them in inhumane conditions, where prison guards abused and ill-treated them with impunity and they lacked access to medical care.

Criminal smuggler networks also abused migrants and asylum seekers and subjected them to forced labor.

Key International Actors

The UN, the United States, EU states, and Egypt, Qatar, Saudi Arabia, Turkey, and the United Arab Emirates (UAE), all played significant roles in the Libya conflict.

The US, United Kingdom, and France issued several statements supporting the UN-led peace initiative.

In February, Egyptian warplanes carried out air strikes against purported ISIS targets in the eastern city of Derna, in retaliation for the alleged killings of 21 mostly Egyptian Coptic Christians by ISIS militants, killing at least seven civilians. In June, the US conducted airstrikes in the eastern city of Ajdabiya in an attempt to kill Mokhtar Belmokhtar, an Al-Qaeda operative. At time of writing, Belmokhtar's death remained unconfirmed.

In March, the UN Human Rights Council agreed to begin an investigation by the Office of the High Commissioner for Human Rights (OHCHR) into ongoing rights abuses in Libya since January 1, 2014 (OIOL).

The first OIOL oral update in September said violations included attacks on civilians and civilian objects, reprisals in the form of destruction of homes, shelling of hospitals, unlawful killings, arbitrary detention, torture, and other ill-treatment, in some cases leading to death. The report also mentioned abductions based on origin and abduction of activists and journalists. It said refugees and asylum seekers remained vulnerable to abuses.

The UN Security Council renewed the mandates of the UN Support Mission in Libya (UNSMIL) and the Panel of Experts on Libya in March, and reaffirmed the international arms embargo on Libya, despite efforts by Libya and Egypt to overturn it. In July, Russia and China vetoed a council resolution that would have imposed sanctions on two individuals for obstructing the UN peace talks.

In May, the EU approved the establishment of EU NAVFOR MED, an air and sea operation empowered to use force against people smuggling networks in Libya. In October, the EU announced that the renamed "Operation Sophia" entered its second phase where it would "conduct boarding, search, seizure and diversion, on the high seas, of vessels suspected of being used for human smuggling or trafficking."

In November, leaked communication alleged the UAE had violated the existing arms embargo against Libya, by supplying weapons to one side of the conflict.

Malaysia

Malaysia's respect for human rights plummeted in 2015, with increased harassment and persecution of human rights defenders, activists, political opposition figures, and journalists. The government reacted to rising public discontent over issues ranging from allegations of corruption to the treatment of former political opposition leader Anwar Ibrahim with a wave of repression, often relying on broad and vaguely worded criminal laws to target its critics.

Freedom of Expression

The biggest threat to free speech remains the Sedition Act, which has been used to prosecute those who criticize the government or the judiciary, or make remarks the government considers to be derogatory toward the sultans (traditional Malay state rulers) or disrespectful of religion.

The Federal Court rejected a constitutional challenge to the law in October. More than 33 people, including seven opposition parliamentarians, have been charged with sedition since 2013. Parliamentarians who receive fines of more than 2,000 Malaysian ringgit (US$475) or are sentenced to more than a year in prison lose their seats and are banned from politics for five years.

In April, the ruling Barisan Nasional, or National Front, coalition passed amendments to the Sedition Act to increase the penalties for violations and to make it easier to use the law against online speech. The amendments created a new offense of "aggravated sedition," providing a penalty of up to 20 years in prison for "seditious" statements that result, even indirectly, in harm to property or bodily injury. The strengthening of the law was a major reversal by Prime Minister Najib Razak, who had repeatedly promised to revoke the Sedition Act and replace it with what he called a Harmony Act.

The government continued to use the Printing Presses and Publication Act (PPPA) to suppress publications and limit content. The PPPA requires all publishers to obtain a license and enables the government to ban publications "likely to be prejudicial to public order," or "likely to alarm public opinion." In July, the Ministry of Home Affairs used the PPPA to suspend the publication of two newspapers for three months after they reported on allegations of corruption involving the government-owned investment fund 1 Malaysia Development Berhad (1MDB), whose board of advisors is chaired by Prime Minister Najib. The High Court overturned the suspension in September.

The government also used the PPPA to ban "any yellow coloured clothing" bearing the logo of the Coalition for Free and Fair Elections (known as Bersih, meaning "clean" in Malay) and any publications about a planned Bersih rally. Despite the ban, which came into effect two days before a major rally Bersih organized in downtown Kuala Lumpur, tens of thousands of people wore yellow Bersih t-shirts to the peaceful 34-hour rally August 29 to 30. The government has instituted criminal investigations of several opposition politicians for wearing Bersih t-shirts.

The government has also used laws criminalizing defamation and statements that could lead to a breach of the peace to arrest and prosecute opposition politicians and activists for critical speech. Article 233 of the Communications and Multimedia Act, which outlaws any communication the government considers "obscene, indecent, false, menacing or offensive," has been used to prosecute users of social media, investigate media, and block websites reporting on the 1MDB scandal or publishing information about the Bersih rally in August.

Lena Hendry, programme manager for the Pusat Komas Freedom Film Fest, was set to go on trial in December for allegedly violating the Film Censorship Act for her involvement in screening the documentary film "No Fire Zone: The Killing Fields of Sri Lanka" in Kuala Lumpur in July 2013. The Malaysian Federal Court in September 2015 rejected Hendry's constitutional challenge to the Film Censorship Act.

Freedom of Assembly and Association

A series of major demonstrations took place in Malaysia during 2015. In most instances, the police did not interfere with the rallies, but subsequently arrested and charged many of those involved with "unlawful assembly" or other offenses under the penal code, or with sedition, for statements they made during the rallies. Authorities declared the rallies "illegal" at least twice before they even took place.

Peaceful Assembly Act
Printing & Press Act
Sedition Act
Communications &
Multimedia Act
Penal Code

**HUMAN
RIGHTS
WATCH**

CREATING A CULTURE OF FEAR

The Criminalization of Peaceful Expression in Malaysia

In October, the Court of Appeals upheld the provision of the Peaceful Assembly Act that allows for criminal prosecution of rally organizers who fail to give police 10 days' advance notice, directly contradicting an April 2014 decision by the same court. After the decision, the government promptly charged opposition politician Nik Nazmi, who had successfully challenged the law in 2014, for failure to give notice of the very rally that was the basis for his constitutional challenge. The authorities also charged two of the organizers of the August Bersih rally with failure to give proper notice, even though Bersih organizers twice met with the police more than 10 days before the rally.

The Societies Act restricts the right to freedom of association by requiring that organizations with seven or more members register with the registrar of societies. The law gives the minister of home affairs "absolute discretion" to declare an organization illegal, and also gives the government supervisory authority over political parties. As of November, the registrar remained locked in a dispute with the opposition Democratic Action Party, refusing to recognize the party's central executive committee or its 120 branch offices after more than two years of investigation. According to the Registry of Societies' website, the registrar rejected more than 38 percent of the applications submitted in 2015 to form organizations.

Political Prosecution of Anwar Ibrahim

The government's politically motivated prosecution of former opposition leader Anwar Ibrahim on sodomy charges—a textbook example of the political use of discriminatory laws—culminated in February, when the Federal Court upheld his conviction and sentence of five years' imprisonment. Since entering prison he has suffered from a variety of health problems, including a shoulder injury and back problems. In October, the United Nations Working Group on Arbitrary Detention determined that Anwar was being arbitrarily detained and demanded his immediate release and reinstatement of his political rights.

Police Abuse and Impunity

Police torture of suspects in custody, in some cases resulting in deaths, and excessive use of force in apprehending suspects continued to be serious problems in 2015. Human rights NGO Suara Rakyat Malaysia documented at least 10 suspicious deaths in police custody in the first nine months of the year, despite promises by Home Minister Ahmad Zahid Hamidi in May 2014 to install closed circuit television equipment in all places of police detention.

The government continues to ignore calls from the Malaysian Bar Council and civil society groups to establish an Independent Police Complaints and Misconduct Commission with the power to receive complaints about police conduct, independently investigate abuses, and sanction those found to have engaged in misconduct. The Yang di-Pertuan Agong appointed a new chairman and new commissioners for the existing Enforcement Agencies Integrity Commission in November 2014.

On November 3, 2015, the commission for the first time issued a report finding that the police were responsible for a death in custody, holding that physical violence during custody and interrogation was the cause of the death of a young man from Johor detained in November 2014. The inspector general of police has stated that the police officers responsible will not be shielded from criminal charges, but at time of writing had done little to implement that promise.

Criminal Justice System

In December 2015, the government rushed through a broad and vaguely worded National Security Council Act that empowers the prime minister to declare security areas within which restraints on police powers would be suspended and the authorities would have the ability to conduct arrests, searches and seizures without warrants.

In April, the government passed a new, restrictive Prevention of Terrorism Act, which gives a government-appointed board the authority to impose detention without trial for up to two years, renewable indefinitely, to order electronic monitoring, and to impose other significant restrictions on freedom of movement and freedom of association, with no possibility of judicial review.

The authorities invoked the similarly restrictive Security Offenses Special Measures Act, which allows for preventive detention of up to 28 days with no judicial review, to detain two people involved in efforts to expose government corruption. Khairuddin Abu Hassan and his lawyer Matthias Chang were arrested on

September 18 and October 8, respectively, for filing police reports about 1MDB in several foreign countries.

They were subsequently charged with attempting to commit economic sabotage of the state under Penal Code section 124L. If convicted, they could be sentenced to up to 15 years in prison.

Malaysia retains the death penalty for various crimes, including drug trafficking, and is not transparent about when and how decisions are made to carry out executions. Nearly 1,000 people are estimated to be on death row.

Refugees, Asylum Seekers, and Trafficking Victims

The discovery of mass graves on the Thai-Malaysia border containing the remains of suspected victims of trafficking highlights the continuing problem of trafficking in Malaysia. Approximately 99 bodies, many reportedly ethnic Rohingya from Burma, were found in May, and another 24 graves were discovered in August. Little information has been made public about progress in identifying and investigating suspects involved in these trafficking camps or government officials who may have aided and abetted operations.

The Malaysian government has failed to effectively implement the amendments passed in 2014 to Malaysia's 2007 anti-trafficking law, in particular by taking the necessary administrative steps to provide assistance and work authorization to all trafficking victims who desire it, while ensuring their freedom of movement. Despite these failures, the United States government in July upgraded Malaysia in its annual Trafficking in Persons Report in what appeared to be a political move connected to the Trans-Pacific Partnership Agreement for trade.

Sexual Orientation and Gender Identity

Discrimination against lesbian, gay, bisexual, and transgender people is pervasive in Malaysia, and that discrimination reaches the highest levels of government. Prime Minister Najib was reported to have asserted at an international seminar on August 18 that sexual and gender minorities pose a threat to Malaysian society, arguing that "groups like the Islamic State and lesbians, gay, bisexuals, and transgenders (LGBT) both target the younger generation and seem successful in influencing certain groups in society."

The Federal Court decided in October to reverse a lower court ruling that the state of Negeri Sembilan's prohibition on "a male person posing as a woman" was unconstitutional. The ruling seriously undermined the rights of transgender people. In June, nine transgender women were convicted by a Sharia court in Kelantan under a similar state prohibition.

On September 10, two men wielding iron bars brutally beat one of Malaysia's most prominent transgender activists, Nisha Ayub, outside her apartment building, requiring her hospitalization. She reported the apparent hate crime to the police, but at time of writing the police had not identified any suspects.

National Human Rights Commission

In November, the Malaysian government announced plans to cut its funding to Suhakam, the national human rights commission, by 50 percent, in what is widely seen as retaliation for the commission's independent reporting.

Key International Actors

Malaysia was the chair of the Association of Southeast Asian Nations (ASEAN) and the East Asia Summit in 2015 and is a member of the UN Security Council. The country positions itself in the UN and the international community as a moderate Muslim state prepared to stand up to Islamist extremism, earning support from the US and its allies. Malaysia also has continued its engagement with China, its largest trading partner.

Mali

The human rights climate in Mali worsened as a result of a significant increase in violence and a marked deterioration in security, notwithstanding the June signing of a peace agreement envisioned to end the military and political crisis in the north. Attacks and violence progressively spread from the north into several southern regions and the capital, Bamako.

Throughout the year there were frequent incidents of banditry and rampant criminality; clashes between armed groups; and deadly attacks by armed Islamist groups on United Nations peacekeepers, Malian government forces, and to a lesser extent, civilians. The violence severely undermined the delivery of humanitarian aid. Government forces responded to the attacks with military operations that on several occasions resulted in arbitrary arrests, executions, torture, and other mistreatment.

Malian authorities made scant effort to investigate and hold accountable those implicated in serious abuses committed during the 2012-2013 armed conflict. The release in 2015 of some 70 men from detention, including some implicated in serious violations, raised concern of a de facto amnesty.

Rule of law institutions countrywide were weak, in part due to unprofessional practices, such as the solicitation of bribes, and inadequate budgetary allocations for the criminal justice system. Corruption, endemic at all levels of government, further impeded Malians' access to basic health care and education. There was little progress in security sector and justice reform or in addressing development challenges, such as the delivery of basic healthcare and education.

Concerns about the deteriorating security situation and the movement south of armed groups allegedly linked to Al-Qaeda generated sustained diplomatic interest in Mali. The French government played a key role in military matters, the European Union (EU) on training and security sector reform, and the UN, through the Multidimensional Integrated Stabilization Mission in Mali (MINUSMA), on rule of law and political stability. However, these actors were largely reluctant to publicly call for investigations into past and ongoing crimes.

Abuses by Armed Groups in the North

Throughout 2015, armed groups linked to Al-Qaeda, along with opposing ethnic Tuareg and Arab groups, engaged in numerous clashes, attacks on Malian soldiers and neutral peacekeepers, and to a lesser extent, on aid workers and other civilians. Many civilians were wounded or killed either in these attacks or by landmines and improvised explosive devices on major roads. Groups arbitrarily detained and often mistreated combatants from opposing sides.

The attacks by Islamist armed groups increased in the north and spread into central and southern Mali. Attacks occurred in Mopti, Segou, Sikasso, and Koulikoro regions as well as Bamako, where Islamist assailants killed five in a March attack on a nightclub, and at least 18, including many foreigners, during a November attack on an upscale hotel. An attack in August on a hotel in the army garrison town of Sevare, in central Mali, killed five civilians including four UN contractors. These groups executed at least 13 civilians accused of being informants for the government, the majority in central Mali.

In 2015, there were at least 30 attacks by armed men on humanitarian agencies, hampering their efforts to deliver aid. In March, a driver with the International Committee of the Red Cross was killed when their clearly marked truck was ambushed by an Islamist armed group.

At least 10 UN peacekeepers were killed in 2015 after being deliberately targeted by Islamist armed groups, bringing the number to 42 killed since MINUSMA's creation in 2013. Armed groups took responsibility for many of these attacks, including an attack in July that killed six peacekeepers from Burkina Faso.

Al-Qaeda in the Islamic Maghreb (AQIM) at time of writing, held two foreign hostages: one from Sweden, and a dual British and South African national. AQIM released a French hostage in December 2014, and French forces freed a Dutch hostage in a military operation in April 2015.

Abuses by State Security Forces

Government forces committed numerous violations against suspected supporters and members of Islamist armed groups. Violations included arbitrary detention, torture and other ill-treatment, and extrajudicial execution. The most frequent and serious abuse was meted out by army soldiers and members of the pro-government militia Groupe Autodéfense Touareg Imghad et Alliés (GATIA), largely targeting men from the Peuhl and Tuareg ethnic groups. In May, GATIA militiamen allegedly executed six Tuareg men including a humanitarian worker in the northern village of Tin Hamma.

The abuse usually stopped after detainees were handed over to government gendarmes, who increasingly fulfilled their mandated role as provost marshal. The military made little effort to investigate and hold to account soldiers or militiamen implicated in violations. Members of the security forces, notably the army, were also implicated in acts of extortion, bribe taking, and theft, mostly from detainees.

Accountability for Abuses the 2012-2013 Armed Conflict

The government made little progress in holding to account those from all warring factions responsible for law-of-war violations committed during the 2012-2013 armed conflict. With few exceptions, judicial authorities failed to investigate over 100 complaints filed by victims and family members. Moreover, the 2012 torture and enforced disappearance of 21 elite "Red Berets," which in 2013 and 2014 resulted in charges against some 25 soldiers, including former coup leader Gen. Amadou Haya Sanogo, had, at time of writing, failed to move past the investigations phase.

During 2015, the authorities freed at least 74 detainees, including several allegedly implicated in serious international crimes during the 2012-2013 armed conflict. The releases, characterized by the government as a "confidence-building measure" in the context of negotiations, were carried out without regard to whether the men might have been responsible for serious crimes. The peace accord lacked provisions to address impunity and the need for justice for serious crimes committed by all sides during the conflict.

On September 18, the International Criminal Court (ICC) issued its first arrest warrant in the context of its Mali investigation. On September 26, Ahmad Al Mahdi Al Faqi was surrendered to the ICC from Niger after being charged with the destruction of historical monuments, the first case of its kind before the ICC. In July 2012, Mali, a state party to the ICC, referred "the situation in Mali since January 2012" to the ICC prosecutor for investigation.

Truth and Reconciliation Mechanism

In 2014, President Ibrahim Boubacar Keïta established the Truth, Justice and Reconciliation Commission by executive order. The Commission will have a three year mandate, covering the period from 1960 to 2013. It is to consist of 15 members and seven working groups. It will function under the Ministry of National Reconciliation and Development of the North. In August, the government appointed Ousmane Oumarou Sidibé as Chair of the Commission; however, his appointment and the credibility of the body were limited due to the government's failure to consult sufficiently with a wide variety of stakeholders on the Commission's membership, mandate powers, and degree of independence.

Judiciary

During 2015, there was some progress in ensuring access to justice for residents of the northern Timbuktu, Gao, and Kidal regions, demonstrated by the continued rehabilitation of local courthouses and jails and the redeployment of prosecutors, judges, and judicial police who had fled during the armed conflict. Their ability to conduct investigations outside major towns was limited by the precarious security situation. Some judicial and corrections personnel fled their posts in central Mali after attacks by armed groups.

Neglect and mismanagement within the Malian judiciary countrywide led to striking deficiencies, including insufficient staffing and logistical constraints. These shortfalls hindered efforts to address impunity for perpetrators of all crimes, contributed to violations of the right to due process, and led to incidents of vigilante justice. For example, in March, two children suspected of planting an explosive device near a police station in Gao were beaten to death by a mob.

Due to the courts' inability to adequately process cases, hundreds of detainees are held in extended pretrial detention in overcrowded jails and detention centers.

Recruitment of Children

Armed groups in the north continued to recruit and use child soldiers, some as young as 12 years old. During 2015, some 15 schools in the north were at various times occupied by members of the armed groups, and, to a lesser extent, government forces. Several children suspected of supporting the armed groups were detained in the Bamako Central Prison, in contravention of a 2013 protocol stipulating that children were to be placed in a care center managed by the UN Children's Rights and Emergency Relief Organization (UNICEF).

Key International Actors

In June, the UN Security Council renewed the mandate of MINUSMA and authorized 12,680 peacekeepers, including 40 military observers. A UN inquiry into the January shooting of three men by UN policemen from Rwanda during a protest in Gao found they had used "unauthorized and excessive force." The UN peacebuilding fund supported reconciliation and justice projects. The UN independent expert on the situation of human rights in Mali, Suliman Baldo, conducted two missions to Mali.

Algeria led peace talks, supported by members from the African Union, the Economic Community of West African States (ECOWAS), the European Union, the UN, and Organization of Islamic Cooperation, as well as regional governments.

The 3,000-strong regional French operation—known as Operation Barkhane—continued operations in Mali as well as in Mauritania, Burkina Faso, Niger, and Chad. The United States military provided logistical support to Barkhane.

The EU Training Mission in Mali continued to train soldiers, and in February established the EU Capacity Building Mission to train the police, gendarmerie, and National Guard.

MINUSMA, the UN Development Programme, the EU, the Netherlands, and Canada took the lead in programs to support the justice sector and address corruption. However, their lack of coordination undermined progress in improving the sector.

Mexico

During the administration of President Enrique Peña Nieto, Mexican security forces have been implicated in repeated, serious human rights violations—including extrajudicial killings, enforced disappearances, and torture—in the course of efforts to combat organized crime. The government has made little progress in prosecuting those responsible for recent abuses, let alone the large number of abuses committed by soldiers and police since former President Felipe Calderón (2006-2012) initiated Mexico's "war on drugs."

In September 2015, an expert group established through an agreement between the Mexican government and the Inter-American Commission on Human Rights (IACHR) exposed serious flaws in the government's investigation into the enforced disappearance of 43 students from Ayotzinapa, Guerrero, refuted key conclusions made by the Attorney General's Office, and called on authorities to pursue fresh lines of investigation. The government subsequently agreed to extend the group's mandate to monitor the investigation for an additional six months. At time of writing, more than a year after the disappearances, the whereabouts of at least 41 of students remain unknown.

Other continuing problems include restrictions on press freedom and limits on access to reproductive rights and health care.

Enforced Disappearances

Since 2006, Mexico's security forces have participated in widespread enforced disappearances.

In August 2014, the government publicly acknowledged that the whereabouts of over 22,000 people who had gone missing since 2006 remained unknown. That number has increased to more than 25,500, according to the National Registry of Disappeared or Missing Persons, which was established by law in 2012. Prosecutors and police routinely fail to carry out basic investigative steps to identify those responsible, often telling the missing people's families to investigate on their own.

Only two of the 43 students from a teachers' college in Ayotzinapa, Guerrero, who were disappeared in September 2014, have been identified among the remains that the Attorney General's Office reports having found. As of August 2015, more than 100 people had been charged for their alleged involvement in the incident, but no one had been convicted at time of writing.

In September, the IACHR expert group convened to evaluate the government response to the incident issued its final report, concluding that the investigation had been marred by the mishandling and possible destruction of key evidence.

The federal government has pursued potentially promising initiatives to find people who have gone missing, but they have produced limited results. In 2013, it created a unit in the Attorney General's Office to investigate disappearances. When consulted in August, officials from the Attorney General's Office said they did not know of a single case in which someone had been convicted for an enforced disappearance committed since 2007.

In April, the legislature approved a constitutional reform that requires the federal legislature to pass general laws on enforced disappearance and torture, which will establish a single nationwide definition for each of the crimes and facilitate their prosecution in all 31 states and Mexico City.

Extrajudicial Executions

Unlawful killings of civilians by Mexican security forces "take place at an alarmingly high rate" amid an atmosphere of "systematic and endemic impunity," according to the United Nations special rapporteur on extrajudicial, summary, or arbitrary executions in 2014.

In January 2015, at least eight civilians were killed at Apatzingán, Michoacán after federal police broke up a demonstration involving citizen self-defense groups. Eyewitnesses reported that federal police opened fire on unarmed civilians, shot two of them in the head while they lay on the ground taking cover, and planted guns next to their corpses. At time of writing, the federal investigation was continuing.

In May, a shootout between federal police officers and civilians in Tanhuato, Michoacán left 42 civilians and one police officer dead. While the federal police commissioner at the time told media that officers were responding in self-defense to civilian gunfire, Human Rights Watch received reports that at least four people were extrajudicially executed after the initial confrontation was over. Federal prosecutors did not open an investigation into the matter until three months after the deadly incident.

Military Abuses and Impunity

Mexico has relied heavily on the military to fight drug-related violence and organized crime, leading to widespread human rights violations by military personnel. Since 2006, the National Human Rights Commission (CNDH) has received about 9,000 complaints of abuse by the army—including more than 1,700 during the current administration—and issued reports in over 100 cases in which it found that army personnel had committed serious human rights violations.

In 2014, Congress reformed the Code of Military Justice to require that abuses committed by members of the military against civilians be handled by the civilian criminal justice system rather than the military system, which had a history of routinely failing to hold members of the military accountable for abuses. Under the reform, abuses committed by military personnel against other soldiers remain subject to military justice.

At time of writing, no military personnel had been convicted in connection with the killing of 22 civilians by soldiers in Tlatlaya, state of Mexico, in November 2014, where witness accounts and a report by the CNDH said that at least 12 civilians were extrajudicially executed by soldiers. According to the CNDH, state prosecutors sought to cover up military wrongdoing by using torture to coerce false testimony from witnesses.

In the state of Zacatecas, three soldiers and a colonel were detained in July for the disappearance of seven people who were subsequently found dead. The four were charged with seven counts of homicide and enforced disappearance and will be tried in civilian courts.

Torture

Torture is widely practiced in Mexico to obtain forced confessions and extract information. It is most frequently applied in the period between when victims are arbitrarily detained and when they are handed over to civilian prosecutors, a period in which they are often held incommunicado at military bases or illegal detention sites.

Common torture techniques include beatings, waterboarding, electric shocks, and sexual abuse. In 2014, the Federal Attorney General's Office received more than 2,400 complaints of torture, more than double the number (1,165) received in 2013. Despite a constitutional prohibition on using evidence obtained through torture, some judges continue to disregard torture complaints and accept allegedly coerced confessions.

Criminal Justice System

The criminal justice system routinely fails to provide justice to victims of violent crimes and human rights violations. Causes of this failure include corruption, inadequate training and resources, and the complicity of prosecutors and public defenders with criminals and abusive officials.

In 2008, Mexico passed a constitutional reform to transform its inquisitorial, written justice system to an adversarial, oral one by 2016. Implementation of the reform has been sluggish. As of August, the new oral system was fully operational—at both the federal and local level—in only two Mexican states.

In 2013, Mexico enacted a federal Victims Law intended to ensure justice, protection, and reparations for victims of crime. As of August 2015, the federal district and 9 of 31 states had not yet enacted implementing legislation in compliance with the Victims Law. Only 10 states had created a state victim's commission, and only five were fully operational.

In April, the Supreme Court ruled that the *arraigo* provision—which allows prosecutors, with judicial authorization, to hold organized crime suspects for up to 80 days before they are charged—is constitutional in cases of "serious crimes," as defined by Mexican law.

Self-Defense Groups

The failure of law enforcement has contributed to the emergence of armed citizen self-defense groups in several parts of the country.

Following concerns about some groups' unregulated security actions, self-defense groups in Michoacán state signed an agreement with the government in 2014 stipulating that their members would register their weapons and incorporate into local security forces. At time of writing, there had been no independent

assessment of how the agreement was implemented or whether it complied with
security force vetting requirements.

Attacks on Journalists and Human Rights Defenders

Journalists, particularly those who report on crime or criticize officials, face harassment and attacks. According to the Special Prosecutor's Office for Crimes
against Freedom of Expression, 103 journalists were killed and 25 were disappeared between 2000 and October 2015.

In 2012, Mexico enacted a law to protect human rights defenders and journalists, resulting in the creation of a national protection mechanism. Protective
measures, however, have been slow to arrive or insufficient in some cases. At
time of writing, authorities had yet to bring charges under the law against anyone believed to be responsible for threats or attacks against human rights defenders.

Authorities routinely fail to adequately investigate crimes against journalists,
often preemptively ruling out their profession as a motive. The CNDH reported in
2014 that 89 percent of crimes against journalists in Mexico go unpunished. As
of October, the Special Prosecutor's Office was conducting 303 investigations of
crimes against journalists or media outlets and had presented charges in only 21
cases.

In August, photojournalist Ruben Espinosa was found dead in a Mexico City
apartment with four female victims, including human rights defender Nadia Do-
minique Vera Perez, all of whom had been tortured before being killed with a single gunshot to the head, according to media reports. Espinosa reportedly had
fled from Veracruz, the state with the highest combined number of killings and
disappearances of journalists in Mexico. At time of writing, the investigation into
the killings was being led by local authorities rather than by the Special Prosecutor's Office.

Journalists are often driven to self-censorship by attacks carried out by government officials or criminal groups. Weak regulation of state advertising can also
limit media freedom by giving government officials disproportionate financial influence over media outlets.

Women's and Girls' Rights

Mexican laws do not adequately protect women and girls against domestic and sexual violence. Some provisions, including those that make the severity of punishments for some sexual offenses contingent upon the "chastity" of the victim, contradict international standards.

In 2008, the Supreme Court affirmed the constitutionality of a Mexico City law that legalized abortion in the first 12 weeks of pregnancy. No other states have laws permitting voluntary abortion.

In 2010, the Supreme Court ruled that all states must provide emergency contraception and access to abortion for rape victims. However, in practice many women and girls face serious barriers to accessing abortions after sexual violence, including inaccurate information and intimidation by officials.

Sexual Orientation and Gender Identity

Same-sex marriage has been legal in Mexico City since 2010 and has since been legalized in the states of Coahuila and Quintana Roo. In June, the Supreme Court ruled that the definition of marriage as a union only between a man and a woman constitutes discrimination and thus violates Mexico's constitution, opening the door for the recognition of same-sex marriage in all 31 Mexican states.

Palliative Care

The Mexican government took a number of important steps to implement legal provisions to improve access to palliative and end-of-life care. In June, it introduced a new system for prescribing and dispensing strong pain medicines that will significantly improve health care for people with advanced illnesses. At time of writing, 29 of 31 states had at least one health facility providing palliative care, up from 24 in 2014.

Despite these significant strides, challenges remain, including the continuing paucity of facilities offering palliative care: in many states, only one hospital does so, leaving most patients without access to palliative care close to or in their homes.

Disability Rights

A January investigation by Disability Rights International revealed that Mexican women with psychosocial disabilities are at high risk of being denied their reproductive rights, with state-run clinics in Mexico City in some cases pressuring such women into being sterilized or, when they become pregnant, undergoing an abortion.

In July, a Disability Rights International report exposed the inhumane conditions of Mexico City's government-funded facilities for people with disabilities. One institution locks children with disabilities in cages. Despite a government "black list" of institutions considered abusive or in very bad condition, they continue to operate and receive government funding. The Ministry for Social Development has called for an immediate ban on restraints and cage beds.

Key International Actors

Since 2007, the United States has allocated over US$2 billion in aid to Mexico through the Mérida Initiative to help combat organized crime. Fifteen percent of select portions of the assistance can be disbursed only after the US secretary of state reports that the Mexican government is meeting human rights requirements. In an unprecedented move, the State Department announced in October that it was withholding $5 million in Mérida aid because it was unable to confirm that Mexico had met the human rights criteria.

In March, a Group of Independent Experts appointed by the IACHR began providing technical assistance to strengthen the search for the students from Ayotzinapa who were disappeared. In October, the government and the IAHCR signed an agreement to extend the mandate of the expert group for an additional six months.

The UN Committee on Enforced Disappearances concluded in February that there exists a "generalized context of disappearances" in Mexico, many of which could be characterized as enforced disappearances. The committee raised concerns about the "serious challenges" Mexico faces with regard to the prevention, investigation, and prosecution of enforced disappearances.

In March, the UN special rapporteur on torture and other cruel, inhuman, or degrading treatment or punishment presented a report affirming that "torture is generalized in Mexico" and that those responsible are rarely brought to justice. The Peña Nieto administration responded by publicly denouncing the special rapporteur as "irresponsible and unethical."

Morocco and Western Sahara

Morocco regressed on human rights in several areas in 2015, and advanced in few. Restrictions tightened on human rights groups, both domestic and international; at least two Moroccans spent the year in prison for "falsely" denouncing torture, and many continued serving long prison terms after unfair trials for politically motivated offenses. Authorities often tolerated protest demonstrations, but in Western Sahara systematically prevented gatherings supporting self-determination for the contested territory.

More positively, a new law took effect that ended military trials of civilians, and authorities for the first time legally recognized a human rights organization in Western Sahara led by people critical of Moroccan rule. Morocco granted temporary legal status to United Nations-recognized asylum-seekers and thousands of economic migrants, pending an overhaul of its laws on asylum and foreigners on Moroccan soil.

Freedom of Expression

Laws that criminalize acts deemed harmful to the king, the monarchy, Islam, or Morocco's claim over Western Sahara limited the rights to peaceful expression, assembly, and association.

Independent print and online media continued to investigate and criticize government officials and policies, but faced prosecution and harassment if they criticized the king or his advisors. The press law mandates prison terms for "maliciously" spreading "false information" that authorities believe may disturb public order, or for speech ruled defamatory.

Authorities arbitrarily imposed administrative obstacles to impede the efforts of journalist Ali Lmrabet to register a new satirical weekly, following his completion of a 10-year sentence banning him from practicing journalism in Morocco. Police in Rabat confiscated tapes from and expelled two French television journalists on February 16 on the grounds that they had been filming in the country without authorization.

Moroccan state television allows some space for debate and investigative reporting but none for direct criticism of the palace or dissent on key issues.

Freedom of Assembly and Association

Authorities tolerated numerous marches and rallies demanding political reform and protesting government actions but forcibly dispersed some peaceful gatherings. In Western Sahara, authorities prohibited all public gatherings deemed hostile to Morocco's contested rule over that territory, dispatching large numbers of police who blocked access to demonstrations before they could even assemble.

Officials continue to arbitrarily prevent or impede many associations from obtaining legal registration, although the 2011 constitution guarantees freedom of association. However, authorities registered the Sahrawi Association of Victims of Grave Human Rights Violations Committed by the Moroccan State (ASVDH) in 2015, nine years after it first applied and eight years after an administrative court ruled that authorities had wrongly refused to register it.

Morocco also registered several, but not all, associations formed to defend the rights of migrants in Morocco. In July, a Tiznit first instance court ordered the closure of the Ifni Memory and Rights Association, partly on grounds that it harmed Morocco's "territorial integrity" by asserting the rights and identity of the population in the Ifni region.

Among the many associations arbitrarily denied legal registration were scores of charitable, cultural, and educational associations whose leadership includes members of al-Adl wal-Ihsan (Justice and Spirituality), a nationwide movement that advocates an Islamic state and questions the king's spiritual authority.

Authorities prohibited dozens of activities prepared by legally recognized human rights associations, notably the Moroccan Association for Human Rights (AMDH) and its branches. After allowing Amnesty International and Human Rights Watch researchers relatively unimpeded access for nearly 25 years, authorities expelled two Amnesty researchers in June and demanded in September that Human Rights Watch suspend its activities in Morocco until officials could schedule a meeting with the organization to discuss its "bias." At time of writing, officials had yet to respond to invitations from Human Rights Watch to meet.

In October, authorities charged historian Maâti Monjib, Hicham Mansouri, and three other associational activists with accepting foreign funding "to harm internal security," punishable by up to five years in prison. The case, set to go to trial in 2016, centers on a foreign-funded workshop to train Moroccans in the use of a smartphone application to practice "citizens' journalism."

Morocco expelled several foreign visitors who arrived on fact-finding missions to Western Sahara, most of them European citizens who openly supported Sahrawi self-determination.

Police Conduct, Torture, and the Criminal Justice System

A new law took effect in July ending military court jurisdiction over civilian defendants. The case of Mbarek Daoudi, a Sahrawi activist facing a military court trial since September 2013 on minor weapons charges, was transferred to a First Instance Court in Guelmine, which sentenced him to three months in prison in March. He remained in custody to face a second trial in an Agadir court, which on December 3 convicted and sentenced him to five years in prison.

Twenty-two other Sahrawis continued serving prison sentences of between 20 years and life that a military court imposed in 2013. The men, who include a few well-known activists, had been charged in connection with violence that erupted on November 8, 2010, when authorities dismantled the Gdeim Izik protest camp in Western Sahara. Eleven security officers were killed in the violence. The military court failed to investigate defendants' allegations that police had tortured or coerced them into signing false statements, and relied almost exclusively on those statements to convict. The new law ending military court trials of civilians did not retroactively benefit these defendants.

In November 2014, Morocco deposited with the United Nations its ratification of the Optional Protocol of the Convention against Torture (OPCAT). At time of writing, it had not designated the National Protection Mechanism that OPCAT envisions for inspecting places of detention.

Courts failed to uphold fair trial rights in political and security-related cases. Authorities continued to imprison hundreds of Islamists suspected of violence arrested in the wake of the Casablanca bombings of May 2003. Many were serving sentences imposed after unfair trials following months of secret detention, ill-treatment and, in some cases, torture.

Police have arrested hundreds more suspects since further terrorist attacks in 2007 and 2011. Courts convicted many on charges of belonging to a "terrorist network," recruiting, undergoing military training, or preparing to join Islamist fighters in Iraq, Syria, or elsewhere. Morocco's 2003 counterterrorism law contains an overly broad definition of "terrorism" and allows for up to 12 days of garde à vue (pre-charge) detention.

Moroccan courts continued to impose the death penalty, but authorities have not carried out executions since the early 1990s.

Prison overcrowding is exacerbated by the tendency of courts to order the detention of suspects awaiting trial. As of August 31, 41 percent of prisoners—or 31,334 out of a total of 76,794—were in pretrial detention, according to the prison administration.

Leftist activist Wafae Charaf continued to serve a two-year prison sentence for slander and "falsely" reporting an offense after she filed a complaint alleging that unknown men abducted and tortured her after a workers' protest in April 2014 in Tangiers.

Oussama Husn, a February 20 youth reform movement activist, was serving a three-year prison sentence imposed in 2014 on similar charges after he put online a video in which he recounts having been abducted and tortured by unknown men. These sentences could have a chilling effect on people wishing to file complaints of abuse by security forces.

Right to a Private Life

Moroccan courts continued to jail persons for same-sex conduct under article 489 of the penal code, which prohibits "lewd or unnatural acts with an individual of the same sex." In October, the UN Committee on Economic, Social and Cultural Rights, in its concluding observations on Morocco's periodic report, urged the "repeal without delay" of article 489.

A Hoceima appeals court upheld on December 30, 2014 a lower-court conviction of two men for homosexuality, sentencing one to six months in prison and the other, who was also convicted on an attempted bribery charge, to 12 months. A first-instance court sentenced three men from Taourirt in May to three years in prison for homosexuality, a sentence that the Appeals Court of Oujda in July reduced to a few months. In both cases, the convictions relied on confessions that the defendants repudiated in court.

After a gay-bashing incident on a Fez street on July 29, Justice Minister Moustapha Ramid said the assailants should be prosecuted but also made homophobic remarks, including a call on homosexuals to refrain from "provoking" society. A court sentenced two men to prison for their role in the assault.

Criminalization of adultery and sex outside marriage has a discriminatory gender impact, as rape victims face prosecution if they file charges that are not sustained. Women and girls also face prosecution if they are found to be pregnant or have children outside marriage.

A Rabat Appeals Court in May upheld 10-month prison terms for adultery and "complicity for adultery" against Hicham Mansouri and a female friend after police broke into his apartment and allegedly caught them in compromising circumstances. The court failed to consider considerable exculpatory evidence. Mansouri's employment at the Moroccan Association for Investigative Journalism (AMJI) raised suspicions that police surveillance and prosecution was retaliation for his associational activities.

In March, police in Casablanca arrested Moustapha Erriq, a senior figure in the Islamist opposition Adl wal Ihsan movement, along with a female friend on suspicion of adultery, but released them three days later after Erriq's wife refused to press charges.

Migrants and Refugees

Implementation continued of a 2013 plan to overhaul national policies toward migrants and asylum-seekers, including by providing them with certain basic rights. Morocco's refugee agency granted one-year renewable residency permits to more than 500 UNHCR-recognized refugees. At time of writing, Morocco had not determined the status it would grant to more than 1,700 Syrians who UNHCR recognizes as prima facie refugees.

Morocco also granted, in the context of a one-time regularization procedure that ended on December 31, 2014, one-year renewable residency permits to thousands of sub-Saharan migrants who were not asylum-seekers but who met certain criteria in the 2013 plan. Some Syrians also obtained one-year residency permits under this procedure.

Rights of Women and Girls

The 2011 constitution guarantees equality for women, "while respecting the provisions of the constitution, and the laws and permanent characteristics of the Kingdom."

The 2004 Family Code, which improved women's rights in divorce and child custody, discriminates against women with regard to inheritance and procedures to obtain divorce. The code raised the age of marriage from 15 to 18, but judges routinely allowed girls to marry below this age. There is no law that specifically criminalizes domestic violence or that establishes protections for domestic violence victims.

Domestic Workers

Despite laws prohibiting the employment of children under the age of 15, thousands of children under that age—predominantly girls—are believed to work as domestic workers. According to the UN, nongovernmental organizations, and government sources, the number of child domestic workers has declined in recent years.

Morocco's labor law excludes domestic workers from its protections, which include a minimum wage, limits to work hours, and a weekly rest day. In 2006, authorities presented a draft law to regulate domestic work and reinforce existing prohibitions on domestic workers under 15 years old. The draft had been modified but not adopted at time of writing.

Key International Actors

France, a close ally and Morocco's leading source of foreign investment, refrained from publicly criticizing Moroccan human rights violations. Morocco and France resumed their bilateral judicial cooperation agreement, which Morocco suspended in 2014 after a French investigating judge served subpoenas on a visiting Moroccan police commander based on a complaint filed by a victim alleging complicity in torture.

The two countries amended the agreement to provide that a judge who receives a complaint about a crime committed in the other country should immediately inform the judicial authorities of the other country and consider transferring the case to that country's courts in priority, an option that, if pursued, would shield Moroccan officials from French justice.

Morocco has a poor record investigating and prosecuting torture and victims have resorted to French courts as a last resort. French President François Hollande visited Tangiers in September for a meeting with King Mohammed VI, declaring that "our difficulties have been ... put behind us," and avoided public mention of human rights.

The United States, another close ally, proffered no public criticism of Morocco's human rights record. In September, the Millennium Challenge Corporation, an independent US state agency that provides grants to countries "that demonstrate a commitment to good governance, investments in people and economic freedom," approved a US$450 million five-year grant to Morocco to support education and land productivity reforms. Morocco is the MCC's second leading aid recipient after Tanzania.

The UN Security Council in April renewed the mandate of UN peacekeeping forces in Western Sahara (MINURSO) without broadening it to include human rights monitoring, which Morocco strongly opposes. The Office of the High Commissioner of Human Rights conducted an investigation in both Moroccan-controlled Western Sahara and the Polisario-run refugee camps near Tindouf, Algeria, in 2015, but did not report publicly on its findings.

HUMAN
RIGHTS
WATCH

"Like We Are Not Nepali"
Protest and Police Crackdown in the Terai Region of Nepal

Nepal

Devastating earthquakes on April 25 and May 12, 2015, left an estimated 9,000 people dead and nearly 20,000 injured. Rescue and relief efforts were slow to get off the ground, in part due to damage to the country's already-weak infrastructure.

Within months of the earthquakes, the four main ruling political parties announced that they had broken through a more than six-year deadlock on drafting a new constitution. Among other reforms, the new constitution contains equal rights and affirmative action clauses for the country's many ethnic minority communities and lower castes, and it outlaws capital punishment.

However, the new constitution, which was put forward for only one week of public consultation, did not address longstanding complaints by historically marginalized communities in Nepal's southern Terai region, leading to months of protests and violence there. The new constitution also fails to guarantee people with disabilities full access to education and work.

While the government made some headway in appointing a Truth and Reconciliation Commission to address longstanding grievances arising from the country's decade-long civil war that ended in 2006, it failed to bring the commission in line with international human rights standards and practices. Courts continued to delay hearings on conflict-era cases.

Post-Earthquake Recovery

The earthquakes in April and May left some 2.8 million people in need of humanitarian assistance. In addition to the tens of thousands of deaths and injuries, several hundred thousand people ended up displaced and many continue to live in temporary settlements or makeshift shelters. Many affected communities live in rural areas which are difficult to access, and have received minimal assistance for emergency housing and other relief. Vulnerable communities including people with disabilities, women, and children remain at particular risk.

Although the government received over US$4 billion for earthquake assistance, none of the funds had been paid out at time of writing, and rehabilitation efforts remained slow.

Constitution-Related Political Unrest

The 2006 ceasefire agreement ending Nepal's civil war contained a promise, enshrined in Nepal's interim constitution, that a new constitution would soon be drafted that, among other things, would provide equality and a greater role in governance for traditionally marginalized communities in the Terai region.

When the main parties hammered out a draft constitution following the devastation of the earthquakes without genuine public consultation and without addressing the grievances of those communities, many groups, particularly along Nepal's southern and far-western belts, declared strikes, blocked roads, and in many cases shut down normal daily activities for weeks at a stretch.

In September, an estimated 45 persons, including 9 policemen, were killed when protests turned violent. In some districts, the government responded by deploying the army and in others by instituting curfews. Most of the protester deaths were attributed to excessive use of force by the security forces.

The ongoing protests led to an effective blockade of trade and transit. By November, fuel and medical supplies were in short supply given that most of land-locked Nepal's goods come in over land through trading posts along its border with India. The Nepali government accused the Indian government of imposing an economic sanction on Nepal, which India denied. Some supplies came in through China, but not in sufficient quantities to meet nationwide demand.

Denial of Citizenship Rights

Due to flawed citizenship laws, an estimated 4 million people are forced to live without official status and at risk of statelessness. Despite promises of reform, many people, particularly women, children born out of wedlock, or children of a refugee or naturalized parent, are ineligible for drivers' licenses, passports, bank accounts, voting rights, higher education, and government welfare schemes. The law makes it particularly difficult for women to secure legal proof of citizenship, especially when male family members refuse to assist them or are unavailable to do so. The citizenship provisions in the constitution do not adequately rectify these problems, and instead raise additional hurdles for children born to a non-Nepali father.

Accountability for Past Abuses

Authorities have made little progress on justice for serious abuses committed by both sides during the civil war. At least 13,000 people were killed and over 1,300 forcibly disappeared during the decade-long conflict.

While Nepal has delivered interim monetary and in-kind compensation to the families of those who were "disappeared" or killed during the conflict, others, such as survivors of sexual violence or torture, have received no compensation from the state.

In March 2015, Nepal's Supreme Court ruled against problematic provisions of the 2014 Truth, Reconciliation and Disappearances Act, striking down amnesty provisions and emphasizing that the Attorney General's Office retains authority to recommend prosecutions, and directed the government to remedy the law.

In February 2015, the government set up legal and institutional frameworks for the Truth and Reconciliation Commission and Disappearances Commission, both called for in the act, and even appointed some initial commissioners without amending the act as directed by the Supreme Court. The work of the commissions remained stalled at time of writing.

Rights of Tibetan Refugees

Tibetan refugee communities in Nepal continue to face a de facto ban on political protests, sharp restrictions on public activities promoting Tibetan culture and religion, and abuses by Nepali security forces including excessive use of force, arbitrary detention, ill-treatment in detention, threats, intimidation, and intrusive surveillance.

Migrant Workers

Although large numbers of Nepali migrants seek work abroad each year, the government has done little to support and protect them. Following reports in 2014 that hundreds of Nepali and other migrant workers had died in Qatar, the government attempted to set up stronger protection measures, but they had not been properly implemented at time of writing.

Nepal continues to ban women under age 30 from traveling to the Gulf states for employment as domestic workers. While motivated by protection concerns, the ban is discriminatory and forces women desperate for work to migrate through irregular channels, putting them at greater risk of exploitation.

Following the earthquake there were fears of increased trafficking. Attention by government and security forces to the increased vulnerability of women and children helped stem some of the potential risks.

Early Marriage and Children's Rights

Nepal has a serious problem with child marriage, with 41 percent of girls married before age 18 and 10 percent married before age 15, often in abusive circumstances. Although child marriage is illegal and the government is reportedly in the process of developing a national action plan to address the problem, authorities so far have done little to prevent child marriage or to assist married children.

Sexual Orientation and Gender Identity

In February, a committee mandated by a 2007 Supreme Court decision published a long-overdue report recommending that the government recognize same-sex relationships. In line with the same Supreme Court decision and a subsequent court order, the government in August began issuing passports in three genders: "male," "female," and "other."

NGOs report that the document application process remains ad hoc, however, and the majority of transgender applicants face discrimination and abuse in the process, including demands from government officials that they produce "medical proof" before being allowed to change their legally recognized gender.

The constitution promulgated in September recognizes that citizenship is available in three genders, and protects "gender and sexual minorities" in clauses related to equality before the law and social justice.

Key International Actors

India immediately deployed humanitarian rescue assistance to Nepal after the April 25 earthquake, with the United Kingdom, United States, and China following shortly thereafter. The United Nations were slower to respond, in spite of years of earthquake readiness preparation. The government came under intense criticism when it refused offers from the UK and others to aid in the relief effort.

The international community remained largely silent on Nepal's contentious constitution drafting process. The call by India, the US, and the UK to engage in broad and transparent public consultations went unheeded by the government.

Cooperation between Nepal and China's border security forces led to increased risk that Nepal will forcibly return Tibetan refugees to China. Tibetans detained by Chinese authorities while attempting to cross the border irregularly from Nepal are routinely imprisoned and physically abused.

Nigeria

Relatively peaceful presidential and gubernatorial elections in March and April 2015 marked a positive shift in Nigeria's history of political violence. However, the inauguration of President Muhammadu Buhari has not diminished the potency of the country's serious human rights challenges. Violence and insecurity persist in the northeast despite the recapture, from the militant group Boko Haram, of dozens of towns and the rescue of over 1,000 hostages by Nigerian and neighboring countries' forces. The name Boko Haram means "Western education is forbidden."

Boko Haram carried out probably its most vicious attacks in January around Baga, a fishing settlement in Borno state, northeast Nigeria, killing at least 2,000 people and sacking the military base of the Multinational Joint Task Force (MNJTF). More than 9,500 civilians have died in the conflict and the number of displaced people has increased from just over 1 million at the end of 2014 to almost 2 million in 2015. Nigerian security forces have neither taken adequate steps to protect civilians during operations against Boko Haram, nor to protect the rights of rescued hostages.

In other parts of the country, frequent violence between farmers and cattle owners in the north-central states remained unresolved in 2015. There have been few investigations or prosecutions against those responsible for the violence. The lack of justice for victims helped fuel reprisal attacks, leading to continuous cycles of violence. Impunity for human rights crimes—such as torture committed by security forces, including police—remained pervasive.

Abuses by Boko Haram

The conflict in the northeast between the militant group Boko Haram and Nigeria's security forces grew more deadly in 2015. By the beginning of the year, Boko Haram had seized control of 17 local government areas (LGAs) across parts of the northeast in Adamawa, Bauchi, Borno, and Yobe states. LGAs are the third and lowest level, after federal and state levels, in Nigeria's administrative structure.

Security forces from Nigeria and its neighbors have since regained control of most of the towns, but the rebels remained active in many rural areas. In July, the governors of Borno and Yobe states said that Boko Haram retained control of a total of five LGAs in their states. An estimated 3,500 died in the conflict in 2015, while most of the 2 million displaced people live with limited access to basic rights like food, shelter, and healthcare.

The horrific attack in Baga and on the nearby MNJTF headquarters was followed by repeated attempts by Boko Haram in January and February to seize military installations in Maiduguri and Monguno, both in Borno state. Increasing cross-border attacks led to an African Union sanctioned renewal of the MNJTF agreement and the mobilization of forces from Nigeria, Cameroon, Chad, and Niger. Boko Haram violence intensified in more than 200 attacks against communities in these countries since February, apparently in retaliation for the involvement of their security forces in military operations.

The group also continued to attack schools, abduct hundreds of women, and increase its use of children as suicide bombers. On July 26, in a style typical of Boko Haram bombings, a 10-year-old girl blew herself up in a busy market in Damaturu, Yobe state, killing at least 15 and injuring 46. Government forces managed to rescue over 1,300 hostages, but none of the 219 missing school girls abducted by the insurgents in April 2014. Some of the rescued people have been held in military facilities since May with little clarity about their status as victims or detainees.

Conduct of Security Forces

Nigerian authorities have yet to open credible investigations into allegations of heavy-handed and abusive response to the insurgency by security forces. Since 2009, hundreds of men and boys in the northeast have been rounded up and detained in inhumane conditions for suspected membership or provision of support for Boko Haram.

There are also allegations of use of excessive force, and inadequate civilian protection measures, including for Boko Haram hostages, by the military in the ongoing operations in the northeast. When the Nigerian army drove at high speed into Sambisa Forest Reserve in late April, some Boko Haram hostages, mostly women and children, were crushed by moving trucks. Survivors said soldiers did not issue instructions on how the hostages could avoid danger.

Abusive conduct by security forces is not limited to the northeast. On April 11, during the gubernatorial elections, soldiers allegedly killed four voters at a polling unit in Bayan Dutse, Kebbi state, northwest Nigeria.

Authorities have rarely prosecuted members of the police and military implicated in abuses. While some soldiers have been prosecuted in military tribunals for offences such as cowardice and mutiny, the pervasive culture of impunity means almost no one has been held to account for human rights crimes.

In apparent recognition of these problems, President Buhari appointed new leadership for the military. He also moved the command and control center of the military from Abuja to Maiduguri—the epicenter of the conflict.

In July and September, the military released 310 people, including women and children, from detention in Borno and Yobe states who had been detained without charges for at least two years. Also, in May, Nigeria endorsed the Safe Schools Declaration, thus expressing a commitment to implement the Guidelines on Protecting Schools and Universities from Military Use.

These steps have fallen short of Buhari's inauguration promise to reform the military. Disappointingly, he claimed during a July visit to Washington D.C. that the application of the United States Leahy Law amendment, which bars US support to abusive units of foreign military forces, has served to aid Boko Haram.

Local vigilante groups assisting Nigerian security forces to apprehend the militants and repel attacks are also implicated in the recruitment and use of child soldiers, as well as the ill-treatment and unlawful killing of Boko Haram suspects.

Inter-Communal and Political Violence

In Nigeria's volatile "Middle-Belt" region, years of economic and political tensions between ethnic and religious communities repeatedly erupted in uncontrolled violence in 2015. The violence is fueled by competition for power and access to land between nomadic and farming communities. Mobs have killed many of their victims based simply on ethnic or religious identity.

Nigerian authorities have failed to address the root causes of the violence and rarely prosecuted those responsible, including the police or military implicated in serious abuses. On May 2, 2015, according to media reports and local sources, security forces killed at least 28 people when they attacked the Langtang and Wase communities following the killings of six soldiers a few days earlier.

Public Sector Corruption

Corruption and weak governance undermine the enjoyment of basic human rights for many Nigerians who live in abject poverty. High unemployment rates—along with public sector corruption and insecurity—were major issues in the March national elections. President Buhari came into power on an anti-corruption platform, promising to confront corruption and lack of transparency in government business.

A number of senior officials in the administration of former President Goodluck Jonathan have been arrested and faced prosecution by the Economic and Financial Crimes Commission (EFCC), since President Buhari's inauguration in May. The agency was in turn controversially accused in August of mismanaging and embezzling funds recovered from people convicted of corruption. On November 9, 2015 Ibrahim Lamorde, the EFCC chairman, was replaced by Ibrahim Mustafa Magu, appointed in an acting capacity.

Sexual Orientation and Gender Identity

The passage of the so-called Same-Sex Marriage Prohibition Act in January 2014—which banned "gay clubs and organizations," support for such organizations, and public display of affection between same-sex couples—has had a chilling effect on freedom of expression for lesbian, gay, bisexual, and transgender people, human rights organizations, writers, and others. Organizations have reported cases of blackmail, evictions, and fear of seeking health care since the law's passage.

Under pre-existing laws, "carnal knowledge against the order of nature" is punishable by 14 years in prison. In 12 northern states where Sharia law is in effect, homosexual acts are punishable by imprisonment, caning, or death by stoning. Activists are unaware of recent cases in which the death penalty has been implemented. Police arrested 12 men on homosexuality charges in Kano state in January and 21 men in Oyo state in May, though all were subsequently released hours later.

Freedom of Expression, Media, and Freedom of Association

While media remains largely free and vibrant, Nigeria retains outdated criminal law provisions that impede freedom of speech and expression. Journalists also frequently suffer intimidation and harassment related to their work.

On May 29, Daily Trust journalist Joseph Hir was beaten, allegedly by supporters of the Nassarawa state governor for writing a "negative" about the governor. A month later, Yomi Olomofe, executive director of Prime magazine, and McDominic Nkpemenyie, a correspondent with Tide newspaper, were severely beaten and injured by a group of people at Seme customs border post in Lagos. The group was allegedly upset by previous unfavorable reports of their activities by the journalists.

Key International Actors

International actors, notably the United Kingdom, United States, and United Nations, have expressed optimism in their support of the new government's reform agenda on security and public sector corruption. The UK, US, UN, and the European Union assisted Nigeria in achieving a peaceful outcome in the March elections.

The UK provides a substantial package of military, intelligence, development, and humanitarian assistance to Nigeria and its neighbors in confronting the Boko Haram challenge. In July, US Deputy Secretary of State Anthony Blinken said the US would deepen its support of Nigeria to develop a comprehensive approach committed to human rights in responding to Boko Haram. Blinken was visiting Nigeria ahead of President Buhari's trip to Washington D.C. later that month.

UN Secretary-General Ban Ki-moon, during a visit in August, noted that "respect for human rights has been most visibly challenged in the context of the Boko Haram threat." He urged the government to ensure its counterterrorism response is not "counterproductive." During an update to the UN Human Rights Council in June, the UN High Commissioner for Human Rights Zeid Ra'ad Al Hussein said in relation to Boko Haram, Nigeria should adopt "a profound policy response that is grounded in the need for accountability and reconciliation."

In January, the African Union approved the MNJTF initiated by Nigeria and its neighbor members of the Lake Chad Basin Commission. The initiative was noted by the UN Security Council in a presidential statement on Boko Haram adopted on June 28.

On November 12, the Office of the Prosecutor of the International Criminal Court (ICC) released a report detailing six possible cases against Boko Haram and two possible cases against Nigerian security forces for crimes against humanity and war crimes in relation to the northeast insurgency. The ICC said it was continuing its "preliminary examination" of the situation in Nigeria with a focus on the adequacy of efforts to ensure accountability for serious crimes before domestic courts.

North Korea

North Korea is an authoritarian state with a dynastic leadership that is among the most repressive in the world. In 2015, his fourth year in power, leader Kim Jong-Un continued to intensify repression, increased control over the North Korean border with China to prevent North Koreans from escaping and seeking refuge overseas, and tightened restrictions on freedom of movement inside the country. The government also punished those found with unauthorized information from outside the country—including news, films, and photos—and used public executions to generate fearful obedience.

The United Nations Commission of Inquiry on Human Rights in the Democratic People's Republic of Korea (COI), set up by the Human Rights Council (HRC), issued a report in 2014 documenting extermination, murder, enslavement, torture, imprisonment, rape, forced abortion, and other sexual violence in North Korea. It concluded that the "gravity, scale and nature of these violations reveal a State that does not have any parallel in the contemporary world."

On December 22, 2014, the UN Security Council added the human rights situation in North Korea to its formal agenda, in line with a COI recommendation. The HRC and the UN General Assembly have both suggested that the Security Council consider referring the situation to the International Criminal Court (ICC).

On March 27, 2015, the HRC adopted a resolution condemning the government's systematic, widespread, and gross human rights violations. On June 23, UN High Commissioner Zeid Ra'ad Al Hussein opened a UN office based in Seoul to help monitor and document rights abuses in North Korea. On November 19, the UN General Assembly 3rd Committee issued a resolution condemning North Korean abuses.

The North Korean government has ratified four key international human rights treaties and signed one other. Most recently, on November 10, 2014, it ratified the Optional Protocol to the Convention on the Rights of the Child, on the Sale of Children, Child Prostitution and Child Pornography. North Korea's constitution sets forth a number of rights protections, but in reality the government quashes all forms of disfavored expression and opinion and prohibits any organized political opposition, independent media, free trade unions, and civil society organizations. Religious freedom is systematically repressed.

The government also violates economic and social rights by criminalizing and arbitrarily punishing market activities, one of the few means by which North Koreans can obtain income needed for food, medicine, and other necessities the government often fails to adequately provide the population. Government officials often require those pursuing market activities to pay bribes and sentence those unable to pay to perform forced labor in penal institutions or reform-through-labor camps.

North Korea continues to discriminate against individuals and their families on political grounds in key areas such as employment, residence, and schooling through use of the "songbun," the country's socio-political classification system that from its creation grouped people into "loyal," "wavering," or "hostile" classes. This classification has been restructured several times but continues to divide people based largely on their family background and perceived political loyalty, though corrupt practices now also influence the system.

The government also practices collective punishment for alleged anti-state offenses, effectively enslaving hundreds of thousands of citizens, including children, in prison camps and other detention facilities where they face deplorable conditions, abuse by guards, and forced labor.

Freedom of Movement

The government uses threats of detention, forced labor, and public executions to ensure obedience and imposes harsh restrictions on freedom of information and movement. It criminalizes leaving the country without official permission, and in some instances state security services actively pursue North Koreans into China, seeking to detain and forcibly return them.

During Kim Jong-Un's rule, the government has significantly expanded efforts to stop irregular crossings of North Koreans into China. The government has increased rotations of North Korean border guards, cracked down on brokers who assist people trying to leave, and prosecuted use of Chinese cell phones to communicate with the outside world. North Koreans who left the country in 2014 and 2015 told Human Rights Watch that the government was tracking down and publicly executing border guards who allowed people to cross into China in exchange for bribes.

Increased patrols, barbed-wire fences, and security cameras on the Chinese side of the border have also made crossings more difficult. Chinese authorities have also targeted broker networks in China, resulting in fewer North Koreans being able to complete the arduous journey through China to Laos or Thailand, from which most are sent on to South Korea.

China continues to label all North Koreans in China as illegal "economic migrants" and routinely repatriates them, despite its obligation to protect refugees under the Refugee Convention of 1951 and its 1967 protocol, to which China is a state party. Concerned foreign governments argue that all North Koreans fleeing into China should be considered refugees *sur place* regardless of their reason for flight because of the prospect of punishment on return. Beijing regularly restricts access of staff of the UN Refugee Agency to border areas where North Koreans are present.

Former North Korean security officials who have defected told Human Rights Watch that North Koreans handed back by China face interrogation, torture, and consignment to political prison camps (known as *kwanliso*, literally management centers) or forced labor camps. The severity of punishments depend on North Korean authorities' assessments of what the returnees did while in China. North Koreans who have fled the country since 2013 or have contacts inside the country allege that the government has started treating all defectors as enemies of the country, sending anyone caught and repatriated from China to political prison camps.

North Korean women fleeing their country are frequently trafficked into forced marriages with Chinese men or the sex trade. Even if they have lived in China for years, these women are not entitled to legal residence there and face possible arrest and repatriation at any time. Many children from these unrecognized marriages lack legal identity or access to elementary education in China.

Freedom of Information

All media and publications are state-controlled, and unauthorized access to non-state radio or TV broadcasts is punished. Internet and phone calls are limited within the country and are heavily censored. North Koreans are punished if found with mobile media such as computer flash drives or USBs containing unauthorized videos of foreign films or TV dramas. As noted above, authorities also actively track, and seek to catch and punish, persons using Chinese mobile phones to make unauthorized calls to people outside North Korea.

Labor Rights

North Korea is one of the few nations in the world that still refuses to join the International Labour Organization. Workers are systematically denied freedom of association and the right to organize and collectively bargain. The only authorized trade union organization, the General Federation of Trade Unions of Korea, is controlled by the government.

In 2003, a special administrative industrial zone at the southern border, the Kaesung Industrial Complex (KIC), was developed in cooperation with South Korea. As of September 2015, the KIC was hosting 124 South Korean companies employing 54,616 North Korean workers, supervised by 809 South Korean managers. A joint North-South Korea committee oversees the KIC, but the law governing working conditions there falls far short of international standards.

Political Prisoner Camps

Persons accused of serious political offenses are usually sent to political prison camps, operated by North Korea's National Security Agency. These camps are characterized by systematic abuses and often deadly conditions, including meager rations that lead to near-starvation, virtually no medical care, lack of proper housing and clothes, regular mistreatment including sexual assault and torture by guards, and executions.

People held in political prisoner camps face backbreaking forced labor at logging, mining, agricultural, and other worksites. These are characterized by exposure to harsh weather, rudimentary tools, and lack of safety equipment, all of which create a significant risk of accident. Death rates in these camps are reportedly extremely high.

United States and South Korean officials estimate that between 80,000 and 120,000 people are imprisoned in the remaining camps: No. 14 and 18 in Kaechun, No. 15 in Yodok, No. 16 in Hwasung, and No. 25 in Chongjin. Pyongyang does not admit the existence of any such camps in the country.

Forced Labor

Forced labor is common even outside political prison camps. People suspected of involvement in unauthorized trading schemes involving non-controversial goods are usually sent to work in forced labor brigades (*rodong danryeondae*, literally labor training centers) or *jipkyulso* (collection centers), which are criminal penitentiaries where forced labor is required and where many women are victims of sexual abuse. Harsh and dangerous working conditions in those facilities purportedly result in significant numbers of injuries.

People whom authorities suspect of smuggling goods from China, trafficking people to China, or committing ordinary crimes or minor political infractions such as watching or selling South Koreans films are often given lengthy terms in detention facilities known as *kyohwaso* (correctional, reeducation centers) where detainees face forced labor, food and medicine shortages, and regular mistreatment by guards.

Key International Actors

Pyongyang's record of cooperation with UN human rights mechanisms remains among the worst in the world. Since 2013, its human rights record has been the subject of more focused UN attention than ever before, including at the Human Rights Council and Security Council, as detailed above.

Japan continues to demand the return of 12 Japanese citizens whom North Korea abducted in the 1970s and 1980s. Some Japanese civil society groups insist the number of abductees is much higher. South Korea has also stepped up its demands for the return of its citizens, hundreds of whom were reportedly abducted during the decades after the Korean War. The North Korean government has also kidnapped individuals from China, Thailand, Europe, and the Middle East.

On September 21, the HRC held a plenary panel on the situation of human rights in North Korea, addressing international abductions, enforced disappearances, and other alleged crimes.

From October 20 to 26, the two Koreas organized reunions of 186 families separated during the Korean War, the first such reunions since February 2014.

In January 2015, United States President Barack Obama issued an executive order imposing sanctions following the hacking of Sony's computers in late 2014, allegedly by groups connected to North Korea. The US sanctions on North Korea included a human rights clause for the first time.

Oman

The government continued to restrict rights to freedom of expression, association, and assembly. Authorities harassed and detained, often incommunicado, several prominent critics and pro-reform activists.

Freedom of Expression and Pro-Reform Activists

The authorities continued to target peaceful pro-reform activists using short-term arrests, detentions, and other forms of harassment. Since mass protests in 2011, authorities have engaged in a cycle of prosecutions of activists and critics on charges such as "insulting the Sultan" that criminalize free speech, leading to prison sentences followed by release under pardons granted by Sultan Qaboos bin Said al Said. According to local activists, the arrests and prosecutions have had a chilling effect on free speech and the expression of dissent.

Articles 29, 30, and 31 of Oman's Basic Law protect freedom of expression and the press, but other laws undercut these safeguards. Authorities continued to restrict online criticism and other content using article 26 of the 2002 Telecommunications Act. It penalizes "any person who sends, by means of telecommunications system, a message that violates public order or public morals."

Authorities arrested pro-reform activists and held them without access to lawyers and their families using a 2011 criminal procedure code amendment that empowers security forces to hold detainees without charge for up to 30 days. The arrests and detentions followed a pattern that has become entrenched since 2011 that has seen the authorities repeatedly arrest and detain peaceful opposition activists and those who use social media and other online outlets to criticize the government.

Security officials arrested Muawiyah al-Rawahi in December 2014, apparently in connection with two tweets in which he criticized corruption and urged people to demand their rights. They released him without charge after four days. In February, he traveled to the United Arab Emirates (UAE), where authorities arrested him on arrival. He remained in UAE detention at time of writing.

In March, a Muscat court convicted 46-year-old Said Jaddad, a human rights activist and pro-reform blogger, of "undermining the prestige of the state," incitement to "illegal gathering," and "using information networks to disseminate news that would prejudice public order" based on his online activities, including a public letter he wrote to United States President Barack Obama asking for human rights improvements in Oman.

The court sentenced him to three years' imprisonment and a fine. He lodged an appeal and was released on bail in April. On September 9, the Appeal Court in Muscat had upheld his three years' prison sentence, suspended for three years, and payment of a 2000 Omani Rials fine (about US$5,200). In November, in a separate case, the Court of Appeal in Salalah upheld his March 31 sentence of one year in prison and a fine of 1000 Omani Rials (about $2,600) for "inciting to break national unity and spreading discord within society" in relation to a blog post he wrote in October 2014 in which he compared the 2011 protests in Dhofar province to the 2014 protests in Hong Kong. Said Jaddad was arrested on November 25 and transferred to Arzat Prison, west of Dhofar province's capital, Salalah, where he continues to be detained.

In March, a court fined Saeed al-Daroudi, a writer and online activist, and sentenced him to one-and-a-half years in prison in absentia after convicting him on charges of disturbing public order and creating discord and hatred. In April, security officials arrested four other online activists, including Majid al-Balushi and Mohammed al-Manai, and detained them incommunicado before releasing them after 14 and 9 days, respectively.

In July, police arrested Mahmoud al-Fazari in July and detained him for three weeks before releasing him without charge after his brother, Mohammed al-Fazari, a prominent blogger and government critic, fled the country despite a travel ban and sought asylum in the United Kingdom.

Authorities arrested Dr. Saleh al-Azri, Ali al-Maqbali, and Talib al-Sa`eedi, all opposition activists, on August 3 and the next day arrested two others, Mukhtar al-Hana'i and Ahmed al-Balushi. They released al-Balushi after questioning him for four hours but detained the others for three weeks before releasing them without charge.

Authorities arrested human rights activist Ismail al-Meqbali on August 29 after summoning him for police questioning, and detained him for six days before releasing him without charge. He has faced repeated harassment, including arrest and detention, by the authorities since police arrested him and two other activists as they traveled to interview striking workers at the Fohoud oil field in 2011.

The new Omani Citizenship Law enacted by decree in 2014 removed citizenship decisions from the jurisdiction of the courts and, under article 20, empowers the Ministry of Interior to withdraw Omani citizenship from any person found to belong to a party or organization that "embraces principles or ideologies that harm Oman's interest" or "works in favor of a hostile country that acts against the interests of Oman."

Freedom of Assembly and Association

All public gatherings require advance official approval; the authorities arrest and prosecute participants in unapproved gatherings. Some private gatherings are also prohibited under article 137 of the penal code, which prescribes a punishment of up to three years in prison and a fine for anyone who "participates in a private gathering including at least 10 individuals with a view to commit a riot or a breach of public order." Authorities sharply increased the penalties under article 137 after the pro-reform demonstrations of 2011.

Authorities continued to imprison Dr. Talib al-Maamari, a former Shura Council member from Liwa. In August 2014, an appeal court in Muscat fined him and imposed a one-year prison term on him for "illegal gathering" and a three-year prison term for calling for anti-government demonstrations. The court also sentenced Saqr al-Balushi, a former Liwa municipal councilor.

The case stemmed from an incident in August 2013 in Liwa, when police used tear gas to disperse people blocking the port's entrance in protest of industrial pollution at the nearby port of Sohar. Authorities arrested al-Maamari two days after the protest, denying him access to a lawyer for over two weeks. Later, a court sentenced al-Maamari and al-Balushi to seven and four year prison terms, respectively, and fines after convicting them of "illegal gathering" and "blocking traffic."

Article 42 of the Civil Societies Law makes it a crime punishable by up to six months' imprisonment and a fine of 500 Rials (approximately $1,300) for any association to receive funding from abroad without government approval. Article 54 makes the Social Development Ministry responsible for legally registering associations; under the law, only associations with at least 40 members are eligible to apply for registration.

Women's Rights

Article 17 of the Basic Law states that all citizens are equal and bans gender-based discrimination. In practice, however, women continue to face discrimination in law—under the Personal Status Law that governs matters such as divorce, inheritance, child custody, and legal guardianship—and in practice.

Oman's penal code criminalizes sexual relations outside marriage and provides three months to one-year imprisonment when the person is unmarried, and one to three years' imprisonment when the person is married. Criminalization of such offenses apply disproportionately to women whose pregnancy can serve as evidence of the offense.

Migrant Workers' Rights

Migrant workers remained vulnerable to exploitation and abuse, due in part to the visa-sponsorship system (*kafala*) that ties migrant workers to their employers and precludes them changing employers without their current employer's consent. Migrant domestic workers, predominantly women, are furthermore specifically excluded from the Labour Law and especially vulnerable to abuse and exploitation.

Many migrant domestic workers complained to Human Rights Watch of long working hours with no rest or day off, denial of salaries, passport confiscation, and in some cases physical and sexual abuse. Oman has yet to ratify the 2011 International Labour Organization (ILO) Convention on Decent Work for Domestic Workers, for which it voted in favor in 2011.

Sexual Orientation and Gender Identity

Oman's penal code provides for six months to three years in prison for consensual sex between men or between women.

Key International Actors

Maina Kiai, the United Nations special rapporteur on the rights to freedom of peaceful assembly and of association, reported on his September 2014 visit to Oman in May. He criticized government efforts to silence dissent and stated that the "legal environment for the exercise of the rights to freedom of peaceful assembly and of association in Oman is problematic." The Omani government rejected the findings of the report and accused Kiai of violating the Special Procedures code of conduct during his visit.

Oman has yet to ratify key international human rights treaties, including the International Covenants on Civil and Political Rights and on Economic, Social and Cultural Rights, although the government pledged to do so when the UN Human Rights Council last considered Oman under its Universal Periodic Review process in 2011.

Both the US and the UK provide significant economic and military aid to the sultanate. Neither country publicly criticized Oman's human rights abuses in 2015, except in annual reports.

Pakistan

Under pressure from the military leadership, the government of Prime Minister Nawaz Sharif ceded significant constitutional and decision-making authority to the armed forces in 2015, particularly in the areas of national security, foreign policy, and human rights.

Parliament passed a constitutional amendment allowing secret military courts to try terrorism suspects. The military assumed control of the implementation of a national plan to address terrorism, largely without civilian oversight. It was also formally given membership in the Apex committees, provincial committees formed to coordinate local counterterrorism efforts and security.

The military muzzled dissenting and critical voices in nongovernmental organizations and media. The Rangers, a paramilitary force, were given complete control over law enforcement in the city of Karachi, where there were reports of extrajudicial killings, enforced disappearances, and torture. The military continued to exercise sway over the province of Balochistan, using torture and arbitrary detention as instruments of coercion.

In December 2014, the Islamist armed group Pakistani Taliban, Tehreek-e-Taliban, attacked a school in Peshawar in northwestern Pakistan, leaving 148 dead, almost all of them children. The government responded with a national action plan to fight terrorism, including tactics that violated basic rights. Authorities established the use of military instead of civilian courts in terrorism cases.

The government ended an unofficial moratorium on judicial executions; the death penalty was carried out 296 times in 2015 at time of writing. Abuses by the security forces led thousands of Afghans living in Pakistan to return to Afghanistan or flee elsewhere. Parliament passed vague and overbroad counterterrorism legislation. The government belatedly acknowledged the need to regulate madrassahs (Islamic schools) and disband armed militias operating in the country, but took few steps to do so. The government officially recognized the need to curb incitement to violence and terrorism financing.

Religious minorities faced violent attacks, insecurity, and persecution, largely from Sunni extremist groups—which the government failed to address. The government continued to use blasphemy laws to institutionalize discrimination against religious minorities. The security forces engaged in extrajudicial killings and enforced disappearances to counter political unrest in the province of Balochistan and in the port city of Karachi in Sindh province. Torture of suspects by the police remained rampant. Large numbers of journalists were killed or injured in attacks, most of which remain unresolved.

Counterterrorism and Law Enforcement Abuses

Suicide bombings, armed attacks, and killings by the Taliban, Al-Qaeda, and their affiliates targeted nearly every sector of Pakistani society, including religious minorities and journalists, resulting in hundreds of deaths. In connection with these attacks, military courts sentenced at least 15 people to death in proceedings shrouded in secrecy, giving rise to fair trial concerns.

Neither the Pakistani government nor the military articulated any criteria for selection of cases to be tried in military courts, giving the impression of arbitrariness. No independent monitoring of the process was allowed, and the news of death sentences was often given by the Interservices Public Relations, a military communications agency, through social media.

Attacks on Minorities and Sectarian Violence

The government failed to take adequate steps to prevent and respond to deadly attacks on Shia and other religious minorities in 2015. In January, at least 53 people were killed in a bomb blast at a Shia mosque in the city of Shikarpur in Sindh province. Jundullah, a splinter group of the Taliban that has pledged support for the armed extremist group Islamic State (also known as ISIS), claimed responsibility for the attack.

In February, 19 people were killed after Taliban militants stormed a Shia mosque in Peshawar. In March, suicide bombers belonging to Tehrik-i-Taliban targeted two churches in the Christian neighborhood of Youhana Abad in Lahore, killing 14. In May, an attack by Jundullah on members of the Ismaili Shia community in Karachi killed 43 people.

The attacks highlighted the threat armed extremist groups to pose to religious minorities, and the government's failure to apprehend or prosecute perpetrators.

Religious Minorities

At least 19 people remained on death row after being convicted under Pakistan's draconian blasphemy law; hundreds awaited trial. The majority facing blasphemy charges were members of religious minorities, often victimized by these charges as a result of personal disputes.

In February, in a welcome move, Punjab's provincial judiciary drew up a shortlist of 50 cases of alleged blasphemy in which the accused was found to be "victimized" by inadequate evidence or lack of legal counsel. The provincial government commited to undertake the legal defense of these defendants—some of them suffering from intellectual or psychosocial diabilities—in special "fast track" trials.

In April, the Sindh provincial assembly enacted a law requiring the mandatory psychological examination of any person accused of blasphemy and allowing judicial discretion to reduce the sentences of those convicted of blasphemy whose medical evaluation produce a diagnosis of a "mental disorder."

Freedom of Expression

Many journalists increasingly practiced self-censorship, fearing retribution from both state security forces and militant groups. Media outlets remained under pressure to avoid reporting on or criticizing human rights violations by the military in counterterrorism operations. The Taliban and other armed groups threatened media outlets and targeted journalists and activists for their work.

In April, Syed Wahidur Rahman, a journalism professor and former journalist, was gunned down in Karachi. Also in April, Sabeen Mahmud, a prominent Pakistani social and human rights activist, was shot dead shortly after hosting an event on Balochistan's "disappeared people" in Karachi. In June, Baloch journalist Zafarullah Jatak was gunned down in his home in Balochistan's capital, Quetta.

In September, in Karachi, Aftab Alam, a senior journalist, was gunned down near his home, while Arshad Ali Jaffery, a TV satellite engineer, was killed by three gunmen. Abdul Azam, a journalist, was wounded after being shot at in the northwestern city of Peshawar.

The National Assembly's Standing Committee on Information Technology and Telecommunication approved the Prevention of Electronic Crimes Act 2015 in September. The bill included abusive provisions that allow the government to censor online content, criminalize Internet users, and permit the government to access metadata without any form of judicial review or privacy protection. YouTube, banned by the government since September 2012 for hosting "blasphemous content," remained blocked in 2015.

The Pakistan government forced the international aid agency Save the Children to suspend operations in June and banned the Norwegian Refugee Council. Independent organizations faced increasing pressure and harassment from the government.

The Pakistani government announced the "Policy for Regulation of INGOs in Pakistan" on October 1, 2015. The new regulations require all INGOs to register and obtain prior permission from the Ministry of Interior to carry out any activities in the country and to restrict their operations to specific issues and geographical areas. The ministry is broadly empowered to cancel registrations on grounds of "involvement in any activity inconsistent with Pakistan's national interests, or contrary to Government policy"—terms that have vague meanings and can be used for political reasons to target critical organizations or individuals.

Balochistan

The security forces continued to unlawfully kill and forcibly disappear suspected Baloch militants and opposition activists in 2015. In January, 13 highly decomposed bodies of ethnic Baloch individuals were found in Khuzdar district. Baloch nationalists and other militant groups also stepped up attacks on non-Baloch civilians. In April, suspected Baloch militants gunned down 20 laborers in Turbat's Gogdan area. In May, 35 people were forced off a bus and kidnapped by members of a militant Baloch nationalist group, the United Baloch Army; 23 of the passengers were killed.

Afghans in Pakistan

The Pakistani government failed to protect Afghans in the country against police extortion, theft, and general harassment in 2015. As a result of threats from local

HUMAN
RIGHTS
WATCH

"What Are You Doing Here?"
Police Abuses Against Afghans in Pakistan

government officials, particularly after the December 2014 Peshawar school attack, increasing numbers of Afghans returned to their country. According to the United Nations refugee agency (UNHCR), over 50,000 refugees were repatriated to Afghanistan, most of whom had resided in Pakistan for more than 15 years. UN Secretary-General Ban Ki-moon noted, and Human Rights Watch research found, that many returnees left because of police coercion and abuse and stated that returning to Afghanistan was their only viable option.

Attacks on Health Workers

Taliban and other religious militant groups carried out violent attacks on health-care workers, mostly women, involved in providing grassroots services. In March, two women health workers and a police guard were killed in Mansehra district in Khyber Pakhtunkhwa province. In May, unidentified militants opened fire on a clinic in Karachi, killing a Shia doctor.

Militants targeted medical providers involved in polio immunization. In February, members of a polio vaccination team were attacked in southwest Pakistan and in Swat. In March, a polio vaccination team was attacked in Bajaur Agency, in the Federally Administered Tribal Areas.

Women and Girls

The government took inadequate action to protect women and girls from abuses including rape, murder through so-called honor killings, acid attacks, domestic violence, and forced marriages. According to local groups, hundreds of honor killings took place. In March, Punjab province passed a law setting tougher penalties for those who arrange or conduct child marriages. The law did not, however, raise the age of marriage from 16 to 18, in line with international standards, as Sindh did in 2014. The government's Council of Islamic Ideology denounced the Punjab reform. The government failed to address the issue of forced conversion to Islam of Hindu and Christian women.

Women were denied the right of vote in various parts of the country. In May, during a parliamentary by-election in Lower Dir, Khyber Pakhtunkhwa, none of the eligible 50,000 women in the constituency voted after warnings reportedly broadcast on mosque loudspeakers. Polling stations were guarded by "baton-wielding men," according to news reports, who blocked the few women who attempted to vote.

Children's Rights

The Pakistani government failed to pass the promised legislation constituting the National Commission on the Rights of the Child, an independent body to protect and enforce child rights in the country. Attacks on schools and the use of child suicide bombers by the Taliban and affiliated armed extremist groups continued.

Rampant sexual abuse of children was exposed in August, when police uncovered a child pornography racket by a criminal gang that had produced and sold more than 400 videos of girls and boys being sexually abused in Kasur, Punjab. These videos had been filmed over a span of 10 years, affecting 280 child victims.

Death Penalty

The Pakistani government had carried out the death sentences of at least 295 people in 2015 at time of writing. After the December 2014 attack on the school in Peshawar, the Pakistani government first moved to rescind a four-year unofficial moratorium on the death penalty for non-military personnel "in terrorism-related cases." In early March, the government lifted the death penalty moratorium for all capital crimes, including kidnapping and murder.

At the end of the year, an estimated 8,300 prisoners remained on death row, one of the world's largest populations of prisoners facing execution. Pakistani law mandates capital punishment for 28 offenses, including murder, rape, treason, and blasphemy. Those on death row are often from the most marginalized sections of society.

Pakistani law forbids the use of the death penalty against children. However, in June, Aftab Bahadur, who was allegedly 15 at the time of his alleged offense, was executed. In August, Shafqat Hussain, who was allegedly 14 or 15 years old at the time of his alleged crime, and whose conviction was based on a confession allegedly obtained through torture, was hanged in a Karachi prison.

Key International Actors

After years of disagreement and mistrust, relations with the United States, Pakistan's largest development and military donor, gradually improved. In March, US Secretary of State John Kerry praised the Pakistani military's operation against militants in the country's northwest, saying the results were "significant," but cautioned that more needed to be done. The US failed to exert any pressure on Pakistan to roll back abusive counterterrorism laws and restrain the injudicious use of death penalty. The US also did not press for a return to the primacy of the civilian government.

Pakistan and China deepened extensive economic and political ties. In April, Chinese President Xi Jinping made his first state visit to Pakistan. China and Pakistan signed agreements worth US$28 billion during Xi's visit, related to the China-Pakistan Economic Corridor.

The United Nations and the European Union expressed concern over the increasing use of the death penalty and urged the reinstatement of the moratorium. As of October, the UN estimated that the 8,300 people on death row included hundreds who were sentenced for offenses committed as children. In June, the UN high commissioner for human rights noted that Pakistan was the world's "third-most prolific executioner."

Historically tense relations between Pakistan and its nuclear rival India further deteriorated in 2015, with both countries accusing each other of facilitating unrest and militancy. Scheduled talks to resolve longstanding disputes over security, territory, and sharing river water resources were stalled.

Relations with Afghanistan, after displaying some initial signs of stabilizing, returned to hostility and mistrust. The Afghan government accused Pakistan of allowing the "Haqqani network", an affiliated group of the Taliban, to operate from Pakistan to carry out attacks in Afghanistan. Pakistan maintained that the network had been dismantled.

HUMAN
RIGHTS
WATCH

BASHED UP
Family Violence in Papua New Guinea

Papua New Guinea

In 2015, Papua New Guinea (PNG) celebrated 40 years of independence. Despite PNG's current extractives-led boom, an estimated 40 percent of the country lives in poverty. Pressing issues include gender inequality, violence, corruption, and excessive use of force by police, including against children. Rates of family and sexual violence are among the highest in the world, and perpetrators are rarely prosecuted.

Women's and Girls' Rights

PNG is one of the most dangerous places in the world to be a woman or girl, with an estimated 70 percent of women experiencing rape or assault in their lifetime. While such acts have long been criminalized and domestic violence was specifically proscribed under the 2013 Family Protection Act, few perpetrators are brought to justice.

The government has started establishing police Family and Sexual Violence Units (FSVUs) and hospital-based Family Support Centres, and initiated a process to develop a gender-based violence strategy. However, the Family Protection Act has not yet been implemented. There is much work remaining to ensure appropriate law enforcement responses and comprehensive access to services for victims of family violence.

Police and prosecutors are very rarely prepared to pursue investigations or criminal charges against people who commit family violence—even in cases of attempted murder, serious injury, or repeated rape—and instead prefer to resolve them through mediation and/or the payment of compensation.

Police also often demand money ("for fuel") from victims before taking action, or simply ignore cases that occur in rural areas. There is also a severe lack of services for people requiring assistance after having suffered family violence, such as safe houses, qualified counselors, case management, financial support, or legal aid.

Reports continue of violent mobs attacking individuals accused of "sorcery" or "witchcraft," the victims mostly being women and girls. In May, a group of men in a remote part of Enga province killed a woman after she was accused of "sorcery." In August, three women and a man were also attacked in Mendi in the Southern Highlands province following sorcery accusations.

Sorcery accusations are often accompanied by brutal attacks, including burning of homes, assault, and sometimes murder. The risks to people accused of sorcery are so severe that the main approach used by nongovernmental organizations seeking to help them is to permanently resettle them in another community.

Government Corruption

In 2015, Prime Minister Peter O'Neill continued to weaken the country's most successful anti-corruption agency, Task Force Sweep, by starving it of funding. Task Force Sweep was briefly disbanded in 2014 when its investigations targeted the prime minister. A court reinstated the agency, but it has not received any government funding since 2013.

In March 2015, the Ombudsman Commission recommended that the minister for public service and the minister for public enterprise and state investments face leadership tribunals over allegations of misconduct in office.

In October, the government sought to suspend Chief Magistrate Nerrie Eliakim, who had issued an arrest warrant against Prime Minister O'Neill on corruption charges in 2014. Attorney General Ano Pala was charged with conspiring and attempting to pervert the course of justice, and with abuse of office. According to police, Pala allegedly tried to frustrate their efforts to pursue official corruption charges against O'Neill.

Death Penalty

In 2013, PNG expanded the scope of crimes eligible for the death penalty and signaled its intention to resume executions. In May, Prime Minister O'Neill publicly announced that the death penalty was under review, which seemed to suspend all pending executions. At time of writing, 13 prisoners remain on death row.

Disability Rights

Authorities launched a National Disability Policy in May 2015, but people with disabilities are often unable to participate in community life, go to school, or work because of lack of accessibility, stigma, and other barriers associated with disability.

Numerous obstacles prevent people with disabilities from being able to leave their homes, including inaccessible infrastructure and the fact that third parties are often put in charge of even basic decisions about their lives. Access to mental health care is limited, and traditional healers are the only option for many people with psychosocial disabilities.

Extractive Industries

Extractive industries remain an important engine of PNG's economic growth, but continue to give rise to serious human rights concerns and environmental harm. In 2014, controversy raged around the environmental impacts of the Ok Tedi mine, and violent clashes erupted around the controversial Ramu Nickel project.

Violence against women and girls committed in the context of PNG's extractive industries remains a pressing human rights concern. In 2011, Human Rights Watch documented gang rape and other violent abuses by private security personnel at PNG's Porgera gold mine, operated by Canadian company Barrick Gold.

Along with other steps, Barrick responded by rolling out a compensation scheme paying out claims to more than 100 women in 2015. The company has commissioned an assessment to evaluate the impact of this remedy program.

Asylum Seekers and Refugees

More than 930 asylum seekers and refugees are currently detained indefinitely in poor conditions at a detention center on Manus Island, which holds asylum seekers transferred by Australia for refugee status determination and resettlement in PNG. Some have been held at the center for more than two years. Since January 2015, 46 men recognized as refugees have been transferred to a transit center, but are prevented from leaving Manus Island and cannot work or study.

Human rights organizations and media are regularly denied access to the detention center. PNG ratified the 1951 Refugee Convention with some reservations, but has never adopted a formal policy for the integration of refugees within PNG.

The protracted and indefinite nature of detention is causing significant mental health problems for those on Manus Island, including depression and anxiety. In January, police detained a large group of asylum seekers for several weeks in crowded cells in the local jail and police lockup following a hunger strike at the detention center. Many of the asylum seekers said the jail experience was traumatizing for them, reporting that at least two asylum seekers had attempted suicide.

In August, following the deportation of two Iranian asylum seekers to Iran, PNG's Supreme Court ordered an interim injunction to stop any more forced removals. In 2015, lawyers mounted a new challenge with the Supreme Court on the constitutionality of detaining asylum seekers on Manus Island, arguing it infringes their right to liberty, freedom of movement, and access to legal representation.

Police Abuse

Police abuse continues to be reported with little accountability even for fatalities or egregious physical abuse. In January 2015, police killed two market vendors in Port Moresby when firing indiscriminately into a crowd after a dispute between vendors and local council officials. At time of writing no one had been arrested for the shooting.

Assistant Commissioner of Police Jerry Frank is reported as having acknowledged that although there is reason to believe police are responsible, they "don't know which ones." Prime Minister O'Neill condemned the use of "unacceptable excessive force," and sacked then-Police Commissioner Geoffrey Vaki, in part for "a litany of cases of police brutality" under his watch. In September, the Ombudsman Commission signed a Memorandum of Agreement with the police force to oversee investigations into police complaints.

Members of PNG's paramilitary police units (Mobile Squads), detention center staff, and local residents were implicated in excessive use of force in quelling protests in February 2014 at the Manus Island detention center. During the incident, at least 51 detainees sustained injuries and one detainee was beaten to death. PNG Deputy Police Commissioner Simon Kauba denied any involvement of police in the violence. An Australian Senate inquiry found that the "mobile squad did not simply fire warning shots into the air, but rather fired dangerously into the centre, possibly directly at transferees." Two staff working at the center are on trial for the murder of Iranian asylum seeker Reza Barati, but no one else has been held to account.

Sexual Orientation and Gender Identity

The PNG criminal code outlaws sex "against the order of nature," which has been interpreted to apply to consensual same-sex acts, and is punishable by up to 14 years imprisonment. Gay asylum seekers on Manus Island have reported being shunned, sexually abused, or assaulted by other men. Some gay asylum seekers are reported to have refused to participate in the refugee status determination process or to move to the transit center because they are fearful of being prosecuted under PNG's laws and are concerned for their safety.

Key International Actors

Australia remains the country's most important international partner, providing an estimated A$577.1 million (US$414.9 million) in development assistance in 2014-2015. Australia has estimated that it will provide approximately A$553.6 million (US$397.9 million) to PNG in 2015-2016.

At time of writing, the Australian Senate was undertaking an inquiry into the delivery and effectiveness of aid in PNG, with concerns raised that corruption is hampering Australia's development objectives. In July, PNG Prime Minister O'Neill announced that advisors from foreign governments would no longer be able to work in the PNG government as of January 1, 2016.

In September, PNG hosted the Pacific Islands Forum Leaders Meeting. In the lead-up to the meeting, O'Neill spoke out against what he called oppression of the indigenous Melanesian population across the border from PNG in the Indonesian provinces of Papua and West Papua, and called on Indonesia to fulfill the promise of its former president, Susilo Bambang Yudhoyono, to reduce the number of troops stationed in the region.

Peru

Security forces, responding at times to violent protests over mines and other large-scale development projects in Peru, continue to use live gunfire that kills and wounds civilians. Official investigations into the deaths and injuries remain inadequate.

Judicial investigations into grave human rights abuses committed during the 20-year armed conflict that ended in 2000 remained slow and limited.

Abuses and Deaths during Protests

During the first nine months of 2015, 12 civilians died from gunshot wounds after police reportedly used live ammunition against protesters. The fatalities occurred despite a police regulation that took effect in January 2015 prohibiting security forces from using lethal weapons during public order operations. In one incident in September, police opened live fire on anti-mining protesters who were trying to get into a mining camp in the southern province of Cotabambas; three people were killed. From July 2011, when President Ollanta Humala took office, through September 2015, 51 civilians were killed during protests in Peru.

In April, police planted evidence on a protester whom police had detained for allegedly engaging in violence during an anti-mining protest in the province of Islay. After local journalists released a video showing that police had planted the evidence, the protester was released and the minister of the interior announced the replacement of the chief responsible for the operation.

Accountability

In January 2014, Law 30151 took effect, providing immunity from prosecution to "armed forces and police personnel who in fulfillment of their duty and using their weapons or other means of defense, cause injury or death." This amendment to the criminal code eliminated language that made immunity conditional on police using lethal force in compliance with regulations. It departs from international standards that require that law enforcement officers use force in accordance with the principles of necessity and proportionality, and that they be held accountable for misusing force.

In July 2015, the Constitutional Court ruled that military courts could not try members of the military accused of committing abuses against civilians in public security operations. In the case, brought by Peruvian human rights activists in 2011, the court provided a restrictive interpretation of a decree adopted by President Alan García in 2010 that had opened the door to trying such cases in military courts. However, Law 30151 continues to restrict police accountability.

In August, President Humala, who signed law 30151, issued a decree that limits the use of force by police. Under the decree, police should only employ lethal force when it is "strictly necessary" in the face of a "serious and imminent risk" of grave harm. But with Law 30151 limiting criminal accountability, it remains to be seen how the decree will affect police behavior.

In cases of excessive use of force against protesters documented by local human rights groups from 2002 through August 2015, not a single official was convicted. Less than one in five cases was being prosecuted at the time of writing, according to local human rights groups.

Confronting Past Abuses

Peru's Truth and Reconciliation Commission has estimated that almost 70,000 people died or were subject to enforced disappearance during the country's armed conflict between 1980 and 2000. Many were victims of atrocities by the Shining Path and other insurgent groups; others were victims of human rights violations by state agents.

In a landmark trial, former President Alberto Fujimori was sentenced in 2009 to 25 years in prison for killings and "disappearances" in 1991 and 1992. Courts have consistently rejected petitions to reverse his sentence. Fujimori's intelligence advisor, Vladimiro Montesinos, three former army generals, and members of the Colina group, a government death squad, are also serving sentences ranging from 15 to 25 years for the assassination in 1991 of 15 people in the Lima district of Barrios Altos, and for six "disappearances."

Courts have made much less progress in addressing violations that occurred under the earlier administrations of Fernando Belaúnde (1980-1985) and Alan García (1985-1990). In a report issued in August 2013 to mark the 10th anniversary of the Truth and Reconciliation Commission's final report, the human rights ombudsman found that, despite initial efforts, Peru had failed to consolidate a specialized judicial system with sufficient staff and resources to bring most cases to court.

As of November 2015, only about 2 percent of the human rights violations committed during the armed conflict had been brought to trial, according to Human Rights Trials in Peru, a project based at George Mason University that monitors human rights prosecutions. In 2015, court hearings continued into their fifth year in two emblematic cases: torture and disappearances at the Los Cabitos military base in Ayacucho in 1983 and a massacre at Accomarca in 1985 in which an army unit killed 62 peasants.

In May 2015, the Attorney General's Office reopened an investigation into forced sterilizations committed during Fujimori's administration. More than 2,000 forced sterilizations have been reported to authorities, but these represent only a small portion of the cases, according to human rights groups. In November, President Huamala signed a decree to create a national registry of victims of forced sterilizations.

At time of writing, President Humala's former minister of interior, Daniel Urresti, was facing trial for his alleged role in the 1988 murder of Hugo Bustíos, the Ayacucho correspondent for *Caretas* magazine. Two soldiers were convicted in 2007 for Bustíos' murder, including one who testified that Urresti had commanded the soldiers who ambushed and shot Bustíos before blowing up his body with a grenade. President Humala appointed Urresti to the cabinet in June 2014 even though he was already facing charges for Bustíos' death; Humala replaced him in February 2015.

In August, the human rights ombudsman concluded that reparations for victims of the country's internal armed conflict, made pursuant to a 2005 law, had been "insufficient" and that some programs called for in the law still had not been implemented—10 years after it was passed.

Torture

The Humala administration has failed to comply fully with its international obligations to prevent torture, which continues to be a chronic problem in Peru. In February 2015, President Humala vetoed a bill passed by Congress in December

2014 that would have created the National Preventive Mechanism Against Torture. He argued that the mechanism's costs had not been included in the 2015 national budget. The bill was returned to Congress. Under the Optional Protocol to the Convention against Torture and Other Cruel, Inhuman or Degrading Treatment (OPCAT), which Peru ratified in 2006, the country should have implemented a National Preventive Mechanism Against Torture by 2007.

Freedom of Expression

Journalists investigating corruption by regional government officials, mayors, and business people are frequent targets of physical attack, threats, and criminal defamation suits.

In March 2015, two unidentified men shot bullets at the building of a local TV channel, Canal 21, in the municipality of Vista Alegre in the southwestern province of Nazca. The owner of the channel said that the attack occurred soon after he had aired allegations that the local mayor had made death threats against two residents of Vista Alegre.

In May 2015, two journalists from the TV channel Cable Vision said they had received several anonymous threats that the police would detain them after they reported on the misuse of force by policemen during protests against the Tía María mining project in the southwestern province of Islay.

Women's Rights

Women and girls in Peru remain at high risk of gender-based violence. In August, the Minister of Women's Affairs reported 96 cases of "femicide" (the killing of a woman in certain contexts, including of domestic violence and gender-based discrimination) in 2014, and 52 between January and July 2015.

In September, Congress passed a law that provides for comprehensive measures to prevent punish and eradicate violence against women. The law builds on existing judicial measures to protect women at risk, and mandates the creation of shelters to provide temporary refuge from abuse. The Committee on the Elimination of Discrimination Against Women, in its review of Peru in July 2014, had called on the country to pass a law against gender-based violence.

Women and girls in Peru have the right to seek abortions only in cases of risk to their health or life. In May 2015, Congress rejected a bill that would have decriminalized abortion when a pregnancy was the result of rape, but another proposal remained pending at time of writing.

Sexual Orientation and Gender Identity

In March 2015, Congress voted down a bill that proposed recognizing civil unions for same-sex couples. The vote sparked one of Peru's biggest public debates on the future of lesbian, gay, bisexual, and transgender rights. Following the vote, thousands of Peruvians took to the streets of Lima to demand marriage equality for same-sex couples.

Key International Actors

In June, the United Nations Working Group on Enforced or Involuntary Disappearances expressed concern about how few cases of "disappearances" had been brought to trial and about Peru's slow progress in the search for victims. The group also noted that most of the recommendations made by the Truth and Reconciliation Commission had not been implemented, 12 years after the commission's final report.

When it was a member of the UN Human Rights Council in 2014, Peru supported resolutions to put human rights violations in North Korea, Sri Lanka, Belarus, Iran, the Occupied Palestinian Territories, and Syria under close scrutiny.

Philippines

President Benigno Aquino III's final full year in office was marked by numerous instances of local intimidation and violence—reminiscent of past election periods—by often unidentified assailants against politicians, their supporters, and outspoken voices in media and civil society groups. The Philippine government took little effective action to hold to account those responsible, including security force personnel.

Aquino's six-year term ends in June 2016. In 2014, he brokered a peace process on the southern island of Mindanao that seeks to bring a measure of autonomy to the region's Muslim minority. His term saw a sharp reduction in extrajudicial executions compared to the prior administration of Gloria Macapagal-Arroyo, though local government-backed "death squads" remained a major problem. His administration has also seen some measure of success in enforcing the reproductive health law passed in 2012. In addition, Aquino deserves some credit for a Supreme Court initiative that addresses the massive backlog of criminal cases, which condemns suspects to often years-long pretrial detention.

Overall, however, Aquino's record on human rights has been disappointing due to the failure to address impunity for the government's rights violations. Among the reasons were lack of political will to investigate and prosecute abuses by state security forces; a corrupt and politicized criminal justice system; and a traditional "patronage politics" system that protects officials and security forces.

Attacks on Indigenous Peoples

Data compiled by indigenous peoples' advocacy groups indicate that assailants often linked to the military or paramilitary groups killed at least 13 tribal leaders and tribal community members in the first eight months of 2015.

On August 26, soldiers raided the tribal village of White Kulaman in Bukidnon province and arrested 17 residents, accusing them of being rebels belonging to the communist New People's Army (NPA). On September 1, gunmen allegedly linked to a paramilitary group killed three tribal leaders in Lianga town, Surigao del Sur province. The paramilitary group Alamara was implicated in numerous attacks during the year, including nine killings in the town of Cabanglasan.

The killings in Cabanglasan followed the evacuation of hundreds of tribal residents from the adjacent Davao del Norte province after the Philippine military deployed in the region to fight NPA rebels.

The United Nations High Commissioner for Refugees has determined that the large-scale military deployment in areas heavily populated by indigenous peoples has contributed to the displacement of 243,000 since January. Military activity against suspected NPA members displaced hundreds of students in several tribal schools in four provinces in Mindanao.

Similar attacks and displacement by the military in tribal domains have occurred in other provinces in the southern Philippines on the grounds of combating the NPA insurgency, as well as acting as paid security for mining and plantation operations.

Paramilitary groups, some of them funded and supplied by the military, are frequently deployed as "force multipliers" against insurgents in these areas, spawning abuses against the local population.

Children's Rights

Hazardous child labor remained a serious concern in 2015. Thousands of children worked in small-scale gold mining at great risk. They dived for gold in underwater mines, dug gold in underground pits, and processed gold with mercury. Child labor laws are poorly enforced. In March, the government banned underwater mining and mercury use for gold processing, but did little to implement it.

In November, authorities rounded up hundreds of poor and homeless children, along with street vendors and homeless adults, and detained them in social welfare facilities in Manila in an attempt to "beautify" the capital for the Asia-Pacific Economic Cooperation summit. The government denied that the arrests were meant to clear the streets of Manila of vagrants. Many of these street dwellers were back on the streets a day after the summit.

Attacks on Media

2015 was another deadly year for Filipino journalists. Eight journalists were killed in the first ten months of the year. August was a particularly bloody month as unidentified gunmen killed three journalists in a span of 10 days.

Victims included Cosme Maestrado, a hard-hitting commentator for DXOC radio station, who was shot dead in front of a shopping center in Mindanao's Ozamiz City on August 28. Eight days earlier, unidentified gunmen killed another broadcaster, Teodoro Escanilla of radio station DZMS, in Sorsogon, a province south of Manila. On August 18, unidentified gunmen killed Gregorio Ybanez, a newspaper publisher, in Mindanao's Tagum City. At time of writing, police had not arrested suspects in any of these killings.

Most victims of media killings in the Philippines are radio broadcasters; many are linked to politics since many radio stations in the Philippines are owned by local politicians or interest groups who hire broadcasters to produce content sympathetic to their employers.

Task Force Usig, a unit created by the Philippine National Police in 2007 to investigate these murders, has not been able to fully investigate most of these killings, mainly due to the lack of witnesses willing to publicly identify themselves and share information with police.

Although the task force has secured the conviction of suspects in eight of the 51 cases it has documented since 2001—a conservative figure since Usig does not classify videographers and producers as "journalists"—no one responsible for planning and executing such attacks has been arrested or convicted.

Death Squads and Extrajudicial Killings

Summary killings are rampant in several urban areas across the Philippines. Popularly known as "riding-in-tandem" killings because they often involve gunmen on motorcycles, Philippine media report such incidents on an almost daily basis.

Many of these killings have been by guns for hire, contracted by local politicians or criminal syndicates, often with the complicity of police to target petty criminals, drug dealers and others.

The Justice Department began an investigation into the "death squad" in Tagum City Mindanao in 2014 after it was reported on by Human Rights Watch and announced that they would file charges against the former mayor and several others. However, at time of writing, the Department of Justice had not filed a complaint, and the suspects had not been detained or brought to trial.

Rodrigo Duterte, the mayor of Davao City, has popularized the perception of death squads as valuable tools of "swift justice" against crime. The Aquino government has failed to investigate Duterte's claims of masterminding the Davao City death squad. Duterte announced his presidential election bid in 2016 on a platform espousing vigilante justice as a crime control technique.

Nearly 300 leftist activists, human rights defenders, and other alleged NPA supporters have been killed since Aquino took office in 2010, with 65 killed in the first 10 months of 2015, according to domestic human rights groups. Killings implicating the military and paramilitary groups almost never result in prosecutions.

Key International Actors

The United States, which in 2009 conditioned some financial military aid to the Philippines on improvements of the human rights situation, resumed aid in 2015 as part of its so-called Asia pivot. That strategy involves engaging the Philippine navy in particular as part of a US counter-strategy to China's incursions into the West Philippine Sea (or South China Sea).

The US, Japan, Canada, and the European Union have continued providing capacity-building assistance, notably to improve local governance and bureaucracy, fight corruption, and institutionalize human rights monitoring. Key beneficiaries of this aid are Muslim areas in the southern Philippines.

Qatar

Labor reforms enacted in Qatar in 2015 failed to provide meaningful protection to low-paid migrant workers. Despite several years of sustained criticism over its mistreatment of migrant workers, who continue to arrive in huge numbers and are acutely vulnerable to trafficking and forced labor, the reforms still require workers to secure their employer's permission to change jobs or leave the country, preventing them from leaving abusive situations.

Having previously placed few restrictions on the activities of international media, authorities detained and interrogated two groups of foreign journalists who were attempting to report on migrant workers' living and working conditions.

Migrant Workers' Rights

Less than 10 percent of Qatar's population of 2.1 million are Qatari nationals, and the country is increasingly dependent on migrant labor as Qatar continues to build stadiums and develop infrastructure as it prepares to host the 2022 FIFA World Cup. In 2015, it had the fourth highest population growth rate in the world; according to the most recent statistics, nearly 80 percent of the population is male.

Low-paid migrant workers, mostly from countries in Asia and to a lesser extent Africa, continue to be abused and exploited. Workers typically pay exorbitant recruitment fees and employers regularly take control of their passports when they arrive in Qatar. Many migrant workers complain that their employers fail to pay their wages on time, if at all.

The *kafala* (sponsorship) system ties a migrant worker's legal residence to their employer or sponsor. The system also requires that foreign workers obtain exit permits from their sponsors when they wish to leave Qatar; in practice, this enables employers to arbitrarily prevent their employees from leaving Qatar and returning to their home country.

Workers can become undocumented when employers report them to the authorities as having absconded, or when they fail to pay to renew workers' annual ID cards. A lack of proper documentation prevents workers from accessing subsidized healthcare and leaves workers at risk of arrest and detention or deportation.

Migrant workers are prohibited from unionizing or engaging in strikes, although they make up 99 percent of the private sector workforce. Accommodation is often cramped and unsanitary.

Domestic workers are explicitly excluded from the Labor Law, and as such are further vulnerable to abuse and exploitation. In addition to labor abuses, many domestic workers face physical and sexual abuse. A law on domestic workers continues to remain in draft form and has not been made public.

In October, Qatar's Emir, Sheikh Tamim bin Hamad Al-Thani, issued Law No. 21 of 2015 on the regulation of the entry and exit of expatriates and their residency. The new sponsorship law refers to "recruiters" instead of "sponsors" but it leaves the fundamentally exploitative characteristics of the *kafala* system in place.

The new law leaves in place a requirement for any foreign workers to obtain a "No Objection Certificate" from their current employer if they want to transfer legally to another employer. The law states that workers who want to change employers before the end of their contracts will need the permission of their employer, "the competent authority," as well as the Interior, and Labor and Social Affairs Ministries. The law does not define who "the competent authority" is.

If the length of the contract is not defined, workers must wait five years to leave an employer. The workers also must still obtain exit permits from their employers to leave Qatar. The new law provides for a grievance committee for workers in cases in which sponsors refuse to grant exit visas, but the arbitrary restriction on the workers' right to leave the country remains in place.

In February, Qatar's Emir, Sheikh Tamim bin Hamad Al-Thani, approved an amendment to Qatar's Labor Law that introduces a wage payment protection system that employers will use to pay workers' salaries directly into bank accounts.

Freedom of Media

Qatar enjoys a reputation as a center for media freedom, due in no small part to its funding and hosting the Al Jazeera news network. However, in 2015, authorities detained two groups of foreign journalists attempting to report on the treatment of migrant workers in the country.

Authorities detained a group of journalists from West German Broadcasting in March, and a group of BBC journalists in May. In both cases, police officers confiscated equipment, including memory cards and phones, and both groups were questioned separately by state security officers and the public prosecutor. Authorities released the German journalists after 14 hours of questioning, but the BBC team spent two nights in detention. Qatar's Government Communications Office said the BBC crew had "trespassed on private property, which is illegal in Qatar."

Qatar's penal code contains provisions that are inconsistent with free speech standards, notably article 134, which provides for five years' imprisonment for anyone convicted of criticizing the emir or vice-emir. Vaguely worded provisions in a draft media law from 2012 and a draft cybercrime law from 2014 pose a further threat to the right to free expression.

Women's Rights, Sexual Orientation, and Gender Identity

Provisions of Law No. 22 of 2006, Qatar's first codified law to address issues of family and personal status, discriminates against women. Under article 36, a marriage contract is valid when a woman's male guardian concludes the contract and two male witnesses are present. Article 57 forbids husbands from hurting their wives physically or morally, but article 58 states that it is a wife's responsibility to look after the household and to obey her husband. Other than general provisions on assault, the penal code does not criminalize domestic violence. Marital rape is not a crime.

Article 34 of Qatar's nationality law does not allow Qatari women, unlike Qatari men, married to non-Qatari spouses to pass on their nationality to their children.

In May, only 2 women out of 29 representatives were elected to the Central Municipal Council. There are no women in Qatar's Shura Council (an advisory body), which has yet to have elections.

Qatar's penal code punishes "sodomy" with one to three years in prison, and under Sharia law, which applies to Muslims, any individual convicted of zina (sex outside of marriage) can be sentenced to flogging (non-married persons) or the death penalty (married persons). According to media reports, dozens of people have been given flogging sentences—ranging from 40 to 100 lashes—since 2004, including at least 45 between 2009 and 2011.

Key International Actors

In September, Qatar sent 1,000 troops to Yemen to assist in the Saudi-led military campaign against Houthi forces, also known as Ansar Allah, which effectively ousted the government of President Abdu Rabu Mansour Hadi in January.

In May, Qatar endorsed the Safe Schools Declaration, committing to do more to protect students, teachers, and schools during times of armed conflict, including implementing the *Guidelines on Protecting Schools from Military Use.*

Russia

The Kremlin's crackdown on civil society, media, and the Internet took a more sinister turn in 2015 as the government further intensified harassment and persecution of independent critics. For the fourth year in a row, parliament adopted laws and authorities engaged in repressive practices that increasingly isolated the country. Against the backdrop of the armed conflict in eastern Ukraine and sanctions against Russia over Crimea, anti-Western hysteria has been at its peak since the end of the Cold War.

Freedom of Association

By the end of the year, the authorities had used a 2012 law that demonizes advocacy groups that accept foreign funding to list as "foreign agents" more than a hundred nongovernmental organizations (NGOs), including the country's leading human rights groups. More than a dozen chose to close rather than bear the stigmatizing "foreign agent" label.

The authorities fined many for failing to display "foreign agent" labels on their publications. In November, the Ministry of Justice informed one of Russia's most outspoken and prominent human rights NGOs, the Human Rights Center Memorial, that the group's work amounted to undermining the country's "constitutional rule," calling for the overthrow of the government, and using foreign funding to harm Russia. The accusations may result in criminal charges against its leadership. They also send a chilling signal to other organizations on the "foreign agents" list regarding the government's readiness to resort to criminal prosecution of critics.

In June, a new law on "undesirable foreign organizations" came into force, authorizing the extrajudicial banning of foreign or international groups that allegedly undermine Russia's security, defense, or constitutional order. Russians who maintain ties with "undesirables" face penalties ranging from fines to a maximum of six years in prison.

In August, the authorities banned as "undesirable" the National Endowment for Democracy, an American donor institution that had funded Russian rights groups. Various politicians urged the government to ban many other groups, further deepening the climate of suspicion and fear. In November, the authorities designated the Open Society Foundation as "undesirable." Two other large foreign donors stopped their Russia funding preemptively.

Freedom of Expression

Russian authorities blocked several independent websites, adopted new laws, proposed measures that would further stifle freedom of expression, and prosecuted critics for speaking out online.

In May, President Vladimir Putin amended Russia's official list of classified information to include information on military losses during peacetime and "special operations," which could potentially include, for example, operations in eastern Ukraine or Syria. Violations draw a maximum eight-year prison sentence.

A law that will enter into force in 2016 allows Russian citizens to request the removal of certain types of information about them from search engine results without a court order. The law requires the censoring of any link providing such information regarding events that took place three or more years previously.

In September 2015, a law entered into force banning the storage of Russian Internet users' personal data on foreign servers and requiring foreign sites that collect such data to store it within Russia. International social network sites, among others, could be blocked for refusal to comply with this new requirement.

In several cases, the authorities prosecuted those who voiced online criticism of Russia's occupation of Crimea. In September, a court in Tatarstan sentenced Rafis Kashapov to three years in prison for allegedly undermining Russia's territorial integrity and inciting hostility towards the Russian people. The allegations stem from several posts he published on VKontakte, a popular social media network, criticizing Russia's actions in Crimea and elsewhere in Ukraine.

In June, a consumer protection group, Public Control, became the target of a criminal investigation after publishing online a memo for tourists that called Crimea "occupied territory." If prosecuted, the group's leader faces up to five years in prison on charges of calling for violation of Russia's territorial integrity.

Political Opposition

In February, political opposition leader Boris Nemtsov was assassinated. Five suspects were arrested and are in custody. Investigative officials have been unable to arrest and question another suspect, Ruslan Geremeev, deputy commander of a battalion under de facto control of Ramzan Kadyrov, the head of Chechnya.

In February, a court upheld a December 2014 conviction against Russian opposition leader Alexei Navalny and his brother, Oleg, on politically motivated fraud charges. Oleg Navalny is serving a three-and-a-half-year sentence; Alexei Navalny, who received a three-and-a-half-year suspended sentence with five years' probation, was released from prolonged house arrest following the February ruling.

North Caucasus

The confrontation between Islamist insurgents and law enforcement agencies continued in the North Caucasus, particularly in Dagestan. Law enforcement and security forces carried out several successful operations against insurgents. At the same time, hundreds of North Caucasus residents reportedly left Russia to join forces of the armed extremist group Islamic State (also known as ISIS) in Syria.

As part of their counterinsurgency efforts, law enforcement and security in Dagestan largely equated Salafi Muslims with insurgents or their collaborators. Police put Salafis on special watch lists, repeatedly detaining, questioning, photographing, and fingerprinting them—often without grounds—and in some cases carried out forced DNA sampling. Police also raided Salafi mosques across Dagestan and conducted numerous, abusive special operations using excessive force in detaining suspects and holding them incommunicado in undisclosed locations. Local residents whose houses had been destroyed or severely damaged in counterinsurgency operations in the villages of Vremenny and Gimry in 2014 and 2013, respectively, did not receive adequate compensation.

The crackdown on activists and journalists reporting on abusive treatment of Salafi Muslims intensified. Several left Dagestan for security reasons. Unknown individuals beat Murad Magomedov, a human rights lawyer in Dagestan's capital of Makhachkala, breaking his jaw, knocking out his front teeth, and causing other injuries. The authorities did not question him as a victim or carry out an effective investigation into the attack.

Authorities in Chechnya viciously cracked down on their critics. Unidentified pro-government thugs destroyed the office of the Joint Mobile Group of Human Rights Defenders in Chechnya (JMG) in December 2014 and again in June 2015. The authorities did not carry out an effective investigation.

The attacks followed a formal complaint the JMG's head had filed regarding public threats by Kadyrov to expel insurgents' relatives and destroy their homes. After these threats, security personnel under his de facto control destroyed more than a dozen homes. In December 2014, President Vladimir Putin publicly stated that the Chechen leadership should act within the law. However, the Kremlin took no steps to rein in Kadyrov.

In mid-January, five men forcibly entered one of the Chechnya offices of Human Rights Center Memorial and pelted the staff with eggs, screaming, "This is for [supporting] Kalyapin [head of JMG]!" Memorial subsequently closed the office for security reasons.

Chechen authorities continued their "female virtue campaign," including by requiring women to wear headscarves. In May, a middle-aged Chechen police chief wed a 17-year-old girl under at least some form of duress in what appeared to be a polygamous marriage, with Kadyrov's public backing. Russian law forbids polygamous marriages and marriage before 18. A prominent Russian investigative journalist received death threats when reporting on the story. Authorities failed to carry out an effective investigation into her complaint.

Sexual Orientation and Gender Identity

Authorities continued to use the country's anti-lesbian, gay, bisexual and transgender (LGBT) "propaganda" law to disrupt pro-LGBT rights events and harass LGBT people and their supporters.

In March, police detained an activist as soon as she unfurled a rainbow flag at a demonstration in Moscow on International Women's Day. In April, Moscow police dispersed a small public event protesting LGBT stigmatization. Also in April,

HUMAN
RIGHTS
WATCH

LICENSE TO HARM

Violence and Harassment against LGBT People and Activists in Russia

unidentified people pepper-sprayed activists from an LGBT group in their office in the city of Murmansk. Police failed to carry out an effective investigation.

In May, several activists applied for a permit to hold three LGBT rights rallies in central Moscow, but local authorities refused to authorize the events. When several LGBT people and activists gathered at a square, they were immediately attacked by homophobic counter-protesters. Police detained around 20, including several attackers. A court sentenced three of the activists to 10 days' detention and a fine for allegedly failing to obey police orders.

Russian authorities continued legal harassment of an online support group for LGBT children, Deti-404. In August, a Russian court banned information published on Deti-404 from distribution in Russia. Elena Klimova, founder and administrator of the online group, is fighting the "propaganda" charges against her in court.

Following a smear campaign, Dmitry Isayev, chief of the clinical psychology department at a St. Petersburg medical school, was forced to resign after a prosecutor visited the university to investigate allegations that Isayev was spreading "gay propaganda." The university also shut down a medical committee headed by Isayev, which authorized access to gender reassignment surgeries for transgender people.

The authorities largely failed to prosecute homophobic and transphobic violence. In May, two men attacked Alexander Ermoshkin, a prominent LGBT activist from the city of Khabarovsk who had been fired from his job for being gay. Ermoshkin received a serious head injury; his attackers have not been identified or caught. In July, Russian state TV aired a smear story alleging that the United States had recruited Ermoshkin to carry out anti-Russian activities, including by organizing LGBT rallies. Ermoshkin subsequently left Russia for security reasons.

Palliative Care

At least 300,000 Russians die from cancer each year, and many of them suffer avoidable, treatable pain. The lack of access to effective pain treatment and palliative care remains a systemic problem. At least 27 cancer patients in several Russian regions committed suicide in 2015 because they reportedly experienced untreated, cancer-related pain. A new law, which entered into force in July 2015, eased some of the many restrictions regulating the prescription and use of opi-oid analgesics for chronic pain. However, access to morphine remained overly restricted for the vast majority of patients.

Russia and Ukraine

Russia provides political and material support to rebels in eastern Ukraine, and mounting evidence, including the capture of several Russian officers, indicates that Russian forces are involved in hostilities. Yet Russia has taken no public steps to rein in abuses by rebels (see Ukraine chapter).

Russia held two high-profile trials against Ukraine's nationals. At time of writing, the trial of Nadezhda Savchenko—a military pilot and a member of Ukraine's par-liament—on charges of premeditated murder in connection with the deaths of two Russian journalists in a shelling attack in eastern Ukraine in 2014, was ongo-ing. Many inconsistencies plagued the investigation, and there are credible alle-gations by Savchenko that she was kidnapped and brought illegally to Russia.

In August, a military court found Oleg Sentsov, a Ukrainian filmmaker, and Olexander Kolchenko, a Ukrainian activist, guilty of operating an anti-Russian "terrorist organization" in Crimea, and sentenced them to 20 and 10 years in prison, respectively. Russian rights groups branded both trials as "political" and reported numerous procedural violations. Sentsov and one of the key witnesses for the prosecution alleged torture in custody, and the authorities failed to carry out an effective investigation into those allegations.

Disability Rights

Adults and children living with various disabilities face discrimination and nu-merous barriers to participating in their communities. Although the government has begun to implement inclusive education, most children with disabilities do not study in mainstream schools due to a lack of reasonable accommodations to facilitate their individual learning needs. Tens of thousands of children with dis-abilities remain isolated at home; others attend specialized schools for children with disabilities, often far from their homes. Hundreds of thousands of people with disabilities live in closed institutions. Most children with disabilities in or-

HUMAN
RIGHTS
WATCH

LEFT OUT?

Obstacles to Education for People with Disabilities in Russia

phanages have at least one living parent, and many face violence and neglect, including inadequate health care, education, and opportunities to play.

Key International Actors

International actors were preoccupied in 2015 with Russia's military intervention in Syria; sanctions against Russia for occupying Crimea; and engagement with Moscow to ensure implementation of the Minsk accords to end hostilities in eastern Ukraine. The murder of Boris Nemtsov caused a tremendous international outcry. Russia's international partners widely condemned the prosecution of Sentsov and Savchenko. Key international actors also deplored some of the new threats to human rights in Russia.

Many governments and intergovernmental organizations condemned the law on "undesirable organizations."

In a July report, Nils Muiznieks, the Council of Europe's human rights commissioner, urged Russia to bring its NGO legislation into compliance with the Council of Europe standards. A July European Union statement said that the "foreign agents" law and restrictions on foreign ownership of media were "crippling civil society" and urged Russia not to implement the "undesirables" law.

In November, Thorbjørn Jagland, the Council of Europe's secretary general, called the Ministry of Justice's accusations against Human Rights Center Memorial "extremely worrying," and urged the government "to protect the activities of human rights defenders in Russia, including the work of Memorial." He also reiterated that "the recently adopted NGO legislation, including the NGO 'foreign agents' law, should be revised." He said, "It brings about a stigmatization of NGOs, can trigger self-censorship, and creates a chilling effect on the society as a whole."

Following on its March review of Russia, the United Nations Human Rights Committee noted some positive developments, especially regarding disability rights, but also recommended that Russia, among other measures, "repeal or revise" the "foreign agents" law; end collective punishment in the North Caucasus; and publicly state that it will not tolerate homophobia.

The UN high commissioner for human rights, Zeid Ra'ad Al Hussein, expressed his "dismay" at the stigmatization of foreign-funded NGOs in Russia. He said that the 2012 law has resulted in "marginalizing and discrediting organizations that contribute to the public good."

In its October review of Russia, the Committee on the Elimination of Discrimination against Women (CEDAW) noted its concern about persistent violence against women, including domestic and sexual violence, and called on Russia to take measures to prevent and address such violence, including through comprehensive legislation, provision of critical services for survivors, and training for law enforcement and judicial officials. CEDAW also raised concern about ongoing early, forced, and polygamous marriages in the Northern Caucasus, and called on Russia to demonstrate political will to end these harmful practices.

Foreign Policy

Russia is positioning itself as a global leader in defending "traditional values and state sovereignty," countering what it has claimed is Western excess in the promotion of the rights of the individual. Several states in Eastern Europe and of the former Soviet Union have, to varying degrees, followed Russia's model and proposed stricter rules for NGOs and bills banning LGBT "propaganda."

Russia joined a core group in the UN Human Rights Council that presented a resolution for "protection of the family," with a narrow, non-inclusive conception of "family," and blocked a proposed amendment to the resolution that would have acknowledged that "various forms of the family exist." Russia voted against a resolution adopted by a committee of the UN General Assembly calling on states to guarantee a safe working environment for human rights defenders.

Russia and Iran are the Syrian government's key allies. In September, Russia began air strikes on anti-government forces and ISIS in Syria, which in some cases caused civilian casualties. Russia rejected allegations that its strikes caused civilian casualties.

In October, Russia's ambassador to the UN, Vitaly Churkin, stated in a media interview that Russia had for years been "speaking with the Syrians to try to [get them to] exercise maximum restraint to avoid civilian casualties." Churkin said barrel bombs were part of the discussion. Russia persistently blocked Security Council action to curb violations by the Syrian government, including its use of barrel bombs in civilian areas. Yet Russia also supported Security Council resolutions threatening UN action against Syria for continued use of chemical weapons and establishing a joint investigation to identify those responsible for past chemical weapons use in Syria.

Russian authorities gave no public indication they had used their influence to curb abuses among the rebels they back in eastern Ukraine. Some new laws and other measures Russia imposed in Crimea since its occupation of the peninsula restrict civic freedoms.

Russia supported numerous Security Council resolutions that favored human rights, such as those condemning abduction and other violations against children in situations of armed conflict. But it vetoed a Security Council resolution that would have condemned the 1995 killings in Srebrenica as a genocide. Russia voted against a UN General Assembly resolution calling on states to guarantee a safe working environment for human rights defenders.

At the Human Rights Council, Russia continued to oppose all country-specific resolutions, including on Syria, North Korea, Belarus and Iran. It also opposed a resolution requesting a regular briefing on Ukraine to the council from the high commissioner for human rights.

Rwanda

Tight restrictions on freedom of speech and political space remained in place. Some radio stations have broadcast more programs expressing critical views of the government than in previous years, but pro-government views dominated domestic media. The government suspended the BBC's Kinyarwanda broadcasts inside Rwanda indefinitely, depriving many Rwandans of an important source of independent information.

The parliament approved amendments to the constitution to allow President Paul Kagame to stand for a third term in 2017, to be confirmed in a public referendum.

Rwanda acceded to the Optional Protocol to the United Nations Convention Against Torture on June 30.

Civil Society

Independent civil society organizations are weak, and few document and expose human rights abuses by state agents. The human rights group LIPRODHOR was taken over by elements sympathetic to the ruling party in 2013. The ousted leaders lost a court case in 2014 to challenge the new leadership, but appealed. On March 23, 2015, the High Court of Kigali upheld the 2014 court decision that the case was unfounded on procedural grounds.

One of the only other active independent human rights organizations in Rwanda, the Human Rights League in the Great Lakes Region (LDGL), suffered serious setbacks as a result of internal disputes, effectively paralyzing its work in late 2015. Its executive secretary, Epimack Kwokwo, and several newly elected members of its management committee were questioned at length by the immigration and police in mid-October, mostly about administrative and organizational matters.

Two policemen accused of the 2013 murder of anti-corruption worker Gustave Makonene, a staff member of Transparency International Rwanda, pleaded guilty at their trial, after initially denying the charges. The High Court in Rubavu sentenced them to 20 years' imprisonment in January.

Freedom of Media

Pro-government views dominated domestic media, but several private radio stations broadcast programs on human rights and other politically sensitive issues. These included debates on proposed amendments to presidential term limits, and discussions on human rights abuses in the Gikondo Transit Center, triggered by the publication of a Human Rights Watch report in September.

The BBC Kinyarwanda service remained off the air since the government suspended it in October 2014 in response to a BBC television documentary, "Rwanda's Untold Story." The Rwanda Utilities Regulatory Authority (RURA), the state body which regulates media, set up a committee, headed by former Prosecutor General Martin Ngoga, to look into complaints about the documentary, including allegations that it had denied the genocide.

The committee's report, published on February 28, concluded that the BBC had, among other things, abused press freedom and violated Rwandan law relating to genocide denial and revisionism, inciting hatred and divisionism. It recommended that the agreement between the Rwandan government and the BBC be terminated and that authorities initiate criminal and civil proceedings to deal with the alleged offenses. On May 29, RURA indefinitely suspended the BBC Kinyarwanda service.

The ability of the Rwanda Media Commission (RMC)—the media self-regulatory body established in 2013—to operate independently was called into question after its chair, Fred Muvunyi, resigned in May and fled Rwanda. Muvunyi had publicly disagreed with the decision to suspend the BBC and had opposed government proposals to transfer some of RMC's functions back to RURA.

Political Pluralism

The ruling Rwandan Patriotic Front (RPF) dominated the parliament. Opportunities for genuine opposition parties to function freely are very limited. Victoire Ingabire, president of the FDU-Inkingi opposition party, remained in prison since 2012, serving a 15-year-sentence for conspiracy to undermine the government and genocide denial.

Parliament initiated a process to amend Rwanda's Constitution to enable President Kagame to stand for a third term in 2017. By July, it had received petitions

HUMAN
RIGHTS
WATCH

"Why Not Call This Place a Prison?"
Unlawful Detention and Ill-Treatment in Rwanda's Gikondo Transit Center

from more than 3.78 million people supporting such a move, and claimed to have validated these petitions. Parliamentarians carried out national consultations and said they found a vast majority of Rwandans were in favor of amending the constitution. In late October, the National Assembly voted to reduce presidential term limits from seven to five years, and to limit these to two terms, but to allow President Kagame to stand for a third seven-year term in 2017. In November, the Senate approved these amendments. The changes have to be put to a referendum before a new constitution is adopted.

The opposition Democratic Green Party of Rwanda (DGPR) launched a case at the Supreme Court challenging proposals to lift presidential term limits. On October 8, the Supreme Court dismissed the case, ruling that amendments to the constitution were permissible. The DGPR announced that it would launch a campaign to persuade people to vote against constitutional changes in a referendum.

On September 4, the United States State Department issued a statement expressing concern about the decision by the parliament and president to establish a Constitutional Reform Commission that may amend or remove executive term limits and allow the president to seek a third term in 2017. The State Department expressed renewed concern following the Senate's approval of constitutional amendments in November. On December 3, the EU High Representative for Foreign Affairs declared that the fact that the constitutional amendments apply to only one person would weaken the credibility of the reform process and undermine the principle of democratic change enshrined in the African Charter of Democracy, Elections and Governance.

Unlawful Detention

Many poor people were detained at the Gikondo Transit Center—which the government describes as a transit or rehabilitation center—in the capital Kigali, including sex workers, street hawkers, homeless people, suspected petty criminals, and others. Detainees were held in deplorable and degrading conditions and beaten by police or other detainees, with the assent or on the orders of the police. Unlike in previous years, children were no longer detained in Gikondo, but adult men and women were held there throughout 2015.

New directives by Kigali City Council were published in the Official Gazette on November 1, setting out the mission and organization of the Kigali Rehabilitation

Transit Center (the official name for the Gikondo center). According to the directives, the center receives people who disturb public order and security. A commission will decide, within 72 hours, whether to keep them in the center for an unspecified "short period" or transfer them to the judicial police, a re-education center, back to their families or another location.Transfers should take place within 14 days of that decision. The directives list the rights of those taken to the center, including the rights to health care, visits and not to be subjected to corporal punishment.

Human Rights Watch continued to receive information on people held unlawfully in other unofficial detention centers, including in military custody. They included at least 23 people detained incommunicado for several weeks in 2014 at Camp Kami, a military camp on the outskirts of Kigali, before being tried by a civilian court for security-related offenses and alleged collaboration with armed groups. A court in Rubavu acquitted some of them and ordered their release in July 2015.

Security-Related Trials

In February, the High Court in Kigali sentenced singer Kizito Mihigo to 10 years' imprisonment for alleged offenses of formation of a criminal gang, conspiracy to murder, and conspiracy against the established government or the president. His co-accused Cassien Ntamuhanga, a journalist at Amazing Grace radio, was sentenced to 25 years, and Jean-Paul Dukuzumuremyi, a demobilized soldier, to 30 years. Agnès Niyibizi, accused of carrying money to assist in the alleged offenses, was acquitted. All four had been arrested in 2014 on suspicion of communicating with exiled opposition groups, among other things. Mihigo was held incommunicado in an unknown location for several days in April 2014 before being formally questioned by the police and brought to trial.

The trial of three military officers—retired Brig. Gen. Frank Rusagara, Col. Tom Byabagamba, and demobilized Sgt. François Kabayiza—which began in 2014, continued in the military high court. The defendants were charged, among other things, with inciting insurrection and public disorder and tarnishing Rwanda's image, accusations believed to be related to their alleged contacts with an opposition group. Hearings were adjourned numerous times on procedural grounds. The trial on the substance of the case began on December 7.

International Justice

The United Nations-run International Criminal Tribunal for Rwanda (ICTR), set up in 1994 to try those responsible for genocide and other serious violations of international humanitarian law in 1994, was due to close at the end of December. The judgment of the last appeal case was due on December 14.

The trial of Jean-Bosco Uwinkindi, referred to Rwanda by the ICTR, was stalled by lengthy procedural delays, more than three years after Uwinkindi's return to Rwanda in April 2012. The trial of Léon Mugesera, who had been transferred to Rwanda from Canada in 2012 and was accused, among other things, of public incitement to genocide, ended in Kigali. The high court is expected to deliver its judgement in April 2016.

Courts in several other countries handled outstanding genocide cases. In January, a Norwegian appeal court upheld the conviction of Sadi Bugingo, who was sentenced to 21 years' imprisonment in 2013 for complicity in murder during the genocide. In October, a French court decided not to pursue the case—transferred to France by the ICTR—of Rwandan priest Wenceslas Munyeshyaka for his alleged participation in the genocide, after the French war crimes unit had stated in August that there was a lack of sufficient evidence to prosecute him.

On June 20, Emmanuel Karenzi Karake, head of the intelligence services, was arrested in London on an European arrest warrant following a request by a Spanish judge. In 2008, a Spanish court had indicted him and 39 other senior Rwandan officials for serious crimes and violations of international law, some dating back to the 1990s.

On August 10, a court in London dropped the extradition case, because it failed to meet the test required by the applicable UK extradition law that the case would have to have been prosecutable in the UK at the time of the alleged crimes, for it to be extradictable.

In October, the Spanish Supreme Court stayed the case against Karake and other RPF officials indefinitely because of changes in the Spanish universal jurisdiction law in 2014. The case is therefore inactive until the conditions for jurisdiction, such as the presence of the accused in Spain, are fulfilled.

Saudi Arabia

King Abdullah bin Abdulaziz died on January 23, 2015, after a nine-and-a-half year reign and his half-brother Salman bin Abdulaziz became king. On April 29, King Salman appointed his nephew Mohammad bin Nayef as interior minister and crown prince, and his son Mohammed bin Salman as defense minister and deputy crown prince. These leadership changes did not lead to significant human rights changes.

Through 2015 Saudi authorities continued arbitrary arrests, trials, and convictions of peaceful dissidents. Dozens of human rights defenders and activists continued to serve long prison sentences for criticizing authorities or advocating political and rights reforms. Authorities continued to discriminate against women and religious minorities. On March 26, a Saudi Arabia-led coalition began an airstrike campaign against Houthi forces in Yemen that included use of banned cluster munitions and unlawful strikes that killed civilians.

Freedom of Expression, Association, and Belief

Saudi Arabia continued to repress pro-reform activists and peaceful dissidents. In 2015, over a dozen prominent activists convicted on charges arising from their peaceful activities were serving prison sentences.

Prominent activist Waleed Abu al-Khair continued to serve a 15-year sentence imposed by Saudi Arabia's terrorism court that convicted him in 2014 on charges stemming solely from his peaceful criticism in media interviews and on social media of human rights abuses. Authorities imposed a foreign travel ban on Samar Badawi, Abu al-Khair's wife, in December 2014; earlier, she had travelled to Geneva to inform the United Nations Human Rights Council of her husband's case.

Saudi authorities publicly lashed prominent blogger Raif Badawi 50 times on January 9, 2015, as part of his 2014 sentence for setting up a liberal website and allegedly insulting religious authorities. On June 7, Saudi Arabia's Supreme Court upheld Badawi's sentence of 10 years in prison and 1,000 lashes.

By September, Saudi Arabia had jailed nearly all the founders of the banned-Saudi Civil and Political Rights Association (ACPRA), and two others—Abdulaziz

al-Shubaily and Issa al-Hamid—were on trial for their peaceful pro-reform activities.

Saudi authorities arrested prominent writer and commentator Zuhair Kutbi on
July 15 after he discussed peaceful reform proposals in a TV interview, and later
referred him to the Specialized Criminal Court for trial.

Authorities persisted in refusing to legally register political or human rights
groups, exposing their members to prosecution for "setting up an unregistered
organization." In December 2015, the Saudi cabinet approved a new law permitting the establishment of civil society organizations for the first time, but authorities had not published the text of the law at time of writing.

Saudi Arabia does not tolerate public worship by adherents of religions other
than Islam and systematically discriminates against Muslim religious minorities,
notably Twelver Shia and Ismailis, including in public education, the justice system, religious freedom, and employment. Government-affiliated religious authorities continued to disparage Shia Islam in public statements and
documents.

Militants affiliated with the extremist armed group Islamic State (also known as
ISIS) carried out five major attacks targeting Saudi Shia from November 2014, including bombings at Shia mosques in Qatif and Dammam that killed 26 people
and injured over 100.

In February 2015, a court sentenced a Saudi man to death for apostasy after he
allegedly filmed himself ripping a copy of the Quran. In November, a court sentenced Palestinian poet Ashraf Fayadh to death for alleged blasphemous statements during a discussion group and in a book of his poetry.

Saudi Arabia has no written laws concerning sexual orientation or gender identity, but judges use principles of uncodified Islamic law to sanction people suspected of committing homosexual or other "immoral" acts. If such activity
occurs online, judges and prosecutors utilize vague provisions of the country's
anti-cyber crime law that criminalize online activity that impinges on "public
order, religious values, public morals, and privacy."

In 2015, for example, an appeals court upheld a sentence of three years in prison
and 100,000 Saudi Riyals (US$70,800) against a Saudi man for using social

media "in order to practice homosexuality." The ruling relied in part on the anti-cyber crime law.

Criminal Justice

Detainees, including children, commonly face systematic violations of due process and fair trial rights, including arbitrary arrest. Judges routinely sentence defendants to floggings of hundreds of lashes.

Judges can order arrest and detention, including of children, at their discretion. Children can be tried for capital crimes and sentenced as adults if there are physical signs of puberty.

Saudi Arabia applies Sharia (Islamic law) as its national law. There is no formal penal code, but the government has passed some laws and regulations that subject certain broadly-defined offenses to criminal penalties. In the absence of a written penal code or narrowly-worded regulations, however, judges and prosecutors can criminalize a wide range of offenses under broad, catch-all charges such as "breaking allegiance with the ruler" or "trying to distort the reputation of the kingdom."

Authorities do not always inform suspects of the crime with which they are charged, or allow them access to supporting evidence, sometimes even after trial sessions have begun. Authorities generally do not allow lawyers to assist suspects during interrogation and sometimes impede them from examining witnesses and presenting evidence at trial.

In 2015, authorities continued to detain arrested suspects for months, even years, without judicial review or prosecution.

Authorities announced three mass round-ups of Saudi and foreign terrorism suspects in 2015, including 93 persons in April, 431 in July, and 74 in August in response to ISIS-related plots and attacks across the kingdom against security forces and, in some cases, mosques, killing civilians.

Saudi Arabia dramatically increased the execution rate in 2015. According to Interior Ministry statements, Saudi Arabia executed 152 persons between January and November, mostly for murder and drug offenses. Sixty-two of those executed were convicted for non-violent drug crimes. Most executions are carried out by beheading, sometimes in public.

In late January authorities said they would prosecute a security official who filmed the January beheading of a Burmese woman in Mecca in which the swordsman required three sword strikes to sever the victim's head. In September, Saudi Arabia's Supreme Court upheld a death sentence against Ali al-Nimr, a Saudi man convicted for crimes related to a 2011 protest movement, allegedly committed before he was 18.

Women's and Girl's Rights

Saudi Arabia's discriminatory male guardianship system remains intact despite government pledges to abolish it. Under this system, ministerial policies and practices forbid women from obtaining a passport, marrying, travelling, or accessing higher education without the approval of a male guardian, usually a husband, father, brother, or son. Authorities also fail to prevent some employers from requiring male guardians to approve the hiring of adult female relatives or some hospitals requiring male guardian approval before undertaking certain medical procedures for women.

Under uncodified rules on personal status, women are not allowed to marry without the permission of their guardian; unlike men, they do not have a unilateral right to divorce and often face discrimination in relation to child custody.

All women remain banned from driving vehicles in Saudi Arabia. In December 2014, authorities arrested two Saudi women who drove a car to the United Arab Emirates-Saudi Arabia border and detained them for 73 days before releasing them without charge.

In a positive move in August, authorities began allowing Saudi women for the first time to both register to vote and to run for office in municipal elections due in December.

Migrant Worker Rights

Over 9 million migrant workers fill manual, clerical, and service jobs, constituting more than half the workforce. Many suffer abuses and exploitation, sometimes amounting to conditions of forced labor.

The *kafala* (sponsorship) system ties migrant workers' residency permits to "sponsoring" employers, whose written consent is required for workers to

HUMAN
RIGHTS
WATCH

DETAINED, BEATEN, DEPORTED
Saudi Abuses against Migrants during Mass Expulsions

change employers or exit the country under normal circumstances. Some employers illegally confiscate passports, withhold wages, and force migrants to work against their will.

In October, labor officials issued directives introducing or raising fines for employers who violate labor regulations. These include prohibitions on confiscating migrant workers' passports, failing to pay salaries on time, and failing to provide copies of contracts to employees.

Faced with a domestic unemployment rate of 12 percent that may rise as the domestic population increases, Saudi authorities have introduced labor reforms since 2011 that create a tiered quota system for the employment of Saudi citizens in the private labor sector that differs according to the nature of the business. As part of these reforms, Saudi labor authorities in 2015 allowed foreigners working in firms that do not employ the required percentage of Saudis to change jobs without employer approval.

Police and labor authorities continued to arrest and deport foreign workers found in violation of existing labor laws, targeting workers without valid residency or work permits, or those found working for an employer other than their legal sponsor.

On March 23, Saudi authorities announced that they had deported 300,000 people over the previous five months, an average of nearly 2,000 a day. Saudi Arabia is not a party to the 1951 Refugee Convention and not established an asylum system whereby migrants can apply to prevent their forced return to places where their lives or freedom may be threatened.

Domestic workers, predominantly women, faced a range of abuses including overwork, forced confinement, non-payment of wages, food deprivation, and psychological, physical, and sexual abuse without the authorities holding their employers to account. Workers who attempted to report employer abuses sometimes faced prosecution based on counterclaims of theft, "black magic," or "sorcery".

Yemen Airstrikes and Blockade

On March 26, a Saudi Arabia-led coalition of states began a campaign of airstrikes against Houthi forces in Yemen and instituted a naval and aerial blockade. The airstrikes struck Houthi targets in the capital, Sanaa, and other cities, but also killed and injured many civilians. Between March and July nearly 2,112 civilians were killed in Yemen as a result of the armed conflict, most from coalition airstrikes.

Human Rights Watch investigated a number of Saudi-led airstrikes that appeared to be unlawful, including the bombing of a dairy factory in the port of Hodaida on March 31 that killed at least 31 civilians, attacks on civilian objects in the northern Houthi stronghold of Saada that killed dozens in April and May, and the bombing of two residential compounds in the Yemeni port city of Mokha that killed at least 65 civilians in July.

The coalition has used cluster munitions, banned by 117 states, in civilian-populated areas in Yemen, wounding and killing civilians.

The coalition-imposed blockade also had a severe impact on Yemen's civilians. According to the United Nations, by September half the population faced food insecurity and 21 million Yemenis—a staggering 80 percent of the population—needed humanitarian assistance. More than 15.2 million people lacked access to basic health care, and over 20 million lacked access to safe water. With commercial imports accounting for 90 percent of Yemen's food and fuel supplies, the coalition-imposed blockade may amount to starvation of civilians as a method of warfare, a war crime.

Key International Actors

The United States largely did not criticize Saudi human rights violations beyond Congressionally-mandated annual reports, but in January 2015 the State Department called on Saudi Arabic to cancel the "brutal punishment" imposed against Raif Badawi and to review his case and sentence.

The US provided logistics and intelligence support to Saudi-led coalition forces conducting airstrikes on Yemen, which may have included assistance with military targeting.

The January lashing of Raif Badawi provoked strong condemnation from some European Union countries. On February 12, the European Parliament adopted a resolution condemning corporal punishment, calling for the immediate release of Badawi and Waleed Abu al-Khair, and urging EU states to "reconsider their relationship with Saudi Arabia." In October, the European Parliament awarded Raif Badawi the 2015 Sakharov Prize for Freedom of Thought.

In March, Saudi Arabia blocked Swedish Foreign Minister Margot Wallström from addressing the Arab League in response to her criticism of Saudi human rights abuses. The same month, Sweden canceled a defense cooperation agreement with Saudi Arabia.

Serbia

There was limited progress in 2015 toward closing the gap between Serbia's human rights obligations and its practice. Serbia struggled in the face of increasing numbers of migrants and asylum seekers, with poor reception conditions, police abuse, and an inadequate asylum system. Journalists operated in a hostile environment that included attacks, threats, and lawsuits for reporting on sensitive issues. The pace of war crimes prosecutions remained slow. The Roma minority continued to face housing discrimination.

Migrants, Asylum Seekers, and Displaced Persons

Serbia saw a dramatic increase in the numbers of migrants and asylum seekers in 2015, many of them from Syria, Afghanistan, and Iraq, seeking to transit through the country en route to Western Europe. Between January 1 and July 31, Serbia registered 66,428 asylum seekers, nearly 10 times the number registered during the same period in 2014 (6,974). Syrians comprised the largest national group (37,970 people). There are no reliable estimates as to the number of unregistered asylum seekers and migrants present in Serbia.

Due to the significant increase in numbers of asylum seekers, Serbian authorities in July opened a new 300-person reception center in the town of Presevo on the border with Macedonia, bringing the total to six reception centers. But capacity remained limited, and many asylum seekers and migrants remained out in the open without shelter. There were credible reports throughout the year of police abuses and extortion against migrants and asylum seekers. In November, Serbia imposed border restrictions on migrants and asylum seekers, allowing only people from Syria, Afghanistan, and Iraq to entry the country from Macedonia.

As of November 1, Serbia had granted refugee status to a total of 16 asylum seekers and subsidiary protection to 14 others in 2015. Beyond the perversely low recognition rates, the office's asylum procedures are inadequate, with thousands of pending claims and delays in lodging intention to seek asylum.

During the first seven months of 2015, the Office of the United Nations High Commissioner for Refugees (UNHCR) registered 4,112 unaccompanied children in

Serbia, the majority from Afghanistan and Syria, compared with only 98 unaccompanied migrant children between January and September 2014. According to UNHCR, Serbia lacks formal age assessment procedures for unaccompanied children, putting older children at risk of being treated as adults and failing to receive special protection. The two institutions in Serbia for unaccompanied children have a total of only 32 spaces.

Serbian authorities made slow progress in finding a durable solution for refugees and internally displaced persons (IDPs) from the Balkan wars living in Serbia. According to data from UNHCR, as of July 1 there were 35,732 such refugees in Serbia, most from Croatia, and 203,140 IDPs, the majority from Kosovo.

Freedom of Media

Journalists in Serbia face attacks, threats, harassment, intimidation, lawsuits, and political and other interference. Between January and August 2014, the Independent Journalists' Association of Serbia reported seven attacks on journalists, thirteen threats, and two cases of attacks on property. Authorities prosecuted two cases during the year involving physical attacks on journalists, apparently related to their work.

The independent online news site Balkan Investigative Reporting Network (BIRN) came under criticism in January and February from Serbian government officials, including Prime Minister Aleksandar Vucic, who accused BIRN staff of being liars and BIRN of receiving money from the European Union to discredit the Serbian government.

The criticism followed an investigative piece in BIRN alleging government corruption. Several pro-government news outlets then engaged in a month-long smear campaign against BIRN and its staff, prompting condemnation by the European Commission and international media freedom groups.

The government commission established to investigate the murders of three prominent journalists in Serbia finally made progress in one case, and a trial began in June of four suspects in the killing of Slavko Curuvija. The commission has made no progress in the other two cases under its mandate.

Accountability for War Crimes

War crimes prosecutions in Serbia are hampered by a lack of support from authorities and weak witness protection mechanisms.

Few high-ranking former military and civilian personnel implicated in serious wartime abuses have been held to account in Serbian courts. At time of writing, 14 war crimes trials were ongoing at first instance and 7 were under appeal in the Serbian courts. Indictments had been issued in 16 cases awaiting trial, including eight people charged in September in connection with the 1995 Srebrenica genocide in Bosnia and Herzegovina, the first indictment for Srebrenica crimes in the Serbian courts. Thirteen cases were under investigation.

In 2015, Serbian courts reached judgments in four cases—one war crimes case at first instance and three on appeal—and ordered a retrial in a fifth case.

In June, the Belgrade War Crimes Chamber convicted two defendants in the 1991 killings of civilians in the city of Vukovar, Croatia. In May, the Belgrade Appeals Court upheld the convictions of three defendants for murder, inhuman and degrading treatment, and torture of non-Serbs during the war in Croatia.

In June, the High Court in Belgrade granted the appeal of six defendants overturning their convictions for the wartime killing of 28 Roma civilians in Bosnia and Herzegovina. In March, the Belgrade Appeals Court annulled the first instance convictions of nine defendants in the wartime killing of 118 Albanians in Kosovo in 1999, ordering a retrial.

The Belgrade Appeals Court in November acquitted a former Serbian volunteer fighter of raping two Bosniak women in the Bosnian town of Bijeljina during the war in 1992, ruling that evidence was insufficient. Three other members of the same volunteer unit were convicted of rape and robbery and sentenced to a total of 43 years in 2012.

In November 2014, Vojislav Seselj, the war crimes suspect and nationalist Serbian Radical Party leader, who had been charged with persecution, murder, forced deportation, illegal imprisonment, torture, and property destruction during the Yugoslav wars against Croats, Bosniaks, and other non-Serbs, was granted provisional release for medical treatment by the International Criminal Tribunal for the former Yugoslavia (ICTY). In March, the ICTY revoked his provisional release and ordered his return to The Hague. Seselj defied the order and remained in Serbia at time of writing.

In July, the ICTY heard oral arguments in the prosecution's appeal of the May 2013 acquittal of former state security officials Jovica Stanisic and Franko Simatovic for war crimes in Bosnia and Croatia during the 1990s. At time of writing, a final verdict was expected in December 2015.

Treatment of Minorities

The Roma minority continued to face discrimination and harassment, particularly in relation to housing.

In July, an informal housing unit in a Romani settlement in the Novi Belgrade municipality was demolished by authorities without prior notification or alternative accommodation for the family living there, according to the European Roma Rights Centre. The remaining 20 families in the settlement faced an ongoing threat of eviction at time of writing.

The planned evictions of 53 Romani families from their homes in Belgrade without alternative accommodation was halted in July after the European Court of Human Rights intervened, issuing an interim order to halt the evictions following a petition from a local human rights organization citing procedural failings and a failure to provide adequate alternative accommodation.

Roma in informal settlements often live in appalling conditions. A May 2015 report on Serbia by the United Nations special rapporteur on adequate housing highlighted the disproportionate number of evictions of Roma, lack of provision of basic services to Roma, and lack of legal security of tenure.

Human Rights Defenders

Human rights defenders continue to work in a hostile environment. Between January and August, the Belgrade Pride Organizing Committee reported between 30 and 50 cases of online threats against LGBT activists to the police. Government officials participated in a successful pride parade in Belgrade in September, amid heavy security and strong statements from top officials that violence would not be tolerated.

A smear campaign against Serbian Ombudsman Sasa Jankovic, which started in late 2014, continued in 2015 when in January the Ministry of Defence described Jankovic as part of an organized campaign to ruin the Serbian army. The campaign against Jankovic followed charges the ombudsman filed against two military police officers for assaulting gendarmerie police at the September 2014 Belgrade Pride Parade. The two military police were escorting relatives of Prime Minister Vucic and the mayor of Belgrade at the time of the incident.

Key International Actors

In March, Federica Mogherini, the European Union high representative for foreign affairs and security, said that Serbia needed to make economic, social, and political reforms, but failed to specifically mention the country's human rights obligations.

EU Enlargement Commissioner Johannes Hahn in February stated that the EU would not respond to allegations of media censorship in Serbia without concrete evidence, despite ample evidence of a poor climate for media freedom. During a May visit, Hahn stressed the importance of continued dialogue between Belgrade and Pristina for the start of accession talks with Serbia. He also called on authorities to respect the institution of the ombudsman.

The European Commission's annual progress report on Serbia expressed concern with respect to the independence of the judiciary. It highlighted restrictions on freedom of expression and media freedom. It also called on Serbia to implement its anti-discrimination framework more effectively in order to promote equality and ensure integration of vulnerable groups and minorities.

The United States State Department 2014 human rights report on Serbia highlighted discrimination and attacks against minorities, especially Roma, threats against media freedom, an inefficient judicial system, and long periods of pretrial detention as key human rights issues facing the country.

Kosovo

Human rights protections progressed slowly in Kosovo in 2015. A new government was formed in May, 13 months after national elections. Parliament finally adopted needed legal changes to establish a special court to investigate allegations of serious war crimes. Early in the year, large numbers of Kosovars, mainly ethnic Albanians, applied for asylum in Germany, and most of them were rejected, prompting Kosovo's President Atifete Jahjaga to appeal to Kosovars to stay.

Kosovo made little progress in implementing programs to integrate increasing numbers of Roma, Ashkali, and Egyptians deported from Germany and other European states. Journalists face threats and intimidation, and prosecutions of crimes against journalists are slow. Tensions between Serbs and Kosovo Albanians continued, particularly in the north. The process of normalizing relations with Belgrade progressed.

Impunity, Accountability, and Access to Justice

The parliament in August adopted constitutional amendments needed to establish a special court to try serious crimes committed during and after the 1998-1999 Kosovo war by former members of the Kosovo Liberation Army (KLA). The court will operate under Kosovo law but with a chamber abroad and internationally appointed judges and prosecutors. At time of writing, Kosovo has yet to sign and ratify a host-state agreement with the Netherlands to operationalize the court.

The special court will adjudicate cases investigated by the Special Investigative Task Force, prompted by a 2011 Council of Europe report accusing some KLA members of abductions, beatings, summary executions, and the forced removal of human organs in Kosovo and Albania during and after the Kosovo war.

In May, the first instance court in Pristina convicted six former KLA members—part of the Drenica Group, made up mostly by former KLA members, including former Skenderaj Mayor Sami Lushtaku—to a total of 65 years in prison for the torture, ill-treatment, and murder of prisoners in the KLA detention center in Likovac. The decision was under appeal as of mid-November.

In June, former Prime Minister Ramush Haradinaj was arrested in Slovenia on a Serbian warrant for alleged war crimes during the 1998-1999 conflict in Kosovo. Slovenia did not extradite Haradinaj to Serbia, but released him later that month.

In April, staff of the European Union Rule of Law Mission (EULEX) exhumed three bodies from a suspected mass grave in the village of Lausa. That same month, Kosovo authorities started searching for suspected mass graves in 20 locations. More than 1,500 people remain missing after the 1998-1999 war.

By the end of September, mixed panels consisting of EULEX and local judges handed down one decision at the first instance level and one case in the Court of Appeals. EULEX has been involved in a total of 35 verdicts since established in 2008.

The Human Rights Review Panel, an independent body set up in 2009 to review allegations of human rights violations by EULEX staff, ruled on two cases during the year. In April, the panel found that EULEX had violated the European Convention on Human Rights by failing to investigate the harm suffered by 116 Roma who spent time in a number of camps for internally displaced persons, some contaminated with lead, during and as a result of the 1999 conflict.

In another case in April, the panel found no violation of the complainants' rights that could be attributable to EULEX. The case involved alleged brutality by Kosovo police against 10 Serbian citizens who attended Christmas celebrations in the town of Gracanica in 2013. Thirty cases were pending before the panel at time of writing.

The Human Rights Advisory Panel, an independent body set up in 2006 to examine complaints committed by or attributable to the United Nations Interim Administration Mission in Kosovo, found violations in 31 out of 36 cases addressed between January and August.

Treatment of Minorities

Roma, Ashkali, and Egyptians continue to face problems acquiring personal documents, which affects their ability to access health care, social assistance, and education. A lack of political will, funds, and cooperation between central and municipal authorities have contributed to the failure to fully implement the 2010 Strategy for the Integration of Roma, Ashkali, and Egyptian communities.

The 2013 strategy on the reintegration of repatriated persons, including Roma, Ashkali, and Egyptians, resulted in the establishment of the Municipal Office for Committees and Return to help provide food and accommodation. Yet those who have been repatriated still face difficulties accessing employment, education, and health care.

Interethnic tensions persisted in ethnically divided northern Kosovo. In April, a 17-year-old Serbian boy was stabbed in the city of Mitrovica by unknown persons. Eyewitness reported that the perpetrators fled to the predominantly Albanian southern part of the city. Police were investigating at time of writing.

In January 2015, violent clashes erupted between riot police and several thousand protesters demanding the dismissal of Aleksandar Jablanovic, a Serb cabinet minister, who earlier that month called Albanians blocking Serb pilgrims from visiting a church in Djakovica "savages." Jablanovic was dismissed from his post in February.

Between January and September 2015, Kosovo Police registered five interethnic incidents.

Asylum Seekers and Displaced Persons

During the first 10 months of the year, the United Nations High Commissioner for Refugees registered 619 voluntary minority returns, including people from outside Kosovo and internally displaced persons, up from 547 during that period in 2014.

Forced returns of Kosovo nationals from Western Europe, most of them ethnic Albanian, but also Roma, Ashkali, and Egyptians, significantly increased. This was due in part to the high number of asylum claims filed mostly by Albanian Kosovars in Germany in the first months of the year, the vast majority of which were rejected.

The Kosovo Ministry of Internal Affairs registered 7,380 forced returns between January 1 and September 30, including 320 Roma, 282 Ashkali, and 68 Egyptians. 1,855 children were among those forcibly deported. Most minorities were deported from Germany and returnees are provided limited assistance upon return.

Freedom of Media

Journalists continued to face threats and intimidation in 2015, and investigations and prosecutions are slow. Journalists who report on radical Islamist groups are particularly vulnerable to intimidation. At least one investigative journalist was forced to temporarily leave Kosovo in 2015 because of death threats. By the end of September, the Association of Professional Journalists of Kosovo registered 22 complaints of threats and intimidation, including four death threats, mainly issued via social media, including Facebook. No physical attacks were reported during the year.

Former KLA fighters allegedly threatened Radio Kosova journalist Serbeze Haxhiaj because she was investigating whether people who were not war veterans were included on war veteran lists to gain significant pension benefits. Radio Kosova, a private radio station, has not aired Haxhiaj's investigation because of what she describes as "censorship." She did not file a police complaint.

Key International Actors

European Union High Representative Federica Mogherini in August said that constitutional changes the Kosovo Assembly passed marked "a crucial step" in addressing "serious allegations" stemming from a 2011 Council of Europe report accusing some former KLA members of war crimes.

The United States government in August welcomed the constitutional and other legal amendments required for establishing the special court. That same month, United Nations Secretary-General Ban Ki-moon issued a report on Kosovo urging authorities to accelerate the establishment of the special court.

Germany in September declared that Kosovo, Montenegro, and Albania are safe countries of origin, meaning that asylum claims from Kosovo will be processed under accelerated procedures with the presumption that claimants do not need international protection.

The October EU Commission progress report on Kosovo stated that the administration of justice is slow, lacking accountability of judicial officials, and that judicial structures continue to be prone to political interference. The report also highlighted the lack of progress in the area of freedom of expression and called on Kosovo authorities to thoroughly investigate physical attacks and other types of pressure on journalists. It stressed that authorities at central and local levels did not do enough to facilitate return and reintegration of refugees and internally displaced persons.

The US State Department Human Rights Report on Kosovo, published in June, raised concerns about freedom of movement and worship by Serbian Orthodox pilgrims, domestic violence against women, and discrimination against ethnic minorities, persons with disabilities, and members of the lesbian, gay, bisexual, and transgender community.

Singapore

Singapore uses overly broad legal provisions on public order, morality, security, and racial and religious harmony to limit fundamental civil and political rights.

On March 23, Lee Kuan Yew, the founding prime minister of Singapore, died at age 91 after a short illness. In September, the ruling People's Action Party (PAP) won 83 out of 89 seats in general elections. The PAP has ruled Singapore since 1959.

Freedom of Peaceful Assembly, Association, and Expression

The government maintains restrictions on the right to freedom of peaceful assembly through provisions of the Public Order Act, which require a police permit for any "cause-related" assembly in a public place or to which members of the general public are invited. Grounds for denial are broad.

Associations of more than 10 people are required to register with the government, and the Registrar of Societies has broad authority to deny registration if it is determined that the group could be "prejudicial to public peace, welfare or good order."

Protests and rallies conducted at the Speakers' Corner in Hong Lim Park do not need a police permit provided that the topics discussed do not touch on religious or racial issues, and the organizer and speakers are Singaporean citizens. Foreigners who are not permanent residents may not participate unless they have a police permit.

During the year, the government continued its prosecution of activists relating to a Hong Lim Park protest on September 25, 2014. Officials charged Han Hui and Roy Ngerng Yi Ling with holding a demonstration without a permit based on authorities' assessment that, although the two had a permit, it allowed speeches but not marching or other protest activities. Ngerng decided to plead guilty and paid a hefty fine; Han's trial was continuing at time of writing. Ngerng and Han, along with four others—Janet Low, Ivan Koh, Goh Aik Huat, and Chua Siew Leng— were also charged with creating a public nuisance. Three of them pled guilty to the charge, but Hui, Low, and Koh were still contesting the charges in court at time of writing.

The government's Media Development Authority (MDA) compels online news websites covering domestic political issues to register under the Broadcasting Act. Registration requires posting a monetary bond, paying fees, undergoing annual registration, and, on notification, immediately removing anything the MDA deems to be against "public interest, public order or national harmony" or to offend "good taste or decency." Registered websites are also prohibited from receiving any foreign funding.

In February 2015, Singaporean police arrested a Singaporean and an Australian who were co-editors of the news portal The Real Singapore, and charged them in April with seven counts of sedition for publishing articles that authorities claimed had a "tendency to promote feelings of ill-will and hostility between different groups of people in Singapore." In May, the MDA decided to suspend the operating license of The Real Singapore. In September, a court sentenced Filipino national Ed Mundsel Bello Ello, who worked in Singapore as a nurse, to four months in prison for comments he posted online disparaging Singaporeans.

The Newspaper and Printing Presses Act requires local newspapers to renew their registration ever year and empowers the government to limit circulation of foreign newspapers.

Government officials continue to use criminal and civil defamation as a means to silence critics. At time of writing, Roy Ngerng Yi Ling was awaiting a court decision on the damages he would have to pay to Prime Minister Lee Hsien Loong for a 2014 blog post criticizing Lee's management of the government's central provident fund. Lee successfully sued Ngerng, arguing that the blog post suggested Lee had criminally misappropriated funds.

The Films Act authorizes the banning, seizure, censoring, or restricting of written, visual, and musical offerings on vague and overly broad grounds. All films and videos to be shown in Singapore must be approved by the Board of Film Censors.

On March 27, Amos Yee Pang Sang, a 16-year-old blogger, released an online video "Lee Kuan Yew is Dead" on YouTube, and then the next day published an image of two cartoon figures having sex, with photos of Lee and the late British Prime Minister Margaret Thatcher superimposed on their heads.

Singapore prosecutors promptly charged Yee with violating penal code article 298 ("uttering words with deliberate intent to wound the religious or racial feelings of any person") for derogatory references to Christianity in the video, and penal code article 292(1)(a) for transmitting obscene materials. Bail conditions—which Yee violated—restricted his right to free expression by stipulating he could not post anything online while his trial was ongoing. In total, Yee spent 53 days in detention and was sentenced in July to four weeks in prison, equivalent to time served. In October, the High Court dismissed Yee's appeal of his conviction.

During legislative debate in parliament, Singapore's Protection from Harassment Act (POHA) was explained as a law designed to protect individuals and civil servants from "indecent, threatening, abusive, insulting words or behavior." In May, a court ruled in favor of the Ministry of Defense, which claimed that it was being harassed by entrepreneur Ting Choon Meng and the directors of The Online Citizen, an online news portal which carried a story about Dr. Ting. The doctor had alleged that that the Ministry of Defense had stolen his patent for an emergency medical care vehicle. On December 9, however, the High Court overturned the lower court decision, ruling that only individuals, not corporations or the government, can seek redress under POHA.

Criminal Justice System

Singapore uses the Internal Security Act (ISA) and Criminal Law (Temporary Provisions) Act to arrest and administratively detain persons for virtually unlimited periods without charge or judicial review.

Singapore retains the death penalty, which is mandated for many drug offenses and certain other crimes. However, judges continued to apply legal provisions that give them discretion to bypass the mandatory penalty and sentence low-level offenders to life in prison and caning where prosecutors attest that offenders have been cooperative.

Use of corporal punishment is common in Singapore. For medically fit males ages 16 to 50, caning is mandatory as an additional punishment for a range of crimes, including drug trafficking, violent crimes (such as armed robbery), and even immigration offenses. Sentencing officials may also order caning for some 30 additional violent and non-violent crimes.

Singapore maintains the archaic offense of "scandalizing the judiciary," which can be imposed for any criticism of the judiciary or a specific judge. In January 2015, a court convicted Alex Au, a popular blogger and lesbian, gay, bisexual and transgender (LGBT) activist, for scandalizing the judiciary in connection with a post on his online blog. The post referenced the court's scheduling of two constitutional challenges to section 377A of the penal code, which criminalizes sex between male persons. Au argued in court that his writings constituted fair criticism consistent with the right to freedom of speech and expression. In March, the court fined him S$8,000 (US$6,000). Au has appealed the verdict.

Sexual Orientation and Gender Identity

In 2014, top government leaders reiterated that Singapore society is not yet ready to accept LGBT rights. In October of that year, the Supreme Court rejected a claim that the ban on gay sex is unconstitutional. The court said the legislature, not the judiciary, needs to address this issue. A constitutional challenge that would have prohibited employment discrimination against LGBT individuals also failed.

The pro-LGBT Pink Dot festival was held for the seventh consecutive year, with an estimated 28,000 people attending at Hong Lim Park in June 2015. However, prior to the event, the MDA banned a Pink Dot promotional advertisement to be shown in movie theaters, ruling that it was "not in the public interest to allow cinema halls to carry advertising on LGBT issues." In May, the MDA ordered TV and radio broadcasters to not air Jolin Tsai's song and music video "We're All Different, Yet The Same" because of the song's lyrics on homosexuality.

Human Rights Defenders

In February, the Law Society of Singapore filed four misconduct complaints against human rights lawyer M. Ravi, demanding he cease practicing until he underwent a medical examination. Ravi—who receives treatment for a psychosocial disability, specifically bipolar disorder and hypomania—frequently takes up causes unpopular with the government, including legal challenges to the death penalty, caning, and anti-LGBT laws. In November, a Law Society disciplinary tribunal ruled against Ravi and sent the matter to a Court of Appeal to decide possible punishments.

Migrant Workers and Labor Exploitation

Foreign migrant workers are subject to labor abuse and exploitation through debts owed to recruitment agents, non-payment of wages, restrictions on movement, confiscation of passports, and sometimes physical and sexual abuse. Foreign domestic workers are still excluded from the Employment Act and many key labor protections, such as limits on daily work hours. Labor laws also discriminate against foreign workers by barring them from organizing and registering a union or serving as union leaders without explicit government permission.

Key International Actors

Singapore is a regional hub for international business, maintains good political and economic relations with both the United States and China, and plays a central role in the Association of Southeast Asian Nations (ASEAN). Singapore has been an increasingly close security ally of the US.

Somalia

Somalia's long-running armed conflict continued to take a heavy toll on civilians in much of south-central Somalia. Warring parties continued to kill, wound, and forcibly displace civilians. Restrictions on humanitarian access exacerbated the human rights and humanitarian crises.

Ongoing political infighting and three government reshuffles in three years, along with political maneuvering around implementation of federalism, detracted from justice and security sector reform progress. Tensions over creation of a new interim regional administration in central Somalia led to open conflict between clan militias and government forces, resulting in abuses against civilians.

The forces of the African Union Mission to Somalia (AMISOM), as well as Ethiopian armed forces, launched a new offensive against the armed Islamist group Al-Shabaab in southern Somalia. While Al-Shabaab lost control of some key towns, it maintains control over large swathes of territory, and many key transport routes. Al-Shabaab carried out targeted attacks on civilians and civilian infrastructure, in the capital, Mogadishu, and other towns under government or allied authority, and increased high-profile attacks on AMISOM facilities. There were credible reports that AMISOM forces killed civilians during operations and in response to Al-Shabaab attacks.

Abuses by Government and Allied Forces

Civilians have been killed at government-manned checkpoints and in the crossfire of fighting between government forces and Al-Shabaab, clashes over the creation of federal states, and in indiscriminate responses to attacks.

The security situation remained volatile in government-controlled towns. Government forces failed to protect civilians, including journalists, clan elders, clerics and lawmakers and other officials from targeted killings by Al-Shabab as well as by unknown gunmen, primarily in Mogadishu, Baidoa, the capital of the Bay region, and Beletweyn, the capital of Hiraan.

In February, as a result of ongoing tensions regarding establishing an interim regional administration in central Somalia, fighting in Guri'el between government forces and the Ahlu Sunna Wal Jama'a, a Sufi militia, resulted in civilian deaths and massive displacement. According to the United Nations, about 90 percent of the estimated population of over 65,000 temporarily fled. Inter-clan fighting, reportedly involving government forces, in Hiraan also resulted in civilians deaths.

Somalia's national intelligence agency, NISA, continued to conduct mass security sweeps despite having no legal mandate to arrest or detain. NISA has occasionally held detainees for prolonged periods without judicial review and beat suspects during interrogations.

The military court continued to try cases that are not legally within its jurisdiction and in proceedings falling short of international fair trial standards. Eleven individuals were sentenced to death by military courts and executed in south-central Somalia and Puntland.

Children continued to be killed, arbitrary detained, and recruited into the armed forces. In January 2015, Somalia ratified the Convention on the Rights of the Child and in November endorsed the Safe Schools Declaration commiting to take concrete steps to protect students and educational institutions.

Abuses by Al-Shabaab

Al-Shabaab regularly targets civilians and civilian structures, particularly in Mogadishu, resulting in numerous casualties. On November 1, Al-Shabaab attacked the popular Sahafi Hotel in Mogadishu, killing at least 15 people, including a journalist covering the attack, other civilians and officials. On December 5, 2014, Al-Shabaab claimed responsibility for a twin attack in Baidoa that killed at least 19 people including three journalists.

Credible reports indicate that Al-Shabaab administers arbitrary justice and severely restricts basic rights in areas under its control, and continued to forcibly recruit children. Al-Shabaab committed targeted killings, beheadings and executions, particularly of those accused of spying. On February 7, Al-Shabaab publicly executed two women accused of working for NISA in Jiliib, Middle Juba. Al-Shabaab controls some supply routes and imposes blockades on towns captured by AMISOM and Somali government forces, notably Wajid, Bulo-Burte and Hudur, severely restricting movement of goods and assistance; on occasion Al-Shabaab killed civilians accused of breaking blockades.

Abuses by Foreign Forces

Reports increased of indiscriminate killings of civilians by AMISOM and other foreign forces, particularly at checkpoints, following attacks on AMISOM convoys and in airstrikes.

In July, local residents in Merka and media accused Ugandan forces working under AMISOM of killing civilians in response to Al-Shabaab attacks on AMISOM supply convoys. On July 31, AMISOM soldiers killed six family members celebrating a wedding. An AMISOM investigation admitted responsibility for the killings, reported three soldiers had been arrested to face prosecution.

On August 8, Ethiopian forces under AMISOM killed five civilians and injured six others at a checkpoint in Halgan, Hiraan. In late May, clashes on the Ethiopian side of the Galgadud border, between the special police of Ethiopia's Somali region, known as "Liyu police," and local pastoralists, resulted in significant displacement and civilian casualties, including women and children.

Sexual Violence

In 2014, the government endorsed an action plan to address alarming levels of sexual violence. However, as in other prioritized reform areas, implementation has been slow and protection of the most vulnerable communities non-existent. While the full scope of sexual violence remains unknown, internally displaced women and girls are clearly particularly vulnerable to rape by armed men, including government soldiers and militia members.

Some soldiers from Uganda and Burundi deployed with AMISOM sexually exploited and assaulted women and girls on their bases in Mogadishu. In some cases women and girls were offered humanitarian assistance, medicine and food in exchange for sex. Few women filed complaints due to fear of reprisals and absence of effective and safe complaint mechanisms. The African Union, and Burundian, and Ugandan authorities investigated specific allegations, although no prosecutions had occurred at time of writing.

Displaced Persons and Access to Humanitarian Assistance

Somalia's 1.1 million internally displaced people, primarily women and children, remained extremely vulnerable and reliant on assistance. Humanitarian agencies faced challenges accessing needy populations due to insecurity, and restrictions imposed by parties to the conflict.

Targeted attacks on humanitarian organizations persisted. Al-Shabaab claimed responsibility for an April 20 attack in which a suicide bomber killed four United Nations Children's Fund (UNICEF) staff and two security guards in Garowe, Puntland. On November 15, a contractor for the UN mine action was killed by armed men in Beletweyn.

Military operations conducted by AMISOM, Kenyan, and Ethiopian forces, and Somali forces against Al-Shabaab, as well as clan-fighting, resulted in significant civilian displacement. More than 350,00 people, including women, children and people with disabilities, who fled to Mogadishu during the 2011 famine remained in dire conditions in the capital and are subjected to forced evictions, sexual violence and clan-based discrimination by government forces, allied militia, and private individuals.

In December 2014, the government passed a displacement policy largely in line with international law, yet large-scale forced evictions, including by government forces, occured in Mogadishu, Kismayo, and Baidoa. During the first two months of 2015, over 40,000 people were forcibly evicted in Mogadishu. Government forces forcibly evicted over 21,000 people during one operation in March, beat some evictees, destroyed shelters, and left them without water, food, or other assistance.

Attacks on Media and Human Rights Defenders

Targeted attacks on media, including attempted killings, harassment, and intimidation continued. On April 20, gunmen killed radio journalist Daud Ali, his wife, and a neighbor at Daud's home in Baidoa. Intimidation by regional authorities is also common, particularly in the context of federal state formation. Similarly, Puntland authorities temporarily arrested journalists, closed media outlets, and banned rebroadcasting of certain programs.

Despite the federal government's commitments to holding those responsible for the killings of journalists to account, impunity prevails.

HUMAN
RIGHTS
WATCH

"Chained Like Prisoners"
Abuses Against People with Psychosocial Disabilities in Somaliland

Somaliland

Somaliland's government at times arbitrarily detained journalists, mainly those reporting on sensitive political issues. Authorities also sometimes arbitrarily arrested and detained political opponents and critics of the government without adequate judicial oversight. In April, the government charged prominent human rights lawyer Guleid Ahmed Jama with "anti-national" propaganda and other crimes, after raising due process concerns in death penalty cases, but eventually the court revoked all charges.

On April 13, the government executed six men convicted of murder, the first death sentences to be carried out in Somaliland since 2006.

Somaliland authorities have also failed to sufficiently control and regulate private mental health centers that have confined patients involuntarily and subjected them to chaining, and, on occasion, beatings.

Key International Actors

Foreign and regional partners continued to provide financial and other assistance to AMISOM, including to mentor and train Somali armed forces engaged in security and military operations against Al-Shabaab. On July 28, the UN Security Council renewed AMISOM's mandate until May 2016, in a resolution that did not underscore the importance of accountability for abuses by AMISOM forces.

Much of the international community—and regional community—has focused on federalism efforts, seen as a prerequisite to political transition in 2016.

In addition to their large military presence in Somalia, Kenya and Ethiopia trained and provided military support to government-affiliated militia. Both focused on the status of border areas, and Ethiopia in particular participated in negotiations over the creation of bordering federal states.

The US has claimed responsibility for three drone strikes since December 29, 2014, against individuals allegedly involved in the September 2013 Westgate mall attack in Kenya, a marked increase in drone usage in Somalia. While the US Defense Department has openly acknowledged involvement, it has consistently failed to make public concrete information regarding civilian casualties.

South Africa

South Africa continued to face a number of human rights challenges, as the government struggled to stop attacks on businesses and homes of refugees, asylum-seekers, and migrants, denying they were motivated by xenophobia or other forms of intolerance.

The report of the Farlam Commission of Inquiry into the deaths of 44 people, including the police killing of 34 miners in 2012, was finally published, but civil society groups and the families of the deceased and injured expressed disappointment with the findings.

President Jacob Zuma continued to face criticism over his handling of a 2014 report by Public Protector Thuli Madonsela about the president's alleged misuse of state funds for a security upgrade to his private residence in Nkandla, Kwa Zulu Natal. Human Rights Watch criticized the government for its failure to realize the right to education for an estimated half-a-million children with disabilities.

In June 2015, South African authorities violated a domestic court order and its international obligations as a member of the International Criminal Court when it permitted President Omar al-Bashir of Sudan to leave the country without arrest. Bashir, who faces charges of genocide, war crimes, and crimes against humanity in connection with the conflict in Darfur, was in South Africa for an African Union (AU) Summit.

Violence against women, including rape and domestic violence, remained very high. Although annual crime statistics released by the South African Police Services showed that sexual offences decreased slightly by 3 percent, many gender activists and human rights groups expressed concerns about the continued under-reporting of rape and the failure of the government to introduce a national strategy to combat violence against women.

Police Conduct

Serious concerns remained about the conduct and capacity of the South African Police Services (SAPS). A number of incidents in 2015 highlighted police brutality and the use of excessive and disproportionate force.

On November 11, a South African judge sentenced eight former policemen to 15 years in prison for the 2013 murder of Mido Macia, a Mozambican taxi driver.

Three months earlier, the Pretoria High Court had found them guilty of murdering Macia, who died in police custody after being tied up by his arms to a police truck and dragged behind along the tarmac road.

In August, 10 police officers were arrested and charged with torturing and murdering Khuthazile Mbedu who was allegedly assaulted and tasered in Tembisa, east of Johannesburg. One of his legs was broken during the incident and he died in police custody four days later. The police officers are on bail pending trial at time of writing.

In August, the Independent Police Investigation Department launched an investigation into a video that showed two police officers in Douglasdale, Johannesburg, on August 18, apparently assaulting a man during a routine stop and search. The two officers have been suspended pending investigations.

Inquiry into Killing of Marikana Miners

On June 25, the government published the report of the Farlam Commission into the deaths of 44 people, including the police killing of 34 miners, between August 11 and 16, 2012, during a strike at the Lonmin mine in Marikana. The commission's report was significantly delayed due to loss of documents (including video evidence), the death of witnesses, and a legal battle over state funding for lawyers representing the families of the miners killed, injured, or arrested.

The commission found that the police had allowed the situation to get out of control and that its plan to deal with the strikers was "tactically defective," adding that the police should not have allowed the operation to proceed and should have been aware that "it would have been impossible to disarm and disperse the strikers without significant bloodshed".

The commission called for a full investigation to determine whether any police officers were criminally responsible and called for an inquiry into whether National Police Commissioner Victoriah Phiyega and North West Provincial Police Commissioner Lieutenant Zukiswa Mbombo were fit to hold office. On October 14, President Zuma suspended Phiyega. The commission recommended that a panel of experts be set up to revise policing methods and investigate new tactics for crowd control that do not involve "weapons capable of automatic fire."

The commission also criticized the mining unions and Lonmin mining company for not doing enough to resolve the original dispute over pay and accommodation.

The commission exonerated Deputy President Cyril Ramaphosa, who was a non-executive director at Lonmin, of any wrongdoing. Lawyers representing injured and arrested mine workers had accused Ramaphosa of using his political influence to press for police action against the striking mine workers. The commission also cleared the then-minister of police and the minister of mines.

Some civil society groups and the families of deceased and injured mine workers were disappointed by the commission's findings. They said the commission ignored key evidence presented by mine workers who testified and instead relied heavily on police description of the events.

Xenophobic Attacks on Foreign Nationals

In April 2015, thousands of people looted foreign-owned shops and attacked non-South African nationals in Durban, KwaZulu-Natal province. Several people died and the United Nations High Commissioner for Refugees said an estimated 2,400 people were internally displaced. The targets of the widespread violence were immigrants of African origin, mostly from Zimbabwe and Somalia. The xenophobic attacks spread to parts of Johannesburg before authorities deployed the army to stop the violence. In October, xenophobic violence displaced more than 500 people in Grahamstown, in the Eastern Cape Province.

Statements by traditional leaders and government officials may have fueled the violence. On March 21, 2015, Zulu King Goodwill Zwelithini told media that foreigners should "pack their bags and go home." The government did not publicly and unambiguously condemn Zwelithini's reckless and inflammatory statements.

Although the police arrested at least 22 people following the violence, authorities neither thoroughly investigated nor successfully prosecuted those involved. No one was held to account for the attacks. Authorities also failed to prosecute those who had incited the violence against foreign nationals.

HUMAN
RIGHTS
WATCH

"Complicit in Exclusion"
South Africa's Failure to Guarantee an Inclusive Education
for Children with Disabilities

Government officials denied the violence was motivated by xenophobia or other forms of intolerance and said it was a result of "pure acts of criminality." Secretary General of the African National Congress (ANC) Gwede Mantashe told media in April 2015 that he believed the solution to xenophobia was to establish refugee camps. Xenophobic violence in 2008 led to the deaths of over 60 people across the country.

Rights of Children and People with Disabilities

The South African government has failed to guarantee the right to education for many children and young adults with disabilities, affecting an estimated half-a-million children. In 2001, the government adopted a policy of providing inclusive education for all children with disabilities, but key aspects of the policy have not been implemented. The majority of the limited budget for learners with disabilities is allocated to special, segregated schools rather than to inclusive education.

Contrary to the government's international and domestic obligations, many children are turned away from mainstream schools and referred to special schools by school officials or medical staff simply because they have a disability. The referrals system needlessly forces children to wait for up to four years at care centers or at home for placement in a special school. Many children with disabilities have to pay school fees to access special schools.

South Africa became the first country to endorse the Safe Schools Declaration at a global conference in Norway in May 2015. By joining the declaration, it agreed to protect students and education in times of conflict, and to avoid using educational building for military purposes.

Sexual Orientation and Gender Identity

South Africa has a progressive constitution that prohibits discrimination on the basis of sexual orientation and protects the human rights of lesbian, gay, bisexual and transgender (LGBT) people. The Department of Justice and Constitutional Development has taken significant steps to improve coordination between government and civil society in combatting violence (including rape and murder) against lesbians and transgender men.

Foreign Policy

South Africa's inconsistent foreign policy once again came to the fore in 2015. While South Africa regularly supports conflict mediation efforts on the continent, it has proven reluctant to protect the rights of victims at the UN Human Rights Council, and at times taken decisions contrary to its stated human rights principles.

In 2015, South Africa continued its peace mediation efforts in a number of conflicts on the continent mainly through Deputy President Ramaphosa, the special envoy to South Sudan and Lesotho. South Africa also used its chairing of the Southern African Development Community (SADC) Organ on Defence, Politics, and Security Cooperation, as well as the African Union Peace and Security Council, to support continental peace and security initiatives.

South Africa firmly supported the establishment of the International Criminal Court (ICC) and has been a key supporter of international justice. But in June 2015, it violated a court order and permitted President Omar al-Bashir of Sudan to leave the country despite South Africa's international legal obligations to arrest him on two ICC warrants.

Bashir, who faces charges of genocide, war crimes, and crimes against humanity in connection with the conflict in Darfur, was in South Africa from June 13 to 15 for an AU Summit. The domestic case was brought by the Southern Africa Litigation Centre (SALC) to compel South Africa to abide by its domestic and international legal obligations. Government officials strongly criticized SALC for this effort.

In September 2015, the North Gauteng High Court rejected the South African government's application to appeal in the Bashir case. The ruling reaffirmed that South Africa was obliged under domestic and international law to arrest Bashir if he was within South African territory. In October 2015, the ruling ANC said the government should seek to withdraw South Africa from the ICC, a call criticized by human rights defenders and civil society groups across the country.

At the UN Human Rights Council, South Africa is a strong supporter of the council's engagement on issues like racism and the council's action on the Occupied Palestinian Territories. It has also participated actively in the Universal Periodic Review process, a review of the rights records of all UN member states. However, its voting record on country specific situations and some rights issues has been considerably disappointing.

Despite country resolutions playing a key role in shedding light on abuses and giving a stronger voice to victims, South Africa has justified its actions in opposing country resolutions by arguing that it does not support the council's work on country-specific situations because such measures and resolutions are perceived as highly politicized and divisive.

South Sudan

South Sudan's civil war, which began in December 2013, continued in 2015 with serious abuses of civilians by both warring parties. Killings, rape, and destruction and pillage of civilian property were widespread, especially during a massive government offensive in Unity state that began in mid-2015. A tenuous peace agreement signed in late August raised hopes of an end to the fighting, which has displaced some 2.2 million people from their homes and plunged much of the population into humanitarian crisis.

The conflict began in December 2013 when soldiers loyal to President Salva Kiir, a Dinka, and those loyal to former Vice President Riek Machar, a Nuer and now the rebel leader, fought in the capital, Juba, following months of growing political tensions. Despite widespread atrocity crimes committed by both sides, the peace deal, if implemented, would put the two men in charge of a transitional government for three years, after which national elections will be held.

A painful history of unaddressed war crimes and human rights abuses committed during decades of conflict in South Sudan helped fuel the atrocities. No serious efforts have been made by either side to end abuses committed by their forces. The peace deal promises a hybrid court established by the African Union Commission to provide accountability for international crimes committed during the recent conflict.

Attacks on Civilians and Civilian Property

A decline in fighting in early 2015 ended abruptly in April, when the government launched one of the biggest and most abusive offensives of the conflict. Government forces and allied militia fighters killed hundreds of people and burned homes and other civilian property in an offensive in opposition-held areas of Unity state, forcing at least 100,000 people to flee their homes. The forces pillaged hundreds of thousands of cattle, as well as other food and property, contributing to severe hunger in an area that humanitarian aid groups have warned could experience famine. Rape of women, including gang rapes, was a common tactic used during the offensive, and many hundreds of other women were beaten, forced to porter goods looted from their own villages, or were abducted

"They Burned It All"

Destruction of Villages, Killings, and Sexual Violence
in Unity State, South Sudan

HUMAN
RIGHTS
WATCH

"We Can Die Too"
Recruitment and Use of Child Soldiers in South Sudan

by the attacking forces. Attacks, rape, and killings of civilians continued into October.

The deliberate attacks on civilians and civilian property during the offensive amount to war crimes, and the killings and rapes may also constitute crimes against humanity.

Clashes also took place in Upper Nile and Jonglei states in 2015.

Use and Recruitment of Child Soldiers

Both the government and opposition forces recruited and used child soldiers in the conflict in 2015. Hundreds of children have been recruited in Unity state by Matthew Puljang, the government's second-in-command in Unity state.

Opposition forces also continued to recruit and use hundreds, probably thousands of children in Unity state. In Upper Nile state, Johnson Olony recruited children in and around the Malakal area in early 2015. Olony fought alongside government forces until April when he defected and later joined the opposition.

Over 1,500 children who had fought under Jonglei state's David Yau Yau in his 2012-3 insurgency against the government, separate from the recent conflict, were released from barracks in early 2015 following a peace agreement between his rebel group and the government. Yau Yau and his commanders have not been investigated for using child soldiers.

Arbitrary Detentions, Torture, and Enforced Disappearances

Since the beginning of the conflict, South Sudan's National Security Service (NSS) and military intelligence detained hundreds of men for alleged connections with opposition forces, some for as long as a year, often in inhumane conditions.

Most detainees were beaten and many tortured. None of the detainees was allowed access to a lawyer or judge. Former detainees held in the NSS Riverside detention site in Juba were held in dark, unbearably hot rooms. Detainees held by military intelligence in Eastern Equatoria and in Juba were tortured including with pliers, suffocation with a plastic bag, or jets of water directed at their faces.

At least three men were victims of enforced disappearances, including two members of Lakes state parliament who were forcibly disappeared for many months after being detained in police custody before eventually being released in August 2015.

Freedom of Expression and Association

The NSS continued to intimidate and detain journalists, further tightening an already restrictive media environment. In early August 2015, NSS officers shut down two newspapers, *Al Rai* and *The Citizen*, and an organization producing radio programs. The print run of another newspaper, the *Daily Nation*, was seized in December 2014 and shut down in January 2015. President Kiir and Information Minister Michael Makuei threatened journalists publicly, and the minister threatened to shut down the UN radio Miraya FM.

In August 2014, journalist Peter Julius Moi was assassinated days after President Kiir publicly threatened journalists. Another journalist, Clement Lochio, last seen in military detention, has been forcibly disappeared. Two more journalists were arrested by MI officers and held in military detention in 2015, one for a month because he interviewed, on the government South Sudan TV, a politician at odds with with the army's chief of staff.

In February, NSS officials shut down the elections for the South Sudan Bar Association in Wau and Juba, allegedly because the organization had not received advance permission from the NSS. A journalist who took photographs at the Juba venue was arrested and detained for about 20 hours in a NSS detention site.

Legislative Developments

NSS officers were given sweeping powers of arrest, search and seizure, and detention without any clear judicial oversight in a National Security Service Act passed by South Sudan's parliament in mid-2014, amid much controversy and procedural confusion.

President Kiir said he would not sign the bill, but in February 2015 the justice minister declared that the bill had become law because the president had not returned it to parliament or provided reasons for withholding his signature for more than 30 days.

In 2015, the government of South Sudan acceded to the Convention Against Torture and its Optional Protocol, the Convention on the Elimination on all Forms of Discrimination Against Women and its Optional Protocol, and the Convention on the Rights of the Child (CRC).

In 2013, South Sudan's parliament passed a bill to ratify both Optional Protocols to the CRC on the involvement of children in armed conflict and on the sale of children, child prostitution, and child pornography. However, neither instrument had been deposited with the UN at time of writing.

South Sudan has neither signed nor ratified the African Charter on Human and Peoples' Rights or the African Charter on the Rights and Welfare of the Child.

Accountability and Justice

The government and opposition leadership have not made any serious effort to hold abusive forces to account. Machar promised to investigate a massacre in Bentiu town, Unity state, by his rebel forces in April 2014, but no findings had been made public at time of writing. Two government reports, one by the police and one by the army, about the involvement of security forces in widespread killings of Nuer men in Juba in December 2013 had also not been made public.

President Kiir also initiated a national investigation into human rights abuses in early 2014; that report had also not been made public at time of writing.

In December 2013, the African Union (AU) authorized a commission of inquiry to document abuses and offer recommendations on justice and reconciliation. The report, made public in October 2015, highlighted the ethnic nature of abuse in the conflict, which it said included war crimes and possible crimes against humanity.

The August 2015 peace deal promises a hybrid court to be established by the AU Commission to investigate and prosecute international crimes committed in the conflict. Details about the court, including where it will be located and how it will be set up, have yet to be decided. The peace deal also mandates a Commission for Truth, Reconciliation and Healing and a Compensation and Reparation Authority.

Key International Actors

The Intergovernmental Authority on Development (IGAD) continued to mediate peace talks in Addis Ababa, and teams of monitors on the ground reported on violations of a January 2014 cessation of hostilities agreement between the two sides. Uganda, an IGAD member, continued to deploy soldiers in South Sudan to shore up the government.

China, the European Union, Norway, the United Kingdom, and the United States continued to support the peace process.

In early March 2015, the UN Security Council adopted a resolution that established a sanctions regime for South Sudan. A sanctions committee has authority to impose travel bans and asset freezes on individuals and entities found responsible for human rights abuses, violations of international humanitarian law, or the recruitment of child soldiers.

Sanctions have been imposed on six South Sudanese commanders from both government and opposition forces. Though the council in the March resolution did not impose an arms embargo on South Sudan, the council expressed its "intent to impose" any measures "appropriate to respond to the situation," including an arms embargo. At time of writing, no Security Council arms embargo has been imposed on South Sudan. In May, the African Union Peace and Security Council called for the Security Council to "urgently consider" establishing an arms embargo on South Sudan.

The UN Mission in South Sudan (UNMISS) continued to shelter tens of thousands of civilians forced to flee their homes because of attacks by forces from both sides. UNMISS peacekeepers struggled to protect civilians outside of their bases.

In June, the UN Human Rights Council passed a resolution that dispatched a UN human rights mission to monitor steps taken to ensure accountability.

Sri Lanka

Elections in Sri Lanka brought about momentous changes after nearly a decade of increasingly autocratic rule. In January 2015, President Mahinda Rajapaksa's government, in power since 2006, lost to a united opposition front led by Maithripala Sirisena, a former health minister. In August, Ranil Wickramsinghe, longtime leader of the largest opposition party, was elected prime minister.

The new government quickly abolished surveillance and censorship of media and civil society groups, embarked on constitutional reforms to restrict executive powers, and took steps to restore the independence of the judiciary. In contrast to the combative approach of the Rajapaksa government, it also initiated a new, more open dialogue with the international community, including human rights organizations.

However, the government took no significant measures to end impunity for security force abuse, including police use of torture. At time of writing, the government also had not yet repealed the draconian Prevention of Terrorism Act (PTA), despite promises to do so, and continued to detain people under it. Following a sustained hunger strike by an estimated 200 PTA detainees, the government in November released some on bail, sent others for rehabilitation, and pledged to charge and try the rest.

In August, the United Nations Office of the High Commissioner for Human Rights (OHCHR) issued a scathing report on abuses committed by all sides during Sri Lanka's 1983-2009 armed conflict with the secessionist Liberation Tigers of Tamil Eelam (LTTE). The report, which was mandated by a March 2014 Human Rights Council (HRC) resolution on Sri Lanka, documented credible accounts of unlawful attacks, killings, enforced disappearances, torture, sexual violence, and attacks on humanitarian assistance .

Following the report, HRC member states endorsed a resolution calling on the Sri Lankan government to implement the report's many recommendations, including to establish a special counsel to investigate and prosecute alleged wartime abuses, and to include foreign judges and prosecutors in a Sri Lankan tribunal.

The government began to investigate some emblematic cases of serious human rights violations during the conflict, including the killing and enforced disappearance of journalists.

Constitutional Reforms

In June, the new government brought in the 19th amendment to the constitution. It places new checks on the power of the executive and seeks to restore the independence of police, judicial, human rights, and election commissions. Although the amendment was not as far-reaching as initially proposed, it limits the presidential term and increases the powers of the prime minister. In September, the government announced that it had established a Constitutional Council which, in turn, will oversee appointments to the independent commissions. Long-time human rights advocates were appointed to the Commission on Human Rights, a body that had been moribund during the Rajapaksa years.

The government has promised to seek further constitutional and legislative changes on electoral reforms and devolution of powers.

Accountability for Past Abuses

In September, the OHCHR, as mandated by a Human Rights Council resolution in 2014, published its report investigating allegations of unlawful attacks on civilians, killings, disappearances, rape and sexual violence, forced recruitment of children, and the intentional denial of humanitarian assistance, and other violations of international law by the government and the LTTE.

The report documented serious violations and called on the government to establish a "hybrid" justice mechanism, including both domestic and international investigators and prosecutors, to adopt legislation criminalizing war crimes, crimes against humanity, genocide and enforced disappearances without a statute of limitations, and to enact command responsibility as a mode of liability.

Based on the OHCHR report, the Human Rights Council, with Sri Lanka's acquiescence, adopted a consensus resolution that recommended establishing a special court "integrating international judges, prosecutors, lawyers and investigators" with an independent Sri Lankan investigative and prosecuting body. The resolution was left with the Sri Lankan government to work out the details for this body, including the role and number of the tribunal's foreign judges and prosecutors. The government has since turned to civil society groups from across the country for their input on this and a resolution-endorsed truth and reconciliation commission.

The Sri Lankan government, through the resolution, accepted many recommendations to improve the country's human rights situation, including a repeal of the PTA and reforms to the Witness and Victim Protection Law. The government also agreed to accelerate the return of land to its rightful civilian owners; to end military involvement in civilian activities in the country's north and east; to investigate allegations of attacks on members of civil society, media, and religious minorities; and to reach a settlement on the devolution of authority to the provinces.

Some key undertakings in the resolution include the establishment of a dedicated office on enforced disappearances; a truth, justice, and reconciliation commission; and an office on reparations. The government also released two sets of presidential commission reports on human rights violations, which included reports that had been completed, but not made public in May 2009.

In November, the government began planning public consultations throughout the country as an initial step towards the establishment of these offices.

In November, the UN Working Group on Enforced and Involuntary Disappearances visited Sri Lanka at the invitation of the government. The group noted the almost complete lack of accountability for disappearances and the lack of sustained efforts to uncover the truth about what happened to the victims. The group also expressed concern that some of the people they had met with on their trip were subsequently visited by members of the security forces and were questioned about their meeting with the group.

In May, the government appointed as its new army chief, a senior officer whose division was implicated in serious human rights abuses. Maj. Gen. Jagath Dias led the Army's 57th Division during the last two years of the civil war, and his promotion created concerns that the new government, like its predecessor, would shield senior military personnel from accountability.

Police Torture and Ill-Treatment

Police in Sri Lanka continued to routinely torture and ill-treat individuals taken into custody to extract "confessions," but also for personal vendettas or to extort funds.

While Sri Lanka has legislation prohibiting torture, the government failed to ensure disciplinary or criminal prosecutions against police officers and their superiors. Many alleged perpetrators remained in active duty or were merely transferred to another police station. Only in a handful of particularly egregious cases in the media spotlight was serious action taken against the offending officers. Even in those cases, superior officers were not held to account as a matter of command responsibility.

Victims of torture and their families faced a daunting path to redress and justice. Those of limited means, particularly from rural communities, often found the various procedural steps overwhelming and prohibitively expensive. Many reported ongoing harassment by the police when back in their villages.

Prevention of Terrorism Act and Politically Motivated Torture

Sri Lanka's new government agreed to review and repeal the Prevention of Terrorism Act, though said it would replace the law with new counter-terrorism legislation. The PTA has long been used to hold suspected LTTE members and others without charge or trial for years. In spite of promises to make the whereabouts of all detainees known to their relatives, many family members received no information about where, or indeed if, their loved ones are detained.

The PTA allows for arrests for unspecified "unlawful activities" without warrant and permits detention for up to 18 months without producing the suspect before a court. The government need not charge the person with an offense; many PTA detainees have been held for years without charge. And the act provides immunity from prosecution for government officials who may commit wrongful acts, such as torture, under the legislation.

The PTA facilitated thousands of abuses over the years, including torture to obtain "confessions," enforced disappearances, and extrajudicial executions. The law has been used since the end of the war, including under the present government, to detain and torture people suspected of links to the LTTE, including

forcibly returned asylum seekers. Many instances of torture, sexual violence, and other ill-treatment occured in the Criminal Investigation Division and Terrorist Investigation Division offices in Colombo and elsewhere, while others occured in unofficial places of detention.

In November, the government announced a plan to deal with the Tamil detainees held under the PTA. At time of writing, authorities had released 39 detainees on bail and sent a further 99 for rehabilitation, although the exact contours of the rehabilitation program remained unclear. The government has pledged to charge and try the rest.

In October, the government decided to issue official certificates to the families of the disappeared affirming their status as "missing" instead of "deceased." This allows for the families to obtain certain benefits while being more sensitive to the families' emotional needs and the need for a continued investigation into their cases.

Migrant Workers

More than one million Sri Lankans are employed overseas and many remained at risk of abuse at every stage of the migration cycle, from recruitment and transit, to employment, repatriation, and reintegration. More than a third of Sri Lanka's migrants are domestic workers, almost exclusively female. The government took some steps to protect their rights abroad, but many continued to face long working hours with little rest, delayed or unpaid wages, confinement in the workplace, and verbal, physical, and sexual abuse.

Sexual Orientation and Gender Identity

Sri Lanka criminalizes "unnatural" sex, acts of "gross indecency," and "cheating the public by impersonation." Police have used these and other laws, such as a vaguely defined "vagrancy" prohibition, to target LGBT people. In 2014, government officials told the United Nations Human Rights Committee that the Sri Lankan Constitution's equal protection clause "protects persons from stigmatization and discrimination on the basis of sexual orientation and gender identities," but neither the constitution nor any other law expressly prohibits discrimination on such grounds.

Key International Actors

The United Nations Human Rights Council in October adopted by consensus a resolution calling on Sri Lanka to establish a credible accountability mechanism, with the involvement of Commonwealth and foreign judges, prosecutors and investigators. The United States, United Kingdom, Macedonia, Montenegro, and Australia, among others, sponsored the resolution.

Since it was adopted by consensus, the resolution brought on board key states that did not support the previous resolution in March, notably India.

However, concerns remained about the failure of sponsoring states to ensure proper provisions for international oversight of implementation of the terms of the resolution. The resolution only calls for an oral update from the high commissioner during the council's 32nd session in June 2016 and a written implementation report at the 34th session in March 2017. The US and other sponors backed away from including language on certain important issues, such as having a majority international judicial presence and command responsibility.

Sudan

Government forces committed serious attacks against civilians, including widespread killings, rape, and destruction of property, in the conflicts in Darfur, South Kordofan, and Blue Nile states. Sudanese authorities restricted civil society and independent media, and suppressed protests and demonstrations. President Omar al-Bashir was re-elected in April 2015 in a poll that did not meet international standards for free and fair elections. Sudan has yet to adopt a constitution since the Comprehensive Peace Agreement's six-year interim period ended in 2011. The ruling National Congress Party and opposition parties remain deadlocked over a national dialogue process that was to pave the way for elections and a new constitution.

Conflict and Abuses in Darfur

In December 2014, President Bashir announced the resumption of "Operation Decisive Summer," a military campaign that began in February 2014 against armed rebel groups in Darfur. The operation was led by the Rapid Support Forces (RSF), a Sudanese government force consisting largely of pro-government militias under the control of its National Intelligence and Security Service.

Between December and April 2015, the RSF and other government forces attacked villages and towns, mostly in the Jebel Marra region. They were responsible for serious abuses against the civilian population—including killings, rape, torture, mass displacement, destruction of property, and looting of livestock—that may amount to crimes against humanity. In January 2015, RSF soldiers raped scores of women and girls in and around the town of Golo.

The government blocked the African Union/United Nations peacekeeping mission, UNAMID, from much of the Jebel Marra region, and from investigating allegations of mass rape and other abuses by government forces that occurred in October and November 2014 in Tabit, North Darfur. Although the peacekeepers were briefly allowed into Tabit, where Sudanese armed forces raped at least 200 women in a 36-hour period, government security forces accompanying the peacekeepers compromised the integrity of their investigation. Neither the UN nor any international aid organizations have been able to access the town and provide victims with medical or psycho-social care.

HUMAN
RIGHTS
WATCH

"Men With No Mercy"
Rapid Support Forces Attacks against Civilians in Darfur, Sudan

UNAMID has been largely ineffective in protecting civilians from violence, hampered by Sudan's denial of access to areas affected by conflict. Jebel Marra, for example, where tens of thousands are still displaced, has not been accessed for several years. Attacks and security threats against mission personnel have also undermined its effectiveness.

Violent intercommunal fighting continued in 2015, especially in South Darfur.

Conflict and Abuses in Southern Kordofan and Blue Nile

Unlawful attacks on civilians by government forces, carried out through aerial bombardment and ground forces in Southern Kordofan caused civilian casualties, including the deaths of at least 26 children in 2014 and 2015, some burned alive or blown to pieces after bombs or shells landed on their homes. Government bombing included what appeared to be targeted attacks on medical clinics.

The fighting and attacks on civilians destroyed homes and property and caused thousands to flee into crowded refugee camps in South Sudan. Government aircraft also dropped cluster munitions on Um Dorein and Delami counties, Southern Kordofan, in February and March 2015. Although the Convention on Cluster Munitions, which enjoys broad international support, prohibits their use, Sudan is not yet a party to this treaty.

In May 2015, government attacks on villages in Blue Nile caused large scale displacement of people from the Bau locality. Sudanese groups reported that at least three villages were burned by government forces, and people were forced to move to government strongholds. Residents were threatened with arrest or were detained if they did not leave.

The government has barred humanitarian agencies from working in rebel-held areas of Southern Kordofan and Blue Nile, and has failed to agree with SPLM-N on terms for humanitarian access, including for a UN emergency polio vaccination campaign. As a result, the majority of children born in rebel-held areas have not been vaccinated against preventable diseases. Health workers received almost 2,000 suspected measles cases during an outbreak in Southern Kordofan between April and December 2014.

Arbitrary Detentions, Ill-Treatment, and Torture

On December 6 and 7, 2014, human rights defender Amin Mekki Medani, political opposition leader Farouq Abu Eissa, and political activist Farah Ibrahim Alagar, were arrested in connection with their support for the opposition declaration, "Sudan Call," and detained for four months. They were held incommunicado for 15 days before being transferred to Kober prison and charged with crimes against the state, which carry the death penalty. They were released on April 9, 2015, after the minister of justice exercised discretionary powers to drop the case.

In the lead up to, during, and after the national elections, from April 13 to 16, 2015, security forces arrested dozens of opposition party members, students, and political activists campaigning for an elections boycott. Many reported they were detained for several days and subjected to harsh beatings before being released without charge.

In mid-April, a well-known female activist appeared in public bruised and beaten after three days' detention. National security denied responsibility and brought defamation charges against her. On April 16, a human rights trainer, Adil Bakheet was detained for 17 days in police custody and charged with crimes against the state for his participation in a voter education training. In May, two activists were detained in connection with speaking about sexual harassment and corruption, then released without being charged.

In August, national security agents continued to detain political activists, including members of the Sudanese Congress Party (SCP) engaged in public demonstrations against government policies. Several were subjected to violence and abuse and required to report daily to NISS.

Freedom of Peaceful Assembly, Association, and Expression

Sudanese security forces used excessive force to break up demonstrations over a range of issues, and prevented or restricted public events, particularly in the lead up to the general elections. In April, police and military fired tear gas and live bullets at protesters at a rally in a displaced persons camp in Central Darfur. Police raided El Fasher University in North Darfur, using tear gas to break up a group calling for an elections boycott, and arresting around 29 students.

Authorities also clamped down on civil society groups. In March, security agents raided the Tracks for Training and Human Development office, seized computers and other assets, and accused staff of supporting an elections boycott. In late December 2014 and January 2015, authorities revoked the licenses of three cultural organizations without providing reasons, and shut down a book fair and cultural event in Khartoum.

On December 21, 2014, agents raided the Sudanese Human Rights Monitor while it was hosting a meeting to prepare for Sudan's Universal Periodic Review at the UN Human Rights Council. The Monitor was founded by Dr. Amin Mekki Medani, who had been detained on December 6 for four months in connection with his support for the "Sudan Call" declaration.

Authorities also continued to restrict media. National security agents seized print runs of 14 newspapers on February 16, and 10 newspapers on May 25, apparently because of articles on sensitive topics. In January 2015, the editor-in-chief of *Al Midan*, an opposition daily, was charged with crimes against the state for articles quoting a rebel commander, and faces the death penalty. In July, three journalists were arrested while covering a doctor's strike in Gedarif.

Legal Reform

The NISS has broad powers of arrest and detention for up to four-and-a-half months without judicial review, months beyond the international standard. Amendments to the constitution in January 2015 further empowered the NISS by designating it as a regular force with a mandate of combatting a wide range of political and social threats and taking precautionary measures against them. The service is known for its abusive tactics, including torture, against real or perceived political opponents.

In February, Sudan made amendments to the criminal code that could reduce the risk of women being accused of adultery when they report rape. However, the government has failed to implement various other reforms, including laws governing media, voluntary organizations, and public order regime.

The authorities continued to apply Sharia (Islamic law) sanctions that violate international prohibitions on cruel, inhuman, or degrading punishment. The penalties are applied disproportionately to women and girls, typically for "crimes" such as adultery or violations of morality codes.

Key International Actors

The AU's High-Level Implementation Panel for Sudan and South Sudan, headed by former South African President Thabo Mbeki, continued to mediate peace talks for Southern Kordofan, Blue Nile, Darfur, and talks on a National Dialogue process.

The ongoing conflict in South Sudan and accusations of Sudan's support to armed opposition there continued to undermine progress on outstanding issues, such as border demarcation, security, and status of the contested area of Abyei, as required in the 2012 cooperation agreement.

Amid Sudan's pressure that UNAMID make plans to leave the country, the UN Security Council reduced the mission's size by almost 5,000 troops in August 2014. In August 2015, despite calls by the government of Sudan on UNAMID to withdraw from "stable" parts of Darfur, the Security Council extended the mission's mandate through June 2016. The Security Council also extended the mandate of the UN Interim Security Force for Abyei through mid-December 2015.

In May 2015, the UN special rapporteur on violence against women traveled to Sudan for the first time in over a decade; her report is expected in 2016. In September 2015, the Human Rights Council extended the mandate of the independent expert for one year and urged the government of Sudan to initiate an independent public inquiry into the shooting of demonstrators in September 2014 and March 2014 and to investigate human rights violations in camps for the internally displaced.

March 2015 marked the 10-year anniversary of the Security Council's referral of the situation in Darfur to the International Criminal Court (ICC). Since then, the ICC has issued arrest warrants for five individuals, including President al-Bashir, for war crimes, crimes against humanity, and genocide in connection with atrocities in Darfur. Sudan has refused to cooperate with the court in any of the cases. In December 2014, ICC Chief Prosecutor Fatou Bensouda told the UN Security Council that she was "hibernating" her investigations on Darfur and urged the council to make "a dramatic shift" in its approach to responding to states that do not cooperate with the court's requests on arresting Darfur suspects.

Al-Bashir remains a fugitive, but his travel has been restricted. A number of anticipated trips abroad have been cancelled, rescheduled, or relocated amid diplomatic and public outcry, particularly by African civil society groups.

Swaziland

Respect for human rights and the rule of law continued to decline in the Kingdom of Swaziland, ruled by absolute monarch King Mswati III since 1986. Political parties remained banned, as they have been since 1973, judicial independence continued to be severely compromised, and repressive laws used to target critics of the government and the king.

As in previous years, Swazi authorities failed to carry out reforms to lift severe restrictions on civil and political rights. The Suppression of Terrorism Act, the Sedition and Subversive Activities Act of 1938, and other similarly draconian legislation provided sweeping powers to the security services to halt pro-democracy meetings and protests and to curb any criticism of the government, however banal, even though such rights are guaranteed under Swaziland's 2005 constitution.

Freedom of Association and Assembly

Severe government restrictions on freedom of association and assembly continued. On February 28, Swazi police broke up a meeting of the Trade Union Congress of Swaziland (TUCOSWA) in Manzini, the country's second largest city, because authorities were unhappy with an agenda item on multi-party democracy.

On March 14, police violently barred TUCOSWA's national executive committee from meeting at the premises of the Swaziland National Association of Teachers (SNAT), one of its members, claiming that TUCOSWA was not a registered entity. SNAT's secretary general, Muzi Mhlanga, was assaulted by the police who knocked out one of his front teeth when he tried to take photographs of the police action. Previously registered in 2012, TUCOSWA was banned in 2013 when it called for a boycott of the 2013 general election, which failed to include opposition political parties. Subsequent attempts to register were denied. TUCOSWA submitted a new application in December 2014 under the country's amended Industrial Relations Act. It was registered on May 12, 2015.

Human Rights Defenders

Political activists faced trial and detention under security legislation and charges of treason under common law. The Suppression of Terrorism Act of 2008 placed severe restrictions on civil society organizations, religious groups, and media. Under the legislation, a "terrorist act" includes a wide range of legitimate conduct such as criticism of the government. State officials used the legislation to target perceived opponents through abusive surveillance, unlawful home and office searches, and arbitrary arrests.

Two leaders of a banned political party, the People's United Democratic Movement (PUDEMO), Mario Masuku and Maxwell Dlamini, were accused under the Suppression of Terrorism Act of criticizing the government by singing a pro-democracy song and shouting "Viva PUDEMO" during a May Day rally in 2014. After more than a year in custody, they were granted bail in July 2015 by the Swaziland High Court. The trial continued at time of writing. If convicted, they could serve up to 15 years in prison. Both men had previously been arrested by Swazi authorities under the same legislation: Masuku in November 2008 for a speech at a funeral and Dlamini in 2010 for his role in organizing student protests. Both men were later acquitted of all charges.

In April 2014, PUDEMO General Secretary Mlungisi Makhanya was also arrested under the Suppression of Terrorism Act along with six other PUDEMO members for wearing a T-shirt protesting the arrest of journalist, Bheki Makhubu, and human rights lawyer, Thulani Maseko. The seven were released on bail after two weeks in detention. His trial also continued at time of writing.

In September 2015, eight trade union leaders and human rights defenders, including Masuku and Dlamini, challenged the constitutionality of the Suppression of Terrorism Act in the High Court of Swaziland. At time of writing the case was ongoing.

Freedom of Expression and Media

Journalists and activists who criticized the government were often harassed and arrested. The Sedition and Subversive Activities Act continued to restrict freedom of expression through criminalizing alleged seditious publications and use of alleged seditious words, such as those which "may excite disaffection" against the king. Published criticism of the ruling party is also banned. Many journalists practiced self-censorship, especially with regard to reports involving the king, to avoid harassment by authorities.

On June 30, the Supreme Court of Swaziland granted an appeal by human rights lawyer, Thulani Maseko, and editor of *The Nation* magazine, Bheki Makhubu, and ordered their immediate release from prison. Maseko and Makhubu were arrested in March 2014 for two articles they published in *The Nation* questioning the impartiality of the judiciary, and sentenced to two years in prison. Civil society groups dismissed the trial as a sham.

In July 2014, *The Nation* and its publishers were fined an equivalent of US$9,500 by the Swaziland High Court for publishing "seditious" information in the two articles that Maseko wrote.

Authorities also barred media from reporting on issues they deemed sensitive. For example, when scores of young girls died in a road traffic accident on August 28 on their way to an annual Umhlanga festival where thousands of virgins dance before the king to celebrate womanhood and virginity, authorities blocked media reporting of the incident. The government later said 13 people had died. Regional and international media disputed the government's figure and estimated the death toll at 65.

Rule of Law

Although the constitution provides for three separate organs of government—the executive, legislature, and judiciary—under Swaziland's law and custom, all powers are vested in the king. The king exercises absolute authority over the cabinet, parliament, and judiciary.

The king appoints 20 members of the 30-member senate, 10 members of the house of assembly, and approves all legislation passed by parliament. The king also appoints judges, and, if he wishes, fires them. On June 17, the king fired Chief Justice Michael Ramodibedi for "serious misbehavior" following allegations of abuse of office and corruption. Ramodibedi, previously a close ally of the king, had presided over a partial judiciary and had played a leading role in the authority's crackdown on human rights.

The constitution provides for equality before the law, but also places the king above the law. In 2011, Ramodibedi issued a directive which protected the king from any civil law suits, after Swazi villagers claimed police had seized their cattle to add to the king's herd.

The government has failed to take the necessary steps to operationalize the Human Rights and Public Administration Commission, established in 2009, which remained ineffective due to lack of funding, human resources, and enabling legislation. In its five years of existence the commission has not produced any report about its work or role.

Women's Rights

Swaziland's dual legal system, where both Roman-Dutch common law and Swazi customary law operate side by side, has resulted in conflict leading to numerous violations of women's rights, despite constitutionally guaranteed equality. In practice, women, especially those living in rural areas under traditional leaders and governed by highly patriarchal Swazi law and custom, are often subjected to discrimination and harmful practices.

Young women and girls are forced to take part in cultural activities like the Umhlanga reed dance. Families of girls and young women who fail to take part in such cultural activities are often punished or fined by their chiefs. Traditional structures and practices prohibit women from speaking in public at men's gatherings and present significant challenges for women's political participation. Violence against women is endemic. Survivors of gender-based violence have few avenues for help as both formal and customary justice processes discriminate against them.

Civil society activists have criticized the widely held view among traditional authorities that human rights and equal rights for women are foreign values that should be subordinated to Swazi culture and tradition.

Sexual Orientation and Gender Identity

Swaziland's common law prohibits sodomy, defined as same-sex sexual relations between men, although no sentence is specified for those found guilty of such an offence. On March 15, a man in Nhlangano (a town 130 kilometers south of the capital, Mbabane) murdered a lesbian after picking a fight with her at a bar and making homophobic comments. Police arrested a suspect, who was charged with murder and is currently on trial. Several months earlier, a gay man was killed for being gay in the same town in another apparent hate crime.

Key International Actors

Neighboring South Africa and regional bodies–the Southern African Development Community (SADC) and the African Union (AU)–have done little to press Swaziland to improve respect for human rights. Instead, criticism has come from outside the continent.

In June 2014, United States President Barack Obama officially removed Swaziland from the list of African countries which benefit from the African Growth and Opportunity Act (AGOA), citing the slow pace of democratic reforms and poor human rights record. The International Labour Organization (ILO) in June 2015 called on the Swazi government to amend the Industrial Relations Act, the Public Order Act, and the Suppression of Terrorism Act, and guarantee labor rights. On July 10, 2014, the Commonwealth initiated political dialogue led by its special envoy to Swaziland, former Malawi President Bakili Muluzi, to move the country towards multi-party elections in 2018.

In May 2015, the European Parliament called on the government of Swaziland to immediately and unconditionally release Thulani Maseko and Bheki Makhubu, and all prisoners of conscience and political prisoners, including Mario Masuku, president of the People's United Democratic Movement, and Maxwell Dlamini, secretary-general of the Swaziland Youth Congress. It further urged Swazi authorities to take steps to respect and promote freedom of expression, guarantee democracy and plurality, and establish a legislative framework allowing the registration, operation, and full participation of political parties.

Syria

In 2015, violence continued to escalate inside Syria amid an absence of meaningful efforts to end the war or reduce abuses. The government and its allies carried out deliberate and indiscriminate attacks on civilians. Incommunicado detention and torture remain rampant in detention facilities. Non-state armed groups opposing the government also carried out serious abuses including attacking civilians, using child soldiers, kidnapping, and torture.

The armed extremist group Islamic State (also known as ISIS), and Al-Qaeda's affiliate in Syria, Jabhat al-Nusra, were responsible for systematic and widespread violations, including targeting civilians, kidnappings, and executions.

According to local Syrian groups, as of October 2015, the death toll in the conflict reached more than 250,000 people including over 100,000 civilians. According to local groups, more than 640,000 people live under long-term siege in Syria. The conflict has led to a humanitarian crisis with an estimated 7.6 million internally displaced and 4.2 million refugees in neighboring countries.

Government Attacks on Civilians, Indiscriminate Use of Weapons

The government persisted in conducting indiscriminate air attacks, including dropping large numbers of improvised barrel bombs on civilians in defiance of United Nations Security Council Resolution 2139 passed on February 22, 2014. These unguided high explosive bombs are cheaply made, locally produced, and typically constructed from large oil drums, gas cylinders, and water tanks, filled with high explosives and scrap metal to enhance fragmentation, and then dropped from helicopters.

Between February 2014 and January 2015, Human Rights Watch determined at least 450 major damage sites that showed damage consistent with barrel bomb detonations. One local group estimated that by February 22, 2015 aerial barrel bomb attacks had killed 6,163 civilians in Syria, including 1,892 children, since the passage of the UN Security Council Resolution 2139.

Airstrikes have indiscriminately hit markets, schools, and hospitals. One of the deadliest air attacks occurred on August 16 when government's air force repeat-

HUMAN
RIGHTS
WATCH

IF THE DEAD COULD SPEAK
Mass Deaths and Torture in Syria's Detention Facilities

edly struck Douma's popular markets and residential areas killing at least 112 people.

Despite its accession to the Chemical Weapons Convention in 2014, the Syrian government used toxic chemicals in several barrel bomb attacks in Idlib governorate in March, April, and May. While Human Rights Watch was unable to conclusively determine the toxic chemicals used, the distinct smell of chlorine reported by rescue workers and doctors indicate that it was probably used. In August, the Security Council adopted Resolution 2235 to establish an independent panel charged with determining who is responsible for chemical attacks in Syria.

The Syrian government also continues to impose sieges, which are estimated by the UN's Office for the Coordination of Humanitarian Affairs (OCHA) to affect over 200,000 civilians. The sieges violate council Resolution 2139, which demands that all parties "immediately lift the sieges of populated areas," including in Homs, Moadamiya, and Daraya in western Ghouta, eastern Ghouta, and the Palestinian refugee camp in Yarmouk in south Damascus. The government has used siege strategies to effectively starve civilian populations into submission and force negotiations that would allow the government to retake territory.

Arbitrary Arrests, Enforced Disappearances, Torture, Deaths in Custody by Government Forces

Syrian security forces continue to detain people arbitrarily, regularly subjecting them to ill-treatment and torture, and often disappearing them using an extensive network of detention facilities throughout Syria. Many detainees were young men in their 20s or 30s; but children, women, and elderly people were also detained. In some instances, individuals reported that security forces detained their family members, including children, to pressure them to turn themselves in.

Despite a general amnesty declared by the government in June 2014, scores of civil society activists, human rights defenders, media, and humanitarian workers remain in arbitrary detention, some of whom are on trial, including before counterterrorism courts, for exercising their rights. Human rights defender Mazen Darwish, and his colleagues Hani al-Zitani and Hussein Ghareer, from the Syrian

Center for Media and Freedom of Expression, were finally released in the summer of 2015.

Activists who remained in detention at time of writing included freedom of expression advocate Bassil Khartabil. Some activists, like the lawyer and human rights defender Khalil Maatouk, whom former detainees reported to have seen in government detention, continued to be held in conditions amounting to enforced disappearance.

Released detainees consistently report ill-treatment and torture in detention facilities, and prison conditions that lead to many cases of deaths in custody. Former detainees, including detained doctors, said that common causes of death in detention include infections, torture, and lack of care for chronic diseases. At least 890 detainees died in custody in 2015, according to local activists.

Security Council Resolution 2139 demands an end to arbitrary detention, disappearance, and abductions, and the release of everyone who has been arbitrarily detained.

Jabhat al-Nusra and ISIS Abuses

Extremist Islamist groups Jabhat al-Nusra and ISIS committed systematic rights abuses, including intentionally targeting and abducting civilians.

On March 31, ISIS deliberately killed at least 35 civilians after they briefly seized the village of Mab`oujeh in Hama countryside, according to local residents. ISIS also deliberately targeted civilians in a June 2015 attack on the northern Syrian city of Kobani (Ain al-Arab in Arabic) killing between 233 and 262 civilians. According to witnesses, the attackers killed civilians using automatic weapons including machineguns and rifles. They also used grenades and snipers fired on civilians from rooftops as they tried to retrieve the dead.

Witnesses told Human Rights Watch that they saw ISIS execute people in public places in towns the group controlled in the governorates of Raqqa and Deir al-Zor. The victims were shot, beheaded, crucified, or stoned to death depending on the charge. Some people were executed for blasphemy, adultery, or treason, the witnesses reported.

ISIS and Jabhat al-Nusra have imposed strict and discriminatory rules on women and girls and they have both actively recruited child soldiers. ISIS continued to sexually enslave and abuse Yezidi women and girls, many of whom are in places under their control, such as Raqqa in Syria.

By September, over 2,000 Yezidi women and girls had escaped, but over 5,200 remained in the hands of ISIS, according to Vian Dakhil, a Yezidi member of Iraq's parliament. Human Rights Watch documented a system of organized rape and sexual assault, sexual slavery, and forced marriage by ISIS forces. Yezidi women and girls told Human Rights Watch how ISIS members forced them into marriage; sold, in some cases a number of times; or given as "gifts" to ISIS fighters.

ISIS also executed men accused of homosexuality. International media has reported the execution of men charged with being gay in ISIS controlled areas by throwing them off the top of buildings. According to the gay activist organization OutRight Action International, 36 men in Syria and Iraq were killed on charges of sodomy.

Abuses by Other Non-State Armed Groups

Non-state armed groups have launched indiscriminate mortar and other artillery strikes from areas under their control that killed civilians in neighborhoods under government control in Aleppo, Damascus, Idlib, and Latakia. These attacks repeatedly hit known civilian objectives, including schools, mosques, and markets.

Armed groups continue to impose sieges around the towns of Nubul and Zahra (Aleppo) and Fou`a and Kefraya (Idlib).

Non-state armed groups including the Free Syrian Army and the Islamic Front also used children for combat and other military purposes. They also put students at risk by using schools at military bases, barracks, detention centers, and sniper posts.

Non-state armed groups have also been responsible for abductions. At least 54 Alawite women and children that were taken hostage during a military offensive in Latakia countryside in August 2013 continue to be held by "the Mujahadeen room in Latakia countryside."

On November 10, 2015 armed opposition groups shelled Latakia killing 23 people and injuring 65 according to international media reports. The Syrian state

HUMAN
RIGHTS
WATCH

"He Didn't Have to Die"
Indiscriminate Attacks by Opposition Groups in Syria

news agency said that the shells were fired by Al-Qaeda's affiliate Jabhat al-Nusra and another armed opposition group, Ahrar al-Sham. The attacks happened close to Tishrin University. The Russian air force has been using a military air base south of Latakia to carry out strikes in Syria.

Armed groups also endangered detained civilians and soldiers in Eastern Ghouta by placing them in metal cages in what they said was an attempt to deter government attacks on the area. Such a practice constitutes hostage-taking and an outrage against their personal dignity, which are both war crimes

Prominent human rights defender, Razan Zeitouneh, and three of her colleagues, Wael Hamada, Samira Khalil, and Nazem Hammadi were abducted on December 9, 2013, in Douma, a city outside Damascus under the control of a number of armed opposition groups, including the Army of Islam. Their fate remained unknown at time of writing.

Areas under Kurdish Rule

In January 2014, the Democratic Union Party and allied parties established a transitional administration in the three northern regions: `Afrin, `Ain al-`Arab (Kobani), and Jazira, which they have declared the Kurdish autonomous region of Rojava. They have formed councils akin to ministries and introduced a new constitutional law. Authorities there have committed arbitrary arrests, due process violations, and failed to address unsolved killings and disappearances.

The Kurdish armed forces known as the People's Protection Units (YPG) is still not meeting its commitment to demobilize child soldiers and to stop using boys and girls under the age of 18 in combat. In June 2015, the YPG wrote a letter to Human Rights Watch saying that it was facing "significant challenges" to stop its use of child soldiers due to the armed conflict but that it had demobilized 27 boys and 16 girls. Concerns remain over the creation of a YPG "non-combatant category" for children aged 16 and 17 where the group will continue to recruit children but not have them perform military duties.

Human Rights Watch received numerous, detailed complaints from Syrian refugees and activists in southern Turkey that YPG troops forcibly displaced a number of Sunni Arabs from areas that the YPG had taken back from ISIS, as well as confiscating or burning their homes, businesses, and crops. Syrian Kurdish authorities have denied any policy of forced displacement or other targeting of Arabs.

Displacement Crisis

The UN Refugee Agency (UNHCR) estimated in 2015 that 7.6 million Syrians are internally displaced and that 12.2 million need humanitarian assistance.

In 2015, humanitarian aid agencies experienced significant challenges in getting assistance to the displaced civilian population and others badly affected by the conflict because of sieges imposed by both government and non-state armed groups, the government's continuing obstacles to allow assistance to come in across the border, and a general failure to guarantee security for humanitarian workers.

In October 2015, UN OCHA estimated that 393,700 live in areas under siege in Syria. As of February 2015, the UN secretary-general named 11 besieged areas in Syria. The Syrian American Medical Society identified 38 additional communities that meet the definition of besieged bringing their total of besieged to 640,000. These besieged areas suffer from constant bombardment, deprivation of adequate aid in forms of nutrition and clean water, and their residents receive poor medical attention.

In July 2014, a Security Council Resolution authorized deliveries of cross border humanitarian aid even without government permission.

As of November had registered over 4.2 million Syrian refugees in Lebanon, Jordan, Turkey, Iraq, and Egypt. In 2015, Iraq, Jordan, Turkey, and Lebanon all implemented measures to restrict the numbers of refugees entering their countries.

All four neighboring countries accepting Syrian refugees have denied Syrians secure legal status.

Palestinians from Syria have faced additional obstacles. They have been refused entry or forcibly deported from Jordan and some Palestinian-Jordanians who had been living in Syria had their Jordanian citizenship withdrawn. Palestinian refugees coming from Syria have also faced additional restrictions in Lebanon following new regulations by the minister of interior in May that limited Palestinians' ability to enter the country or renew their residencies if they already were in the country.

In 2015, more than 440,000 Syrians attempted to reach Europe by sea. While some European Union countries offered them safety, as the year progressed, and particularly in the aftermath of the November 13 Paris attacks, barriers were increasingly erected to prevent entry of all migrants, including Syrians. Hungary erected fences and imposed high penalties for irregular entry, while pushbacks were reported from Bulgaria and Greece, sometimes violently, at their borders or from their territorial waters without allowing people to lodge asylum claims.

Countries that do not neighbor Syria, including in the West, continued to accept only small numbers of refugees for resettlement, though a few, such as Canada and most notably France, reiterated their commitments in the wake of the Paris attacks

At time of writing, only 45 percent of UNHCR's appeal for the regional refugee response was funded, leaving a budget shortfall of more than US$2.5 billion. As a result, UNHCR, the World Food Programme, and others have cut assistance to refugees, including the provision of basic goods and health care subsidies.

At time of writing, only 51 percent of UNHCR's appeal for the regional refugee response was funded, leaving a budget shortfall of more than $1.8 billion. As a result, UNHCR, the World Food Programme, and others have cut assistance to refugees, including the provision of basic goods and health care subsidies.

Key International Actors

Efforts to push the UN Security Council to take more meaningful action in Syria failed. The French sought to pass a resolution banning barrel bombs and introducing a more robust reporting mechanism but their efforts stalled amid Russian opposition and a preference among a number of countries to prioritize negotiations.

Key regional and international actors in Syria, but not Syrian parties themselves, met in Vienna in October in an attempt to restart political negotiations. While the meetings did not result in any tangible outcomes regarding the protection of civilians, the parties agreed to launch direct negotiations between the warring parties in early 2016.

The Syrian government continued to violate Security Council Resolution 2139 from February 2014 demanding safe and unhindered humanitarian access—including across conflict lines and across borders; that all parties cease "indis-criminate employment of weapons in populated areas, including shelling and aerial bombardment, such as the use of barrel bombs," and an end to the prac-tices of arbitrary detention, disappearance, and abductions, and the release of everyone who has been arbitrarily detained.

In addition to persistently blocking Security Council action to curb violations by the Syrian government, Russia, along with the Iranian government, continued to provide the Syrian government with military assistance in 2015, according to in-ternational media reports.

The Human Rights Council renewed the mandate of its independent International Commission of Inquiry on Syria in March 2015 for one year.

Russian forces began a joint air operation with the Syrian government at the be-ginning of October claiming it was targeting only ISIS locations but in fact were also striking other armed group in areas like Idlib and Homs. Human Rights Watch recorded a number of civilian casualties where people said they were vic-tims of Russian airstrikes.

The United States continued leading coalition to bombard ISIS in Iraq and Syria. France promised to increase its airstrikes in ISIS controlled areas after the armed extremist group claimed a series of attacks in Paris in November. The United Kingdom and Germany also voted to begin airstrikes against ISIS in early Decem-ber.

Tajikistan

Tajikistan's already poor rights record dramatically worsened in 2015, as authorities declared the country's leading opposition party a terrorist organization and banned it, imprisoned approximately 200 opposition activists, extradited and kidnapped government critics abroad, arrested several lawyers and at least one journalist, and harassed workers at nongovernmental organizations (NGOs) with onerous checks.

As in previous years, the government regularly blocked numerous Internet sites and continued a campaign to enforce severe restrictions on religious practice. NGOs reported several cases of torture and ill-treatment in pretrial custody and prisons. Domestic violence against women also continues to be a serious problem.

Government Opposition and Detention of Activists Abroad

In 2015, Tajik authorities expanded repressive measures against the political opposition. In January, a court sentenced rights lawyer Shukhrat Kudratov to nine years in prison following a politically motivated trial. Kudratov, who is also deputy head of the opposition Social Democratic Party, was found guilty of fraud and bribery.

A few months before being imprisoned, Kudratov served as counsel for Zayd Saidov, an opposition figure sentenced in December 2013 to 26 years in prison in a prosecution that appeared to be retaliation for his intention to run in the November 2013 presidential election. In August 2015, prosecutors brought additional charges against Saidov, resulting in an additional three years to his sentence.

On March 5, assailants shot and killed opposition figure Umarali Kuvvatov in Istanbul. Kuvvatov headed Group 24, an opposition group that called for democratic reforms and accused President Emomali Rahmon and the ruling elite of corruption. Three Tajik citizens are on trial in Turkey for Kuvvatov's murder. The circumstances of the shooting, and previous efforts by Tajik authorities to detain Kuvvatov in various countries, led many observers to suggest Kuvvatov's killers may have been acting on orders from or with the approval of Dushanbe.

Since October 2014, authorities have actively sought to arrest anyone associated with Group 24, convicting several people in Tajikistan on vague charges of extremism and seeking the extradition of activists for the group who live in Russia, Belarus, and Moldova.

In July, a Dushanbe court sentenced Maksud Ibragimov, leader of the opposition group Tajikistan's Youth for Revival, to 17 years' imprisonment for extremism. Ibragimov said that Tajik security services kidnapped him off the street in Moscow, where he had lived for more than 10 years, and forced him onto a plane bound for Dushanbe, where he was immediately arrested.

In another case, on July 15, Belarusian authorities detained peaceful Tajik activist Shabnam Khudoydodova as she was crossing the Russian-Belarusian border. A member of Group 24 who lived in St. Petersburg, Khudoydodova publicly called for reforms in Tajikistan. After learning that security services might be preparing to forcibly return her to Tajikistan, Khudoydodova fled to Belarus, where she sought refugee status. At time of writing, Tajik authorities were seeking her extradition on extremism charges.

Sobir Valiev, deputy head of the opposition group the Congress of Constructive Forces, and Group 24, was detained in August for several weeks by Moldovan migration police in the Moldovan capital of Chisinau. The Moldovan police detained him on a request from the Tajik government, which sought his extradition on similar extremism charges.

In the run-up to Tajikistan's parliamentary elections, the government sought to suppress the activities of the Islamic Renaissance Party of Tajikistan (IRPT), the country's leading opposition party. In March, for the first time in Tajikistan's modern history, the party was unable to win any seats in parliamentary elections. Monitors from the Organization for Security and Co-operation in Europe said the vote was marred by ballot-stuffing and government intimidation.

In June, IRPT's leader, Muhiddin Kabiri, went into exile, fearing prosecution on bogus charges. That same month, 20 videos appeared online of IRPT members saying they were "voluntarily" abandoning the party. Mahmadali Hayit, the IRPT deputy head, said members were acting under pressure from officials. In public statements and sermons, some officials and state-controlled imams have also tried to link the IRPT to Islamic terrorism.

The Justice Ministry banned the party in August.

In September, following clashes between government forces and militants loyal to Abduhalim Nazarzoda, the deputy defense minister, which left at least 17 fighters and 9 police officers dead, authorities arrested dozens of IRPT members, accusing them of involvement in the violence, despite a lack of evidence.

By November, authorities had arrested or detained approximately 200 IRPT members as well as at least 3 lawyers—Buzurgmehr Yorov, Nouriddin Mahkamov, and Dilbar Dodadzhonova—who sought to represent the detained IRPT members. The charges brought against them for fraud appeared to be trumped-up and retaliatory for their attempts to represent the detained IRPT members.

Freedom of Expression

Authorities' restrictions on media freedoms and access to independent information, including on the Internet, and the intimidation of journalists and NGOs, violated Tajikistan's obligations on freedom of expression.

On July 20, authorities announced a rule barring media outlets from reporting "official news" without citing Khovar, the state-run news agency. Nuriddin Karshiboev, head of Tajikistan's National Association of Independent Media, condemned the move, saying the regulation violates the constitution's guarantee of equal access to official information.

Other news outlets known for reporting critical views told Human Rights Watch they have been subjected to increasing pressure in 2015, with security services frequently interrogating staff and demanding advance notification of any potentially critical stories.

Under the pretext of protecting national security, Tajikistan's state telecommunications agency regularly blocks websites that carry information potentially critical of the government, including Facebook, Gmail, Radio Ozodi, the website of Radio Free Europe's Tajik service, and opposition websites.

In August, a Dushanbe court convicted journalist Amindzhon Gulmurodzoda of forgery, sentencing him to two years' imprisonment. Gulmurodzoda is editor of the news site faraj.tj.com and works for the Center for Investigative Journalism. Security services accused Gulmurodzoda of obtaining falsified documents in 1989, when he would have been five or six years old. They claimed his passport, which he obtained in 1998, 17 years before the criminal charges were laid, was a forgery. Gulmurodzoda maintained he acquired the documents legally.

Numerous NGOs reported increased government harassment during 2015. As of July, 22 NGOs had reported that various authorities, including the Tax Committee, Ministry of Labor, and Ministry of Justice, were conducting intrusive checks into their activities, and threatening them with steep fines.

The Justice Ministry introduced a bill that, if adopted, would require NGOs to register grants from foreign donors in a state registry prior to accessing them. The move raised concerns that the government planned to adopt measures to restrict the activities of independent NGOs similar to the "foreign agents" laws adopted in Russia and Azerbaijan.

In July, Nota Bene, an independent think tank, announced that Justice Ministry officials had filed a suit to liquidate the organization for failure to properly register activities.

Criminal Justice and Torture

Authorities took some positive steps in recent years to bring the criminal code's definition of torture into line with international law and provide compensation for some torture victims. But torture remains widespread in the criminal justice system. Police routinely use torture to coerce confessions and deny detainees access to counsel.

In April, officers of Tajikistan's Drug Control Agency detained 25-year-old Shamsiddin Zaydulloev. Visiting him the following day in custody, his mother told a local NGO: "When I petted his head, he said I shouldn't touch the back of [it] because it was swollen and painful. I asked him in a low voice whether he was beaten and he nodded." For the next three days, authorities prevented her from seeing him under various pretexts. On April 13, the family learned Zaydulloev was dead. His parents told their lawyer that when they saw his body in the morgue, it was covered in bruises. An initial autopsy by authorities stated the cause of death was pneumonia. The family's lawyer has petitioned for a new autopsy and investigation into torture allegations.

Freedom of Religion

Tajikistan severely restricts religious freedom, regulating religious worship, dress, and education, and imprisons individuals on overbroad charges of religious extremism. Authorities ban several peaceful minority Muslim groups and Christian minority denominations, such as Jehovah's Witnesses.

Regulations also restrict the naming of children, headscarves are banned in educational institutions, and beards are prohibited in public buildings. On September 3, 22-year-old Vakhdat resident Umar Bobojonov died in hospital of injuries he sustained during a police beating on August 29. Bobojonov's relatives accused police of detaining him because of his beard. The Ministry of Internal Affairs stated it was investigating the incident, but no results have been made public.

Authorities suppress unregistered Muslim education throughout the country, control the content of sermons, and have closed many unregistered mosques. Authorities kept in place a Parental Responsibility law, which requires parents to prevent their children from participating in religious activity until they turn 18.

Domestic Violence

Authorities took some steps to combat domestic violence against women and children in 2015, establishing several police stations staffed by female police inspectors who received training in gender-sensitive community policing. However, survivors of domestic violence, lawyers, and service providers reported that Tajikistan's 2013 law on the prevention of violence in the family remains largely unimplemented and that victims of domestic violence continue to suffer inadequate protection. Impunity for severe acts of domestic violence and a scarcity of critical services for survivors remain the norm.

Social and Economic Rights

Tajikistan's Rogun Dam and Hydropower Plant stand to displace over 42,000 people before they become operational. Since 2009, authorities have resettled 1,500 families to regions around Tajikistan. Despite commitments to comply with international standards on resettlement that protect the rights of the displaced, the government has not provided necessary compensation to displaced families to replace their homes or restore their livelihoods. Many families have suffered serious disruptions in access to housing, food, water, and education.

Key International Actors

During a June visit to Tajikistan, United Nations Secretary-General Ban Ki-moon urged the government to strengthen "national coordination mechanisms and [implement] UN human rights recommendations holistically and in cooperation with civil society," emphasizing the importance of Tajikistan's second Universal Periodic Review, coming in April 2016.

In June, the European Union held its annual human rights dialogue with Tajikistan, raising concerns about torture and restrictions on freedoms of expression and religion.

For the third year in a row, the United States Commission on International Religious Freedom recommended that Tajikistan be designated a "country of particular concern," highlighting "systematic, ongoing, [and] egregious violations of religious freedom," but the Obama administration elected not to make that designation.

Thailand

The ruling National Council for Peace and Order (NCPO)—led by Prime Minister Gen. Prayut Chan-ocha—took power in a coup in May 2014. Despite initial promises to restore democracy within one year, the junta in 2015 exercised increasingly dictatorial power and continued to systematically repress fundamental rights and freedoms.

Deepening Authoritarianism

Instead of paving the way for a return to democratic civilian rule as promised in its so-called "road map," the junta has created a political system that seems designed to prolong its grip on power.

On March 31, 2015, nationwide enforcement of the Martial Law Act of 1914 was replaced with section 44 of the interim constitution. Section 44 provides unlimited administrative, legislative, and judiciary powers to Prayut in his capacity as the NCPO chairman without any oversight or accountability. The interim constitution also absolves anyone carrying out actions on behalf of the NCPO of all legal liability.

Growing opposition to military rule prompted junta leaders to claim that Thailand was not ready for a constitutional referendum or a general election. The National Reform Council rejected the draft constitution on September 6, 2015, extending the junta's rule to at least until 2017. In November 2015, the NCPO proposed that the new constitution should guarantee blanket amnesty for the use of military force to "protect national security."

Freedom of Assembly and Expression

The NCPO has banned political gatherings of more than five persons. Since the coup, at least 80 people have been arrested and sent to military courts for organizing or taking part in peaceful public gatherings.

At time of writing, at least 27 people had been arrested and charged with sedition for criticizing military rule and violating the junta's ban on public assembly, including 14 activists from the New Democracy Movement in Bangkok arrested in June 2015. On December 8, Thanakorn Siripaiboon, a 27-year-old factory worker, was arrested and charged with sedition and computer crimes for sharing Facebook infographics alleging corruption by Prayut and other junta leaders in the army's Rajabhakti Park project.

The junta has also aggressively restricted free expression, using section 44 of the interim constitution.

In April, authorities suspended broadcasts by Peace TV and TV 24, accusing the stations of violating the NCPO's ban on criticism of the military. In November, Fah Hai TV was shut down by authorities on the same grounds. Human Rights Watch's Thailand webpage remains blocked in the country because authorities deem it a threat to national security.

Military units in Bangkok and other provinces forced the cancellation of more than 60 political events, seminars, and academic panels on political and human rights issues in 2015 on grounds that the events threatened stability and national security. The police and military enforced an NCPO order canceling report launch events by Human Rights Watch, Amnesty International, and the Thai Lawyers for Human Rights at the Foreign Correspondents Club of Thailand (FCCT) in Bangkok.

In September 2015, Prayut ordered the revocation of former Deputy Prime Minister Chaturon Chaisaeng's passport to punish him for his criticisms of military rule.

Criticizing the monarchy is a serious criminal offense in Thailand, and Prayut has made *lese majeste* (insulting the monarchy) prosecutions a top priority of the NCPO. Since the coup, 56 *lese majeste* cases have been brought, 43 against individuals for online commentary. Military courts have imposed harsher sentences than civilian courts did prior to the coup. In August 2015, the Bangkok Military Court sentenced Pongsak Sriboonpeng to 60 years in prison for alleged *lese majeste* Facebook postings (later reduced to 30 years when he pleaded guilty). It was the longest recorded sentence for *lese majeste* in Thailand's history.

In December, the junta announced that individuals who share, comment on, or click "Like" on Facebook contents that authorities deem offensive to the monarchy would be prosecuted for *lese majeste*. Junta leaders also strongly criticized foreigners who commented on Thailand's increasingly harsh and arbitrary enforcement of the *lese majeste* law, including remarks by the United States ambassador, deeming the commentary interference in Thailand's domestic affairs.

Arbitrary Detention

At time of writing, the NCPO had summoned at least 751 people for questioning since the coup. Most were affiliated with the ousted Pheu Thai Party and the activist group United Front for Democracy against Dictatorship (UDD), known as the "Red Shirts," but they also included politicians, activists, and journalists accused by the junta of involvement in anti-coup activities or insulting the monarchy. Failure to report to authorities following an NCPO summons is considered an offense subject to trial in military court. The junta has issued arrest warrants and revoked the passports of at least 10 exiled dissidents for failing to report to the authorities when summoned.

Under the provisions of martial law and, later, section 44 of the interim constitution, the military can secretly detain people without charge or trial and interrogate them without access to lawyers or safeguards against mistreatment. The NCPO has summarily dismissed allegations that the military has tortured and ill-treated detainees but has provided no evidence to rebut those serious allegations.

Human Rights Watch submitted a letter to the Thai government on November 24, raising serious concerns regarding conditions at the 11th Army Circle military base after the recent deaths of fortuneteller Suriyan Sucharitpolwong and Police Maj. Prakrom Warunprapa—both charged with *lese majeste*—during their detention there.

The use of military courts, which lack independence and fail to comply with international fair trial standards, to try civilians—mostly political dissidents and alleged *lese majeste* offenders—increased significantly in 2015.

Impunity

Prime Minister General Prayut has frequently stated that soldiers should not be condemned for violence connected to the military dispersal of UDD street protests in April and May 2010—in which 90 people died and more than 2,000 were injured—despite evidence that most casualties resulted from unnecessary or excessive use of lethal force by soldiers. No military personnel have been charged for killing and wounding civilians at that time.

The government, however, has expedited investigations into cases in which persons connected to the UDD used violence in 2010, and UDD leaders and supporters face serious criminal charges. In contrast, there has been little progress in investigating or prosecuting alleged rights abuses and criminal offenses committed by the People's Alliance for Democracy (PAD), the so-called "Yellow Shirts," and by the People's Democratic Reform Committee (PDRC) during political confrontations in 2008 and 2013-2014, respectively.

Violence and Abuses in Southern Border Provinces

Since January 2004, more than 6,000 ethnic Malay Muslims and ethnic Thai Buddhists have been killed in armed conflict in Thailand's southern border provinces.

Even though there was a drop in violent incidents after a peace dialogue started in August 2015 between the Thai government and Barisan Revolusi Nasional (BRN) and other armed separatist groups in the loose Majlis Syura Patani (Mara Patani) network, both sides have committed serious human rights abuses and violations of the laws of war.

Separatists have killed at least 175 teachers during 11 years of insurgency and continued to target civilians in bomb attacks, roadside ambushes, drive-by shootings, and assassinations.

Thai security forces have not been prosecuted for numerous illegal killings, torture, and other abuses against ethnic Malay Muslims. In many cases, Thai authorities provided financial compensation to the victims or their families in exchange for their agreement not to pursue criminal prosecution of abusive officials.

Enforced Disappearances

There has been no progress in the police investigation to locate ethnic Karen activist Por Cha Lee Rakchongcharoen, known as "Billy," who was forcibly disappeared after officials at Kaengkrachan National Park arrested him on April 17, 2014, in Petchaburi province.

Until today, Thai authorities have failed to satisfactorily resolve any of the 64 enforced disappearance cases reported by Human Rights Watch, including the "disappearance" and presumed murder of prominent Muslim lawyer Somchi Neelapaijit by a group of police officers in March 2004.

Thailand signed the International Convention for the Protection of All Persons from Enforced Disappearance in January 2012 but has not ratified the treaty. The penal code still does not recognize enforced disappearance as a criminal offense.

Human Rights Defenders

In September 2015, the Phuket Provincial Court acquitted Chutima Sidasathian and Alan Morison—journalists from the online newspaper *Phuketwan*—who had been put on trial for criminal defamation and breach of the Computer Crimes Act for publishing a paragraph from a Reuters special report on Rohingya boat people that the Thai navy alleged had implicated their personnel in human trafficking.

In June 2015, the Yala provincial prosecutor issued a non-prosecution order in a criminal defamation case against Pornpen Khongkachonkiet and the Cross Cultural Foundation, ruling that their open letter calling for an investigation into torture allegedly committed by paramilitary troops of the 41st Taharnpran Unit had been published in good faith.

Despite positive outcomes in the above-mentioned cases, Thai authorities and private companies have continued to use defamation lawsuits to retaliate against those who report human rights violations. On August 24, 2015, the Southern Bangkok Criminal Court indicted migrant rights activist Andy Hall on criminal charges in a lawsuit filed by Natural Fruit Co. Ltd., one of Thailand's biggest pineapple processors, for a report alleging serious labor rights abuses at one of its factories.

Refugee Rights

Thailand is not a party to the 1951 Refugee Convention and its 1967 Protocol. Asylum seekers are treated by Thai authorities as illegal migrants, and subject to arrest and deportation.

Thai authorities continue to violate the international prohibition against refoulement (forcible return) by forcing refugees and asylum seekers back to countries where they are likely to face persecution. On July 9, 2015, defying pleas to the contrary from the United Nations Refugee Agency (UNHCR) and several foreign governments, Thai authorities forcibly returned at least 109 ethnic Uighurs to China. Their current whereabouts and well-being are unknown. In November, the Thai government repatriated human rights activist Dong Guangping and Jiang Yefei, both recognized as refugees by UNHCR and accepted for resettlement in Canada, to China.

In May 2015, Thai authorities discovered at least 30 bodies at an abandoned human trafficking camp in Songkhla province close to the Thai-Malaysian border. Police reports indicated the dead were ethnic Rohingya from Burma and Bangladesh who starved to death or died from abuses or disease while held by traffickers who were awaiting ransom payments before smuggling them into Malaysia.

The case led to the arrest of army Lt. Gen. Manas Kongpan together with 52 local politicians, community leaders, businessmen, and gangsters for trafficking. In November, Police Maj. Gen. Paween Pongsirin—the chief investigator in the case—resigned and left Thailand to seek asylum in Australia, claiming he was fearful of retaliation and that he had received no protection from his supervisors.

On May 22, Thailand hosted an international meeting to address the thousands of Rohingya asylum seekers and migrants stranded at sea in small boats, but, unlike Malaysia and Indonesia, refused to work with UNHCR to conduct refugee status determination screenings or set up temporary shelters for those rescued.

Despite the peril faced by those on the boats, Thai authorities regularly took action to prevent boats carrying Rohingya from landing in Thailand. On many occasions, boats were intercepted and pushed back to sea after receiving rudimentary humanitarian assistance and supplies from Thai authorities.

Migrant workers from Burma, Cambodia, and Laos are vulnerable to abuses by police and government authorities and to exploitation by employers and criminals, including sexual violence and extreme labor exploitation. Trafficking of migrants into sex work or onto Thai fishing boats remained pressing concerns in 2015.

Thailand also continues to detain unaccompanied children and families with children, in violation of international standards.

Anti-Narcotics Policy

The junta has shown no interest in investigating extrajudicial killings related to past anti-drug operations, especially the more than 2,800 killings that accompanied then-Prime Minister Thaksin Shinawatra's "war on drugs" in 2003.

Drug users are sent to "rehabilitation" centers, mostly run by the military and Interior Ministry, where "treatment" consists mainly of military-style physical exercise with little or no medical assistance for drug withdrawal symptoms.

Health

Residents of lower Klity Creek in Kanchanaburi province continue to be exposed to toxic lead from a now-defunct lead processing factory. On January 10, 2013, Thailand's highest administrative court ordered the government to remove the lead from the creek, but Thailand's Pollution Control Department has yet to begin a proper clean-up.

Sexual Orientation and Gender Identity

Thailand's Gender Equality Act, a national non-discrimination law that specifically protects against discrimination on the grounds of gender expression, came into effect in September.

Key International Actors

The UN and Thailand's major allies—including the US, European Union, and Japan—continued to urge the junta in 2015 to respect human rights and return the country to democratic civilian rule through free and fair elections as soon as possible. However, no international action has been taken against the junta for its failure to do so.

In November 2015, an international accrediting body recommended downgrading the status of Thailand's National Human Rights Commission based on concerns about its lack of independence, ineffectiveness, and flawed processes for

HUMAN RIGHTS WATCH

TOXIC WATER, TAINTED JUSTICE
Thailand's Delays in Cleaning Up Klity Creek

selecting commissioners. A downgrade would result in the commission losing its privileges to present views at the UN Human Rights Council.

After an August 17 bomb attack in Bangkok killed at least 20 people and wounded 125 others, Thai authorities arrested Bilal Muhammed and Meiraili Yusufu, ethnic Uighurs from China. The two suspects were put on trial in a military court trial for offenses including murder and illegal weapons possession.

The Trafficking in Persons Report of the US State Department kept Thailand in Tier 3 for another year for failing to combat human trafficking. In April 2015, the European Commission put Thailand on formal notice for not taking sufficient measures in the international fight against illegal fishing.

Tunisia

Tunisia experienced several deadly attacks by Islamist extremists in 2015 that left dozens of people dead and others injured. On March 18, two gunmen attacked the Bardo Museum, adjacent to Tunisia's parliament, killing 21 foreign tourists and one Tunisian security agent. On June 26, a gunman rampaged through a beach resort in Sousse, killing 38 foreign tourists. On November 24, a suicide attack on a bus killed 12 presidential guards and wounded 20 others, including four civilians. The attacks prompted the government to invoke a 1978 decree to declare a state of emergency that empowered authorities to ban strikes or demonstrations deemed to threaten public order, and to prohibit gatherings "likely to provoke or sustain disorder."

Constitution

The 2014 constitution guarantees key civil, political, social, economic, and cultural rights. Tunisian authorities made little progress in overhauling legislation that fails to comply with the constitution, particularly the penal code and code of criminal procedures.

Article 29 of the constitution affords detainees "the right to be represented by a lawyer," but the code of criminal procedures allows detainees to consult a lawyer only after they appear before an investigative judge, up to six days after arrest. Parliament has yet to debate a draft law to reform the Code of Criminal Procedures that the previous government submitted in April 2013.

If enacted, the proposed law would affirm the right of detainees to access a lawyer promptly after arrest and to have their lawyer present during their interrogation and court hearings.

The penal code, the Code of Military Justice, and the Telecommunications Law still include articles that punish with imprisonment speech offenses, such as defamation of public officials, harming public order and public morals, and spreading false information.

Freedom of Expression

In 2015, authorities prosecuted several people for alleged defamation or "insult" of state officials and on charges of "harming public order" or "public morals."

Authorities also used counterterrorism legislation to prosecute a few journalists and bloggers for publishing information or their opinions.

Judicial authorities charged Noureddine Mbarki, chief editor of *Akher Khabar online*, with complicity in terrorism on July 8 for publishing a photograph of gunman Seifeddine Rezgui getting out of a car driven by another person shortly before he killed 38 foreigners in the June 26 Sousse attack.

Authorities also detained Abdelfattah Saied, a teacher, on the same charge on July 22 after he posted a video on Facebook that accused the security forces of planning the Sousse attack and duping Rezgui into carrying it out. He also faced the charge of "defaming a public servant" for publishing a caricature of Prime Minister Habib Essid on his Facebook page.

On March 2, a military appeals court sentenced Yassine Ayari, a prominent blogger, to six months in prison for Facebook posts that criticized the army and its top echelons. Several posts in August and September 2014 had criticized the minister of defense for refusing to appoint a new head of military intelligence, and accused him of weakening military institutions. Ayari spent four months in prison before his release on April 16, 2015.

Transitional Justice and Accountability

On December 24, 2013, the National Constituent Assembly (NCA) adopted the Law on Establishing and Organizing Transitional Justice.

The law sets out a comprehensive approach to addressing past human rights abuses. It provides criminal accountability via specialized chambers within the civil court system to adjudicate cases arising from past human rights violations, including abuses committed by military and security forces.

The law also established a Truth and Dignity Commission (TDC) tasked with uncovering the truth about abuses committed between July 1955, shortly before Tunisia's independence from France, and the law's adoption in 2013. The NCA elected 15 of the TDC's members on May 15, 2014, and in August 2015, the TDC said it had received 16,000 complaints from people alleging human rights abuses and had begun processing them.

On July 14, however, the government approved a draft Law on Economic and Financial Reconciliation, strongly supported by President Essebsi. If enacted, the

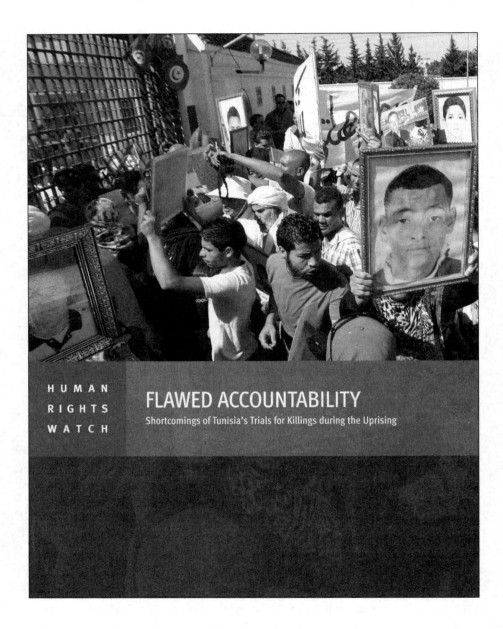

HUMAN
RIGHTS
WATCH

FLAWED ACCOUNTABILITY
Shortcomings of Tunisia's Trials for Killings during the Uprising

law will offer broad amnesty to officials of the former Ben Ali regime and will terminate prosecutions and trials of, and cancel any sentences against, corrupt business executives who submit a reconciliation request to a state-run commission.

The proposed law would threaten the TDC's role, mandated under the transitional justice law, to mediate cases relating to corruption and economic crimes, which were endemic during the 23-year rule of former President Ben Ali.

Counterterrorism and Security

Tunisia's parliament adopted a new counterterrorism law on July 25 that imperils human rights and lacks adequate safeguards against abuses. The law, which replaced the 2003 counterterrorism law enacted by the Ben Ali administration, affords the security forces broad and vague monitoring and surveillance powers, extends incommunicado detention from six to up to 15 days for terrorism suspects, and permits courts to close hearings to the public and allow the identities of witnesses to be withheld from defendants.

A Human Rights Watch study from July found that Tunisian authorities, under the guise of fighting terrorism, were arbitrarily banning persons under age 35 from travel to countries including Algeria, Libya, Morocco, and Turkey unless they obtain their father's authorization to travel, even though Tunisian law does not require adults to obtain such authorization.

Judicial Independence

The constitution guarantees judicial independence. On May 15, parliament approved a law to create a constitutionally mandated Supreme Judicial Council (SJC). Its functions will include making judicial appointments and overseeing judicial discipline and the career progression of judges.

A week after its adoption, 30 members of parliament challenged the new law before the Constitutional Council, itself a temporary body, arguing that its composition and mandate failed to implement the constitutional chapter on the judiciary. In June, the council issued a decision invalidating the law and sent it back to the parliament for revision. On November 13, the parliament adopted the final version of the law, upholding the Constitutional Council's request to remove membership of the general prosecutor of military justice as an ex-officio member.

Torture and Ill-Treatment

In May 2014, the UN special rapporteur on torture said that Tunisian prosecutors and judges had taken "very little action" to pursue torture complaints dating from the Ben Ali era and since the 2011 revolution.

This failure continued through 2015. Although the National Constituent Assembly approved legislation to create a 16-member High Authority for the Prevention of Torture in October 2013, by September the parliament had yet to select any members. Under its mandate, the High Authority will carry out unannounced inspections of detention sites.

In 2015, Tunisian law still allows police to deny those they arrest access to a lawyer for the first six days of their detention, typically the period when detainees face the greatest pressure to "confess." The counterterrorism law adopted in July extended this to a maximum of 15 days in the case of terrorism suspects, increasing the risk of torture.

There were several documented incidents of torture and other mistreatment in 2015. On August 4, seven men detained on suspicion of terrorism filed formal complaints of torture upon release. Shortly after, officers of the police counterterrorism unit they had accused rearrested them. The men underwent forensic medical examination that concluded that five of them bore marks consistent with their torture allegations. On August 10, the prosecutor of the First Instance Tribunal in Tunis opened an investigation but had yet to reveal its outcome at time of writing.

Earlier, the prosecutor of the First Instance Tribunal of Sidi Bouzid opened an investigation into the case of Abdelmajid Ejday after he died on May 13 while held at the city's National Guard headquarters. Ejday had filed a torture complaint four weeks earlier against officers from the same police unit force who had detained him in February. A forensic medical examination reported finding injuries on his body. At time of writing, the prosecutor had not announced the outcome of his investigation.

Women's Rights

The 2014 constitution provides improved protection for women's rights and obligates Tunisia to work towards achieving gender parity in elected assemblies.

Tunisia has a personal status code that gives women greater rights within the family than those allowed by other states in the region, but the code retains some discriminatory provisions. These deny women an equal share with men of any inheritance and prohibit a mother who has remarried, unlike remarried fathers, from having her children live with her.

Tunisia's parliament adopted a new law on November 10, which will allow women to travel with their minor children without getting permission from the children's father.

Sexual Orientation and Gender Identity

Tunisia's penal code punishes consensual same-sex conduct with up to three years in prison. In March, Shams, a lesbian, gay, bisexual, and transgender group, was permitted to operate. On September 22, a 22-year-old man was sentenced to one year in prison on homosexuality charges, after being subjected to a forced anal exam, a practice that amounts to torture.

Key International Actors

Several United Nations agencies and foreign governments have committed to support Tunisia's transition since the 2011 revolution, focusing on technical and financial assistance to the economy and private sector, security sector support, and support for civil society and democratic practices.

In July, US President Barack Obama and President Essebsi signed an agreement in Washington making Tunisia a Major Non-NATO Ally, thereby enhancing Tunisia's eligibility to receive training on security and military financing of certain defense equipment.

In July, the UN Working Group on the use of mercenaries visited Tunisia, and concluded that some 6,000 Tunisians had left the country to join extremist armed groups in Syria, Iraq, Mali, and Libya. The group urged the government to urgently stop the flow of Tunisians to join extremist groups abroad, dismantle recruitment networks, and devise and implement a comprehensive solution to the problem.

Turkey

The environment for human rights in Turkey deteriorated in 2015 with the break-down of the Kurdish peace process, a sharp escalation of violence in the southeast, and a crackdown on media and political opponents of the ruling Justice and Development Party (AKP).

There were two general elections in 2015. In the June 7 election, the AKP lost its overall majority polling at 41 percent, while the left-leaning pro-Kurdish Peoples' Democracy Party (HDP) polled 13 percent, for the first time passing the 10 percent threshold for entering parliament. Failure among the four main political parties to agree the formation of a coalition government precipitated a second general election on November 1, which the AKP won with 49 percent. The run-up to the November election was marked with violence, including an October 10 double suicide bombing in Ankara by individuals linked to the armed extremist group Islamic State (also known as ISIS). The bombing was the worst single attack in Turkey's modern history, killing 102 people.

Turkey continued to host large number of refugees, asylum seekers, and migrants, primarily from Syria but also from Afghanistan, Iraq, and other countries. The number from Syria surged in 2015, bringing the total to 2.2 million. Conditions and rights protections for refugees, asylum seekers and migrants remain uneven at best, including in relation to education and employment.

Turkey was the main transit route in the European Union for asylum seekers and migrants in 2015, prompting Brussels to agree to a migration action plan with Ankara in November. A lack of effective protection in Turkey for Syrians and others, existing border restrictions with Syria imposed by Turkey, and Turkey's record of police abuse gave rise to concerns that the deal could deny people access to asylum, trap people in Syria, and lead to police abuse and detention of asylum seekers who try to travel to the EU.

The war in Syria also had a growing impact on Turkey's domestic politics. The AKP publicly advocated the overthrow of the Assad government and creation of a "safe zone" in northern Syria to house Syrian refugees. The latter proposal was strongly opposed by refugee and rights advocates who feared that Syrians could effectively be denied the ability to seek protection outside the country or returned to Syria while becoming easy targets for armed forces. The most notable shift in Turkey's Syria policy came after the July Suruç bombing when Ankara reached an agreement with the United States to open a Turkish airbase for coalition airstrikes against ISIS and to play a limited role in airstrikes.

Renewed Violence in the Southeast

The breakdown in 2015 of the government-initiated peace process with Abdullah Öcalan, the imprisoned leader of the armed Kurdistan Workers' Party (PKK), was accompanied by an increase in violent attacks, armed clashes, and human rights abuses in the second half of the year. The latter included violations of the right to life, arrests of non-violent protesters and activists on terrorism charges, and ill-treatment of detainees.

Hundreds of attacks on HDP offices took place in the run-up to both elections, and two of its offices were bombed in the run-up to the June election. A bomb attack on a Diyarbakır HDP election rally on June 5 killed four. A former ISIS fighter is under investigation for the Diyarbakır bombing.

The most serious escalation of violence followed the June general election. The government held ISIS responsible for a July 20 suicide bombing that killed 32 students and activists from Turkey who had traveled to the southeast town of Suruç to join efforts to rebuild Kobani. The PKK blamed Turkish authorities for the bombing, and local PKK associates killed two police officers in nearby Ceylanpınar. In response, the Turkish air force repeatedly bombed PKK camps in northern Iraq and later in Turkey. The PKK countered with a series of deadly attacks on police and army conveys.

In early September, Turkish security forces placed the southeast town of Cizre under blanket curfew for eight days to conduct a military operation against the PKK's youth wing, which reportedly had sealed off three neighborhoods. The government estimated that 40-42 militants were killed in the operation; the Diyarbakır Bar Association reported 21 civilians dead, 16 from firearm injuries. The authorities have not made the circumstances of the deaths public at time of writing, fueling concerns that they continue to be unwilling to ensure effective investigations and criminal accountability for alleged security force abuses. During further curfews and military operations in towns with neighborhoods sealed off by the PKK youth wing—including Silvan, Nusaybin, and Diyarbakir's Sur district—civilian deaths were regularly reported by media and human rights organizations. There was a rise in credible reports of serious ill-treatment in detention.

On November 28, Tahir Elçi, a human rights lawyer and head of the Bar Association, was shot dead in Diyarbakır. The circumstances of his killing were under investigation at time of writing; it followed an attack on the police by individuals reported to be members of the PKK youth wing in which two police officers died and several police officers opened fire in response.

Starting in July, authorities launched a new wave of investigations into hundreds of Kurdish political party officials and activists, including mayors, detaining many on terrorism charges, including in cases where the evidence consisted of non-violent political association and involvement in peaceful protests or press conferences.

Despite thousands of killings and enforced disappearances of Kurds by security forces in the 1990s, only a handful of military personnel have faced criminal trial; in four cases in 2015, military personnel were acquitted, and in no case convicted. Turkey's 20-year statute of limitations on the prosecution of unlawful killings remains a major obstacle to justice.

Freedom of Expression, Association, and Assembly

Government-led restrictions on media freedom and freedom of expression in Turkey in 2015 went hand-in-hand with efforts to discredit the political opposition and prevent scrutiny of government policies in the run-up to the two general elections.

In May, the Istanbul prosecutor's office launched a terrorism and espionage investigation of Cumhuriyet newspaper for posting a video and news report showing trucks laden with weapons allegedly en route to Syria. President Recep Tayyip Erdoğan subsequently made speeches strongly condemning the newspaper and filed a separate criminal complaint. In November, the newspaper's editor Can Dündar and journalist Erdem Gül were arrested and jailed pending trial.

In October, police raided the İpek Media group, including TV stations and newspapers, two days after the government had appointed trustees to run the parent company, Koza İpek Holding. Firing the staff and appointing new editors, both TV stations and newspapers are now pro-government organs. The government alleges the Koza İpek group is supportive of US-based cleric Fethullah Gülen—the head of a religious movement whose followers in Turkey are subject to an unprecedented crackdown—and has effectively seized the company's assets. The government similarly moved against the Samanyolu Broadcasting Group, known for its support for the Gülen movement, by ending distribution of its TV channels on the state-owned Turksat satellite dish distribution platform.

Prosecutions of journalists, judges, prosecutors, and police for membership of an alleged "Fethullah Gülen Terrorist Organization" were ongoing at time of writing, although there is no evidence to date that the Gülen movement has engaged in violence or other activities that could reasonably be described as terrorism.

In November, the publisher Cevheri Güven and editor Murat Çapan of weekly news magazine *Nokta* were arrested and jailed pending trial for "inciting an armed insurrection against the government" for a satirical picture of Erdoğan and report. A court ordered all copies of the issue to be confiscated. The editor faces earlier charges of insulting the president and terrorist propaganda for a September cover of Nokta.

In September, the building of Hürriyet newspaper and its owner the Doğan Media Group came under direct attack by crowds, including a parliamentarian from the AKP, hours after Erdoğan had accused the newspaper of misrepresenting comments he made in a television interview. One week later, an Istanbul prosecutor initiated an investigation of news reports in Doğan media outlets. On September 30, a leading *Hurriyet* journalist, Ahmet Hakan, was attacked and beaten by four men who followed his car. Seven men were subsequently detained, one placed in pretrial detention, and the other six released pending completion of a criminal investigation.

Journalists continued to be fired from mainstream press outlets in 2015 for critical reporting, commentary, and tweets. Social media postings critical of the president and politicians by ordinary people also led to criminal defamation charges and convictions. A new trend in 2015 saw courts in several cases order pretrial detention of people for several months for allegedly insulting Erdoğan via social media or during demonstrations.

Three foreign journalists were deported in 2015 for their news reporting activities in the southeast, and a fourth, Mohammed Rasool, was in pretrial detention facing investigation on terrorism charges at time of writing.

In the first six months of 2015, Turkish authorities were responsible for almost three quarters of requests to Twitter worldwide for removal of tweets and blocking of accounts. In March, parliament passed new legislation allowing ministers to request the Communications Directorate (TİB) to block online content or remove it within four hours to "protect life and property, national security, the public order, [or] to prevent crime and to protect general health." A court must approve the decision within 48 hours.

The authorities frequently impose arbitrary bans on public assemblies and violently disperse peaceful demonstrations, in some cases using powers conferred by a new domestic security law passed in March. For the first time ever, the Istanbul governor's office banned the annual Istanbul Gay Pride march in June 2015, citing vague concerns about counter-demonstrations. Police dispersed groups who had assembled peacefully using tear gas and water cannons.

In a rare positive development, the five organizers of Taksim Solidarity and 21 co-defendants were acquitted in April of criminal charges relating to the 2013 Gezi park protests. The group was charged with forming a criminal gang, inciting and participating in unlawful demonstrations, and refusing orders to disperse. The court decision cited at length Turkey's obligations to uphold the right to peaceful assembly under the European Convention on Human Rights.

Judicial Independence

Long-standing defects in Turkey's justice system include threats to judicial independence, a pattern of ineffective investigation into abuses by security forces and other state actors, excessively long proceedings, and politically motivated prosecutions.

The AKP government in 2015 continued efforts to purge the police and judiciary of alleged supporters of the Gülen movement. During 2015, prosecutors, judges, and police officers with perceived links to the Gülen movement were jailed and charged with plotting against the government and membership of a terrorist organization. The main evidence being cited against judges and prosecutors at time of writing was decisions taken in the course of their professional duties rather than any evidence of criminal activity.

Refugees and Migrants

As of October 2015, according to official estimates, Turkey hosted 2.2 million refugees from Syria, 250,000 of them in camps, as well as more than 80,000 asylum seekers and refugees from other countries, notably Afghanistan and Iraq.

While Turkey has been generous in hosting large numbers of Syrian refugees, the government only grants Syrians temporary protection rather than refugee status, while other nationalities of asylum seekers do not receive that.

Turkish government schools are officially available to all Syrian primary and secondary school-age students registered for "temporary protection," but at time of writing more than 400,000 children—over two-thirds of all Syrian children in Turkey—were receiving no form of education. Child labor is rampant among the Syrian refugee population as well as among other refugee groups in Turkey. Syrians and other refugees and asylum seekers are not legally allowed to work.

A growing number of refugees, asylum seekers, and migrants attempted to cross by sea from Turkey to the Greek islands in 2015, making it the main transit route into the European Union. This prompted Brussels to agree to a migration action plan with Ankara in November. Under the plan, Turkey agreed to curb migration flows to the EU, in exchange for €3 billion and the prospect of visa-free travel for its citizens in most EU countries and reinvigorated talks on EU membership.

More than 627 of people had died trying to make the crossing from Turkey to Greek islands at time of writing. The death of three-year-old Syrian Kurdish toddler Aylan Kurdi drew international attention to the crisis, but more than 100 children died trying to make the crossing since then, underscoring the lack of safe and legal routes to the EU.

In September, Turkish authorities prevented thousands of asylum seekers from attempting to cross the land border into Greece. At time of writing, Turkey had all but closed its borders to Syrian asylum seekers and was summarily pushing back Syrians detected as they try to cross.

Women's Rights

Despite Turkey's ratification of the Council of Europe Convention on Preventing and Combating Violence against Women and Domestic Violence, violence

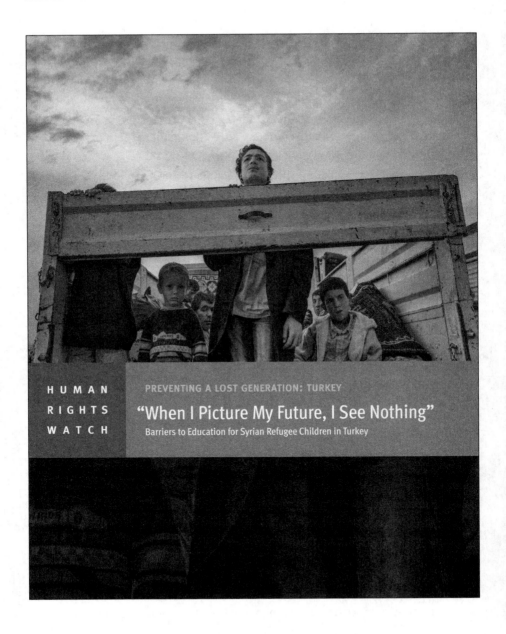

against women remains a significant concern in Turkey. The murder and attempted rape of Ozgecan Aslan in Mersin in February sparked mass protests calling for government action to stop the killing of women, including by their partners.

Key International Actors

The EU, EU member states, Council of Europe, and the US expressed serious concerns about Turkey's record on media freedom and judicial independence, while commending Turkey for hosting nearly 2 million refugees from the war in Syria.

The decision by the European Commission to postpone publication of a critical annual report on Turkey's human rights progress until after the November elections; the absence of a reference to human rights in an EU-Turkey summit statement when the migration action plan was agreed; and comments by Commission President Juncker that the EU should not "harp" on about Turkey's rights record all raised concerns that the EU-Turkey migration cooperation may come at the expense of strong EU pressure on Turkey's rights record.

The Council of Europe Committee of Ministers urged Turkey in March to comply with a group of European Court of Human Rights rulings by amending its Law on Meetings and Demonstrations to address restrictions on the right to peaceful assembly and to ensure effective investigation of excessive use of force "to ensure the accountability of all, including senior law enforcement officers."

Turkey accepted recommendations made during its Universal Periodic Review at the Human Rights Council in January 2015 to create a fully independent national human rights institution but rejected recommendations to improve its legal framework for the protection of minorities.

In a May 2015 follow-up report on recommendations made to Turkey during his 2012 country visit, the UN special rapporteur on extrajudicial, arbitrary, and summary executions criticized the expanded power given to police to use firearms against demonstrators in Turkey's new domestic security law, saying it was "in direct contradiction to the special rapporteur's recommendation" and expressed concern at Turkey's failure to prosecute military personnel for a 2011 air force bombing on the Turkish border near Uludere that killed 34 Kurdish men and boys.

Turkmenistan

Turkmenistan's atrocious rights record worsened in 2015. The country remains extremely repressive and is virtually closed to independent scrutiny. The government imposes harsh restrictions on media and religious freedoms and exerts total control over access to information. Independent critics face constant threat of government reprisal. Authorities continue to impose informal and arbitrary travel bans on various groups, including students leaving for study abroad, activists, and relatives of exiled dissidents. The government continues to use imprisonment and bans on foreign travel as tools for political retaliation.

For the first time in 12 years, Turkmenistan sent a delegation to the annual Human Dimension Implementation Meeting of the Organization for Security and Co-operation in Europe (OSCE) and continued to expand relations with foreign governments and international organizations in 2015. However, this did not result in any meaningful outcomes for human rights reform.

Cult of Personality

Despite plans for constitutional reform and the establishment of an ombudsman institution, President Gurbanguly Berdymukhamedov and his associates enjoy unlimited power and total control over all aspects of public life in Turkmenistan.

The Turkmen government often forces people to gather for hours for events attended by Berdymukhamedov. They are not permitted to leave or use the toilet. According to the Turkmen Initiative for Human Rights (TIHR), a Vienna-based group, on August 5, many were forced to wait for almost seven hours in the sun in heat of 41 degrees Celsius (105.8 degrees Fahrenheit) to welcome Berdymukhamedov for the opening of a new stadium in Ashgabat. Three of them died the same day.

Civil Society

The repressive atmosphere makes it extremely difficult for independent groups to operate.

Local activists reported the fiercest government pressure against them in recent years. In the lead up to the November visit to Ashgabat by the United States secretary of state, authorities warned local activists to stay home or otherwise face retribution.

Websites tied to the government published smear articles against several human rights defenders in the country and in exile.

Turkmenistan's first Law on Assemblies came into force in July. It allows for peaceful assemblies if local authorities approve the venue in advance and bans protests near government buildings and other areas. The exceedingly repressive atmosphere makes it unlikely that people can participate in independent, peaceful gatherings without government reprisal.

Freedom of Media and Information

The total absence of media freedom in Turkmenistan remains unchanged. The state controls all print and electronic media, and foreign media outlets often cannot access Turkmenistan. Authorities have repeatedly targeted Radio Azatlyk, the Turkmen service of Radio Free Europe/Radio Liberty (RFE/RL), the only source of Turkmen-language alternative news available in the country.

A court sentenced Saparmamed Nepeskuliev, a freelance correspondent for RFE/RL and Alternative News of Turkmenistan, an exile-run news website, to three years of imprisonment on August 31, although the charges for which he was prosecuted and on which he was convicted are not known even to his family. Police had arrested Nepeskuliev in July for alleged narcotics possession.

In 2015, government pressure eventually forced three other correspondents to cease working for RFE/RL.

Starting in March, authorities have forced residents to dismantle privately owned television satellite dishes, which could also receive Radio Azatlyk, offering to replace them with government-controlled cable packages. Thugs destroyed satellite dishes belonging to many residents who refused to comply.

A new Internet law requires government agencies to maintain websites. However, it also introduces even more thorough government controls on the Internet, such as by banning the transmission of computer data that does not go through official providers.

Internet access in Turkmenistan remains limited and heavily state-controlled. Many websites—including social media and messenger services—are blocked; Internet cafés require visitors to register their personal data, and the government monitors all means of communication.

Freedom of Movement

In September, authorities allowed Geldy Kyarizov, a prominent horse breeding expert who fell out of favor with the government, to leave the country for medical treatment. They had barred him, together with family members, from doing so in December 2014 and August 2015. In October 2015, unknown persons speaking Turkmen assaulted Kyarizov in the Moscow metro, making clear they were retaliating for his family having spoken out about his ordeal in Turkmenistan.

In July, authorities barred Aitzhamal Rejepova and her two children from leaving the country and told her that they are on a list of people permanently banned from foreign travel. Rejepova's father is an exiled former politician. In August, Turkmenistan's Supreme Court upheld the migration service's arbitrary banning of the Ruzimatov family—relatives of an exiled former official—from traveling abroad. The ban has been in effect since 2002. Throughout 2015, as in previous years, migration authorities told Aidogdy Kurbanov, son of an exiled Turkmen businessman, that he was banned from foreign travel.

In May, airport officials barred participants in an exchange program from traveling to the US. In September, authorities barred a number of students from traveling to Kyrgyzstan to commence their studies.

Freedom of Religion

Unregistered congregations and religious groups are banned. Religious literature is subject to compulsory state censorship.

According to Forum 18, an independent religious freedom group, in February a Protestant leader, Narmurad Mominov, was fined 100 manat (US$29) after participating in a family gathering at home and allegedly giving the family a copy of the New Testament. Local authorities forced a person at the gathering to renounce their Christian faith and publicly repent in a mosque.

In February, security police beat three of four Jehovah's Witnesses they arrested. A court found all four guilty on trumped-up hooliganism charges and sentenced three to 15 days in jail, and one to a 100-manat fine.

Also in February, prison guards of Seydi labor camp severely beat five Muslim prisoners serving sentences for so-called religious extremism offenses.

In May, a court sentenced Bahram Hemdemov, a Jehovah's Witness, to a four-year prison term for allegedly inciting religious hatred. According to Forum 18, security personnel beat Hemdemov in pretrial detention.

Political Prisoners, Enforced Disappearances, and Torture

Many people continue to languish in Turkmen prisons on what appear to be politically motivated charges.

Political dissident Gulgeldy Annaniazov, arrested in 2008, remains imprisoned following a conviction on charges that are not known even to his family. He is serving an 11-year sentence.

Several dozen people, many of whom were imprisoned under former President Niyazov, remain victims of enforced disappearance—including former Foreign Minister Boris Shikhmuradov, his brother Konstantin, and a former ambassador, Batyr Berdiev. For more than a decade, the government has refused to allow them any contact with their families and their fates remain unknown. In 2014, the United Nations Human Rights Committee recognized Boris Shikhmuradov as a victim of enforced disappearance and stated that the Turkmen government must release him. At time of writing, the Turkmen government had not replied to the committee, missing the one-year deadline to do so.

Torture remains a grave problem, particularly in high-security facilities. The government has persistently denied independent human rights monitors access to the country, including international nongovernmental organizations and 10 UN special procedures.

Sexual Orientation and Gender Identity

Homosexual conduct is punishable by a maximum two-year prison sentence. Criminalization and social prejudice create widespread homophobia, and medical institutions and judicial authorities often regard homosexuality as a disease. Gay men, lesbians, and transgender people have to hide their sexual identity, fearing persecution, harassment, and discrimination.

Key International Actors

Several international actors continue to seek to leverage Turkmenistan's energy wealth, sidelining concerns about the government's human rights record.

In June, on the occasion of the annual human rights dialogue before the European Union and Turkmenistan, the EU raised a wide range of concerns, including enforced disappearances, the forced dismantling of satellite dishes, and forced evictions.

However, the upgrading of relations between the EU and Turkmenistan, in the form of a Partnership and Cooperation Agreement (PCA), remained pending, with the European Parliament postponing the agreement's final ratification on technical grounds. None of the EU's institutions or member states have made any known efforts to secure concrete rights improvements as a condition for its conclusion.

In June, at the 29th session of the UN Human Rights Council, the EU expressed concern about restrictions on civic freedoms, reports of torture, and the use of incommunicado detention in Turkmenistan, and urged authorities to engage with UN treaty bodies. The US expressed similar concerns.

In its March concluding observations, the UN Committee on the Rights of the Child expressed concern about restrictions on media and civil society organizations and "the continued practice of mass mobilization of school children and students for various festive events…." The Committee urged Turkmenistan to ratify the International Convention for the Protection of All Persons from Enforced Disappearance and the Optional Protocol to the Convention against Torture and other Cruel, Inhuman or Degrading Treatment or Punishment.

During his June visit to Turkmenistan, UN Secretary-General Ban Ki-moon delivered a forceful speech in which he made a strong case for respect for human rights and the rule of law as essential to development. Marking concern about a deterioration in rights, he stressed, with respect to the government's creation of an ombudsman post, that the institution needs to meet internationally agreed standards.

The World Bank and Turkmenistan continued discussions of a new strategy of partnership for fiscal year 2016-2017. The bank said that it held discussions with civil society leaders as part of this process, although it is unclear how it was able to do so given the severe repression in Turkmenistan.

Uganda

Concerns about violations of freedom of association, assembly, and expression are increasing as Uganda prepares for presidential and parliamentary elections in early 2016. Police obstruct some candidates' access to media and public meetings. President Yoweri Museveni has been in power for 30 years and remains his party's sole presidential candidate. Former Prime Minister Amama Mbabazi left the ruling party to vie for president and has faced arrest, detention, and obstructions during his campaigns, as have other opposition candidates.

A new nongovernmental organizations (NGOs) bill, passed by parliament in November, includes vague and undefined "special obligations" of independent groups, provisions that could make organizations vulnerable to politically motivated charges for legitimate work. Although the Anti-Homosexuality Act was overturned by a constitutional challenge in 2014, government officials continue to voice support for its discriminatory provisions.

Freedom of Expression and Assembly

The 2013 Public Order Management Act grants police wide discretionary powers over the content and management of public meetings. The law has been used largely to obstruct civic meetings and opposition rallies and as a basis to arrest opposition members and their supporters, posing a serious threat to freedom of assembly.

The law's uneven implementation in the run-up to the 2016 elections has led to numerous accusations of partisan policing, where police prevent opposition gatherings while protecting activities deemed partial to the incumbent. In July, police arrested two opposition presidential candidates, Dr. Kizza Besigye and Amama Mbabazi, as they tried to hold meetings in Kampala and Mbale, respectively. Seven youth activists holding a press conference to condemn the arrests were arrested and charged with unlawful assembly. Meanwhile, police escorted Museveni supporters during a mock funeral for Mbabazi as they marched through Gulu, Northern Uganda with a coffin bearing his photos.

In September, police used teargas, rubber bullets, and brutality to disperse people gathered to hear Mbabazi, despite the absence of public disorder. In some instances, police fired teargas canisters directly at people, turning the canisters into projectiles that caused injury. In Jinja, Eastern Uganda, police lobbed teargas canisters onto the grounds of a primary school, harming children during one opposition gathering.

In January, police arrested six activists from the Unemployed Youth, a protest group, on charges of inciting violence after they brought chickens to a central Kampala square as a "retirement gift" for President Museveni to protest high unemployment. Charges of criminal trespass and conspiracy are still pending against two activists from another group, the Jobless Brotherhood, for protests in June and October 2014 in which they highlighted unemployment and government corruption by releasing pigs painted yellow—the ruling party's color—in public spaces in Kampala. In August, the group's founder, Norman Tumuhimbise, was forcibly disappeared for eight days. The group has said police abducted, detained, and tortured him. Police have denied the allegations.

In June, police charged blogger Robert Shaka with offensive communication under the Computer Misuse Act. Police argued that Shaka violated the president's right to privacy by questioning his health on Facebook. Shaka spent four days in prison, was charged and released on bail.

Freedom of Association

The government has increasingly sought to curtail the work of NGOs working on topics considered sensitive by the government, such as governance, human rights, land, oil, and the rights of lesbian, gay, bisexual and transgender (LGBT) people. Tactics include closure of meetings, threats, and heavy-handed bureaucratic interference. In July, the internal affairs minister ordered an investigation and suggested possible deregistration of the Great Lakes Institute for Strategic Studies. The minister argued the organization was opposing government programs and recruiting young people into political opposition parties.

In April, the government tabled the Non-Governmental Organisations bill. The repressive and controversial bill was significantly improved during parliamentary debates, but the version that was passed by parliament in November remains troubling. The bill includes vague "special obligations" of NGOs, including a requirement that groups should "not engage in any act which is prejudicial to the interests of Uganda or the dignity of the people of Uganda." Another provision criminalizes any activities by organizations that have not been issued with a permit by the government regulator, fundamentally undermining free association rights. A separate provision provides criminal sentences of up to three years for any violations of the act. It is not clear when the bill will reach President Museveni for signature.

No ruling has been issued in the Feburary 2014 constitutional challenge to the current laws regulating organizations. Activists contend that some provisions violate the constitution and international human rights law.

Sexual Orientation and Gender Identity

Although the Constitutional Court nullified the Anti-Homosexuality Act on procedural grounds in 2014, there are concerns that a similar bill or similar repressive measures could become law. Given widespread homophobia and transphobia, the NGO bill could, if signed into law, provide a legal basis for restricting advocacy on the rights of LGBT people on the grounds that such work violates the "dignity of all Ugandans."

Same-sex conduct remains punishable with life imprisonment under Uganda's colonial-era law prohibiting "carnal knowledge against the order of nature."

Police subject some men arrested on homosexuality charges to forced anal exams, a discredited method of seeking "proof" of homosexual conduct that amounts to torture.

There has been no hearing in the appeal of a July 2014 High Court ruling upholding the government's forced closure of a 2012 LGBT rights workshop on the grounds that participants were "promoting" or "inciting" same-sex acts.

In August, Ugandan LGBT activists held a pride rally with minimal police presence.

Corruption and Land

Lack of accountability for public sector corruption remains a serious problem, as misuse of government funds affects health services and infrastructure projects. Communities have voiced serious fears of land grabs, environmental damage, and lack of information as to if and how they can receive fair compensation for encroachment on their land when companies, such as those in mining or extractive industries, arrive.

Government officials, including President Museveni, have labeled those protesting investment projects as "development saboteurs" and argued for lethal force. In Amuru, Northern Uganda in September, soldiers shot at least five people during protests against a land sale to create a private hunting reserve.

Killings of Muslim Clerics and Allied Defence Forces (ADF)

In July, Jamil Mukulu, the leader of the Allied Democratic Forces, was extradited from Tanzania to face trial for multiple counts of murder. The ADF is a Ugandan, largely Muslim, rebel group that has been fighting the government since 1996. Since 2012, 12 Muslim clerics have been killed in Uganda. Police leadership has blamed the killings on the ADF. Although there have been some arrests, none has proceeded to trial.

Accountability for Past Abuses

In protests in 2009 and 2011, police and military police killed at least 49 people, but police have not conducted serious or meaningful investigations. Relatives continue to search for justice through civil cases. In December 2011, police disbanded the Rapid Response Unit but there have been no investigations into killings or torture by the unit. The Ugandan army has also not investigated cases of those tortured or killed while in the custody of the Joint Anti-Terrorism Task Force (JATT).

In August, a military court in Kasese, in western Rwenzori region, sentenced 11 people to 25 years in prison for carrying out the July 5, 2014 attacks on a military barracks and some police posts. There has been no accountability for the violent aftermath of the attacks in which civilians were tortured and killed. The government has committed to exhuming the mass graves in the area for investigations.

The Lord's Resistance Army

The rebel group the Lord's Resistance Army (LRA) remains active in central Africa but with allegations of killings and abductions on a significantly lesser scale than in previous years.

In January, former LRA commander Dominic Ongwen came into the custody of US forces in southeastern Central African Republic and was transferred to the International Criminal Court (ICC) to face charges of four counts of war crimes and three counts of crimes against humanity committed in 2004 in northern Uganda. Warrants for four other LRA commanders have been outstanding since 2005, but three are believed to be dead. LRA's leader Joseph Kony is the group's only remaining ICC suspect at large.

Former LRA fighter Thomas Kwoyelo, charged before Uganda's International Crimes Division with willful killing, taking hostages, and extensive destruction of property, has been imprisoned since March 2009, but his trial has yet to begin. In April, the Supreme Court unanimously agreed that Kwoyelo should face trial and not receive amnesty.

Key International Actors

Ongoing concerns of increased corruption, especially the October 2012 theft of US$12.7 million from the Office of the Prime Minister, and the passage of the Anti-Homosexuality Act prompted differing approaches among development partners.

The European Union, among others, continues to provide direct budgetary support, while the United Kingdom, Ireland and Germany have stopped, either cutting back on funding or channeling funds through civil society groups. In 2014, Belgium temporarily withheld 11 million euros ($12.05 million) for the health sector until Uganda reversed plans to send 300 health workers to Trinidad and Tobago in return for oil sector support.

The United States provides over $440 million annually to support the health sector, particularly anti-retrovirals. The Ugandan army continues to receive logistical support and training from the US for counterterrorism activities, its leading role in the African Union Mission in Somalia (AMISOM), and counter-LRA operations in the Central African Republic. One hundred US military advisors remain deployed to support anti-LRA efforts.

Ukraine

Throughout the year, international and domestic actors struggled to end the armed conflict in eastern Ukraine, but the situation has remained unstable. Parts of Donetsk and Luhansk regions remain under de facto control of Russia-backed fighters. All sides in the conflict violated international humanitarian law. Travel restrictions introduced by the government in January 2015 contributed to severe delays in delivery of humanitarian assistance, including medicine, to conflict-affected areas, resulting in a dire humanitarian situation for civilians.

As of fall 2015, according to estimates by aid groups, over 5 million people in eastern Ukraine needed humanitarian assistance, with over 3 million most vulnerable. In August, violence broke out in Kiev after the parliament voted to consider constitutional reform giving more autonomy to rebel-controlled areas. During clashes between far right-wing protesters and police, a protester threw a grenade that injured more than 100 people, including a policeman who later died from his injuries.

In October, local elections were held in government-controlled territories of Ukraine. Rebels postponed elections in territories they control until February 2016, requesting in return that the government grant those territories special autonomous status.

Hostilities in Eastern Ukraine

As of fall 2015, more than 6,500 people had been killed and over 17,000 wounded in the conflict. By September, an estimated 1.4 million people were internally displaced in Ukraine and more than 600,000 had fled abroad, mainly to Russia.

Although the September ceasefire largely held, sporadic fighting continued. Both sides violated the laws of war. They committed indiscriminate attacks that injured and killed civilians, including through the use of cluster munitions. Government forces and Russia-backed rebels deployed within or near densely populated areas, endangering civilians and civilian objects, including schools, hospitals, and apartment buildings. There was significant evidence that several types of antipersonnel landmines have been used in eastern Ukraine, although at time of writing it was not possible to determine the responsible party or parties.

Both rebel and government forces were implicated in credible reports of torture and cruel and degrading treatment of detainees.

Thousands of civilians remain in rebel-held areas of Donetsk and Luhansk regions. Travel restrictions, introduced by the Ukrainian government in January 2015, severely impede the ability of civilians in rebel-controlled areas to reach safety and access life-saving services available in Ukraine-controlled territory. The restrictions also impede the delivery of humanitarian aid, causing a severe shortage of medicine and medical supplies in rebel-held areas. The resulting health crisis is having a devastating effect on some of the most vulnerable groups of patients, in particular those receiving treatment for tuberculosis, HIV, and drug dependence.

Rule of Law, Accountability for Past Abuses

No significant progress has been achieved in accountability for perpetrators of abuses during the 2014 Maidan protests, in which more than 100 protesters and 13 law enforcement officers died and many were injured. In its March report, the Council of Europe's International Advisory Panel criticized the slow progress and poor quality of the investigation, noting a "widespread perception of impunity" on part of law enforcement agencies.

Among positive steps, in December the authorities established a Special Investigation Division within the Prosecutor General's Office tasked specifically with Maidan-related investigations. The prosecutor's office claimed that it had identified all senior government officials who took part in decision-making during Maidan events, but at time of writing, it was unclear whether any had been charged. Authorities detained several riot police officers suspected of killing protesters from February 18 to 20, 2014. At time of writing, the trial of two of the officers remain ongoing. Many of the alleged perpetrators have reportedly left Ukraine.

At least eight people remain missing in connection to the Maidan events.

Trials are ongoing regarding some aspects of the May 2, 2014 political violence in Odessa, in which 48 people died and more than 200 were injured. Law enforcement bodies, however, have been either unable or unwilling to bring many of those responsible to justice.

In a positive development, in September, Ukraine issued a declaration accepting the jurisdiction of the International Criminal Court (ICC) for crimes committed in the country since February 20, 2014. Although Ukraine is not yet an ICC member country, this declaration paves the way for the ICC prosecutor to consider whether the court should investigate abuses committed during the armed conflict.

A February parliamentary resolution that prompted the government's declaration attempted to cast the ICC's potential inquiry as limited to alleged crimes committed by Russia or Russia-backed forces, but the ICC prosecutor will be able to consider conduct by all sides to the conflict. The government had also accepted the court's jurisdiction for the time period covering the Maidan protests during the period of November 21, 2013, to February 22, 2014. In November, the ICC prosecutor reported that based on the information available, the abuses committed during that period did not amount to crimes against humanity, but that the prosecutor could reconsider this in light of any additional information.

Freedom of Expression and Freedom of Media

Positive developments included an open data law, passed in April, which encourages government agencies to open their records and regularly share information with the public. In June, the parliament passed a law to make public archives of Ukraine's Soviet-era KGB files.

However, Ukrainian authorities, citing the "information war" with Russia, took controversial steps restricting freedom of expression. In December 2014, the government's creation of the Ministry of Information Policy coincided with independent reports of Ukrainian forces' abuses in eastern Ukraine. Ukrainian bloggers and journalists protested the new ministry, fearing it could lead to censorship.

In April, Ukraine banned all films made in Russia after January 2014 and all films post-1991 that portrayed the Russian military in a positive light. In August, authorities introduced a list of 38 books, mostly by Russian authors, banned from being imported to Ukraine, and also "blacklisted" several Russian singers and actors for their views on the conflict. In September, the government expanded the list of persons banned from entering Ukraine to 382. Among them were 35 journalists and bloggers from several countries, including Russia, Israel, and Great Britain.

In June, a package of laws entered into force that ban Nazi and communist symbols and criminalize denial of the "criminal nature of the communist totalitarian regime," punishable by up to five years in prison. "Propaganda" of either ideology is punishable by up to 10 years in jail. Another law recognizes as "fighters for independence" nationalist groups that fought Germany during World War II but also collaborated with the Nazis. The law also criminalizes questioning the legitimacy of their actions.

The armed conflict and the political tension caused by the information war between Russia and Ukraine have jeopardized journalists' safety. A prominent pro-Russian journalist was shot and killed in Kiev in April. At time of writing, the trial of two men charged with the murder was ongoing. Nearly all pro-Ukrainian journalists fled eastern Ukraine and Crimea and relocated to government-controlled parts of Ukraine, fearing repercussions from local authorities. Rebel authorities in eastern Ukraine deny accreditation to foreign correspondents whose reporting is "unfavorable." In June, rebel authorities in Donetsk region expelled a journalist from the independent Russian newspaper *Novaya Gazeta*, and rebel forces beat him in retribution for his reporting.

Sexual Orientation and Gender Identity

The authorities have been more supportive of the lesbian, gay, bisexual, and transgender (LGBT) movement than in previous years, but homophobia and intolerance remain widespread.

In June, the March for Equality took place in Kiev, and although the city's authorities expressed concerns that they would not be able to provide protection to the participants, President Petro Poroshenko publicly supported the idea of the march. On the day of the march, several dozen far-right activists attacked around 300 participants of the gathering, shouting abuses and throwing flares at them. Police tried to block the attackers, but nine policemen were injured in the clashes and one was seriously injured.

In November, the parliament passed an amendment to the labor code that bans discrimination based on sexual orientation and gender identity, a precondition for instituting a visa-free regime with the European Union. LGBT activists voiced concerns that a newer version of the amended labor code being developed at time of writing did not include the same anti-discrimination provision.

In June, a Kiev court overturned the government's rejection of a transgender man's application to have his gender fully recognized, ruling that the applicant did not have to prove he had been sterilized to receive documents in his preferred gender. The ruling represented a major victory in the struggle against the existing gender change process in Ukraine, which is lengthy and humiliating and violates rights of transgender people, including the right to health and the prohibition on inhuman and degrading treatment or punishment.

Crimea

The human rights climate in Crimea under Russian occupation remains repressive. People who decline Russian citizenship and retain their Ukrainian citizenship experience serious difficulties in accessing education, employment opportunities, or social benefits. The authorities did not conduct meaningful investigations into the 2014 enforced disappearances of Crimean Tatar and pro-Ukrainian activists.

They continue to silence critical voices and pressure Crimean Tatars, the ethnic minority which openly criticizes Russia's actions in Crimea. In April, ATR-TV, a Crimean Tatar television channel known for its critical reporting that lead to Russia's occupation, was forced to cease operating because it was not able to re-register under Russian law within the deadline set by authorities. Meydan radio station and Lale, a children's television channel, which are part of the same media holding company as ATR-TV, also had to discontinue. In May, Crimean authorities once again refused to allow public events in Simferopol to commemorate the 1944 deportation of Crimean Tatars.

From September until time of writing, Crimean Tatar activists, backed by Ministry of Interior troops, border guards and the far-right group Right Sector, blocked roads connecting Crimea to mainland Ukraine to prevent food deliveries from Ukraine to Crimea to protest Russia's occupation of Crimea.

Key International Actors

Moscow continues to deny its direct involvement in the conflict in eastern Ukraine, despite mounting evidence to the contrary, such as accounts by Russian soldiers captured in Ukraine, and observers from the Special Monitoring Mission of the Organization (SMM) for Security and Co-operation in Europe (OSCE).

Ukraine's international allies frequently speak out against Russian aggression in Ukraine but rarely publicly criticize abuses by the Ukrainian government. Still, key international actors, including the United Nations, the Council of Europe (CoE), OSCE, the United States, and the EU have repeatedly called on all parties to the conflict to honor the ceasefire laid out in the Minsk agreements. Several European leaders have warned the government of Ukraine against trying to regain territory militarily, fearing increased military involvement from Russia and further escalation of the conflict.

In March, in a joint initiative with the Ukrainian government, the CoE launched a two-year action plan to support Ukraine in fulfilling its human rights obligations.

Through 2015, several rapporteurs of the Parliamentary Assembly of the Council of Europe, conducted fact-finding visits to Ukraine. The CoE's human rights commissioner conducted numerous visits to eastern Ukraine to look into the human rights consequences of the conflict, and issued detailed reports on his findings, repeatedly calling on both sides to respect international humanitarian law. In June, the Parliamentary Assembly adopted a report on missing persons, calling on both sides of the conflict to join efforts to resolve the problem of persons reported missing during the conflict.

The United Nations Human Rights Monitoring Mission in Ukraine and the OSCE's SMM continue to monitor and regularly report on the human rights situation in the country. In May, the SMM published a report highlighting concerns about the protection of civilians and freedom of movement in the Donetsk and Luhansk regions, and recommended the Ukrainian government review whether its permit system's impact on civilians is proportionate to the government's security needs.

In January, the EU Foreign Affairs Council adopted conclusions on Ukraine condemning the escalation of fighting and calling on Russia to use its influence with the rebels to stop their hostile actions. It also called on Ukraine to accept full jurisdiction of the International Criminal Court for abuses committed in 2014 and 2015.

In January 2015, the European Parliament adopted a resolution condemning Russia's "aggressive and expansionist policy" in Ukraine and calling on the government of Ukraine to continue efforts to eradicate corruption.

In July, the UN Human Rights Council adopted a resolution welcoming the technical assistance to Ukraine provided by the Office of the United Nations High Commissioner for Human Rights, acknowledging further need for such assistance and establishing a process for the high commissioner to regularly brief the council in interactive dialogue on each report of the monitoring mission. The first such briefing took place at the September council session.

United Arab Emirates

The United Arab Emirates (UAE) continued in 2015 to arbitrarily detain and in some cases forcibly disappear individuals who criticized the authorities, and its security forces continued to face allegations that they torture detainees in pre-trial detention. The UAE passed an anti-discrimination law that further jeopardizes free speech and is discriminatory in that it excludes references to gender and sexuality. Authorities denied access to the country to activists who criticized the UAE's mistreatment of migrant workers.

Arbitrary Detentions, Enforced Disappearances, and Torture

Authorities forcibly disappeared and detained incommunicado individuals who criticized the government or its allies. Three Emirati sisters, Asma, Mariam, and Al Yazzyah al-Suweidi, spent three months in incommunicado detention after authorities called them to a police station in Abu Dhabi on February 15. The three, whom authorities eventually released without charge, had posted comments criticizing the UAE authorities' unlawful imprisonment of Emirati dissidents, including their brother, Dr. Issa al-Suweidi.

In August, 13 security officers in civilian clothes arrested Emirati academic Nasser bin Ghaith. He had made comments on social media criticizing the Egyptian security forces' mass killing of demonstrators in Cairo's Rab'a Square in 2013 on the two-year anniversary of the massacre. Egypt is a key ally of the UAE government. Bin Ghaith's whereabouts remained unknown at time of writing.

Six Libyan nationals remained in detention without charge, more than a year after their arrests. Individuals who were arrested at the same time but subsequently released alleged that authorities tortured them in an attempt to secure confessions and said they heard other detainees being subjected to torture. The Libyans said their interrogators asked them about supposed links to the Muslim Brotherhood, which the UAE has designated a terrorist organization, and described being subjected to beatings, forced standing, and threats of rape, electrocution, and death.

Freedom of Expression

People who speak with rights groups remained at serious risk of arbitrary detention and imprisonment. The 2014 counterterrorism law provides for the death penalty for people whose activities are found to "undermine national unity or social peace," even if these acts do not include an element of violence or intended violence.

In May, local media reported that the Federal Supreme Court sentenced a UAE national, Ahmed Abdulla al-Wahdi, to 10 years in prison for "creating and running a social media account that insults the UAE's leadership and the country's institutions." In June, local media reported that the Federal Supreme Court found that Nasser al-Junaibi, a UAE national, had "spread rumors and information that harmed the country" and "insulted government entities," and sentenced him to three years in prison.

Authorities cited "national security" grounds as the reason for denying activists who have criticized the UAE's mistreatment of migrant workers entry to the UAE.

Federal Decree Law no. 2 of 2015 on anti-discrimination and anti-hate contains numerous broadly worded provisions that further jeopardize free speech. Enacted in July, the law provides for a minimum of five years in jail for anyone who commits "an act that may instigate any form of discrimination, using any forms of expression or any means." Article 3 of the law says that freedom of expression cannot be invoked as a defense in cases relating to acts or statements "that may incite the contempt of religions that offend them."

Freedom of Association and Movement

Family members of political detainees imprisoned in a mass trial in 2013 complained of repeated harassment by the authorities, including the freezing of assets, the denial of government security clearances required to secure employment, and the imposition of foreign travel bans that they cannot challenge.

HUMAN
RIGHTS
WATCH

MIGRANT WORKERS' RIGHTS
ON SAADIYAT ISLAND
IN THE UNITED ARAB EMIRATES
2015 Progress Report

Migrant Workers

Foreigners account for more than 88.5 percent of UAE residents, according to 2011 government statistics, but despite labor reforms, low-paid migrant workers continue to be subjected to abuses that amount to forced labor. Domestic workers are particularly vulnerable to abuse since they do not enjoy even the minimal protection afforded by UAE labor law.

The *kafala* sponsorship system, which operates in all Gulf Cooperation Council states, ties migrant workers to individual employers who act as their visa sponsors. In practice, the system severely restricts workers' ability to change employers. The system gives employers inordinate power over workers by entitling them to revoke migrant workers' sponsorship at will, thereby removing their right to remain in the UAE and making them liable to deportation.

Under new regulations from 2010, workers covered under the labor law can switch employers in certain cases. However, domestic workers—who are excluded from this reach—cannot transfer employers before their contract ends or before they receive their employer's consent.

Women's Rights

Discrimination on the basis of sex and gender is not included in the definition of discrimination in the UAE's 2015 anti-discrimination law.

Federal law No. 28 of 2005 regulates matters of personal status in the UAE, and some of its provisions discriminate against women. For instance, the law provides that, for a woman to marry, her male guardian must conclude her marriage contract; men have the right to unilaterally divorce their wives, whereas a woman who wishes to divorce her husband must apply for a court order; a woman can lose her right to maintenance if, for example, she refuses to have sexual relations with her husband if she does not have a lawful excuse; and women are required to "obey" their husbands. A woman may be considered disobedient, with few exceptions, if she decides to work without her husband's consent.

Domestic violence is permitted under UAE law. Article 53 of the UAE's penal code allows the imposition of "chastisement by a husband to his wife and the chastisement of minor children" so long as the assault does not exceed the limits prescribed by Sharia, or Islamic law. In 2010, the UAE's Federal Supreme Court issued a ruling—citing the UAE penal code—that sanctions beating and other forms of punishment or coercion by husbands on their wives, provided they do not leave physical marks.

LGBT Rights

The UAE's penal code does not explicitly prohibit homosexuality. However, article 356 of the penal code criminalizes zina offenses with a minimum sentence of one year in prison. Zina offenses include consensual sexual relations outside heterosexual marriage and other "moral" offenses, including same-sex relations. The UAE courts could convict and sentence people for zina offenses under article 356 which criminalizes but does not define "indecency," punishable by at least one year in prison.

Key International Actors

The UAE sent thousands of ground troops to Yemen in July to assist in the Saudi-led military campaign against Houthi forces, also known as Ansar Allah. The same month, the United States and the UAE launched an online counterterrorism messaging program, which they said "will use direct online engagement to counter terrorist propaganda rapidly and effectively."

United States

The United States has a vibrant civil society and strong constitutional protections for many civil and political rights. Yet many US laws and practices, particularly in the areas of criminal and juvenile justice, immigration, and national security, violate internationally recognized human rights. Often, those least able to defend their rights in court or through the political process—members of racial and ethnic minorities, immigrants, children, the poor, and prisoners—are the people most likely to suffer abuses.

Harsh Sentencing

The United States locks up 2.37 million people, the largest reported incarcerated population in the world. About 12 million people annually cycle through county jails.

Concerns about over-incarceration in prisons—caused in part by mandatory minimum sentencing and excessively long sentences—have led some states and the US Congress to introduce several reform bills. At time of writing, none of the federal congressional measures had become law.

Thirty-one US states continue to impose the death penalty; seven of those carried out executions in 2014. In recent decades, the vast majority of executions have occurred in five states. In August, the Connecticut Supreme Court ruled the state's death penalty unconstitutional, barring execution for the 11 men who remained on death row after the Connecticut legislature did away with the death penalty in 2007.

At time of writing, 27 people had been executed in the US in 2015, all by lethal injection. The debate over lethal injection protocols continued, with several US states continuing to use experimental drug combinations and refusing to disclose their composition. In March, Utah passed a law allowing execution by firing squad. In June, the US Supreme Court ruled that Oklahoma's lethal injection protocol was constitutional. Two prisoners executed in Oklahoma in 2014—Clayton Lockett and Michael Wilson—showed visible signs of distress as they died.

HUMAN
RIGHTS
WATCH

A PRICE TOO HIGH
US Families Torn Apart by Deportations for Drug Offenses

Racial Disparities in Criminal Justice

Racial disparities permeate every part of the US criminal justice system. Disparities in drug enforcement are particularly egregious. While whites and African Americans engage in drug offenses at comparable rates, African Americans are arrested, prosecuted, and incarcerated for drug offenses at much higher rates. African Americans are only 13 percent of the US population, but make up 29 percent of all drug arrests. Black men are incarcerated at six times the rate of white men.

A US Department of Justice report on the police department of Ferguson, Missouri, commissioned after the 2014 police killing of unarmed African American teenager Michael Brown, found that African Americans were disproportionately impacted at all levels of Ferguson's justice system—a problem that persists in justice systems throughout the country.

Drug Reform

The federal government has begun to address disproportionately long sentences for federal drug offenders. At time of writing, President Barack Obama had commuted the sentences of 86 prisoners in 2015, 76 of them drug offenders. Yet more than 35,000 federal inmates remain in prison after petitioning for reconsideration of their drug sentences. In October, the Bureau of Prisons released more than 6,000 people who had been serving disproportionately long drug sentences; the releases resulted from a retroactive reduction of federal drug sentences approved by the US Sentencing Commission.

Police Reform

Once again, high-profile police killings of unarmed African Americans gained media attention in 2015, including the deaths of Freddy Gray in Baltimore and Walter Scott in North Charleston, South Carolina. The federal government does not maintain a full count of the number of people killed by police each year. The Bureau of Justice Statistics revealed in 2015 that it tracks only 35 to 50 percent of arrest-related deaths on an annual basis. A new federal law incentivizes the collection of data regarding deaths in police custody, but does not require states to provide that data and so fails to ensure reliable data on people killed by police.

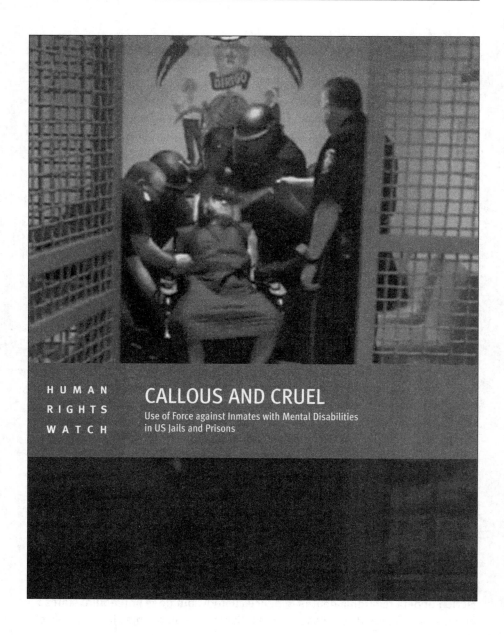

In May, Obama's Law Enforcement Equipment Working Group released recommendations to better regulate and restrict the transfer of Defense Department equipment to local law enforcement.

Prison and Jail Conditions

Momentum against the use of solitary confinement continued in 2015, but according to a new report, an estimated 100,000 state and federal prison inmates are being held in isolation.

In July, President Obama ordered the Department of Justice to review the practice of solitary confinement. Several states are currently considering legislative or regulatory reforms to reduce the use of solitary confinement. In New York, a proposed bill would limit the time during which an inmate could be held in isolation, and would ban solitary confinement for people with mental illness and other vulnerable groups. California settled a lawsuit brought by prisoners and agreed to eliminate the use of indefinite solitary confinement at the Pelican Bay State Prison—a supermax facility—as well as significantly reduce the length of time prisoners in California can be kept in solitary. However, California's legislature failed to pass a bill that would have eliminated solitary confinement for children.

Jail and prison staff throughout the US use unnecessary, excessive, and even malicious force against prisoners with mental disabilities. Although no national data exists, research—including a 2015 Human Rights Watch report—indicates that the problem is widespread and may be increasing in the country's more than 5,100 jails and prisons.

Poverty and Criminal Justice

Poor defendants nationwide are subjected to prolonged and unnecessary pretrial detention because they cannot afford to post bail. Kalief Browder committed suicide in June, two years after being released from the jail complex on New York City's Rikers Island, where from age 16 he had been held for three years in pretrial detention, mostly in solitary confinement, because he could not afford to post $3,000 in bail. His case catalyzed renewed criticism of money bail, prompting the New York City Council to announce creation of a bail fund and city officials to embrace new pretrial detention programs.

A new lawsuit challenging money bail was filed in October in San Francisco, and the governor of Connecticut has called for review of money bail in that state.

State and municipal practices that prey on low-income defendants to generate income gained increased attention after the Justice Department's report on Ferguson, Missouri described that town's municipal court system as little more than a revenue-generating machine targeting African Americans, with the Ferguson police as its "collection agency."

The privatization of misdemeanor probation services by several US states has also led to abuses, including fees structured by private probation companies in ways that penalize poor offenders or lead to the arrest of people who genuinely cannot afford to pay. In March, Georgia passed a law that imposes important new limits on the practices of such companies. Other states where private probation is widespread have thus far not taken similar steps, though awareness of probation-related abuses seems to be rising.

Youth in the Criminal Justice System

In every US jurisdiction, children are prosecuted in adult courts and sentenced to adult prison terms. Fourteen states have no minimum age for adult prosecution, while others set the age at 10, 12, or 13. Some states automatically prosecute youth age 14 and above as adults. Fifteen states give discretion to the prosecuting attorney, not a judge, to decide whether a youth is to be denied the services of the juvenile system. Tens of thousands of youth under the age of 18 are being held in adult prisons and jails across the country. The US remains the only country to sentence people under the age of 18 to life without the possibility of parole.

In 2015, there was some movement toward reducing the number of children tried as adults. In Illinois, a new law ended the automatic transfer of children under 15 to adult court. New Jersey increased the minimum age to be tried as an adult from 14 to 15. California, for the first time in 40 years, improved the statutory criteria judges use in transfer hearings, which could reduce the number of youth tried as adults.

Rights of Non-Citizens

The US government continued the dramatic expansion of detention of migrant mothers and their children from Central America, many of them seeking asylum, though it announced some reforms mid-year. Human Rights Watch has documented the severe psychological toll of indefinite detention on asylum-seeking mothers and children and the barriers it raises to due process.

In June, the Obama administration announced it would limit long-term detention of mothers and children who pass the first step to seeking refugee protection, and cease detaining individuals as a deterrent to others. A federal judge ruled in July that the US government's family detention policy violates a 1997 settlement on the detention of migrant children. While detention of families continues, most are released within weeks if they can make a seemingly legitimate asylum claim.

A federal lawsuit halted implementation of the Obama administration's November 2014 executive actions to provide a temporary reprieve from deportation to certain unauthorized immigrants, which could have protected millions of families from the threat of arbitrary separation. Legislative efforts toward legal status for millions of unauthorized migrants in the US continued to founder.

Human Rights Watch documented in June how the US government targets for deportation lawful permanent residents and other immigrants with longstanding ties to the US who have drug convictions, including for old and minor offenses. State and federal drug reform efforts have largely excluded non-citizens, who face permanent deportation and family separation for drug offenses.

Labor Rights

Hundreds of thousands of children work on US farms. US law exempts child farmworkers from the minimum age and maximum hour requirements that protect other working children. Child farmworkers often work long hours and risk pesticide exposure, heat illness, and injuries. In 2015, the Environmental Protection Agency banned children under 18 from handling pesticides. Children who work on tobacco farms frequently suffer vomiting, headaches, and other symptoms consistent with acute nicotine poisoning. After Human Rights Watch reported on hazardous child labor in US tobacco farming, the two largest US-based

tobacco companies—Altria Group and Reynolds American—independently announced that, beginning in 2015, they would prohibit their growers from employing children under 16.

Right to Health

Stark racial disparities continue to characterize the HIV epidemic in the US, as
the criminal justice system plays a key role as a barrier to HIV prevention and
care and services for groups most vulnerable to HIV, including people who use
drugs, sex workers, men who have sex with men, and transgender women.

A large outbreak of HIV and Hepatitis C infection occurred in rural southern Indi-
ana in 2015, affecting more than 180 people who inject drugs. A state law allowing needle exchange programs in response to outbreaks was passed but
maintains prohibitions on state funding for such programs as part of a broader
prevention approach.

Rights of People with Disabilities

Corporal punishment in state schools is still widely practiced in 19 US
states. Children with disabilities receive corporal punishment at a disproportionate rate to their peers, despite evidence that it can adversely affect their physical
and psychological conditions. In contrast, 124 countries have criminalized physical chastisement in public schools.

Women's and Girls' Rights

Despite Defense Department reforms, US military service members who report
sexual assault frequently experience retaliation, including threats, vandalism,
harassment, poor work assignments, loss of promotion opportunities, disciplinary action including discharge, and even criminal charges. The military does little to hold retaliators to account or provide effective remedies for retaliation. In
May, Human Rights Watch released a report that found both male and female
military personnel who report sexual assault are 12 times as likely to experience
some form of retaliation as to see their attacker convicted of a sex offense.

In June, the US Supreme Court ruled that housing policies and practices with a
disproportionate and negative impact against classes protected from discrimina-

HUMAN
RIGHTS
WATCH

EMBATTLED
Retaliation against Sexual Assault Survivors in the US Military

tion violate the Fair Housing Act, regardless of whether the policy was adopted with the intent to discriminate. The ruling is important for domestic and sexual violence victims who can face eviction due to zero-tolerance policies—where an entire household may be evicted if any member commits a crime—or municipal nuisance ordinances that subject tenants to eviction if they call the police frequently.

Sexual Orientation and Gender Identity

The US Supreme Court issued a landmark decision on June 26, 2015, that grants same-sex couples throughout the country the right to marry.

At time of writing, 28 states do not have laws banning workplace discrimination based on sexual orientation or gender identity, while three states prohibit discrimination based on sexual orientation but not on gender identity.

In July, the federal Equal Employment Opportunity Commission ruled that discrimination on the basis of sexual orientation is prohibited under the existing definition of discrimination based on sex in Title VII of the Civil Rights Act of 1964.

In June, US Immigration and Customs Enforcement (ICE) introduced a policy providing certain protections for transgender women in immigration detention. Nevertheless, transgender women in ICE custody continue to receive inadequate medical care and report verbal and sexual harassment in detention.

National Security

The practice of indefinite detention without charge or trial at Guantanamo Bay entered its 14th year; at time of writing, 107 detainees remained at the facility, 48 were cleared for release, and the Obama administration had in 2015 transferred 20 detainees to their homes or third countries.

The administration continued to pursue cases before the fundamentally flawed military commissions at Guantanamo. In June, a federal appeals court overturned the 2008 conviction of Ali Hamza Ahmad Suliman al-Bahlul, the alleged Al-Qaeda "public relations director" who was found guilty of conspiracy, soliciting murder, and providing material support for terrorism. As a result of the decision, at least five of the eight convictions imposed by the military commissions are now no longer valid.

Some detainees continued hunger strikes to protest their detention, including Tariq Ba Odah, who has been force-fed by nasal tube for several years and whose lawyers and doctors say is near death. The Obama administration opposed Odah's legal request for a court-ordered release, even though the administration had cleared him for release five years ago.

Congress and President Obama signed into law the annual National Defense Authorization Act (NDAA), which in recent years has included provisions on Guantanamo detentions. In 2015, the law tightened existing restrictions on the transfer of detainees out of Guantanamo. The provisions will make it more difficult, though not impossible, to transfer detainees home or to third countries, and maintains the complete ban on transfer of detainees to the US for detention or trial.

The release in December 2014 of a summary of a Senate Intelligence Committee report on the Central Intelligence Agency (CIA)'s detention and interrogation program uncovered new information on the methods and extent of torture and Bush administration efforts to avoid culpability. The summary sparked calls by Human Rights Watch and others for new Justice Department criminal investigations into CIA torture and other violations of federal law, and, should the US fail to act, for action by other governments, including renewed efforts in Europe where a number of cases related to CIA torture already have been filed.

In response to the Senate summary, Congress included a provision in the NDAA that requires all US government agencies except law enforcement entities to abide by rules in the Army Field Manual on interrogation, and provide the International Committee of the Red Cross with notification of, and prompt access to, all prisoners held by the US in any armed conflict. The provision will bolster existing bans on torture, but without credible criminal investigations into CIA torture it is unclear how effectively the provision will guard against future abuse.

In June, Congress took a first small step toward curbing the government's mass surveillance practices by passing the USA Freedom Act. The law imposes limits on the scope of the collection of phone records permissible under section 215 of

HUMAN
RIGHTS
WATCH

NO MORE EXCUSES
A Roadmap to Justice for CIA Torture

HUMAN
RIGHTS
WATCH

SECRET AND UNACCOUNTABLE
The Tribal Council at Lower Brule and its Impact on Human Rights

the USA Patriot Act. It also puts in place new measures to increase transparency and oversight of surveillance by the National Security Agency (NSA).

The law does not constrain surveillance under section 702 of the FISA Amendments Act or Executive Order 12333, the primary legal authorities used by the US government to justify mass violations of privacy of people outside US borders. The law also does not address many modern surveillance capabilities, from use of malware to interception of all mobile calls in a country.

US law enforcement officials continued to urge major US Internet and mobile phone companies to weaken the security of their services to facilitate surveillance in the course of criminal investigations. In May, the UN special rapporteur on freedom of expression called on all countries, including the US, to refrain from weakening encryption and other online security measures because such tools are critical for the security of human rights defenders and activists worldwide.

Foreign Policy

In July, the US and other countries reached a comprehensive deal with Iran, restricting its nuclear weapons program in exchange for sanctions relief.

Although a full drawdown of US troops from Afghanistan was planned for the end of 2014, Obama ordered 9,800 US troops to remain in Afghanistan through the end of 2015 and 5,500 to remain into 2017.

Throughout the year, the US conducted airstrikes against the forces of the armed extremist group Islamic State (also known as ISIS) in Iraq and Syria and led a coalition of Western and regional allies in what Obama called a "long-term campaign" to defeat the group. A US program to train and equip "moderate" Syrian rebels—costing hundreds of millions of dollars—only produced approximately 60 fighters, a number of whom were promptly captured or killed. The US continued to call for a political solution to the conflict in Syria without a role for President Bashar al-Assad.

In March, a Saudi-led coalition of Arab states began a military campaign against the Houthis in Yemen. The US provided intelligence, logistical support, and personnel to the Saudi Arabian center planning airstrikes and coordinating activities, making US forces potentially jointly responsible for laws-of-war violations by coalition forces.

US drone strikes continued in Yemen and Pakistan, though at reduced numbers, while US strikes increased in Somalia.

The US restored full military assistance to Egypt in April, despite a worsening human rights environment, lifting restrictions in place since the military takeover by President Abdel Fattah al-Sisi in 2013. Egypt resumed its position as the second-largest recipient of US military assistance, worth $1.3 billion annually, after Israel. In June, the US lifted its hold on military assistance to the Bahraini military despite an absence of meaningful reform, which was the original requirement for resuming the aid.

In July, President Muhammadu Buhari of Nigeria met with Obama in Washington; the US then pledged broad support for counterterrorism efforts and the fight against the militant Islamist group Boko Haram, as well as collaboration on economic development and tackling corruption. Obama in July traveled to Kenya and Ethiopia, where he urged respect for term limits across Africa.

More than 50 years since trade and diplomatic ties were severed during the Cold War, the US officially reopened diplomatic relations with Cuba in August. Obama also called for the lifting of the economic embargo, which would require an act of Congress.

In September, Obama waived provisions of the Child Soldiers Prevention Act to allow four countries—the Democratic Republic of Congo, Nigeria, Somalia, and South Sudan—to continue to receive US military assistance, despite their continued use of child soldiers. Obama delegated authority to Secretary of State John Kerry to make determinations under the act regarding Yemen, where child soldiers are used by all sides to the conflict; at time of writing, all US military aid to Yemen was suspended because of continuing instability there.

Uzbekistan

Uzbekistan maintained its appalling human rights record in 2015. A decade after government forces massacred hundreds of largely peaceful protesters in the city of Andijan, the Uzbek government continues to deny justice to the victims. In March, authoritarian President Islam Karimov's 26-year rule was extended by another five years in elections international observers found lacked any meaningful choice and violated Uzbekistan's constitution. The government denies citizens the freedoms of association, expression, and religion, using the country's pervasive security services to maintain rigid control over the population.

Thousands of people are imprisoned on politically motivated charges, torture is endemic, and authorities regularly harass human rights activists, opposition members, and journalists. Muslims and Christians who practice their religion outside strict state controls are persecuted. Authorities force millions of adults to harvest cotton every fall under harsh conditions, netting enormous profits for the government.

Despite continuing abuses, the United States and European Union failed to condition ties with Uzbekistan on improvements in human rights.

Freedom of Expression, Pluralism

In authoritarian Uzbekistan, citizens are not able to freely express their opinions on elections, form political parties, field any independent candidates, or otherwise ensure a transparent, democratic electoral process.

In the March presidential election, President Karimov stood for a fourth five-year term, despite the constitution's prohibition on serving more than two consecutive terms. In its final report, the Office for Democratic Institutions and Human Rights of the Organization for Security and Co-operation in Europe noted the election's absence of meaningful "political debate and genuine competition," stating that the fundamental freedoms of association, assembly, and expression were effectively curtailed.

Imprisonment and Harassment of Critics

The government has imprisoned thousands of people on politically motivated charges, mostly religious believers, but also human rights and opposition activists, journalists, and other perceived critics. Authorities frequently subject detainees to torture and arbitrarily extend their sentences. Many prisoners suffer from poor health.

Human rights activists in prison include Azam Farmonov, Mehriniso Hamdamova, Zulhumor Hamdamova, Isroiljon Kholdorov, Gaybullo Jalilov, Nuriddin Jumaniyazov, Matluba Kamilova, Ganikhon Mamatkhanov, Chuyan Mamatkulov, Zafarjon Rahimov, Yuldash Rasulov, Bobomurod Razzokov, Fahriddin Tillaev, and Akzam Turgunov. Journalists in prison include Solijon Abdurakhmanov, Muhammad Bekjanov, Gayrat Mikhliboev, Yusuf Ruzimuradov, and Dilmurod Saidov.

Opposition activists behind bars include Samandar Kukanov, Kudratbek Rasulov, and Rustam Usmanov. Imprisoned religious figures and other perceived government critics include Ruhiddin Fahriddinov, Akram Yuldashev, Nodirbek Yusupov, Dilorom Abdukodirova, Botirbek Eshkuziev, Bahrom Ibragimov, Davron Kabilov, Erkin Musaev, Davron Tojiev, and Ravshanbek Vafoev.

Imprisoned rights defender Azam Farmonov's nine-year prison term was due to end in April. Weeks before Farmonov's release, officials accused him of unspecified "violations of prison rules"—a practice authorities have used to arbitrarily extend political prisoners' sentences—and kept him in prison. In May, authorities extended his sentence by five years.

In May, police officers in the town of Chinaz detained Elena Urlaeva, head of the Human Rights Alliance of Uzbekistan, a local human rights group, as she was interviewing doctors and teachers forced to pick cotton. The police and medical staff forcibly sedated Urlaeva, and then subjected her to a body cavity search, X-rays, and other cruel and degrading treatment during an 11-hour interrogation, saying they were looking for a memory card from her camera.

Uzbekistan still requires exit visas for citizens to travel abroad, and authorities often withhold the visas as a tool to punish dissidents. Authorities prohibited artist Vyacheslav Okhunov from traveling abroad in 2015 after he equated Gulnara Karimova, President Karimov's daughter, with a monkey in his works of art. Many others have been banned from traveling abroad in recent years, including activists Shukhrat Rustamov, Sergei Naumov, Saida Kurbanova, Elena Urlaeva, and Uktam Pardaev.

In August, a Tashkent court upheld a lower court's finding that rights defender Shukhrat Rustamov, a longtime member of the Human Rights Alliance, was insane and should be involuntarily committed for forced psychiatric treatment. Rustamov is currently appealing the ruling. In recent years, authorities have subjected rights activists Elena Urlaeva, Jamshid Karimov, Alikul Sarymsakov, and others to forced psychiatric treatment as a form of punishment for their peaceful work.

In November, authorities allowed Murod Juraev, one of the world's longest-imprisoned political activists, to leave prison after 21 years. A former member of parliament accused of seeking to "overthrow the constitutional order," Juraev was repeatedly tortured and had his original nine-year sentence arbitrarily extended by twelve years on absurd charges, including "improperly peeling carrots" in the prison kitchen.

In December 2014, Uznews.net, a Germany-based independent news website focused on Uzbekistan, closed down. A month earlier, the names of a dozen of the site's Uzbekistan-based contributors were publicized when editor Galima Bukharbaeva's email account was hacked. She accused Uzbek security agents of responsibility.

Torture

Torture is widespread and unpunished in Uzbekistan. Detainees' rights are violated at every stage of criminal investigations and trials, despite habeas corpus amendments that went into effect in 2008. The government has failed to meaningfully implement recommendations to combat torture made by the United Nations special rapporteur on torture, the Committee against Torture, and other international bodies. The state-controlled bar association has disbarred lawyers that take on politically sensitive cases.

Following the forced return of six Uzbek asylum seekers from Norway to Uzbekistan in December 2014, authorities arrested, tortured, and tried the asylum seekers on charges of terrorism, accusing them of viewing "extremist" videos in Norway. In February 2015, state-sponsored television aired a film containing excerpts of the defendants confessing, in which the men displayed visible signs they had been tortured.

Andijan Massacre

May 13 marked 10 years since government forces killed hundreds of largely peaceful protesters in the city of Andijan. Defying numerous calls to allow an independent investigation into the massacre, Uzbek officials continued to state that the matter is "closed." On the massacre's 10th anniversary, both the Office for Democratic Institutions and Human Rights and former UN High Commissioner for Human Rights Louise Arbour renewed calls for an independent investigation.

In 2015, Human Rights Watch interviewed dozens of Uzbeks, many outside the country, who expressed fear about speaking on the record about Andijan, citing threats to themselves and family members who remain in Uzbekistan. They stated that authorities still regularly call their relatives in for questioning, and force them to sign statements saying that those who fled abroad after the massacre are terrorists. The wife of one Andijan refugee said that since the massacre, officials have interrogated her monthly, including about her husband's whereabouts, and threatened to force her into prostitution in retaliation for his participation in the protest.

Forced Labor

State-organized forced labor of adults in the cotton industry remains widespread. In 2015, authorities compelled farmers to meet an annual production quota and forced millions of adults to harvest cotton in the fall.

Teachers, doctors, nurses, civil servants, and private sector employees were forced to pick cotton under threat of dismissal from work or loss of salary and pension and welfare benefits, and authorities detained and threatened citizens attempting to report these abuses.

In September, police detained and ordered body cavity searches of activists Elena Urlaeva and Malohat Eshonqulova over the course of a 14-hour detention. On October 20, authorities filed administrative charges against activist Dmitry Tikhonov in connection with his human rights work. The same day, in circumstances that appear orchestrated by authorities, Tikhonov's home was burned down, destroying his archive of evidence of forced labor. Unknown assailants stole additional materials from a room in his home untouched by the fire.

At least six people died as a result of the unsafe working conditions during the 2015 cotton harvest, according to independent monitors.

Following a decade of global pressure, authorities did not mobilize children to harvest cotton in 2015, as in 2014, and instead increased the number of forced adult laborers. In several regions, officials also forced children to help toward the end of the harvest.

Freedom of Religion

Authorities imprison religious believers who practice their faith outside state controls. In August, the Initiative Group of Independent Human Rights Defenders estimated that more than 12,000 persons are currently imprisoned on vague charges related to "extremism" or "anti-constitutional" activity, several hundred of them convicted in the previous year. Authorities also arbitrarily detain and fine Christians who conduct religious activities for administrative offenses.

Sexual Orientation and Gender Identity

Consensual sexual relations between men are criminalized, with a maximum prison sentence of three years. Activists report that police use blackmail and extortion against gay men, threatening to out or imprison them. Lesbian, gay, bisexual, and transgender community members face deep-rooted homophobia and discrimination.

Key International Actors

During a June visit to Tashkent, UN Secretary-General Ban Ki-moon urged the Uzbek government to deliver on its international rights commitments, stating that "there can be no peace and development without human rights."

In a July 2015 review, the UN Human Rights Committee was highly critical of Uzbekistan, including concerns about politically motivated imprisonment, lack of accountability for the Andijan massacre, persistent torture, and lack of cooperation with UN human rights mechanisms. Since 2002, the government has ignored requests by at least 13 UN rights experts to visit the country.

The United States deepened its military cooperation with Uzbekistan, despite human rights concerns and a reduced need to rely on Uzbek assistance in transiting US troop supplies out of Afghanistan. In January, the State Department announced that Uzbekistan would receive more than 300 armored utility trucks, known as mine-resistant ambush protected (MRAP) vehicles, and 20 armored recovery vehicles—the largest single arms transfer ever made by the US to any Central Asian nation.

Two Congressional human rights bodies and the State Department marked the 10th anniversary of the Andijan massacre. US Secretary of State John Kerry met with President Karimov in Samarkand in November as part of a five nation Central Asia tour. While Secretary Kerry argued in a speech in Kazakhstan that Central Asian governments should uphold human rights, he did not make any specific public remarks on Uzbekistan's human rights record during the Uzbek leg of his tour.

In July, the State Department upgraded Uzbekistan's placement in the Trafficking in Persons report, a global human trafficking report, from the lowest category—Tier III—up to Tier II, despite acknowledging the government's responsibility for widespread adult forced labor. For the seventh consecutive year, the State Department designated Uzbekistan as a "country of particular concern," due to its serial violations of religious freedom, but the White House waived the sanctions envisaged under the statute, citing national security grounds.

The European Union raised concerns regarding rights abuses in Uzbekistan in the March and June sessions of the UN Human Rights Council, but the EU's overall stance on human rights remained disappointingly weak. The European External Action Service failed to publicly mark the tenth anniversary of the Andijan massacre—an event that had triggered EU sanctions between 2005 and 2009. In contrast, the European Parliament marked the anniversary by referring to an October 2014 resolution highlighting ongoing abuses in Uzbekistan, and calling for the establishment of a special rapporteur on Uzbekistan at the UN Human Rights Council.

Venezuela

Under the leadership of President Hugo Chávez and now President Nicolás Maduro, the accumulation of power in the executive branch and erosion of human rights guarantees have enabled the government to intimidate, censor, and prosecute its critics, leading to increasing levels of self-censorship.

Leading opposition politicians were arbitrarily arrested, prosecuted, convicted, and barred from running for office in legislative elections scheduled to be held in December 2015. The government prosecuted dozens of lesser-known opponents for criticizing the government.

Police abuse, poor prison conditions, and impunity for abuses by security forces—including arbitrary arrests, beatings, and denial of basic due process rights for largely peaceful protesters in early 2014—remain serious problems. Other concerns include lack of access to basic medicines and supplies—the result of problematic government policies—and continuous harassment of human rights defenders by government officials.

Security Force Abuses

In early 2014, the government responded to massive anti-government protests with brutal force. For several weeks, security forces routinely used unlawful force against unarmed protesters and bystanders. They also tolerated and sometimes collaborated directly with armed pro-government gangs that attacked protesters with impunity. Detainees were often held incommunicado on military bases for 48 hours or more before being presented to a judge, and in some cases suffered a range of abuses during detention that included severe beatings; electric shocks or burns; and being forced to squat or kneel without moving for hours.

The Attorney General's Office reported that it had opened 189 investigations into alleged security force abuses committed during the protests and that 42 law enforcement officials had been charged with improper use of force and firearms and ill-treatment of citizens. It did not give information on convictions.

Protesters continue to be subject to criminal prosecution for participating in peaceful demonstrations. In January, National Guardsmen detained Raúl Virgilio Quintero García, a university student, for taking a picture of people waiting in line to purchase goods at a supermarket in Caracas. Six demonstrators who had been peacefully protesting against the long lines, and a cameraman filming them, were also detained. Quintero was charged with several crimes and released, but remains subject to criminal prosecution.

Starting in July 2015, President Maduro deployed more than 80,000 members of security forces nationwide in "Operation Peoples' Liberation" to address rising security concerns, as well as illegal sales of scarce products. During these operations, security forces violated fundamental rights through arbitrary detentions, illegal home searches, and verbal and physical abuse. The government reported dozens of killings during the operations; in several cases, there have been credible allegations that some victims were extrajudicially executed.

Arbitrary Deportations

In August, the president declared a state of emergency in six municipalities in Táchira State near the Colombian border. Between August and late September, Venezuelan security forces deported more than 1,700 Colombians. At least 22,000 more left Venezuela fearing abuses or deportation. Hundreds of Colombians claim to have suffered forceful eviction from their homes, which were subsequently destroyed; verbal and physical abuse by Venezuelan security forces; and forceful separation of families. Some deported Colombians had legal permits to live in Venezuela but were not allowed to challenge their deportations.

Judicial Independence

Since former President Chávez and his supporters in the National Assembly conducted a political takeover of the Supreme Court in 2004, the judiciary has ceased to function as an independent branch of government. Members of the Supreme Court have openly rejected the principle of separation of powers, publicly pledged their commitment to advancing the government's political agenda, and repeatedly ruled in favor of the government, validating its growing disregard for human rights.

Judge María Lourdes Afiuni remains under criminal prosecution as a result of a 2009 ruling in which she authorized the conditional release of a government critic. Although Afiuni's ruling complied with a recommendation by international human rights monitors and was consistent with Venezuelan law, a provisional judge who had publicly pledged his loyalty to Chávez ordered her to stand trial on charges of corruption, abuse of authority, and "favoring the evasion of justice." After a year in prison and two under house arrest, she was released but remains subject to criminal prosecution.

Prosecution of Critics

Venezuelan authorities have repeatedly abused the justice system's lack of independence to arrest and prosecute prominent political opponents.

In September, a judge convicted Leopoldo López, an opposition leader, and sentenced him to more than 13 years in prison for crimes that include "public incitement" to commit crimes during a demonstration in Caracas in February 2014. Three students whose cases were linked to López's were also sentenced, two to four-and-a-half years, and one to more than 10. The judge ruled all three could serve their sentences in conditional liberty.

During Lopez's trial, the prosecution failed to provide credible evidence linking him to a crime, and the presiding judge, who is a provisional judge and lacks security of tenure, had not allowed his lawyers to present evidence in his defense. In October, one of the prosecutors fled Venezuela and claimed the case had been a "farce."

Authorities have also brought or threatened to bring criminal charges against dozens of Venezuelans for criticizing the government. For example, in February, National Bolivarian Intelligence Service (SEBIN) agents detained a medical doctor and threatened him with prosecution for criticizing shortages of medicines on television. In April, SEBIN agents detained an engineer after a local newspaper quoted him criticizing government policies that regulate access to electricity. In July, SEBIN agents detained a businessman a day after he criticized on television the government's economic policies.

Lawyers have been prosecuted for providing legitimate legal assistance to clients. Marcelo Crovato was detained in April 2014 while advising a neighbor whose home was being illegally searched during the protests. He was charged with crimes that included "instigation to disobey the law" and belonging to an "association to commit crimes." Even though prosecutors did not provide any credible evidence against him, Crovato spent nearly 10 months in prison until February, when he was granted house arrest for medical reasons. At time of writing, Crovato remained subject to criminal prosecution.

Freedom of Expression

Over the past decade, the government has expanded and abused its powers to regulate media and has taken aggressive steps to reduce the availability of media outlets that engage in critical programming. While criticism of the government is articulated in some newspapers and on some websites and radio stations, fear of government reprisals has made self-censorship a serious problem.

In 2010, the National Assembly amended the telecommunications law to grant the government power to suspend or revoke concessions to private outlets if it is "convenient for the interests of the nation." It also expanded the scope of a restrictive broadcasting statute to cover the Internet, allowing the arbitrary suspension of websites for the vaguely defined offense of "incitement." Previous amendments to the criminal code had expanded the scope and severity of defamation laws that criminalize "disrespect" of high government officials.

In April, Diosdado Cabello, the pro-government National Assembly president, filed civil and criminal charges of aggravated defamation against 22 "shareholders, editors, editorial boards, and owners" of the Venezuelan newspapers *Tal Cual* and *El Nacional* and the news website La Patilla for reproducing an article by the Spanish newspaper *ABC*. The article included statements allegedly made by Cabello's former bodyguard, who the reports said was collaborating with United States authorities to investigate whether Cabello had links to a drug cartel.

Human Rights Defenders

Venezuela's government has sought to marginalize the country's human rights defenders through repeated unsubstantiated allegations that they are seeking to undermine Venezuelan democracy. During his weekly show on state-run television in 2015, Cabello repeatedly characterized human rights groups' participation in hearings before the Inter-American Commission on Human Rights (IACHR) or United Nations human rights monitoring bodies as attempts "to destabilize the government."

In October, three unidentified individuals kidnapped for several hours and robbed Marino Alvarado, a well-known human rights defender who works at the Venezuelan nongovernmental organization Provea. Before the incident, Alvarado had requested the intervention of the IACHR, fearing for his life and physical integrity after Cabello and President Maduro openly questioned Alvarado's and Provea's activities and sources of funding. The IACHR ordered the government two weeks later to protect Alvarado and other Provea staff.

In 2010, the Supreme Court ruled that individuals or organizations that receive foreign funding could be prosecuted for "treason." In addition, the National Assembly enacted legislation blocking organizations that "defend political rights" or "monitor the performance of public bodies" from receiving international assistance.

Prison Conditions

Corruption, weak security, deteriorating infrastructure, overcrowding, insufficient staffing, and poorly trained guards allow armed gangs to effectively control the prisons in which they are incarcerated. The Venezuelan Observatory of Prisons, a human rights group, reports that 6,472 people died and 16,387 were injured in prisons between 1999 and 2014. As of July, 63 percent of the more than 50,000 people in prison were in pretrial detention, and more than 100 people had died in prison, according to the Observatory.

Right to Health

The government has failed to ensure that basic medicines and supplies are available and accessible to all Venezuelans without discrimination. It has failed to provide the public health care system with medicines and supplies, and at the same time its currency exchange rules and price controls interfere with the import of medicines and health care products, resulting in a grossly inadequate supply of essential medications and medical supplies.

In March, a network of medical residents working in public hospitals throughout the country reported that 44 percent of the nation's operating rooms were not functional and 94 percent of labs did not have the materials they needed to operate properly. They also found that 60 percent of medicines or supplies routinely stocked in hospitals elsewhere were entirely or partially unavailable in Venezuelan ones, and that essential medicines were not available in pharmacies.

Labor Rights

Labor legislation adopted in April 2012 includes provisions that limit the freedom of unions to draft their statutes and elect their representatives. In practice, the National Electoral Council (CNE), a public authority, continues to play a role in union elections, violating international standards that require that these elections be held without government interference.

Key International Actors

The UN high commissioner for human rights and several UN rapporteurs have expressed concern regarding the deteriorating human rights conditions in Venezuela, including the government's harsh responses to criticism and peaceful expressions of dissent, intimidation campaigns against human rights defenders, and mistreatment and torture of detainees.

The UN Human Rights Committee and the UN Committee on Economic, Social, and Cultural Rights expressed serious concerns regarding a range of violations, including the process to appoint and remove judges, which undermines judicial independence; limited access to information held by the government; the critical situation of Venezuela's health care system; and violence and intimidation against union leaders.

In July the Inter-American Court of Human Rights (IACrtHR) ruled that Venezuela had violated free expression rights when it arbitrarily took off air the critical TV station RCTV in 2007, and ordered the government to reinstate the channel.

Due to the government's decision to withdraw from the American Convention on Human Rights, Venezuelan citizens and residents are unable to request the intervention of the IACrtHR when local remedies are ineffective or unavailable for abuses committed since September 2013. The IACHR has continued to monitor the situation in Venezuela, applying the American Declaration of Rights and Duties of Man, which does not require states' ratification.

Regional bodies such as the Union of South American Nations (UNASUR) and the Common Market of the South (MERCOSUR) have failed to call on Venezuela to address abuses. Although some Latin American governments—including Chile, Colombia, Costa Rica, and Paraguay—publicly commented on López's conviction, most regional leaders have remained silent regarding the human rights situation in Venezuela.

In November, Organization of American States Secretary General Luis Almagro broke the silence by publishing a letter criticizing the jailing of López and other Maduro administration abuses of power. Days later, Argentine President-Elect Mauricio Macri stated that once in office he would request that Venezuela be suspended from MERCOSUR pursuant to a provision in the regional body's founding treaty that allows state parties to suspend others when there is a "breach" in their "democratic order."

In December 2014, the US adopted legislation that allows it to freeze assets and ban visas for those accused of committing abuses against anti-government demonstrators during the 2014 protests. In March, President Barack Obama issued an executive order imposing targeted sanctions against seven Venezuelan government officials.

Venezuela is currently serving on the UN Security Council where it is the chair of the sanctions committees for Sudan, Somalia, and Eritrea. As a member of the UN Human Rights Council, Venezuela regularly voted to prevent scrutiny of serious human rights situations around the world, voting against resolutions spotlighting abuses in North Korea, Syria, Iran, Belarus, and Ukraine. Venezuela's October 2015 campaign for a second term on the Human Rights Council was successful.

In November 2015, President Maduro addressed the Human Rights Council at a special meeting convened at his request. In a taped statement, the UN high commissioner for human rights noted that he shared concerns expressed by the UN Human Rights Committee about intimidation, threats, and attacks against journalists, human rights defenders, and lawyers in Venezuela. Despite repeated requests, Venezuela has not allowed any UN special procedures to visit the country since 1996.

Vietnam

Despite renewed economic growth and progress on a number of social indicators in 2015, Vietnam's record on civil and political rights remained dismal. The ruling Communist Party has a monopoly on political power and allows no challenge to its leadership. Basic rights, including freedoms of speech, opinion, press, association, and religion, are restricted. Rights activists and dissident bloggers face constant harassment and intimidation, including physical assault and imprisonment. Farmers continue to lose land to development projects without adequate compensation, and workers are not allowed to form independent unions.

Analysts suggested that the government was trying to keep the number of political arrests and trials to a minimum in 2015 because it faced scrutiny from the United States Congress as negotiations over the Trans-Pacific Partnership (TPP) neared completion. Even so, there were many notable instances of government persecution of critics.

Police abuse received increasing attention from local media in 2015, but police still frequently torture suspects to elicit confessions and sometimes use excessive force in responding to protests over evictions, land confiscation, and other social issues. The government took no steps in 2015 to repeal laws criminalizing peaceful expression.

Government Critics and Activists

The government's crackdown on independent writers, bloggers, and rights activists deemed threatening to Communist Party rule continued in 2015.

Bloggers Nguyen Huu Vinh (known as Anh Ba Sam), Nguyen Thi Minh Thuy, and Nguyen Dinh Ngoc (known as Nguyen Ngoc Gia), arrested in 2014, remained in police custody and had still not been put on trial at time of writing.

In February 2015, the People's Court of Dong Nai province put rights activists Pham Minh Vu, Do Nam Trung, and Le Thi Phuong Anh on trial for "abusing the rights to freedom and democracy to infringe upon the interests of the state," an offense under penal code article 258. They were sentenced to 18, 14, and 12 months in prison, respectively.

In April, the authorities arrested Nguyen Viet Dung for participating in a "pro-tree" peaceful march at Hoan Kiem lake in Hanoi and charged him with disrupting public order under article 245 of the penal code. In August, police in Thanh

Hoa province arrested Dinh Tat Thang for sending out letters criticizing provincial leaders and police. He was charged under article 258. In September, police in Thai Binh province arrested former political prisoner Tran Anh Kim for "activities aiming to overthrow the people's administration" under penal code article 79. Tran Anh Kim had recently finished a five-year, six-month prison sentence in January 2015, also under article 79.

In September, the government temporarily suspended the sentence of prominent blogger Ta Phong Tan, who was then escorted directly from prison to Noi Bai airport for the US. As with legal activist Cu Huy Ha Vu and blogger Nguyen Van Hai (known as Dieu Cay), who were similarly exiled to the US in 2014, Ta Phong Tan would have to serve the rest of her 10-year sentence were she to return to Vietnam.

During the first nine months of 2015, at least 40 bloggers and rights activists were beaten by plainclothes agents. They included Pham Doan Trang, Nguyen Tuong Thuy, Nguyen Huu Vinh, Tran Thi Nga, Nguyen Chi Tuyen, Trinh Anh Tuan, Dinh Quang Tuyen, Nguyen Ngoc Nhu Quynh, Chu Manh Son, and Dinh Thi Phuong Thao. No one involved in the assaults was held accountable.

Freedom of Religion

The government restricts religious practice through legislation, registration requirements, harassment, and surveillance. Religious groups are required to gain approval from and register with the government, as well as operate under government-controlled management boards.

While authorities allow many government-affiliated churches and pagodas to hold worship services, they ban religious activities that they arbitrarily deem contrary to the "national interest," "public order," or "national great unity." In 2015, authorities interfered with the religious activities of unrecognized branches of the Cao Dai church, the Hoa Hao Buddhist church, independent Protestant and Catholic house churches in the central highlands and elsewhere, Khmer Krom Buddhist temples, and the Unified Buddhist Church of Vietnam.

In January 2015, UN Special Rapporteur on Freedom of Religion or Belief Heiner Bielefeldt issued a report identifying "serious problems" in Vietnam's approach to religion, notably "legal provisions that tend to give broad leeway to regulate, limit, restrict or forbid the exercise of freedom of religion or belief."

In April 2015, the Ministry of Interior published the fourth draft of a Law on Belief and Religion, scheduled to be approved by the National Assembly in 2016. Although the draft contains a few marginal improvements on the existing legal framework, it maintains mechanisms allowing authorities to persecute religious groups they dislike and could even give such mechanisms greater legal force.

Members of ethnic minorities in the Central Highlands continue to be accused of religious "evil ways" and politically "autonomous thoughts" and subjected to intimidation, forced renunciation of faith, arbitrary arrests, and mistreatment in custody.

In January, April, and July, police prohibited unsanctioned Buddhist Hoa Hao groups from commemorating the anniversaries of the birth and death of Hoa Hao founder Huynh Phu So and of his establishment of the Hoa Hao faith. Participants were intimidated, harassed, and assaulted.

In January 2015, local authorities prevented members of an independent Mennonite church in Ho Chi Minh City from gathering to pray. Mennonite Pastor Nguyen Hong Quang was repeatedly assaulted during the year. Thugs also attacked other religious figures, including Mennonite pastors Huynh Thuc Khai and Le Quang Du, Hoa Hao Buddhist activist Vo Van Thanh Liem, and Buddhist monk Thich Khong Tanh.

Criminal Justice System

Vietnamese courts remained firmly under the control of the government and Communist Party, and trials of political and religious dissidents consistently failed to meet international fair trial standards. Police regularly intimidated and in some cases detained family members and friends who tried to attend trials.

Deaths in police custody continued to be reported in 2015. In July, Vu Nam Ninh died in Detention Center No.1 (Hanoi). According to the victim's family, "there were serious injuries all over his body; his face, chest and arms were swollen; his nose, collarbone and fingers were broken ... there was a deep stab on his left leg and blood in his nose. There were serious bruises on the shoulders, nape and underarms." The police told media that the case is under investigation.

People who are dependent on drugs, including children, continued to be held in government detention centers where they are forced to perform menial work in

HUMAN
RIGHTS
WATCH

PERSECUTING "EVIL WAY" RELIGION
Abuses against Montagnards in Vietnam

the name of "labor therapy." Violations of center rules and failure to meet work quotas are punished by beatings and confinement to disciplinary rooms where detainees claim they are deprived of food and water. In 2015, the government reduced the overall number of detainees, but confirmed plans to leave some 15,000 detainees in the centers by 2020.

Key International Actors

Vietnam's most important foreign relations were with China and the US, but linkages with Japan, Cambodia, the European Union, the Association of Southeast Asian Nations, and Australia were also significant.

Vietnam's relationship with China continued to be complicated by maritime territorial disputes, though perhaps more important for both was the shared commitment by each country's communist party to maintain its rule. Chinese President Xi Jinping visited Vietnam in November 2015.

The US continued to deepen ties with Vietnam across the board. It made some efforts to press Hanoi to improve its human rights record, but the issue was not prominent in the meeting between President Barack Obama and Communist Party General Secretary Nguyen Phu Trong during Trong's visit in to the US in July 2015, the first-ever White House visit by the head of the Vietnamese Communist Party.

The EU made few efforts to promote respect for rights. In August, the EU and Vietnam reached an agreement in principle on a free trade agreement. Japan failed to use its status as Vietnam's largest bilateral donor to publicly press for reforms even as, in July, it completed TPP bilateral negotiations with Vietnam.

Australia's relationship with Vietnam continued to grow, also with little attention to human rights. The two countries signed the Declaration on Enhancing the Australia-Vietnam Comprehensive Partnership in March and held their 12th human rights dialogue in August.

Vietnam maintained close security ties with Cambodia, despite some border friction between the two countries. Vietnam successfully pressured Cambodia to refuse to register hundreds of Vietnamese Montagnards as asylum seekers and to return dozens of Montagnards back to Vietnam where many have been subjected to persecution.

Yemen

In January 2015, Houthi forces, also known as Ansar Allah, effectively ousted Yemeni President Abdu Rabu Mansour Hadi and his cabinet; he subsequently re-located to Saudi Arabia and re-established a government there.

In March, after Houthi and allied forces advanced south, threatening the port city of Aden, a Saudi Arabia-led coalition of Arab countries, with the participation of the United States, began a campaign of airstrikes against them. On March 26, coalition warplanes attacked Houthi forces in Sanaa, the capital, and other locations. The airstrikes continued throughout 2015 as fighting occurred across the country, with Bahrain, Sudan, Saudi Arabia, and the United Arab Emirates sending ground troops to battle Houthi and allied forces.

Dozens of coalition airstrikes were indiscriminate, violating the laws of war and killing and wounding thousands of civilians. The coalition also used cluster munitions, banned by international treaty. Houthi forces also committed serious laws-of-war violations by firing indiscriminate rockets into southern cities and Saudi Arabia, killing dozens of civilians.

They also laid banned antipersonnel mines in eastern and southern Yemen before withdrawing. Southern forces, supported by the Saudi-led coalition, also committed serious abuses, executing Houthi prisoners in Aden. None of the warring parties carried out meaningful investigations into their forces' alleged violations.

Airstrikes

Human Rights Watch documented dozens of coalition airstrikes that appear to have been unlawfully indiscriminate, causing civilian casualties, some of which may have amounted to war crimes. They include a March 30 airstrike on a camp for internally displaced persons near Yemen's border with Saudi Arabia that killed at least 29 civilians; a March 31 airstrike on a dairy factory outside Hodaida that killed at least 31 civilians; a May 12 airstrike on a market and neighboring lemon grove in the town of Zabid, south of Hodaida, killing at least 60 civilians; a July 4, airstrike on a village market in Muthalith Ahim, south of the

HUMAN RIGHTS WATCH

TARGETING SAADA
Unlawful Coalition Airstrikes on Saada City in Yemen

Saudi border, killing at least 65 people; and a July 24 airstrike on homes in the port city of Mokha that killed at least 65 civilians.

In the Houthi's northern stronghold of Saada, Human Rights Watch examined a dozen coalition airstrikes that destroyed or damaged homes, five markets, a school, and a gas station, but found no evidence of military targets. The strikes killed 59 people, all reportedly civilians, including at least 35 children, between April 6 and May 11.

Cluster Munitions

Human Rights Watch documented the use by coalition forces of three types of cluster munitions in Yemen in 2015, while Amnesty International documented the coalition's use of a fourth type of cluster munition in November 2015. A fifth type of cluster munition has been used, but the actor responsible is unclear. Yemen, Saudi Arabia, and other coalition states are not party to the 2008 Convention on Cluster Munitions.

In May, following Human Rights Watch's second report on the use of CBU-105 sensor fuzed weapons in Saada, the Saudi military acknowledged that coalition forces had used the weapon.

In August, the Saudi military responded to a new Human Rights Watch report that documented the coalition's use of M26 cluster munition rockets at least seven times in Hajja governorate, killing or wounding at least 35 civilians. A Saudi coalition spokesperson denied use of the M26 cluster munition rockets.

In August, a US Defense Department official, speaking on condition of anonymity, told media that "the US is aware that Saudi Arabia has used cluster munitions in Yemen."

The United Nations, International Committee of the Red Cross (ICRC), and more than 15 governments have condemned the use of cluster munitions in Yemen, as did the European Parliament in a July 9 resolution.

Landmines

Houthi forces laid numerous landmines, including banned antipersonnel mines in Yemen's southern and eastern governorates of Abyan, Aden, Marib, Lahj and

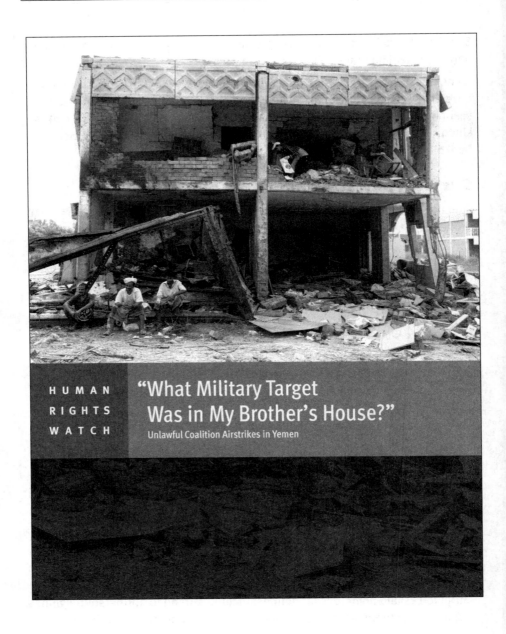

HUMAN
RIGHTS
WATCH

"What Military Target
Was in My Brother's House?"
Unlawful Coalition Airstrikes in Yemen

Taizz since July. Landmines and explosive remnants of war killed at least 23 people and wounded others, including two deminers, according to Yemeni mine clearance officials, medical professionals, and media reports.

Antivehicle mines accounted for nine of those killed and five injured, although whether the mine is antivehicle or antipersonnel is often not detailed in reporting. Human Rights Watch believes that the actual number of mine victims in Yemen may be much higher.

Indiscriminate Attacks

Before and since the coalition air campaign, Houthi and allied forces have used artillery rockets in indiscriminate attacks in the southern cities of Taizz, Lahj, al-Dale`a, and Aden, killing dozens of civilians. Houthis have also launched artillery rockets into the southern Saudi Arabian border city of Najran and areas of Jizan province.

Attacks on Health and Humanitarian Workers

During 2015, at least three ICRC staff and two Yemen Red Crescent Society (YRCS) staff were killed while engaged in humanitarian operations. On July 31, the British Red Cross reported that a wounded patient died when a YRCS ambulance came under fire in Taizz.

Houthi and allied forces engaged in military operations around Aden, Taizz, and other areas and opposing Southern forces repeatedly exposed hospitals, patients, and health workers to unjustified risk. In one case in Aden, Southern forces sought cover in a hospital, putting its staff and patients in jeopardy. At least two civilians died and a nurse was wounded.

According to the United Nations Office for the Coordination of Humanitarian Affairs (OCHA), as of September 2015, at least 160 health facilities had closed due to insecurity caused by the conflict.

In at least four instances, Houthi forces unlawfully detained aid workers attempting to deliver medical supplies to healthcare facilities.

Children and Armed Conflict

In 2015, the Houthis and other armed groups, including tribal and Islamist militias such as Al-Qaeda in the Arabian Peninsula (AQAP), increased their recruitment, training, and deployment of children. According to UNICEF, by August 2015, armed groups had recruited 377 children, more than double those they recruited in 2014. At least 398 children were killed and 605 wounded between late March and August as a result of the fighting in the country.

Under Yemeni law, 18 is the minimum age for military service. In 2014, the government signed a UN action plan to end the use of child soldiers. Without an effective government in place, the action plan has not been implemented.

In September, the Yemen Sanctions Committee and the Working Group on Children and Armed Conflict held informal joint consultations on the conflict in Yemen.

According to OCHA, as of September 18, approximately 140 schools had been destroyed, and another 390 damaged by the fighting. In August 2015, UNICEF estimated that at least 3,600 schools were closed, affecting 1.8 million children.

Terrorism and Counterterrorism

Both AQAP and armed groups loyal to the armed extremist group Islamic State (also known as ISIS) claimed responsibility for numerous suicide and other bombings that killed dozens of civilians. AQAP claimed responsibility for the January 7 attack that killed 11 people associated with the French satirical magazine *Charlie Hebdo* in Paris.

On December 6, 2014, two hostages held by AQAP were killed during a rescue effort by US special forces in southeastern Shabwa governorate.

The US continued its drone attacks on alleged AQAP members; independent research groups reported 15 to 20 strikes by mid-November. AQAP confirmed that a strike on June 12 killed its leader Nasir al-Wuhayshi.

The US remained unwilling to publish basic data related to the drone strikes, including the number of civilian casualties and information on unlawful strikes. Research groups estimate the strikes—one in 2002 and at least 210 since 2009— have killed 700 people. It is not known how many were in violation of interna-

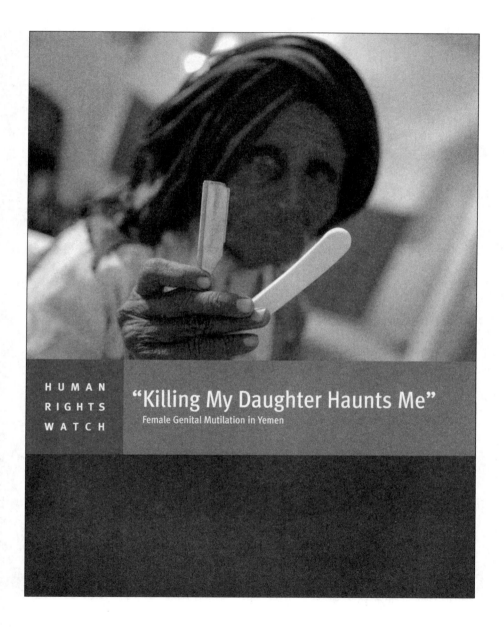

HUMAN
RIGHTS
WATCH

"Killing My Daughter Haunts Me"
Female Genital Mutilation in Yemen

tional law. On June 8, a Yemeni citizen filed a lawsuit in US federal court seeking formal US acknowledgement that a US drone strike in August 2012 killed two of his relatives, including a cleric who preached against AQAP. The suit sought an apology but no compensation.

Harassment of Critics

After Houthi and allied forces seized control of Sanaa, they cracked down on dissent. Between January 25 and February 11, these forces beat peaceful protesters against the takeover with sticks and rifle butts. They arbitrarily detained at least 46 protesters, some for 13 days.

On February 8, Yemen's Interior Ministry ordered Sanaa police to prevent all unauthorized demonstrations due to "the exceptional circumstances" in Yemen, and on February 11, the Houthis detained three men attempting to join a protest and tortured them, in one case to death.

The Houthis arbitrarily detained activists, tribal leaders, and political opponents incommunicado for months. They also committed enforced disappearances.

The Houthis also targeted critical journalists. The Freedom Foundation, a Yemeni group that monitors press freedom, reported at least 49 attacks on media in January 2015 alone, while the Yemeni Journalists' Syndicate reported that Houthi forces beat at least 10 journalists, cameramen, and photographers as they covered the January and February 2015 protests, arbitrarily detaining seven and seizing or smashing equipment. Human Rights Watch documented seven attacks on media in early 2015.

In May, Houthi forces arbitrarily detained Abdullah Qabil and Yousef al-Ayzari, journalists who had criticized the Houthis. Both journalists died when a coalition airstrike hit the building in Dhamar where they were detained.

Women's and Girls' Rights

Women in Yemen face severe discrimination in law and practice. They cannot marry without the permission of their male guardian and do not have equal rights to divorce, inheritance, or child custody. Lack of legal protection leaves them exposed to domestic and sexual violence. In the absence of a functioning government, no advances were made to pass a draft constitution that includes provisions guaranteeing equality and prohibiting discrimination based on gender, and a draft Child Rights Law that would criminalize child marriage and female genital mutilation.

Sexual Orientation and Gender Identity

Yemen's penal code prohibits same-sex relations. Sex between women is punishable by up to three years in prison and 100 lashes, while sex between men is punishable by whipping, imprisonment, and death by stoning.

Key International Actors

The United Kingdom is responsible for preparing first drafts of all United Nations Security Council resolutions on Yemen. The Security Council issued resolutions on the crisis in February and April 2015. In September 2015, UK International Development Secretary Justine Greening warned that "the lack of international action on the crisis in Yemen shows worrying parallels with the delayed response to the famine in Somalia."

In September, the high commissioner for human rights recommended establishing an independent, international, and impartial mechanism to investigate alleged abuses committed in Yemen. In a joint statement in September, the UN special advisor on the prevention of genocide and the UN special adviser on the responsibility to protect issued a joint statement that endorsed the high commissioner's conclusion and underscored the "urgent need to establish credible and independent investigations" to hold perpetrators accountable and secure reparations for victims.

Reporting to the Human Rights Council in September, the high commissioner for human rights recommended the "establishment of an independent, international, and impartial mechanism to investigate alleged violations" committed in Yemen. Yemen responded by announcing the creation of a purely domestic mechanism.

An initial draft resolution presented by the Netherlands would have requested the OHCHR dispatch a mission to monitor and report on violations. The Dutch text was withdrawn in the face of a competing draft, presented by Saudi Arabia on behalf of the Arab Group, together with Yemen, which merely requests that the high commissioner provide "technical assistance" and assist the national commission of inquiry in meeting international standards. The Arab Group text was adopted by consensus.

The high commissioner is requested to report to the council in March and September 2016, and a number of states highlighted that the council should remain ready to press for a greater international investigative role if civilian casualties continue and the national process is inadequate.

Zimbabwe

Zimbabwean President Robert Mugabe consolidated his grip on power and failed to introduce any meaningful human rights reforms in 2015. In December 2014, Mugabe fired reformist Vice President Joyce Mujuru, apparently because he considered her disloyal, and replaced her with two co-vice presidents, Emmerson Mnangagwa and Phelekezela Mphoko. Both are implicated in serious past human rights abuses.

Mugabe secured the endorsement of the ruling ZANU-PF party to be the 2018 presidential candidate (when he will be 94), appointed his wife to head the party's women's wing, and amended the party constitution to allow him to make all senior party appointments.

The government faced severe socioeconomic challenges and did not invest in desperately needed public services such as water, education, health, and sanitation. About 82 percent of the national budget was allocated to civil service salaries, much of which appears to have disappeared through corruption. The International Monetary Fund (IMF) estimated that Zimbabwe's external debt obligations were over 80 percent of the country's gross domestic product.

Those who criticized Mugabe or his government, including human rights defenders, civil society activists, political opponents, and outspoken street vendors, were harassed, threatened, or arbitrarily arrested by police and state security agents. The authorities disparaged lesbian, gay, bisexual, and transgender (LGBT) people. There was no progress toward justice for past human rights violations and political violence.

Attacks on Human Rights Defenders

Itai Dzamara, a pro-democracy activist and human rights defender, was forcibly disappeared on March 9, 2015. Dzamara, the leader of Occupy Africa Unity Square—a small protest group modelled after the Arab Spring uprisings—had led a number of peaceful protests concerning the deteriorating political and economic environment in Zimbabwe in 2014 and 2015. He had petitioned Mugabe to resign and for reforms to the electoral system. Police ZANU-PF supporters assaulted him on several occasions, including during a peaceful protest in Novem-

HUMAN
RIGHTS
WATCH

HOMELESS, LANDLESS, AND DESTITUTE
The Plight of Zimbabwe's Tokwe-Mukorsi Flood Victims

ber 2014, when about 20 uniformed police handcuffed and hit him with batons until he lost consciousness. When Kennedy Masiye, his lawyer, tried to intervene, the police beat him up, breaking his arm.

Zimbabwe authorities denied any involvement in Dzamara's abduction, but state authorities have not conducted any meaningful investigation. When Dzamara's wife, Sheffra Dzamara, approached the high court in Harare to compel state authorities to search for her husband, government officials failed to comply with the court order to report on the investigation's progress.

On April 25, activists organized a car procession to raise awareness about Dzamara's case. Police arrested 11 activists and detained them for six hours, then released them without charge.

On January 27, 2015, five community leaders representing 20,000 Tokwe-Mukorsi dam flood victims (see below) were sentenced to five years in prison for public violence after they organized a demonstration to protest the government's failure to compensate them for the loss of their land and the dire conditions in which they lived. Authorities had arrested the community leaders in August 2014, including Mike Mudyanembwa, the chair of the victims' Chingwizi Camp Committee, who did not participate in the demonstration. Their lawyers alleged that they were tortured in prison.

On July 24, police wrongfully arrested three activists—Edgar Gweshe, Charles Nyoni, and Don Makuwaza—who they said had taken photographs at Harare Remand Prison, which is prohibited under the Protected Places and Areas Act. On July 25, police arrested three more activists—Mfundo Mlilo, Nixon Nyikadzino, and Dirk Frey—on trumped-up charges of organizing a meeting outside Harare Remand Prison in violation of the Public Order and Security Act (POSA).

Government Opponents and Other Critics

Police and state security agents targeted perceived govenrment opponents and critics. They threatened, kept under surveillance, and arbitrarily arrested supporters of former Vice President Joyce Mujuru after she was removed from her post and considered forming an opposition party.

In November 2014, police arrested and detained former leader of the war veterans and key Mujuru supporter, Jabulani Sibanda, on charges of undermining Mugabe's authority. Sibanda was released on bail after five days in detention. He said he received death threats from state security agents after he was released from detention. In February, April, and June 2015, police arrested and briefly detained Temba Mliswa, another expelled senior ZANU-PF official, on spurious charges.

On July 14, police beat and arrested 16 street vendors, including Sten Zvorwadza, Samuel Wadzanai Mangoma, and Lucy Makunde, leaders of the National Vendors Union of Zimbabwe (NAVUZ), and brought trumped-up charges of inciting public violence against them. The arrests were part of a violent crackdown on unlicensed street vendors—mostly women living in extreme poverty—in the capital, Harare, during a government "clean-up" campaign. The crackdown was marked by beatings, destruction of goods, and arbitrary arrests.

Internally Displaced Persons

The government ignored the plight of the 20,000 people who fled their homes because of massive flooding at Zimbabwe's Tokwe-Mukorsi dam in February 2014. It coerced the flood victims to resettle onto one-hectare plots at a farm with close links to the ZANU-PF party, without paying them fair compensation. The flood victims lacked adequate shelter, safe drinking water, and access to sanitation and health services.

According to the governmental Zimbabwe Human Rights Commission (ZHRC), the flooding "was not natural, but [a] man-made disaster" and could have been avoided. It urged the government to protect the basic rights of all the flood victims. In July 2015, the flood victims sent a desperate plea to Mugabe to provide them with basic services, adequate compensation for the loss of their land, and full consultations about their future resettlement. He did not respond.

Rule of Law

Mugabe's government continued to ignore human rights provisions in the country's 2013 constitution, neither enacting laws to put the constitution into effect nor amending existing laws to bring them in line with the constitution and Zimbabwe's international and regional human rights obligations. The government has yet to repeal or amend the Access to Information and Protection of Privacy

Act (AIPPA) and the Public Order and Security Act, among others, whose provisions severely restrict basic rights and are contrary to the constitution.

The government lacked comprehensive strategies to curb the rising practice of child marriage. The United Nations Children's Fund (UNICEF) said nearly one-third of girls in Zimbabwe marry before their 18th birthday and 4 percent marry before they turn 15. In June, the prosecutor general said girls as young as 12 can marry if they give their consent, undermining efforts to curb the harmful practice. He later denied making the statement. Two former child brides launched a legal appeal at the Constitutional Court of Zimbabwe in January to declare child marriage illegal and unconstitutional. The court was still considering the case at time of writing.

There was no progress on establishing the constitutionally mandated National Peace and Reconciliation Commission (NPRC) for post-conflict justice, healing, and reconciliation. To date, no independent mechanism has addressed serious past human rights crimes, including widespread election-related violence and the massacre of an estimated 20,000 people in the Matebeleland and Midlands provinces in the 1980s.

Sexual Orientation and Gender Identity

Authorities continued to violate rights of LGBT people. A Zimbabwe Human Rights Commission report published in July showed continued hostility and systematic discrimination by police and politicians against LGBT people, driving many underground.

Police did not conduct serious investigations or arrest any suspects in the December 2014 attack at a Christmas party organized by the activist group Gays and Lesbians of Zimbabwe (GALZ), during which 12 armed men invaded the private party and seriously injured 35 people with chains, sjamboks, and long sticks.

Key International Actors

In February, the European Union announced it would resume development aid to Zimbabwe after 12 years of sanctions with an aid package of €237 million

(US$252.37 million) over five years. EU officials said they would closely monitor the funds to ensure they were not misused.

In April, the European Parliament issued a resolution strongly condemning Itai Dzamara's forced disappearance and calling for his immediate and unconditional release. The EU urged Zimbabwean authorities to take all necessary measures to find Dzamara and bring those responsible to justice. In July, the United States issued statements registering deep concern over the government's failure to properly investigate his forced disappearance.

The UN resident and humanitarian coordinator told Human Rights Watch that UN agencies and their partners supported the government in providing humanitarian assistance to Tokwe-Mukorsi flood victims. The aid included basic health care, food, shelter, water, and emergency sanitation facilities. He said UN assistance was guided by humanitarian principles premised on accountability to beneficiaries by providing humanitarian response in a humane, impartial, neutral, and independent manner.

In August, Mugabe concluded his one-year tenure as chairperson of the Southern African Development Community (SADC); his tenure as president of the African Union will end in January 2016. Neither institution criticized or engaged with his government on human rights violations.